JAYNE MANSFIELD

Also by Eve Golden

Platinum Girl: The Life and Legends of Jean Harlow (1991)
Vamp: The Rise and Fall of Theda Bara (1996)
Anna Held and the Birth of Ziegfeld's Broadway (2000)
The Brief, Madcap Life of Kay Kendall (2002)
Vernon and Irene Castle's Ragtime Revolution (2007)
John Gilbert: The Last of the Silent Film Stars (2013)

JAYNE MANSFIELD

———

THE GIRL COULDN'T HELP IT

EVE GOLDEN

UNIVERSITY PRESS OF KENTUCKY

Scholarly publisher for the Commonwealth,
serving Bellarmine University, Berea College, Centre
College of Kentucky, Eastern Kentucky University,
The Filson Historical Society, Georgetown College,
Kentucky Historical Society, Kentucky State University,
Morehead State University, Murray State University,
Northern Kentucky University, Spalding University,
Transylvania University, University of Kentucky,
University of Louisville, and Western Kentucky University.
All rights reserved.

Editorial and Sales Offices: The University Press of Kentucky
663 South Limestone Street, Lexington, Kentucky 40508-4008
www.kentuckypress.com

Unless otherwise noted, photos are from the author's collection.

Library of Congress Cataloging-in-Publication Data

Names: Golden, Eve, author.
Title: Jayne Mansfield : the girl couldn't help it / Eve Golden.
Description: Lexington, Kentucky : University Press of Kentucky, [2021] |
  Includes bibliographical references and index.
Identifiers: LCCN 2020053334 | ISBN 9780813180953 (hardcover) | ISBN
  9780813180977 (pdf) | ISBN 9780813180984 (epub)
Subjects: LCSH: Mansfield, Jayne, 1933-1967. | Motion picture actors and
  actresses—United States—Biography. | Publicity—United
  States—History—20th century.
Classification: LCC PN2287.M37 G65 2021 | DDC 791.4302/8092 [B]—dc23

This book is printed on acid-free paper meeting
the requirements of the American National Standard
for Permanence in Paper for Printed Library Materials.

Manufactured in the United States of America.

Member of the Association
of University Presses

For Keith Greene (1954–2020),
my Uncle Mame and my Sebastian Flyte

Contents

Contents

Contents

Photos follow page 214

A Note on Sources

This has been one of my most difficult books when it comes to distinguishing truth from fiction. I am serious about getting my facts right, but Jayne has proved to be very frustrating: a performance artist, she told reporters whatever she thought would entertain them and their readers and cement her persona as a delightfully ditzy movie star. What's more, as the years went on, she began to believe some of her own stories.

Additionally, many quotes said to be "from Jayne" were written by her press agents and sent out to fill newspaper and magazine space.

What was written in those newspapers and magazines is also potentially unreliable. Jayne's life and career were covered extensively by such syndicated columnists as Louella Parsons, Harrison Carroll, Jim Bishop, Dorothy Kilgallen, Walter Winchell, Earl Wilson, Hedda Hopper, and Sheilah Graham—some of them reliable reporters, some of them shameless storytellers.

Finally, Jayne's biographers, friends, coworkers, and family all had their own agendas and told often contradictory or biased (good or bad) tales.

What to believe? I have tried to be as cynical and suspicious as possible, double-checking sources, citing them in the notes, and telling the reader how much faith I have in quotations. I *hope* I have done a good job.

1

Sometimes I think it's just flightiness—and sometimes I think it's because, at heart, she despises the things she's trying for. And it's the difficulty of deciding that makes her such an interesting study.

Edith Wharton, *The House of Mirth*

April 12, 1957, Romanoff's, Beverly Hills

Marilyn Monroe was the biggest star in Hollywood in 1957, certainly the biggest on the 20th Century-Fox payroll. The blonde bombshell had been trouble from the start, though—her latest film, *Bus Stop,* had been a long, hard shoot, and her current production, *The Prince and the Showgirl,* was mired down in England.

But there was a new girl in town, nipping at Marilyn's heels, and she seemed like a sure bet. Signed less than a year before by Fox, she was climbing quickly to the top of her game: unlike Monroe, Jayne Mansfield had been a Broadway star, playing a featured role in *Will Success Spoil Rock Hunter?* Also unlike Monroe, she seemed to enjoy the hell out of being a star.

That April Mansfield was in the midst of shooting the film version of *Rock Hunter.* Her first Fox film, *The Girl Can't Help It,* had opened the year before, showing her to be not only a stunning beauty but a smart, savvy comic actress—and a real threat to Marilyn Monroe. She had just finished filming John Steinbeck's drama *The Wayward Bus,* which was due to open in May. Rough cuts proved she was equally impressive as a dramatic actress—playing a former pin-up trying to hide her past, she gave a low-key, Oscar-worthy performance. It looked like Fox had picked a winner.

Fox had also just signed Italian bombshell Sophia Loren, whose US debut, *Boy on a Dolphin,* was to premiere later that month. The studio threw Loren a huge bash at Romanoff's restaurant in Beverly Hills, inviting its stars and the press to meet the new acquisition. As Loren chatted with tablemate Clifton Webb, in swanned Jayne Mansfield, her hair like whipped cream, her face like an angel's—and wearing a dress cut so low you could see her knees.

She wiggled toward the guest of honor's table, squealing happily, making her way through the stunned crowd. She leaned over—*way* over—to greet Loren, who was unable to hide her shock: "I'm so frightened that everything in her dress is going to blow—*BOOM!*—and spill all over the table," she said decades later. Webb politely averted his eyes, concentrating on his food, as delighted photographers crowded around. Jayne sat herself down next to Loren and beamed at the cameras, as Loren gave her what was to be history's most famous side-eye. "Look at the picture. Where are my eyes? I'm staring at her nipples because I am afraid they are about to come onto my plate. In my face you can see the fear."

That photo was enduring. It made all the papers in 1957; it made book covers years later; it was the subject of parodies and tributes; in 1993 Anna Nicole Smith—fittingly enough—re-created the moment for a Guess? ad.

20th Century-Fox executives, however, were not happy. They wanted their stars to be stars, to be in the public eye, but it began to dawn on them there might be something a little . . . *off* about their new blonde bombshell. Without proper handling and oversight, their new Marilyn Monroe might become more problematic than their *old* Marilyn Monroe.

If Jayne Mansfield had died in 1957, she'd be remembered as one of the most promising and talented young stars of her generation. But over the next ten years, she went from being the "new Marilyn Monroe" to "the poor man's Marilyn Monroe."

2

I shielded her from every unpleasantness and built a sort of
pink lollipop world for her.

Vera Palmer

Jayne Mansfield was born on the Philadelphia Main Line, an area with a
reputation for low-key, old-money gentility. She is, in fact, the only
movie star born on the Main Line. Grace Kelly—Hollywood's epitome of
sexy elegance—was from East Falls in Northwest Philadelphia. Katharine
Hepburn, star of *The Philadelphia Story* and a Bryn Mawr graduate, was
from Connecticut. But Jayne was actually born in Bryn Mawr—the Bryn
Mawr Hospital, to be precise. Yet Jayne was the least "Main Line-y" star one
can imagine: she was brash, gaudy, and socially unacceptable.

Why Jayne was born in Bryn Mawr is a mystery, as her parents lived
in Pen Argyl, a small, middle-class town in Northwestern Pennsylvania
about halfway between Scranton and Allentown. *Nowhere* near the Main
Line. None of her parents or grandparents were from Bryn Mawr; nor did
any aunts or uncles live there. While the Bryn Mawr Hospital is an excellent institution, it's hardly worth the nearly eighty-mile drive. Perhaps her
parents, Herbert and Vera Palmer, were en route to Philadelphia or Atlantic City and got caught short, or maybe they had some now-unknown
friend or relative nearby who could look after the new baby and her parents. Jayne was born by cesarean section, so perhaps the Palmers knew of a
Bryn Mawr doctor who specialized in that sort of complicated delivery.

In any case, a few days after her birth on April 19, 1933, Vera Jane Palmer was on her way back home to Pen Argyl with her parents. Her father, lawyer Herbert William Palmer, was born in 1904 into a slate-industry family. Her mother, elementary schoolteacher Vera Jeffery Palmer, was born in 1903 and came of Cornish stock (though both were named Palmer, Vera Jane's parents were not related—or not closely, at any rate). At least three of the baby's grandparents were quite wealthy, which would come in handy for their granddaughter when they started dying.

Herbert and Vera Palmer had married in 1928, and Vera Jane was their only child. They set up home in Phillipsburg, New Jersey, only a half hour from Pen Argyl, handy for visiting grandparents and Vera Palmer's two sisters. Vera Jane had three first cousins—Richard, Cynthia, and Doug Milheim—to play with.

Herbert had a flourishing law practice, but his 1935 run, as a Republican, for Warren County assemblyman was unsuccessful. Vera gave up teaching when her daughter was born, devoting her time to her daughter, on whom she doted: "I shielded her from every unpleasantness and built a sort of pink lollipop world for her," she recalled in the early 1960s. As little Vera Jane began to walk and talk, she not only turned into a beauty, she became the girliest little girl who ever lived. She loved ribbons and bows and everything pink, and her parents indulged her; if the Depression afflicted Phillipsburg, it didn't affect Vera Jane.

That life came to an end in 1936. While out for a drive with his wife and daughter, Herbert Palmer—only thirty-two years old—suffered a massive heart attack and died at the wheel. Vera managed to steer the car to safety. Vera Jane was only three years old—the same age her daughter Mariska would be when she lost her mother in a car accident.

Jayne rarely talked about his death, but her third husband, Matt Cimber, recounted that her father told her, "The doctor said, 'Jump on this foot, now jump on that foot, your heart is fine,' and they walk out the door and the guy drops dead."

The young widow and her daughter were lucky to have a large, supportive family nearby. Vera Palmer remained single for three years before meeting a strong, commonsensical Dallas native, Harry Peers, who was in Phillipsburg working for Ingersoll-Rand. The two married in St. Louis in 1939, and the new family moved to Dallas that summer, when Vera Jane was six. How this upheaval—losing one father, gaining another, moving from the Northeast to Texas—affected her can only be guessed, as she never dwelt on the experience in public. Vera Jane was leaving not only her East Coast home but her large network of supportive friends and family—grandparents, aunts, cousins. For a six-year-old, this must have been an awful jolt.

She seems to have had a normal childhood; Harry Peers was strict and Vera overprotective and hovering, but no more so than many parents. The Dallas kids made fun of Vera Jane's New Jersey accent, but "I wasn't shy long," she said. "In the third grade they voted me queen of my class. If you want something in life, go after it. I believe in hard work." Like many children, Vera Jane escaped to the movies. Her favorite star was Shirley Temple, the preternaturally talented girl who sang and danced her way through more than forty features and shorts in the 1930s (and who also displayed great acting talent in her nonmusical moments).

She was also mischievous, in an adorable Shirley Temple way. Reading in *Ladies' Home Journal* that a free case of soap was being sent to anyone with newborn triplets, nine-year-old Vera Jane wrote in that she had just given birth to Jammy, Sammy, and Pammy ("It's a good thing I'm not a writer, I'd have never been successful," she later admitted), and "one morning a postman came with all the soap in the world." A panicked Vera Jane hid the soap, and it was some time before her parents discovered it.

By the time she'd reached her teens, Vera Jane was tall and skinny and attending Highland Park High School; she still loved movies but had graduated from Shirley Temple to Betty Grable (she also had a crush on John Lund, a handsome actor best known for *A Foreign Affair*). Classmate and good friend Ann Wedgeworth (who also grew up to be a successful actress) recalled Highland Park as "a real snob school." Vera Jane, said Ann, "was very sweet, and neither of us had a lot of friends. . . . There was the 'in' group, and we were *out*. That bothered her some."

Another school pal, Charlsa Wolf, agreed that Highland Park was "upper-class and upper-middle-class. They were *not* blue-collar workers. . . . We didn't know what was going on in the outside world, nor did we care." Vera Jane was "always smiling. She was never nervous." Charlsa added that Vera Jane "was not popular in high school. She really didn't have a lot of dates, and the dates she had were with kind of tacky fellows."

The girls were almost comically typical 1940s teens, right out of Archie Comics. They were fashion-mad, boy-crazy, and obsessed with their figures. "She would come over to our house," Charlsa Wolf told biographer Martha Saxton, "and mother would buy tins of fruit, and we would set in the bowl six peaches and [a] whole thing of cherries and Lord only knows what else, and we would take it up to my room. We would sit up all night and eat this fruit."

As a student, Vera Jane was average, but she excelled in languages, played the violin in the school orchestra (as well as the piano), and took horseback-riding lessons. In later years a story circulated that Jayne had an IQ of around 164 (the number varied by a point or two in the retelling). It sounds like publicity fluff, but by the 1960s Jayne seemed to believe it herself. IQ tests are arguably meaningless, little more than a parlor game. But Vera Jane was certainly a quick, bright child—learning foreign languages, reading music, playing two instruments, and becoming very eloquent and articulate, which showed more about her intellect than any IQ test number. Her musical skills were such that her mother paid for private tutors, and Vera Jane developed into a really impressive amateur. She kept up her piano and violin lessons well through her twenties. Later offers for her to play with orchestras or in concerts came only because she was a movie star—and none of the offers were serious—but Jayne was justly proud of her musical talents.

She auditioned for—but did not make—the drama club.

In late 1949 romance came into Vera Jane's life. Paul Mansfield, born in Galveston, Texas, in 1929, was a sophomore at the University of Texas in Austin when the two met at a Christmas party (Jayne later claimed it was at midnight Mass, but her friend Charlsa Wolf told Jayne's biographer Martha Saxton that the party was at her house). "Jaynie was crazy about him," said Ann Wedgeworth.

Paul Mansfield was tall, slim, and pleasant-looking; he was also smart, funny, and down-to-earth. He was a good piano player, but not in the least artsy or show-biz struck. He later recalled Vera Jane as "a real vision of loveliness. I was not bad-looking in those days, either. I began calling her, and we began dating; I felt very proud when I'd walk down the street with this gorgeous thing on my arm. I was young and in love, and I guess she was, too." He added, "She was a very smart woman—she had street smarts, too."

In a 1957 interview with Ray Parker, Jayne recalled, "My parents were very strict about my hours and with whom I associated. They were part of the reason I married so young. One month and three days [after we met] we were married secretly in the Baptist church in Fort Worth, where I gave my age as 18 [she was actually sixteen]. I was afraid to tell my parents."

That secret wedding took place on January 28, 1950. The couple took a $35-a-month apartment, but they never had a honeymoon—in fact, they barely had a marriage at all. Terrified to tell her parents that she was married, Vera Jane returned to her family home every night by 11:00; Paul continued at college and Jane worked toward her high-school diploma, planning to go on to the University of Texas in the fall of 1950. "I feel very strongly about that college bit," Jayne told Parker. "What could I say to my daughter if she ever asked, 'Mommie, where did you go to college?'" As for that daughter: by the spring of 1950, it was obvious to Vera Jane that she was pregnant, and the marriage couldn't be kept a secret any longer.

Three months' pregnant and just getting over the nausea she suffered with every baby, Vera Jane had to confess to her parents before she started to show. They were disappointed—they had no objection to Paul, but the idea of their teenage, pregnant daughter marrying while still in high school was quite a blow. The Peerses and the Mansfields gathered for a second, public wedding on May 10, 1950, and the next month Jayne Mansfield graduated from Highland Park High School.

She was "Jayne" now: she liked the sound and look of "Jayne Mansfield," and already had her eye on a movie-star name that would look good in lights. Right from the start, she made no bones about her ambitions, telling Paul that "someday she'd be going to Hollywood and would become a movie star. And she said it in a way that I believed her."

Jayne Marie Mansfield was born on November 8, 1950, at St. Paul University Hospital in Dallas, and her mother enrolled for the spring 1951 semester at the University of Texas, alongside her husband. In later years, Jayne joked and bragged about her dual role as college student and mother. She was the same age as her classmates, still in her late teens. But being a wife and mother must have set her apart, making it difficult to form friendships and join the social scene that's so important to college life. She frequently made light of her college days, so that it seemed like a lark: "We took Jayne Marie to chemistry class, and whenever she needed it one of us would stick a bottle in her mouth or change her diaper." But she and Paul were juggling classes and homework with weekend and evening jobs to pay the rent and buy groceries.

And there was a baby to take care of—at least sometimes. According to Vera Palmer, when she was a little girl Jayne used to tell her that "she was going to get married, have her babies, give them to me to take care of and go to college. I just laughed it off. . . . Well, she almost *did* that." Childhood friend Charlsa Wolf found the situation rather sad when she came to visit. The Mansfields' two-room apartment was shabby, and they ate out a lot—mostly at Someburger's—because Jayne couldn't cook. While Jayne never admitted that life wasn't fun and exciting, Charlsa said, "She kind of came into her own when she got to college, which was kind of sad because it was too late because she had all that responsibility."

Jayne worked evenings as a receptionist at the Gregg Scott Dance Studios, and briefly got a job at a veterinarian's clinic, though that didn't last long: "People used to bring dogs to be destroyed because of old age or illness," she recalled. "But I took them home with me, rather than see them put away. Whenever one died I had a funeral for it and buried it with flowers and prayers." Paul swept floors and sold ice-cream cones and magazines; between the two of them, they managed to pay the rent and keep themselves in Someburgers. Although the Peerses looked after Jayne Marie, Jayne claimed they did not chip in financially "because I insisted on studying dramatics and becoming a movie star."

Paul was happy with his little family. "I think she was a good mother," he said of Jayne decades later. "She was very careful with Jaynie Marie. She had schedules, just like a lot of mothers do, and she had it pretty much together. She certainly loved Jayne Marie, and Jayne Marie brought a lot of happiness to both of us."

❤

Jayne was happy, too, but marriage and motherhood did not put a dent in her acting ambitions. In an April 1951 University of Texas production of *Much Ado about Nothing,* she worked on the set crew and played a lady-in-waiting.

She and Paul also managed to land roles with the Austin Civic Theater —an impressive feat, considering their course load, pay-the-rent jobs, and parenthood. Over the next several decades the Austin Civic Theater (ACT) alternately bragged about and apologized for giving Jayne Mansfield her professional start. Founded in 1932, the theater (renamed the Zachary Scott Theater in 1968, after another famous Austin alumnus) is still active today—besides Jayne, others to appear on that stage were Tex Ritter, Eli Wallach, Walter Cronkite, Pat Hingle, Barbara Barrie, Rip Torn, and Mary Louise Parker.

It was still a small, semi-amateurish company when Jayne and Paul made their debuts in September 1951 in the revue *Playhouse Varieties*. Paul played the piano, and he and Jayne did a song-and-dance number, which must have been bliss for the young bride—her photo (flirtatiously lifting her skirt) was featured in the *Austin-American* and held an honored place in the first of her many scrapbooks. The show went over so well that two additional performances were added. "Paul could have been a marvelous entertainer, but he didn't work at it," Jayne later reminisced, baffled by her husband's lack of interest in show business. "He didn't like animals, either," she added darkly.

In October Jayne was cast in *The Drunkard; or, The Fallen Saved*, a nineteenth-century temperance melodrama that was rewritten as a camp comedy in the 1930s (this version can be seen in the 1934 W. C. Fields film *The Old Fashioned Way*). Jayne (wearing terrible character makeup) played Mary Middleton, the long-suffering wife of the titular drunkard; between acts, Paul "tears the piano apart in a boggie-woogie [*sic*] number," as one reviewer noted. That the actress and the pianist were college students with a baby at home was notable enough to gain mention in the reviews: "Jayne Mansfield, the drunkard's wife, is the off-stage wife of Paul Mansfield, a talented guy.... Jayne and Paul married in high school and came on to the university, Jayne to major in drama and Paul in music. There's a little Mansfield in the family, and the parents have their classes staggered so that one stays home and baby sits while the other's on the campus."

Though best known as a movie actress, Jayne really shined onstage, and she loved interacting with a live audience. Both *Playhouse Varieties* and *The Drunkard* enjoyed decent runs and enthusiastic receptions. Every audience was different, and Jayne was learning the art of playing up or down to a crowd that might be lively or apathetic. In her nightclub act and in summer stock, she thrived on walking out into the crowd and chatting, flirting, and joking with audience members. If she hadn't been so set on becoming a Movie Star, she might have developed into a deft stage actress.

Though she had grown out of her teen gawkiness and was now a curvaceous young lady, Jayne had not yet developed—or exploited—her future startling figure. In her college days Jayne was a wholesome girl-next-door type: fresh-faced, with a big girlish smile and dark-brown hair—more "teen Natalie Wood" than a future Marilyn Monroe.

❤

War intruded on the lives of Jayne and Paul Mansfield. US troops had been fighting in Korea since 1950, and in 1952, upon graduating from college, Paul was commissioned a second lieutenant, with two years to serve in the army. He joined the Reserve Officer Training Corps and shipped off to Camp Gordon in Georgia, not far from Augusta. Jayne tagged along, leaving Jayne Marie parked with her grandparents. "He promised to take me to Hollywood and let me try for a movie career if I accompanied him during his military duty," Jayne told Ray Parker. The couple lived in the married officers' quarters.

Being an army wife did not slow down Jayne's plans: "I took ballet and seven singing lessons a week." After she became a public personality, Jayne spun colorful tales about her time at Camp Gordon. She never let the truth stand in the way of a good story, so her memories of practicing her ballet lessons "on the lawn while barefooted and dressed in a black leotard" may be a total fabrication. "People began to notice that the troops had stopped drilling on the parade grounds and were marching and countermarching around the Mansfield house. A major's wife—it's *always* a major's wife—paid me a call for tea. She said, 'Mrs. Mansfield, leap-frogging about in a leotard is just not done by officers' wives in military establishments.' So I had to give up dancing in the sun and the troops went back to drilling on the parade ground."

According to Jayne, she also preferred to use the enlisted men's swimming pool as it was bigger and closer to her quarters. "Another call from another major's wife. 'Mrs. Mansfield,' she said, 'that is a very becoming velvet bikini, but don't you think it is a little unfair to use facilities reserved for enlisted personnel?'"

When she wasn't appalling her betters, Jayne acted in several stage productions in Georgia, including playing the lead, Reno Sweeney (originated by bullhorn belter Ethel Merman), in *Anything Goes*. With her light, as-yet-untrained voice, Jayne sang such Cole Porter songs as "I Get a Kick out of You," "You're the Top," and the title number.

In the summer of 1952—possibly run out of town by officers' wives—Jayne enrolled for a semester at the University of Southern California, tantalizingly close to Hollywood. She took as many drama classes as she could squeeze in and lived in the women's dorms. Again, the storyteller in Jayne had fun with her brief stint at USC: "I kept nine hamsters in the women's dormitory," she claimed. "I drilled holes in the bureau drawer. The expulsion nearly came about when I put a hamster in the housemother's bed. I can still hear her screams." When she left, her dorm mates gave her two hamsters as a going-away gift.

One of her stories can be disproved. When, years later, rumors of her modeling nude for art classes circulated, Jayne insisted, "That is not true. I always wore a leotard." But photos do exist of a dark-haired Jayne, naked as the day she was born, with a guitar covering her nether regions. She did admit—very early in her career, in 1955—to the *Boston Globe*, "We weren't living very high on the hog and I was trying to make a few extra pennies; so once or twice I modeled nude, but mostly in a leotard with nothing under it so they could see the body structure." But by the time she became famous, she backtracked—even after she did pose nude, for *Playboy.*

Jayne also applied for the Miss America contest while at USC and claimed to have gotten as far as winning Miss Southern California. She told two stories about the upshot of that; in one she was disqualified when she confessed that she was a Mrs. A few years later, when she was divorcing Paul, Jayne gave a different reason, claiming that he had objected: he "put his foot down and made me withdraw . . . he sent me a special delivery letter threatening to expose me as a married woman and, therefore, ineligible for the contest."

Jayne left USC after just one semester and returned to her parents and Jayne Marie, but for the rest of her life she reminisced fondly about her college days. She told one reporter that she was "a student of psychology" and had studied "lots of things. A lot about animals. Animals always intrigued me. You know, monkeys. Psychological stuff." Aside from her dizzy-blonde act, Jayne made a very good point about school: "What you've got to remember is you don't go to college to print indelibly each medical term on your mind," she told the reporter. "You go to learn to *think.*"

His ROTC training at Camp Gordon completed, Paul shipped off for Korea in 1953 (in July of that year, US involvement wound down as the demilitarized zone was created and North and South Korea began their long Cold War). Jayne moved back in with her parents and Jayne Marie, and enrolled at Southern Methodist University in her old Highland Park neighborhood.

Much to the annoyance of her fellow students and professors, she often took Jayne Marie to class with her to give her parents a break. "I used to think, 'this is terrible! Here I am, married woman, and a husband in

Korea, and I'm cutting up frogs!'" She brought a purse full of candy with her, and baby bottles of milk, to quiet Jayne Marie—who sat on the floor under her chair—when she started getting fussy.

Jayne also took acting classes, and had a bit part in a production of *Death of a Salesman* at the Knox Street Players in October 1953. Her director was Polish-born Yiddish theater actor Baruch Lumet, whose son Sidney later became a top film and TV director. Another early acting coach, Bob Glenn, recalled, "She was quiet in those days, a little dumpy. And very serious about a career in the theater. And she had a little talent too, for comedy in particular." Glenn said that the last advice he gave Jayne before she left his class was "Never, but never, try to play a dumb blonde. You're not equipped for it."

When the Korean conflict ended—for the United States, at least—Paul Mansfield returned to his family late in 1953 to pick up normalcy. As he already suspected, though, "normalcy" was not on his wife's agenda. He had promised she could go to Hollywood and seek an acting career and she was holding him to it, baby or no baby. "I said, okay," Paul recalled. "I saw the Los Angeles area as good as any to establish myself, too." As all of Jayne's husbands were to learn, there was no contradicting her: what Jayne wanted, Jayne got. "I always said Jaynie had more guts than most men," Paul later admitted. "Jaynie wanted to be a movie actress—not just an actress, but a *star*. I was playing my role, I told her I would take her to California, and I would stand by, and give her opportunity."

And so, in late 1953, Jayne Mansfield was finally on her way: after a couple of years of acting classes and a handful of college and community theater productions, stardom was waiting.

Though they were willing to help the couple settle, neither the Peerses nor the Mansfields were willing to finance Jayne's unrealistic dreams. The couple rented a small apartment on Fulton Avenue in Van Nuys and took what work they could find; neither of them was lazy, and their early days were a round of one dead-end job after another.

Jayne sold candy and photo albums door to door. "We had a combined income of about $150 a month," Jayne later recalled. When asking for a divorce, she denigrated Paul's jobs, which ranged from "sweeping out in the grocery, to selling cement, to selling radio time, to selling vibrators." But it sounds as though he was working very hard to support his family, and getting very little thanks for it. "Within a couple of weeks, she was out calling all the studios," said Paul. "I didn't feel at home in the movie business. I couldn't see myself being a Mr. Jaynie Mansfield for the rest of my life."

And Jayne *was* going to become "Jayne Mansfield," no one doubted that. "She talked about it constantly" was daughter Jayne Marie's early memory. "Very sure of herself, Mother. She had so much enthusiasm, nothing could stop her."

Somehow—probably with the begrudging help of her family after all—Jayne bought a red Buick. Even in centrally located Van Nuys, a car was a necessity for a woman who wanted to arrive at film studios looking crisp and stylish.

As 1953 turned into '54, the Mansfield marriage finally fell apart. "I knew it wasn't going to work almost from the beginning," Jayne told Ray Parker. "Paul was trying to find himself and he deeply resented any part I would have in show business. He believed a wife's place was in the kitchen. He would sulk when agents called me to talk about possible jobs and he didn't like the modeling I did. He would tell me, 'I don't want a million men looking at my wife.'"

Paul, looking back decades later, agreed that this marriage couldn't be saved. "I had begun to not like what I saw, and I told her that this really wasn't what I bargained for. I could see that she was going places, and that was good for *her*. I just couldn't stand the attention she was receiving from other men." He also had—rightly so—concerns for his daughter: "I didn't know how we were going to care for Jaynie Marie in a family atmosphere with that going on. Of course, you could say my leaving didn't help *that*, but still it just wasn't right, it seemed wrong to me."

In the spring of 1954, Paul packed up and moved to San Francisco. Jayne and Jayne Marie were on their own, and with no one to hold her back, Jayne tackled Hollywood with more obsession and enthusiasm than any unknown starlet ever had.

3

I saw myself on the screen for the first time and it was love at first sight.

Jayne Mansfield

As nightclub comics later pointed out, when Jayne arrived in Hollywood she had two big things going for her. Not what they meant, though: she had searing ambition and a total lack of doubt in herself.

She had looks, too, but not the drop-dead beauty of a Marilyn Monroe or a Kim Novak. Jayne's face was an agreeable, baby-like affair, its best feature her large mouth with perfect teeth and pillowy lips. She had small, sparkling brown eyes, a tiny blip of a nose, not much chin to speak of, and no camera-friendly bone structure. But somehow it came together in a pleasing whole.

Her figure was not the advantage one would think, at least not at first—she later claimed she was turned down for roles for being too distractingly curvy, and that's not hard to believe. Even in the background of a scene, modestly clothed, Jayne's hourglass figure drew all eyes away from the star (Jayne herself was later accused of firing too-curvy showgirls from her movies). Her breasts—so soon to become her trademark—were not freakishly huge. But her large rib cage and cup size, combined with her tiny waist, required careful costuming. When she first hit Hollywood, Jayne was just another voluptuous starlet. Within a few years—with the help of foundation undergarments akin to a Gothic cathedral's flying buttresses—she became a human sight gag.

One of the first things Jayne did after landing in L.A. was to go platinum blonde, pretty much stamping what kind of movie star she wanted to be. Jean Harlow was not the first platinum blonde, but she had popularized the color in the early 1930s—and almost instantly it became the halo of the gum-chewing floozy. Harlow herself, recognizing this, cut her hair short and grew back her own honey-blonde color in 1935. Natural-looking blondes could be bucolic girls next door or elegant Park Avenue swans, but platinum blonde shouted "chorus girl" or "two-bit tart." Still, it was (more or less) the hair color of Marilyn Monroe, Kim Novak, Betty Grable, Lana Turner, Judy Holliday—even, briefly, Rita Hayworth—so Jayne went with it. Until 20th Century-Fox got its hands on her in 1957, though, she kept her dark eyebrows (sometimes even penciling them in darker), giving her a rather alarmingly intense appearance.

Bleaching is death to hair: more so in the 1950s, when the chemicals were even harsher than they are today. A dark brunette like Jayne might have to go through one or two rounds of bleaching to get all the color out of her hair, followed by another dye to achieve whatever ash or buttercup blonde she wanted. Then there were the regular touchups, necessary in the days before the inexplicable "two inches of black roots" vogue took hold. By the early 1960s Jayne's once-healthy hair was straw-brittle and thinning, her scalp dry and probably itchy—leading to an increasing reliance on wigs and hairpieces as the years rolled on.

Jayne spent most of 1954 spinning her wheels. Hollywood was overflowing with pretty blondes, many of them prettier and more talented than Jayne—some were even curvier. Every one of them was ambitious and hopeful and convinced that she would be the next Betty Grable or Marilyn Monroe. Most of them never got as far as a casting agent; some of them managed to land extra work or bit parts or TV commercials. Some even got what they thought was their Big Break—a speaking role in a movie or TV show. Look at the cast list of any 1954 movie or TV series, and you'll see the names of actresses every bit as talented and full of dreams as Jayne Mansfield, but unknown to modern audiences. They did their turn in front of the camera, but for all their hard work and hopes, they faded away into marriage or a "civilian" career.

Jayne turned twenty-one in April 1954, and fell heir to $6,000 when her father's mother, Alice, died. She made a down payment on her first house, an $18,000 bungalow at 9840 Wanda Park Drive in Beverly Hills (since demolished), which she dubbed Mansfield's Madness. It was on a hillside, surrounded by flowers, and Jayne eventually added a small pool and patio. She also traded in her Buick for a pink Jaguar: "I have a pink mink stole, a black mink and a silver mink," she bragged, "and I've almost paid for a Jaguar. I'm just about the happiest girl in the world." She also owed $17,000 on all those purchases—even in 1954, $6,000 only went so far.

Even though she was a mother and soon-to-be divorcée, Jayne was a somewhat sheltered and trusting young lady, the kind whom show business eats up like hors d'oeuvres. Jayne encountered the same casting-couch dilemma that has plagued actresses—and actors—since the business began. According to Leo Guild, who ghosted her memoirs in 1963, "A rather handsome young man met Jayne on the street and asked if she'd like to meet a motion picture producer. Absolutely naïve, she agreed she would. He led her to his car and they started to drive. He drove with one hand and unzipped himself with the other, meanwhile making vulgar comments and gestures. Crying, Jayne managed to switch off the ignition key and broke away from the man, screaming as she ran." Another time, Jayne said, "A director who promised me a bit part reneged on his promise because I wouldn't have dinner at his house. I had heard about what he demanded for dessert."

In 1956 she told writer Ray Parker, "I haven't met the wolf I couldn't handle. With a figure like mine, a girl is certain to attract attention—and I find it pleasing and necessary that men look at me. But when they get too attentive I give them the Mansfield 'routine A.' I tell them how much I trust them and value their advice and friendship. This startles the wolfiest of wolves and almost immediately he becomes fatherly, or even brotherly." She shrugged off what she considered to be an unavoidable hazard of the game: "Sure, some little girls get lost in Hollywood, but they would have been lost in their hometowns, or anywhere else."

Like other newcomers to the business, she found herself shut out by the unions, which were—and are—closed shops. It's the classic catch-22: you can't even *audition* for a union show or movie unless you have a union card, and the only way to get a union card is to have a part in a union show or movie. Jayne went to Republic Studios where, she told Leo Guild, "I was asked if I were a member of the Screen Actors' Guild or the Screen Extras' Guild or even AFTRA [American Federation of Television and Radio Artists]. I wasn't. That was a big problem right away. . . . From there I went to Universal Studios where I went through the same experience. At Warner Bros., my next stop, they had certain hours for interviewing talent and I was there at the wrong time."

One of the most retold and silly stories about Jayne actually has the ring of truth. She told Canadian interviewer Joyce Davidson in 1957, "I called Paramount Studios and said, 'I'm Jayne Mansfield, and I want to be a movie star.' They said, 'Well, thank you, Jayne Mansfield, but we already have a movie star!'" It sounds too good to be true, but that's exactly the sort of disarmingly bold-as-brass tactic Jayne was to employ for the rest of her life.

She expanded on this tale to Ray Parker that same year. "I don't know why I picked Paramount," she said, "except, perhaps, that I had been hot driving through the desert and I thought of Paramount's snow-capped peak trademark. I was connected to a secretary in talent chief Milt Lewis's office and told her, 'I'm Jayne Mansfield and I want to be a star. I just arrived from Dallas where I won a beauty contest.' There was a pause on the other end of the line and then the secretary laughed. 'This is the first time the direct approach has been used in Hollywood in 20 years. I'll set up an appointment with Mr. Lewis for you,' she told me."

In another version, Jayne left out the phone call and recounted that her old Texas director Baruch Lumet, now in Los Angeles, got her the Paramount audition and screen test in April 1954. Jayne chose a scene from Maxwell Anderson's highly dramatic *Joan of Lorraine*—one cannot imagine what she could have been thinking. Lumet coached her on her scene, but in the 1960s he wisecracked, "Don't hold me responsible for her acting today." Still, Paramount was interested (or amused) enough to test her again, on May 8—this time, more wisely, she did the piano scene from *The Seven Year Itch,* then starring Vanessa Brown on Broadway, and already earmarked for Fox's Marilyn Monroe. The "*Rachmaninoff*—it *shakes* me! It *quakes* me!" scene was perfect for Jayne, but Paramount sent her home without a contract.

"I wanted, needed and had to succeed. So I did," she told Leo Guild. If she had never gotten a break, "maybe I would have married again. Maybe I would have been some V.I.P.'s mistress. I don't know, but it is strange that I never considered failure."

Running from studio to studio, begging for auditions or even a glimpse of a casting director, was getting Jayne nowhere: "I was learning painfully that my breaks wouldn't fall in my lap." So she approached her career in a way that showed those street smarts that Paul had acknowledged—she got a job at Ciro's as a photo girl. The West Hollywood nightclub had been a gathering place for stars and studio executives since it opened in the early 1940s. Jayne could not afford to be a patron, but even better was this chance to get paid for table-hopping and meeting the famous and influential. "My job was to roam around the club with a camera, smile prettily and ask if people would like their picture taken. . . . As the evening progressed and as the drinking went on, I would do better and better." The pretty, smiling photo girl had only one thought: "a movie job. I hoped some picture star or producer would see or talk to me and decide I was perfect for a picture."

Through the long summer of 1954, Jayne and Jayne Marie—now three years old—somehow managed to scrape by. She tested at Warner Bros., again doing that piano scene from *The Seven Year Itch*. Again, she went home empty-handed.

Then, in October 1954, came Jayne's first real break, small as it was: a bit part on a TV show. NBC's hour-long anthology *Lux Video Theatre* cast her in *An Angel Went AWOL*, which aired on October 21. Starring (fairly) big names George Nader and Joanne Dru, it was a fantasy about a young actor and his supernatural wife. Jayne's blonde hair and big bust did not get her the role—her piano-playing skills did. She had a few lines, played the piano at a party scene, and would not be seen on TV again for another two years. "I had ten lines," she recalled. "I got $300. I was very thrilled about it—at last I was acting for money. I even wore my own dress in the show!"

Her first real press coverage came that same month when she was named "Miss Four-Alarm Fire" for Fire Prevention Week and was photographed at a Junior Chamber of Commerce breakfast honoring L.A. city fire chief John H. Alderson; she posed sexily with a fire pole. The story and photo ran alongside an article in the *L.A. Times* on Marilyn Monroe's divorce suit against Joe DiMaggio.

In late 1954 the Ciro's job—not Jayne's rounds at the studios—paid off; she landed a major role in a minor movie. Jayne told Leo Guild that she spotted tough-guy (on- and off-screen) actor Lawrence Tierney at a diner and eavesdropped on his conversation, about his upcoming project *Female Jungle*, a low-budget crime thriller. She barged right in on Tierney—which took some nerve; he was known for his barroom brawls—and asked to see the script he had with him. "In the cast of characters, which I turned to first, was this notation: 'Girl—busty, attractive, sexy, outgoing alluring.' Hey, that was me! I told Tierney I was an actress and I thought I was right for one of the parts. He just nodded as if he had heard this story a thousand times. He suggested I get through to the producer [Burt Kaiser] and talk to him."

That, Jayne already knew, "sounded easy but it wasn't. But I called his office and told his secretary Ciro's was on the line. She put me through. I told him I was the photographer at Ciro's and I had seen him there a few times. He was very cordial but confused. Then I told him I thought I would be fine as the sexy girl in *Female Jungle*. He remembered me from Ciro's and suggested I come up and see him." P.S. She got the part.

Female Jungle, "introducing Jayne Mansfield," fourth-billed, is a tidy little thriller, despite a clunky script and some wildly overacting supporting players. The plot, involving the murder of an actress, follows three suspects: a troubled police detective (Tierney), a creepily suave gossip columnist (an excellent John Carradine), and a struggling artist (producer and screenwriter Burt Kaiser, in his only major acting role). Jayne plays a broken blossom sleeping with at least two of the suspects, and she is excellent: she starts out light (amusingly answering her phone, "Who is this, honey?") and becomes increasingly desperate as the killer closes in on her.

Although a project of the independent Burt Kaiser Productions, the film was shot on the Warner lot. The director and co-screenwriter, Bruno VeSota, was better known as a character actor in scores of movies and TV shows; he (over-) plays a role in *Female Jungle* as well. VeSota not only directed Jayne's first movie, but he was also to have a role in one of her last, *Single Room Furnished* (his directing career was not quite as successful—he went on to helm *The Brain Eaters* and *Invasion of the Star Creatures* before deciding to stick with acting).

Jayne worked on *Female Jungle* for only two weeks—in November– December 1954—at $250 a week. "It was made in a very poor section of Los Angeles," she told columnist Earl Wilson. "Warehouses and little children who should have gone to bed at night but were up watching us shoot night scenes. . . . The kids didn't know who I was, but they asked for my autograph."

"It wasn't *Gone with the Wind,*" she admitted, "but as far as I was concerned it was even better and bigger. Everyone thought I did well." And her work paid off: "On the last day of shooting, Solly Biano, Warner Bros.' casting head, came in. . . . 'We all like you here and we think you have great potential. We've decided we'd like to have you under contract.'" After only a year in Hollywood, Jayne had scored herself a seven-year Warner Bros. contract, at $250 a week with thirteen-week options.

Dress designer Walter Emerson told reporter May Mann—later Jayne's friend—that Jayne had approached him before her Warner's contract meeting, looking shabby and desperate. She asked him for free clothes, promising to pay him back with her first studio check. Either charmed or bulldozed, Emerson "took Miss Mansfield to the bookkeeper and asked her to fill out a credit card. I took her into the dressing room, where she removed the man's white shirt and torn, old blue jeans she was wearing. . . . I chose a sexy, fitted black jersey with a high turtleneck collar and long sleeves with the whole back bare. She was delighted. Then she said, 'But what can I do for shoes and gloves and a bag?' 'A knock-out,' I thought. I decided I'd have to go all of the way." Jayne did indeed pay Emerson back after getting her Warner's contract. He added, "She never sold her clothes to thrifty gown shops. Instead she'd send them to Goodwill shops. 'Maybe some girl trying for a career, who has no clothes—like me, when I first came to Hollywood—will find these lucky for her,' she'd say generously."

"I saw myself on the screen for the first time and it was love at first sight," Jayne later said of *Female Jungle*. The film received only a limited release (mostly at drive-ins) and few reviews in January 1955, but after Jayne's fame hit, it played nationwide for years, with her billing bumped up. Her few reviews were good ones: The *Hollywood Citizen News* wrote, "In her own right, Miss Mansfield is very appealing . . . her uninhibited love scenes are sizzling." *Picturegoer* agreed: "As a jaded good-time girl who just wants the bad-time guy, she registers as something more than a vigorous blonde with spectacular statistics." If *Female Jungle* had been a better, higher-budget movie, it might have channeled Jayne into a career as a noir anti-heroine like Lizabeth Scott or Gloria Grahame.

Thus the year 1954 ended hopefully, and 1955 would be a major turning point in Jayne's career: she gained a press agent, a film contract, and a lot of press. In December 1954, she signed with publicist Jim Byron. Jayne told Leo Guild that one of her diction-school classmates introduced her to Byron—but he was a promoter for Ciro's, and she probably met him through her job there. Byron told her: "If you'll gamble, I'll gamble. I'll take 5% of your income. If you make a lot, I'll make a lot. Otherwise, I'll be out of luck." Bryon related to biographer Martha Saxton that "I was looking for a chick to prove that I was the world's greatest living press agent."

And so, like Faust making a deal with the devil, Jayne signed with the man who would transform her into "Jayne Mansfield." He helped her become a working actress, but he would also turn her into a walking punch line, a caricature of a movie star. "She never refused the press," Byron recalled with admiration. "You could call her up at 4:00 a.m. and she would give you a story."

Byron introduced Jayne to agent Bill Shiffrin, who had guided Victor Mature and Robert Stack to stardom a decade earlier. Shiffrin agreed to take another 5 percent off Jayne's paycheck for whatever help he could provide. Bryon advised Jayne not to take that Warner's contract, claiming that 20th Century-Fox was considering her for *The Seven Year Itch,* as Marilyn Monroe was giving them such a headache. But Shiffrin, realizing she was never going to land that part, told her to grab Warner's offer. She did, but later groused that Warner's "promised me the star treatment and gave me little bit walk-on parts as a dumb blonde or a gangster's sweetie."

Bill Shiffrin directed Jayne to show-business lawyer Greg Bautzer, who became her legal advisor (not that she ever took advice from anyone). Bautzer, a handsome, dashing forty-something when he met Jayne, had already romanced such Hollywood stars as Lana Turner, Joan Crawford, Ginger Rogers, and Ava Gardner. He was also known for brushing off legal fees owed by friends. Bautzer did not take 5 percent, as did Byron and Shiffrin, and never sent Jayne a bill for his advice. According to his biographer, B. James Gladstone, "Some inferred that he received another form of payment. He denied it, saying he didn't find her attractive." Bautzer told Martha Saxton that Jayne "was an honest dame . . . I found her simpatico. She just got involved later with too many people, four lawyers, four agents. You can only operate with one trusted advisor."

Jim Byron hit the ground running and found Jayne a willing partner in crime. He sent her to the shared press room of the *Los Angeles Times* and *Mirror* on Christmas Eve 1954, dressed as a sexy Santa and bearing gifts of liquor. She went over like gangbusters, and soon friendly newsmen were making sure her photo was featured, even if there was no story to go along with it. She told columnist Sheilah Graham in 1956, "The quality of making everyone stop in their tracks is what I work at. It's a case of dog eat dog—if I don't do it, someone else will."

Jim Byron earned his 5 percent right out of the gate, turning Jayne from an unknown starlet to front-page (entertainment) news overnight. He also set the template for the rest of her career: the cheerfully brazen, camera-hungry pin-up girl.

The launch pad was a press event for the adventure film *Underwater!*, a Howard Hughes production distributed through RKO, starring Gilbert Roland and Richard Egan as sunken-treasure hunters and featuring shapely Jane Russell as Egan's wife (occasionally displayed in form-fitting swimsuits). The film's premiere was the pinnacle of movie silliness: it was held in Silver Springs, Florida, and a few moments of the film were actually to be shown underwater, on a submerged movie screen. Guests were invited to wear swimsuits, and scuba gear would be provided. Debbie Reynolds, Mala Powers, Gordon Scott, and Peggy King attended, along with reporters and photographers from *Look, Time, Life, Parade, McCall's*, and *Collier's*.

Bryon managed to get Jayne on the guest list, advising her to wear her most attention-getting bathing suit. It "wasn't even my own suit," recalled Jayne. "I was in such a rush to get on the plane [to Florida] that I didn't have a chance to shop. I borrowed the suit from Peter Gowland, the still photographer, who kept it in his studio for models. It was red lamé and skin tight. It covered everything but didn't hide a thing." The suit looks modest by today's standards, and it didn't hike up Jayne's cleavage, as her later costumes did—but it got the job done. "When I took off my robe I thought I'd forgotten to put it on. The men just stared and stared. Then there was a wild rush and I was surrounded by photographers."

But it wasn't Jayne at the pool who got all the press coverage—it was Jayne on the plane. Byron already recognized that Jayne was naturally chatty and friendly and genuinely interested in other people. He made sure to tell her to sit with the press, not with the other celebrities, and to be her sunniest, most flirtatious self. "On the planes, coming and going, the males played a version of musical chairs taking turns sitting beside Miss Mansfield," wrote the *Arizona Republic*. "The question on everyone's lip was, 'where has this gal been, why hasn't a studio signed her?' For a week after the *Underwater!* junket every Hollywood reporter who wrote about it mentioned Jayne Mansfield, pointing out in every form of elegant and inelegant expression that she was quite a dish."

Reporter Jean Yothers of the *Orlando Sentinel* recalled that, as photographers and stars were prepping themselves poolside, "almost unnoticed at first, a curvaceous blonde strolled out and seated herself casually on the sand. Suddenly, one photographer after another glanced over, then rushed wildly in her direction, leaving the stars in amazement. It's as simple as that, girls. Just pour yourself into a red bathing suit, stroll out to the Silver Springs beach and seat yourself casually on the sand, but be sure it's casually. Hollywood will get you if you don't watch out."

It wasn't as simple as that, of course: Jayne had been schmoozing and chatting and sitting on laps and asking about wives and children and pets all the way from Los Angeles. She wasn't photographed at poolside and on the beach because she was prettier or sexier than Debbie Reynolds, Mala Powers, or Peggy King—it was because every man on that plane was now her friend.

It paid off, too: the next day, Jane Russell and *Underwater!* got only nominal coverage in the entertainment pages; Jayne and her red one-piece garnered photo after photo, even if the captions had to explain who the unknown starlet was (they often mentioned her 40-21-35½ measurements as well). Readers—and casting directors—got their first real eyeful of Jayne Mansfield.

That *Underwater!* premiere became the stuff of Hollywood legend: in later retellings, Jayne wore a teeny-weeny bikini and lost the top half in the pool, playfully squealing and tossing it to photographers. That never happened, though after a few years Jayne herself was telling that version. Reporters were still a little vague on what a "bikini" was in 1955: two-piece swimsuits had been popular since the 1930s, but were dubbed "bikinis" only in 1946. To non-fashion-conscious reporters, any sexy bathing suit was a "bikini." But photos of the event show Jayne only in her borrowed red suit, so the "Oops, I lost my top!" story was a later fabrication (repeated even in Jayne's ghosted 1963 memoirs).

Jayne also made her first appearance in *Playboy* in February 1955, as their Miss Valentine Playmate. Wrapped in a white shortie robe and pink pajamas, she showed modest side-boob and bottom-boob, but not much below the waist. Only two years old in 1955, *Playboy* was still a work in progress. Jayne was the closest thing to a "name" actress to pose for the magazine. (Marilyn Monroe was in the first issue, but it was an old photo and she certainly did not give permission for its use.)

Now-famous pin-up Bettie Page had appeared in the issue right before Jayne's, but Page did not become a cult goddess until the 1980s. Playmates of 1954 included Joanne Arnold (a starlet who made Jayne look world-famous by comparison) and a bevy of models. Over the next year or two, floodgates hardly opened: Eve Meyer, Marla English, and Meg Myles were the only working actresses to pose for Hugh Hefner's camera till Jayne reappeared in February 1956 (she was also Miss Valentine in the 1957 and '58 issues, in equally teasing but not explicit poses).

Posing for *Playboy* was certainly daring in the mid-1950s, but not as scandalous as it would later become when the photos became far more explicit. It was still "naughty" but not a career-ending shocker. Through the 1950s, Tina Louise, Mara Corday, Brigitte Bardot, Kim Novak, and Sophia Loren appeared in *Playboy* (some as Playmates, some featured in articles), with little or no damage to their careers. "I wouldn't like to see my daughter do cheesecake pictures," said Jayne, "but a certain amount is necessary. Had I not done that, I might still be doing Little Theater in California without any reaction."

Warner's did not seem to object to its rising young starlet getting that kind of exposure; indeed, she was so low on the studio's list of worries that executives may not have noticed. The studio did put out some publicity on Jayne (and on her fellow new hire Dennis Hopper, "the 18-year-old actor who aroused the attention of the entire industry with a powerful performance on the TV *Medic* show"). "Under the stepped-up talent grooming program," Warner's announced, "the new discoveries will be given intensive studio training, as well as being introduced in important pictures. We feel that our intensified new program will introduce to world motion picture audiences many fresh personalities with extraordinary qualifications for enduring stardom."

John Bustin, the amusements editor at the *Austin American,* did not display the hometown-girl spirit about Jayne that one might expect. "Out at the Austin Civic Theater, she was regarded more as a personality than a budding young actress," he wrote. "She sang a little, danced a little, on an occasion or two, even acted a little. But mainly she just looked pretty. . . . But audiences seemed to be of the opinion that she was worth keeping an eye on, no matter what she was doing or not doing on the Playhouse stage."

Jayne was also in the news in April for what would be the first of many car accidents, on West Sunset Boulevard near Hollywood High School. She suffered minor neck and back injuries, and of course her car needed repairs—she later sued the other driver for $10,500, though we don't know how much—if any—money she got. Intriguingly, newspapers reported that her maid, Irene Bluford, was also injured and sued for

$10,000—exactly what a still-struggling starlet was doing with a maid is anyone's guess.

In the very first film under her new contract, Jayne had a small but good supporting role in *Illegal,* a crime film starring Edward G. Robinson (an art collector, he loaned his own Degas and Gauguin paintings as set dressing). Robinson was going through a nasty divorce from his first wife and was being hounded by the House Un-American Activities Committee for his longtime left-wing sympathies. In his early sixties, he was still a busy actor in films and on TV, though not the top star he'd been ten years earlier.

Jayne filmed *Illegal* from February through early April 1955. It's a black-and-white B-film but a relatively good one, starring Robinson as Victor Scott, a tough district attorney who sends an innocent man (DeForest Kelley, in his pre–*Star Trek* days) to the chair. Demoralized, Scott resigns to become a crooked lawyer working for gangster Frank Garland (Albert Dekker). Jayne plays Angel O'Hara, Garland's piano-playing moll; she looks lovely, with light-blonde, shoulder-length hair and beautifully tailored wardrobe by Marguerite Royce; tight fitting but not slutty. She already has her whispery Marilyn-voice down pat. For a pianist, she does a very unconvincing job faking it in her first scene. Through various tortured plot twists, Scott finds himself turning against Garland in a murder case— Jayne's character is the surprise witness in the film's courtroom finale, doing a very nice job till Robinson's character upstages her by keeling over with gunshot wounds in the middle of her testimony.

James Bacon, an entertainment reporter for the Associated Press and the *Los Angeles Herald-Examiner,* began his long, sometimes tortured relationship with Jayne around this time. He gave her plenty of press over the years, but he veered from fawning adoration to spiteful disdain. Jayne told him in April 1955, "I want to be known as an actress—not as a girl with a big bust. How can I get producers and columnists to realize this? All my life I've wanted to be an actress, a good actress." Jayne raved about shooting the movie: "It's a key role and I get a chance to act all right, but who will notice it? I wear a low-cut gown and there is nothing so distracting for a girl who wants to act." She also called Edward G. Robinson "the *most,*" and the feeling seems to have been mutual, as Robinson helped get her a part in her next film.

By the time *Illegal* was released in late 1955, Jayne was already a Broadway star, so she got a lot more attention in the reviews than most debuting starlets. The *Boston Globe*'s Marjory Adams wrote that "gorgeous Jayne Mansfield, the honey baby of the gangster chief's lighter moments, helps give the film importance." John Chapman in the *New York Daily News* gave her a rave ("Miss Mansfield is splendid as a sexy but typically dumb broad"). Not everyone was enchanted: Frank Custer of the *Capital Times* dismissed her as just "a blonde" and said "what her sisters, Monroe and Russell, have she also has abundantly." And Red Leiter of the *Indianapolis News* wrote, "You'll see, briefly, Jayne Mansfield, now the toast of Broadway. She doesn't do much acting, but that doesn't matter. You probably won't be able to keep your mind on her acting, anyway."

Edward G. Robinson told her during the *Illegal* shoot, "I thought you were just another blonde trying to wiggle her way into pictures. But you can act, too," much to Jayne's delight. As soon as *Illegal* had wrapped, he got her another role—though this time only a bit—in his next film, *Hell on Frisco Bay*, shot in early April in San Francisco. It was a run-of-the-mill crime film, starring Alan Ladd (who also produced it) as Steve Rollins, a bitter ex-cop who was framed for a murder. Out of jail, he's looking for the rat who sent him up—unfortunately, Rollins is the dullest character in the film. The real color and excitement come from the supporting cast: heartless mobster Vic Amato (Robinson), his reluctant hit man Joe (Paul Stewart), his handsome thug nephew Mario (Perry Lopez), and Kay, Joe's girl, a "washed-up, has-been old broad of 35" (Fay Wray, who was actually forty-eight). Even the bit players shine in comparison to poor Ladd: future leading man Rod Taylor as a hired killer, silent-film great Mae Marsh as Rollins's landlady, and Jayne (in a black evening gown) as Mario's dancing partner at a nightclub. She's on-screen for maybe a minute and has half a dozen lines; that scene, however, is stolen by a frustratingly unbilled Asian actress playing a flirtatious jitterbug.

It all ends in gunfire and a very silly fistfight aboard a runaway motorboat—sadly, stuntman Louis Tomei (who had competed in the Indianapolis 500 in the 1930s and '40s), doubling for Robinson, was thrown against a metal fitting on the boat and died a few hours later. The *New York Times* brushed off *Hell on Frisco Bay* as "just the usual murders, mayhems and intrigues," while *Variety* complimented most of the cast by name—though not bit-player Jayne, of course.

Jayne was on a roll in the spring of 1955, and went right into *Pete*

Kelly's Blues—though just in another walk-on. The story of a 1920s speakeasy cornet player and bandleader, *Pete Kelly's Blues* was written, directed, and produced by Jack Webb, who'd been playing Sergeant Joe Friday in *Dragnet* on the radio since 1949 and on TV since 1951. This film was an attempt to break free of Joe Friday. The project and character were kind of an obsession for Webb; he actually played the cornet, though he was dubbed in this film. *Pete Kelly's Blues* was originally a 1951 radio series starring Webb, and much later, in 1959, a short-lived TV series produced by Webb and starring William Reynolds and the singer Connee Boswell.

This 1955 film version had an impressive cast: Janet Leigh, Lee Marvin, Peggy Lee (deservedly nominated for an Oscar), and Ella Fitzgerald; Edmond O'Brien played a gangster, presaging his *The Girl Can't Help It* role opposite Jayne. It's a lush, high-budget, great-looking film; cinematographer Hal Rosson and costume designer Howard Shoup were top drawer. It was produced by TV company Mark VII (familiar to viewers for its blacksmith-hammering logo) and released by Warner Bros. It's a step above most 1950s gangster films; the Jazz Age is not played as "cute," and the plot goes effectively dark. While the Oscar-nominated soundtrack is 1950s, not 1920s, it boasts great Lee and Fitzgerald numbers.

Jayne has a bit part as a cigarette girl who politely (and unsuccessfully) flirts with a disinterested Webb. With her hair medium-brown, she has half a dozen lines in the first half of the film and can be glimpsed in the background of a few other scenes. When *Pete Kelly's Blues* was released in July (Jayne's third-filmed but first-released Warner's movie), the critical reaction was a blow to Jack Webb. Only *Variety* liked it; other critics called it "a jazzed-up version of *Dragnet*" and "*Dragnet* with a trumpet." Webb was locked into Joe Friday for the rest of his life.

While making her early films—and all through that spring and early summer—Jayne gave interviews, appeared at charity benefits, and managed to get named Miss Four Alarm (for fire prevention week). Her other purported titles included Miss Photoflash, Miss Third Platoon, Miss Queen of the Chihuahua Show, Miss Nylon, Miss Orchid, Miss Negligee, Miss Blue Bonnet of Austin, Miss Texas Tomato, Miss Electric Switch, Miss Cotton Queen, Miss Freeway, Miss July Fourth, Miss Standard Foods, and Gas Station Queen. "I think the only thing I ever turned down was Miss Roquefort Cheese, because it didn't sound right," she told reporters, batting her eyes innocently. Most of these titles were probably just press handouts from Jim Byron on slow news days.

Jayne gave a talk at a business club, and when she asked the audience for questions, she was asked what her measurements were. She was so annoyed and flustered she nearly missed the chair when sitting back down. She appeared at the opening of a new hotel in Las Vegas (in an actual bikini this time) along with Jeffrey Hunter, Cesar Romero, and Tab Hunter. She was at the Sportsman's Vacation Boat and Trailer Show at the L.A. Pan-Pacific Auditorium. She presented Edmond O'Brien with the Foreign Press and Foreign Correspondent's Best Supporting Actor Award for *The Barefoot Contessa*. She and Debbie Reynolds were cigarette girls at the Biltmore Bowl benefit for the Jewish Home for the Aged.

Warner Bros. Television announced that she would be starring as a "sexy Mata Hari" in the series *Casablanca* (the show ran for one season, sans Jayne). She told the *Long Beach Independent* that "I want to be known for my acting, not my bust," while posing playing ping-pong in a low-cut leotard.

And she gave interview after interview, displaying a great ability to talk to anyone about anything, or about nothing at all. Her stream-of-consciousness monologue to Vernon Scott in March 1955 sounds like Gracie Allen all hopped up on goofballs:

> My dog's name is Byron. I named him after my press agent, who loaned me the $25 down payment for him. I guess I'm the only person in town buying a dog on the installment plan. He looks wonderful riding around in the Jag—the dog, I mean. I love animals. I have two dogs and three cats at home. My house, by the way, is done in pink and charcoal. I don't have a pool yet, but I will someday. It'll have a little island in the middle with a tree and live monkeys crawling around. Don't you think that'll be nice? I worry about my neighbors, though. I wear a black leotard every day to practice ballet on my front porch. The men don't mind, but the women do. I feel like I've lived in Hollywood all my life—it's so unusual. People say I am, too.

Scott — and other reporters — were simultaneously charmed and dumbfounded.

Jayne was a little less dizzy and more on point when talking to the *Los Angeles Times*'s beauty columnist Lydia Lane in May 1955. Jayne had diet tips ("A diet is no good if it makes you feel so hungry that you break down and cheat. I put myself on a high-protein diet of 750 calories a day. This diet allowed lots of raw vegetables and things which were filling but not fattening. For example, a cup of shredded cabbage has only 28 calories; two stalks of celery just 10; a sliced cucumber with vinegar only 7"), career advice ("I've always believed in preparedness—not just trusting to luck. If you are prepared you stand a much better chance of achieving your goal"), and classic 1950s-era dating tips ("Men like their women to be not only feminine but interesting and interested. Often a pretty girl will spoil things for herself because she talks too much. There are times when a good listener is called for. Then there is the other extreme—the girl who simply looks beautiful and does nothing to hold up her end of the conversation. One more thing, I think men are always attracted to a girl who has a bright outlook on life").

In 1955 Jayne met fan-magazine writer May Mann, who was to become a lifelong friend (as well as an afterlife friend: Mann claimed that Jayne's ghost was very chatty after her death). To hear Mann tell it, Jayne said of her: "God always sent me help. This time it was a kind friend, who was a very powerful columnist. . . . She was pretty and popular. She looked like a movie star herself. I always told her she was the prettiest gal of them all." By the time this was printed, Jayne was no longer around to say any different (but to be fair, Mann *was* a looker in her day).

Gossip also slipped through that Jayne was pursuing a divorce. She filed papers in June, charging cruelty; by then Paul was living in San Francisco and had not seen Jayne or Jayne Marie for nearly a year. "He tried to back her in it [show business] for a while, but it wasn't his thing," recalled Jayne Marie years later. "So he was out of the picture, and it was just me and her. She tried to make it as normal as possible, as far as the living went, and having me always around her, so there was a close bond."

In the summer of 1955, Warner Bros. loaned Jayne out for a costarring role in a cheap indie film, a harbinger of how 20th Century-Fox would later handle her. Filmed by Samson Productions and released through Columbia, the crime drama *The Burglar* was directed by Paul Wendkos. It was his first directing job, but he went on to have a long career in films and TV (several *Gidget* movies, *The Untouchables, I Spy, Honey West*). The screenplay was by David Goodis (who wrote some of the best pulp-magazine stories and noir novels of the 1940s and '50s); both men were Philadelphia natives, so that's where the film was shot, with some location scenes in nearby Atlantic City.

No movie studio for *The Burglar:* it was filmed at the WCAU-TV studios on Chestnut Street, a breathtaking 1922 Art Deco building (thankfully, on the National Register of Historic Places). Wendkos told reporters that Jayne "was not a dumb blonde, she knew her lines, knew the background of the scene, understood what we were striving to achieve. Those are not the manifestations of a dumb blonde."

There was a tiny accident on set that Jim Byron blew up into two days of newspaper coverage: on July 27, Jayne's character was making tea on the cramped kitchen set when the kettle boiled over and steam shot out: she was very mildly scalded on the face and arms, and a dermatologist (who happened to be filming a show at WCAU) applied cortisone cream. Jayne was back at work two days later, but she got some dramatic newspaper stories out of it.

It was a gritty shoot, and Jayne had a difficult, layered role to play. The plot concerns a small, ragtag group of crooks, played by Dan Duryea, Mickey Shaughnessy, Peter Capell, and Jayne. Nat (Duryea) and Gladden (Jayne) are childhood friends, a sibling relationship with romantic undertones. Her character is needy and moody, trapped in a cheap lodging house, fighting with Shaughnessy and Capell. Looking more like an incipient Shelley Winters or Joanne Woodward than "Jayne Mansfield," she's dressed in off-the-rack clothes, her medium-blonde hair messy and her face cleaned of makeup (director Wendkos was neither blind nor stupid, so he does send Gladden off to Atlantic City in a bikini). And her acting is impressive—not given the best of scripts, she is nonetheless free of affectations, her voice low and expressive; she *listens* and *reacts* in a way that would delight any acting coach. Veterans Capell and Martha Vickers, on the other hand, overact wildly.

The Burglar is well directed but awkwardly written, with a meandering plot. There are precious glimpses of a rinky-dink, pre-casino Atlantic City, including Steel Pier, Ripley's Believe It or Not Museum, and the famed diving horse. Jayne called it "the best thing I've ever done. Sex is played down and it's the sort of thing I want to do in the future." She was already a star by the time *The Burglar* was released—it floated around in movie limbo till the summer of 1957—and critics were Monday-morning quarterbacking her. *Box Office:* "It's a quietly effective portrayal, even if some fans may scarcely recognize her." *Motion Picture Herald:* "There's a sufficient talent shining forth to indicate adequate grasp of what is apparently the main feminine role." The *Monthly Film Bulletin* kindly called Jayne and Duryea "competent."

Jayne in *The Burglar* was at a turning point in her career: sincere and unglamorous, she gave as good a turn as Marilyn Monroe had in RKO's 1952 *Clash by Night* before 20th Century-Fox Marilyn'd her up. Had Jayne been bought by Columbia from Warner Bros., the studio's notorious Harry Cohn might have put her into the roles played by Gloria Grahame, Eva Marie Saint, or Kim Novak in their mid-'50s films. But Jayne was destined for a brighter, sillier, and more colorful future.

4

Jayne Mansfield is undoubtedly the Broadway Gal of the Year.

Earl Wilson

A t the same time Jayne was filming *The Burglar,* she had another iron on the fire, though she had very mixed feelings about it. Her agent Bill Shiffrin managed to get her an audition for a major Broadway show, set to start rehearsals on August 18.

Will Success Spoil Rock Hunter? was written by George Axelrod, who'd recently had a huge hit with *The Seven Year Itch;* it was to be produced by Jule Styne (who produced *Pal Joey* and also wrote the scores of *Gentlemen Prefer Blondes, Bells Are Ringing,* and *Funny Girl*). This would be Axelrod's first directorial attempt, so he was understandably picky about the cast. Axelrod was inspired to write this skewering of Hollywood, agents, and success by his experiences with *The Seven Year Itch,* which ran on Broadway from 1952 to 1955 and which was twisted and rewritten (to Axelrod's financial advantage but professional dismay) as the more-famous 1955 movie starring Marilyn Monroe.

Anyone who has seen the movie version of *Rock Hunter* will be baffled by the play, which bears no resemblance to it at all. *Will Success Spoil Rock Hunter?* was actually a terrible title. It stemmed from the first big story of the hero (a fan-magazine writer), "Will Success Spoil Rock Hudson?" Hudson's agent threatened to sue (though Hudson himself thought it was funny), and after "Hudson" became "Hunter," the title no longer made sense. *Will Success Spoil Rock Hunter?* was a Faust story in which neophyte writer George MacCauley (played by Orson Bean) sells his soul to the devil (agent Irving "Sneaky" LaSalle, a jab at real-life agent Irving "Swifty" Lazar, played by Martin Gabel). George becomes an Oscar-winning screenwriter and wins the love of Marilyn Monroe-esque movie star Rita Marlowe. Other characters include playwright Michael Freeman (Walter Matthau) and Rita's football-star husband Bronk Brannigan (William Thourlby). Bit parts were played by Carol Grace (divorced from writer William Saroyan, she went on to marry costar Matthau in 1959) and Tina Louise, the future Ginger on *Gilligan's Island.*

Jayne, of course, was to read for the part of Rita Marlowe—Bill Shiffrin arranged for her to take a train to New York and meet Jule Styne on July 28, the day after her steam-scalding on *The Burglar* set (indeed, the dramatization of that story may have been an excuse to get her a day off). Styne was charmed by her and could see that she looked the role, so he arranged for her to audition for George Axelrod.

"My problem was whether to get an actress to play a broad or a broad to play a broad," said Axelrod. "When an agent brought in Jayne Mansfield . . . the question was answered. She was not the girl to make boys write clean words on clean fences." Jayne auditioned in a red leotard, "swinging her hips, smiling widely, lips glistening." Styne's biographer recalls his reaction: "Sold on first sight. An absolute click." Styne jumped up and told her, "Don't read anymore. You'll spoil the illusion. You look the part. You are the part. You're hired, if Mr. Axelrod agrees." Mr. Axelrod agreed.

Jayne was signed at $350 a week and professed herself very happy—a leading role in a major Broadway show, after all—but her eyes were still set on movie stardom. Bryon and Shiffrin had to convince her this show was a step in that direction, and of course they were right. A few months later, Jayne admitted, "My movie career didn't seem to be hitting out too well, and Warner Bros., who had my contract, looked like they might drop me any day. . . . The really great thing about this deal, though, is that I'm being recognized as an actress instead of just as a body. You know, blondes with big bosoms have a hard time." Jayne went on, "A lot of girls wanted the role," naming Sheree North, Barbara Britton, and even—ridiculously— Marilyn Monroe. "That trip to Florida started everything," she realized. "I don't mind posing for leg art; I think it's good for your career. If you get too Grace Kellyish, you're overlooking a large audience of men."

Shiffrin secured her release from Warner Bros. (which had pretty much lost interest in her by that point), and rehearsals started, aiming for two weeks in Philadelphia and two weeks in Boston before opening on October 12 at the Belasco Theater on Broadway (actually, on West 44th Street).

"Jayne took her big chance and romped off with it," said Axelrod, though "whenever we wanted her for rehearsal she was opening a supermarket in Westchester or spending the afternoon as Miss Cantaloupe in southern Jersey." Sylvia Herscher, the show's associate producer and manager, agreed that "she'd get up early in the morning and drag herself out to the Bayside supermarket opening. She was the queen of the supermarkets. There wasn't a supermarket in New York she didn't open that year."

Herscher told Martha Saxton that she found Jayne a trial: she "was always late and had no discipline. She thought she was being sweet and adorable, but she wasn't. She wasn't professional." But, Herscher admitted, "You couldn't dislike her. She just always gave you a lot of trouble. She insisted on running around backstage nude."

Jayne was late once too often, and Herscher quite rightly called her on the carpet for it: "I got up and said she could leave. There was dead silence. She turned green. She shaped up for about three weeks." On the plus side, "She had no stage fright. She never lost her temper. She said, 'I'll try, I'll be better. I promise.' . . . She was just a crazy lady."

When the show moved to New York, Jayne and Jayne Marie (along with a menagerie of dogs) took up residence at the Gorham Hotel on West 55th Street, two blocks east of Broadway. As the years passed, hotel managers learned to dread the approach of Jayne Mansfield and her traveling zoo of animals, children, and press parties, but the Gorham was taken by surprise. Eventually, it sued Jayne for $10,000 for the damages, and the Gorham was far from the only hotel to curse her name.

The out-of-town reviews were promising, though that never assures a Broadway hit. The *Philadelphia Inquirer* praised "a cast which hardly could be improved upon. . . . Jayne Mansfield plays the movie queen with the right note of ingenuousness which allows her to explode some of the play's more potent lines." The *Boston Globe* called *Rock Hunter* "a fast and racy comedy," adding that it did need some cutting and rewriting. "Jayne Mansfield as the platinum job with swivel hips . . . does not speak with precisely the jeweled tones of a Katharine Cornell, but her endowments drown her voice, anyway," wrote the *Globe*'s critic.

Will Success Spoil Rock Hunter? opened on Broadway on October 13,

1955, in the midst of a near-record season of new shows. Stars competing with Jayne for audiences included Claudette Colbert, Tyrone Power, Carol Channing, Boris Karloff, and Lunt and Fontanne; other shows debuting that year were *A View from the Bridge, The Diary of Anne Frank,* and Rosalind Russell in *Auntie Mame;* the press also gave a passing mention to a musical version of *Pygmalion* starring Rex Harrison and Julie Andrews, which was preparing to open early the following year.

While *Rock Hunter* didn't get unanimously good reviews, it was acknowledged to be one of the most fun, glittering evenings in town, and Jayne became that fabled creature, the Overnight Star. Walter Winchell called her a "talented actress. The town's only sunshine during the three-day deluge." The International News Service's review was headlined "Jayne Mansfield Outdoes Marilyn in Latest Show"; critic Joan Hanauer mentioned that she "spends almost the entire first act in nothing but a Turkish towel, and in part of the third act wears a sequined evening dress that's so tight the wardrobe mistress must have to cut her out of it after each performance. . . . Such celebrities [in the audience] as Margaret Truman, Clifton Webb, Phil Silvers and Gloria Vanderbilt [were] laughing so hard they stopped the show." John Chapman of the *New York Daily News* summed Jayne up as "a masterpiece of architecture." He also singled her out not for her curves but her talent: "Jayne Mansfield plays a stock role of a dumb Hollywood broad—a type; but she does it with some humor of her own and therefore rates as a comedienne." (Not everyone loved the show; Bob Thomas of the AP felt that it was "mighty slim" but "brightened by Orson Bean and Jayne Mansfield.")

Jayne graced her first *Life* magazine cover on September 11, along with other promising young "Broadway Cinderellas" Judy Tyler (*Pipe Dream*), Diane Cilento (*Tiger at the Gates*), Lois Smith (*The Wisteria Trees*), and Susan Strasberg (*The Diary of Anne Frank*). Jayne was given the most coverage inside the magazine: photos and a profile of "the buxom Jayne Mansfield . . . who came out of nowhere to grab what could be one of the plums of the season."

John Bustin of Jayne's hometown *Austin-American,* who had been so nasty to her earlier that year, continued to make his opinion known: "Since displaying her limited but appealing talents on the local Playhouse boards," he wrote, "the bosomy Miss Mansfield has undoubtedly developed into one of Hollywood's most outstanding figures—a accomplishment wrought more by a heady dose of cheesecake pictures than by her work in only three movies. . . . At any rate, Miss Mansfield's Broadway debut is being eyed with considerable interest. And if you don't think the reasons are obvious, take another look at that picture accompanying this column."

Through the autumn of 1955, as *Rock Hunter* continued doing well at the box office, Jayne's fellow cast members and backstage crew tried to adjust to her scatty work habits. When she later became a film star—both in big studio projects and cheap indies—Jayne was always praised for her professionalism. But in the first rush of Broadway fame, she could be infuriating. George Axelrod said, "There is absolutely no chance, whether by design or coincidence, that Jayne will ever do two shows alike."

Orson Bean said in 2019, "I loved Jayne," but he admitted that "the other guys in the cast, Walter Matthau and Martin Gabel, did not. I think they were jealous of her. She was the reason everyone came to see the show. In the wings one night, waiting to go on, Matthau grumbled, 'the bitch upstaged me again last night.' I said, 'Walter, she does it by accident, she's an amateur.' He snarled, 'Yeah? How come she never once *down*-stages me?'"

Bean remembered her as "a sweet, simple girl. With incredible boobs. She was the toast of the town and loving it. She was darting about the stage like a little kid. She'd call me into her dressing room: 'Orsie—look through the crack in the curtain and see if anybody famous is out front.' If there was a celebrity in the house, Jayne always gave a better performance. If there wasn't one, I made a name up."

And—as always—Jayne made herself available to the press. When she wasn't posing for photos or attending benefits, she was giving interviews. Most of them were the usual chatty fluff about her role and her career. Jayne told Jack Gaver of the *Paterson News* that her character Rita Marlowe "is a little naïve—but not dumb—kittenish, friendly, ambitious, and with a sense of humor. I'm somewhat like that myself." She told Louella Parsons that she had duly registered with the Actors Studio, where all "serious" New York actors had to genuflect to Lee Strasberg, but "I haven't had a chance to attend class yet." To Joe Hyams of the *New York Herald Tribune,* she mused about dropping the bombshell image: "With brown hair, my face and figure would look like 16. Well, my figure not so much maybe, but my face. I could play down my lips and wear loose clothes and I'd be a natural for serious TV."

She did make some significant missteps. She told Dorothy Kilgallen, "It's my responsibility to pick up the play if anything happens, and sometimes I have to carry the whole play." And Joe Hyams portrayed her as bragging, "It's nothing, really nothing. Why, anyone can do it. After ignoring me for so long now all the movie studios are giving me a rush. Instead of them doing me a favor by seeing me I'm doing them a favor and seeing them." She may have been quite right, but one does not say such things out loud, and Jayne must have gotten the cold shoulder and a severe talking-to from her coworkers, as she never came off as such a self-important bitch again. Columnist Kaspar Monahan took her to task, writing, "Miss Mansfield should not let Manhattan scribblers' reporters on her Broadway debut go to her head. That part of her anatomy is not too impressive, comparatively speaking."

But mostly Jayne just reveled in her fame and her future movie prospects; as Orson Bean noted, she was having the time of her life. "It's great, it's just great. And I love it, every minute of it," she told Jack Geyer of the *L.A. Times.* "I'm happy as a lark." She rejoiced that "I've grown so much," at which Geyer admitted to eyeing her breasts. "Career-wise, I mean," she added wearily. "No matter what happens just keep fighting. Ever since I was a little girl I knew I was going to be a great star. I'm not there yet, but I'm still trying. You've just got to keep going." She told Joan Hanauer of the International News Service that she wasn't going in for Shakespeare or Ibsen, like Marilyn Monroe was rumored to obsess about, "but I'd like good, solid, meaty roles. But I do love Shakespeare—or maybe I better say I love George Axelrod and Shakespeare."

She even agreed to reminisce about her Austin Civic Theater days with the ever-snide John Bustin. "Mel Pape—is he still the director?" she asked. "You know, Mel really gave me a lot in the way of stage training. Without that experience, even though I didn't do much, I couldn't have been able to go from movies to the stage. I suppose you might even say that the Civic Theater is in part responsible for whatever success I'm having here in New York."

As autumn turned to winter and Jayne continued to light up the stage, movie studios did indeed come sniffing around, with Bill Shiffrin's encouragement. Newspaper columns got word out (with a strong push from Jim Byron) that "Buddy Adler has flown to New York to talk to Jayne about *Bus Stop,* as Marilyn was being so difficult"; "Dore Schary of MGM is talking to Jayne about a contract"; "Jayne to be tested for a Harlow bio-pic"; "Jayne had a meeting at MGM's New York offices"; and "Four studios are after her for movies."

It escaped no one's notice that this blonde upstart was doing a hilariously vicious Marilyn Monroe parody. "Whether Marilyn will see her attorneys about it all is a new $64,000 question," wrote Erskine Johnson of the National News Agency. "She is as beautiful as Marilyn Monroe (in every department) and effortlessly delivers the most devastating impression in years," said Walter Winchell, and Martin Starr on Texas radio KBWD even called her "the rich man's Marilyn Monroe." Joan Hanauer headlined her review, "Jayne Mansfield Outdoes Marilyn in Latest Show," going on to write that "the boys in the balcony will never believe it isn't Marilyn Monroe. The very blonde Miss Mansfield, who could give Miss Monroe a real battle in a bathing suit contest . . . outdoes Marilyn as she copies the Monroe trademarks—the wiggly walk, the shoulder shrugs, the diction and the exaggerated lip movements."

But Jayne insisted she wasn't doing a Marilyn: "No. It's a composite of all the glamour girls," she told Earl Wilson. She added, to Aline Mosby of the United Press, that "Marilyn and I are completely different." Jayne also mentioned up-and-coming Sheree North, rather contemptuously calling her "a very competent little actress. We don't compete for the same parts."

Jayne also threw some major shade at Marilyn. "I've always thought, since I was a little girl, that she was the most beautiful woman in the world," she smiled demurely. "You know, I really don't look like her at all. You can take practically any fairly shaped girl, bleach her hair, wet her lips, put her into a tight dress and have her walk a little wiggly and—well, we all look a little alike."

Marilyn and Jayne never actually met, though they brushed past each other on December 12, 1955, at an Actors Studio Benefit premiere of *The Rose Tattoo*. All of Broadway and much of Hollywood was at the Sheraton-Astor Roof in Times Square that night: Helen Hayes, Marlon Brando, Joan Crawford, Leslie Caron, Mary Martin, Orson Welles, Tennessee Williams, Michael Redgrave. But Jayne—in a spaghetti-strap dress, rather demure for her—had eyes only for one star. Marilyn was seated at a table, wearing a black dress (also "sex-symbol demure"), and Jayne hovered behind her like the moon orbiting the Earth. For once Jayne looked nervous and shy, as Marilyn—purposely?—ignored her, smiling at the camera and chatting with her tablemates, Jayne too abashed to actually tap her on the shoulder.

❤

Through the holiday season, Jayne kept as busy as her performance schedule would allow. She put in an appearance at the Knickerbocker Ball (along with the elite of society and the arts, including the Viscountess de Ribes, Mrs. David Gimbel, and John Raitt); she attended the Artists and Models Ball, and went to the Night of Stars Benefit at Madison Square Garden. She guested on the *Make Up Your Mind* radio show, talking about "how to cut down the ranks of bachelors."

She was named—astonishingly—on the list of best-dressed men and women chosen by the nation's stylists. Even more astonishing, Vice President Richard Nixon was named best-dressed man (others to make the list included Conrad Hilton, Eddie Fisher, Grace Kelly, and Claire Booth Luce). Jayne Mansfield 1956 calendars were more requested than Marilyn Monroe calendars (western pin-up girls, religious themes, Maxfield Parrish paintings, and household tips rounded out the top sellers).

Louella Parsons, who would be a champion of Jayne's throughout her career, proclaimed her "the toast of Broadway with three studios standing in line to sign her up for pictures. . . . I believe that when she returns to Hollywood you can look to see her zoom to the top the way she has in her Broadway play." This clipping had pride of place in Jayne's growing scrapbook collection, as those prophecies echoed her hopes exactly. Jayne was having a great time, but couldn't wait to shake the dust of Broadway off her shoes and return to Hollywood.

"The whole town's talking about her," wrote M. Oakley Stafford in the *Hartford Courant.* "She's the rave of the hour." Young actress Cloris Leachman, appearing on Broadway in *The Rack,* called Jayne "the most amazing phenomenon on Broadway." The influential Earl Wilson proclaimed her "the Broadway Gal of the Year. . . . She and the new Coliseum are New York's biggest buildups, and builds, of 1955." The *New York Daily News* noted that Jayne "receives fan letters with cash enclosed ('Go out and buy something and think of me when you use it')." She told the paper that "I know I'm getting ahead because they're naming dolls after me, there's a song called the 'Mansfield Mambo,' Steve Allen wants me on his program, and there are two books about me. Not only that but I'm shadowed around by Ernie Havemann of *Life* magazine for a story they're getting ready to do."

Newsman Ed Reardon attended a party for comic Joey Adams's new joke book. "'Jayne Mansfield,' someone shouted, and the stampede was on," Reardon reported. "A year ago nobody in the room would have lifted an eyebrow at the mention of the name, but Miss Mansfield has come a long way since then. . . . In the twinkling of a flashbulb Miss Mansfield was rang-ing her statuesque figure alongside Joey Adams, Joe E. Lewis and anybody else who could manage to fight his way into the picture."

As 1955 turned into 1956 and Jayne continued to be one of the shining lights of Broadway, five-year-old Jayne Marie whiled away her days at the Gorham, attended to by hired nannies, hotel staff, and Jayne's friends. Jayne was photographed reading her bedtime stories ("I always rush home to put Jayne Marie to bed and help her say her prayers. We turn on the picture of Jesus by her bed and she says her prayers") and at ballet class with her ("Sometime during the day we try to squeeze in our dancing lesson—we take ballet and tap lessons together"); the two took part in the New York Easter Parade in April 1956.

But Jayne's description of the day-to-day life of a Broadway gadabout does not leave much room for motherhood: "We get up around eight and there's always somebody here to take pictures by nine. I'm always being named Miss This or Queen of That. So we take pictures for an hour or so. I'm a guest or something at some sort of luncheon for some cause or another. In the afternoon there are generally interviews or more pictures or radio shows or something. Then I generally have to go to some dinner or some kind of affair. It's a hectic life. I need a lot of energy. So does Jayne Marie."

What Jayne Marie needed was to be back with her father in San Francisco or her grandparents in Texas, but to Jayne, being a "good, loving mother" meant having your children with you always, everywhere. This was to become more of an issue as Jayne produced sibling after sibling for Jayne Marie.

That *Life* cover Jayne had spoken of was published just after her twenty-third birthday. This time it was a solo shot, a lovely, elegant image of Jayne in a scoop-necked pink dress and dangly earrings, her hair swept back, posing in front of the lights of Broadway as if she owned the street. Writer Ernest Havemann was prescient about her career, saying that she was "only in what might be called the larval stage. Her face has not yet been metamorphosed by Hollywood's makeup and lighting experts, nor has her mind by exposure to the Actors Studio, poetry and imaginative movie producers."

But what he wrote about Jayne in early 1956 was to hold true for the rest of her life: he noted that she was "friendly and frank, perhaps even somewhat naïve in her own calculating way. Miss Mansfield does not even obey cliché No. 1 of the movie queen, which is to act bored with success. No teenager ever exhibited so much tenacity at seeking autographs as she does at signing them; she will stand in the wind, rain or snow until her last admirer is satisfied."

She was ubiquitous through that Broadway run in 1956, giving so many interviews that she was already becoming a joke; reporters didn't know whether to feel grateful or used. "Jayne Mansfield didn't pose for a picture all day," wrote Earl Wilson. "Some people said New York suddenly seemed a ghost town and things certainly were abnormal." (Journalist Marj Heyduck noted wryly that the reason Jayne was in Earl Wilson's column almost every day was because her character in *Rock Hunter* bragged about how she was in Earl Wilson's column almost every day.) The *Davenport Daily Times*'s Tom O'Malley and Bob Cuniff professed themselves "fed up with Jayne Mansfield. The girl's publicity-insane, appearing on some show every day, it seems." Reporter Mel Heimer noted that more serious, less successful, performers were jealous, "making snide, lofty remarks about her. 'So, she gets her picture in the paper all the time,' they carp. 'Surely she doesn't think that'll make her a success in the acting profession, does [she]?'"

And the Jayne Mansfield jokes started. Eventually they centered on her figure, but in early 1956 they were about her publicity: "The newest cocktail is the Jayne Mansfield. While you're drinking it the bartender takes your picture." The *New York Daily News* kept a tally of the wisecracks about her: (1) she's mad at her press agent because he hasn't gotten her name in the obits columns, (2) she broke the steak-broiling record at the Charcoal Room using photographers' flashlights, (3) they've invented a new camera that comes with a picture of Jayne Mansfield already in it.

In April, Ben Gross of the *New York Daily News* interviewed "the retiring little woodland flower" at the Gorham. She wore slacks, a red sweater, and no shoes. Jayne Marie was being babysat by one Faithful Charity, a follower of Philadelphia-based religious cult leader Father Divine. "Not so busy today," Jayne told Gross. "I only had a matinée and evening performance and only attended three or four parties. Of course, during my six months of Broadway, my picture has been snapped at least 10,000 times. I've appeared at hundreds and hundreds of affairs—luncheons, charity events, cocktail parties, get-togethers, premieres, supermarket openings, fashion shows and what-have-yous. I never refuse. I guess that's why your darling newspaper, the *News*, called me The Girl Who Can't Say No."

Jayne went on talking, nonstop, veering between delightfully silly dumb-blonde pronouncements and thoughtful theories about her career.

She told Walter Winchell that her favorite things were "steak, mink, pink Jaguars and going to the Stork Club," and that "I'm just the same as anyone else. I like good music and good literature and all that stuff. I'm well-rounded, you see." (Winchell added, "Uh-huh.") She insisted to Ben Gross that she was "a good dramatic actress. I proved it down in Texas while at the university and now I want the chance to prove it in television. I've got more than a figure, even though, when I go into the movies, they're going to play me up—I fear—as just another sexy gal . . . do me a favor. Just tell everybody that I'm a good actress, emotional stuff and all that, you know."

Jayne insisted,

> My personality is entirely different from the pictures. They don't show the real me. They make me out to be a kind of character. I'm not a character at all. Actually, I'm a person living life and having fun. I'm uninhibited. I try to be inhibited, but it never works that way. I know where I am all the time. I've got my feet on the ground. I have a mission to accomplish, but I'm not going to turn into a stuffy individual. In show business, there are artists and personalities. Artists dedicate themselves to their art. Personalities include people like Gable and Monroe, and I suppose I fall in that category. I'm still in the personality class, but I hope to be an artist soon. I'd love to make a picture with Gable. He's my dream. People say I have the propensities of Marilyn Monroe, but I wouldn't want to be a second anything.

She had a 3D portrait painted of herself (the mind boggles) by Canadian artist Arthur D'Artois. "It's *divoon*," cooed Jayne. "I want to be a sex symbol; that is, a pure sex symbol. Nothing lewd or cheap. Another thing, I just love newsstands, don't you? I love to see myself on magazine covers." (An etymological note: Jayne popularized but did not coin *divoon*. The first use in print was by Walter Winchell, calling Jean Harlow "too, too divoon" in 1934—a bit of gay slang from the 1920s "pansy craze" that filtered down to Winchell's column.)

And when not talking to reporters, Jayne was courting them—and her ever-growing public—by appearing everywhere and doing everything. It's amazing she ever made it onstage, and goodness knows Jayne Marie was seeing a lot more of her babysitter Faithful Charity than she was her own mother. The *Philadelphia Inquirer* noted in March 1956 that "Jayne Mansfield does get around, especially where cameramen are present. In the past few days she was photographed at a dozen places, including two movie premieres—although she obviously couldn't stay to see the films without missing her own performance in *Will Success Spoil Rock Hunter?* Be it charity, dog show, or supermarket opening, Miss Mansfield is there, ready and posing."

Jayne attended an Adlai Stevenson rally at Sardi's; Martha Raye's thirtieth anniversary in show business party at Danny's Hide-a-Way; the opening of Eartha Kitt's Roxanne Dressmaker shop in Harlem (and the after-party at Smalls' Paradise); a Joey Adams "brawl" at Gilmore's on East 54th Street (other attendees were Dagmar, the McGuire sisters, Rocky Marciano, and Mike Wallace); the Red Cross Fiftieth Anniversary Parade in Brooklyn; and the opening of a Paramus, New Jersey, bowling alley (she showed up forty minutes late, with two Chihuahuas, Charles and Phillip, both in red sweaters). She was grand marshal of the Junior Chamber of Commerce Parade in Newark (waving from a convertible at the "sparse crowd," she was followed by a giant chicken float for the Vineland Poultry and Egg Festival; on its return to Vineland the chicken burned down).

She appeared at the Coliseum ball, borrowing a violin from Meyer Davis and shocking everyone by competently playing two pieces. Jayne, Sammy Davis Jr., David Wayne, Shelley Winters, and others performed at Madison Square Garden for the Gustave Hartman Home for Children benefit; she made "one of her rare public appearances" (the *New York Daily News* being sarcastic) at Palisades Amusement Park: "The actress and a corps of professional models will be the focus point for an outing of amateur photographers." Jayne (looking "shiny-faced, wind-blown and rather unappealing") attended the New York Dress Institute hat show; a bored Tina Louise escaped halfway through, muttering, "Whew, what a relief."

When Jayne appeared as the Mystery Guest on *What's My Line?*, wiseacres suggested the title be changed to *What's My Neckline?* Jayne, Judy Tyler, and Elise Rhodes judged an all-male beauty contest at Larry Matthews's Beauty City; she ushered at the premiere of *Doctor at Sea* at the Trans-Lux on 52nd Street to raise money for the Heart Fund; unveiled a plaque at Roseland Ballroom with the names of couples who'd met there and gotten married; was queen of the Artists and Models Ball (Gene Rayburn was her king); dined at Chez Vito with George Jessel; and showed up at LaGuardia Airport to be photographed with the Oscar statuettes, which were in transit. All this in the spring of 1956 while starring nightly—twice on matinée days—in a Broadway show. Not surprisingly, she ranked among the ten most photographed Americans in 1956 (for the record, the other nine were President Eisenhower, Marilyn Monroe, Princess Grace, Cardinal Francis Spellman, Adlai Stevenson, Estes Kevauver, Billy Graham, Vice President Nixon, and Secretary of State John Foster Dulles).

As *New York Daily News* columnist Robert Sylvester deadpanned, "If Jayne Mansfield doesn't watch her step, people are gonna start talking about her."

❤

The dream of a good majority of New Yorkers is to star in a Broadway show, but for Jayne this was just a step in the right direction: the fame and fun of *Rock Hunter* was all very well and good, but she was a modern girl who had her sights set on *movie* stardom. She had Jim Byron, Bill Shiffrin, and Greg Bautzer making phone calls, contacting whatever influential people they knew on her behalf.

In February 1956, 20th Century-Fox tested her for the upcoming film *The Wayward Bus,* and according to Louella Parsons, "They're all very high on Jayne, and it looks very much as if she'll get an exclusive contract at that studio." Parsons—a fan of Jayne's—added that "Marilyn Monroe is only making four pictures in four years on a non-exclusive contract, and Jayne looks like Marilyn without even trying."

George Axelrod directed Jayne's *Wayward Bus* test, and she—for some unfathomable reason—wanted to do a scene from *A Streetcar Named Desire.* He pointedly and not very nicely told her, "Unless people are prepared for what's coming, they might figure you're imitating Judy Holliday imitating Marilyn Monroe trying to play Blanche."

In July, *Will Success Spoil Rock Hunter?* moved from the Belasco Theater to the Shubert (*Too Late the Phalarope* replaced *Rock Hunter* at the Belasco; it opened and closed like a camera shutter). Bowing to the obvious, the producers put Jayne's name in lights on the Shubert marquee: "I'm a full-fledged star now," Jayne enthused to Louella Parsons. She insisted to Charles Mercer of the AP, "My whole career has been revamped. I'm launched on a new policy of 'don't do anything.' Now I'm turning down everything—cocktail parties and guest appearances and all that. I got where I am by promoting myself. I did just about everything. But not anymore. I don't miss the parties at all." If Mercer laughed in her face, he politely left that out of his article. Reporter Claire Cox did find her remarkably dressed down for her interview, though, in a baggy flannel shirt, blue jeans, gray socks, and no shoes. Cox did note a pile of minks on the table, including a pink stole: "A girl needs mink, and it might as well be pink," Jayne reasoned.

5

I see a girl, blonde hair. . . . And she had a *milkshake.* I fell in love! And so did she. Both of us.

Mickey Hargitay

Jayne did not limit her off-hours to just publicity, benefits, and interviews—or at least, she incorporated those into her social life. Jayne was a very pretty young woman, unattached, and in love with love. Every heterosexual man in New York was after her phone number, as were many a gay man who wanted an amusing friend and his name in the paper.

Some of the dates were just publicity exercises set up by Jayne's public-relations people, or by her date's, but at least one turned into a genuine romance. And one man cynically toyed with Jayne: director Nicholas Ray. Ray was in his mid-forties, reasonably handsome, and the director of such dark, offbeat films as *They Live by Night, In a Lonely Place,* and *Johnny Guitar.* He also had a very colorful private life: he was divorced from actress Gloria Grahame, who'd been having an affair with Ray's teenage son (she and Tony Ray later married and divorced).

Early in 1955 Ray was preparing for what would become his most famous film, the teen-angst drama *Rebel without a Cause,* which was filmed that spring. Up-and-coming James Dean would play the title role, with Sal Mineo, Dennis Hopper, and Nick Adams in support. The female lead, troubled but sympathetic Judy, was not yet cast—Natalie Wood, a seventeen-year-old former child star, was eventually cast, but Ray was not sold on her at first, feeling she was too squeaky-clean.

He began dating Jayne, teasing her with the possibility of playing Judy. The *New York Daily News* named them as an item in February; they went to the Photographers' Ball at El Morocco (he was "a perfect gentleman," said Jayne), and in March Louella Parsons tagged the relationship as "serious."

In early February Ray tested Jayne for *Rebel without a Cause,* but she was never in serious consideration for the part; nasty rumors later circulated that there was not even film in the camera. Hedda Hopper duly noted Jayne's screen test, along with those of Wood, Debbie Reynolds, Pat Crowley, and Lori Nelson. Jayne called Ray a "rare combination of brawn, brains and achievement," but he seems to have seen her as nothing more than arm candy. Decades later, he told interviewer Mel Neuhaus that he "freaked out" at the thought of Jayne playing Judy: "She's supposed to be the girl next door. Not the girl next door to a strip joint!" *Rebel without a Cause* opened in October 1955, and both Jayne and Nicholas Ray went on to other romances, but they still hooked up as late as January 1956.

Through the first half of 1955, Jayne was seen on the town with press agent George Bennett, *Limelight* magazine editor Chet Whitehorn, actors Jacques Sernas and Lance Fuller (who took her to a twenty-second birthday dinner at the Mocambo), Gregory Peck (who was conveniently between wives), Robert Wagner, Hugh O'Brian, Vince Edwards, and Race Gentry (that last actor was John Gentri, rechristened by agent Henry Willson). She was also seen dancing and dining with her lawyer Greg Bautzer, who made it quite clear years later that matters were strictly platonic.

When quizzed by the *Sydney Morning Herald* on her ideal men, Jayne named Adlai Stevenson ("He is a strong, powerful man, and so sure of himself. I admire his strength of character"), actor Richard Egan ("I like his deeply spiritual side"), fashion designer Oleg Cassini ("One of the romantic ones who sends boxes of flowers—I like that"), and singer Johnnie Ray ("He just makes me want to listen to him and get caught up in that little old white cloud"). But her big romance in late 1955 and early '56 was Merle Roy "Robbie" Robertson.

The tall, silver-haired, and very handsome Robertson was an American Airlines pilot whom Jayne met in transit. "I took one look at him and swooned, and I said to myself, 'I must have that!'" said Jayne. "I did something I've never done in my life. I gave him my telephone number and asked him to call me." Call he did, and soon Jayne was sighing dreamily, "I don't think success means as much unless you have somebody to share it with. When things go wrong it's nice to have somebody say, 'Darling, I love you anyway.'" He gave her a $500 watch, which is also nice to have.

Jayne being Jayne, she also gave out amusing quotes she knew would get used: "My beau, Robbie Robertson, has handsome charcoal gray hair! And you should see the Italian silk suit he has to match it. He always wears pink socks. I like men with charcoal gray hair, charcoal gray suits, pink socks and pink tie. You see, my pink house has charcoal gray furnishings. And my pink Jaguar is upholstered in charcoal gray." However, when quizzed about marriage by Sheilah Graham, Jayne admitted, "I rather don't think I will. I don't see any sense in marrying when I'm getting the glamour buildup."

Jayne introduced Robertson to her childhood friend Charlsa Wolf, who approved: "I liked him," she told Martha Saxton. "A very nice guy. He was smart and had Jayne's best interest at heart." But the romance—as genuine as it seemed to be—did not last past May 1956, at which time Robertson transferred his affections to actress Linda Darnell, whom he married in 1957. (Robertson and Darnell split in 1963, and both died young—she in a 1965 house fire, and he of a heart attack that same year.)

The most embarrassing of Jayne's suitors was "Broadway playboy" Count Stephano V. Tirone, whom Jayne called "very sweet, very courtly and refreshing. Italian counts are *so* friendly that I tried to have protection along when I was with him." He turned out to be one Stephen Vlahovitch of Long Island, a church sexton with a wife and two kids, which was revealed after he died in a car accident in April 1956 on his way home from a date with Jayne at Toots Shor's.

❤

On May 13, 1956, the course of Jayne's life changed—that night, she and Jule Styne attended Mae West's show at the Latin Quarter. In 1954 Mae—her film and theater career on the wane—began touring nightclubs in a music and comedy act, backed by eight musclemen dressed in diaper-like shorts. Though tales of Mae's casting couch were probably overstated, she did run her chorus boys' lives like a strict schoolmistress: they had to stay tanned and muscle-bound, and they were certainly not to be seen with any other women.

By 1956 one of her musclemen was Miklós "Mickey" Hargitay, who had been born in Budapest in 1926. He immigrated to the United States in 1947 to avoid serving in the army (the Hungarian Communist Party had just won that year's parliamentary elections). Mickey settled in Cleveland and married Mary Birge in 1948; the following year, their daughter Tina was born.

Mickey earned his living as a plumber, carpenter, and contractor, also learning landscaping. He was excellent at those trades and thoroughly enjoyed them. But he was sidelined into show business in 1952: "This guy talked me into entering a weight-lifting contest in Indiana," Mickey told the *Oakland Tribune*'s Bill Fisit. "I won the contest. I could see myself getting muscular, so I decided to try to get absolutely as big as I could get. I was aiming at the Mr. Universe title and in 1956 I went to London to compete, against 120 others. I won. It was a very touching moment, for I knew I'd reached the top."

With the body of a Tom of Finland drawing and a handsome, boyish face, Mickey was just what Mae West was looking for. He was also good-natured (*too* good-natured at times) and wore his heart on his sleeve. But—as Mae and Jayne and the first Mrs. Hargitay would discover—Mickey Hargitay could only be pushed so far.

The meeting of Mickey and Jayne was no freak of fate; Mickey's fame as Mae's handsomest chorus boy ("the male Jayne Mansfield") was already widespread, and Jayne told Jule Styne she wanted two things that night: an introduction to Mr. Universe and a $6 steak for her dog. She got both.

Mickey—decades later—recalled their first meeting. "I was singing a song, 'Everything I Have Is Yours,' and I was looking down there, and I see a girl, blonde hair, just like Mae West. And she had a *milkshake*. I fell in love! And so did she. Both of us." The two briefly met after the show, phone numbers were exchanged, and the game was on.

Both Jayne and Mickey were working in shows, so meeting proved difficult: performances, rehearsals, and (for Jayne) publicity and benefit appearances took precedence. But within a week or two, gossip columnists took notice of the eye-catching couple. "Jayne Mansfield admits she's found her dream man in Mickey Hargitay, the muscular chap who is almost better known as 'Mr. Universe of 1956,'" wrote Dorothy Kilgallen. "They only managed to squeeze in a few dates before he had to leave town, but that was enough to convince Jayne they were made for each other." Earl Wilson wrote that Mickey "phones Jayne three times a day. . . . 'This could develop into something,' says Jayne, whose build is equally famous; 'he's so modest, and never says anything about his muscles. He's really divoon.'"

Mae West, who had appeared on Broadway before Jayne or Mickey were born and who was now in her fourth decade of playing the sex symbol, pitched a fit and told Mickey to drop Jayne—at least in public. "Rather than embrace the relationship we had, she was against it," said Mickey. "Miss West, she give me hell, she say, 'how dare you go out there and make a spectacle of yourself with that cheap blonde,' and I said, 'Miss West, that is not so—I *love* this girl . . . and I'm gonna marry her.'"

Dorothy Kilgallen reported, "Mae West is furious. . . . She complains that after Jayne met him, she—Mae—scarcely saw him except on the stage of the club where they were working, because Jayne used to come and pick him up as soon as his bicep-flexing chores were finished." Jayne and Mickey took off for dates on the beach—where they gave the other sunbathers horrendous inferiority complexes—and journeyed to the Catskills in upstate New York, where they were photographed nuzzling in a gondola. Jayne (or perhaps Jim Byron) came up with one of her best wisecracks at this time, telling Harrison Carroll, "We don't have so much fun dancing. Mickey has a 50-inch chest and I have a 40-inch chest, and we both have short arms." It got such a great reception that she repeated the gag for years.

The mid-1950s were boom years for headline-grabbing show-business romances: Debbie Reynolds and Eddie Fisher, Natalie Wood and Robert Wagner, Grace Kelly and Prince Rainier, Marilyn Monroe and Arthur Miller, Kay Kendall and Rex Harrison, Elizabeth Taylor and Michael Wilding and Mike Todd and Eddie Fisher. Jayne and Mickey were like a neon caricature of star romance—they knew it and they played it up. Mickey, who had a great sense of humor, occasionally signed fans' autograph books "Arthur Miller."

Jayne and Mickey had something else in common besides their stunning good looks: they were both still legally married, and each had a daughter. And as much as she loved Mickey, Jayne continued seeing Nicholas Ray, who made flying visits to New York that May.

Mary Hargitay, finding none of this amusing, filed for divorce in early June 1956. Later that month she also filed an alienation of affections suit against Jayne, which could very well endanger her future film career. "I had heard the rumors about my husband going out with Jayne Mansfield," Mary testified years later during a child-support hearing. "I asked him about it and he said it was true and that since his first love was show business, and Jayne had promised him a part as her leading man—he would like a divorce. He said if I would quietly get a divorce without the mention of names, he would take care of Tina."

The case made its way quietly through the courts, all parties keeping a low profile, and in September 1956 Mary Hargitay was granted a divorce. She got custody of their daughter and a shockingly stingy $20 a week child support. Jayne, however, remained bound to Paul Mansfield—that divorce would have to wait another year.

Mickey remained with the Mae West company in early June, despite hard feelings all around: his contract stated that there had to be a Mr. Universe in her cast, and until the next contest in a few weeks, he was it.

The whole situation blew up spectacularly on June 6 in Washington, DC, where Mae opened at the Casino Royale. Between the first and second shows, the press crowded in to interview Mae, who held court with two of her favorite musclemen, George Eiferman and Chuck Krauser (who later changed his name to Paul Novak and became Mae's companion till her death in 1980).

Mickey pushed his way into the room, hoping to put his case to the press, he said. All hell broke loose: the musclemen went feral, Mae started yelling, and Krauser decked Mickey. "I was knocked out for a minute," Mickey told the *New York Daily News*. I was falling all over chairs. I never had a fight in my life." Sounding hurt and surprised rather than angry, he went on, "If I had been looking, I could have held my hands up. Or if Chuck said, 'let's fight,' I would have said that we are friends and should not fight."

George Eiferman said that he didn't see Mickey threaten Krauser, adding that Krauser was "emotionally involved with Miss West." Asked if this was the first time men ever fought over her, Mae said, "No, but not in public before," purringly adding (she *was* Mae West, after all), "I prefer doing things behind closed doors."

Mickey filed assault charges against Krauser, who in turned claimed that Mickey made a "threatening gesture" and he hit him in self-defense. Krauser was arrested, and Mae paid his $300 bail. Contract or no, Mae fired Mickey, who pulled off his sunglasses to reveal a black eye: "I am an actor. I have suffered damage."

The case was eventually dismissed, though not before Mae testified before Judge Armand Scott that Mickey had always been professional and cooperative till he got mixed up with Jayne. "She's a dangerous publicity seeker," snapped Mae. "Maybe if she went to school and learned how to act she wouldn't have to do that."

There was no way that Jayne was going to let that go. "There is no truth that I'm having a feud with Mae West," she said. "I admire her—as a *performer*. She just didn't like Mickey having outside dates. She doesn't like any of her muscle boys having dates. People don't like to think romances can be sincere. They always suspect publicity stunts." Building up steam, she let Mae have it with both barrels: "I must say she looks good for her age, even better offstage than on. I hope I can look that good when I'm her age."

In 1964 press agent Irving Zussman claimed the dressing-room fight had been a publicity gag set up by him, though Mickey was an innocent besieged. "Mae's muscle-man show needed business. So I called a press conference and told Mr. California to slug Hargitay. I wanted it to look like the real thing, so I didn't tell Mickey what was coming. He got a real wallop. It made all the papers."

Being jobless did not cool Mickey's love, nor Jayne's. He flew back to New York from DC on June 9, and Jayne met him at Idlewild Airport. "We haven't seen each other for five days," she cooed. They dined at the Bird 'n' Glass on East 47th Street to celebrate her Chihuahua's birthday and chatted with reporters. "We met three weeks ago, didn't we, darling? I got so flustered, he was so beautiful, you know," she chattered, as Mickey looked hugely embarrassed. "I asked him how he kept in such good shape but I don't know what he answered because I was looking at the way he said it. You know?"

The next week Earl Wilson interviewed Mickey, quoting him in rather insulting dialect. Mickey complained about being a sex symbol: "The vomans vait for you and grab you and kiss you. Some nights I get so aggravated with them! They wait for you at nightclubs and dey say, 'let me feel you muscles.' Dey send you telegrams and give you telephone numbers. I always velt it should be the man who do dose things." As for his show-business career, "I had some studio offers but I didn't grabbed it, instead I vorked with Miss Vest. Now maybe they take me. Maybe I could make some Hungarian vesterns!"

Even after she had hooked up with Mickey—"the love of her life"— Jayne continued dating other men. Mickey was a bolt of lightning, but he was also out of town a lot, and still an unknown quantity. She and Jack Haley Jr. were a couple at Gary Crosby's birthday party at Ciro's; she was seen out with Martin Milner; Dorothy Kilgallen reported that "colorful real estate millionaire Henry Epstein is putting on a big campaign for the affections of lush Jayne Mansfield"; she went out four nights in a row with game-show host Robert Q. Lewis (Jayne's Great Dane and Chihuahua accompanied them to at least one restaurant); and she was spotted strolling through Central Park with hot, rough-trade actor Steve Cochran. When Louella Parsons wrote that Jayne was dating actor Laurence Harvey (who was engaged to actress Margaret Leighton at the time), he was visibly annoyed: "I never met her but once in my life, and I never expect to see her again," Harvey snapped.

❤

Jayne had many wild enthusiasms and obsessions: movie stardom, love (both from men and from her fans), her children (though her mothering skills were better in the abstract than the concrete). Way up on the list of her lifelong loves was animals. As soon as she had her first home, Mansfield's Madness, she began filling it with a zoo-full of pets, to the alarm of Jayne Marie, her neighbors, and skittery visitors. Mind you, she also wore fur and leather and loved digging into a steak dinner—and like many a well-intentioned animal hoarder, Jayne occasionally overloved them to death.

She babbled to Louella Parsons in 1955, "All I have now is a Great Dane, a Chihuahua, three cats named Sabina, Romulus and Ophelia, and a rabbit. I had a pink poodle which just died after I had it dyed pink to match my pink Jaguar, although that wasn't the cause of its death. I also had some mice, but somebody let them out."

That pink-dyed poodle predictably got her into hot water. Earl Wilson ran a letter from a Mrs. J. E. Willis of Sewickly, Pennsylvania, complaining it was "an insult to animal lovers. It only points out the cheap publicity-seeking tactics of would-be Hollywood actresses of today. Somebody should dye Jayne Mansfield (whoever she is!). Poor pink poodle, he must have died of shame." Jayne responded that the poodle didn't die of the harmless vegetable dye but of a virus, "so she hopes the ASPCA'll lay off. I broke down and got hysterical. It hurt me so much that anybody would think that. I was so heartbroken."

When Jayne moved to New York in 1955 she had her 180-pound Great Dane Lord Byron (named after Jim Byron) shipped by air to the Gorham Hotel, to the horror of the staff. He promptly peed on the rug. "He's so attached to me," she said, while feeding him four or five pounds of hamburger. "He's going to be a wonderful watchdog; he'll weigh 200 pounds before he stops growing." Damage charges were added daily to her hotel bill.

Jayne eventually owned—sometimes fleetingly—an ocelot, house-cats, a monkey, a water buffalo, a burro, and any number of dog breeds—but her real love was Chihuahuas, the tiny (four to six pounds, six to ten inches), bug-eyed, shaky, inbred but adorably baby-like dogs. Jayne preferred the short-haired breed. If not well trained and well treated, a Chihuahua can be aggressive and neurotic, chewing clothes, furniture, and friends; and of course, like all dogs, they need to be housebroken and walked.

Jayne's Chihuahuas were *not* well trained.

Canadian TV talk-show host Joyce Davidson asked Jayne in 1957 why she preferred Chihuahuas, to which she replied that they were good with children, and "contrary to the general belief, a little Chihuahua is the sweetest, cuddliest, most endearing, adorable animal you'll ever find. They're just like a little stuffed toy for a child, terribly cuddly and awfully sweet, they even have good temperaments, good dispositions."

Anyone who encountered Galena—Jayne's most notoriously bitey Chihuahua—might beg to differ. Several TV hosts were snapped at on the air, sometimes to the point of bloodshed. Bill Soberanes, one of Galena's victims, recalled that Jayne referred to the incident when they met years later. "She cautioned me about Chihuahuas. 'Let them make up to you first,' she said. 'You're tall and they think you're a giant. You'd bite, too, if a giant man put his hand on you. Let the little dog get used to you first. Pretty soon he'll like you, and you can't help liking him in return.'"

Soberanes was much fonder of Jayne than he was of Galena. Jayne "did not have fits of temperament," he recalled in 1983, "and she was sympathetic to the problems of others. She had plenty of problems of her own, but she tried not to burden her acquaintances with them."

Galena died in 1964, en route to Milwaukee on one of Jayne's summer-stock tours. She was buried in a pet cemetery, Jayne photographed kneeling grief-stricken over the grave. No one but Jayne was sorry to see Galena safely under the sod.

Jayne did more than interviews, dates, and Broadway—New York was still a center for TV production in the 1950s, and Jayne managed to fit in several appearances while acting in *Rock Hunter.*

On May 4 she was interviewed on the prestigious *Person to Person* (she shared the half-hour show with Mickey Rooney—each got twelve minutes). The *San Francisco Examiner*'s Dwight Newton called Rooney dull and Jayne dazzling, though the *Petaluma Argus-Courier* could only say of Jayne, "Blimey, what a dumbell!" The "Jayne Mansfield jokes" were beginning to turn from her publicity to her figure: one reporter joked that when technicians put the microphone in Jayne's cleavage, all you could hear when she talked was a distant echo.

Her biggest production was *The Bachelor,* a ninety-minute musical comedy, aired on NBC on July 15, for which she was paid $4,500. Hal March—best known for hosting the soon-to-be scandalous game show *The $64,000 Question*—starred as an ad executive trying to decide between three women. Jayne played one of them, a model who wants to be taken seriously for her mind (the other two ladies were Carol Haney and Julie Wilson). "This is the first time I'll be singing in public, and it may be the last," she told Harry Harris of the *Philadelphia Inquirer.* "I used to take singing lessons, and I've started again, with Bernie Wayne." Her schedule would have cowed anyone with less energy and ambition: "Saturday, I did the matinee of *Will Success Spoil Rock Hunter?* from 2:30 to 5, I rehearsed *The Bachelor* from 5 to 7, I appeared on *Down You Go* [a game show] from 7:30 to 8, and I was back in *Rock Hunter* at 8:30. I think it's all just terrific!" She told Harris that "TV is my second favorite medium. It's a wonderful means to an end." The end? "The movies!"

"I've had to turn down lots of shows," she told reporter Steven H. Scheuer. "I did appear on some interview shows and on *Person to Person,* but they don't count. My agents tell me what to do, so now audiences will only see me on big, exploited, planned TV shows."

The Bachelor turned out to be a rather silly, lightweight affair, none of the songs or comedy really standing the test of time. But it—and Jayne—got great reviews (as did Hal March: "among the best demonstrations of the art of featherweight farce I've ever seen, in any medium," wrote Donald Kirkley of the *Baltimore Sun*). Kirkley also felt that Jayne "fully justified her recent elevation to stardom on Broadway in *Will Success Spoil Rock Hunter?* Her portrayal of the girl who aspired to culture was a hilarious thing, and no accident, there was considerable intelligence and a sound knowledge of the art of acting behind it."

Larry Wolters of the *Chicago Tribune* thought *The Bachelor* was "a diverting 90 minutes. . . . Jayne Mansfield gave an adequate demonstration of why Marilyn Monroe forsook our shores for those of England." Jack O'Brian of the International News Service (INS) wrote that all three actresses "attacked their targets liltingly and engagingly," and Richard F. Shepard of the *New York Times* wrote that Jayne "shone in her portrayal of the traditional dumb blonde." Her best notice was from Peg Simpson of the *Syracuse Post-Standard:* "Biggest scene-stealer and laugh-getter of the evening was curvy, saucer-eyed Jayne Mansfield, who displayed her flair for comedy to the hilt."

But then came the disaster of *Atlantic City Holiday,* a bizarre variety turn, also on NBC, on August 12. Created as a showcase for the already waning resort town, it featured, in the words of the Newspaper Enterprise Association's Dick Kleiner, Jayne "as a visitor from outer space, who learns about America through such teachers as Bill Haley and the Comets, Pat Boone, Jack Carter, Polly Bergen, Rocky Graziano, Jonathan Winters and the new Miss Universe, Carol Morris."

It was so awful it was wonderful; unlike *The Bachelor, Atlantic City Holiday* has jaw-dropping camp appeal: Jayne and Rocky Graziano portrayed two Venusians who travel to Earth to complain to "Miss Universe" that there are more planets to be heard from. Jack Carter and Polly Bergen prove to Jayne and Rocky that Earth is indeed the pinnacle of all planets by introducing them to Pat Boone, the 500 Club, eccentric passersby played by Jean Stapleton and Jonathan Winters, and hot dogs. In one of the slyest bits, Jayne (in a bubble bath) sings an excellent version of "Heat Wave," which had been Marilyn Monroe's big number in *There's No Business Like Show Business* two years earlier.

Critics were not impressed. Jack O'Brian of the INS complained that "its writing was cheap, its comedy performances were cheap, Jayne Mansfield's dancing was cheap and Jack Carter's glib-and-shallow emceeing boasted the very best third-rate taste and talent. . . . The shy Miss Mansfield started her jelly-shaking precisely as she came into TV view, a bit of progressive Minsky for the 7:30 p.m. children in NBC's coast-to-coast audience."

A summer guest spot on *The Today Show,* in honor of George Bernard Shaw's centennial, did not go over well. Jayne and Jack Lescoulie (who intermittently hosted the show in the 1950s and '60s) did a scene from *Caesar and Cleopatra,* a play that is hard to take done straight or not. "It was richly rewarding to those students who have watched Vivien Leigh, Claire Bloom and other lesser actresses struggle with this role," snarked John Crosby for the *Boston Globe.* "Miss Mansfield got through the passage all right, staring limply into the cameras and knitting her brows only over the hard words. . . . Shaw probably would have loved it, too. He was a clown in his own rights, and, like Miss Mansfield, he would go to almost any length to attract attention."

She was more successful on the word-play quiz show *Down You Go,* "disillusioning many who have regarded her as a mere dumb, bosomy blonde," as Ben Gross of the *New York Daily News* wrote. Jayne's natural playfulness, quick intelligence, and sheer sense of joy made her a natural for talk and game shows, and she would spend both the high and low points of her career guesting on them.

"Television is fabulous! It's the quickest way to get to the heart of the public. And I love cameras so much," Jayne enthused that summer. "I'm not sure if I should stick to dramatic and comedy roles on TV, or do an occasional emcee or hostess type of thing. What I'm afraid of is that a hostess role might take away something that's very important to all actresses—you know, the illusion of mystery." But still, it was not the movies, which "I prefer to anything, because I love to see what I've done. I mean, it's possible in movies to look at your performances and correct yourself next time. You can't do that in the theater."

6

Of course she cannot act. Who wants her to act? . . . Go and see
her move, stand, speak, look, kneel.

Birmingham Daily Post

In September 1956 Jayne sent all the newsmen she knew a note reading,
"I feel you have boosted my career so much. It is people like you who
make a star out of a starlet." She told reporter Jack Fitzgerald, "To get ahead
these days you must have 60 percent determination and 10 percent natural
resources. Determination is nothing more than hard work."

Jayne was nothing if not determined (some felt she was nothing *but*
determined), and from the moment she'd signed her *Rock Hunter* contract,
she'd been angling for a movie deal. As early as September 1955, there were
rumors that 20th Century-Fox wanted the rights to both *Rock Hunter* and
Jayne, but of course the show's producers were not letting their big attraction get away. Fox was preparing a comedy tentatively called *Do-Re-Mi,*
about a gangster trying to turn his moll into a singing star, and its producer, writer, and director, Frank Tashlin, was interested in Jayne for the lead,
with Bing Crosby as the washed-up agent who falls in love with her.

Jule Styne and Fox haggled as Jayne fretted: Hedda Hopper reported
that Fox producer Buddy Adler was flying to London to sign Marilyn for
the film version of *Rock Hunter.* Finally, Fox bought the film rights for
$100,000, along with $20,000 to be distributed among the play's backers.
And—best of all—the studio also got Styne to release Jayne from her

Eve Golden

Broadway contract. In early May 1956 Jayne signed a seven-year deal with Fox, starting at $60,000 a year; she left *Rock Hunter* in September. She was euphoric. "It's exactly what I want to do," she told Louella Parsons. "I've talked with a number of people at 20th, and I like what they promised me. I'm studying dancing, singing and dramatic acting. Twentieth has promised to build me as one of their most important stars." And when she got back to Hollywood, "I want the horn and the trumpets—the whole works." She was not exaggerating, as Hollywood soon learned.

In September 1956—a year after *Rock Hunter* had previewed out of town—Jayne left the show that made her a star, replaced as Rita Marlowe by Jane Kean (who went on to a respectable career as a character actress in films and TV). Just a little over two years since arriving in Hollywood as an unknown, with a daughter in tow, Jayne had pushed her way into a promising little film career, Broadway stardom—and now she was to be the new Marilyn Monroe.

She left New York a Jayne-battered town. Show-biz columnist Mel Heimer wrote that "the storm was over," that Jayne had conducted what "must have been the greatest publicity campaign in history. . . . If a delicatessen opened in the Bronx, Jayne showed up and was photographed sitting on a stool with a sturgeon sandwich in hand. I am not kidding. I am not sure I can remember a cocktail party or Scrabble session I attended in the last year in which Jayne didn't arrive sooner or later to say 'hello, everybody,' and make that pretty, open-wide smile for the birdie." Heimer joked that "city editors were afraid to pick up their phones, lest another Mansfield p.a. would be there to inform him Jaynie was opening a dog kennel in Brooklyn. At least one editor announced tiredly that there would be no more Mansfield publicity in his paper unless Jayne knifed someone." Now that Jayne was safely on her way to the West Coast, "editors are beginning to come out from behind locked doors. Wondering, of course, who the next one will be. If you wonder why newsmen drink. You now know."

The Hollywood Jayne returned to in late 1956 was pretty much identical to the one she'd left a year and a half before, but this time she was a welcomed, fêted star, not a desperate, climbing nobody.

At 20th Century-Fox, executives, makeup, hair, and wardrobe people took a good hard look at what they'd bought in this twenty-two-year-old acquisition. Most of the biggest stars had slightly quirky looks, and Jayne was pretty enough to pass for star material. Then, of course, there was that figure. A little over average height (just above five feet six), Jayne possessed a rib cage like a football player's, with large (probably E-cup) breasts. She reported her exact measurements differently from interview to interview, but her bust was probably forty or forty-one inches. She had a tiny waist-line—but also small hips and backside, not an hourglass figure at all. Her biggest figure problem were her birdie stick-legs, so thin she looked as though she might topple over. Pants and long dresses were the answer—but when miniskirts came in ten years later, Jayne had to hide her legs with go-go boots.

Jayne's new home, 20th Century-Fox, was the result of a 1935 merger between the Fox Film Corporation (founded by William Fox in 1915, it had made superstars of Theda Bara and Tom Mix) and Twentieth Century Pictures (a short-lived studio run by United Artists' Joseph Schenck and Warner Bros.' Darryl F. Zanuck). The new studio turned out Charlie Chan and Mr. Moto B-mysteries, and in the World War II years it really came into its own with a series of bright, candy-colored musicals starring Betty Grable, Alice Faye, John Payne, Carmen Miranda, and Don Ameche.

By the 1940s, 20th Century-Fox was a winner, competing with the majors MGM, Paramount, and Warner Bros. Each studio had its own personality, and Fox (sometimes shortened to "20th," depending on what producer was talking) specialized in light musicals, romances, westerns, and of course, dramas. Fox made stars of Jayne's childhood and teen idols Shirley Temple and Betty Grable as well as Tyrone Power, Loretta Young, Jeanne Crain, Linda Darnell, and musical star turned character actor Clifton Webb.

20th Century-Fox's first "prestige" film was the Oscar-nominated *The Grapes of Wrath* in 1940; it won its first Best Picture Oscar for 1941's *How Green Was My Valley*. Other Big Serious Pictures followed with increasing success through the 1940s and '50s (*Lifeboat, The Ox-Bow Incident, Laura, A Tree Grows in Brooklyn, Leave Her to Heaven, Gentleman's Agreement, Pinky, The Snake Pit*). But whether comedy, musical, or drama, 20th Century-Fox films had a well-deserved reputation for being smart and fun, thanks largely to the hands-on involvement of the vice president of production, Darryl F. Zanuck. He cared deeply about his films, and he also knew what would sell. In addition to those great wartime musicals—classics of their kind—many Fox movies are as enjoyable today as they were at their premiere: *Miracle on 34th Street, Kiss of Death, The Ghost and Mrs. Muir, All about Eve, The Day the Earth Stood Still.*

After its wartime stars Grable, Faye, and Darnell began to fade (at least in Zanuck's opinion), Fox began signing up promising new starlets to take their place: Vivian Blaine, Sheree North, June Haver, Marion Marshall, Bella Darvi (Zanuck's mistress), Dana Wynter. Their biggest find was Marilyn Monroe, who had briefly been a Fox starlet in 1946 and was re-signed in late 1950.

Marilyn's career took a few years to really blossom. In the early 1950s she was just another cute, unremarkable young hopeful, as she worked her way up in silly B-films. It was in 1953 that she became "Marilyn"—the hairstyle, the makeup, the affectations (half-closed eyes, sleepy, whispery voice)—in *Niagara, Gentlemen Prefer Blondes,* and *How to Marry a Millionaire.* She proved herself a brilliant light comedienne and a surprisingly good singer, and by 1956, when Jayne joined Fox, Marilyn was the biggest game in town. Marilyn was "in town" as infrequently as she could manage, though. She loved New York and hated Hollywood as much as Jayne did the reverse. She'd recently wrapped filming on *Bus Stop,* which she hoped would make her a major dramatic star, and had married playwright Arthur Miller. When Jayne arrived at Fox, Marilyn was in London filming *The Prince and the Showgirl* (which turned out to be a huge headache and disappointment for all concerned).

Marilyn may have been the biggest star in the industry, but she was not the only blonde bombshell Jayne had to contend with. Kim Novak was a rising star over at Columbia, Anita Ekberg had just been imported from Sweden, and the icily ambitious Gabor sisters, Eva and Zsa Zsa, both well into their thirties by 1956, had been climbing the TV and movie ladder for more than a decade, both with increasing success. Judy Holliday, at Columbia with Kim Novak, was pretty enough to be a sex symbol, but her smart, off-kilter comedy skills typed her more as a character actress.

Then there were the B-blondes, the actresses who were "the poor man's Marilyn Monroe," "the poor man's Jayne Mansfield," "the poor man's Kim Novak." There was the sweet-faced Joi Lansing, who had been struggling along for nearly ten years and was still playing bit parts; kazoo-voiced Jean Carson, who played hilariously tough broads; long-legged Sheree North, also being pushed by Fox as a new find; cheap-looking but quiet and intelligent Cleo Moore, who'd just had a hit with the low-budget *Women's Prison;* and chromium-bright Mamie Van Doren, whose laser-focused ambition mirrored Jayne's own. One of the most talented of the whole crop was versatile Barbara Nichols, just as good as a comic floozie (*Pal Joey, The Pajama Game*) as she was heartbreaking in dramatic roles (*Sweet Smell of Success*).

And there was Dagmar, a category unto herself. Not so much an actress as a "presence," the Amazonian blonde (real name Virginia Ruth Egnor) became a sensation on TV variety shows, playing straight woman to such leering comics as Milton Berle, Jerry Lester, and Bob Hope. Before Jayne Mansfield came along, "Dagmar" was shorthand for "big-breasted blonde."

The British film industry was incubating its own small army of blondes as well, most notably Diana Dors, who was constantly annoyed at being called "the British Marilyn Monroe." The classically beautiful Belinda Lee made a great start, but by the late 1950s she was already being shipped off to Italy and Germany to make B-films. And there was "the British Dagmar," the hourglass-shaped Sabrina (born Norma Ann Sykes), a funny, admittedly talentless performer who good-naturedly poked fun at herself.

♥

Jayne's new workplace was located at Santa Monica and Pico Boulevards in West Los Angeles, later dubbed Century City. The studio was in the midst of a shakeup in early 1956: Darryl F. Zanuck had been frustrated over his increasing lack of creative control. "Until a few years ago," he told Bob Thomas, "I was able to devote myself to the creative end entirely. . . . But this business has changed. I found I had less and less time to work on stories." In February 1956 Zanuck stepped down as head of production—replaced by Buddy Adler—remaining at Fox as an independent producer. Studio president Spyros Skouras would now have more sway over the studio's output, which made everyone nervous—it had been Zanuck's eccentric, creative touch that had set Fox apart from its competitors.

"Everything was hunky-dory, everything was just great," enthused Mickey Hargitay. Jayne "had a contract, she had a film to walk into—everything was working just like clockwork." Everything was hunky-dory for Mickey, too: "I felt like I made it, everyone knows me! I came to America in '47, nobody knows me—everybody knows me now!"

"I haven't got a dime in the bank and I'm $2,000 in debt," Jayne cheerfully told reporter Olga Curtis. "Jim Byron, my press agent, gets 5 percent. Bill Shiffrin gets 10 percent as my agent. All together, the government gets another 20 or so, and I get what's left. I spend $50 a month to stay blonde, $25 a month for a fan-mail service, $200 for a maid." But she had no complaints: "I said when I started that I'd do anything and work harder than anybody to make good. Well, I've got a seven-year movie contract and I'm going to be a star—and that's all I ever wanted to be. I run on a publicity schedule, like a train. The boys line up something, tell me where to go and what to wear, and I go."

Jayne, Jayne Marie, and Mickey breezed back into Hollywood in September. "It's wonderful to come back as an established actress," Jayne told the *Los Angeles Times*. "It's so nice to know you've settled down to a long-term contract in a place you really love. I'm not here to play around. I'm reporting to 20th Century-Fox first thing in the morning to start on *Do-Re-Mi* with Tom Ewell. I'm anxious to see my pink Jaguar, though." She tried not to brush off New York; she knew she still needed her friends there: "I'm grateful to New York for what it did to me, but now that I'm back here I want to stay 99 years. It's too wonderful to be back. I haven't words to express it."

She glowed with exhilaration at her dreams coming true. "This has been the happiest, most exciting week of my life. I was resigned to staying with the play for the rest of its New York run and going on tour with it. Then the deal came through and I've been on air ever since."

Fox put her right to work: "I won't even have a breathing spell. The designers are already making my clothes. I had to airmail my two favorite bras to the studio this week so they could get an idea." *Do-Re-Mi*—retitled *The Girl Can't Help It*—was still being tinkered with (the studio was hoping newcomer Elvis Presley would make his film debut in it), but Jayne knew the outline of the plot and her role. "I like rock 'n' roll and I'm looking forward to doing a picture with Elvis Presley. Elvis and I haven't met as yet, but we have something in common—Jaguar cars."

The Girl Can't Help It was the brainchild of Frank Tashlin, loosely based on a novel by Garson Kanin. Tashlin directed, produced, and wrote the script (with Herbert Baker). The wildly eccentric but highly professional Tashlin was forty-three when he and Jayne first worked together, and he already had quite a résumé. A cartoonist and animator, he headed animation production at Columbia and Warner Bros., creating many Porky Pig and Private Snafu cartoons.

Tashlin turned to live-action films with Bob Hope's comic western *The Lemon Drop Kid* in 1951, working with Hope again on *Son of Paleface* and with Jerry Lewis and Dean Martin on *Artists and Models* in 1955 (Tashlin went on to make another seven films with Lewis) and *The Lieutenant Wore Skirts* with Tom Ewell, who'd be costarring in *The Girl Can't Help It*.

Coming from the animation world, he became tagged as a cartoony director, which he resented, but there was some truth there. Tashlin's films tended to be fast moving with exaggerated characters, bright colors, and larger-than life stars (Jayne, Hope, Lewis). In a 1971 interview, Tashlin noted that "all the reviewers—Truffaut, and Godard, and all these people, when they were reviewers on *Cahiers du Cinema,* they always treated my films . . . as a cartoon." He also laughed about the pretentious overthinking that his films inspired. Speaking of *The Girl Can't Help It,* he said, "As far as they were concerned, that was a Tom and Jerry cartoon, and the fact that his name was Tom, and hers was Jerry [*sic*]—which I never thought of— they said, 'She is the cat, and he is the mouse.' And they wrote, you know, all this philosophical double-talk."

As the picture took shape, Broderick Crawford dropped out as Jayne's gangster lover; Fox wanted Orson Welles, but wound up hiring Edmond O'Brien. The film was to be shot in Cinemascope, which worried costume designer Charles Le Maire, who felt that Jayne "could look out of proportion, so we devised a startling new effect—widening instead of deepening the bustline. It was a problem, but a delightful one."

Le Maire was paid $35,000 to make eighteen costumes for Jayne. He wisely padded out her hips and backside to balance out her figure. Later, many less talented costume designers put Jayne in tight skirts and pants and uplifted her bust, which did her no favors. Le Maire actually put tassels and a modified bustle on Jayne's backside. "You should see the rushes of a scene where Jayne walks up the street," he said. "Wow! Even Buddy Adler couldn't understand it when I went to his office and discussed Jayne's wardrobe for the film. I told him about the buttons and bows in the back and he said, 'do we have to *add* things to Jayne Mansfield?' I assured him it was high fashion to have a little movement in the back, too. Jayne has the greatest shape of any gal I've ever dressed. She'll bring back the hourglass figure." Jayne herself told the *Los Angeles Times* that "I thought maybe my costumes might be designed to hide my hips, but the couturiers have all said, 'why deemphasize something so unusual?'"

The Girl Can't Help It shot through September and October, and everyone was impressed with (and happily surprised by) Jayne's talent and professionalism. She dropped the antics she'd pulled during her Broadway run, and was always on time, with lines and business learned, eager to cooperate. "This girl can handle a five-page scene of dialogue and hit it on the nose every time," Tashlin told Harrison Carroll. "Everybody on the set has respect for her ability as a performer." Veteran actor Tom Ewell said, "She's a very smart girl. She knows exactly what she's doing."

Frank Tashlin told Jayne's friend and biographer May Mann, "She always arrived on the set on time, letter perfect in her lines. She always knew every bit of business in the script, even the timing of picking up a cup of tea or whatever. I was amazed at her complete professionalism." Fox hairdresser Helen Turpin was not as impressed. She told Mann, "She always arrived with a couple of her dogs and sometime a child or two. That we didn't mind so much, but she was always on the telephone every second, or calls were coming in for her. It was constant interruption and bedlam . . . she always had a thousand things going at once."

Jayne happily told a reporter that Tashlin had said "my acting gave him goose pimples. He told me when the film started, 'Jayne, you've gotten all this publicity with cheesecake photos. . . . Now you have to prove you are an actress with close-ups of your face. . . . In two years you'll be one of the biggest stars in Hollywood, with the pictures and the build-up you'll get at 20th.' So I'm glad I signed for seven years. At the end of it I'll still only be 30."

The Girl Can't Help It—released on December 1, 1956—is an absolute delight, perhaps Jayne's best film. The plot is simple: washed-up gangster Fats Murdock (Edmond O'Brien) hires washed-up agent Tom Miller (Tom Ewell) to make a singing star out of his girlfriend, Jerri Jordan (Jayne). Jerri can't sing (. . . or *can* she? Jayne later does a number, dubbed by Eileen Wilson). Miller and Jerri fall in love, of course, and hijinks ensue. The whole movie is a cinematic marvel: "I could try my whole life and never get a movie to look that beautiful," says writer and director John Waters. "It symbolized what I wish all my movies could look like: garish, beautiful."

And Jayne gives a great comic performance: her Jerri is silly but far from dumb; Jayne alternately plays her as warm, romantic, sad, angry, resigned, and giddy, and for a lightly trained actress in her first major role, she shows real promise. This was not the kind of role considered for an Oscar, but she put in just as good comic work as Grace Kelly and Debbie Reynolds did that same year (1956 was a drought year for comedy).

The supporting cast, too, is flawless. Ferret-faced Tom Ewell manages to be both creepy and sympathetic; tough-guy actor Edmond O'Brien is unexpectedly hilarious; the always-wonderful Henry Jones is, well, wonderful, as Fats's sentimental right-hand man.

But the real draw of the film is musical numbers, performed by some of the top rock, pop, and soul greats of the mid-1950s: "Be-Bop-a-Lula"

(Gene Vincent), "Blue Monday" (Fats Domino), "Spread the Word" (Abby Lincoln, wearing one of Marilyn Monroe's *Gentlemen Prefer Blondes* costumes), "You'll Never Know" (the Platters), "Twenty Flight Rock" (Eddie Cochran), "Cry Me a River" (Julie London, appearing as a *Vogue*-gowned apparition in an increasingly hilarious sequence). Tashlin wanted Elvis Presley to do a number, too, but his manager Tom Parker demanded $100,000 so Fox dropped him without a second thought.

The real star act is Little Richard, singing the title song and "She's Got It." Jayne struts her stuff to both Little Richard numbers: in a nightclub, past goggle-eyed managers to "She's Got It," and down the street to "The Girl Can't Help It"—a scene encompassing some of the great sight gags of the era. As she wiggles past, the iceman's entire supply melts, the milkman's bottles obscenely boil over, a neighbor's eyeglasses shatter. John Waters hilariously parodied the scene in *Pink Flamingos,* as Divine strolls down a Baltimore street to the same number, while secretly filmed passersby react in stunned horror.

Waters credits Tashlin as having both a sense of humor and great cinematic style: "I don't think you can work with Jerry Lewis and Jayne Mansfield all those times and not love it, unless you're a masochist. But there's also moments in this film that remind me of Douglas Sirk, in a way of visual similarities. He understood irony—it was an early ironic movie. He saw the extreme taste. He understood that."

The film is indeed a Big Hollywood Movie, and looks it: Jayne is presented as a work of art, looking like she is made of spun glass and whipped cream. La Maire's costumes, Helen Turpin's hairstyling, Ben Nye's makeup, Leon Shamroy's cinematography—Jayne never looked lovelier. But she doesn't actually look *sexy,* or like a real human being: Tashlin and his crew turned her into a human cartoon, which is what she remained the rest of her life. Pointed breasts and padded hips jutting, waist cinched in till it looked like a spinal column; audiences literally gasped when Jayne threw off her fur coat, but it was a gasp of shock, not lust.

In a 1962 interview with Peter Bogdanovich, Tashlin said, "Imagine a statue with breasts like Mansfield's. Imagine that in marble. We don't like big feet or big ears, but we make an idol of a woman because she's deformed in the breasts. There's nothin' more hysterical to me than big-breasted women—like walking leaning towers."

The rock numbers (with a few wince-making exceptions, such as Ray Anthony's "Rock around the Rock Pile" and the Chuckles' "Cinnamon Sinner") had 1956 audiences dancing in the aisles. John Waters is also impressed with the quality and realness of the rock stars featured. Some were manicured and croony, but "Gene Vincent was *scary*—they looked rockabilly. They weren't even regular rock and roll, they were *Southern,* and they scared people. To put it in this Hollywood lighting, that's what made it cartoonish and almost freakish. Little Richard is *beyond* what you could ever hope for."

The movie was also quite naughty, and the censors had several fits. A lot was cut, but a lot got through, too: the phallic milk-bottle explosion; Jayne picking up groceries and holding two milk bottles in front of her breasts, leaning over Tom Ewell and complaining, "Everyone figures me for a sexpot! No one thinks I'm equipped for motherhood!" Jayne told Erskine Johnson of *Hollywood Today,* "After all, the censors can't condemn a girl if she sticks out a little. Besides, I play a sweet, honest girl unaware of her sex appeal."

The reviews for both Jayne and the film were mostly ecstatic. The hypercritical Dorothy Kilgallen wrote that Jayne "is just liable to be a big star. She turns in a genuinely funny performance in the classic 'dumb blonde' style." The *News Chronicle* critic raved, "I burn my critical boats and hail her as the most majestic vamp of the decade." And John L. Scott of the *Los Angeles Times,* admitting he was sick of rock and roll films, called this one "Grade A quality. . . . Jayne Mansfield outdoes Marilyn Monroe in some respects, and makes, I must say, a successful featured debut. . . . The plot doesn't amount to much, but rock and rollers won't care; neither will the boys who plunk down their money at the box office to ogle Miss Mansfield's charms. . . . Male whistles fill the air at her every appearance, which means she has 'arrived.'"

When the film opened in England in early 1957, reviews were mixed and rather discerning; they could see America, rock, and Jayne from a distance. The *Birmingham Daily Post* summed up Jayne by quoting George Bernard Shaw's evaluation of Mrs. Patrick Campbell: "Who wants her to act?—who cares tuppence whether she possesses that or any other second-rate accomplishment? On the highest plane one does not act, one is. Go and see her move, stand, speak, look, kneel . . . and then talk to me about acting, forsooth!" Princess Margaret—a very hep twenty-six-year-old—caused something of a stir with her public glee. "I was rockin' and rollin' with Princess Margaret last night and may I tell cats everywhere that this royal chick is cool, real cool," wrote reporter Robert Musel. "The princess hopped in her seat. An usherette reported that she also knew how to laugh at double entendre and she didn't miss one of the script writers' intentions. In fact she was way ahead of them."

Harold Heffernan of the NANA (North American Newspaper Alliance) cheered: "Any doubts about the permanency of shimmering Jayne Mansfield were thunderously dispelled. . . . Jayne was given a continuously roaring vote of approval. Definite feeling among curbstone critics was that Hollywood has a new face that should be around a long, long time." Frank Custer of the *Capital Times* (Madison, Wisconsin) was more begrudging, but realistic, in his appraisal: "Her endowments, as expected, exceed her ability as an actress, but undoubtedly the film's producers don't care as long as she moves attractively."

Jympson Harman of the *London Evening News* wrote that Jayne "walks like Marilyn Monroe, lacks her prettiness, and has a good deal of the tough sex appeal of Diana Dors. . . . I never saw a girl go in and out so dramatically." Harman foresightedly added, "Where does Jayne Mansfield go from here? She is no better at burlesquing Miss Monroe than Marilyn herself is. And she reveals no saving natural wit. Can she get out of the gimmick class?"

❤

Jayne was finally a real Hollywood star, and for the rest of her career, she was ballyhooed, criticized, and advised by the syndicated columnists who still held sway in the nation's thousands of newspapers, big and small. Hedda Hopper and Louella Parsons were the feuding queens of the genre: Louella loved Jayne, so naturally Hedda hated her. Harrison Carroll, Sheilah Graham, Jim Bacon, and Mike Connolly were generally fans of Jayne and treated her gently—though all of them piled on with glee when she made one of her frequent missteps. Walter Winchell and—particularly—Dorothy Kilgallen looked down their noses at Jayne and took every opportunity to be unpleasant to her.

The dilemma with these columnists is whether to believe what they wrote. As seen most baldly in the novel and movie *Sweet Smell of Success,* much of what was printed in these columns was fluff: silly jokes, obviously planted press-agent nonsense, years-out-of-date "breaking news." Some columns had stories about Jayne's "current" doings in Italy when she'd been back in the US for months. Every man she was seen with in passing was her new great love and future husband.

Some interviews with Jayne were obviously planted gags: she supposedly met Wilt Chamberlain, "the basketball king," and asked him, "How many baskets do you weave?" He said, "I don't weave them, I throw them," and Jayne asked, "How many games have you thrown?" When asked about her acting method, she supposedly said, "If I want to look happy I think about some happy event in my life. If I want to look sad, I think of some sad scene. Of course, in some photos I look somewhat mysterious. That happens when I think how cold I am." The problem is Jayne was just savvy enough to have actually *said* that, knowing full well it would get a laugh.

The interviews are the hardest things to parse. Jayne's speaking style—as seen in candid interviews on YouTube—could range wildly from eloquent and thoughtful to bubbleheaded silliness. Louella Parsons was surprisingly accurate in her quotes, though she too must be viewed with a critical eye. Jayne spoke in person to Harrison Carroll and Mike Connolly, but Jim Bacon and even the once hard-hitting journalist Dorothy Kilgallen printed as gospel quotes and facts that were obviously fabrications.

The Associated Press (AP) and United Press International (UPI) were two other major sources of news stories on Jayne, and they too must be approached gingerly. They also used out-of-date and highly dubious items. Both agencies had thousands of employees in hundreds of worldwide bureaus, and not all those employees were trustworthy or immune to bribery, boredom, or desperation to get items used and get paid.

One must carefully weigh every news story on Jayne and every newspaper and magazine interview with her: how likely is it? Are the quotes actually hers? Is the breaking news five years old and tossed in to fill up space? With someone as press-mad as Jayne, it's a real conundrum telling truth from fiction even in reputable newspapers.

❤

The Girl Can't Help It made Jayne the blazing superstar of late 1956. A newspaper clip that season claimed that "she has so many offers and requests for her time that she would have to be four girls to accept them all. [Josh Logan] wanted her to do a lead for two weeks in *Mr. Roberts* at New York's City Center. . . . Meanwhile, says Jayne, boyfriend Mickey Hargitay has a new project, too. He wants to become a builder."

Jayne settled happily into life in Los Angeles, moving back into her Mansfield's Madness home while shopping for a bigger one. Jayne Marie was enrolled at a West L.A. public school; Jayne said that "I could afford to send her to a private school, but there isn't much point in it. I wanted Jayne Marie to have the same friends and playmates in school as in the neighborhood where we live, so she wouldn't feel left out of anything." Jayne added amusingly—and unconvincingly—that "I try to keep active in the PTA at her school. We were in California only a few days when I went to the first meeting with the other mothers. I rushed from the studio where we were working and didn't get a chance to remove my makeup. I didn't want to be conspicuous what with my figure and all, so I covered up with my sapphire mink coat."

In December, in the first flush of *The Girl Can't Help It*'s success, Jayne made the first of several appearances on *The Jack Benny Program.* Wearing a startlingly tailored dress, she does a cute cameo in which she reclaims her purse from Benny: "I was just walking outside, passing the studio, and an usher ran out and grabbed my purse! I think it's a pretty sneaky way for you to get guests up here on the stage." Benny was impressed with Jayne's talents as a comic's straight woman. "She was a delight to work with," Benny later said. "She knows her lines, she has a great sense of comedy timing. Oh, yeah, she looks marvelous, too." Benny, Red Skelton, Bob Hope, Milton Berle, George Jessel, and Jackie Gleason all found Jayne a good line-feeder, a talent often overlooked by audiences but prized by comedians.

As her next film, *The Wayward Bus,* prepared to go into production, Jayne said of her Fox contract that "I was offered $75,000 a picture, to make four of them, on a freelance basis. But it meant more to me to have a big studio behind me. I was offered one of the leads in Clark Gable's picture *The King and Four Queens,* but I'd have been lost in the shuffle." If this quote is accurate, she was right: Gable's costars in this dull western, Eleanor Parker, Jean Willes, Barbara Nichols, and Sara Shane, were given little to work with.

Jayne said she was professionally ambitious, but that another ambition was "to feel satisfied with myself, to know that I have arrived. To be a good actress. To be liked. To be a big personality." She was to succeed in all of these, to varying degrees. "The real stars are not good actors or actresses. They're personalities," she realized, also being self-aware enough to admit that "I was colorful even before I landed in show business. In fact, my only problem is being *too* colorful."

Reporter John Crosby consulted orchestra leader Vincent Lopez (who also dabbled in predicting the future) on his guesses for 1958. "Princess Grace will have a boy" (correct), "Jayne Mansfield will hit a great peak in 1957 and that will be it." A little harsh, but not totally inaccurate.

As 1958 dawned, both Jayne Mansfield *and* Mickey Hargitay pin-up calendars hit the stores. But the real eyebrow-raiser was the Jayne Mansfield hot-water bottle. "You'll be amazed at the hundreds of unique Gift Items we now have in stock," read an ad for Happy's Package Store in St. Petersburg, Florida. The *Petaluma Argus Courier* was indeed amazed, noting that the hot-water bottle was "billed as 'good for the grouchy boss,' but why a grouchy boss would like the bottle isn't made clear. Suppose your boss is a woman?" The reporter also noted a ball-point pen shaped like a woman's leg and a beer mug that "'has a cute nude lass molded right into the bottom of it' gazing up at you when you tilt the mug to drink. 'A real surprise for guests.' They'd probably be so surprised they'd head for the door after the first sip."

Jayne told Harrison Carroll that "a manufacturer offered me a $20,000 advance and a guarantee of $70,000 in one year" for rights to the hot-water bottle. "I hesitated at first" but, she quite sensibly asked, "who can turn down that much money?'" Her agent Bill Shiffrin rather wished she had resisted. "She got involved with the rotgut of Hollywood," he later said, "and they made those Mansfield rubber dolls. She went through the whole gamut of Hollywood nonsense."

That "rotgut of Hollywood" was actually Don Poynter, an amusing and very nice fellow who also came up with an Uncle Fester light-up light bulb, talking toilet seats, and whiskey-flavored toothpaste. Today, Poynter says that Jayne did not get $20,000 for the initial deal, though "I think she eventually got more than that."

When Poynter came up with the idea for a starlet hot-water bottle, Jayne was naturally the first subject he thought of. "Fox was opposed to this," he admits. "They did not want her to do this, because they were trying to make her into a serious actress. She said, 'hey, you've got to be kidding! I don't want to be a serious actress—I'm *Jayne Mansfield!*' So above their head, she went ahead and signed the contract."

When Poynter showed up at Jayne's house on a Sunday morning to discuss the project, he found she was away at church and "Mickey Hargitay was out spraying the lawn with water. I was so shocked that they were living together—where I came from, you had to be married before you could do that!" Poynter hired a photographer to take preliminary shots for the model, and Jayne suggested someone who charged $500 a photo: "In Cincinnati I could have pictures taken for $15," says Poynter. "I had no choice, because I had to act like a big cheese. I asked her if she had a little nightie with a pair of panties that we could use, and she said, 'oh, no, I sleep nude.' So I had to go out and shop—I finally found a very flimsy blue gown that came with a pair of panties. I took them and showed them to her press agent, and he said, 'oh my God, you can't use that, you can see right through it!' I showed it to her, and she fell in love with it and told the press agent to go jump in the lake."

At the photographer's studio, Jayne posed in her nightie (though the end product wound up having her in just a black painted-on bikini). "She was very straightforward," recalls Poynter. "Nothing unusual. She was wonderful—not only that, but I thought she was pretty bright. After the pictures were taken, she took her gown off and was standing in front of me nude! Which I thought was rather interesting."

While her career and her love life were heating up, Jayne had old business to take care of. Paul Mansfield, living in San Francisco, had been out of Jayne's life for years, but they were still legally tied together. He, wanting to move on with his life, was as unhappy about this as she was. As her career skyrocketed in 1955, he reiterated that Jayne's ambitions "are not compatible to our marriage." Jayne replied, "When I married Paul, he was the most popular boy in high school [*sic*], a football player and a wonderful pianist. I thought, of course, that he would follow me in show business, but when he didn't, I don't see how I could do anything else but divorce him."

Although Paul was granted a divorce decree in Texas, Jayne still needed one valid in California before remarrying. Paul sounded sad but resigned about the situation: "No man wants to be second choice," he said. "If she should come back I would be second choice to her career." He contested Jayne's custody of Jayne Marie, claiming she was an "unfit mother." "I'm a very stainless character," Jayne angrily replied. "My petticoats are clear. Those pictures in *Playboy* magazine I posed for to get milk and bread for the baby. Paul was so jealous of my career. He calls up now every so often and cries for me to go back to him. This is his last contact with me, and I guess he's going whole hog." She added, "I read little Bible stories to her every night and she is a well-balanced and intelligent child." She had lots of motherly photos taken with Jayne Marie, but some papers elected to print pin-ups of her instead.

It got ugly, as these things tend to do. Jayne got an interlocutory decree of divorce, at which point Paul countersued, accusing her of causing him "pain, anguish and distress" with her "harsh, cruel and tyrannical conduct." "I have no idea why he would do such a thing," said Jayne. "All I can say is I hope he has fun." In October 1956 Paul agreed to drop the "unfit mother" accusations, and Jayne appeared in the Los Angeles Superior Court to testify. Paul "did not make enough to pay household bills and I had to work for bread and butter money," she said. "He believed a woman's place was in the home, and most especially in the kitchen from 5 a.m. to 5 p.m."

The divorce was granted (it became official a year later, on January 28, 1958): Jayne would keep Jayne Marie (Paul was never to play any role in her life); Jayne of course kept the Mansfield name and was awarded a token $1 a year alimony, plus $20 a week child support; she also got $25,000 out of their joint bank account and one of their two cars.

Safely divorced, Jayne calmed down and spoke more kindly of Paul and their marriage. "I hope he eventually finds the type of wife he wants. [He did—Paul and his second wife, Mary Sue Greer, remained married until his death.] I want him to be happy. I don't regret my early marriage, although I know now that a girl of 16 doesn't know her own mind when she imagines she is in love." As for her future, Jayne told Aline Mosby of the United Press (UP), "I want a husband and six children and a complete life and I bet I get 'em. I want movie stardom more than anything in the world, and I hope two years will be enough to get my career established. Then if I feel the same way in two years about Mickey as I do now, we'll get married."

Mickey was proving himself no Paul Mansfield, and was as happy to show off his attributes as Jayne was hers. He told Aline Mosby, "I'm just an average guy. But here in Hollywood I regret sometimes I acquired muscles and won the Mr. Universe contest. People think I can't carry on a conversation. Why am I supposed to be dumb just because I have a build? Around swimming pools here you'll find me with a shirt on. I don't want people to think I'm showing off."

In October 1956, he and Jayne attended the Publicists' Association Ballyhoo Ball. As it could double as a Halloween party, attendees were asked to come in costume. Jayne and Mickey essentially dressed as themselves: in tiny, skin-tight leopard-print swimsuits. Mickey's was cut so high and so low that he flirted with disaster; Jayne wore a bikini accessorized with arm and ankle bracelets. Mickey picked Jayne up and flung her about; she perched on his shoulders and balanced on his thighs as photographers snapped away and other guests faded into the background. Kathryn Grant came as a circus performer, Valerie Allen as a dance-hall girl, and Cleo Moore as an American Indian. No one noticed—nothing short of Garbo on roller skates could have deflected attention from Jaynie and Mickey.

7

I work just as hard at my acting as I do at being a personality. I think too many people have tried to take the showmanship out of show business.

Jayne Mansfield

As Fox prepared *The Wayward Bus* (and yes, there were many "Wayward Bust" jokes), Jayne took time off from wardrobe and makeup tests to be Jayne. Lydia Lane, interviewing her in November, found her in a reflective mood. "When I left Hollywood I was so broke I couldn't treat my daughter to 10-cent rides on the merry-go-round," she said, "and now I have a pink mink stole, a black mink coat, and my own home." Jayne Marie was now enrolled at school, and "when I saw her walk off with her lunch to join the other girls without looking back it was a sad feeling because I knew from then on she was on her own."

She talked about the changes Fox had made in her looks, apparently on board: "My hair is a different color, my hairline is higher and my black eyebrows have been bleached. I believe in doing everything you can to make yourself look great. This doesn't mean you have to be all dressed-up every time you go out, but even casual clothes, your pedal-pushers, sweater and shoes, should be carefully chosen and you should be neatly groomed. I used to hate some of the dresses my mother picked out for me and it affected my personality for that day. I take my daughter shopping and encourage her to tell me what she likes."

Jayne insisted—despite photographic evidence to the contrary—"I don't wear a girdle. I think a girdle ruins your figure. You should learn to hold your stomach in without it. And I don't wear a brassiere, but I work every day with five-pound dumbbells. I stand up, stretch my arms apart shoulder height and make little circles first in one direction and then the other. I lie on a slant board the wrong way so my shoulders are off the floor and I raise my arms close together above my face and I slowly lower them and sweep them up. . . . These chest muscles need exercise to stay firm and keep your bust line high."

As for her diet—newly influenced by Mickey—"I never let my eating get out of hand. I love pizza, spaghetti and all that fattening Italian food, but it makes me feel terrible afterward. And it isn't worth it. Sometimes I indulge myself and when I gain I go on my favorite diet of steak, tomatoes and apple juice three times a day."

Jayne splurged for Christmas, getting her mother a mink stole, Mickey gold and pearl cuff links, Jayne Marie a bike, new clothes, and a strand of pearls, and furniture and a washing machine for Jayne Marie's dollhouse. She also kept up her social whirl, usually accompanied by Mickey: she appeared at the Los Angeles Press Club in December, carried in by Santa Claus and placed under the tree. "I like you people. Where would I be without you?" she told the reporters. Iowa sophomore quarterback Randy Duncan said he wanted Jayne Mansfield for Christmas, and he got her— she showed up at the Iowa Big Ten Club dinner at the Biltmore in Los Angeles and gave Duncan a big kiss for the cameras.

Jayne and Mickey showed up at the premiere of *Around the World in 80 Days,* both dressed all in white (fellow attendee Adolphe Menjou sighed resignedly, "This could ruin my whole evening"). In February veteran photographer and self-described "tough old billiard" Arthur "Conky" Conkwright dropped dead of a heart attack right after taking a photo of Jayne at a charity ball in Palm Springs; although the obits were respectful, most of them hinted broadly that a look at Jayne Mansfield was more than his heart could take.

Hollywood columnist Bob Thomas named Jayne and Tony Perkins as the "most promising newcomers," also giving Diana Dors a nod for "biggest publicity splash." A poll of 122 Louisville teenagers revealed that their favorite actresses were, in order, Jayne, Natalie Wood, Kim Novak, Marilyn Monroe, Anita Ekberg, Elizabeth Taylor, and Esther Williams (it was noted that girls preferred Natalie, boys Jayne). Jayne made another TV appearance with Jack Benny in January, in a courtroom scene defending Jack before Judge Liberace. Jayne even spoke up for Marilyn Monroe when Joan Crawford blasted her for vulgarity, though she deftly managed a passive-aggressive jab at Joan: "Joan Crawford has always acted like a star should act," Jayne told the *Chicago Tribune*'s Jack Eigen, "and she should continue to act like one."

In January she sat for Canadian photographer Gabriel "Gaby" Desmarais wearing a modest, high-necked dress from *The Girl Can't Help It*, looking demure and ladylike, but with an annoyed glint in her eyes. Desmarais was equally annoyed. "The movie people pose too much," he told reporter Aline Mosby. "Jayne kept telling me what her best side was. I had to fight all the way through the sitting to bring out her real beauty and not just bust, legs and hips. I try to get them for what they are themselves, not for what the public sees. They are used to photography here which is like making candies—one picture the same as another and over-retouched." He added, "Business and society women are much more beautiful than the actresses. That makeup they have to wear is bad for the skin. After a while it begins to show. Glamour is just a state of mind, anyway. If you look for beauty, you find it. Everybody has something beautiful about them."

Jayne usually went over well on talk shows, but she had a dire experience on *Tonight! America After Dark*, hosted by Jack Lescoulie. Hollywood columnist Vernon Scott, cohosting, interviewed Jayne; he dwelt on her figure and leeringly wondered how many people could fit in the heart-shaped bathtub she wanted. Press and public reaction was quick and sharp: "I didn't encounter anybody who had anything good to say about the mishmash," wrote Will Jones in the *Minneapolis Star Tribune*. "Reactions to an interview with Jayne Mansfield, conducted by Vernon Scott, ranged from disbelief to disgust."

John Crosby added that Jayne spoke "in a sepulchral whisper that may have been her dying breath or may on the other hand be the way she thinks busty blondes have to talk." Crosby was not amused when fellow guest Irv Kupcinet asked her about weightlifting and she said, "It's brought out quite a few of my finer points. It straightens things and puts things in the right places." The show's producer, Richard Linkroum, admitted that "the Jayne Mansfield thing got a little bit out of control," but "I believe our show has been cruelly treated. And despite all the criticism by the critics, maybe we're lucky. Everybody is talking about us." Jack Lescoulie was out as host after seven episodes.

Jayne was well known enough by early 1957 that companies were cashing in on her name, with or without her cooperation. The Molly Ann shop in Indiana, Pennsylvania, ran a hilarious Washington's Birthday "truth" ad in the local paper, offering "beautiful, luscious cashmere cardigans made with Jayne Mansfield in mind. Jayne didn't come in to buy them for $24.95 and neither did Marilyn so you can have them for $17." The copywriter (who, one hopes, got a bonus) also plugged Molly Ann hats ("These are too punk to even laugh over. You'll look your worst but feel your best!") and scarves ("These scarves will never go out of style—they'll just look ridiculous year after year! Why, oh why did our buyer buy so many?").

She was also being name-checked on TV and in books: the 1957 best seller *Gidget* (a lot racier than the films made from it) included a scene in which randy surf bums pore over the new *Playboy* issue, one of them crowing, "I'd fertilize that Mansfield any day!"

Also in early 1957 came the first mention of Jayne's purportedly high IQ, in a syndicated article by Ray Parker: "Let it be stated for the record at this point Miss Mansfield boasts an I.Q. of 163 and attended three universities." The factoid took off: by the summer of 1957 Scott Thurston of the *Scranton Times Tribune* was repeating it, and eventually Jayne was declaring herself a genius-level intellect. By the time she wed Matt Cimber in 1964, Jayne was claiming a 164 IQ, noting that Matt's was 165.

Jayne's actual IQ scores have not yet surfaced: it's quite probable that she was given a Stanford-Binet or Wechsler test in school (most mid-century students were), but it has yet to be uncovered. The important point is that Jayne was genuinely smart, whatever her IQ score. She played the violin and piano competently, could converse fairly well in several languages, learned her scripts and stage business quickly, and—as filmed interviews show—she was witty, quick on her feet with a wisecrack, and eloquent, with an impressive mastery of the English language. Jayne may have made some jaw-droppingly stupid decisions, both in her career and in her private life, but she was not stupid.

When *The Wayward Bus* began shooting in February 1957, Jayne was awarded Victor Mature's old dressing room at Fox. "After work I go home, have a fast steak, cream my face, and then to bed," she told Hedda Hopper. "I have to be up at 5 a.m., and at the studio by 6." She added that "I give my evenings to" Jayne Marie.

The Wayward Bus is based on John Steinbeck's enjoyably lurid 1947 novel about the unhappy marriage of a bus driver and his diner-running wife, their unhappy employees, and the unhappy customers who come into their lives. Jayne plays Camille, a weary stag-party dancer and pin-up model. She wasn't the only cast member out of her usual mold: British sex kitten Joan Collins (first-billed, right above Jayne) plays the hash-slinging wife, a blowsy alcoholic role originally planned for Susan Hayward. The overbearing novelties salesman who puts the moves on Camille is played by Dan Dailey, a song-and-dance man who also excelled at smarmy character roles.

Steinbeck's Camille is described as a blonde knockout, resigned to being reduced to her obvious charms: "It was nice to always get the best seat, to have your lunches bought for you, to have a hand on your arm crossing the street. Men couldn't keep their hands off her. But there was always the trouble. She had to argue or cajole or insult or fight her way out. All men wanted the same thing from her, and that was just the way it was. She took it for granted and it was true." If any actress could get inside Camille's head, it was Jayne.

The shoot was not an easy one, though numerous photos exist of the cast palling around in a comradely way. Jayne caught a painful, maddening case of poison oak while filming on location on the hills outside Los Angeles (of course, one story was amusingly but unsympathetically headlined "Jayne Mansfield Covered with Bumps"). At the Hollywood Foreign Press Awards dinner in early March, Jayne was all bundled up in mink to hide her still red and itchy rash. In her memoirs, Joan Collins recalled walking in on Jayne having her pubic hair bleached and hurriedly backing out of the dressing room. "Oh, Joan, you English are so prudish!" laughed Jayne.

Most of Jayne's scenes are with Dan Dailey, and the two have great on-screen chemistry. His hard-boiled salesman and her damaged, shy dancer softened each other. Both give wonderful performances, hers low-key and his tightly wound. Their terrible off-screen relationship showed what professionals they really were. Jayne never said a bad word about Dan Dailey, but when he was slated for another film with Jayne, he told Sheilah Graham, "It was the kiss of death as far as the studio and I were concerned. . . . I'm not against bosoms as such. But you're doing a scene with a girl, and all she's conscious of is whether her bra is being used to the best advantage, you might as well be doing a documentary for a girl's underwear company."

The Wayward Bus wrapped in March and premiered in late May. It is too dreary and depressing a film to have become a big hit—though it does its dreary and depressing source book proud. Director Victor Vicas (who mostly worked in German films and French TV) did an excellent job, pulling good performances from his cast. Jayne, looking movie-star beautiful, gives a superb performance as the cynical, tired-of-life Camille, trying to hide her past from nosy fellow passengers. No squealing, no baby voice, just a good, stripped-down acting job, one that might have pointed her career in another direction had it been in a hit film.

There's no real plot, except for the titular bus getting stuck in the mud and approaching a washed-out bridge (the special effects, by *Planet of the Apes* and *Fantastic Voyage* master L. B. Abbott, are superb). Mostly—like the book—it's a series of character studies: will the bus driver (handsome Rick Jason) and his wife split up? Will the lonely passenger (Dolores Michaels) make it with the driver? Will Camille be outed as a nudie model? Will she and the pushy salesman fall for each other? (They do, and we're supposed to be happy about it.) Happy endings were tacked on because producer Charles Brackett felt the book was too depressing for movie audiences.

Jayne did get some well-deserved good reviews. The *Anniston Star* wrote that "rock-n-roll star Jayne Mansfield of *Girl Can't Help It* fame emerges as a real dramatic actress!" But most of the compliments were backhanded: "Miss Mansfield can do little with this stock role" (*Pittsburgh Press*); "Although Miss Mansfield contributes a capable acting job, Joan Collins is outstanding" (*Fairbanks Daily News-Miner*). Harold V. Cohen in the *Pittsburgh Post-Gazette* wrote that "as Mansfield performances go, it isn't too bad. As a matter of fact, there are even moments when the suggestion of an actress comes through hiding behind the hour-glass figure, those long lashes and that even longer straw blonde hair. Of course, there isn't a lot Miss Mansfield or anyone else can do with Mr. Ivan Moffatt's script, which is as wayward as Mr. Steinbeck's bus."

None of the critics loved *The Wayward Bus*. Some liked it ("All things considered, it is an entertaining film well worth seeing") and some hated it ("All the persons involved strike me as shallow and hardly worth dramatizing"). It was nominated for a Golden Bear Award at the Berlin International Film Festival, lost, and pretty much sank without a trace. Jayne was bitterly disappointed in *The Wayward Bus,* and rarely mentioned it in future interviews (she spoke of *The Burglar* as her best dramatic performance). Joan Collins, too, felt let down: she told Louella Parsons in 1958 that it "was one of my favorite pictures, but I doubt if this picture ever made the production cost back." Of her costar, Collins said, "If Jayne would stop trying to be so glamorous all the time, she would be a good actress."

With terrific comedy and dramatic performances to her credit, Jayne was the rising star of 1957—but there was always someone younger pushing her way ahead of this year's sensation. In March, Sheilah Graham reported that "Jack Warner was impressed with the rough cut of *Untamed Youth* in which Mamie Van Doren comes through as a singer. Warner, who once had Jayne Mansfield under contract and let her get away, now has commanded his publicity crew to give Mamie the Mansfield build-up." Graham also noted that at the Hollywood Foreign Press Awards dinner (the one where poor Jayne was still nursing her poison oak rash), Van Doren was called "Miss Mansfield," to the amusement of her husband, bandleader Ray Anthony. Belgian actress Monique Van Vooren "maintains a Jayne Mansfield-ish publicity pace," wrote columnist Hy Gardner in March 1957. "I had five dates with Elvis Presley while I was making a movie in Hollywood," said Van Vooren, "but it's nothing serious. He's too young for me now and maybe in about five years I'll be too young for him."

Another high-profile star that year was Liberace, who was sometimes called "the male Jayne Mansfield" (as she was called "the female Liberace"). Their exuberant sense of camp and the sheer fun they had with their public images ensured that they would become friends. Show-business writer Bob Thomas approved, feeling that both performers brought a necessary sprinkle of glitter to Hollywood. "The movie business at mid-century is entering middle age," he wrote. "The madcap days are over; respectability has set in. The seriousness of this trend is best illustrated by those who counter it. Examples: Liberace and Jayne Mansfield. Both Liberace and Mansfield have been targets for derision in Hollywood. Yet Liberace is merely a throwback to the era when Tom Mix dressed entirely in white from his 10-gallon hat to his shoes and drove an all-white limousine. And Mansfield harks back to when Dolores Del Rio slept in a bedroom with four walls and ceiling completely mirrored."

Erskine Johnson compared Jayne to another high-intensity show-biz character, Mike Todd, who had just married Elizabeth Taylor. "For all their publicity-madness, Jayne Mansfield and producer Mike Todd have the right idea," wrote Johnson. "Jayne's living it up in the big tradition of movie queens—and she's selling tickets." Jayne was delighted that some people "got it," telling Johnson that "I work just as hard at my acting as I do at being a personality. I think too many people have tried to take the showmanship out of show business. I see nothing wrong about driving around in a white convertible, walking a leopard, wielding a bejeweled trowel in the garden, ordering pink champagne and dragging a mink to help sell yourself as a movie star. They're all props that help sell tickets."

A few years later, Arthur Helliwell of the *People* chimed in with his admiration for Jayne's showmanship. "The real truth is that Jayne, gorgeous, sexy, extravagant and slightly larger than life, was born about three decades too late," he wrote in 1961. "Today she is the ONLY girl in Hollywood who lives like an old-time movie star. . . . Jaynie gets such an obvious kick out of playing the glamorous film star, it becomes infectious. . . . I think Hollywood could do with a few more Jayne Mansfields. She represents the carnival candy floss, the icing on the cake, the diamond-bright glitter and the stardust that makes show business exciting."

Just before the film version of *Rock Hunter* went into production, Jayne made a very public appearance that resulted in her most famous photo and that tipped off both Fox and the public that Jayne was no ordinary movie star—that there just might be something a little too crackpot about this new star to blend into the Hollywood crowd.

There were already signs, of course: the night before, Jayne and Mickey had showed up at the *Spirit of St. Louis* premiere; Jayne wore a pleated gold lamé gown, and Mickey lifted her above his head in an airplane pose: "Isn't that what this picture is all about?" she said. One fellow attendee, the very ladylike Greer Garson, sighed, "Who could follow that?"

Then came what was to be the most talked-about welcome party in Hollywood history, Sophia Loren's elegant, all-star bash at Romanoff's. Loren—in a modestly low-cut black gown—was seated with Clifton Webb; other guests included Barbara Stanwyck, Gary Cooper, Shelley Winters, Eva Marie Saint, Rita Moreno, Fred MacMurray, and Jeanne Crain, all drifting around making conversation and smiling for the cameras.

Then Jayne wafted in, trailed by 20th Century-Fox executive Roy Craft (described by the *Los Angeles Times* as "a little page"). Jayne was wearing a silver mink coat (which she declined to check at the door) and carried, of course, a Chihuahua. Then—just as Marilyn Monroe would doff her fur coat to gasps at President Kennedy's 1962 birthday party—Jayne handed Craft the Chihuahua (he was heard to mutter, "Luckily she didn't bring the Great Dane") and shimmied out of her mink to reveal a form-fitting silver silk gown "cut so dangerously low that it made a mockery of the word neckline," in the words of the *Philadelphia Inquirer*.

Reporter Andrew Carthew of the *Daily Herald* recalled, "She undulated over to the bar and stood next to me. She explained in a loud voice that she was wearing nothing underneath. I'd noticed already. Suddenly she said, 'Watch this!' and wiggled her way over to the Loren table." Reports varied on what happened next. Carthew said that Loren "refused to reply when Jayne spoke, and deliberately turned the back of her head to her. Which was lucky for Jayne, if looks can kill." Photos—and there are many of them—belie Carthew's account, though.

Jayne leaned over—*way* over—to chat with Loren and position herself for photographers, while Loren politely smiled and laughed and chatted with her. Tablemate Clifton Webb concentrated very hard on his food and did not look up; restaurateur Michael Romanoff hovered nervously in the background, looking as if he wanted to hustle Jayne off as quickly and politely as possible. Rita Moreno, then a rising young Fox starlet, did a Jimmy Finlayson–worthy double take, captured by one photographer, that echoed what everyone else was thinking. Louella Parsons noted that "the photographers who wanted solo pictures of Sophia had to ask Jayne to step aside."

Parsons had been sitting between Loren and Webb, but when she abandoned her post (perhaps to call in the story), Jayne plunked herself down next to Loren. As Jayne smiled dazzlingly and ingenuously at the cameras, Sophia Loren executed a side-eye for the ages, nervously glaring at Jayne's breasts as they peeked out to say "hello."

Andrew Carthew, whose version of events is, as mentioned above, somewhat untrustworthy, wrote, "Undaunted, Jayne came back to the bar and said: 'That's a silly girl. She wouldn't speak to me—and I only wanted to make her welcome.' Somebody pointed out to her that she had ruined Sophia's public debut in Hollywood—stolen her limelight, so to speak. Said Jayne innocently: 'Did I really do that? All I wanted was to show Sophia that we also have bosoms in Hollywood.'" On her way out, as Roy Craft helped her back into her coat, he "called Jayne a doll. Ann Miller called her something else later."

It was a party that went down in history, alongside Truman Capote's Black and White Ball and the time Norma Shearer wore red to Carole Lombard's 1936 White Ball (a faux pas immortalized in *Jezebel* and *Gone*

JAYNE MANSFIELD

with the Wind). While Rita Moreno may have been amused, few others were—well, nearly everyone was, but none would admit to it. "I have been one of Jayne's best boosters and defenders ever since she came to town," wrote Louella Parsons, "but she is going to lose me in her corner if she continues to wear those daringly low gowns and courts publicity with silly actions, as she has been doing lately." Hedda Hopper pulled a "We were not amused," and Joan Winchell of the *Los Angeles Times* wrote that "Jayne has two obvious gimmicks, neither of which was more obvious than our blushes. Mercy me, she makes Marilyn Monroe look like Mona Lisa!" Italian newspapers refused to publish any photos of Jayne at the event. Actress Vera Miles's agent, Milt Rosner, snootily said, "She doesn't lend herself to spectacular publicity, like Jayne Mansfield."

Some reporters got the joke and cheered Jayne on, including Bob Thomas: "Pish-tush! Jayne is doing a yeoman job in her one-woman campaign to restore some excitement to this tired old town." The *Philadelphia Inquirer* declared that Jayne "wins by a neckline," quoting Loren as sniffing, "I would never wear a dress like that," and Jayne purring back, "Maybe she can't afford to wear dresses like this. You know, if you raise a flag it has to have something to hold it up." Several papers noted that Sophia Loren had appeared nude in the 1954 Italian film *Due Notti con Cleopatra*.

Over the years, various quotes from Jayne were printed; their veracity can only be guessed at (even if they did come out of Jayne's mouth, she never let the truth get in the way of a good story). She told her ghostwriter Leo Guild in 1963 that "I chose to wear a gown that was low cut in front. It was the only presentable gown I had which wasn't in dry dock for repairs or cleaning. True, I didn't wear a bra—I never do—but then many girls don't wear bras with an evening gown. . . . I really had no idea how much of me was showing. I only realized how much was exposed when I saw the expression on Miss Loren's face and I noticed that she was staring down my dress." In a summation that Anita Loos's Lorelei Lee would admire, Jayne added prettily, "It is situations like this which I seem to become involved in that accounts for so much publicity that some people frown at."

With a mixture of good common sense and double entendre, she was also quoted as saying, "If you're a Bernhardt or a Shakespeare but no one knows about it, you might as well just kind of act in your own home, which doesn't do too much good if you want to be a successful star. So I feel that the right balance of publicity, coupled with talent, brings forth a giant star that cannot be toppled over."

20th Century-Fox's press department immediately called Jayne on the carpet and stipulated "no more semi-nudes," instructing her that she would have to have all her photos and dresses okayed by the studio. She tried to atone by having a public checkup (dressed in a towel) for the American Cancer Society.

Somewhat chastened—or at least smart enough to appear so—Jayne made the Louella Parsons Apology Tour. Parsons was one of the more powerful columnists who actually liked Jayne, so it was a wise move. "When I saw the photographs I knew my dress was too low," Jayne said during a phone conversation. "It was only too low when I bent over and posed the way the photographers requested. I had worn the dress before with no adverse comment. Do you think I ought to go to any premieres at all?" Parsons told her that "she didn't have to go into a convent but not to lend herself to any more cheap publicity. 'You don't have to do it.'"

A week later Jayne made more Stations of the Cross with Parsons, sitting down person-to-person and insisting—straight-faced—"I am normally a very quiet, home-loving girl and really shy. I would much rather stay at home with my little daughter, Jaynie, and have a little dinner before a fireplace." Jayne "looked younger than her years in blue slacks, blue jacket and matching shoes. She had difficulty restraining the tears, because for the first time Jayne, who has always been such a good Joe with the newspaper people, had been held up to ridicule and bitter criticism and this was new to her."

Parsons had been a show-business columnist since 1914, so this was nothing she hadn't heard before. "But when I came to Hollywood," Jayne went on, "I was told you have to get in the limelight and if I wanted to succeed I had to go to all the previews and happenings. I know now I must pick and choose the places I go and I must not wear dresses too low, and try to attract too much attention. I would like to explain about that dress I wore. I paid $200 for it and I have worn it several times at various affairs and there was never a word said."

Proving herself a better actress than critics gave her credit for, Jayne pleaded to Parsons, "'Tell me, what's wrong with me?' 'Nothing,' I told her, 'that a little common sense can't cure. Why did you let Mickey Hargitay take you in his arms and hold you up to the last row in the bleachers so you could sign autographs?'" Jayne had an excellent answer to that one: "The fans never get the autographs of stars at premieres." Parsons scolded her, "If you are going to be a great actress, you are going to have to have dignity. Don't always be on stage."

The following week Jayne appeared at a party for Hedy Lamarr and kept her full-length mink firmly closed, even indoors. Then at one point she "dropped her mink coat to reveal a dress that hadn't quite made it to the party with Jayne. She flirted with the maharaja of Baroda and told him she'd love to visit his country if she could ride a pink elephant." The maharaja was heard to mutter, "Charming, utterly charming. We shall supply pink tigers, too."

8

Jayne Mansfield can't get on *I've Got a Secret* because she doesn't.

Louella Parsons

Two years after she was hired for *Will Success Spoil Rock Hunter?* on Broadway, Jayne was set to begin the film version. The shoot—during the summer of 1957—went well, as Jayne and Frank Tashlin (who wrote, directed, and produced) had a good working relationship, and costars Tony Randall (in a part originally meant for Tom Ewell), Joan Blondell (originally Thelma Ritter), and Henry Jones were thoroughgoing professionals. Tashlin even threw a small supporting role to Mickey, who plays Rita Marlowe's TV Tarzanesque boyfriend, Bobo Branigansky. Tashlin also tried to get Jerry Lewis for a surprise end-of-film cameo, but wound up with Groucho Marx.

There is nothing about the film version of *Rock Hunter* that even vaguely resembles the Broadway show (George Axelrod saw this coming a mile away, shrugged, and took the money). Tashlin rewrote it as a satire of advertising and television, two subjects that were sore points with movie executives. "Rock Hunter" became a real person in this version, an eager young ad exec played by Tony Randall. To keep his job, Hunter has to save the company's Stay-Put Lipstick account and get movie star Rita Marlowe to endorse it. Rita is written as both a bubblehead (who thinks every word she doesn't understand is dirty) and a wily businesswoman who knows exactly how the publicity and stardom games work.

"My day starts at 5 a.m. and it's a full grind of picture-making, lessons and rehearsals before I fall asleep exhausted at 9 p.m.," Jayne said during the filming of *Rock Hunter.* "Weekends and what free hours I can squeeze out of the work week I spend with my daughter Jayne Marie." She also showed herself to be a real-life Rita Marlowe, not one of the new breed of jeans and T-shirt actors: "When I do go out in public it's a full-scale production. I'm dressed in my best. I believe the movie fan expects glamor and is entitled to it. I don't believe in this new fad of blue jeans and sweaters worn by some actresses and I wouldn't allow myself to be seen on the streets with my hair up and no makeup."

Dress designer Elgee Bove said, "I don't always agree with her studio. They built her up as a scantily-clad sex goddess, and now 20th Century-Fox wants to *dress* her. I think it would be a terrible mistake." Bove added that Jayne "is a dream to work with. She leaves herself in the designer's hands. Jayne and I see eye to eye."

Her costars took great delight in needling her, sometimes rather nastily, perhaps resenting this newcomer who coasted to fame on publicity and her measurements. Tony Randall laughed that Mickey "carries her everywhere. At the studio, he carried her from her dressing room to the set every day. He carried her across streets. I went to a party with them once and he even carried her around the living room." Jay Sayer, who played a bit part, reminisced to film historian Tom Weaver that Joan Blondell *loved* to poke fun at Mansfield. "People keep saying Mansfield was really a very intelligent, bright woman pretending to be a ditz. Uhn-uh! She was *such* a ditz . . . you don't start with Blondell, she really was a bright, tough lady." Blondell would make some veiled wisecrack at Jayne, said Sayer, and Jayne "started laughing . . . *halfway* knowing she was getting it, but the other half thinking, '*what* is she saying?'"

Will Success Spoil Rock Hunter? is a delightful follow-up to *The Girl Can't Help It,* giving Jayne two great comic showcases in a row. While the stage play was dark and cynical, the movie is bright and silly right from the first frame (the opening credits contain TV commercial parodies: "If you're like me, with six filthy children and a big dirty husband . . ."). Tashlin created ninety-some minutes of delightful jokes, sight gags, and jabs at TV, advertising, corporate culture, and sex. While the ad execs treat the pretty secretaries (one of them a young Barbara Eden) like baubles, there's also some scrutiny of sex roles, both male and female: Rita makes the female supporting characters feel flat and inadequate, and Rock is also shown to be a sexless nebbish compared to Mickey's Bobo. In a 1962 interview, Frank Tashlin said that *Rock Hunter* was about "the difference between living and *earning* a living. I know it's no new thing. The picture is really saying that success is a lot of nonsense."

Rita is clearly Jayne; references are made to *The Girl Can't Help It, The Wayward Bus,* and her upcoming *Kiss Them for Me.* Marilyn Monroe is also a target—Rita plans to open her own production company in New York, as Marilyn did in 1954, and Marilyn's desire to play Grushenka in *The Brothers Karamazov* is echoed with Rita appearing in "that Russian drama about two Russian brothers."

The script is sharp and funny and naughty; Tashlin must have thrown in a lot of sacrificial dirty jokes to get the censors to pass the ones they did. There's a reference to Rita's ex-boyfriend, "that Academy Award winner who had you polishing his Oscar"; Rock feels inadequate because he can't keep his pipe lit; and when Rock tells Rita she will be the "titular" head of her production company, she squeals with delight and kisses him (at which the bag of popcorn in his pocket pops lewdly). The film makes much use of Jayne's ear-splitting helium squeal.

Tashlin being Tashlin, there are lots of great sight gags, many of them incorporating Jayne: dressed head to toe in leopard skin, wearing the world's largest sunglasses, she proclaims, "I'm just a perfectly normal American girl!" She's seen in a Roman-sized bubble bath, reading *Peyton Place;* she walks a polka-dot poodle (to match her dressing gown); she exits a plane to a scrum of fans and reporters, throwing off her hooded white fur to reveal a bathing suit. She's gorgeous and silly and a bright, lovely carica-ture of '50s glamour. (The poodle, by the way, is named Shamroy, after *The Girl Can't Help It* cinematographer Leon Shamroy).

She's also sharp and funny; any doubt that Jayne was a smart, talented comic actress was laid to rest with *Rock Hunter.* She switches from dizzy to cynical in a blink, and her comic timing is spot-on. Tony Randall is also perfect as a fey fussbudget, a role he would basically play to the end of his long career.

Rock Hunter was released in July, and critics who screwed up the play's name had no better luck with the film, sometimes calling it *Will Suc-cess Ruin Rock Hunter?* or *Will Success Spoil Rock Hudson?* (Then again, for years newspaper ads ran for *The Girl Couldn't Help It, A Girl Can't Help It,* and *Girls Can't Help It.*)

The film was a hit; everyone seemed to enjoy Tashlin's bright, silly fun. The *Los Angeles Times*'s Philip K. Scheuer called it "hilarious" and "merciless," noting, "The burden of laughs is carried mainly by Randall and, with surprising sparkle, by Miss Mansfield." Art Cullison of the *Akron Beacon Journal* complimented her "increased skill as a comedienne." Marjory Adams of the *Boston Globe* wrote that Jayne's "shrill, gurgly squeal alone is worth the price of admission. . . . Miss Mansfield shows she is more than just a girl with a handsome figure—she manages her comedy lines so cleverly that she could be making them up as she goes along." Best of all, Marjorie Rutherford of the *Atlanta Constitution* wrote, "Up to now, we had believed that Jayne Mansfield's principal claim to fame was her ability to smile into the lens of a newspaper camera. After seeing *Rock Hunter* we are convinced that she has other talents. She is a comedienne of no small stature . . . it's topnotch with loads of laughs."

Other critics' compliments were somewhat backhanded: "Miss Mansfield is a good 'straight' woman for Randall. . . . Fortunately, Miss Mansfield had simple lines" (*El Paso Herald-Post*); "Miss Mansfield, with a wiggle here and a waggle there, is Miss Mansfield. Here is typecasting to the Nth degree" (*San Francisco Examiner*). Kaspar Monahan of the *Pittsburgh Press* let loose: "I felt as though I'd go mad—mad, I tell you—if I heard just one more of Jayne Mansfield's idiotic squeals . . . the squeal, indicative of ineffable delight, is overworked. So is Tony Randall's mugging."

The film itself came in for praise. Hortense Morton of the *San Francisco Examiner* said that the Broadway version of *Rock Hunter* had been "silly, sloppy and smutty. On screen, it is smart, saucy and has a high old time needling television." Carolyn Stull of the *Oakland Tribune* agreed: "What 20th Century-Fox has done for *Will Success Spoil Rock Hunter?* is a delightful surprise and, incidentally, far more than playwright George Axelrod's original deserved . . . the obnoxious vulgarities of the play have been converted into a farce on vulgarity itself which is madly comic from start to finish. Not the least surprise contained in the movie is the performance of Jayne Mansfield . . . a take-off on every such performance by every such film figure of those well-publicized proportions."

The same month that *Will Success Spoil Rock Hunter?* was released, Jayne's *Life* magazine cover companion Judy Tyler died in a car crash, at the age of twenty-four. Tyler's was one of those frustrating "What if?" stories—like Jayne, she had shoved her way to the top with steely ambition, starred in a Broadway musical, and gone on to Hollywood. But Judy Tyler never got the chance to go on to fame.

♥

Even during the long days of shooting, Jayne kept up her social and publicity schedule. She and Mickey—both wearing brief swimsuits—accepted "American Health Awards" from Bert Goodrich, Mr. America 1939, for being "outstanding examples of American health and physical attractiveness." Mickey told reporter Lee Belser, "I know men are always making eyes at Jayne. But it doesn't bother me. We both know the score."

As for their relationship, Jayne said, "Until next October 21, I am a married woman. Mickey and I have no plans to run off to Mexico or Texas. If we did I couldn't return to live in California." And Mickey added, "We have a lot of things in common. We both like outdoor life. We also like barbecued steak. As a matter of fact, Jayne is really a wonderful cook. But I hate to see her do it after working so hard at the studio all day. I like to cook simple things like steak, but Jayne is the one who can really go to town with the macaroni and cheese."

Money was certainly no worry: after her maternal grandfather's will was settled (Thomas Henry Palmer died in 1954), Jayne would clear $120,000 after taxes ($60,000 right away, another $30,000 when she turned twenty-five, and $30,000 when she reached thirty).

♥

At the peak of her stardom, studio executives, fans, foes, and reporters pretty much knew what they had in Jayne Mansfield, and that she was not going to change. Many were exasperated by her over-the-top exhibitionism and glittery, childlike persona. But even those who thought she was a terrible actress and an example of the worst caricature of Hollywood stardom had to admit she was one of the most upbeat, likable people in town.

Reporters who came to scoff found themselves won over. Barbara Flanagan of the *Star Tribune* was surprised to find that "Miss Mansfield on film and Miss Mansfield in the flesh are two different beings. Big on the screen and little in person, Miss Mansfield has a soft, cozy voice and sweet manners. She is alert, pleasant and friendly and seems perpetually surprised at your interest in her." And Herb Kelly of the *Miami News* wrote that during a one-on-one interview out of the public eye, "When she's dressed properly and talks like a woman should, Jayne's an interesting personality. She wore a loose-fitting coat instead of the skin-tight dress which is her show-business trademark. The giddy baby-talk was absent."

Jayne loved the press, even when writers were mean to her, as they often were. "The press and photographers have put me where I am. So I never turn them down. I just can't find it in my heart to say no." Daughter Jayne Marie agreed decades later, "She would do anything for the press. I mean *anything*—the adoration that came back, the attention, meant so much to her."

And as much as she loved the press, Jayne loved her fans even more. "I can remember when I had all sorts of time to myself," she said in 1957. "I'd sit by the telephone and no one ever called. I remember my first fan letter. I was so excited I rushed out and spent $100 just to have pictures taken to send to the fan." Like Joan Crawford, Jayne embraced her fans, answering their letters, signing autographs, stopping to chat with genuine interest. While Garbo, Katharine Hepburn, and Rex Harrison fled from their fans or even insulted them (Hepburn was known to wield her walking stick against autograph seekers), Jayne said of hers, "Some of them, they actually build their lives around me. That's sweet, I think. I have a lot of love in my life. Love is so important, I think."

"Every time she did a play, after the show, she drove producers crazy, she would sit out there and sign every autograph," says her third husband, Matt Cimber. "She was always wonderful to people, on a one-to-one basis. I never saw her put anybody down. She was so un-Hollywood. She never, never, in private or anywhere said anything derogatory about anybody." Nelson Sardelli, her beau in 1963, recalls, "A few times we almost missed a plane because she would stop and make time to talk to everyone and sign all requests for autographs. People really loved her. She wanted and needed to be loved."

Even being interrupted on a dinner date didn't faze her, as diners at Ruby Foo's restaurant found out: "She's not only intelligent but she talks directly to you, giving you her undivided attention," recalled one fan who barged up to Jayne's table. "Unlike some stars she didn't keep looking around to see who was staring at her." In 1963 high-school student Charlene Peters and her sister met Jayne on the street and asked for her autograph. She didn't have any photos on her so, to their amazement, she invited them up to her hotel suite. "She didn't talk about herself at any great length," recalled Peters. "Most of the conversation was directed to my sister and me. She asked us about our family, where we were from, our ambitions in life, what we liked and didn't like. Talking with her wasn't any different than talking to a good friend. She was very down-to-earth."

The pushing, frenzied mobs at the opening of the Chicagoland Consumers Mart of America in 1962 would seem to most people like a nightmare: shouting lewd remarks, shoving cameras, photos, and autograph books in Jayne's face. But Jayne loved every minute of it, and loved every last fan—or at least that's the impression she worked hard to give. "It was a friendly, captivating face which later turned patiently and often toward the amateur shutterbugs without a trace of impatience or annoyance," wrote Jim Davies of the *Arlington Heights Herald.* "'Oh, it's really kind of fun,' she said. 'I'm enjoying it as much as I hope everyone else is.' And there was no trace in her voice or smile of the phoniness almost expected of a publicized product of the Hollywood glamour factory."

Jayne also had an astonishing memory for names and faces. Kenneth MacDonald had interviewed her during a 1960 USO tour, and when he met her two years later at a premiere, "she remembered me. And she invited me and the girl who's now my wife backstage while she made her appearance." The following year when he was in California, Jayne took MacDonald to lunch and invited him to her film set. "She was down to earth and intelligent, not like the dumb-blonde act she puts on."

And if the saying "You can tell a lady by how she treats the help" is true, Jayne was Hollywood royalty, according to Esther Massen, a maid at the Hotel Algiers in Florida. "The staff of a hotel fast finds out what a guest is really like, and it didn't take long for us to get to know Miss Mansfield," Massen said in the mid-1960s. "We all loved her. She never saw me or any of the other maids without coming over, smiling, and asking how we were. She never seemed stuck-up or self-centered. Her rooms were always straight and neat. She kept her clothes hung up and her shoes in place; better than most people, I can tell you." When Massen admired a framed photo of Jayne, "she was delighted. You would have thought it was the first time anybody had said such a thing. A few weeks after she left, I got one in the mail—autographed, too."

9

The average teenager knows Jayne Mansfield's statistics better than he does the First Commandment.

Billy Graham

*K*iss *Them for Me,* Jayne's next assignment, was the film version of a 1945 dark comedy about three war heroes on leave, and it was to star Cary Grant (at fifty-three a little too old to be a war hero). The thought of costarring with Grant overwhelmed Jayne. The Broadway show had starred newcomers Richard Widmark and Jayne Meadows as the romantic leads, with bright young Judy Holliday as the female comic relief—Holliday, as she pretty much always did, stole the show. Louis Sobol wrote, "What could have been a tawdry part was illuminated by the great performance of Judy Holliday in the role of a sympathetic tart." Holliday's part, of course, went to Jayne, which meant she has limited on-screen time with Cary Grant. Jayne had been thrilled at costarring with Grant, but was less than happy when she saw how few scenes she had, and how uninspiring the role was. Matt Cimber recalls Jayne saying, "'They wanted me to costar with Cary Grant—I never made a film where I'm not the only name above the title.' Unbelievable. She wasn't even *in* the film, she was only in it very sporadically. You know when the studio system changed, there weren't people who were writing scripts deliberately for her."

Shooting started in late March and continued through June, which means Jayne was dashing from *Rock Hunter* to *Kiss Them for Me.* It sounds like an impossible schedule, but her *Kiss Them for Me* scenes were so limited that it was easy to work around her—not a good sign for her new film.

Another bad sign was Suzy Parker, who was signed for the female lead, Gwinneth Livingston, a snooty society girl who falls for Cary Grant's Commander Andy Crewson, a bitter navy pilot in the throes of what would now be called PTSD. Parker, a twenty-five-year-old supermodel, made a splash appearing as herself in *Funny Face;* this convinced producer Jerry Wald that she was a sure bet for stardom, so he flew her in from Paris for screen tests. Somehow she was signed, despite possessing no discernable acting talent. "They were building the other girl up, she was terrible," says Cimber. The cast was filled out by Ray Walston (yanked out of Broadway's *Damn Yankees*) and rising young TV actor Larry Blyden. Fox had wanted Dan Dailey for the Walston role, but he made his disdain for Jayne known and walked out on his contract.

Though most of the film was shot on the Fox lot, a couple of weeks were spent on location in San Francisco. In early May—two weeks after her Sophia debacle—Jayne, in the words of the *San Francisco Examiner*'s Herb Caen, "swished into the Blue Fox restaurant in a low-cut gown, bent over a little too far and—well—good morning, all! Cool Jayne merely cooed 'Oops' and got things back under control." Jayne was accompanied by her Chihuahua Philip, who wore a mink collar. (Jayne also lunched with Igor Cassini, the brother of her former beau Oleg, to Mickey's consternation.)

Filming wrapped in early July, and Bill Shiffrin met with Fox executives to discuss a raise and her upcoming films; as Sheilah Graham noted, Jayne had "made four movies for $60,000 during the past twelve months. That makes her the biggest bargain in town." But *Kiss Them for Me* would be the last film Jayne would make for Fox that was not a loan-out. Her tenure in Victor Mature's dressing room was over.

Kiss Them for Me, released in December 1957, is a dispiriting film, veering between bitter wartime drama and forced comedy, and never finding its level. The three navy pilots, Crewson (Grant), McCann (Walston), and Mississip' (Blyden) are on leave in 1944 San Francisco. There's a lot of girl chasing, drinking, claustrophobic partying, and the three men coming to terms with their war experiences. "Treating women abominably" was expected, both in 1944 and 1957, but things do get surprisingly nasty (particularly one moment early in the film, when a perfectly lovely but insufficiently glamorous WAC—Barbara Gould, who'd been in *The Girl Can't Help It*—is thrown out of the men's suite in favor of the curvier Jayne).

Jayne plays Alice Kratzner, a Rosie the Riveter who's madly keen to entertain the troops (for much of the film she wears a lovely yellow-patterned frock by Charles Le Maire, who really knew how to dress her by now). She's the comic relief, and is sorely needed: when Grant compliments her on her lovely hair, Jayne replies, "It's natural, except for the color," and at one point she proclaims, "I only dance with servicemen and civilians." It's a one-note role, except for a scene toward the end that she and Walston really nail: a married man, he feels guilty about fooling around with her, and Jayne—dropping all comic affectations—explains that she flirts with on-leave servicemen for all the boys over there who have no girls (and yes, she does say "Kiss them for me").

Cary Grant grumpily walks through his role, and Jess Stearn of the *New York Daily News* noted that he was at least twenty years too old for the part—and that Gary Cooper, Gene Kelly, and Clark Gable were all romancing significantly younger women on-screen that year as well. But Grant, he conceded, "is charming and youngish enough to bowl over a couple of twenty-ish beauts, Jayne Mansfield and Suzie [*sic*] Parker, and make it stick." The film has some great bits from comic pros Frank Nelson, Richard Deacon, and Nathaniel Frey, who is a delight as tongue-tied Chief Petty Officer Ruddle; in one of the film's best moments he and Jayne flirtatiously chuckle and squeal at each other.

The lovely monkey wrench in the works—besides the script and Stanley Donen's listless direction—is poor Suzy Parker, thrown in completely over her head. Parker was a very talented model (and being a good model is much harder than many people realize), but she never found her footing as an actress. This was her big-screen acting debut, and the role called for more than she had. Parker looks beautiful—she was incapable of looking otherwise—but as far as acting goes, she says all her lines in the right order, and when she is supposed to be angry she says them very loudly. But she and Grant grind the film to a halt whenever they are together on-screen. "I was lousy in my first picture," Parker later admitted. "Everyone was bad in it, even Jayne Mansfield. If you can imagine that."

Poor Parker was eviscerated in the reviews: "Has looks and poise but needs a lot of tutoring in speaking her lines"; "Her acting, unfortunately, is as wooden as some of her poses in *Vogue*." Vernon Scott wrote, "The reviews of Suzy's emoting were so severe there were no barbs left for Jayne Mansfield's acting." Sadly for Jayne, this was not true. Dorothy Masters in the *New York Daily News* wrote that Jayne "is allowed, or probably encouraged, to do a particularly inane caricature of the dumb blonde." Herb Kelly wrote that "the platinum-haired and over-sized woman still does nothing except swivel, squeal and simper." William Mootz of the *Louisville Courier-Journal* described Jayne's character as a "giggling nymphomaniac" and added, "Her simpering, exaggerated caricature of Marilyn Monroe gets increasingly tiresome, picture by picture. She is striking proof that larger-than-life dimensions do not an actress make." Walter Winchell called Jayne "an inept female impersonator." Which is not only unkind, it's inaccurate: Jayne was a *brilliant* female impersonator.

The reviews weren't all bad—Helen Bower of the *Detroit Free Press* felt that "laugh-minded audiences will probably get their money's worth. . . . Miss Mansfield has good comedy sense and a manner of innocent merriment like a playful kitten," and the critic at the *Valley Morning Star* in Texas wrote that Jayne "proves herself not only exceedingly lovely to look at but comes through a fine comedienne as well."

Jayne and Mickey took off for a vacation in Acapulco as soon as filming ended, and with her agent talking to Fox, Jayne had unrealistically rosy plans for her career. "What I want to do more than anything else is the life of Jean Harlow," she said. "I have seen parts of some of her pictures and I think she is just wonderful." All through the late 1950s, Fox had been dangling *The Jean Harlow Story* over Jayne's head (though Harlow had been an MGM star). Marilyn Monroe, Lee Remick, and Natalie Wood were also mentioned as possibilities, as the studio wrangled with Harlow's mother over rights. The project was eventually dropped at the time, but was picked up in 1965 by Paramount (starring Carroll Baker) and Theatrofilm (starring Carol Lynley). Both versions are jaw-droppingly awful, even worse than the cinematic defilements of Cole Porter, Rudolph Valentino, Jeanne Eagels, and Pearl White committed by major studios.

While filming *Kiss Them for Me,* Jayne made a valiant effort to be taken seriously in an appearance on *The Ed Sullivan Show* aired on May 26 (other guests that night included Dolores Gray, Red Skelton, and 1920s pop star Gene Austin). Rather than singing or doing a comedy sketch, Jayne decided to play the violin and piano.

That sort of act usually works, if just for the shock value: newsman Edwin Newman belting out a tune on *Saturday Night Live,* Christina Hendricks playing the accordion on *Mad Men,* politicians Bill Clinton and Condoleezza Rice busting out their saxophone and piano skills. Jayne had not had time to keep up her musical training, but she had years of lessons behind her, and she convinced Sullivan to let her give it a try. A week before the broadcast, she got up at the Little Gypsy restaurant on Sunset Boulevard and played the violin for patrons (including Mickey).

On Sullivan's show, wearing a glittering gown and a scared but determined expression, Jayne played the violin in a quite respectable rendition of Vivaldi's "Concerto in A Minor," then returned to play Ernesto Lecuona's lively "Malagueña" on the piano. She did herself proud, and the audience was appreciative; she even good-naturedly quoted Samuel Johnson's line about dogs that walk on their hind legs—"It is not done well, but you are surprised to find it done at all."

Reviews ranged from lukewarm ("She did prove that she can do more than just stand around and look beautiful," from the *Los Angeles Times* and "She's better than Jack Benny, not as good as Yehudi Menuhin" from the *Orlando Evening Star*) to vicious ("Nobody expects her to have talent. She ought to leave well enough alone," from the *Ottawa Citizen* and "Her piano playing should have stood in the audition hall of Ted Mack's Original Amateur Hour" from the *San Diego Examiner*).

Ben Gross of the *New York Daily News* liked her violin recital, but called her piano playing cold and mechanical. Jim Gilmore of the *Vancouver Sun* made the obvious joke that the "violin and piano playing may not have been good, but it certainly wasn't flat." James Devane of the *Cincinnati Enquirer* was coldly savage: "With that mannequin-like hair as perfect as ever and her better-known attributes showily encased, Jayne determinedly worked away on a fiddle. For good measure, she also sat down at the piano and resolutely fingered through 'Malagueña.' She went at them with the intensity of a studious child, too, becoming so involved with her labors that she even forgot that glamour-girl smile. . . . Jayne was an adequate parlor performer in no danger of setting the concert world afire."

Jayne was undeterred, and though she rarely played the piano in public again, she incorporated her violin skills into future stage and nightclub performances.

❤

Sexy actresses in the 1950s were usually divided into two groups: the

"Marilyns" and the "Audreys." The exception who proved the rule was Kim Novak, who careened back and forth from Audrey to Marilyn throughout her career, even playing both in *Vertigo*.

The Audreys (Miss Hepburn herself, and her acolytes Grace Kelly, Kay Kendall, Eva Marie Saint, and Dina Merrill) were ladylike swans: slim, elegant, sophisticated. "I feel so vitriolic about ladies with enormous bosoms," said the tall, willowy Kendall in 1957. "They give anyone who is my height and slightly flat-chested a bad name." Many Audreys wanted to be Serious Actresses, and some succeeded. But none of them wanted to be Marilyns. In 1958 modeling agent Roz Foy noted, "A fashion model can't be voluptuous—Marilyn is too abundant. So is Anita Ekberg. So is Jayne Mansfield. In the world of fashion, they're regarded as freaks of nature. As a matter of fact, if there is a trend it is this: bosoms are on the way out, and legs are back in."

Upcomer Anne Francis, who'd had recent hits with *Blackboard Jungle* and *Forbidden Planet,* said. "I'm not the Marilyn Monroe type at all. I just can't loll around in bathing suits with my mouth hanging open and my eyes half closed. Every time they ask me to get a sexy look on my face when I'm posing in the picture gallery I break up. To me that idiotic look is funny, not sexy."

Jayne denied any similarity to Marilyn and resented comparisons to Columbia's Kim Novak, insisting, "I don't wiggle. I walk. The movement is all my own. We have certain assets in common, along with Ekberg, Diana Dors and that girl at Columbia, but we measure up differently. Why, I could dye my hair and play a serious role."

Some of the Marilyns—including Marilyn—were not all that happy about being Marilyns, either. Sophia Loren, Elizabeth Taylor, and Shelley Winters were bosomy, overtly sexy, and delightfully vulgar, but they were talented and lucky enough to break out as character actresses. But Jayne reveled in her status. While most Marilyns vied for dramatic, dressed-down roles, Jayne wore lower-cut dresses and happily grabbed all the publicity she could while the grabbing was good.

She made a show about wanting to be taken seriously, but she did it with such deadpan comic subversiveness that everyone just laughed along. She told the *Baltimore Sun,* "From now on I want to be the real me. I want to project the inner qualities, not the outer ones." She planned to recite Hamlet's soliloquy soon on television, she claimed: "'You know,' she explained, 'the one that goes, O! what a rogue and peasant slave am I.' 'Don't you think,' asked the reporter, 'considering the problem of your outer qualities, you ought to do the first soliloquy instead? You know, the one that goes, "O! that this too, too solid flesh would melt."' She looked at us. We looked at her. Nothing happened."

❤

"Sex appeal made me famous, but where will it get me ten years from now?" Jayne asked Marie Torre of the *Philadelphia Inquirer* in May 1957, at the height of her career. "Even my studio is aware of that. I had a chat the other day with Buddy Adler—he's head of production at Fox—and he told me that in about a year the studio is going to start giving me serious parts. He said that right now I'm the sex symbol of the world, and that's where he wants me to be. But he knows there's no future in being a sex symbol. He was very encouraging." She told Sheilah Graham that agents were trying to steal her away from Bill Shiffrin: "They promise me more money for my pictures and big personal appearances in Monte Carlo, London and Las Vegas."

That summer she told Earl Wilson, "*The Girl Can't Help It* is making a fortune. The studio's trying to rewrite my contract. It's got six years to go, but they want me for another year besides. They didn't even do that with Marilyn!" Still living at Mansfield's Madness, "Bouncety-bouncety, she trotted out in a two-piece playsuit," related Wilson, "fetching me orange juice, a handful of newborn Siamese kittens, and information about how she and her neighbor down the road a piece, Muscle Man Mickey Hargitay, plan to get married—eventually—and raise beautiful Great Danes together." Mike Connolly added that when Jayne held her poolside interviews, she "has swimsuits in nearly all sizes for guys and dolls scribes to enjoy the pool with her."

She had dined with Fox president Spyros Skouras, she told Burt Boyar of the *Philadelphia Inquirer*. "Two years ago if I had met Spyros Skouras I would have frozen. It's different now. Tomorrow we're going to his country home for dinner. And he's—well—a friend." She was enjoying the hell out of her success and her fame: "You're treated as if you're really someone. People suddenly bend over backwards for you. I guess my success can be measured by the fact that I don't have a minute to myself, all day long anymore, and I love it."

She and Mickey kept busy over the summer: they visited Jayne's relatives in Pennsylvania and Texas. (Jayne told a Texas newspaper, "Everyone should try to be the best—the best lawyer, the best doctor, the best anything. A woman should be as feminine as she can. . . . I'm glad I grew up in Dallas. I want to visit all my old schools. . . . I was a brunette then, and covered up. Men whistled at me, but that's all. I decided my body was an asset, and I'd use it.")

Jayne signed fifty photos for Boy Scout Jack King (described rather cruelly as "chubby Jack King") for him to trade at the Valley Forge scout jamboree. "I had to leave a few prints at home for my family and friends," said budding entrepreneur King, "but the rest I swapped for troop patches and neckerchiefs. . . . I want to dicker for a horned toad, but I figure my mother wouldn't want me traipsing home with one of those."

Jayne attended the Minneapolis Aquatennial Star Night and Coronation Show along with James Stewart, Eddie Fisher, TV's Fran Allison, and "15 Visiting Queens." While in Minnesota (which she liked because "it's green and has a cute shape. I remember it from the days when I was little and had to put it into a jigsaw puzzle"), Jayne gave an extended interview to Barbara Flanagan of the *Minneapolis Tribune*. "Hollywood to me is synonymous with heaven. If I'd stayed the little brown-haired girl I was, I wouldn't be here today. I'd like to have dark hair again someday and will have for a dramatic role, I know. I'm really quite a serious girl and I want very much to win an Academy Award for my acting ability."

She insisted that

Hollywood is a very good influence on Jayne Marie. I shouldn't brag, but she is the happiest, sweetest, normal—and I don't believe in that word, normal—little girl in the world. She doesn't know much about the movies except every once in a while when some other little girl tells her that her mother is in the movies. We have daily tea parties at home for seven or eight children. We have *such* fun. They have the most beautiful public school in Beverly Hills and that's where she goes. Right now we're trying to decide if she should be a Brownie or a Bluebird. I was a Campfire Girl, you know, and of course a Bluebird before that. I usually cook on weekends, when the maid is off. We love outdoor barbecues. Steaks and home-made ice cream made in an electric freezer. Jayne Marie and I usually race to see who gets to lick the scoop.

From *Leave It to Beaver* suburban motherhood Jayne veered into left field: "I really love to bathe in pink champagne," she cooed. "It isn't as expensive as it sounds because I have a friend who provides the champagne. Usually I take a regular bath first and then I get into the cool champagne and romp around. It bubbles and makes me feel good, just like a little pink kitty-cat. But hot champagne sounds nice. I might warm it up sometimes."

But the bubbly, always, *always* happy and upbeat Jayne did admit, "The only negative thing about me is that I'm slightly nervous. Every once in a while, I get so excited that I just have to retire and rest. But not very often." Within a few years she would start to rely on drinking, and later pills, to alleviate her career and personal anxieties. But that was still some time off.

The photo ops continued (Mickey in Palm Springs lifting Jayne's fourteen-hundred-pound Renault Dauphine car so she can change the tire), as did the lewd jokes: ventriloquist Edgar Bergen said at a dinner, "I see Jayne Mansfield over there—or is that two Yul Brynners?" And Jayne's *Kiss Them for Me* costar Ray Walston recalled that Jayne looked down on set and complained that she couldn't see her mark.

A feud was also cooked up between Jayne and Zsa Zsa Gabor—possibly cooked up by Jayne and Zsa Zsa. Mike Connolly claimed to have overheard the two sniping at the Cocoanut Grove:

JAYNE: "I may make a movie in Paris."

ZSA ZSA: "They *love* me in Paris, dollink—I'm the toast of the town when I'm there!"

JAYNE: "How nice."

ZSA ZSA: "I'm European you know, so I understand them and they love me for it."

JAYNE: [looking at Mickey] "I'm European by proxy."

ZSA ZSA: "Dollink, you must have that long hair of yours cut before you go to Paris. You must be terribly chic. You can't be flashy over there. Jane Russell tried it and they criticized her for it. As for your dresses, well, *really,* dollink!"

MICKEY: "Now look here, don't you dare compare Jayne Mansfield with Jane Russell! Jayne is a much bigger star over there!"

JAYNE: "Yes, Fox says I'm bigger at the box office, too."

Zsa Zsa (who had just opened in *Queen of Outer Space*) told Vernon Scott,

"There's no feud with Jayne Mansfield. I just don't like her. If I want a feud I find someone bigger." Had Zsa Zsa ever met her? "How can you miss meeting her? She goes everywhere. After all, her only claim to fame is that she took a man away from Mae West."

Erskine Johnson reported Zsa Zsa as saying, "This Jayne Mansfield. She's just sexy. Not glamorous. Someone should teach her to be glamorous. Like Ingrid Bergman. There is a glamorous woman. So is Marlene Dietrich and Anita Ekberg." Jayne replied, "She has a perfect right to her opinion. Some people seem to think I'm glamorous. I'm happy that fans do. I'd be willing to put my fan mail up to hers any day."

Matt Cimber recalls, "Zsa Zsa Gabor was always trying to be her big buddy. She wanted to hang out with Jayne, because Jayne would draw all the money guys. That's all Zsa Zsa was ever interested in." When Jayne guested on Jack Paar's show in the early 1960s, "we were standing in the wings. And Zsa Zsa, Jayne's 'great friend,' is being interviewed, and Paar says, 'You know who's out there, your buddy Jayne Mansfield, she's gonna come out soon.'" Cimber says that Zsa Zsa "went on this rant about how, 'Well, Jaynie is a sucker for men, she falls in love, she doesn't look to the practicalities,' she started putting Jayne down, in a comical way."

Standing in the wings, fuming, Cimber told Jayne, "When he calls you out there, put your arms out and say, *Mother!*" He went on, "We stood there and—as happened very often between us, it was the best part of our relationship—we started laughing; Jayne was laughing so hard she was crying. We knew Zsa Zsa would stand there with her mouth open and not know what to do. So they were ready to announce her, and she said, 'Oh, Matt, I can't do that, it's not nice. I would be putting her down.' Here, she would have gotten a laugh you wouldn't believe, but she wouldn't go for it."

Jack Paar quickly caught on that Jayne and Zsa Zsa's "frenemy" act was delighting audiences, so he booked them together four times between 1961 and 1963. Of a 1962 appearance, Jayne said that "I enjoyed it, although I didn't know Zsa Zsa was going to appear with me. I think Jack thought we would have a hair-pulling, but when his back was turned, Zsa Zsa whispered the same thought to me, and we kept matters on an even keel."

Patricia Costa of the *Democrat & Chronicle* found the Zsa Zsa/Jayne feud "grossly unfunny," and Paar downright offensive. She complained that he called them "broads" and talked about smut. Jayne, "who was attired in something that looked like mattress ticking with matching hairdo, was less subtle, more ludicrous" than Zsa Zsa, she felt. Harry Harris of the *Philadel-*

phia Inquirer also raised his eyebrows as "the chatter stressed double and, with Paar's crafty help, triple entendres. Amid talk of husbands, sex and children, Zsa Zsa reported that she discusses with her daughter 'the boys and the bees.'"

And speaking of feuds, there was good news for Jayne and bad news for Mae West. In 1940 an inflatable life vest was named after West by the Royal Air Force, for obvious reasons. In July 1957 a press release from the Shaw Air Force Base in South Carolina stated that they were updating their old Mae Wests with "Jayne Mansfields," which "have the advantage of being inflated prior to wriggling out of the parachute harness. In the old style Mae West jacket, the pilot down at sea had to first shed his parachute before inflating the vest."

Jayne made a return appearance on *The Ed Sullivan Show* on August 11, this time leaving her musical instruments at home but pulling an equally eccentric act, singing "The Army Goes Rolling Along" with winners of the Army Talent Contest. Matt Messina of the *New York Daily News* noted that Jane Russell and Dagmar were also appearing on TV that week. "Daggie proved to be the most entertaining of them all," he wrote. "With a sly tongue-in-cheek approach, she revealed herself as a person of common sense and a hilarious comedienne." When asked about Jayne, Dagmar said, "Honestly, I think she has a lovely body and I think her brains have been very important in her rise to fame. She's a nice little girl."

It wasn't all fun and photo ops that summer; indeed, some of the press caused Jayne and Mickey much chagrin. Since its first issue in 1952, *Confidential* had been annoying celebrities with its sordid tell-all stories and photos about sex, drinking, drugs, and general misbehavior. *Confidential* and other such entertaining rags as *Star* and *Whisper* ran stories that June Allyson was a "hubby-snatching" flirt, Mae West was getting cozy with a "negro boxer," Anita Ekberg and her husband "played house long before the wedding bells rang out," both Eddie Fisher and John Carroll cavorted with numerous cuties, and Liberace made a pass at a male press agent.

Whisper, in a June 1957 issue, ran: "Jayne Mansfield's Overnight Mickey! If you're wondering what these two atomic anatomies do to keep the shapes they're in, wonder no more." On the night of November 23, 1956, according to *Whisper,* Mickey "went up the steps of Jayne's front porch like a husband sneaking home after a wild night with the boys and disappeared inside the doll's front door. Whatever they did, they did till half-past midnight. If they did anything after that, they did it in the dark—because that's when the lights went out." Mickey had rented a one-room bungalow a block from Jayne's house, but he spent little time there.

Even in the supposedly straitlaced Eisenhower 1950s, stories about Liberace or Tab Hunter being gay, Rory Calhoun having been a convicted car thief, and stars actually having sex with one another drew little more than slightly raised eyebrows. Far better scandals than these had been bandied about since the dawn of the film industry. But in August 1957, *Confidential, Whisper,* and their publishers and distributors were sued for criminal libel about stories on Dorothy Dandridge (interracial outdoor lovemaking), Liberace (gay), Errol Flynn (voyeurism), and Maureen O'Hara (sex in a movie theater). Two witnesses died before they could testify: private eye Polly Gould and Mae West's purported lover Chalky Wright, who drowned in his bath after having a heart attack.

Jayne was also asked to testify but, perhaps at the behest of Fox, she haughtily brushed off the whole distasteful affair: "I know nothing about it, and I am certainly not going to appear [at the trial]. The whole story is untrue. My life has been too full of wonderful things to think of disgusting things like that."

The *Confidential/Whisper* lawsuit ended in a mistrial, but *Confidential* publisher Robert Harrison bowdlerized his magazine, turning it into just another *Photoplay*. By the time *Confidential* went out of business in 1978, few people knew it was even still around.

Southern Baptist super-evangelist Billy Graham was not brushing off *Confidential* or Jayne. Graham complained at a Madison Square Garden revival meeting that "the average teenager knows Jayne Mansfield's statistics better than he does the First Commandment." Jayne replied to Graham, via her press agent, "I can't help it if I'm on their minds. It's a free country and a free world and I'm flattered that the youth of the world is thinking about me."

10

The British press did its best to make Jayne Mansfield sound like an idiot.

Sheilah Graham

It wasn't only Billy Graham getting all in a lather over Jayne. She was so in-your-face—in *everyone's* face—that it seemed impossible for critics, columnists, and fellow stars to keep their opinions about her to themselves. The Associated Press called Jayne "Hollywood's greatest natural acting talent since Lassie," and Erskine Johnson described her as "a caricature from a forgotten era, wiggling in and out of tight-fitting gowns as she plays 'The Star.' The 'glamour queen' with her $10,000 mink and her dyed poodle is as out of date as pie-in-the-face comedy."

Inez Robb of the *Arizona Daily Star* "would love to know why every editor in the United States believes the American public can't live through any given 24-hour period if it is deprived of pictures of Miss Jayne Mansfield proving what no one in his right mind has ever doubted, i.e., that she is a mammal. . . . It is only too obvious that adenoids is the occupational disease of all glamour girls whose chief distinction is the large, economy-size façade. I do not ever recall seeing a picture of the Misses Mansfield, Monroe or Dors with their respective kissers closed. These ladies obviously are forced to breathe through their rosebud lips, which are eternally ajar or at half-mast. This gives each the piquant air of a gaffed trout fighting for breath in epic cinemascope."

105

Hedda Hopper quoted "one of the world's best photographers and a big coward" who wouldn't let her use his name. He called Jayne "the most overrated girl in the business—her bovinity appalls me." The cantankerous photographer also had a thing or two to say about Doris Day ("pedicured, manicured, deodorized, completely 'look-but-don't-touch'"), Debbie Reynolds ("if they pump one more quart of cuteness into her, she'll explode"), Grace Kelly ("she leaves me cold"), and Natalie Wood (she "can take off with the rest of them . . . a product of press agentry").

While Joan Crawford was known for dissing the younger set, Barbara Stanwyck also weighed in. "Miss Mansfield is a member of that falling shoulder strap school of acting that very often never gets beyond the publicity stage," the then fifty-year-old Stanwyck said. "At this point the most that she can do is lean over. If she would stop all this publicity right now and concentrate on her acting, she might make the grade. Marilyn Monroe started out in much the same way, but she was smart. She knew when to stop being the clown and get down to work. Of course," Stanwyck added cattily, "Marilyn has class."

Actress Polly Bergen also dived in: "Men who gape at the likes of Miss Mansfield must be sick. The way she flaunts sex—well, it's downright shameful! I'm not quite an Audrey Hepburn, but what a relief not to be like Jayne!" Bawdy Sophie Tucker sang in her nightclub act, "Jayne Mansfield— you call that charm? You can see the same thing on a dairy farm!"

Harry Harris of the *Philadelphia Inquirer* quoted appalled letter writer Gwen Schoch: "Jayne Mansfield's appearance [on *What's My Line?*] was disgusting and revolting. . . . She is vulgar in her tastes—hair style, makeup and her entire ensemble. . . . Let's keep her element out of TV. At the Troc [Philadelphia's burlesque palace], she would be sensational." But Dee Rankin wrote to Harris, "I think that both Kim Novak and Jayne Mansfield are more talented than Marilyn Monroe . . . from what I've read, both Novak and Mansfield are more professional than Monroe—always on time, know their lines, etc."

Columnist Michael Sean O'Shea, filling in for Dorothy Kilgallen, wrote in 1958, "Given to giggling and squealing when she isn't spouting inane quotable quotes, Jayne's rise to Hollywood stardom has been based on her startling physical dimensions. The grotesque posturings have found favor with moviegoers." But he gave her the benefit of a doubt, conceding, "She's a lot smarter than half her contemporaries and twice as kind to people than most of her co-workers. Her intelligence might be the very thing to hasten her decline in popularity if she let it show, but those who know her and have a sincere regard for her, regret that the real Jayne Mansfield is kept out of sight."

Jayne wasn't the only actress annoying columnist James Bacon; in early 1957 Marie McDonald claimed to have been kidnapped at gunpoint and dumped on the side of a road. Her story couldn't be proved, and—despite McDonald's protestations—police dropped the case. Bacon believed she did it for publicity, and also complained that "stars like Jayne Mansfield, Marilyn Monroe and others pose in revealing photos that can't help but excite the appetites of sex deviates."

In what one hopes was a parody of a think piece, psychiatrist Dr. J. E. Schmidt of Northwestern University spoke to an interviewer about Jayne. He started out intelligibly enough—"American males form the most susceptible group for mass hypnotism on earth, at least, where female guiles are concerned"—then went off the rails with a Professor Irwin Coreyesque rant: "The pseudoluscious and exaggerated Miss Mansfield is the possessor of a pretty face, but figure-atively, she is a super-paramorph, or bag, poured into a prefabricated shell of textile," Schmidt said to the presumably gobsmacked reporter. "Mansfield spreads like a soggy dough to fill every desirable curve of the ideal gown. But sans gown and sans deceptive convexities, paramorph Mansfield would droop and overflow into an amorphous mass of tissue resembling, roughly, a cone topped by a melting dip of ice cream."

Happily, Jayne had as many champions as she did detractors, one of them the painfully honest and outspoken talk-show host Jack Paar. In 1958 Paar called Mamie Van Doren "dull," said Marilyn Monroe (with whom he'd costarred in *Love Nest*) "was a nice big little girl, one who was constantly carrying books of poetry with the titles visible, so you could see what she was reading. . . . She was always late. She kept me waiting for those still pictures and by the time she arrived I was burning. I had to hug her for the cameras but under the circumstances I didn't enjoy it." But when it came to Jayne, the easiest target, Paar said, "She has about the best mind of all these big-breasted beauties. That girl's no fool."

Andrew Carthew of the *Daily Herald* also came to Jayne's defense. "I now rate Mansfield as the cleverest woman I have ever met in show business," he wrote. "Some of the things she says are outrageous. Most of the things she says are funny. And all of the things she says are calculated to extract the maximum publicity. . . . She has become a professional flutter-head of rare quality and she is happy in her success. . . . Where most people think sex is sexy, Mansfield thinks sex is FUNNY."

Jack Major of the *Akron Beacon Journal* interviewed Jayne in 1963 and began unpromisingly, "I still think—don't we all?—that Jayne is a terrible actress. That she hasn't contributed much to the world, or to the world of entertainment. That she really isn't very pretty. That her days in the spotlight have been marked by some of the dumbest behavior ever attributed to an actress." But he admitted that "the off-stage Jayne Mansfield is something else. She showed me gracious and intelligent sides of her that made the conversation memorable simply because of the surprise of it all."

And writer/director John Waters far prefers Jayne to Marilyn.

> In my world, Jayne Mansfield is the ultimate movie star. Divine was my Jayne Mansfield, only put together with Godzilla. I marvel at how she looks. She must have done the roots for her hair every day. She never had a root, not even for one second. And anyone that has a bar that is open 24 hours a day for the press is a girl after my own heart. People *liked* Jayne, she was a comedienne. She was a parody of Marilyn Monroe—she went beyond parody; she was an insane Marilyn Monroe. Jayne Mansfield was an animated character—she's not a real person. She's from outer space, basically. . . .
>
> I never got over Jayne Mansfield. I still think that's how women should look. She looked to me like she was happy being completely out of her mind, an Extreme Glamour Paerson. Jayne Mansfield has always looked a little like a drag queen—but no drag queen can pull it off like Jayne could. Because she's in on the joke, that's the thing that makes it so endearing.

As Waters notes, looking like Jayne Mansfield was a 24/7 job, and throughout her career she was happy to give out diet, beauty, and exercise advice, much of which was self-contradictory and which she followed herself only when she was in the mood.

Being Mickey Hargitay's girlfriend was the best exercise tip anyone could offer: he ate right, he exercised, and he encouraged Jayne to do the same. "I have light weight barbells and I do my exercises every day," she told Lydia Lane in 1959. Jayne's advice still holds true today: "You get so much better results with a diet, if you exercise. If you don't eat when you are not hungry and if you stop eating when your appetite is satisfied, your weight takes care of itself." Jayne felt that she looked her best at 118 pounds, but the doctor's weight charts had her ideal weight at 130. "This is something you have to decide for yourself," she said. "The size of your bones—whether large or small—makes a big difference."

More sensible advice, and equally hard to follow: "I think eating can get to be a habit, more or less. You look at the clock and say, 'it's time for lunch,' and you eat, whether you're hungry or not. That's silly." This should be printed out and attached to the door of every refrigerator in the world.

She added prettily that the best beauty secret was love: "It does wonderful things to a face. It's not just romantic love, but any love—that of a mother for her children, a person for his fellow man."

As for her outré figure, Jayne told Lane that "I think most men find big bosoms exciting when they are pointing forward and upward . . . if a girl isn't born with the kind of figure that men admire, she can develop it with hard work and the right diet and exercise. And as for women losing their charm when they become aggressive, my experience is that men find it stimulating for women to be competitive—it bores them to have a placid ornament around the place."

Regarding diet, Jayne veered back and forth between vegetarianism and digging into a nice thick steak. She smoked and drank—moderately at first—but so did nearly everyone else in the 1950s and '60s.

Bob Considine happened to encounter Jayne during one of her vegetarian periods. "It's bad to kill to eat," she said over a salad. "Once I saw a field of tuna swimming through a turquoise sea and you know what I said to myself? I said, 'it wouldn't be one-quarter the pleasure to eat them than watching them swim.' They were like beautiful blue angels. I don't believe in eating creatures that have mothers, fathers, children and brothers."

❤

By late summer 1957, it was obvious that 20th Century-Fox did not have the slightest idea what to do with Jayne. There were so few good vehicles in pre-production that loan-outs were being considered. At this point, the studio certainly had no notion of dropping her. Jayne was so good with the public and with reporters, and she so loved pressing the flesh, that it decided to send her off on a US publicity tour, and if this went well, maybe an overseas, Eva Peron–like Rainbow Tour of the world.

All through late July and August Jayne and her entourage (Mickey, a pack of dogs, Jayne Marie, and a flurry of press agents and hair, makeup, and wardrobe people) toured the East Coast and Midwest, with a stop in Toronto, plugging *The Girl Can't Help It, The Wayward Bus,* and *Will Suc-*

cess Spoil Rock Hunter?, all still in wide release (she was able to do advance press for *Kiss Them for Me* as well).

She hit the Cincinnati Twin Drive-In, danced with Mickey at Chicago's Pump Room, sporting her pink mink and drinking pink champagne, and appeared onstage at Detroit's Fox Theater, "perfect as a cooing parody of every 'love goddess.'"

She made lightning-quick stops at the Wilmington and Philadelphia train stations, signing autographs and wearing a boxy Chinese jacket and black satin trousers: "High necklines, that's what I'm wearing now," she said. "I want to depend on my face, my emotions, my eyes, my ability as an actress, my feelings from inside. A woman has as much sex appeal in her face as in her bosom. And sex appeal isn't everything. It suits only a very small audience. I'm not teasing," Jayne insisted, "I'm serious about this. I want to play to women as well as men, I want women to like me, to be on my side."

Then it was into "a tight blue sweater and pink skirt and teetering white sequin-trimmed spike-heeled shoes," in Washington, DC, where she caused a huge sensation. She toured the US Capitol, even managing to flummox Senate Majority Leader Lyndon Johnson, not a man easily shaken. Jayne shimmied up to him, proclaimed her loyalty to Texas, and complimented his shirt and tie. He was heard to mutter, "Thank you very much, ma'am," and one paper reported that he blushed.

House Speaker Sam Rayburn "grinned like a schoolboy," Senator Estes Kefauver offered her one of his trademark coonskin caps, and Senator Mike Mansfield fled in a panic when she called him "cute." Someone suggested that all the Texas politicians be summoned for a photo op, and Representative William Robert Poage, called without explanation off the House floor, found himself shoved into a group photo with Jayne. With a blank expression he turned to a friend when the flashbulbs had ceased popping and asked, "Who in the world is she?"

Later, when Sam Rayburn was asked "Don't you think it was terrible letting Jayne Mansfield cause all that commotion in here?" he snapped, "I don't think it was terrible at all. The only people I've heard complain are cranky old women."

Jayne did not impress Judy Rushin of the *Montgomery Advertiser* when she appeared at the star-studded Aquatennial: "The Mansfield face, although a secondary factor, is not beautiful," wrote Rushin. "Close-up it does not compare with Marilyn. Her figure is sloppy, mainly because of the way she carries herself. . . . Even the other two celebrities on the bill, Jimmy Stewart and Eddie Fisher, seemed to be steering clear of her." Rushin did, however, fall hard for Mickey: "The saving factor was Mickey Hargitay, her number one boyfriend and a former Mr. Universe. In fact, La Mansfield's press agent would be wise to switch his attentions to Mickey entirely."

But she was a hit in Boston, where a huge crowd greeted her at the train station—despite Jayne being so publicly available, mobs still turned out as though she made an appearance only once a decade. Leo Shapiro of the *Boston Globe* reported that "hundreds of persons of all ages, many teenagers and many women among them, jammed the plaza. . . . Boys lined the railroad bridge overhead for a better look-see . . . the crush was almost like a whirlpool, sucking in those who happened to be caught anywhere near it."

Jayne did not have time to schedule a stop in her birthplace, but she did say that "I would love to go back to Bryn Mawr. I was born at Bryn Mawr, on the Main Line. I'm a Pennsylvanian, and my dad might have been governor of New Jersey." One reporter sarcastically noted, "To illustrate how she fit into the Bryn Mawr picture, Jayne posed for photos in shorts, sweaters and evening gowns—just like the Bryn Mawr girls wear at proms at the Merion Cricket Club."

Jayne journeyed north of the border to Toronto for her last stop in the tour, and was interviewed on the TV show *Tabloid*. She looked lovely (though she needed some face powder in the hot studio), wearing a jewel-trimmed sweater from *The Girl Can't Help It*. She came off very sweet and low-key, and host Joyce Davidson had a good rapport with her.

Jayne was very thoughtful and eloquent in this interview, pausing to think over her answers and find just the right words. "The personality I portray is not the personality I am," Jayne told Davidson. "I'd rather be a star *and* an actress but if I had my choice, I'd rather be an actress. I'd like to win an Academy Award, at least one; I'd like to fulfill many serious roles as well as many comedy roles, like I have been doing. Now I'm at the point where I feel I can relax with the cheesecake publicity and go much farther dramatically." Davidson asked about those cheesecake poses: "I used it as a means to an end," said Jayne. "I don't know if I should say I *liked* it, but I felt that it would do me some good as far as being recognized. You can have a lot of ideas, but if the press, the photographers, the public, isn't nice to you, then the ideas are no good."

Did Jayne ever long to be just an ordinary, everyday housewife? She looked momentarily stunned. "No. No, I really haven't. I've wanted a home and family, and I think I'll get that, too, but I like acting, I like everything connected with it. I like my family and my home, along with my career." As for that career, Jayne repeated, as she often did, that "I feel very, very fortunate, everyone's been very nice to me and I wouldn't want to take the credit myself. Everyone's been good to me—the press, the photographers, the studios—I'm just a very fortunate girl. I love my fans, they're all wonderful people. If it weren't for them, there would be no Jayne Mansfield."

❤

Fox was delighted—or perhaps just relieved—that Jayne had done so well on her US tour. She hadn't fallen out of her clothes, she'd plugged her movies, she'd been a pleasant and thoughtful ambassador for the studio. Fox decided it was safe to send her off on her worldwide tour—especially as it had no film projects ready for her, so there was no sense having her sit around her swimming pool getting paid for nothing. While in London, she would also meet with Angel Productions about a possible British film, to be released through 20th Century-Fox in the US.

Jayne threw a going-away party for herself at Mansfield's Madness. Some papers printed that she filled her swimming pool with pink champagne for the event, but she wisely just poured a bottle in for photographers to commemorate (photographer Earl Leaf found this out firsthand when she pulled him into the pool with her).

Art Ryon of the *Los Angeles Times* was surprised that the house, "instead of being the marvelous marbled mansion we all expected, turned out to be a very modest hillside bungalow in the boondocks end of Benedict Canyon." The fifty or sixty guests found a charmingly thrown-together affair, much like any suburban pool party: "There was plenty of California pink champagne on ice in wash buckets, a huge bowl of popcorn, a drastic shortage of glasses, and that was it. Jayne, bulging in a dotted bathing suit and with sopping-wet hair, graciously posed with everyone for pictures. There were frequent sudden outcries when someone stepped on one of the horde of tiny puppies or kittens underfoot." Ryon decided that "Jayne is truly a wonderful, forthright gal. But her party was pretty much of a bust."

Then she was off on a breakneck tour of fourteen European cities (including Frankfurt, Amsterdam, Antwerp, Paris, London, Stockholm, Rome, Brussels, Oslo, and Copenhagen), from late September through early November. Mickey was left behind, on Fox's orders. Jayne was given lessons on "English manners and mores" by Fox executive Ben Lyon. Lyon was the perfect man for this assignment: he and his wife, Bebe Daniels, film stars in the 1920s and '30s, had moved to England just in time to become "beloved Yanks" during World War II, performing in London through the worst of the bombing. Lyon knew Hollywood, and he knew the Brits.

Jayne managed to put her foot in it on her first stop. Landing at Shannon Airport in Ireland, she told reporters, "I just love you English, and your English fields are so green." When it was pointed out that she was in Ireland, she backtracked, "Oh, I'm sorry, I mean I like the Irish." Then on to London, trailing her hairdresser, maid, publicity agent, and a retinue of movie executives. "I think London and British people are wonderful," she said, hoping that Britain and London were the same place.

When she appeared at the London premiere of *Rock Hunter* in a skin-tight zebra-print dress with matching cape, she was mobbed by three thousand fans. "She was crushed and bruised and reached the foyer almost in tears," reported one paper. On the way from the theater to the 400 Club, her car was in a minor accident, and she was thrown to the floor.

But worst of all, some photographer managed to get a rear-view picture of her bending over, and it made the front page of the trashier tabloids. "Whisper it softly," said the *People*. "Jayne is putting on weight!" Fox publicists insisted the photo was taken with a fish-eye lens to make her backside look bigger, and columnist Arthur Helliwell thought it might be payback because Jayne's press agents had refused to let her pose beside Britain's own entry in the busty sweepstakes, the ubiquitous Sabrina. Jayne was "scared of the competition," Helliwell insisted. "Sabrina may be three times as dumb—but she is twice as lovely." Sheilah Graham stood up for Jayne—the columnist had been born in England, and she knew how really vicious British newspapers could get. "The British press did its best to make Jayne Mansfield sound like an idiot," she wrote. "I wasn't there, but I'd bet that Jayne did not ask, 'Is Sir Winston Churchill still Prime Minister?'"

John Godley, 3rd Baron Kilbracken of Killegar and a dashing thirty-seven-year-old war hero and journalist, was paid £100 plus expenses by Fox to shepherd Jayne around London and keep her out of trouble. Plus, being seen with a lord would impress her fans and—maybe—reporters. Godley needed the cash to keep up his crumbling 1808 family home, so he grabbed the offer, accompanying Jayne to the Tate Gallery (she preferred Picasso to Monet, he noted), fashionable clubs, and public events. He also snagged another £100 writing an article about all this for the *Daily Express*.

Godley was struck by Jayne's Jekyll and Hyde personality: she was either "a gentle, sympathetic, shy, very human person, easy to speak to, very easy to get on with, and full of active interest in the world and people," or she was Hyde—"the glamourous, busty, vulgar, effervescent, pin-up prototype." And she could snap back and forth between these personalities in a second—whether on purpose or in self-defense, he could never decide.

He found a "strange, unexpected closeness and real same-way thinking" with Jayne when the two of them were in a quiet spot, no fans or photographers around. She wanted to do typical tourist things: go to a pub, explore Chelsea and Soho, ride on top of one of those double-decker buses, "wander through lampless streets and escape from the ballyhoo which is what Hyde-Jayne lives for." Godley did not find Jayne sexy at all; he thought her persona was "as artificial as the icing-sugar decorations on a Christmas cake. But as a movie-star, since this is the nature of movie-stars, she's the success-phenomenon of 1957."

After appearing on Val Parnell's *Sunday Night at the London Palladium* (reciting Shakespeare and playing the violin and piano), Jayne was off to Paris. "The Eiffel tower is most impressive," she said, a statement no one was able to take issue with. When asked to compare nationalities, she did some fancy footwork: "British men are charming and right to the point. The French are more flowery in their language and have more icing on top." Asked what she thought of Paris as the City of Sin, she deftly answered, "You can commit sins anywhere you want to. Anyway, I won't have time here." Jayne visited Les Halles, viewed the Venus de Milo and the *Mona Lisa* at the Louvre, and attended a Christian Dior fashion show (his last— Dior would die on October 24). Leaving Godley behind in England, she was escorted through Paris by Gilbert Pineau, son of the French minister of state (the younger Pineau went on to be a successful TV director).

Jayne had not forgotten Mickey on her journeys: she announced that the two would marry in California in January. Mickey denied any rift with Jayne, despite romantic newspaper photos of her with her paid escorts. "Jayne and I have talked many times on the phone since she left for Europe," he told Harrison Carroll, "and when she gets back, I am going to surprise her with a diamond ring. I had a little business and sold it to buy the ring." Not that it would be much of a surprise since he had just told a newspaper columnist about it. Mickey was house-sitting, looking after animals and pasting clippings in Jayne's scrapbooks, as papers snidely noted. And it was true that even though Mickey had not even married her yet, he was beginning to feel like Mr. Jayne Mansfield.

The indefatigable Jayne traveled on: in Rotterdam, the crew of the US carrier *Tarawa* formed the name JAYNE! on the deck of the ship to welcome her; she entertained American GIs in Frankfurt, and was escorted by Private Robert Keifer through the army hospital, where she greeted patients one by one; at the Dusseldorf racetrack, she presented the winning jockey with a beer mug. At an airport in Geneva, she crossed paths with director Roberto Rossellini, and the two were photographed chatting. "I hope this is not going to start still another rumor," said Rossellini, who was married to Ingrid Bergman but linked with actress Sonali Das Gupta.

In Holland Jayne was interviewed on TV by Wim Sonneveld, a star of musicals and cabaret. Looking both sexy and demure in a low-cut dress but little makeup, her hair done back in a chignon, she comes across as soft-spoken, intelligent, and thoughtful. Did she think a Rita Marlowe could exist in real life? asked Sonneveld. "I think so—but I think for a person to exist as a star is one thing, and a person to exist as an actress is another. A person has to carry on where publicity leaves off. It's a 24-hour-a-day job, and I love every minute of each hour each day." Sonneveld brought up her famous squeal, asking her to demonstrate. "Is your squeal spontaneous or something fabricated for the purpose of the career?" "No," Jayne said, after attempting an only partly successful example. "It's quite spontaneous, you have to feel it, you have to have some kind of an inspiration." When asked if she wanted to do more serious roles, Jayne repeated her standard line of "I want to do all kinds of parts. I want to do as many serious roles as I do comedy roles. I as a person am much different than the comedy roles I portray on the screen, and also much different from the serious ones."

Jayne arrived in Milan in late October, and the crowds were too much even for her: Italian riot police had to rescue her, trembling and barefoot, from a mob, and speed her away in a truck. "The near riot in which fans made off with her $1,000 diamond-studded garter, her matching gold earrings and her shoes climaxed a hectic day," reported one paper. Earlier that day, three thousand people rushed her at the Ariston Cinema "in a scene reminiscent of the Oklahoma land rush," and a news conference descended into chaos when Italian actress Angela Guy burst in, whipped off her fur coat to show off her undies-clad figure, and shouted, "What's all this fuss about a foreign star? What has she come here to do? Does she think there is nobody here to out-shape her? Look here, gentlemen!" Jayne told reporters after Guy was hauled off by police, "I am very sorry for her. If she wanted to pose for photographers beside me and let the people judge which one was better, of course I would have accepted—but only if both of us were fully dressed."

Fleeing Italy (a country she would later grow to love), Jayne excitedly returned to London for the thrill of her lifetime. Back in early October, it was reported that Queen Elizabeth had invited Jayne to a Royal Command Performance in November. Jayne wanted to meet the queen, "but I never thought for a moment it would be possible." What will she wear, everyone wondered? Especially as she would have to bend down and curtsy? "I can tell you my Hollywood designer is already working on a sensational dress for the occasion," she said. "It should outdo anything the girls have worn on past occasions." Fox executives fainted dead away, then called her and ordered her to wear the high-necked gown from *The Girl Can't Help It* in which Gaby Desmarais had photographed her. Leonard Lyons reported, "Buckingham Palace officials are trying to keep Jayne Mansfield from being presented to the Queen. They suspect that Miss Mansfield may do something to get publicity."

On Monday, November 4, the two queens met at the annual Royal Film Festival at London's Odeon Theatre (the film on show that night was *Les Girls*). When the queen reached Jayne in the presentation line, Jayne bobbed a pretty curtsy and the two embarked on the pleasant, empty conversations to which royalty is confined. "I have just come back from your country," said Elizabeth. "I enjoyed America very much." Jayne: "I'm enjoying it even more over here, your majesty. You're looking so beautiful." Elizabeth: "Thank you so much. You're so kind. So are you. I understand you have been traveling on the continent. Did you come here to meet me especially?" Jayne: "Yes, ma'am. I was never so excited in all my life." "How long are you staying?" "I'm going tomorrow." "We hope you will come back and see us." And the queen moved on to the next in line, leaving Jayne overwhelmed with delight.

Several papers noted that the queen's dress was cut lower than Jayne's. What wasn't mentioned but is obvious in photos and newsreels: as Jayne rose from her curtsy, the queen pulled a Sophia Loren and stared, as if briefly hypnotized, right at Jayne's breasts (they, hefted by a bullet bra, stared right back).

"The Queen is beautiful. She is regal and gracious," Jayne later told reporters. "I was shivering and trembling with ecstasy." She thought Prince Philip "was quite stately, but I was so in awe of the beautiful Queen that I had my eyes glued on her."

The British papers weren't quite through with Jayne yet, razzing her when newsreels of the event hit the theaters: "On the basis of audience response, the funniest film of the year must have been the newsreel of the Royal Film Performance," wrote the *Londonderry Sentinel.* "The sight of Jayne Mansfield attempting to curtsy in a dress that fitted her as if she were going to be mummified in it got the biggest laugh of the year." And famed society hostess Elsa Maxwell told Jack Paar that Jayne was "vulgar and over-busted. I think it's disgraceful that she was allowed to meet the Queen. I'll say this, she may have been received in London, but Paris, my dear, wouldn't have her."

Upon returning to the US in November, Jayne took two steps that were to change her life and define her as a star and a personality: she and Mickey Hargitay became officially engaged, and they bought a Mediterranean-style Holmby Hills house that would evolve into the camp wonderland known as the Pink Palace.

11

We called it the House of Love. She just hugged me, tears in
her eyes, and said, "We're sitting on top of the world."

Mickey Hargitay

When Jayne disembarked from her plane in California, Mickey and
Jayne Marie were waiting for her. "I saw the man I love and I guess
I just went crazy," said Jayne. "All the photographers met me at the airport
. . . and then I spied Mickey in the crowd. Everything went black and I
screamed, 'no more pictures, please.' The photographers were all old
friends, too, and you should have seen their faces. They couldn't have been
more stunned if I had smashed their camera. I hadn't seen Mickey or my
daughter in seven weeks. I wanted to stay home, cook dinner for my
daughter and the man I love."

A year and a half of Jayne Mansfield had not discouraged Mickey: he
knew she was a publicity and fan magnet; he knew her career was everything to her; and he at least suspected by now that his role would be gentle-
man-in-waiting to the queen as much as husband. "If people are going to
call me Mr. Mansfield, let them. I'm happier for her success than mine. I
don't have any male ego about that. Besides," he added with unwarranted
optimism, "acting is only incidental with me. I have business interests on
the side."

Jayne and Mickey genuinely loved each other. In early November
they showed off her ten-carat engagement ring, with photographers and

reporters present. No poolside bathing-suit event this time: Jayne and Mickey were dressed like any normal young couple, he in slacks and a plaid shirt, she in a simple blouse and skirt, as they showed off the ring, and hugged and kissed. Jayne Marie was presumably nearby, rolling her eyes as only an embarrassed seven-year-old can do. "I didn't think anything would top meeting Queen Elizabeth, but this surpasses even that great thrill," said Jayne. "I never expected to own a ring like that. And it wasn't necessary. I told Mickey long ago that a plain gold band would be enough for me."

In the days before huge elaborate proposals, Mickey managed to be offhandedly romantic. A few days before the press event, "we were driving back from the airport talking about how much we love each other," said Jayne, "when Mickey said very casually, 'oh, that reminds me, I've got a little something for you.' He reached into his pocket and got out something wrapped in pink tissue paper. I thought it must be some old earring I asked him to get repaired for me. When I opened the package, I couldn't believe my eyes. I'm the happiest girl in the world!"

Of course there were wisecracks about these two perfect specimens marrying; the best came from James Bacon, who wondered about Jayne, "Will rock spoil success hunter?"

That same month Jayne had her first brush with Las Vegas, a town that would play a large role in her career. Jayne and several other stars appeared in a Saturday-night TV variety special, *Holiday in Las Vegas,* which impressed few. But Jayne stood out as one of the show's bright spots, which boded well for her future Vegas act. "Most of it was rigorously routine," wrote Harry Harris of the *Philadelphia Inquirer.* "Ann Sothern modeled luxurious furs, crinkled her nose and sang. Sammy Davis Jr. expended bursts of energy. Vic Damone sleep-walked through a few numbers. The show perked up, however, when Tony Randall, representing lots of class, and Jayne Mansfield, representing lots of lass, were involved in comedy shenanigans. Jayne scored as not-so-straight woman for comedian Randall, playing wartime mademoiselle, British deb and dimwitted gangster's moll to Randall's Yank, cad and mugg." Dwight Newton of the *San Francisco Examiner* gave her a more mixed review ("Jayne Mansfield overcame her histrionic shortcomings with uninhibited verve and good humor. . . . One thing about unplain Jayne: she never stops trying"), while Bob Foster of the *San Mateo Times* outright slammed her with "She displayed about as much talent as a rock. In fact, she's not even pleasant viewing any more. Wonder when casting people will realize this."

❤

After a quick vacation in Acapulco, Jayne and Mickey joined Bob Hope on what would the first of many USO tours (and yes, "Battle of the Bulge" jokes were made). Hope had begun his involvement with the United Service Organizations in 1939, and since then had traveled the world—beginning with World War II and continuing through to the Persian Gulf War in the early '90s, when Hope himself was pushing ninety. He took with him comics, singers, dancers, and pretty girls, and though his humor was anvil-subtle, the troops appreciated his efforts.

Hope's Operation Santa Claus tour would play in the Far East in the last two weeks of December 1957—joining Jayne would be Mickey, Hope's reliable comic sidekick Jerry Colonna, singers Erin O'Brien and Carol Jarvis, Les Brown and His Orchestra—and gossip columnist Hedda Hopper, never a fan of Jayne's. (Hedda was along to hand out gifts, tell Hollywood jokes, and remind the soldiers of their moms.) The troupe would travel in five military transport planes carrying eighty-three performers and support staff.

Their first stop was Honolulu, where "a rip-roaring audience of 6,000 service boys shook the rafters of Bloch Arena. . . . When Jayne Mansfield wove her way onstage the boys became men." She wasn't there to sing, just to show herself off and politely play straight woman to Hope's lewd jokes about her.

The troupe arrived in Japan on December 15, presenting its first show on the aircraft carrier *Ticonderoga* in Buckner Bay, Okinawa. The performers went on to play for airmen at Tachikawa, Johnson, and Itazuka airbases in Japan, and at the Osan and Kimpo airbases in Korea, as well as for soldiers in Yokahama and near the 30th parallel in Korea.

In Seoul, it was reported, Jayne's "autographed photo hangs next to M-1 carbines in the place of honor; when the troupe arrived at Haneda Airport in Tokyo, two hundred photographers pushed over a fence and mobbed Jayne, who graciously posed for shots and said how lovely Japan was." Japanese fans were wild about Jayne; she was mobbed again at the Gekijo Theater in Tokyo. On Christmas Day, the troupe performed two shows for sixty-five thousand servicemen on the "truce-silenced" front lines in Korea, after which Jayne and Hope had lunch with the visiting Cardinal Francis Spellman.

Bringing Mickey along turned out to be a misstep. Servicemen wanted to see Jayne Mansfield, not Mickey Hargitay (well, *some* of them wanted to see Mickey, but they had to keep quiet about it in 1957). They booed him, held up "Go Home, Tarzan" signs, and yelled, "Someone put a uniform on him!" He also made a faux pas in Okinawa when he refused to escort a colonel's wife to dinner, saying, "Somebody should have asked me first. I'm going with my fiancée."

Jayne even won over Hedda Hopper, who grudgingly admitted that Jayne "stood in the rain for the photogs with water soaking her open-toed shoes as long as anyone wanted a shot of her. She's being a perfect doll." Years later, though, Terrence O'Flaherty of the *Honolulu Star-Bulletin* recalled Hopper glaring at Jayne's cleavage and snapping, "Oh, for God's sake, Jayne, we've all seen those things. Why can't you cover them up?" And there was a nasty crack from Hal Humphrey of the *Oakland Tribune,* who wrote that "Jayne Mansfield doesn't require a passport, since she comes under the heading of 'props.'"

The whole trip had been filmed, and was seen on *The Bob Hope Show* on January 17, 1958. The *New York Daily News* wrote, "It was a joy to share in the laughter of the marines in Guam, in the hilarity of the sailors on a battlewagon, and in the gaiety of the airmen near Tokyo. . . . [Jayne] brought forth howls and wolf whistles in equal proportions. I don't care what Elsa Maxwell says about this gal, the new Mrs. Mickey Hargitay [which she was by the time the show aired] was the sweetheart of the expedition."

Exhausted but buoyed by the adulation, Jayne arrived back home on December 29, giving Jayne Marie a hug at the airport and heading home with her and Mickey to collapse and prepare for the wedding.

The new year began with a slam from Dan Valentine of the *Salt Lake Tribune,* who wrote that the Duchess of Windsor and Claudette Colbert had made 1957's best-dressed list, but not Jayne, because "most of the time she isn't dressed."

❤

On January 4, Jayne (wearing a leopard-skin cape, hat, and muff) told Louella Parsons, "We are going to have a very quiet wedding and then we'll fly to Dallas where my mother plans to give a reception for our friends there."

Then everyone had a good laugh and went to work on the real plans.

The happy couple held another press event, showing off her ring and trousseau. They sent out one hundred invitations (on pink paper, of course).

"This is one time I don't want a lot of publicity," Jayne unconvincingly told the assembled reporters and cameramen. ("It just happens that most of her friends are newspapermen," said Jim Byron.) Charles Le Maire, of course, was asked to design her pink lace gown. Jayne and Mickey chose January 13 for their wedding date, "because Mickey and I met on the 13th. He won the Mr. Universe contest on the 13th and got his American citizenship on the 13th. I just love that number." Jayne added, "I'm so happy. We're both on a pink cloud."

Mickey balked at the one hundred invitations: "I said, 'honey, I don't want 100 people,'" he recalled years later. "A hundred invitations turned out to be thousands. I almost didn't make my wedding, the crowd was so heavy." The Reverend Kenneth W. Knox would perform the nondenominational rites; Jayne's mother was to be matron of honor, the best man Ross Christina, an old friend of Mickey's from Indianapolis.

Jayne picked the Wayfarer's Chapel in Palos Verdes for the wedding—designed by Lloyd Wright (son of Frank Lloyd Wright) in the 1940s, it was a modernistic glass and wood building that looked like the skeleton of a church. Glass was the key factor here: people who couldn't get into the wedding could still see it—and photograph it. The only concern being would they crash through the walls in a disaster of blood and shards?

"I want the ceremony to be serious and serene," Jayne reiterated. "It's going to be entirely free of photographers. Except maybe just one, from the studio. Well, I don't suppose I can keep the photographers away if they want to come." Andrew Carthew of the *Daily Herald* wrote that Jayne described the wedding, "with some slight irreverence, as the Greatest Publicity Stunt in History."

It took place as planned on Monday, January 13—none of the many celebrities invited showed up, which had to have hurt, but scores of reporters and hundreds—fifteen hundred to two thousand, depending on the source—of fans did. Jayne, in her skin-tight fishtail-cut pink lace gown, and Mickey, in a somber black tux, fought their way into the church early that evening. The ceremony had been set for 8:00 p.m. but was slightly delayed due to the mobs. "But through it all, Jayne was the perfect bride," wrote Bill Dredge of the *Los Angeles Times*. "Trembling, smiling, even blushing a time or two in the long minutes of delay. . . . There were photographers on ladders taking pictures through the glass roof, others crouched amid the shrubbery, photographing through glass walls, and more than a score of others, tightly jammed together at the church entrance. . . . The flashing floodlights of newsreel cameras sent streams of light cascading through the church. Screams of fans (some of them being hauled off by cops) were heard from inside, and someone even bounced a rock off the glass walls." "All I heard was Mickey saying 'I do,'" said Jayne.

Columnist Gus Weill's heart was not warmed. "Did you see Jayne Mansfield in her wedding gown?" he wrote. "It is fortunate that she has a body. She certainly had not one drop of human dignity. We think that she is the best example today of a human being reduced to the level of an animal. Perhaps she is the missing link. When civilization dies, it will be in all probability her type that will stand triumphant over the ruins of a library or a concert hall."

Brushing off the chance that she might instigate the demise of humanity, Jayne planned her honeymoon. "I wanted the reception to be in my home town," she said, "because I wanted the first wedding cake I cut to be the one Mama baked." Mickey said to her, "We won't be alone until tomorrow night," and Jayne replied, "I'm alone now with you, darling." It was all too saccharine to be spoken straight-faced and sincerely by anyone but Jayne and Mickey.

Wearing a pink jersey dress and "just a little old white mink," Jayne flew to Dallas with Mickey and her parents. At the airport she told reporters who asked about her upcoming films, "Everything is secondary to my marriage. This is what we've wanted for 20 months." The two spent their first married night in a guest cottage behind the Peerses' house. Jayne cooked Mickey breakfast the next day (eggs and pink champagne). About eighty friends and family showed up for the backyard reception; police cordoned off the block. Then the Hargitays flew to Miami for their honeymoon at the Eden Roc Hotel. Jayne wore a demure black one-piece bathing suit on the beach.

During her Miami honeymoon, Jayne of course consented to be interviewed. Jean Sprain Wilson of the *Miami News* went in wanting to write a hatchet piece but wound up admitting, "I was not prepared to do so. It isn't sophisticated of me to admit it, and apparently is not the standard procedure among newspaper women, but . . . I like Jayne Mansfield. I feel sorry for her." Wilson went on to describe the crush of pushy reporters and rude questions Jayne had to face during her press sessions, and Jayne's attempts to be open and nice. "She is pretty, more so than her pictures. She isn't dumb, just a little too honest, too cooperative for her own good," wrote Wilson. One reporter asked her about nude photos she'd posed for, and another called her a lousy actress right to her face. Wilson winced in sympathy. Jayne "was still trying to be sweet to reporters, but this man had hit hard." Jayne, in an even and unemotional tone, replied that "I have never, never had any bad notices about my acting." "There were things she could have left unsaid," wrote Wilson. "I hadn't asked. But she is utterly candid even though it hurts."

Jim Bishop, that same month, was not as kind or understanding. A coffee-table book titled *The Movies,* by Richard Griffith, had been published in 1957, and Bishop snidely recommended that Jayne give it a good hard read. "She is too new, as a star, to be in this book, but she is too old and wise to think that her career is going to last forever," Bishop wrote. "John Wayne and Clark Gable can grow old. Jayne Mansfield cannot," he said, in a masterpiece of both sexism and unwitting prescience. "The price of beauty is that no one is allowed to keep it. . . . Forty years from now, someone will be writing a hundred-year history of the movies. In it, the fans will learn that once upon a time, in grandpa's day, there was a girl named Jayne Mansfield. They will study the outrageous figure, the thick lips, the crinkly eyes, and they will say: 'Oh brother!'" Film fans of 1998 did indeed say, "Oh, brother!" at photos of Jayne Mansfield, but Jim Bishop had died in 1987 and was not around to know the exclamations were generally affectionate nostalgia.

Jayne and Mickey flew back to California and to Jayne Marie the night of January 19 from what Jayne called the first week of their "80-year honeymoon." No sooner had Jayne landed, it seemed, than semi-nude photos of her were featured in the February *Playboy,* in a five-page pictorial, for her now-annual Valentine's spread.

The newlyweds went house-hunting; Mansfield's Madness not big enough for the family Jayne had planned. In late 1956 she told Harrison Carroll that "Mickey has fixed my present home up so much that it looks like a different place. He put in plants, flowers and shrubbery, he built me a brick patio and dog house for my five dogs. We are painting it pink like the main house. Before I buy another house, I guess there is something else that should really come first. I have my eye on a white mink coat with the skins running horizontally."

By early 1957 she was "mulling construction of a heart-shaped house with two heart-shaped pools. Beside one pool would be an undraped statue of her own ample figure. Beside the other, a nude of her rippling-muscled boyfriend, Mickey Hargitay." Mickey seemed to jump right into the spirit of things, seeing the chance to do the construction and landscaping work he loved. "She wanted nostalgia, Sunset Boulevard," he said years later. "That's what it's all about, being a movie star in Hollywood! Let's play the game. It was the goal of a big house, a palace—we called it the House of Love. She just hugged me, tears in her eyes, and said, 'We're sitting on top of the world.' And that's the way it was. And it's a pity sometimes people don't stay there, isn't it?"

In March 1958 the newlyweds put down $76,500 (though Lawrence Block Realty) to buy a home at 10100 Sunset Boulevard, in Holmby Hills. On the corner of Sunset and Carolwood Drive, the Mediterranean-style house had been built in 1930 for a Texas oilman, then bought by singer and actor Rudy Vallee—who never lived in it (apparently his second wife, whom he wed in 1931, did not find it her style). Sitting on three and a half acres, it contained twenty-five rooms, including eleven bathrooms.

This was to be no ordinary movie-star home: it grew like a coral reef, and was just as colorfully breathtaking. Though Jayne and Mickey called it their House of Love, it was better known as the Pink Palace. Over the next few years, it became the Xanadu, the Taj Mahal, the Barbie's Dream House of Hollywood. Jayne and Mickey lived in it only for about five years, and for the last few years of Jayne's life it was all but abandoned; it stood—in all its Jaynified glory—only a little over forty years.

"We're going to decorate the house and put in white satin draperies," Jayne enthused to Vernon Scott. "And I'm going to use as much pink as Mickey will let me get away with." As it turned out, she was not exaggerating, and Mickey let her get away with a *lot* of pink. "Just look at all that wonderful grass," Jayne delightedly said of her expansive property. "I've never had a real lawn of my own. It will be perfect for Jayne Marie and all our pets. I think pink iron gates would look nice on the driveway. We're going to install a heart-shaped swimming pool. It will be pink, too." Mickey jumped in, saying hopefully: "We will decorate it in good taste. We'll take our time and do it right." His optimism was admirable but misplaced.

Mansfield's Madness was sold to a businessman for $30,000 (it was eventually demolished). On March 27 Mickey carried Jayne over the threshold of their new home and they started on as much decorating and planning as they could before Jayne had to leave for Las Vegas, and then England on her next film assignment. Some "Texas chums" (actually Bob

Fink of the Buccaneer Day Commission) started things off nicely by giving them two enormous beds, installing a kitchen, and giving Mickey a lawn-mower. Dorothy Kilgallen noted that Jayne, "never a shy one, is making no secret of the fact that she hopes to furnish her new Hollywood house by endorsing all the manufacturers involved and thus getting the merchandise free." And that is exactly what Jayne did.

❤

By the time Jayne and Mickey started moving into their not-yet-Pink Palace, they had already made their Las Vegas debut, in late February. Back in August 1957, Jayne got an offer from the recently opened Tropicana in Las Vegas for $25,000 a week. "The studio's going to flip!" she accurately told Earl Wilson. It took months to iron out the details, but she was granted leave to do a revue (called *Tropicana Holiday*) from February 12 to March 19, in the Tropicana's huge Theater Restaurant.

By the late 1950s, Las Vegas had become a lifeline for performers whose Hollywood careers were either losing steam or had not yet picked it up, as well as for stars looking for a little work and a lot of money. The Vegas Strip was home to the El Rancho, the Sands's Copa Room (most famous for its Rat Pack shows of the early '60s), the Silver Slipper, the Pioneer Club (with its famed Neon Cowboy sign), the Sahara, the Riviera, the Flamingo, the Stardust, and other clubs, big and small.

The same week that Jayne and Mickey were scheduled to open, other clubs were featuring Jimmy Durante, Rudy Vallee, Buster Keaton, Sophie Tucker, Ginger Rogers, Marlene Dietrich, and Jayne's *Wayward Bus* costar Dan Dailey. Fading film stars Betty Grable and Ann Miller moved house and home to Las Vegas, finding lucrative second careers there. "It's no longer necessary, or even advisable, to journey to New York for the tops in entertainment," wrote the *Los Angeles Times*'s Tom Cameron in 1958.

Tropicana Holiday was directed by Monte Proser, the British-born impresario of not only the Tropicana but the Copacabana, Beachcombers, La Conga, and—he claimed—some fifty other clubs. "A lotta people are gonna come up here to laugh at her," Proser told Mike Connolly of the *Philadelphia Inquirer*. "I think they'll be in for a big surprise." Nightclub producer Dave Siegel told James Bacon that Proser was planning to "surround her with a big show good enough for a Broadway musical," and that Jayne would be onstage only "maybe 20 out of the 90 minutes." She did comedy skits and sang (one of her onstage personas was "Trixie Divoon"—

Jayne managed to become a drag version of herself), sometimes with Mickey, sometimes solo, sometimes with backup singers and dancers.

Jayne checked out the competition, catching Marlene Dietrich's act at the Sahara. Jayne rushed backstage and enthused, "I just don't know what to say. You were great." Marlene replied, "Thank you, my dear. There *is* nothing more to say."

One highlight of Dietrich's act was her "illusion gowns" by Jean Louis—he later made a version for Marilyn Monroe's famous "Happy Birthday" number for President Kennedy. The gowns looked as though Dietrich—and Marilyn—were naked and covered in diamonds, but of course the dresses were as structured as a hazmat suit, and covered their wearers just as much. Dietrich, tightly corseted, wore a thin chiffon overlayer sewn with countless shimmering rhinestones.

Jayne was determined to out-gown Dietrich. She hired dressmaker David Berman to make her a "molten gold" gown, at a reported cost of between $25,000 and $30,000. It was made of 3 million (according to Jayne) tiny gold discs and links, which from a distance looked like liquid gold poured over her form. It weighed fifteen pounds, and Berman begged Jayne not to stress the links and seams. "I told her she could walk and turn around in it, but not to let Mickey Hargitay swing her all over the stage." Nevertheless, of course, she and Mickey did a dance move every night in which she put her arms around his neck and he spun her like a pennant, then flipped her up in the air and caught her (amazingly, he slipped only once—they both crashed to the floor but sustained only minor bruises). To Berman's annoyance, the gown had to be repaired every single night, at a cost of $250 (which he charged against her salary). "They did that *every night,* so we had to keep a man in Las Vegas for four weeks to put the dress back together after every show," recalled Berman.

Tropicana Holiday opened on February 12, holding a $50-per-plate benefit for the March of Dimes (two of Jayne's backup dancers were Bing Crosby's niece Cathy and George Chakiris, who went on to costar in *West Side Story*). Audiences loved the show—crowds were lined up for tickets, and there was never an empty seat throughout the run—and even critics begrudgingly admitted that they'd been properly entertained. "Jayne Mansfield's Las Vegas act is a hit and boss Monte Proser may hold her over," wrote Earl Wilson, and Herb Stein of the *Philadelphia Inquirer* called it a "mop-up."

Far from being exhausted after her last show, Jayne held "a jolly early-morning open house" in her dressing room every night, according to the *Boston Globe*'s Harold Heffernan. "Seldom does one witness such sincere graciousness on the part of a top Hollywood performer as Jayne displays toward the hundreds of plain everyday mill-run fans who tag after her." The night Heffernan stopped by for an interview, fans from Portland—total strangers to Jayne—knocked at her door with their five-year-old son (one hopes this was an early-evening show). While Jayne and Mickey searched for photos to autograph, "hesitant greetings came from the Oregon folks, but Jayne's exuberant personality quickly put them at ease." The five-year-old climbed right up on Jayne's lap, looked her straight in the eyes, and announced, "I wish I had you for my mommy." (One hopes, again, that his actual mommy took this well.)

Heffernan brought up Jayne's professed Christian faith and asked what God would think of the Tropicana. "Oh, I'm sure God is against gambling, and so am I," Jayne admitted. "I mean, you can't win. But it's not my responsibility what other people do. God is on the side of people who do their work conscientiously, and that's what I do."

Earl Wilson was right: Jayne's run was extended two weeks to meet demand, earning her a $5,000 bonus over her regular salary. The only sour note was on closing night: the star was expected to give the backstage crew a cash bonus, but she cluelessly handed out autographed Jayne Mansfield hot-water bottles. When everything was tallied, Jayne complained, income taxes took everything but $15,000 of her Vegas earnings.

Brilliant comic Ernie Kovacs and his gorgeous, talented wife Edie Adams followed Jayne and Mickey at the Tropicana, and in one sketch, Edie was tossed around by a muscleman while Ernie nonchalantly narrated. Edie did a dead-on imitation of Jayne in her act, but after the two women got to know each other, Adams cut it out of her repertoire. "It just comes out as a dumb blonde," said Adams, "and I can't put my heart in it, because I've found out from knowing her that Jayne is one of the smartest girls in Hollywood."

❤

Honeymooning, moving into a new home, Las Vegas, and planning for a new film were not the only things going on in the lives of the happy couple. Ex-spouses reared their heads and hit both Jayne and Mickey with particularly nasty child-support claims, which did their adorable America's Gilded Couple image no good. None of the four people involved came out smelling like a rose. In April 1958 Paul Mansfield filed a petition to stop Jayne from taking Jayne Marie to Europe for her next film; he told the court he wanted Jayne Marie to come stay with him and his second wife in Chattanooga. Paul added pointedly that he'd not seen his daughter since Christmas 1956, and would like her to spend six weeks with him every summer.

Jayne—who had a very healthy salary from Fox and spent it freely—responded that Paul owed her $1,000 in back alimony, and she would make him pay it if he didn't allow her to take Jayne Marie to Europe. Paul quietly dropped his suit, stipulating only that Jayne Marie have a tutor with her and keep up her schoolwork.

"It's always in a child's best interest for her to be with her mother," Jayne told reporters. Of course, it's *not* always in a child's best interest, and this episode points out Jayne's insistence on always having her own way, convincing herself that her own way was best for everyone. Jayne Marie deserved to know her father and stepmother, and spending a few months in Chattanooga having a normal childhood would have been far better for her than being part of Jayne's entourage. But giving up custody of Jayne Marie—even for a few months, even while she was working overseas—would have punctured Jayne's self-image as the perfect loving mother, surrounded by adoring fans, pets, husband, and daughter. Jayne would have been genuinely shocked and hurt had anyone suggested that maybe Jayne Marie would be better off without her, if only for a few months.

Jayne Marie admitted later that she and her mother were close, but that it was not the healthiest kind of closeness. She was an only child till she was eight years old and "having eight years difference till the next one was born kind of affixed that closeness. I then became her best friend, confidante, you name it, I kinda played the role."

Mickey, too, had issues with child support. He'd originally agreed to pay $20 a week to his ex-wife Mary to support their daughter Tina, but considering his new income, Mary asked for $5,500 a week. Mickey said that his ex-wife's request "came like a stab in the back." Jayne—who had just threatened her own husband—added, "That's the way they do things in Hollywood, but it's not very nice."

During his child-support hearings, Jayne and Mickey cried poverty, bringing reporters into their unfinished Pink Palace: they slept on mattresses on the floor—not Jayne Marie, Jayne was quick to add—had no rugs, no furniture, and they cooked on a gas stove in the basement. "We spend about $45 to $50 a month on food and $15 a month on [Jayne Marie's] clothing. Don't worry about us," Jayne added bravely. "Mickey and I are happy." The articles were accompanied by sad photos of the couple on their mattresses and cooking in the basement, like Okies fleeing the Dust Bowl.

Bob Fink of the Buccaneer Day Commission, who had given Jayne and Mickey two enormous beds and installed a kitchen in their new home, reasoned, "If they have so many rooms in that house, they may have lost those beds." A Laguna policeman posted a joking notice in his station reading, "Attention all officers: Please be advised that we shall each donate $10 from our next paycheck to Jayne Mansfield for the purchase of bedroom furniture." A sarcastic fan mailed Jayne and Mickey two feathers "as a starter set for a pillow." Florabel Muir of the *New York Daily News* visited the couple's "palatial hardship mansion" and saw "two rattan chairs and Mickey's barbells" in the living room, "elsewhere, a few lonely chairs and end tables . . . no curtains, no carpets."

Mickey's child-support case finally arrived in court in September 1958. He claimed his only income was $125 a week for acting as Jayne's personal manager, plus 10 percent of her earnings. He also claimed to be in debt, still owing $4,000 on Jayne's engagement ring, $3,000 on his Cadillac, and $40,000 for his investment in the Pink Palace.

L.A. Superior Court judge John Oliver was having none of it: "He is more interested in his own pursuits than his own flesh and blood," Oliver said. "It's a sad commentary that in the time this man had $69,000 pass through his hands, he has paid $800 for his child, whom he testified he hasn't even seen since December of 1956." When Jayne testified in court, "it became apparent that the only resemblance between Jayne and her 'dizzy blonde' label is her peroxide job," wrote Hazel K. Johnson of the UPI, marveling at "the attorney firing the questions in quick succession and a non-flustered Jayne answering them with a heretofore concealed intelligence . . . the attorney couldn't conceal his own amazement. 'This is a very bright girl,' he whispered to a colleague. 'I didn't know.'"

Judge Oliver ruled that Mickey was to pay $300 a month child support. Louella Parsons reported that Jayne Marie Mansfield and Tina Hargitay had some playdates in Griffith Park, though the children seem to have parted company thereafter.

The day after Judge Oliver's ruling, displaying awe-inspiring gall, Jayne and Mickey invited reporters into the Pink Palace to talk about their plans, which included a heart-shaped pool and fireplace, pink-fur-covered bathroom, and pink iron gates out front—all to the tune of $75,000. "It's so—oh, so *regal*," said Jayne. "Oh, I'm so excited. Every couple wants to build their own dream house, don't you think?"

Inez Robb of the *Scranton Tribune* was not going to let that get past her. "It seems terrible that we are sending all that money overseas to absolute strangers when Jayne and Mickey are down to their last $76,000 mansion, their last Cadillac, their last two servants and a $7,500 diamond engagement ring on which they are heroically trying to meet the payment," she wrote. "Tina ought to be helping Mickey, not vice-versa. Here she is, nine years old and still jobless! A drain on her father."

12

I sometimes regret it all, but I've no right to. It's what I wanted, after all. . . . But it does get a bit tiring.

Jayne Mansfield

After two hit comedies, a great dramatic performance, and agreeably taking a second lead in a Cary Grant starrer, Jayne might have hoped for a gift from Fox. But there wasn't much to go around. Other Fox actresses in 1958 were getting big roles in big films, although it was not always great art: Joanne Woodward (*Rally 'round the Flag, Boys!* and *The Long, Hot Summer*), May Britt (an ill-advised remake of *The Blue Angel*), Deborah Kerr (*Beloved Infidel*). Jayne would have made a great Gregg (a flashy, untalented, self-deluded actress) in *The Best of Everything*, but that role went to Suzy Parker. Much of what Fox was putting out in 1958 either had no good female roles or was B or C level: *Thundering Jets, The Barbarian and the Geisha, The Alligator People, Hound-Dog Man.* Even Marilyn Monroe had a long hiatus between the awful *Prince and the Showgirl* (1957) and the brilliant *Some Like It Hot* (1959).

Fox had a film lined up for Jayne—with a top director and a rising costar—but it was a western, on loan-out, to be shot in Spain on the cheap. Back in early 1957 Fox was already mulling over sending Jayne to England to film *The Respectable Widow Froy* with Vittorio de Sica and Walter Chiari. Instead, in February 1958 she was assigned to the distressingly titled *The*

Sheriff of Fractured Jaw. "I want to do the picture, but when will I be able to move into my new house?" Jayne sulked.

She was also required to do publicity on her way from Los Angeles to location filming in Spain. She and Mickey flew to Indianapolis for a Press Club Gridiron dinner—Jayne, in a tight black dress with white lace bodice, said, "I don't think the sack dress is here to stay. It seems to me women shouldn't be covered like that. I think they should take advantage of their figures. They weren't intended to be straight lines, but otherwise." She put her footprints in the cement in front of the Tower Terrace before the Indianapolis 500 race, beside such previous honorees as Barbara Stanwyck, Loretta Young, and Linda Darnell—now married to Robbie Robertson, Jayne's ex-boyfriend. Jayne never did make it to the forecourt of Grauman's Chinese Theater—indeed, no one did in 1957, and only producer Elmer C. Rhoden Jr. and actor Richard Bakalyan were so honored in 1958.

Jayne and Mickey next flew to Love Field in Dallas for her appearance at the Corpus Christi Buccaneer Days celebration (perhaps to reassure Bob Fink that the kitchen and beds had indeed arrived). Jaycees dressed as pirates "kidnapped" Jayne from Mickey at the airport, to Jayne's amusement and Mickey's annoyance. A hundred-piece band greeted Jayne and Mickey at Austin's Cliff Maus Airport, and the Hargitays judged a male beauty contest (Jerry Williams of Waco was awarded the "Mr. Corpus Christi" prize) and led a parade through Corpus Christi.

Finally, in late April Jayne, Mickey, and Jayne Marie—along with her tutor—took off for Europe. Before shooting started, Jayne did the rounds. She professed optimism as she landed in Copenhagen en route to Spain: "I'm so happy that I'm not going to be a dumb blonde," she told reporters. "This will be my first really dramatic part [forgetting all about *The Burglar* and *The Wayward Bus*]. I'm quite sure that I'm now at the crossroads of my career," she added, with unknowing prescience.

Jayne and Mickey attended the Cannes Film Festival, along with Yul Brynner, Sophia Loren, Orson Welles, Jean Marais, Gina Lollobrigida, and Mitzi Gaynor. She was mobbed by fans on her way from the airport to the hotel, and assigned police protection after a photographer was found hiding in the closet of her hotel room. Jayne and Mickey met the Begum Khan, wife of Aga Khan III, who invited them to splash around her private pool (with photographers present, of course), and she attended a party with Russian actress Tatiana Samoilova (whose film *The Cranes Are Flying* was featured at the festival); they toasted each other with vodka and exchanged polite translated compliments.

"She has become a kind of Pied Piper, this Mansfield girl, ever since she descended on Cannes a few days ago," wrote the *Liverpool Echo*. "A flock of adulators gathers in her wake like so many sheep—with expressions to match. Unkind souls suggested that the authorities of the recent film festival here sent out an urgent summons for her to liven up the proceedings."

Jayne prettily pretended to be flustered by all the attention—as she splashed around in a bikini and attended as many press parties as she could squeeze in. "Gee! Those people! I just can't behave like an ordinary person any more, life's so frantic. When I got here they named a cocktail after me: La Mansfield, they called it. Sorta sweet, lots of fruit and with a kick in it. Nothing connected with me is weak, you see."

She also engaged in some unusually thoughtful self-analysis. "The trouble is, every so often you get kinda human," Jayne told one reporter after a day of bikini-splashing. "Then all I feel is that I'm just a girl who wants to hide somewhere and live a life of my own. But it's just not possible. I've been a sex symbol too long to turn the clock back. But I've worked out a solution. I create in my mind the illusion that nobody knows me. So if I go to a public place and want to dance and have fun and be like any normal girl, I pretend I'm quite unknown." She admitted that "I sometimes regret it all, but I've no right to. It's what I wanted, after all. And I believe I've grown more intelligent by it, by all the travel and meeting people I'd never have done otherwise. But it does get a bit tiring."

The Cannes Film Festival out of the way, it was off to the Spanish highlands, where *The Sheriff of Fractured Jaw* was to be shot. "Spain looks so *American*," squealed Jayne. The film was produced by the British company Daniel M. Angel Productions, burning off Fox money frozen in Europe. Much was made in the press of a western being shot in Spain, especially since Jayne's leading man was to be forty-four-year-old Kenneth More, a British star who'd recently had successes in *Genevieve, Doctor in the House,* and *A Night to Remember.* Columnist Mike Connolly noted that a lot of Hollywood stars were filming in Europe that summer: Bette Davis, Jack Palance, Ingrid Bergman, Audrey Hepburn, Errol Flynn, and Orson Welles, mostly because production costs were so much cheaper (unions were laxer in Europe as well).

It was a mixed British/American cast, with a few Spaniards thrown into bit parts, and Cree tribesmen Joe Buffalo and Jonas Applegarth imported from Canada to play generic "Indians." "The bulk of the Indians were Spanish gentlemen with feathers in their hair," explained Jayne.

It was one of director Raoul Walsh's last films, and a big step down for him—in a career stretching back to the 1910s, he'd directed such classics as *The Thief of Bagdad, High Sierra, They Died with Their Boots On,* and *White Heat.* In comparison, *Fractured Jaw* must have been a dull, painful assignment (his lack of interest shows in some blindingly obvious rear-projection shots). Walsh wanted to darken Jayne's platinum hair to a more realistic color, but Fox objected.

Jayne and Kenneth More were both corseted throughout production, More because of a recent skiing accident. "Kenneth is such a sweetie. I've never enjoyed a film so much," said Jayne. But her feelings were not reciprocal—just as her *Wayward Bus* costar Dan Dailey had bad-mouthed her, Kenneth More gave a nasty interview right after filming was complete: "Her talent is very limited," he said of Jayne, and complained that busty stars were killing off the careers of such "sophisticated" actresses as Lauren Bacall, Rosalind Russell, and Barbara Stanwyck. He did admit that Jayne was "always on time and always knows her part. She knows all the other parts, too. She never fluffs," then made the obvious breast joke: "People are still wondering how I got close enough to kiss her." More also had a few choice words for Sophia Loren ("I don't see much in this woman at all") and Marilyn Monroe ("She's like Lassie—one bark and she steals a scene"). So much for international relations; while he remained a big star in England, More's US career never really took off.

Production went smoothly and quickly, with no drama, though Hedda Hopper got in some jabs: "Raoul Walsh, putting Jayne Mansfield through her paces, threatens to kick her where it'll do the most good if she wiggles or shakes. So maybe he'll succeed where others have failed. It would be funny if she had to go all the way to Spain to learn how to act." The loyal Sheilah Graham shot back, "Jayne Mansfield has one big advantage over the rest of her company now shooting in Spain: Jayne can speak Spanish."

Location shooting was finished by the beginning of July, and the cast and British crew members returned to Pinewood Studios in Buckinghamshire for interior shots. Jayne hoped to be home by the end of the month, after a stop in the Middle East to entertain troops. But she and Mickey were refused visas when Iraqi army officers overthrew their monarchy and replaced it with a republic, and US Marines and British Special Forces landed in Lebanon and in Jordan to monitor the situation—so it was right back to California.

What no one knew except Jayne and Mickey was that Jayne was in the early stages of pregnancy during filming. "I wore wasp-waisted dresses and it was the sickest part of my pregnancy," she later said, "but if the studio had known, it might have taken a whole lot of unnecessary precautions that would have delayed the picture until I never would have fit into those dresses I had to wear. I even rode horseback in one scene because my stand-in, who was also pregnant, wasn't feeling well. When the picture opens, we're going to take the baby to see it, even if he's just a few days old. Not many people make their picture debut that young."

The Sheriff of Fractured Jaw—released in late 1958 in the UK and early 1959 in the US—is a lightweight, silly film, enjoyable despite itself. The plot is as old as westerns: a misfit outsider becomes sheriff of a lawless town, and somehow manages to tame it and win the heart of the local saloon gal. It was the same plot that served *Destry Rides Again, My Little Chickadee,* and *Blazing Saddles*—but Jayne was no Marlene Dietrich, Mae West, or Madeline Kahn (and more to the point, she wasn't given the brilliant scripts those ladies received). She plays Kate, the town's hotelier and saloon keeper, with More as Jonathan Tibbs, a naïve Brit who comes west to sell his family's guns. Tibbs manages to conquer feuding ranchers and hostile Indians, and of course he and Kate ride off into the sunset together.

Jayne is a bright spot in the film (literally, with her platinum hair and neon-hued 1880s costumes). She plays a tough, smart, capable woman who doesn't swoon and require rescue; shotgun at the ready, she chases down the ranchers and Indians and saves Tibbs's skin. The one real dent in her performance is the shaky southern accent she affects—a particularly bizarre misstep for a Dallas girl.

She sings two catchy saloon numbers and a love ballad, and was proud enough of her work to give interviews about maybe signing a recording contract. But when the film opened, Jayne was humiliated to find that she'd been dubbed by a young, up-and-coming singer, Connie Francis.

Reviewers were lukewarm about the film, though Kenneth More came in for raves. "It would be as ridiculous to criticise *The Sheriff of Fractured Jaw* as to criticise the conduct of a children's party," wrote the *London Observer,* "and if you think of it as a big children's party, you won't go far wrong." The *Pittsburgh Press* called it "just a series of exaggerated events which are meant to be satirical but which fail to strike sparks of humor," and the *Baltimore Sun* felt it was a "gentle, almost affectionate parody . . . on the whole, refreshingly hilarious."

Jayne's reviews ranged from mild to scathing: "Jayne looks more like a caricature of Jayne Mansfield than ever"; "Jayne Mansfield also is in the film, but doesn't hurt it very much"; "A caricature of Marilyn Monroe is permissible, but a poor imitation of her is sad." Still, some critics, at least, didn't outright hate her: "Jayne Mansfield, pretty and pink and demonstrating a passable acting ability, is a pleasant foil for More's comedy," said one, and she was given a nice backhanded compliment by Sara Roberta Getty of the *Daily American:* "Whether you like her acting or not is beside the point. You're going to like Jayne, she's that type." Coventry's *Evening Telegraph* was kind enough to call Jayne "splendid" in her role. She won one of her few awards for *The Sheriff of Fractured Jaw,* a Museum of Modern Art Golden Laurel for Top Female Musical Performance (Connie Francis must have fumed at that).

No matter how poor the reviews, Fox had no reason to complain: *The Sheriff of Fractured Jaw* cost only $700,000 to make, and by the summer of 1959 had taken in $2,300,000.

Jayne loved being pregnant, despite the morning sickness she suffered with each baby, and as soon as *The Sheriff of Fractured Jaw* wrapped she happily talked about it to the press. "It's a wonderful time in the life of woman when she's expecting a baby. It's really her happiest time," she told the *Pasadena Independent Star-News.* She added that Mickey "almost died" when she told him she'd worn corsets and ridden horseback while pregnant, "but I assured him, it was very light riding and just for a minute."

From London she said that she and Mickey "are delighted. We want nothing so much right now as a baby." Whether it was a boy or a girl "really doesn't matter in the slightest—to either of us. . . . I love Europe, but my baby will be born in California. California is a great place for babies." They already had names picked out: "If it's a boy, we'll name him Miklós after my husband, and if it's a girl we'll call her Camille Yvonne." Jayne added that she wanted five children, one of her few predictions to come true. "If you plan properly, having a family doesn't affect an actress's career."

While in London, Jayne traded pleasantries with C. Avery Mason, the bishop of Dallas. They commiserated about Alaska's becoming the forty-ninth state, leaving Texas no longer the biggest, but Mason consolingly told Jayne, "Texas may be smaller, but we're louder." She also sold her grandfather's Pen Argyl house for $12,500, assuring that she and Mickey would be able to afford lots of baby furniture.

Just before leaving London, Jayne gave one of her most deliriously bubbleheaded interviews. She spoke with British journalist Thomas Wiseman, who uncharitably described her as "a large girl, with a protruding mouth, prominent teeth, thickish lips and off-white hair. She is a little on the plump side. Her eyes are brown. So are her eyebrows and the roots of her hair."

Perhaps sensing his hostility, Jayne went full Rita Marlowe on him, bubbling over about her plans for her new home: "It's all very beautiful and artistic, and we're putting in a heart-shaped swimming pool and a private cinema. We're going to have a little private chapel where we can go to iron out our spiritual problems. Don't you think that's a beautiful idea? Oh yes, we've also got a couple of waterfalls. I think they're nice."

When asked if she was going to have leopard-skin rugs, she shrugged prettily, "No, I think they're old-fashioned, and they're not feminine, are they? I got through my leopard-skin phase three years ago. I'm going to have a real home. Nothing flashy. I do think homes are just the most wonderful places." She built up steam: "Oh, yes, I forgot to tell you, we're going to have maribou curtains—that's a kind of feathery fox fur, you know. It's not as staid as mink, but it has the same connotation as champagne, very light and fluffy."

Jayne went on to discuss her public image: "I'm a very religious person. I'm afraid people sometimes have the wrong idea about me. Because of those pin-up pictures I posed for. Well, a girl has to eat, doesn't she? But I'm absolutely against lust, it's very immoral, in my opinion. What you've got to have is inner sexiness and inner cleanliness. . . . I think people could be cleansed by healthful thinking."

Even for Jayne it was daffy cluelessness. But that very same month, Burt Boyar of the *Philadelphia Inquirer* noted that "I have spoken with almost every star of importance who has come to New York in the last three years. Not one of them has had the quality which is Jayne Mansfield's alone. She has a mind like a columnist. She can talk you a column in five minutes. She has a feeling for provocative comments."

So was it an act, or was it for real? Andy Warhol, Mae West, Salvador Dalí—their schtick was a part of their real personality, which they used in their act. Eventually the schtick took over and possessed them.

Stepping off the *Queen Mary* on her return to the US, Jayne was questioned about the newest blonde bombshell, Brigitte Bardot, whose *Mam'zelle Pigalle* had just made a big splash. *Life* magazine wrote that Bardot "has forced Hollywood queens Marilyn Monroe and Jayne Mansfield off into a sort of technicolored limbo where they seem to be hardly more dangerous than suburban housewives painted-up for the local Junior League Follies." Jayne batted her eyes when Bardot was mentioned: "Who is she? I've never heard of her, although I've heard it said abroad that some French girl is a miniature of me."

In late August Jayne had her first appointment at Fox in six months; she was given three scripts to look over. She complained to the *Boston Globe* about her loan-outs: "If I made a picture outside of Fox they'd have to pay $300,000 for me. Per film. But as I'm under exclusive contract to Fox, I only get $75,000 a year."

Mickey was offered the lead in *Tarzan's Greatest Adventure,* which eventually went to Gordon Scott. Mickey insisted—quite sincerely—that he wanted to give up acting to open a chain of health studios. This was to become an issue in their marriage: Mickey wanted to settle down, get a job, and be a normal person, and Jayne wanted to be Jayne Mansfield. Less than a year after their wedding, the ending had been written.

As her pregnancy progressed, Jayne continued to hit the hot spots, wherever a photographer was present. She and Mickey attended a party with Natalie Wood and Robert Wagner, Guy Madison, and Art Linkletter; she showed up at the Del Mar racetrack to decorate the winner, How Now; she and Mickey went to the premiere of *The Big Country* and the after-party at Romanoff's with Clark Gable, Cary Grant, Claudette Colbert, and Eva Gabor; UCLA's Nu Beta Epsilon law fraternity voted Jayne "the girl we'd most like to defend in court," so she opened her still-in-progress Pink Palace to their rushing party. Also held at the Pink Palace was Jayne's baby shower (Elizabeth Taylor's gift was a music box shaped like a pig).

Jayne kept a sharp eye on her publicity, issuing a cease-and-desist order to the delightfully sleazy mail-order clothing company Frederick's of Hollywood for using her name and photo to advertise their padded bras and underpants. "It's ridiculous," she fumed. "I wasn't padded by Frederick's. My curves came from nature." Besides, when she did an endorsement, it's for "a beautiful fee or percentage. I wouldn't sign my name and likeness over for charity's sake."

There was nothing she could do about the store-brand knockoffs using her name to advance their careers. Lasa Saya, advertised as "the Jayne

Mansfield of Japan," was appearing at Honolulu's infamous Club Hubba Hubba, and the raunchy B-film *Girl with an Itch* starred Kathy Marlowe, who "makes Jayne Mansfield look like a boy!" All Jayne could do was shrug and take it as a compliment.

And the interviews continued—always, the interviews continued. She proved once again that her calculated dumbness paid off with a double joke that made scores of newspapers: "If, for example, a journalist asks me who wrote *Othello*," she deadpanned, "I answer without hesitation Louis XVI or Eisenhower. The journalist immediately publishes a page-long article." Then the punch line: "Obviously if I told the truth, that it is Dickens, the effect would be nil."

In 1958 Vernon Scott mused about the Big Three blondes in Hollywood—Jayne, Marilyn Monroe, and Kim Novak (who appeared in *Vertigo* and *Bell, Book and Candle* that year). "Marilyn's blue eyes are wary and reflect a feminine desire to be protected from the rigors of being a movie star," wrote Scott. "Jayne, on the other hand, flirts shamelessly from behind her long eyelashes, and protection seems the farthest thing from her mind. Kim's hazel eyes are penetrating, outrageously sad."

He continued, "Marilyn carefully steers the conversation. Her personal life, husband Arthur Miller and past marriages are taboo. Kim is a soul-searcher. She fixes you with a bewitching smile and talks freely and intelligently about her thoughts." Jayne, on the other hand, "boasts about her Mickey and will discuss anything from sex to Texas." As for their beauty, "Up close, where you can see through the makeup, Kim rates highest for pure facial beauty, augmented by warmth and naturalness. Marilyn weaves a spell of mystery, and her four-alarm figure would probably win a bathing-beauty contest among the trio." And then the payoff, which must have made Jayne's month: "When it comes to swinging glamour, a cute (unrehearsed) quip and outright good company, Jayne takes over. She might well score highest in an I.Q. test, too."

"Mostly I want to rest until the baby comes," Jayne insisted between parties and premieres. "Mickey and I have been on the go since our marriage and have not had a chance to do anything" as far as home renovations went. "It's a big house with two acres and completely in need of everything." In December she showed the *Daily Mirror*'s Lionel Crane around the grounds, and as he later wrote: "We were walking along a steep garden path when Jayne slipped on the concrete. One of her slippers came off and she was about to fall down a slope at the edge of the path when I grabbed her. We swayed on the brink for a moment or two before Jayne found her feet again—and we BOTH sighed with relief." She told Mickey, "You can thank the *Daily Mirror* for saving your baby."

Miklós Jeffrey Palmer Hargitay Jr. was born on December 21, 1958, after nine hours of labor, at St. John's Hospital in Santa Monica. Jayne was on the phone to Louella Parsons forty-five minutes after the birth ("They gave me a spinal so I could watch"). The new family spent Christmas Day at the Pink Palace, with Jayne's parents (and a photographer, of course). By January 1, Mickey Jr. was already being used as an adorable little prop: his first outing was to the Los Angeles Eastside Boys' Club, where he was made an honorary member.

13

Jayne Mansfield had a bad scare when they ripped off her clothes in Brazil: the photographers almost didn't show up!

Myron Cohen

Finally back home in early 1959 with her husband, new baby, and eight-year-old Jayne Marie (who, for the first but far from last time, was conscripted as babysitter), Jayne threw open her doors and gave the press a tour of her work in progress. Jayne and Mickey got their mattresses and bedsprings from Powers and Pittenger of Indianapolis, with the understanding that they mention in every interview that they got their mattresses and bedsprings from Powers and Pittenger of Indianapolis.

She told Bob Thomas that her new bed would be "Texas-sized—that's bigger than king-sized. There will be a heart-shaped red canopy over the bed. On the wall above the bedstead will be cupids and arrows in marble. All around the bottom of the bed will be pink fluorescent lighting. Come see my bathroom, it's divine." Thomas duly noted that the heart-shaped tub had a gold-mosaic bottom, and the separate shower was studded with jeweled tiles. "Mickey tore out the tile in all eleven bathrooms," explained Jayne. "They were just too dreary. We'll put pink fur on the floor." The new baby's room was painted with a fairy-tale mural. Thomas reported with undisguised consternation that "the rabbits in the design even had heart-shaped noses and navels."

Barbara Flanagan of the *Star Tribune* also got the grand tour. "The front door with its pink Christmas wreath was open. In the front hall was a pink satin 'thing.'" Jayne explained to Flanagan that it was a baby bed sent by a thoughtful fan in Georgia. "It was the only sittable object in sight except for barrels, ladders and sawhorses. . . . The master bedroom held only a pink bed—big and roomy with a pink mirrored heart-shaped headboard." That headboard was a work of Mickey's art: "Mickey is sub-contracting the work himself and doing a lot of it," said Jayne. The headboard was made of mirrored glass—lozenge-shaped, antique, and pink—worked into more of a floral design than a heart. The bed was topped by eight candelabra, in the center of which was an angel nestled in a heart.

As the house took shape, neighbors, tourists, and reporters realized this was no ordinary Hollywood mansion; it was an apotheosis of mid-century interior design that veered wildly from shrieking kitsch to genuine charm. The original house was a Spanish hacienda gone 1920s Hollywood, with tiled roof, arches, a two-story living room with a dark wood-beamed ceiling. Mickey had the white stucco exterior painted pink, mixed with glittering quartz grains. It shone in the sunlight against the surrounding greenery in a way that managed to be quite lovely.

In the den Mickey built a fireplace from petrified wood and added a copper ceiling. That room also boasted a bearskin rug as well as curtains that appeared to be made from molten copper. The main stairway—leading from the living room to the upstairs bedrooms—was made from Swedish-looking painted wood and Spanish tiles, with a banister of metal grillwork.

The most disturbing rooms were the office and Jayne's bathroom. The office's desk, ceiling, walls, and drawers were made from bright-red tufted "leather" (probably vinyl), giving the claustrophobic feeling of being inside a human heart. Jayne's bathroom was not covered in pink fur, as she'd wanted, but the end result was just as distressing to any maid who had to clean it. The floors, walls, ceiling, and the sides of the heart-shaped tub were covered in pink shag rugs—this in a house overrun with small children and poorly housebroken pets. "It makes you feel you were being hugged by teddy bears," said Jayne.

Then, of course, there was the swimming pool, perhaps the Pink Palace's most famous feature. It was heart-shaped, with blue tiles and two small heart-shaped inset islands, which Mickey was wiring up as fountains. Next to the main pool was a small heart-shaped kiddie pool. The pièce de résistance was "I Love You Jaynie" written in tiles between the two heart islands. Mickey also built a bathhouse next to the pool, with a copper-topped fireplace inscribed, "My love for you flames forever."

Over the next couple of years, Mickey worked hard on the landscaping, adding waterfalls, trees, and pathways, labor he enjoyed much more than acting in films, performing at Las Vegas, or trailing Jayne from movie set to movie set.

❤

In early February, a little over a month after giving birth, Jayne took off for what she hoped would be a combined vacation and publicity event. She and Mickey left Jayne Marie and Mickey Jr. with Jayne's mother, and took off for Rio de Janeiro, where she would publicize *The Sheriff of Fractured Jaw* and attend several parties. Rio's pre-Lent carnival makes New Orleans's Mardi Gras look like an Emily Post tea party; Jayne and Mickey had no idea what they were in for.

It was 101 degrees when they arrived, so the couple took off for the beach—wearing the briefest of swimsuits—where the expected photographers and fans gathered. Jayne later wore a white dress as she gave a press conference in her hotel room, insisting, "Sex appeal has nothing to do with bodily proportions. It's all in the mind. It's what you have inside. The rest is all tinsel."

Then came Jayne's Night of the Locust, February 9, when she saw for the first time how dangerous a crowd of frenzied fans could get. That night Jayne put on a $400 black dress, its bodice covered with sewed-on roses. She and Mickey headed for a packed, rowdy carnival ball at the Copacabana Hotel. Accounts vary as to what happened next: Jayne either got up on a chair and did a "shimmy," or she merely climbed up on the chair so her fans could see her.

See her they did: "I had these little red roses on the bosom of my dress," she later recalled. "They started picking them. When the flowers were gone, they went after the dress. I thought I'd be completely stripped. I was frightened for a few moments." Photos show that she was terrified, in tears. Ripping the top of her dress off, men in the mob groped and pinched her. Mickey fought his way through the crowd, threw his coat over Jayne, and powered her out of the room.

The next morning, the stories and the photos were international news. Jayne shrugged off the attack: "I'm black and blue all over, but I'm not sore. The boys just got a little excited. I really think Brazilians are wonderful, the salt of the earth." Even the protective Mickey said, "They meant well, it was just the carnival spirit." Did Mickey ever take a sock at men for getting fresh with his wife? one reporter asked. "Nah, it's never happened," Mickey insisted. "I could have killed a hundred people by now, but why? Jaynie would never be in business if I acted that way. People come up to her 1,000 times a day and tell her she's beautiful."

Undaunted, the couple planned to attend another party, at the Quitandhinha Hotel. That night Jayne wore green shorts and a white blouse. At one point she got up on a table with Mickey to dance, but she remained unmolested, though some in the crowd yelled, "Take it off!"

The press, of course, made a huge joke of the whole affair, and Jayne got not one ounce of sympathy. Walter Winchell quoted comic Myron Cohen's quip: "Jayne Mansfield had a bad scare when they ripped off her clothes in Brazil: the photographers almost didn't show up!" Eleanor Rice of the *Arizona Daily Star* wrote, "Isn't it great to have Jayne Mansfield back in the news again? They jolly well did a good job of it down in Rio. Seems these festivals are pretty giddy go 'rounds." The Associated Press said that Brazil is "where men are men and a woman's dress is in the nature of impediment." Dorothy Kilgallen was particularly nasty: "Jayne Mansfield's headlines out of Rio de Janeiro, where she 'suffered' the loss of her dress top, was just what the press agents ordered." Other comedians besides Cohen went to town; Corbett Monica said he bought a Jayne Mansfield convertible: "The top comes down in a crowd."

The press coverage led to a deluge of letters to various editors: not complaining about how lightly Jayne's mob assault was taken, but literally blaming the victim. A *Minneapolis Star Tribune* reader objected to the paper's coverage: "The front page story describing Jayne Mansfield's disgraceful conduct is a sad commentary on our country's public relations abroad . . . she should be censured and advised to stay at home until she learns to conduct herself as becomes an American citizen." One reader of the *Vancouver Province* came right out and said, "She was asking for it. If she wants to be a real lady I suggest she go to Vancouver or Toronto to see how a lady acts."

To be fair, by 1959 standards, Jayne *was* asking for it. She'd made her name as an open, unapologetic exhibitionist, falling out of her dress in Sophia Loren's face, parading about in bikinis at every opportunity. She did herself no favors when she got home and immediately released photos of herself bubble-bathing in her new heart-shaped tub; they were printed widely. So no one blamed that crowd in Rio: it was, after all, just Jayne Mansfield.

Three years into her Fox career, she was already "just Jayne Mansfield." Frank Tashlin, according to May Mann, said that "Jayne had everything—beauty, talent and drive—but she blew her career at Fox with too much publicity. No one could get through to her that she was hurting herself with this constant barrage of daily publicity in the papers and press. She would call her own press conferences for the most intimate detail or happening."

There was a lot of publicity and many happenings through the first half of 1959, but none of them were coming from Fox. The studio was not doing well financially and had bigger problems than Jayne Mansfield. She collected her salary, waited in vain for a film project—anything, even a loan-out—and made sure her name stayed in the public eye.

Jayne spun her wheels professionally while vague rumors filled the papers: she might make a film on loan-out in Mexico with that country's popular star Cantinflas. After Jayne met Sophie Tucker at a benefit, the idea of her playing Soph's life story was floated about. Dorothy Kilgallen wrote that Jayne was available for summer stock, but only if "her darling Mickey Hargitay" was in on the deal—but that might just have been a nasty jab. Vernon Scott printed that Fox had signed Jayne to a recording contract—pretty unlikely, considering her recent dubbing by Connie Francis.

"All the studio can see me in is comedies," Jayne complained to Bob Thomas. "In my earlier career, I did serious roles almost entirely. One of the best pictures I did was a little movie called *The Burglar,* which was a drama." She wanted to do another Vegas act, "but the studio won't let me go. They say they have other plans for me. One of them is to go to Australia to publicize *The Sheriff of Fractured Jaw.*"

Even not working, Jayne was newsworthy: when she showed up at a formal dinner in leopard-print stretch pants, it made headlines around the nation. She attended the Municipal Opera House Ball in Rio and tossed her shoes to fans pleading for souvenirs; she was the honorary queen of the Lions Club Sports Car races in Stockton. She showed up at the Screen Writers' Guild Awards in March along with Shirley MacLaine and Jack Benny, and the new scandalous couple of the season, Elizabeth Taylor and Eddie Fisher.

She told Ben Gross of the *New York Daily News,* "I go to all the PTA meetings and I'm also a Brownie leader. I'm very serious about it all. The only trouble I have is at the PTA, where lots of the men are present, some of them are always saying to me, 'Jayne, how about squealing for us?'"

Vacationing in Fort Lauderdale and looking like a "tousled well-developed teenager," Jayne talked to reporter Dick Hoekstra. On getting her post-pregnancy figure back, she said, "If your body muscles are tight and in good health, you don't need anything else to hold you in. I hate girdles, they make your muscles lazy. I'd like to put the girdle-makers out of business because they put your muscles out of work."

Then Jayne said something that may have been true of many women in 1959: "I love being dominated. I think a man should dominate his wife in every respect. It's no good if the wife tries to be the man and vice-versa, if you know what I mean." But this wasn't true, not for Jayne, though she may actually have believed it herself—Jayne was a master at self-deception. She may have put on a public face of girlish submissiveness, but she was a hurricane, blowing away everyone else's advice, wishes, and opinions. All three of her husbands, her parents, her children, her bosses at Fox—no matter what they told her, Jayne went along only if it was what Jayne wanted. Her headstrong personality won her stardom, but it also ruined her marriages, hurt her children, and wasted what very real talent she had.

That spring Jayne had the best public exposure she'd had in a long time, but it was on TV, not the big screen (though she probably reached a larger audience). On March 1 she appeared on *The Steve Allen Show,* her first appearance since the Rio debacle, and gave a thoroughly charming performance. Wearing a blindingly metallic gown, she hauls out her violin and plays a passable rendition of "Alice Blue Gown" while she—in dubbed voice-over—insults Steve Allen ("I came 3,000 miles for *this?* . . . It looks like I'm gonna miss *Maverick* tonight").

Then they do a parody *Person to Person* interview, showing both her comic skills and her amiability about poking fun at herself. She is interviewed in her dressing room ("Jayne, what do you think of Marilyn Monroe?" "Who's he?"), in her kitchen ("Mickey's so helpful when we're rearranging the furniture—I lifted the piano, while Mickey moved the living room"), and writing in her library ("I was recently honored by the Massachusetts Institute of Technology, for pronouncing it").

She is relaxed, low-key, and very funny, but the few reviews were dismissive: "Jayne Mansfield showed up to play a violin. Signor Stradivarius could be heard turning over in his grave" (*Orlando Evening Star*); "Jayne

Mansfield also appeared. And she was—well, she was Jayne" (*New York Daily News*).

She was also seen on the April 6 Oscars broadcast—not as a presenter but modeling for the Best Costume nominees. Wearing one of Eva Gabor's corseted gowns designed by Cecil Beaton for *Gigi,* she was the last model down the runway, following Victoria Shaw (in a dress from *Bell, Book and Candle*), Inger Stevens (*The Buccaneer*), Christine Carere (*A Certain Smile*), and Joanna Moore (*Some Came Running*). When *Gigi* won the Oscar, Jayne joined presenters Wendell Corey and Ernie Kovacs at the podium as producer Arthur Freed accepted the award.

But there were no real job offers, either on TV or in the movies, so Jayne asked Fox again if she could take a temporary leave to appear in Las Vegas. The late 1950s were the end of the big studio era, with stars signed to long-term exclusive contracts—but only the beginning of the end. Asking Fox to loosen the chains indicates that Jayne saw problems looming, and that both her career and her finances were becoming real worries. Fox did give her a month-long leave of absence so that she and Mickey could perform at the Tropicana in May.

Mickey was also branching out—while he would continue performing for several years, he knew his future did not lie with acting. For one thing, he just wasn't very good at it—he was visibly embarrassed and awkward on-screen—and he didn't much enjoy it, either. He'd worked as a contractor and builder since long before he'd met Jayne, and remodeling the Pink Palace and its grounds reminded him of what he loved. For the past few years, Mickey had sold workout equipment and attached his name to a string of gyms. Now he and Jayne incorporated a pool-building company—not all of the pools were heart-shaped, but Mickey was happily on his way to what would become his life's work, building and landscaping.

The help-wanted ad was certainly eye-catching: sandwiched between ads for "Sales Engineer" and "Executive Training Program" in the *Los Angeles Times* was "JAYNE MANSFIELD immediately requires 5 division managers for her new multimillion dollar dream swimming pool corp. Experience in sales, advertising, public relations helpful, but not essential." Jayne Mansfield Dreampools showrooms opened in Los Angeles and Inglewood—with Jayne appearing in person, of course—in late March. "With Dreampools' new Permaflex method, your pool will be installed within 7 days."

Attaching her name, rather than Mickey's, to the ads would bring in business—but Marilyn Monroe and Kim Novak weren't hawking side enterprises. It was a smart business move, perhaps, but not a harbinger of acting success. Jayne Mansfield Dreampools managed to get a few distributors and contractors, but faded away in a flurry of lawsuits because of unfinished work and unfulfilled contracts within a couple of years.

Mickey also promoted Hargitay's Health-Glow, "The Aristocrat of Exercise Equipment." The equipment came with an exercise booklet showing photos of bikini-clad Jayne and swim-trunk-clad Mickey doing exercises (the booklet was used for more than physical fitness purposes, one imagines).

Over the next few years, both Jayne and Mickey threw money and energy into various businesses, none of which became successes. She and Mickey bought a corner lot in Beverly Hills and two in Palm Springs to open a chain of Mickey Hargitay Health Clubs, which never came to anything. In 1962 Jayne sold her name to Celebrity Merchandisers, which advertised Jayne Mansfield Health-Tan Sun Lamps ("the only sun lamp that CAN'T BURN") and Jayne Mansfield Tan-Thru Sun Hats ("tested and endorsed by doctors, institutions and authorities").

An influx of cash came from a second Las Vegas booking, again at the Tropicana, for $25,000 a week. Jayne managed to get Fox to rewrite her contract for a two-picture-a-year deal that would allow her to do Vegas as well as any indie pictures offered her.

She showed Rick Du Brow of the UPI around the still-evolving Pink Palace, which was growing ever pinker and more eccentric with the help of the new Vegas money. "Rock 'n' roll music blared into all the rooms over a loudspeaker system," wrote Du Brow. "Nine dogs of assorted shapes and sizes scampered all over the place, yelping."

Jayne hired the decorator of the Tropicana to design Mickey Jr.'s nursery. Added to the aforementioned heart-adorned bunnies were paintings of Jayne, Mickey, and Jayne Marie skipping hand in hand. The curtains were lavender and the carpets pink; the heart-shaped bassinet was pink and purple. Dorothy Kilgallen reported that Jayne and Mickey were sending out letters that "solicit free loot for their new house, on an endorsement deal, and imply that plugs in the media will follow." Proving the point, that same day Mike Connolly noted in his column that Republic Water Heaters was supplying fixtures.

The living room got its focal point on April 19, when Mickey gave Jayne a nine-foot concert grand piano for her twenty-sixth birthday. It was a Steinway concert model, painted ivory with little cherubs floating about on it. The huge, airy living room also contained two purple sofas facing a glass coffee table, and multicolored throw pillows scattered around. Overlooking it all were two small Venice-style balconies on the second floor, from which Jayne and Mickey could (and did) wave and blow kisses at each other.

❤

The ready money was in Vegas, and Jayne knew it. "Three weeks' salary, the house was paid for," Mickey recalled. She and Mickey headed back to Vegas for a late May–early June run. With Jayne in town again, the old Mae West feud heated up. Mae had been booked for a four-week engagement at the Sahara Hotel, which was cut short one week (because of illness, said Mae). When Jayne too sweetly expressed her sympathy, Mae snapped, "That woman doesn't even exist as far as I'm concerned. I don't know her, I never met her." Jayne purred, "I never feuded with Miss West. I just fell in love with Mickey, who happened to be in her show. In fact to me she was our cupid."

Jayne opened one night early, as a favor to Eddie Fisher. He wanted to close his own act early so he could marry Elizabeth Taylor on May 12. Jayne's new Vegas show, called *French Dressing,* was produced by Lou Walters, best known today as the father of journalist Barbara. Lou Walters was one of the top names in nightclubs from the 1940s into the early '60s; his Latin Quarters in New York and Miami were hugely successful. But by the time he took on Jayne's show, Walters's luck was running out. His Café des Paris clubs drove him toward bankruptcy, and just the previous year he'd attempted suicide. His work with Jayne was something in the way of a comeback.

Jayne and Mickey previewed their act for a local Alcoholic Anonymous chapter before opening: as one paper noted, "stage actors have learned that the AAers, because of the no drinking, are there to enjoy the show."

French Dressing audiences left the show humming the costumes. Jayne's opening-number dress was so shocking that descriptions of it took up most of the press coverage, leaving very little room for her performance. It "brought a gasp from first-nighters who had been watching scantily clad French and German beauties for months on the other side of the strip," wrote one reviewer. Photos show Jayne seemingly nude from the knees up, covered only by transparent, clinging netting, with spangles and sequins covering strategic spots; from the knees down (covering her least-flattering features, her legs), was a foaming petticoat of ruffles. Columnist Bill Vaughan wrote, "Jayne Mansfield's Las Vegas costume comes along just in time; we were about to run out of things to view with alarm."

Jayne performed some sketches with comic Don Williams, and invited audience participation, which would become a big part of all her live acts. Jayne loved her audiences, and she needed them to love her—she walked among them, up close and personal, with racy but never nasty jokes, sitting on men's laps and admiring women's jewels—they enjoyed it, and so did she. (Jayne got a little too up-close to audience member Katherine Walker, who went into labor during her show and was hustled into Jayne's dressing room—she walked in just as Mrs. Walker's daughter was being born.)

Reviewers noted that, as usual, Mickey picked Jayne up and tossed her around, and that she did a lot of singing and dancing: "She is no Dinah Shore or Cyd Charisse," wrote James Bacon, "but with that gown and the shape she doesn't have to be." When Rick Du Brow of UPI asked her how this new Vegas act squared with her wanting to do serious movie roles, she admitted frankly, "I'm getting $25,000 a week, plus expenses, to appear. So I figured it would be worth delaying my chance a little longer."

Reporter Bill Crawford interviewed Jayne on a 104-degree day in Las Vegas. She lounged poolside in a bikini with Mickey and the children, who had come to join them from California, and held forth on publicity ("I'd rather pose for a six-year-old boy than for *Life* magazine"), children ("I really want seven kids, but I'll settle for five—I have lots of time in the next 20 years"), Las Vegas ("I prefer movies to either stage or dinner-club performances. But nightclub work is the most monetarily lucrative"). She also answered questions about her measurements ("41½-18-35½") and her pet peeve ("People asking me my measurements").

French Dressing did so well that it was held over an extra two weeks; when Jayne closed on June 24, she was followed by Betty Grable (whose husband Harry James was playing at the Flamingo). Right below Erskine Johnson's syndicated review about Jayne's new show ("'It's a real swingin' show,' says Jayne, 'and I don't just mean Mickey swinging me around'") was an ominous story about 20th Century-Fox selling off its back lot to a New York syndicate for $59 million.

14

She's got every blue ribbon in Europe for making personal appearances, from opening a can of sardines to a flower show. They love her.

Bob Goldstein

In the midst of her Vegas show, Jayne was taking quick trips to Fox. She went on suspension for one week, unhappy with the film the studio had finally cast her in, a crime drama called *Too Hot to Handle,* to be filmed in London. She finally agreed to do the film, and managed to get Fox to pay for Mickey and her children to accompany her; she was to report for work at the Borehamwood studios by the end of July. She'd be working on loan-out to the Associated British Picture Corporation, which meant that 20th Century-Fox simply had no suitable films for her. Fox wouldn't even be distributing and promoting *Too Hot to Handle;* that would be left to the Topaz Film Corporation, whose previous films included such C-grade fare as *Fire Maidens of Outer Space.*

Jayne—and entourage—arrived in London in late July 1959, with Jayne enthusing, "The role will be a dramatic one, and I am very excited about it." She and her family were put up in the home of actor Hubert Gregg at Gerrards Cross, Buckinghamshire; they hired a cook and a butler. Jayne loved old-fashioned British service, pondering whether she could take them home with her: "The butler will double as a chauffeur, and the cook as housekeeper, and they'll serve tea on the terrace every afternoon." She met former prime minister Clement Attlee at a London premiere. (He had no idea who she was: "Who? You had better ask my wife, she knows more about these things than I do.")

Too Hot to Handle ran into difficulties almost immediately. Jayne didn't like the script, and columnist and writer Robert Ruark flew from his home in Spain to rewrite it—it took a week and cost the production company $25,000. Then she was ordered to bed with a touch of the flu (of course this provided the opportunity for newspapers to headline "Jayne Mansfield Has Chest Trouble"). Technicians on another film at the studio went on strike, and the *Too Hot to Handle* crew also walked out. Worse yet, the film ran through its $784,000 budget, and cast and crew members walked out again when the paychecks stopped coming. Director Terence Young explained, "By British law if a man has a stroke six weeks before he signs anything, he is ruled incompetent and the deal is canceled. Our financial backer had a stroke three weeks after the picture started." Scrambling, Young found another backer and the production was dark for only thirty-six hours.

It was not a happy set. Costar Karlheinz Böhm, who played a sympathetic reporter, had been told he'd be making a gangster thriller with his idol Leo Genn, and enthusiastically signed on. "When I showed up, the producer said they had just signed Jayne Mansfield for the feminine role," he later said. "Suddenly, the whole movie was changed. This is nothing against Miss Mansfield. She's a lovely girl, but I refuse to see the picture."

Even less happy was rising young actress Barbara Windsor, who was dancing in a club at night while filming during the day. While she was later a delight in *Carry On* films, *EastEnders,* and in West End theaters, she was still a gawky newcomer in 1959. One of the few people who did not get along with Jayne, she recalled in her memoirs, "It took Jayne Mansfield only a few minutes to upset me. She walked on to the set as though she had a nasty smell under her nose, gave me one look and told the director to get make-up to tint my hair light brown. 'You can't do that, I'm afraid,' I said. 'My boss at the club will go insane if I'm not blonde tonight. I'll get sacked.'"

Perhaps intimidated by the well-established London cast, Jayne was unusually standoffish. "She was non-communicative with almost everyone, crew as well as cast," said Windsor. "It's a great feeling when the star walks on to a set and says, 'Good morning, how are you, everyone?' It makes the company feel good and encourages a good working atmosphere."

Late in life, Windsor reasoned that "although she had been a big star, by this time her career was on the wane, and maybe this was part of the problem." But the chorines had their revenge: "We would all meet up for lunch in the dining room, and I'd have them in fits with funny stories on how Jayne Mansfield's 'bristols' [Cockney rhyming slang: "Bristol City" = "titty"] had to dominate every scene, even if it meant putting us behind schedule." For all her complaining, Windsor had a good supporting role in the film, including a scene in which Jayne gives her motherly (and unheeded) advice about not going home with the customers.

This was not the first time Jayne played the diva and had a distracting actress "taken care of." Showgirl Felicia Atkins recalled that during one of Jayne's Las Vegas runs, Jayne took one look at her and suggested to the management that maybe she was due for a vacation. A "source" said, "You couldn't blame Jayne. Suppose Marilyn Monroe had been the headliner. Would she have wanted a figure like Jayne's in the chorus?"

Even if her *Too Hot to Handle* costars weren't thrilled with her, assistant director Frank Nesbitt was impressed with her talent, recalling "a particular scene in which Jayne Mansfield simply walked across the set and picked up a rose. She had been jilted by Leo Genn, and the way she moved was really touching. There was absolute silence, and after the scene the 'atmosphere' lingered on the set."

Too Hot to Handle (released in the UK as *Playgirl After Dark*) sat on the shelf for months—it was first released in West Germany in April 1960, and not in the US till early 1961. Reviews were vicious. "Perhaps the least uncomplimentary thing to be said about it is that it is very tedious," said the *Guardian*. "The story has a familiar pattern: that of a mixture of sex and gang warfare. But the sexiness—as personified, chiefly, by Jayne Mansfield—is chromium-plated and fabricated and the gang warfare is puerile. Miss Mansfield conforms to her usual standard." The *Sydney Morning Herald* wrote that "critics agreed it was so terrible it could not possibly have been released."

Don Morrison of the *Indianapolis Star* wrote, "When the British make an American-type movie, it is always laughably out of date," referring to it as an "English-made crumpet, starring that leaden American biscuit, Jayne Mansfield." The scene that so impressed Frank Nesbitt was brushed off with "Miss Mansfield is called up to display depth of tortured emotion. Tears flow but I think it must have been hay fever." Colin Bennett of the *Age* wrote that Jayne "wobbled through the picture in a dozen outlandish ensembles, like a Mae West of the 'sixties," and the *Philadelphia Inquirer* cracked that Jayne "has better proportions as a person than as an actress."

The British paper the *People,* however, gave Jayne "nine out of ten for her work. . . . She gets this high rating for the big, blazing personality she is. Jayne is dead right as a strip-tease crooner who can put over a number with plenty of zip and charm. She knows how to use that purring voice and flutter those ice-blue [*sic*] eyes—and if she waggles her hips, what show girl doesn't?"

The *Daily Mirror*'s Donald Zec had savaged Jayne in print (and would do so again). He recalled that shortly after Jayne's British film outings "we bumped into each other on a plane at Dallas, Texas. She looked daggers at me and said 'I'll never speak to you again after that really horrible notice you gave my picture.' And I walked away with my head down thinking what a quiet and peaceful New Year it was going to be when she rushed over, hugged me and kissed me on both cheeks. 'I love you really,' she said, 'let's be friends again.'"

For all its bad reviews, *Too Hot to Handle* is not at all a bad film, and Jayne is excellent in it. It's a run-of-the-mill crime drama about the Pink Flamingo, a Soho strip joint. Jayne is cast as Midnight Franklin, the star performer and mother hen to the other dancers; she's in love with the sketchy owner, Johnny Solo, played by handsome, velvet-voiced Leo Genn. He, in turn, is being extorted by a competing club owner and his own money manager (Christopher Lee, still a few years away from stardom). Solo is no hero: he pimps out his girls (including the underaged Ponytail, played by Barbara Windsor) to menacing letches.

Director Terence Young—who later went on to helm the James Bond films *Dr. No, From Russia with Love,* and *Thunderball,* as well as the thriller *Wait until Dark*—got an excellent performance out of Jayne: quiet, world-weary, and underplayed. She also sings (undubbed this time) two quite catchy numbers, the title tune and "You Were Meant for Me."

Jayne's wardrobe does her no favors, however—most of it is unflatteringly tight. One dress, by Beatrice Dawson, caused a scandal. While singing "Too Hot to Handle," Jayne wears a transparent net gown with spangles covering her breasts and crotch, similar to her recent Las Vegas outfit. Two versions of this gown were made: for American and British release, she is fairly decently covered; for French audiences, her breasts are totally visible. Jayne later claimed that additional spangles were painted on frame by frame for British release, but this seems unlikely from a production standpoint, and is not obvious in the release print.

Additional audience-reaction scenes had to be shot in the Pink Flamingo showing women in the audience, to prove it wasn't just a strip club—a waste of money, as there was an electric "Striptease!" sign right over the club's front door. As it turned out, it was released in England with an X rating, for adults only. *Too Hot to Handle* opened slowly around the US, winding up second-billed to *I Spit on Your Grave* at the Trail Drive-In in Tampa in January 1963.

Jayne being Jayne, she did not spend her off hours wandering around Buckinghamshire or showing her children London. She did the exhausting publicity-appearance and interview tour; 20th Century-Fox exec Bob Goldstein bragged, "She's got every blue ribbon in Europe for making personal appearances, from opening a can of sardines to a flower show. They love her."

Jayne appeared on ITV's *Saturday Spectacular* with Cliff Richard, and she attended a charity fair in Ilford, where Mayor Harold Root, feeling snubbed by her fans, stormed off (the mayor was "neither a realist nor a gentleman," wrote the *Indianapolis Star*). She and Mickey attended the races at Sandown Park, where Mickey jovially picked up two jockeys, one on each arm. Jayne, standing in for the minister of transport (who was off electioneering), opened a cloverleaf intersection between the Great West Road and the Cromwell Road. Dudley Smith, conservative politician campaigning for MP, complained, "It is an insult to turn such a fine achievement into a stunt for an American film star." Jayne (along with Petula Clark, Leo Genn, Sylvia Simms, and Tommy Steele) took part in the Variety Club charity show at Billy Smart's Circus on Clapham Common, during which Jayne gamely lay down on the floor as an elephant stepped over her.

Jayne and family moved to actress Pat Kirkwood's house at Gerrards Cross, which had just been bought by songwriter Paddy Roberts (Roberts laughed, "I'm going to have a plaque made to hang over my bed. It will say, 'Jayne Mansfield Slept Here'"). Even when confined to bed with a bad cold, Jayne invited reporters in to see her: Arthur Helliwell gave her a silver Victorian goblet while she reclined in a pink negligee. "Cheer me up. I feel awful," she laughed weakly. Just as Helliwell was sitting on her bed giving her a good-bye kiss, Mickey walked in. Helliwell related that Mickey "picked up my hat and put it on my head and opened the door. 'What a pity you can't stay.'"

❤

Jayne's second British film, *It Takes a Thief* (released in the UK as *The Challenge*), was made at Twickenham Studios in Middlesex, in late

November through mid-December. It was produced by Alexandra Productions (the company's first, and practically only, film) and distributed by J. Arthur Rank. In the US, it was shunted off to Valiant Films, which had released such foreign and/or low-budget films as *The Sword and the Dragon, Go, Johnny, Go!* and *Terror Is a Man.*

Jayne called Louella Parsons to tell her she'd been made a co-producer on the film. "Sol Lesser and Cy Weintraub are producing, and have been negotiating with Paramount and UA for its release." "I love the excitement Jayne gets in her voice. I haven't heard her as happy in months," reported Louella.

But England was getting bored with Jayne by this time, so the publicity was meager and strained. It was announced that she would dye her hair dark for the role; it turned out that she wears a dark-brown wig for the first few scenes.

Jayne did give interviews, of course: "I feel that a star owes it to her public to bring the public into her life," she said while filming *It Takes a Thief.* "The fans feel that they kind of own you, and if you kept your life a complete secret it wouldn't be fair to them. But my private life is always very private." When asked what sex appeal was, she expounded, "It comes only from inside, it's nothing that's manufactured, it has nothing to do with measurements or lipstick color. To me, it's cleanliness and youth and an effervescent desire to enjoy life. The vibrancy you'd find present in a young kitten."

Jayne collapsed on set after a fight scene with Anthony Quayle and was ordered home to bed with exhaustion and a sprained ligament. She was interviewed in a fresh white nightie, rather bizarrely explaining that "babies always like to see their mothers in simple, fresh clothes. I adore black nighties and negligees. But Miklós will never see me in them. It isn't nice for babies to be conscious of their mothers as being sexy."

It Takes a Thief is a hard-boiled crime drama with a slow-moving, convoluted plot. Wearing that dark, shoulder-length wig, Jayne plays Billie, the cold-hearted head of a crime ring. Her hapless lover and cohort, Jim (an excellent Anthony Quayle), is a widower with a small son. Jim is nabbed after burying a large haul; he does time, getting out to find Billie now platinum blonde and wealthy. Jim wants to go straight; Billie and the gang want that buried loot and kidnap his little boy, though Billie draws the line at child murder. The plot eventually involves trucking explosives, double crosses, police raids, and lots and lots of punching. For absolutely no reason Jayne sings a torch song in a nightclub in the middle of the film, although at no point is it suggested she works in a nightclub (according to the *Stage,* her singing was dubbed by Joan Small).

Jayne looks lovely in the film, although she is saddled with one of the most hilariously ugly dresses ever seen on the British screen, courtesy of costumer Beatrice Dawson (*The Roman Spring of Mrs. Stone, The Importance of Being Earnest*). It's a kind of Heidi meets *The Sound of Music* horror, with a puffed-sleeve peasant top, acres of pouffed skirt (with appliquéd hearts all over it), and a kind of Bavarian cumberbund. She and Quayle act out a very dramatic scene, but all one can focus on is that appalling dress.

As in *Too Hot to Handle,* Jayne is actually quite good in this film, rising above her material. She shows real promise as a hard-bitten tough gal. Had she managed to stay in England—gotten a contract with a movie or TV studio, with a good manager—she might have had a nice little career as the queen of the crime genre. But Jayne had had enough of low-budget, badly received British movies, no matter how well they stretched her dramatic muscles.

It Takes a Thief was released in May 1960 in England, and throughout Europe in 1961 and '62. It never had an official premiere in the US, playing in New York in August 1963—nearly four years after it was made—and showing up in small towns and drive-ins through the mid-1960s.

Most of the reviews were nasty and unfair. Critics saw what they wanted to see, not the performance Jayne actually gave. "The singularly untalented Jayne Mansfield . . . is still Miss Mansfield and then some—undulating beneath a brunette wig and snarling like a fury"; "Jayne Mansfield who, confronted with a part in which she is required to act, has at last met something bigger than herself"; "The sight of Jayne Mansfield as the brains . . . provides at least one good laugh." Only the *Motion Picture Herald* was able to really look at her with unbiased eyes: "Miss Mansfield emerges as a dramatic actress of considerable impact here; she has a role into which she can finally project far beyond the usual Mansfield showings." But by the time these reviews, good and bad, were printed, Jayne had long since gone on to other, and worse, projects.

Before leaving England in mid-December, Jayne fulfilled her obligations to Fox, her fans, and herself by displaying herself at every opportunity. British-born Sheilah Graham, under no illusions about her homeland's press, lamented that Jayne "talked to the writers and reporters of the cheaper press. Jayne was chopped into mean little pieces . . . one of the most venomous reporters murdered her more ruthlessly in print than he had ever done before."

What was supposed to be her biggest honor blew up in her face. Jayne was invited to switch on Blackpool's annual autumn lights display on September 6: these stretched a quarter mile and depicted, among other things, giant butterflies, the birth of Venus, and portraits of the royal family.

It started out well enough: Jayne, Mickey, Jayne Marie, and little Mickey Jr. were mobbed by fans. As the *Stage* reported, "Lancashire folks love kiddies, and they took Jayne's eight-month-old son, Mickey, straight to their hearts. . . . All things considered, Jayne was the appropriate person to switch on those lights." Despite Mayor Ernest Machin calling her "Jean" Mansfield, everything went perfectly. Jayne and Mickey signed countless autographs, posed for photos, and were back in Buckinghamshire in time for Jayne Marie and Mickey Jr. to get to bed by 10:00.

But by the next day, things had gone downhill. Jayne was reported to the National Society for the Prevention of Cruelty to Children for bringing Mickey Jr. to the event: "The baby blinked in the glare of TV lights and was startled by exploding fireworks. It was 10 p.m. before he was tucked in bed," the complaint read. Inspector Frank Seviere scolded, "No child of that age should take part in publicity stunts, especially at that time of night." Jayne defended herself, saying that "Blackpool is a wonderful family town and I thought everyone would love to see my baby." Mickey added, "We are hurt and disgusted at the allegation that we don't look after our baby properly. Jayne is shocked and upset."

The American press, for a change, rushed to Jayne's defense—foreigners were not welcome to make fun of *our* joke celebrity. The *Moline Dispatch* wrote, "If that Blackpool bluenose is going to start interfering with proud mothers displaying offsprings, he is due for a short, miserable career." Walter Winchell added, "Everybody thinks being a celeb is fun, except the celeb. Miss Mansfield was hit by an ugly headline, simply because she is Jayne Mansfield." Mayor Machin, perhaps to make up for his "Jean" slip, pointed out, "There were hundreds of children of all ages in the audience. The love of Miss Mansfield and her husband for the child was apparent to all. They are a delightful and devoted family."

Jayne stood up for herself in a hurt and angry interview with the AP: "I've had a very nasty trick played on me and it just isn't true what's been said," she told the reporter. "I follow a strict plan with my baby. I have him put to bed every afternoon at 4:30. He sleeps until 7:30—when I get home from the studios. I have two hours with him, and then he's put to bed again at 9:30. If I didn't follow this plan, I'd hardly ever see my son."

Jayne's name was bandied about by member of Parliament (and future prime minister) Harold Wilson in October; he said that "the Soviets have photographed the reverse side of the moon. The summit of western achievement is to photograph the reverse side of Miss Jayne Mansfield." The *Daily Telegraph* called this joke "monumental bad taste. He was striving, with fatal success, to impart some liveliness into his economic arguments."

As Jayne prepared to leave England, her professional future was in doubt; Sheilah Graham wrote on December 1, "I checked with 20th Century-Fox for the rumor that Jayne has parted permanently the studio. Not so. Although there was a vagueness about future movies, except loan-outs." On the 19th, Jayne returned to L.A. with twenty-six bags and four dogs. She and Mickey were planning a trip to Italy, and Bob Hope called to ask her to join his Christmas USO show in Alaska.

"I've changed my whole approach to acting," she told Joe Finnegan of the AP while still at home. "The cheesecake stuff has been really overshadowed. You see, in England I was given my first chance to play a real dramatic part. I do hope the picture gets past the censor."

On December 20 Jayne left on her second USO tour, covering six military bases in eight days. Jerry Colonna was along, of course, as well as singer Frances Langford and bandleader Skinnay Ennis. Dancer Neile Adams—who'd just made a hit in Vegas—joined the group with her husband, rising young actor Steve McQueen, currently starring in TV's *Wanted: Dead or Alive.*

They flew from Ladd Air Force Base near Fairbanks to a naval installation in Kodiak, and played Christmas Day at Elmendorf Air Base in Anchorage. The weather rarely got above twenty degrees below zero ("When it was that warm, you'd think it was time for a swim," said Jayne). Jayne did comedy sketches with Hope and sang "I've Got a Crush on You"—she and Hope also talked to far-flung troops who couldn't get to the shows via short-wave radio. There were fears for Bob Hope's health: he'd had a blood clot earlier in the year and suffered dizzy spells during the tour (Hope, of course, lived to be one hundred).

The tour was shown as a TV special on January 13: "good, familiar fun," read a typical review, and "This year [Hope] took Jayne Mansfield along, so you can write most of the gags yourself." Dwight Newton of the

San Francisco Examiner called Jayne's singing "somewhat sweeter than a howling coyote," adding that she "fulfilled the great expectations of the servicemen when she skillfully balanced and/or juggled the twin targets of all assembled eyeballs." One of Hope's more cringe-making jokes was "Jayne Mansfield toured the Far East with us two years ago and left the population of Korea and Japan round-eyed."

Jayne arrived back home just in time to celebrate the end of the 1950s with her family.

15

The excitement Jayne Mansfield puts into her voice when she telephones is something! She always sounds as if the most wonderful thing in the world has happened, and that's not bad to get that much joy out of life.

Louella Parsons

On January 2, 1960, Earl Wilson published his "Fearless Forecast about the Sizzlin' Sixties." Thank goodness for everyone, he had no idea what was coming. Jayne, he predicted, "will be photographed all over (watch your language, Wilson!)." He went on to guess that Marilyn Monroe "will be rumored divorced, pregnant, rebellious, lazy, crazy and temperamental, but actually she'll make two pictures in six months, and one of them will make a star out of her leading man, Yves Montand." That picture was *Let's Make Love,* possibly Marilyn's worst; it sent Montand scurrying back to France (though he did indeed make love with Marilyn, much to the displeasure of his wife, Simone Signoret).

Jayne's brief career as an A-star was essentially over by 1960. So were the careers of Marilyn Monroe, Kim Novak, Diana Dors, Mamie Van Doren, and Barbara Nichols—they all still had a few good years of work ahead of them, but as the 1960s rolled on, they became yesterday's main course. Rising to the top—and taking their roles—were such sex kittens as Yvette Mimieux, Ann-Margret, and Jane Fonda, all of whom launched their movie careers by the early 1960s. The 1960s Youthquake was about to begin, and womanly femme fatales were about to be replaced by "girls."

In retrospect, one can see Jayne's decline beginning, but in 1960 she still seemed to be a major star with a promising career and studio backing. Bob Thomas summed up the 1950s as "a decade colored by Kim Novak's lavender, Jayne Mansfield's pink, and Liberace's gold lamé." Joseph Alsop wrote in early January that after Kennedy and Hubert Humphrey announced their long-expected presidential bids, "one hopes Miss Jayne Mansfield will call a press conference to announce, breathlessly, that she is a member of the female sex. If she does, it will be more unexpected, but no inherently funnier than the antiquated rituals of American politics in an election year."

Despite being loaned out to England for low-budget films (and getting only her regular salary while Fox pocketed $200,000 per picture), Jayne expressed confidence in her studio. "They take good care of me," she insisted. "We've been negotiating for two years to try and get me a deal for one outside picture. I'm sure that sooner or later the studio will give it to me."

But she made not one single film during 1960. She kept busy: through the early part of the year, Jayne was the queen of the Palm Springs Rodeo (Dennis Weaver was the king); she hosted the Pre-Olympic Press Party at the Tahoe Harrah's (others attending were Victor Borge, Miss Nevada of 1959 and future "Mary Ann" Dawn Wells, Ernie Kovacs and Edie Adams, and Art Linkletter); she was crowned empress of the Carioca Ball at the Astor in New York (clutching her Chihuahua, alternately called Csopy or Schoppy); she was named honorary chair of the Hollywood Chamber of Commerce.

Jayne appeared on a tribute to Bob Hope for TV's *Arthur Murray Party,* which aired in March, with Dorothy Lamour, Tony Bennett, Alan King, Mickey Mantle, Ethel Merman, Jane Russell, and others. Jayne sang a duet with Lamour ("Her Junoesque figure contrasting oddly with her thin, piping voice," wrote the *Pittsburgh Press*). Jayne and Mickey stayed at Manhattan's Drake Hotel while filming the Hope tribute, and had as relaxing a tourist week as any vacationing couple: they got into their pajamas, drank champagne, and watched the *Late, Late Show* in bed.

❤

Jayne was in her twenties at the perfect time in terms of fashion: the New Look hourglass figure popular in the 1950s flattered her curves and deemphasized her thin legs. The twentieth century featured so many different silhouettes for women, and one was lucky indeed to be young and suitably equipped at the right time: the curvaceous Gibson Girl of the

1900s, the slim Tango Girl of the 1910s, the tubular flapper of the 1920s (with a heart-shaped face—the only kind that looked good in bobbed hair and a cloche hat), the subtle curves of the 1930s and '40s, back to the girlish waif of the 1960s.

Jayne's time had passed: the Marilyns gave way to the Audreys as the decade turned. As early as January 1960, Yves Saint-Laurent and Guy Larouche were showing flat-busted lines and proto–Jackie Kennedy suits with short jackets and knee-length skirts. Jayne was not happy: "I wish him [Yves Saint-Laurent] luck—he'll have to get men to wear them," she told a fashion reporter, adding, "My mother was in that era [the 1920s] and she has a large bosom. She bound herself up so she'd look flat-chested and tore down all her bosom muscles, which is not normal. It was a tremendously barbaric thing to do." Several fellow actresses agreed: Janet Leigh (slim and angular herself) said, "You can't hide the fact that we have bosoms," and Mamie Van Doren insisted that "I'm going to wear clothes as sexy as I can."

"I love avant-garde fashion," Jayne said, an admirable understatement. "I wear mostly French and Italian clothes. There's Fontana in Rome, Mr. Blackwell in California, Oleg Cassini in New York. They're all great on fit, and that's the most important thing in clothes. It can always be adapted to the individual." She also insisted that she was a simple sweater-and-slacks girl at home, that "my own clothes taste has nothing to do with the gowns I have to wear for public appearance. I like things simple, covered-up, in sedate colors. I follow the best of fashion rules. After I am all dressed, I stand in front of the mirror and remove the bracelet. Or the earrings—something!" Columnists noted that Jayne indeed was known for "removing something."

Hairstyles, too, changed with the 1960s, and Jayne was at the forefront. Through the 1950s, Jayne had worn her hair in lustrous, shoulder-length waves, sometimes pinned up into a loose chignon. She also owned a wig and hairpiece wardrobe, as many stylish women did well through the 1970s. As early as 1956, the *New York Daily News* noted her chignons and falls in silver white, honey yellow, bamboo blonde, and blue ash, depending on what tint her hairdresser used that week, "with a gay disregard for nature . . . the pin- and paste-on rage is for everybody." But in 1960 Jayne followed the trend to shorter, softly waved hair and had it cut into a chin-length bob (more of a Jackie Kennedy look, this one was also sported by Marilyn Monroe, Doris Day, and Hope Lange). She also began to supplement her hair with some outside help.

Human-hair wigs are heavy and expensive, but by the 1950s, lightweight synthetic wigs—made of nylon, dynel, acetate, Kanekalon, or Elura—came in every color of the rainbow. Fake hair actually holds a curl longer than human hair, and with lightweight honeycomb caps, you could forget you were wearing it. Most department stores had wig departments (right next to hats); wigs could be ordered through magazine ads; and specialty stores were available in most cities.

Jayne—and many other actresses—favored Larry Mathews's Beauty World, which had branches in New York and L.A. As early as 1958, Jayne bought six different-colored wigs from Beauty World. In 1961 Mathews bragged that Jayne came in and bought blonde and red wigs, and an orange one for Halloween. Larry's wife Norma Mathews enthused over the selection available, citing "orchid, frosted and tutti-frutti" wigs tipped in twelve colors. Mathews even offered a limousine pickup service: "A chauffeur will pick up the woman's wig at her home in the morning, and we set it and comb it, so she can wear it that night."

"Wigs are only chic when they are undetectable," wrote Genevieve Antoine Dariaux in her delightful 1964 book *Elegance*. "A wig can be a most practical accessory when traveling, for example, or during vacations when you are on the beach or in a sailboat all day long and yet wish to be well-groomed for a party in the evening." She also warned, "A wig that is badly made or obviously artificial is not at all elegant."

Wigs are also *fun*, and Jayne was all about having fun with her appearance. In the summer of 1961, she decided to go back to her natural brown hair color, by way of Beauty World. She bought several flattering, medium-brown wigs in a chin-length bob, and of course called in reporters and photographers to show off her new "serious" look. Within a couple of months, she was back to blonde: "My fans don't want it," she sighed. "They wanted me like I was. After all, I can do serious roles with blonde hair. Then I can make my fans and myself happy at the same time."

But there was a more serious reason for Jayne to patronize Beauty World: by the early 1960s, her own already fine and silky hair was thinning and brittle from over-bleaching. She also wanted to save her hair from the constant teasing, curling, and spraying public appearances required. "When I am on personal appearance tours, I often wear a wig the exact color of my hair and no one ever knows it," she said in 1962. "Wigs are so light and well-ventilated today that they do not harm your hair at all."

Jayne's third husband, Matt Cimber, recalls a hair disaster around

1965, when the two were touring in stage shows. Jayne was playing a theater in Boston, and Matt was at a small motel in Nebraska; he asked the woman at the front desk to put through a call for him. "So the next thing I know [Jayne's] calling me late at night and she said, 'Who are you fucking around with? Who was the woman who answered the phone?' I said, 'No, that's the woman who's running the place!' While we were there talking, in the background, I hear her hairdresser saying, 'Miss Mansfield, you have to come here,' and she didn't. He had the bleach in her hair, and all her hair fell out."

It must have been traumatic for a woman so conscious of her appearance to lose her hair. For the last six years of her life, she was never—never—photographed without a wig. Only her family saw her *au* naturel, and even they rarely did. She (quite rightly) was paranoid about paparazzi, and never went outdoors, even in her own backyard, with her thinning hair showing. Her breasts, yes, and sometimes her lack of underpants—but her scalp, never.

As the 1960s wore on, Jayne's wigs were the type that Genevieve Antoine Dariaux would have frowned upon. Huge, immobile bouffants and towering "showgirl chignons" by 1963–1964, and long, straight, strawlike numbers in the groovy, Carnaby Street years of 1966–1967. Goodness knows what her real hair looked like by then.

The Pink Palace was nearing its breathtaking final form as the 1960s dawned and Jayne and Mickey were between assignments. She called Louella Parsons with the latest updates, and Parsons wrote, "The excitement Jayne Mansfield puts into her voice when she telephones is something! She always sounds as if the most wonderful thing in the world has happened, and that's not bad to get that much joy out of life."

The house had a new sound system, paid for by Jayne's opening the Los Angeles High Fidelity Show at the Pan Pacific Auditorium. "I just love to bathe in stereophonic sound," she said—and indeed, her rock music was pumped into every room of the house as well as outdoors. Jayne Marie, nine years old at the dawn of the decade, was already reaching the end of her rope. "*Everything* was pink," she recalled with exasperation decades later. "I mean, pink doilies, and the pink curtains, and the pink *everything*. She even made my room pink. I didn't want it pink, but *everything* was pink."

In February Jayne gave James Bacon a tour. "In the mammoth living room is a huge sofa and chair in purple," he wrote. "It has to be seen to be believed. 'I think if you're going to be a movie star, you should live like one,' says Jayne. The house is unfinished but already makes Liberace's piano-shaped mansion in Sherman Oaks look like a Quonset hut. For instance, the living room has a fountain. It shoots water now but plans call for it to spurt champagne. A downstairs room is reached through a hallway plastered with hundreds of magazine covers of Jayne." Outside, Mickey had dug three small ponds and surrounded them with tropical foliage: "Waterfalls drip between them, reminiscent of a Dorothy Lamour movie set. . . . Hargitay is building a waterfall to drop over his man-made mountain to the pool. 'Mickey said he would build Niagara Falls if I wanted it,' says Jayne, beaming."

Jack Scott of the *Vancouver Sun* found the Palace a sad commentary on Jayne and Mickey's inner lives. "The whole place has a rather recreational atmosphere," he wrote in 1960. "A carping critic might note that there appears to be not a single book, or place for books, in evidence, but the Hargitays are so preoccupied otherwise, under the influence of their interior decorator, that there could scarcely be time for reading." On the pool and its motto, he wrote, "Well, nobody's going to top that. Oh, I thought of substitutes. I could put blinking pink lights over our mantle, flashing out the message 'Keep Fighting, Gracie,' or 'Don't Give Up, Gracie,' but it might look cheap without a fountain in the living room."

Jayne told Joe Finnegan of the UPI of some plans which, mercifully, were never fulfilled: "We're getting a beauty parlor for me with a gymnasium," she said. "Then, we've got a room down near the pool that's going to be used for keeping our monkeys. We just love monkeys. I've been in Europe so much lately that a real estate man is trying to sell me a castle in England. It's completely furnished with shields, rugs and armor. And, as castles go, it's not expensive, only $80,000. It only has five bathrooms. We have 13 here."

Not everyone sneered; one syndicated architectural critic wrote admiringly that the "bold of pink paint on the house and surrounding walls makes it stand out against its surroundings as much as its occupants do in a crowd of people. . . . The house has many artistic features that have generally been overlooked. . . . It is in the use of tiles that the Hargitays reveal their originality and good taste. Large quarry tile covers the entry way and stairway to the second floor. Ceramic mosaic, glazed wall and non-skid tile floors are dramatically featured in six large bathrooms."

And as Bob Thomas had smiled upon Jayne's old-style Hollywood glamour, so did James Bacon. "The town frowns on the antics of Jayne Mansfield and Elvis Presley," he wrote. "A generation ago their behavior would have been commonplace. . . . If a member of the press wants to tour Miss Mansfield's shocking-pink mansion, done in early Mae Murray motif, all he has to do is ring the doorbell. Jayne makes a crazy guide."

As she prepared to leave for Italy for her next film assignment, Jayne sighed to Bacon, "I love this house, but we never live in it."

16

None of the pictures today follow history closely. It's good to put glamour in a picture, don't you think?

Jayne Mansfield

In April 1960, Jayne headed overseas to make another loan-out—to Italy this time. There was a Writers Guild of America strike from January 16 to June 10. The Screen Actors Guild joined the picket lines on March 7, so Jayne and Mickey got dispensation from SAG to film overseas, as all the other actors in the film were foreign non-union members. Numerous major productions skidded to a halt during the strike, including Elizabeth Taylor's *BUtterfield 8*, Gina Lollobrigida's *Go Naked in the World*, Jack Lemmon's *The Wackiest Ship in the Army*, and Marilyn Monroe's *Let's Make Love*.

The unpromisingly titled *The Loves of Hercules* was financed by three production companies, and never did find a US distributor—despite collecting Jayne's loan-out money, Fox washed its hands of it. It was directed by Carlo Ludovico Bragaglia, an old hand at comedies and sword-and-sandal epics (this would turn out to be both, though not intentionally). It was written by Sandro Continenza, who had scripted eight Sophia Loren films, and Luciano Doria, who started in silents and had not written a film in nearly ten years.

Mickey, of course, played the titular Hercules, and Jayne was to play one of his three loves. "When I first read the script I felt my part was too small because there were two other women in the picture chasing Mickey," she said. "Mickey solved all that, though. He suggested I play all three parts." Mickey rather wished she could play Hercules as well; he was not happy about doing this film. "I'm funny about pictures. One star in the family is enough," he said.

Accompanied by Jayne Marie (on summer vacation) and Mickey Jr., Jayne and Mickey were all but absent from the press during filming—they were far from large cities and reporters, and Fox was certainly not eager to publicize this film. For the first time since 1956, newspapers had to rely on old Jayne Mansfield jokes and dubious stories—some of them years old—to prevent an unthinkable Jayne vacuum. In late May Sheilah Graham finally came through with the news that "there's never a dull moment" during filming: "Jayne has Sanka going all the time, with gallons of certified milk in the fridge for Mickey, little Mick and Jaynie, her three loves."

Jayne got $75,000 for the role. The multinational cast spoke whatever language they were comfortable with, their dialogue later dubbed for various countries (Jayne by Carolyn De Fonseca, who would later voice her in *Primitive Love* and *The Wild, Wild World of Jayne Mansfield*).

Harrison Carroll reported that *Hercules* was going so well that Jayne was mulling over offers for *Queen of the Caribbean, Giant of Babylon,* and *Scheherazade and the Giant,* all to be shot in Europe and all, luckily for Jayne, destined for other actresses. The *Indianapolis Star* reported that Italians were "struck dumb over curvaceous Jayne Mansfield's preoccupations with domesticity, her baby son's diet, his pasteurized milk, Mickey Hargitay's meals, calories, setting up exercises and 'good clean living.'"

Mickey later said that he was called on to kill a bull during filming, but refused. "The bull was given a sleeping pill and he slept like he was dead. It looks like I plunge a knife in his neck, but I actually miss him by two inches. When the bull woke up, he seemed to want to say thanks."

The Loves of Hercules (released in Italy as *Gli Amori di Ercole* and also known as *Hercules vs. the Hydra*) is Jayne's first "so bad it's good" film. Indeed, it's the best of the worst—*The Fat Spy, Primitive Love,* and *Las Vegas Hillbillys* are so bad they're depressing and a bit infuriating. But *Loves of Hercules* is a nonstop roller-coaster ride of deliciously bad acting, writing, directing, and special effects.

Mickey, of course, plays the Roman half god/half mortal Hercules, whose wife Megara (Lidia Alfonsi) is killed by evil Ecalian soldier Licos (a wonderfully hammy Massimo Serato). Understandably annoyed, Hercules rides off to seek vengeance against Ecalian queen Deianira (Jayne in a black wig), who offers up her own life in compensation. Hercules thinks this is awfully nice of her, and the two of them fall in love.

As the film rolls on, Hercules encounters an extremely leisurely cattle stampede; the Hydra (a three-headed dragon that basically just stands there and weakly waves its heads around as Hercules gamely chops away at them with an axe); Hippolyta, the evil queen of the Amazons (Tina Gloriani—like most movie Amazons, these all dress like hat-check girls at the Copa), who magically transforms herself into Jayne in a red wig; and a forest of screaming tree-men (all ex-boyfriends of the Amazon queen).

Our hero Hercules, having forgotten his just-murdered wife and fallen in love with Deianira, now forgets Deianira and falls in love with Hippolyta. It all comes to a rousing finale as Hippolyta is hugged to death by one of her tree-exes ("Die! Die! You die!"), Licos is killed by a Sasquatch (played by six-foot-nine Aldo Pedinotti), Hercules kills the Sasquatch by throwing a papier-mâché rock in his general direction (it misses him by a good two feet, but the Sasquatch obligingly falls dead anyway), and Hercules and Deianira ride off together atop what must be the world's strongest horse. During one fight scene, two bit players exclaim, "Oh, it's *awful*," and "Don't worry—it's almost over," echoing the thoughts of the audience.

Mickey actually does a good job, as all he has to do is look concerned and manly and in love with Jayne, and his voice is dubbed by a Christopher Lee sound-alike. Jayne comes off less well—she pouts and scowls and snarls and vamps; without a good script and a good director, her years of training evaporated. While *Loves of Hercules* may have helped torpedo Jayne's career, it boosted Mickey's: he went on to star in such 1960s sword-and-sandal epics and spaghetti westerns as *Revenge of the Gladiators, Stranger in Sacramento, Three Graves for a Winchester,* and *Cjamango.*

Sheilah Graham predicted accurately that *Loves of Hercules* "will never be seen as a picture in this country. Producer Joe Levine included the epic in a batch of pictures recently sold to television."

After filming wrapped in late May, the family took off for Rome, a city that would play a large, sometimes vexing, part in Jayne's life over the next few years. She said that Rome might as well be Hollywood, there were so many Americans there. "Mickey and I were invited to as many as three parties a night." She also announced her third pregnancy, joking that her "baby bump" might "just might be the spaghetti and all that rich Italian food."

They arrived back in the US on May 28, Mickey reporting that their experience had been "just great. We were like a couple of kids playing a game." Jayne added, "I'm spoiled now. I don't want any other leading men, just Mickey."

As her pregnancy progressed healthily through the spring and summer of 1960, Jayne kept busy. She took part in the Indianapolis 500 Festival Parade, also featuring actors Nick Adams and Ty Hardin as well as bandleader Fred Waring. Polly Cochran of the *Indianapolis Star* noted that the weather for the race veered from hot to cold, and no one was comfortable no matter what they wore. Jayne stood barefoot on some newspapers, wearing frosted-frame glasses and a rose-beige maternity dress. One nasty photo caption referred to her as "blond (?) movie star (?) Jayne Mansfield."

Next it was on to the Tournament of Roses parade; Jayne rode on a Hollywood Boosters float, escorted by the delightfully named officers Sinner and Rich, "obviously pleased with their assignment." Then Mickey and Jayne flew to Minneapolis for the premiere of Fox's *Can-Can*. The Texas Press Convention was held in Mexia (where Anna Nicole Smith grew up); Jayne crossed paths there with Vice President Richard Nixon. A *Mexia Daily News* reporter wrote, "Many newsmen, who are probably the hard-boiled type behind their desks back home, crowded around to get her autograph. Did you ever hear of anything so silly?" The reporter added, "Want to see the autograph I got? It's on my convention program."

Then back home to California in late June to award dog-show blue ribbons for Best of Breed (winners included Great Dane Peter of Guilderdane and toy poodle Little Sister). A sadder event was Buddy Adler's funeral; Fox's production chief, he was largely responsible for Jayne's career at the studio. Actress Anita Louise (Adler's widow), Spencer Tracy, Dick Powell, Gary Cooper, and David O. Selznick were also in attendance.

As the birth of her next child approached, *Family Weekly* elected Jayne "Most Pretentious Star," the runner-up being Zsa Zsa Gabor. Gregory Peck was voted "Most Lacking in Humor," Marlon Brando "Worst Dressed," John Wayne "Most Overpaid," and Dean Martin "Most Fun to Be With."

Vernon Scott polled movie stars on their presidential favorites—as the primaries approached, Kennedy and Pat Brown led the Democrats, and Nixon had the Republican vote sewed up. Most stars kept mum, not wanting to offend fans. Doris Day said, "I have my political convictions, but they are my business. I don't think my support would help any candidate, so I never even state whether I am a Republican or Democrat." Jayne said, "I like 'em all. They're all very nice men and I think it's a shame each and every one of them can't be president."

In late July, a month before her due date, Jayne was rushed to St. John's Hospital in Santa Monica, "awfully uncomfortable and worried," with what doctors feared was an infection. Over the next few days, Jayne had way too much time to research—she apparently had access to medical books—and worry. She said, "Ninety-five percent of all women who start the premature delivery symptoms I had last Friday night gave birth within 48 hours. But I've already gone 92 hours. And obstetrical records show that 75 percent of women with premature distress like mine have their babies within just four hours. Just think of that." "All we can do is pray and pray," said Mickey.

Zoltan Anthony Hargitay, five pounds, was born on August 1, 1960, a month premature. "I'm so thrilled, I'd love to have 500 more babies," Jayne enthused. "We have a very large home, and I want to fill it with children. He is named for my husband's brother. Zoltan is being kept in an incubator, but he is a beautiful, perfect baby and looks exactly like Mickey. And by the way," she added, as if this even needed to be said, "we are allowing pictures to be taken of the baby this afternoon."

The new family went home on August 9. "I've never won an Oscar but Zoltan is the best thing I've ever done!" (One can imagine how Jayne Marie must have felt upon hearing that.) Jayne told Harrison Carroll, "We want to have a bunch more kids, but I may wait about a year and a half before the next one. Mickey and I are caring for him ourselves. Mickey, bless his heart, takes the night shift."

Late that summer and into the fall, Jane might have stayed home in her Pink Palace and relaxed with her new baby, her two other children, and her husband—but then she wouldn't have been Jayne. Instead, she dove into a Silly Season of personal appearances—none of which made her any money or advanced her career. She just needed love and attention and the feeling that she still mattered.

Jayne hosted a barbeque for two hundred Southern Methodist University alumni at the Pink Palace. She attended the annual Sheriff's Rodeo at the Coliseum to benefit widows and orphans of the sheriff's department men. She modeled furs and jewels at a Beverly Hills benefit for Israel Bonds. She went to the sports-car races at Cotati, sponsored by Corvette. She celebrated Natural Gas Day in Eugene, Oregon, lighting a flame to inaugurate a 120-mile gas pipeline (music was provided by the Eugene Highlanders Bagpipe Band); then she and Mickey went to a Natural Gas banquet (one longs to see the menu). Then she was off to ride a float in the New

Mexico State Fair and attend an open house at the Brown Pipe and Supply Company in Albuquerque, after which she and Mickey stayed with the "Pipe and Supply" Browns themselves. The local newspaper ads trumpeted her appearance: "The latest ideas in plumbing, heating and air conditioning products for your home! Come Early! Stay Late! Fun! For the Entire Family!" She raised funds for the Flying Tiger Airline Community Chest, and yes, the obvious "community chest" jokes were made.

In early September Jayne participated in one of the most charming bits of puff publicity of the year, now long forgotten: Melvin Miller Week. It all started when Marine captain Joe Gestson, through a crossed-wire mix-up, accidentally called factory foreman Melvin Miller in Peoria on the phone and the two became phone pals. Just for the fun of it, Gestson somehow arranged for all of California to honor Miller in a weeklong riot of festivities. Miller was serenaded by the Marine band, attended a bullfight in Tijuana, and tossed out the first ball at the Coliseum for the Dodgers–San Francisco game. His story was featured in *Life* magazine, he was a guest on *Truth or Consequences,* and he headed a parade.

Miller was also Jayne's guest at 20th Century-Fox; this was just the sort of "Why not?" event she loved. Fox put up a WELCOME, MELVIN MILLER banner, at which he laughed, "Why all this fuss over an ordinary Joe? Don't get me wrong. I'm having a lot of fun going to the races and everything. But sometimes I wonder about the sense of it. Take a fellow like Desi Arnaz. Why, he's done something with his life, that television series with his wife, lotsa things. I'm having a good time out here—but getting back to Peoria is just fine with me." Jayne greeted him at her Jayniest, wearing a low-cut dress, kissing him for the press. When Joe Gestson, host and originator of the gag, complained about not getting any kisses himself, Jayne cooed seductively, "You're not Melvin Miller."

Then Melvin Miller went home and was promptly forgotten by all but his family and friends.

Jayne was interviewed for a second time on *Person to Person,* this time as a last-minute replacement for Richard Nixon (headlines proclaiming "Jayne Mansfield to Replace Richard Nixon" raised both eyebrows and hopes for many readers). Jayne and Mickey led interviewer Charles Collingwood on a tour of the Pink Palace, "which looked pink even in black and white," noted one TV critic. The *Oakland Tribune* wrote, "The visit with Jayne Mansfield was everything you may have expected. Everything. A funny thing, television. Millions of dollars are spent turning out comedy programs and yet which show is the funniest? *Person to Person.*"

When Juliet Prowse dropped out of the Fox film *It Happened in Athens*—a tale of the 1896 Greek Olympics—it was assigned to Jayne: the first of her films actually produced by Fox since *Kiss Them for Me.* Not on the Fox lot, however; it was filmed on location in Athens. Jayne complained, "I don't want to return to Europe now to make a picture. All my dogs are pregnant. I want to be here when the pups are born. My Chihuahua probably will have to have a Caesarian."

But work was work, and in late October she and Mickey consoled themselves with a week on Aristotle Onassis's yacht before filming began. Her three children flew over with a nurse to join her when she started filming.

Unlike filming in the wilds of Italy for *Loves of Hercules,* Jayne was able to enjoy the social scene in Athens. She was invited out to dinners, where she daintily nibbled steaks, chicken, and kebabs, then took the rest home for the four Chihuahuas, which she had managed to smuggle into the country after all.

This time she was also available to talk to the press, and did so with a vengeance, pulling out some of her better fluff-headed humor. Jayne told Joe Hyams, "This particular Greek actress I play has platinum hair because she has been to Paris and is up on the latest fashions among film actresses." Hyams pointed out that there weren't any film actresses in 1896. "Oh, I didn't know that. Well, what she has done is to copy Jean Harlow and Mae West." Hyams then brought up that they came along a bit later, too. "Oh, dear. Well, I don't know who was around then, but let's face it—none of the pictures today follow history closely. It's good to put glamour in a picture, don't you think? There's no way of knowing what the Greeks had. Perhaps they invented platinum hair dye."

In what might be called a "whopper," Jayne said, "This actress is different from other types of actresses I have portrayed in films. She's not a sexpot. She's just a strikingly beautiful woman. This is a serious picture."

Asked if she did any research on ancient or 1890s Greece, she said, "I research all day long. I've been to the Acropolis three times for picture sessions. And today I was shopping and came back loaded with research material. Don't ever admire something a Greek has or he'll give it to you. The Greeks can't say 'no.' They're a fabulous people." She bought a nine-foot chandelier and a statue of herself, from the hips up, done by Catherine Helepa. "It's in the nude. That's the only way she could show all the lines." A reporter who saw the chandelier wrote, "It was a monstrous affair—originally intended for a church. If she ever switches it on I am convinced that the major portion of Sunset Boulevard must inevitably be plunged into darkness."

Asked about her acting technique, she told Hyams, "As far as acting is concerned all you have to do is react. If you react seriously then your acting comes through sincerely. But you must react with your whole heart. If you go before the camera trying to act you end up nothing but a ham. I have techniques all my own, but I won't display them in public. How do I know you won't put on a tight suit and blonde wig and try to replace me?"

One journalist asked her if she would do a striptease in front of Nikita Khrushchev if she thought it would benefit world peace. "Of course I would," said Jayne, unfazed. "I'm all for world peace. Isn't everybody?"

In mid-November Dorothy Kilgallen wrote that "20th Century-Fox is ready to release a dozen films, but they're counting on the Jayne Mansfield picture, *It Happened in Athens,* to become the biggest money maker. It's caused a flutter among exhibitors, and Jayne is considered a box-office draw while many a more polished actress is bombing with the customers." The Italian co-producer, Alex Pavesoulous, president of Alfa Films, was not so optimistic. The production was burdened with middlemen and cost overruns; he complained that "a brassiere for Jayne Mansfield cost $130—and then didn't fit."

Jayne's role turned out to be more of a supporting than starring one, and she was not happy that a younger actress played the hero's girlfriend. But she tried to keep her spirits up, and philosophically told a reporter that "Mickey and I miss our lovely home but we brought all the children here with us so we are not as homesick as we might have been without them. Little Jayne Marie has learned to speak a little Greek—isn't that something?"

A reporter from the *Sydney Morning Herald* she met with in early December came to the interview armed to the teeth. "After the savage mauling given her last picture, *Too Hot to Handle,* by the critics (they agreed it was so terrible it could not possibly have been released; it must have escaped), I assumed she must wisely have stocked up with nuts and gone to earth," he began unpromisingly. And then it got worse: "For what does she really stand today? She is not taken seriously as an actress, and most women tell me she is not taken seriously as a woman either. What, then, is she taken seriously as? Is she a sex symbol? I do not believe it. She has always struck me as rather a pathetic combination of Goody Two-Shoes and the Michelin Man; a caricature of sex hardly likely to inflame hidden hungers even in the breast of a 10-year castaway."

If she sensed his hostility, Jayne breezed right past it. "I know in my last film, the plot wasn't all it should have been," she admitted, "but I'm told it's doing all right on the Continent. And that's all I worry about. My money's going up since I made it, so why should I worry?" The Sydney reporter suggested she do more comedy and engage in fewer publicity stunts. "Her eyes opened wide. 'Publicity stunts? I've never taken part in a publicity stunt in my life.' I thought I must have misheard her, so I asked her to repeat it, and she did, and I wrote it down on the edge of my menu. For posterity." Jayne explained, "I've done things, of course, which have resulted in publicity—but I've never been asked; I've never promoted them myself. Mind you, I believe in publicity in building up a star. Mere talent isn't enough."

Then she bombarded the reporter with common sense and her always-surprising cheerfulness. "I'm not unhappy about my career. Or my life. Every morning I wake up and say, 'Gosh—aren't I lucky?' Mickey and I live a good, clean life. We don't go drinking or carousing or spending money uselessly. We've got three lovely children, and we want ten. We're wonderfully happy."

It Happened in Athens is a picturesque film—lots of lovely location scenery and Greek dancing—but not terribly interesting. The plot concerns a shepherd who wants to run the marathon in the 1896 Olympics—he's encouraged by his girlfriend and the kindly American team. The character was very loosely based on Spyridon Louis, a water carrier who became a national hero after winning the marathon in the first modern-era Olympic games.

Jayne, as in *Kiss Them for Me,* has the secondary female role—she plays Eleni Costa, "the greatest actress in Greece" (actually a publicity-chasing sexpot, and Jayne is quite convincing in the part). The leading lady is Xenia Kalogeropoulou (billed, for the benefit of non-Greeks, as Maria Xenia). Fresh and natural, she gives the best performance in the film. She went on to have an impressive career in Greek films, TV, and theater.

The film's hero is played by New Jersey boy Louis Morelli, who was discovered by agent Henry Willson and renamed Trax Colton. Willson was also responsible for such hilariously butch names as Rock Hudson, Dirk Rambo, Race Gentry, Tab Hunter, and Clint Walker (these were brilliantly lampooned on *The Beverly Hillbillies* with such characters as Dash Riprock, Biff Steel, Crunch Hardtack, and Bolt Upright). Trax Colton was handsome and ingratiating, but acting was not his métier, and after this film he quickly bowed out of the profession. Real-life gold-medal Olympian Bob Mathias (sporting a handsome handlebar moustache) gives a surprisingly good performance as the American coach, but he too dropped out of acting, becoming a member of the House of Representatives from California. Mickey Jr. also has a role—cute as a button, he plays the shepherd's baby brother, splashing soup at the dinner table.

The plot is obvious, and the ending can be seen a mile away; the script is earnest to the point of silliness. The only really funny line comes when Jayne—who has promised to marry the winner of the marathon—is told the Hungarian is in the lead. "A *Hungarian?* Ohhh . . ." she sighs disappointedly. Mickey may have laughed at that in-joke, but—on set as baby-sitter and gopher—he must have winced to hear the actor playing her boyfriend snarl at her, "You take away everything I have, but don't take away my pride—not ever."

It Happened in Athens wrapped in early November 1960 but was not released in the US till the summer of 1962. Most of the reviews seem to be studio press releases, describing the plot and cast, but nowhere giving any kind of critique. Only Aline Jean Treanor in the *Daily Oklahoman* really had her say: "Jayne's appearances in the film are relatively brief, but at that, they may seem longer than they are. As the movie-wise know, her histrionic repertoire consists chiefly of baring her formidable breastworks to the low water line." Treanor went on to say that the US circulated Jayne Mansfield films such as this "to our friends and would-be friends abroad. And still we wonder that the world turns against us."

Jayne was back in the US by November 20; she told Harrison Carroll that she hoped to return to Europe in March to make *Mars, God of War* with Mickey, adding that she'd also met with producer Arthur Cohn about filming *Act of Violence* in Yugoslavia. "Mickey and I want to have a bunch of kids," she said, "but we'd like to wait just a little while before the next one. I have too many pictures to do."

Jayne Marie turned ten on November 8, and Jayne took her and twenty-five classmates to Fox's screening room to see *The Sheriff of Fractured Jaw* (probably leading to a month's worth of teasing for Jayne Marie in school), then back home for a wienie roast. The family also went to Disneyland; Jayne said, "I'm really looking forward to it. It'll be the first time I've taken those rides when I wasn't pregnant."

❤

Person to Person was all very nice, but in December 1960 Jayne was the surprised honoree of *This Is Your Life,* intermittently broadcast on radio and TV from 1948 through to a few specials in the 1980s. Many of the shows were about ordinary folks with extraordinary stories, but it's the celebrity tributes that made *This Is Your Life* must-see viewing. Some of the broadcasts are horrifying, as when host Ralph Edwards "sympathetically" harangues guests Frances Farmer and Buster Keaton on their miserable, washed-up lives. The show is mostly remembered for highlighting such has-beens as Mack Sennett, Gilda Gray, Helen Kane, and Francis X. Bushman, but many stars at the height of their careers were also set upon by Edwards: Jerry Lewis, Bobby Darin, Debbie Reynolds, Rock Hudson. Not everyone was happy to be honored by the attention: when Ann Sheridan and Angie Dickinson found out they were to be featured, they refused to show up; Bette Davis and Stan Laurel were visibly furious when Ralph Edwards leaped out at them.

Jayne, of course, was thrilled to be singled out: she screamed and doubled up with glee when Edwards shouted, "Jayne Mansfield—*this is your life!*" at her. As guests Edwards dragged out gossip columnist Jimmie Fidler (who said the glory days of old Hollywood "have been revived in the person of Jayne Mansfield and her way of life"), her mother and stepfather, Southern Methodist University teacher Harold Chapman ("Jaynie was in one of my psychology classes—she was a serious-minded, hard-working student"), and *Rock Hunter* costume mistress Rose Caully ("Jayne hasn't a nerve in her—I remember opening night, Jayne was sitting in her dressing room pasting pictures in her scrapbook"), along with Mickey, Jayne Marie (nervously rehearsed), Mickey Jr., and Zoltan. Jayne cried and hugged all of her guests with unaffected delight and was obviously having the time of her life.

17

If one wants success, one must be ready to accept the pressure accompanying it. You have to try to keep your feet on the ground as much as possible.

Jayne Mansfield

$\mathbf{A}$s 1960 drew to a close, Fox had no projects lined up for Jayne—so it was back to her third (and, as it turned out, last) engagement in Las Vegas. This time it was at the Arabian Nights–themed Dunes Hotel, at $35,000 a week, for an eight-week run. "There will be a proper amount of clothing in the proper places," Jayne promised, or threatened (the Dunes was known for its topless dancers). She would wear a leotard adorned with $16,000 worth of diamonds, later to be made into pins and bracelets, she claimed. The club spent $65,000 on sets for her show (titled *The House of Jayne*), including a huge heart-shaped bed.

The House of Jayne opened on December 29, and thanks to a recording made of the act, we know pretty much how it went. The show was expensive and glitzy and well produced; Jayne and Mickey poke good-natured fun at themselves and send up their public images. But the writing (by Sid Kuller, who did comedy material for Jack Benny) is not up to par—the jokes are anvil-subtle, the song lyrics generally witless. Jayne—like Liberace—was already aiming at a dual audience: both middle-aged, middle-class marrieds and gays. Drag performer and celebrity impersonator Arthur Blake joins several numbers, and the words *camp* and *queer* were worked winkingly into several songs.

Musical numbers include the amusing "Just Playne Jayne" with Blake (whose Louella Parsons impression sounds exactly like Truman Capote), "I Think I'm Gonna Like It Here" (a tribute to the Pink Palace: "The lounge is lazy, the carpet's crazy, I dig the chandelier—the lights are spooky, the love-seat's kooky—I think I'm gonna like it here!"), and "Let's Do It" ("I know the squares and the boppers do it, it's as simple as that—Why, Louella saw Hedda Hopper do it, but she still wore her hat!"). The most cringe-making number is "We're Cultural, Not Physical," in which Jayne and Mickey sing-talk to "Noel Coward" (Blake again) about their intellectual pursuits: Jayne: "I would rather go to bed with Proust." Mickey: "You must have deduced, she can't be seduced." Poor Mickey is audibly embarrassed—singing and acting were just not his strong points—but he was a good sport and mustered up enthusiasm.

Jayne's first number was "A House Is Not a Home without Love," and on opening night her mike went dead. "Tonight I learned a lesson," she laughed after it was fixed. "It isn't diamonds at all. It's a microphone that's a girl's best friend."

When Harold Heffernan of the North American Newspaper Alliance came backstage to interview Jayne, he found her dressing room a frenzied mob of Mickey, "two-year-old Mickey, Jr. (playing on the dressing-room floor), five-month-old Zoltan (asleep in his cradle), and Jayne Marie, ten, dashing out with a girl friend for a game of handball. Meanwhile, Sam, a miniature palm-sized monkey, dozes in Jayne's lap, and Do Mo, a toy Dachshund, and Blue Bell, a Chihuahua, cuff one another in a friendly battle to get closer to their mistress."

As usual, the Vegas money was poured right into the Pink Palace, and Jayne threw open the doors for the press, which, also as usual, was more than eager to make fun of her. It was as though the house was morphing into an architectural version of Jayne. *Here's Hollywood* host Dean Miller took viewers on a tour that played like an insane drag version of Jacqueline Kennedy's TV tour of the White House a year later. Jayne wore gold lamé pajamas; she introduced Mickey, who excused himself, in Miller's insulting dialect, "Eyef got to go to me ahfice to type out a few tings." In the nursery, Mickey Jr. announced, "I want to go," to Miller's embarrassment—he quickly segued into "I'm sure our audience would like to see your bathroom and the heart-shaped, uh . . . bathtub that's in there."

Jayne bragged to Hy Gardner, "We have a remote control [TV] set in our bathhouse; one remote control set in our bedroom; one in Jayne Marie's room, one in the playroom, the servants have one in their living room and we have one in our TV room, a mammoth color set. Our lives are so packed with other goodies we don't watch many TV shows, but our two older children certainly make up for it." Reporter Mike Tytherleigh spent a few hours in the Pink Palace, finding Mickey "busy in the yard sloshing cement around like any other do-it-yourselfer." He wrote that the house "is a glamorous house, but then Jayne Mansfield is the last of the glamour queens and it suits her. . . . She has charm and, when I first met her, an almost shy quality which, when combined with beauty, is immediately appealing to men. She is by no means the dumb blonde that Hollywood used to put before us. The dumb blondes skyrocket briefly but Jayne has lasted on personality and warmth."

Rick Du Brow of the UPI agreed that the Pink Palace was a brilliant marketing ploy, "probably the most spectacular home in Hollywood history. Extravagant? Absolutely not, from a professional point of view, because extravagance is Miss Mansfield's stock in trade. She doesn't claim to be a great actress—but she has spread the image of old-fashioned Hollywood glamour around the world as much as anyone."

Jayne updated the public on the latest home improvements:

> In front Mickey has created a scene of Roman ruins, just gorgeous, with pink flowers growing out of them. There's a marble entrance hall and a marble walkway that leads out to a statue of Christ over a fishpond with pink water lilies. There's a bridge which overlooks our heart-shaped pool. . . . In the pool, there are two heart-shaped mosaic islands upon which are two receptacles. On each receptacle is a statue of a maiden holding a jug of water, and a fountain comes out of each. We also have a white sand beach by the pool. The sand was imported from Acapulco. Surrounding the pool is a pink wall with about ten statues representing the four seasons.

She came up for air and remembered, "Oh, yes, there's a three-story waterfall leading down from the living room into a water pond. And we have every kind of palm tree in the world. And a badminton court. And we're building a replica of the all-glass chapel we were married in, with a wishing-well fountain in front of it. Of course, some of our flower beds are heart-shaped, too."

Just when it seemed the Pink Palace had reached its culmination, that not one more staggering addition was possible, the chandelier that Jayne had bought in Greece arrived. Unassembled, with instructions in Greek. "Our living room is 50 feet long and about 225 feet wide, and we've got that chandelier spread all over the place," Jayne sighed. "There are more than 150 glass candles. I have no idea how long it will take us to put it together. Maybe our dinner guests can help." The chandelier was eventually assembled and somehow suspended from the two-story ceiling, but was so *Phantom of the Opera* terrifying that few people had the nerve to stand under it.

After Vegas, Jayne and Mickey took off to Miami, were they hit the beach and attended the boxing matches; Jayne and Sophie Tucker joined Tony Martin onstage at the Eden Roc. "She wore a loose-fitting coat instead of the skin-tight dress which is her show-business trademark," wrote Herb Kelly. "When she's dressed properly and talks like a woman should, Jayne's an interesting personality. The giddy baby-talk was absent." She and Mickey had been out fishing, and Jayne said, "I can't stand to see anything hurt, even a fish. I was nauseated when someone hooked a big one."

She later expounded to actress and beauty columnist Arlene Dahl that "I really don't like meat, so I always have to have it extremely well done. I don't approve of animals being killed for food, but Mickey says that I must eat meat for the amino acids, and so I do. When we are at home for dinner, we always have a salad made of lettuce, tomatoes, hard-boiled eggs, freshly ground black pepper, and mustard with an oil and vinegar dressing, home-made pickles, and always steak. I never eat potatoes or drink coffee, just very weak tea, in fact it's mostly lemon. I do like a cocktail, like a pink lady, before dinner, and I smoke occasionally but never inhale." She realized that not everyone should—or could—follow her diet tips, "but I have disciplined myself to eat this way. . . . Everything is just a matter of habit. I think you do your best work when you are a little on the hungry side, rather than overly full."

Having been a success at the Oscars, Jayne was invited to present a Golden Globe award in March 1961, and she came through with a performance that almost outdid her Sophia Loren party appearance—thank goodness, it was captured on film. That year, Golden Globes went to Burt Lancaster, Jack Lemmon, Shirley MacLaine, Janet Leigh, Tony Curtis, Rock Hudson, and Gina Lollobrigida. But the moment that stays in everyone's mind is when Jayne presents a Golden Globe to Mickey Rooney, collecting it on behalf of Mexican actor Cantinflas.

When the category is announced, Jayne saunters down the aisle toward the stage in high heels and a low-cut black gown, every little movement exaggerated by her wiggle and her dress. At the podium, the five-foot-two Rooney looks at her, looks away, then goes into a flustered act, and the audience falls out of its chairs laughing. As good a straight woman as Margaret Dumont, Jayne smiles innocently, puts one arm around Rooney, and draws his face closer to her cleavage. The laughter goes on for a full forty-five seconds before Rooney stammers out, "Who wants to be *tall?*" During Rooney's subsequent speech on behalf of Cantinflas, Jayne loses a shoulder strap (more gasps and laughs from the audience), kisses Rooney on the forehead, and generally steals the show.

While Jayne was presenting awards, showing off her home, and hunting for new acting projects, Mickey (Hargitay, that is, not Rooney) was finally trying to come out from behind her overwhelming shadow. In the spring of 1961, he developed what was actually quite a brilliant idea: an exercise TV show along the lines of Jack LaLanne's, which had been running since 1951 (and which would continue into the 1980s). Mickey was sexier, younger, and—in 1961—more famous than LaLanne, and his idea would still work today. "It's strictly a family show," Mickey told Joseph Finnegan of the UPI. "I will do exercises for 15 minutes of the show and then explain diets. We will also have guests tell us what they have accomplished. I feel that moderate exercises are the best thing you can do for your health."

The show started out small, only in the Los Angeles area (beginning with station KTLA), but was rated among the top ten in that market. Eve Starr of *Inside Television* wrote that "Mickey's syndicated exercise series is catching on. His letters from televiewers rave about his daily weight losing and fitness programs."

For the first time Mickey was giving interviews about himself, not about Jayne or Mae West. "I like fresh fruit, fresh vegetables and fresh meat," he told Bill Fisit of the *Oakland Tribune*. "I eat my one meal at whatever time of day I'm hungry, and if I get hungry at other times I'll eat a little fruit or perhaps a small salad." He recommended swimming: "Swimming keeps a person limber. It takes weight off fat people and puts weight on thin people. The body is like an automobile. You maintain it properly and take care of it and it will be in as good condition 20 years from now as it is today."

Tragedy hit the show in 1962, when Darbi Winters, a sixteen-year-old singer and dancer who appeared as one of his exercise assistants, was murdered in her Van Nuys home by her stepfather, the manager of the Peppermint Twist club. The killing did not reflect badly on Mickey or his show, but he still struggled in the ratings.

"I'm not a fanatic," he sensibly told the UPI. "I think to be a fanatic you overdo it. I'll just do exercises and have people follow me. My English is lousy. I don't try to be a television star, that's not my aim. I know I'll have extreme criticism for my English." Mickey was no actor, but he was charming and friendly and funny, very good company for TV viewers. "Just the other day on the show I mentioned that ever since I was a boy in Hungary I liked to chew on grass," he told Vernon Scott. "My mother used to tell me it was good for me. I said you never saw a cow with a bad complexion, so grass must be good for the complexion. I got hundreds of letters from other grass eaters who said I was absolutely right. It's things like that that make me feel good."

Sadly, Mickey's show ran for only thirteen weeks before getting cancelled. Hal Humphrey of the *Los Angeles Times* believed that Mickey "tried to please both male and female physical culture fans by stripping to the waist himself and leading a bevy of shapely young models in a series of exercises. Either he didn't regard what he was doing in a religious enough fashion, or the exercises were too intricate."

With both Jayne's and Mickey's careers struggling, they needed to keep money coming in—and Jayne needed to be in front of an audience to feel the love of her fans. As far back as her Broadway days, she had attended ribbon cuttings, store openings, every local parade and promotion that would have her. Now she did so for the money—and quite unashamedly so.

"She seems to turn up at everything new, to turn the spade or cut the ribbon or push the button to start wheels turning," wrote Hubbard Keavy of the AP in 1961. He asked her point-blank, "Why do you go to all of these openings? Can't you say no? Or do you want your fans to see you? It must be exhausting and expensive in time and clothes." Jayne smiled prettily at his naïveté. "Oh, you're kidding aren't you? I do it for money." She went on to explain—like a businesswoman at a board meeting—that she asked for $10,000 per appearance: "We average about one appearance a week. Our fee is $5,000 in cash and $5,000 in merchandise. Last Tuesday, I picked up a lot of sheets—orchid ones—and pillow cases and towels and blankets. They're always handy. We get washing machines or deep freezes or whatever. Some store called—some little town like Pomona or Tucson—and wanted us to appear, but they could pay only $7,500. We turned it down."

All through the early and mid-1960s—as long as anyone would have her—Jayne marketed herself as the queen of the store openings. When she opened Tucson's Thrift City she nearly caused a riot. "Somebody hollered, 'here she comes!' and Jayne & Co. arrived to the tune of squeals and screeches and 'Wows' and whistles," wrote the *Tucson Daily Citizen.* "She was all gussied up for the festivities. Miss Thrift City USA, in a white, painted-on dress, and wearing the pink mink on her shoulders and Mickey on her arm, undulated past the crowd and into the store. Draping her shape on a two-piece divan ('regular $189.95, our price $88'), Miss Mansfield told the newsmen: yes, she has about 200 dresses; no, she is not thrifty; yes, she has about 400 pairs of shoes; and no, she doesn't remember how many fur pieces she owns."

The Thrift City team directed Jayne around the store to show off whatever they thought needed the exposure, "telling her just what to do when the cameras began grinding. She made her way up and down the aisle, admiring the merchandise and talking with assorted employees. Everything was '*gorrrr*-juuuus,' Jayne said." One dejected shop girl sighed to a reporter, "This is my very best dress and next to her I look like an immigrant or a peasant or something."

Jayne and Mickey drew a crowd of fifty thousand when they opened the Mansfield, Ohio, Giant Tiger department store; in Phoenix it was the CMA Shopping Center, and in Cincinnati the FAME department store (with "76 big departments—100,000 items—super-food market—gasoline service station").

That summer Jayne (and slightly over-the-hill singer Snooky Lanson) opened Atlanta's Thrift City Super Discount Department Store on live TV. *The Jayne Mansfield Spectacular* was "a new low," wrote Paul Jones of the *Atlanta Constitution.* "This hour-long telecast was nothing more than a tasteless commercial broken up now and then by songs and patter featuring night club entertainers, a hillbilly pianist and Snooky Lanson. . . . The program carried Miss Mansfield on a tour of the shopping center . . . at frequent intervals the announcer solicited Miss Mansfield's opinion of various articles of merchandise on display. Miss Mansfield more often than not expressed her enthusiasm this way: 'Oh, isn't it *wonderful!*'"

Jayne traveled as far as Montreal to open a new discount store, and Bill Bantey of the *Montreal Gazette* was more impressed than Paul Jones had been. "She handled questions with the skill of a diplomat and became the movie Jayne again only when the photographers were at work," he wrote. Jayne dropped the "Oh, isn't it *wonderful!*" act long enough to tell Bantey, "There is a lot of pressure on an international personality. But if one wants success, one must be ready to accept the pressure accompanying it. You have to try to keep your feet on the ground as much as possible." Jayne didn't miss a trick: she even brought a book on French to Montreal to show she was trying to brush up on her grasp of the language.

By 1963 Jayne had dropped all pretense and was beginning to sound slightly desperate. She placed ads around the country reading "Opportunity to join JAYNE MANSFIELD (star of stage, movies & TV) in a new business as her local distributor. If you have some business ability, can follow simple instruction and have approximately $4,000 capital to cover rotating inventory, you can qualify." It is not known how many people followed simple instruction and took her up on the opportunity.

Jayne earned huge amounts of money from Fox and Las Vegas, and not inconsiderable hauls from her public appearances. She put some of it into real estate, some into jewelry—but too much of it went into the Pink Palace and maintaining her star lifestyle (children and pets don't come cheap, either). While rarely actually broke, Jayne never learned to manage her money efficiently. Years later, daughter Jayne Marie laughed and rolled her eyes affectionately, recalling that "in some respects she was very thrifty, she got that from her mother. On the other side, it was, 'I gotta have that 20-foot chandelier.'"

❤

It's important to note that Jayne not only took, but she also gave. Most stars appeared at benefits, telethons, and charity shows, visited hospitals and orphanages, entertained the troops, raffled off items (or kisses) for charity, championed pet causes. Jayne, soft-hearted and with no concept of scheduling, said yes to everything, often resulting in missed dates and assistants pulling their hair out.

As early as May 1956 Jayne appeared at Madison Square Garden with

Sammy Davis Jr., David Wayne, and Shelley Winters for the Gustave Hartman Home for Children benefit; later that year she performed in a charity show for the Variety Club. Through the 1950s she was indefatigable: arthritis telethons; the Golden Nugget Ball benefit for the Desert Hospital; a tenhour multiple sclerosis telethon with Eddie Cantor, Lawrence Welk, Ann Blyth, Peggy Lee, and Dean Martin.

In 1958 Jayne, Mickey, and Jayne Marie were photographed getting their Salk polio vaccines from Dr. L. V. Morrill, husband of actress Rhonda Fleming, in an effort to encourage others to get vaccinated. Jayne and Mickey attended a rally at a Boys' Club, Mickey entertaining the "urchins" with weightlifting. In Miami Jayne raised $250,000 for the Israel Bond Drive by offering to pose for photos with fans, for donations. While shooting a film in England, she performed at a benefit for flood victims (a dam broke on the French Riviera, killing twenty-three people) along with Margot Fonteyn, Michael Redgrave, Peter Sellers, and Paul Robeson.

Her charitable ventures continued through the 1960s, right up till her death (she had visited a veterans' hospital on the day she died). In 1961 Jayne went to Johns Hopkins University in Baltimore for a United Cerebral Palsy benefit, and the Gateway Associates for Mental Health named her Woman of the Year for her work with mental patients in veterans' hospitals. The following year she was at benefits for the Children's Asthma Research Institute and Hospital; recorded books for the blind; was mistress of ceremonies at the Fantasy Ball benefiting the Muscular Dystrophy Association; appeared for the USO Jewish Welfare Board; went to a party benefiting the Lytton Center of Visual Art in Beverly Hills; and made a presentation at the Joint Defense Appeal meeting in Palm Springs, "reviewing the contributions of the motion picture industry to the cause of democratic understanding."

Over the next few years, Jayne appeared at, and contributed to, events for the Marine Corps' Toys for Tots program, the March of Dimes, the Foundation for the Junior Blind (whom she hosted at the Pink Palace), and the John F. Kennedy Memorial Hospital; she manned the phones at the Federation of Jewish Philanthropies during a fund-raising drive; performed at a 1966 cerebral palsy telethon (along with Tony Bennett, Diahann Carroll, Totie Fields, Sammy Davis Jr., Señor Wences, and the Shirelles); along with actors Nick Adams and Tommy Noonan, she appeared at a benefit for the family of Sergeant George Davis, who had been killed during a bank robbery.

Most of all she loved visiting hospitals, especially to see children and veterans (though she was often reduced to helpless weeping for hours afterward, as can be seen in photos and newsreels). After her death Jayne's stepfather Harry Peers asked that donations be made in her name to muscular dystrophy, heart disease, and cancer funds, "as throughout her career she assisted these organizations in their efforts to raise money to overcome these diseases."

❤

While 20th Century-Fox had no projects for Jayne, 20th Century-Fox Television—formed in 1949—found assignments for her. The studio had produced such popular fare as *The Many Loves of Dobie Gillis* and *Adventures in Paradise,* though it didn't really hit its stride till the mid-'60s.

In the summer of 1961 and February 1962, 20th Century-Fox Television plopped Jayne into two series that needed her star power. *Monte Carlo* (also known as *The House of Rue Riviera*) was a pilot shown on the *Kraft Mystery Theater* on August 30 (late summer was—and is—the place to dump a doomed show). *Monte Carlo* starred Richard Anderson (later of *The Six Million Dollar Man* and *The Bionic Woman*) and John Ericson (soon to costar with Anne Francis on *Honey West*) as "a pair of American private eyes loose among the international crooks at Monte Carlo," as the *Los Angeles Times* recounted.

Jayne was paid $4,000 for two days' work, some of it in a bathing suit (she did not get to go to Monte Carlo for the few location shots). "Jayne would rather make movies but this is a studio assignment," wrote Mike Connelly. The *Paducah Sun* called *Monte Carlo* "an entertaining enough mystery loaded with contrivances, good Riviera backgrounds, and an intriguing storyline," while Carl Hooper of the *Victoria Advocate* complained, "The only thing left out was a good script. Cheese was sold by the megaton." The *Atlanta Constitution* noted that "Jayne says about a dozen words in one of her two scenes, and even those three sentences seemed to be an effort." Anderson and Ericson went on to their busy careers, but *Monte Carlo* sank from sight.

Early in 1962 Jayne guested on another 20th Century-Fox Television series. The hour-long comedy/drama *Follow the Sun* starred Barry Coe and Brett Halsey as handsome bachelor magazine writers in Hawaii (not too far a stretch from handsome private eyes in Monte Carlo). In "The Dumbest Blonde" episode, Jayne and Brian Keith appear as a *Born Yesterday*–type couple: he is a bellowing blowhard oilman; she's his put-upon mistress. Like *Born Yesterday*'s Billie Dawn, she educates herself; but unlike Billie, she exposes her abusive lover's crooked business partner. Jayne gives an excellent, low-key performance, convincing as both the wily investigator and the enthusiastic tourist (it takes place in Hawaii, so of course they put Jayne in a bathing suit—a one-piece, as 1962 TV censors would never allow a bikini). She looks trim and lovely, sporting a huge bouffant and a wardrobe that ranges from chic and flattering to cheap and flashy.

Jayne managed to spoil the plot in a January interview, calling her character "a girl who is thought of as dumb and has a childlike wonder about her. And that's a very nice thing to have. She even saves the boyfriend's life and he's supposed to be the intellect. I feel you have to be smart to play a dumb blonde." *Follow the Sun,* toward the end of its first (and last) season, "is going in more for light comedy," she said. "That's why they called on me."

She told the *Philadelphia Inquirer* that Fox was considering a sitcom that, in retrospect, sounds like a modern-day reality show. "The studio has put an OK on a Mickey Hargitay–Jayne Mansfield comedy series," she said, although no other evidence of this actually exists. "Even our three kids will be in it. There's no title yet, but Mickey plays a strongman, and I'm a health faddist. I don't know yet if we'll be a married couple. I like the idea of doing more TV and a series, because I don't like to travel anymore. I like my husband, children, animals and my blue pool."

The Kardashians, Anna Nicole Smith, *The O.C.,* and *The Osbournes* were still decades away—but if anyone was born to be a reality star, it was Jayne, who was a living piece of performance art. Even the reluctant husband, embarrassed children, and camera-hungry hangers-on would later become staples of reality TV. Jayne's tragedy was that she was born too late to be a Hollywood star, and too soon to be a reality-TV star.

In May 1961 Jayne was loaned out again, this time at least within the US. She was signed for *The George Raft Story,* produced and distributed by Allied Artists Pictures, a successful low-budget operation that grew out of the Poverty-Row Monogram Pictures, the last career stop for faded stars.

This was a bio-pic of onetime gangster hanger-on turned dancer turned movie star George Raft, who by 1961 really needed the money. He was still doing cameos (most notably in *Some Like It Hot*) and TV (the '50s cop show *I'm the Law*), but was happy to sell his life story for even a B-film.

Raft told Lloyd Shearer that a lot of juggling was done with the truth: "I don't know who's playing who. The truth of the matter is this movie is semi-fictional. Parts of it are true, and parts of it are fiction. The parts concerning the dames are fictional. They've got to be, for two reasons: one, I'm not the kind of a guy who kisses and tells no matter how much the dough, and two, if we were going to use real identifiable people, we'd have to pay them clearance fees for invading their privacy, and those dames would probably want millions."

Raft is played by Ray Danton, a charming actor but only a barely competent dancer. The women in Raft's life are played by best-selling singer Julie London (who proves an excellent actress), Barbara Nichols (brassy and wonderful, as always, as speakeasy queen Texas Guinan), dancer Barrie Chase (as a movie extra who helps launch Raft's career), and Margo Moore (a top model and not a bad actress who left show business to run the Toy Robot and Pig Museum with her husband in Pennsylvania). Barrie Chase had no illusions about the script. "We say, 'Georgie,' and he says, 'Baby,' and we say, 'Georgie,' and he says, 'Baby,' and that's about the way the roles are."

Jayne plays the Betty Grable character, renamed Lisa Lang (Raft and Grable were an item in the 1930s, when he was married and she was underage; the two remained close, off and on, into the 1940s). Jayne sports the first truly awful wig of her career, a huge pillowy affair with a very 1961 flip for scenes taking place in the 1930s. She doesn't show up till an hour into the film, and does the best she can with the awkward dialogue she's given, but she's out-acted by that wig.

The movie was filmed in Los Angeles and New York in July and August 1961 (Zoltan had his first birthday party on set) and released in early 1962. It garnered few reviews (Lynn Hopper of the *Indianapolis Star* accurately wrote, "The film is made well enough, and there are moments of excitement . . . but Raft never falls down enough for pity, and there is never any real reformation of character"). It didn't do a thing for the careers of anyone involved in it.

❤

The most frustrating part of Jayne's Fox contract was that, while she was doing *The George Raft Story*, the studio actually was making weak moves to put her into bigger films, and then letting her down. In May 1961 20th Century-Fox finally came through for Jayne. Despite the fact that Fox was, as per Sheilah Graham's column, "clearing out all their expendable people under contract in order to trim the studio's huge operating costs," the studio picked up Jayne's option, with a salary bump to $2,500 a week. She had four films in limbo (*Too Hot to Handle, It Takes a Thief, Loves of Hercules,* and *The George Raft Story* had not had US premieres), but Fox recognized Jayne as a marketable public figure and a "company player." Jayne's recent films had been disappointing, but they were also cheap to make. Jayne was professional, did as she was told, and caused not one moment of trouble on the set, as even her severest critics admitted. And calling her "enthusiastic" would be a huge understatement.

So she was given two major assignments. In late May Jayne was cast in *The Chapman Report,* a steamy drama about a *Kinsey Report*–like examination of the sex lives of married women. Based on a best-selling novel, the film also featured Jane Fonda, Shelley Winters, Claire Bloom, and Efrem Zimbalist Jr. Jayne would play a faux-intellectual who picks up a hot beach boy (up-and-coming beefcake Ty Hardin). The director, George Cukor, had countless hits to his credit, but was just coming off the appalling bomb *Let's Make Love.*

By September 1, though, Jayne was off *The Chapman Report,* replaced by thirty-eight-year-old British actress Glynis Johns. Show-biz columnist Mike Connelly explained that "George Cukor is a perfectionist who admires what he calls 'professional actresses.' He considers Jayne more of a clotheshorse than an actress." Connolly publicly stood up for Jayne: "I don't go all the way with George. I think he could have drawn a great performance out of Jayne, who is studying dramatics and who desperately wants to be a good actress." Cukor had directed such challenging, opinionated actresses as Katharine Hepburn, Greta Garbo, Joan Crawford, Norma Shearer, Judy Holliday, and Judy Garland, and had gotten some of their best work out of them. Watching Glynis Johns in the role, it is easy to see how Jayne might have done just as well in the part, which is dramatic with comedic overtones.

Jayne had not been a threat to Marilyn Monroe at Fox since 1958, but their careers still jolted into each other. Marilyn had been a pain in Fox's neck since the mid-1950s, turning down assignments, showing up late and/or unprepared on set. But audiences still lined up to see her, so her job was fairly safe. Her last hit had been 1959's *Some Like It Hot,* made on loan-out through United Artists. *Let's Make Love* was a critical disaster, though it did make a small profit, and the angsty western *The Misfits* was a disaster in both categories. Now, Jayne's and Marilyn's careers collided again.

In late 1961 Jayne got some more promising news: she was assigned to a medium-budget comedy, to be directed by her old champion Frank Tashlin, costarring Bob Hope and Joan Collins. It was a comic take on Tennyson's poem *Enoch Arden,* about a man lost at sea, who returns to find his wife remarried. It had already been made into a film several times, including two 1940 comedies, *My Favorite Wife* and *Too Many Husbands.* In this version—titled *Something's Got to Give*—Jayne would have played Ellen Arden, the mother of two small children, who comes home to find husband Hope about to wed Collins. It would have given Jayne a great role in a lightweight comedy, showing off both her comedic and dramatic skills.

Then it all went to hell: the studio bumped the project up to a bigger budget and cast Marilyn Monroe in it—Frank Tashlin was not on her list of approved directors, and he was replaced by George Cukor. According to Mike Connolly, by January 1962 Marilyn had read the script (admittedly not a very good one), tossed it in the air, and walked out. Fox tried to recast Jayne in the role, but Cukor once again refused to use her.

Billy Wilder (who directed Marilyn in *Some Like It Hot*) famously said, "I've got an old aunt in Vienna. She's going to be there at five in the morning and never miss a word. But who wants to look at her?" It might have behooved Cukor to remember that Jayne would also be there at 5 in the morning and never miss a word, and *everyone* wanted to look at her. But, for the second time in a year, George Cukor pulled the rug out from under Jayne's comeback chances.

As it turned out, *Something's Got to Give* was a disaster. Filming didn't begin till the spring of 1962, and Marilyn was a hot mess: though looking her loveliest, she rarely showed up on the set, and when she did, she could barely get through a scene. Cukor may have wished he'd stuck with Jayne. Marilyn was fired in June, rehired in August, and died before filming could recommence in September. *Something's Got to Give* was reworked as 1963's pallid *Move Over, Darling,* starring Doris Day and directed by Michael Gordon—Cukor was busy with *My Fair Lady* by then.

Certainly, Jayne's career would have been revived by *The Chapman Report* and *Something's Got to Give,* at least in the short run. Fox, still in serious trouble, would have dropped her by the mid-1960s, but with the "street cred" of starring roles in two major (if lightweight) films behind her, directors and producers would have taken her more seriously. But instead of starring for George Cukor alongside Jane Fonda and Shelley Winters, Jayne was cutting ribbons at supermarkets.

❤

After finishing *The George Raft Story,* Jayne found herself at loose ends for the rest of 1961. She told Bob Thomas in July that she was going to clean up her act and become a normal person. Sounding like Marilyn Monroe wandering out of the Actors Studio in a scarf and cardigan, she told Thomas, "Being an international sex symbol is fine, but limiting. My career got waylaid by the sex-pot bit. I've enjoyed it, but that's just one branch of the tree." She dragged out her three universities again, and sighed reflectively: "I can always have the glamour, but I think you should fill your life as full as you can. My talent has been somewhat obscured by my fluffy blonde hair and my sexy publicity. I don't intend to put a tent over my head. But I do want to be my real self. I think a girl looks sexier without a low-cut dress."

This went exactly nowhere. It got the expected headlines (more than sixty of them throughout the country), and by the next week Jayne was waving from a float, as grand marshal of the La Mirada Junior Chamber of Commerce Parade, bumptious as ever. Jayne's reverting to type also garnered nationwide headlines, so for her this was win-win.

She and Mickey visited her family in Pen Argyl. Then they were off to New York for Jayne to film some *Candid Camera* pranks, which didn't work, because everyone in New York recognized her. (She tried more successfully in New Orleans, for a show broadcast in January 1962.) While in New York, Jayne and Mickey attended Elsa Lanchester's cabaret act. Jayne had to leave halfway through, but politely went backstage during intermission to tell Lanchester how much she'd enjoyed what she saw. As Dorothy Kilgallen gleefully reported, "Elsa bawled her out in tones that could be heard far outside the star dressing room, and as a result Jayne sat through the entire performance in tears. Jayne's post mortem: 'No one's ever talked to me like that before.'"

Jayne and Mickey took off for the Berlin International Film Festival in late June, stopping off in Montreal, where "she obliged photographers by posing any way they wanted and even posed with some of the more forward ones so other photographers could take their picture. Reporters threw question after question at her—she answered every one."

In Berlin Jayne joined fellow celebs Marcello Mastroianni, Jeanne

Moreau, Jean-Luc Godard, and Toshiro Mifune at the festival (Michelangelo Antonioni's *La Notte* won that year, as did actress Anna Karina and actor Peter Finch). Jayne met Mayor Willy Brandt and German starlet Regine Sieffert, who claimed to have a 46.85-inch bustline. This set off what, yes, was called a Battle of the Bulge (that joke got dragged out a lot), with other starlets vying to outdo one another.

This did not go over well in Berlin. One official said, "After all, Berlin is not Cannes. No one has anything against Jayne Mansfield displaying her curves in proud naïvete. We are amused when she strains to pull in her stomach to fill out her bikini better. But we get angry when career-seeking women, shady ladies and certain starlets and actresses of riper years use every opportunity to display their anatomy unmasked." One festival party turned into a bacchanal of starlets hopping up on tables and posing to display their charms (singled out was actress Laya Raki, described as a "former strip-teaser" but actually a dancer and actress with a dozen or so films and TV shows to her credit). Mickey calmly lifted Jayne up over his head, and the competition slunk away. Jayne told Harrison Carroll, "I didn't even notice the others. This sort of thing happens all of the time."

After Berlin, Jayne and Mickey paid their first visit to Hungary since he'd left in 1947. Jayne met his parents and two brothers, while state-run TV covered the reunion. Jayne—carefully coached by Mickey—said, "I love you both, Mama and Papa" in Hungarian, and Papa replied, "I could keep this golden little woman here forever." Visiting behind the Iron Curtain was a big deal in 1961, and Jayne noted that "although Mickey is now an American citizen, the officials there don't recognize him as such. I imagine if we weren't movie celebrities they would have detained us indefinitely, and possibly drafted Mickey into the Hungarian army."

Back in the US that fall, Jayne appeared on *The Red Skelton Show* as Laurelie Lovely, movie queen, with Red as Clem Kadiddlehopper. The *Minneapolis Star* opined, "It's nothing you haven't seen before, but fun," and Jack Marsters noted that Jayne and Red "were laughing so much they nearly fluffed their regular lines." She also helped celebrate the premiere of a new season of *The Bullwinkle Show* on NBC. Creators Jay Ward (in a baseball uniform) and Bill Scott (dressed like Teddy Roosevelt) had a thirty-foot Bullwinkle statue erected on Sunset Boulevard; Jayne pulled a cord to unveil it. A sign in the crowd read, "Watching *The Bullwinkle Show* helps fight Communism."

Jayne and family (plus her mother) vacationed in Honolulu; she had her photo taken cooking on a Southern Counties Gas Company range, in exchange for a Southern Counties Gas Company range. "It had to happen," said one editor who was asked to run the photo. "We've had pictures of Jayne with Aspirin tablets, Baby blankets, Clock radios, Dance bands, Electric fans, Fur coats . . . she has just worked her way down the alphabet to R for Ranges, that's all."

When artist Eva Prager did (not very good) portraits of Jayne's children in September she also sold a nice long article about them. "She is gentle but firm with her children and demands immediate obedience," Prager said of Jayne, and for the first time a hint of Jayne's somewhat oddball and obsessive mothering came across. "She has an inter-com set up in the house so when she is in the garden she can be in constant touch with everyone in the house, including the children. And she knows the moods of her children very well. Once, for example, I was painting Mickey, 2½, in the nursery. Just when he began to get restless his mother's voice came over the inter-com. 'Mickey, are you being a good boy?' she asked. 'Sit up straight and behave yourself.' Mickey immediately stopped his squirming and did what he was told." Prager reported that Mickey Jr., who referred to himself as Mickey-Boy, "was very curious as to whether or not the way he behaved with me would have any effect on what Santa Claus would bring him next Christmas."

Prager summed up, "The one strange thing about the Mansfield home is that no one is allowed to enter the house wearing shoes." Somehow, Prager has managed to alight on possibly the *least strange thing* about the Mansfield home. "But after I got accustomed to this, and thought it over, I came to the conclusion that this is a most sensible and hygienic rule."

That fall Jayne appeared in a benefit show for the Thalians, raising money for mental health services for children by acting with Carl Reiner and Broderick Crawford in a parody of *La Dolce Vita*. That parody—which one longs to see—brings up yet another lost chance in Jayne's career. As wonderful as Anita Ekberg was as overblown, dizzy movie star Sylvia, the role seems to have been written for—or about—Jayne. Indeed, it's hard to look at Ekberg in the role and not think of Jayne Mansfield. *La Dolce Vita* was filmed in Italy in 1959; Fox would have had no problem loaning Jayne out for it. But there is no hint that Jayne was ever on Fellini's radar for the part.

By the end of 1961, Eve Starr of the *Allentown Morning Call* was asking, "When was the last time you saw Jayne Mansfield in anything even remotely resembling a creditable piece of film?"

❤

Bob Hope called upon Jayne again in December 1961 for another USO tour, this time to Iceland and Greenland, accompanied by Mickey, Jerry Colonna, Dorothy Provine, and "Miss World," Rosemary Franklin. Once again Hope was "warned by his doctors to avoid undue exertion." Also on the tour was beauty queen and singer Anita Bryant, later notorious for her homophobic crusades. Bryant told Dorothy Kilgallen that "my husband and I shared two-family cottages with Jayne Mansfield and Mickey Hargitay in Goosebay, Labrador, and Thule, Greenland. If you've read Jayne's publicity it may come a surprise that she couldn't have been sweeter or more down-to-earth if she had been one of the Army wives who usually occupied the quarters."

The fifty-nine-person troupe arrived at US Harmon Field Air Base, Newfoundland, and played to a crowd of eight thousand (including Royal Canadian Mounted Police), en route to the US-Canadian radar station at Baffin Island; then the company went on to two bases in Greenland. On-stage, Hope joked about Jayne's figure, soon-to-be-sworn-in President Kennedy, beatniks, and Cuban prime minister Castro. Jayne danced the twist and did a *Romeo and Juliet* sketch with audience volunteers. An ice storm in Thule delayed travel, and the troupe had to shelter in the air force quarters and share emergency K-rations till the weather cleared; Jayne managed to skin a knee in a jeep accident during the storm.

Jayne missed Christmas and New Year's at home again; as soon as she landed back in the US, she was off to open Detroit's Concourse Room lounge and the Thunderbowl bowling alley on December 31.

Worse than the weather, a skinned knee, and missing the holidays with her family was reporter-photographer Alan Stensvold, who accompanied the USO tour. Stensvold told Hal Humphrey of the *Marion Ohio Star* that he "protects the gals as much as he can," offering as proof the fact that when he noticed "a little roll" over the top of Jayne's Capri pants, he made sure to point it out to her. "As soon as I mentioned the roll, she held her breath the rest of the trip."

18

That poor girl will have to die to prove she's on the level.

Dorothy Kilgallen

Everything began to unravel in 1962. Up till then, Jayne had been able to pretend that her life and career were still a big pink bubble of perfection—but as the year careened on, forces from inside and outside wore her down: 20th Century-Fox's financial problems, the death of Marilyn Monroe, Mickey's increasing annoyance at being treated like one of her Chihuahuas—plus a near-death experience laughed off by the press, and a difficult film shoot during which she was physically attacked. Even Jayne couldn't shrug off 1962 with her usual *insouciance*, and her cheerful public face began to appear a little more strained.

The year started off well, with Jayne and Mickey vacationing in Fort Lauderdale. "I doubt if we'll go to the beach in front of the hotel," said Jayne. "That would just turn into one long autograph session. Don't get me wrong, I'm grateful fans come and talk to me. Yet, sometimes a person has to be by herself, so Mickey and I have a private beach picked out." Jayne then went out and stopped traffic by walking across the highway in a bikini to go to the beach near her hotel.

In February Jayne and Mickey decided to extend their vacation before heading off to Italy to shoot Jayne's next film. They went to Nassau, where on Wednesday, February 7 they took a water-skiing jaunt, along with Jack Drury, public relations man for the Gill Hotel Group in Fort Lauderdale.

It did not go well.

The trio spent a pleasant afternoon boating and water-skiing and gazing out at the water. None of them were wearing life jackets. About five miles from Nassau, Jayne fell off her water skis, twisting her leg. Mickey jumped out of the boat to help her back aboard. Then Jack Drury called out to them that he thought he saw sharks (local hotel owners later huffily stated that there were no sharks anywhere near that area, never had been, and never would be).

Jayne—like most people—was terrified of sharks, and she was not a brave little soldier when she heard Drury's warning. She began flailing around in a panic, screaming and swallowing water, while Mickey tried unsuccessfully to calm her down and guide her back to the boat. With one arm around Jayne and one on the gunwale, he managed to capsize the seventeen-foot outboard motorboat, sending Jack Drury into the water. Jayne knocked her head against the boat, lost consciousness, and went under.

"It was terrible," recalled Mickey. "She was knocked out, she was in the water, I couldn't find her. I dived under, somehow I find her and put her on the capsized boat top." The three—atop the overturned boat—drifted for about an hour. Around dark they came within sight of a small coral reef near Rose Island, a small, largely uninhabited island that is a popular day trip from Nassau.

Mickey and Drury managed to pull a struggling Jayne atop the tiny reef. It was in sight of Rose Island—"about two blocks," Drury estimated—but the tide was high and the still-panicked Jayne could not be persuaded to get into what she was convinced were shark-infested waters. "The water kept getting higher and higher," Jayne recalled. "It kept coming up until I thought it was going to take us. Sitting there like that you think you are going to die." "All I can remember is the cold and the drag of time," Drury said years later. "We were all huddled together that night but believe me, all you could think of was trying to keep warm."

By 4:00 a.m. the tide was receding, and the men "dragged her into the water" (Drury's words) off the reef and over to Rose Island to await the sunrise and—they hoped—rescue.

Back on shore, panic took hold. When the trio failed to return, the Coast Guard was called, but by then it was dark and the search and rescue planes would not set out till daybreak. Small boats—fishermen, locals, news crews—sailed off in the dark waters to search. Then a fisherman found the overturned boat, the steering-shaft bracket broken, and presses around the nation were stopped.

Headlines on that Wednesday morning discussed President Kennedy resuming nuclear tests, a buildup in the "advisory group" in South Vietnam, and a German mine explosion that killed at least 246 people. But by the evening editions, front pages all over the world proclaimed that Jayne and Mickey were most likely dead: "Movie Beauty Missing at Sea," "Jayne Mansfield Missing—Lost off Nassau," "Jayne Mansfield Feared Lost in Boating Mishap," "Jayne Mansfield Lost at Sea." James Bacon even penned what read like a memorial, headlined "Self-Made Bombshell Loved Her Publicity."

The family and friends of Jayne, Mickey, and Jack Drury kept up a vigil, telephoning local police and hotels all night. Then, at 8:39 a.m., the castaways were spotted by a Nassau Development Board plane, whose pilot notified the Coast Guard. A fishing boat picked them up, sunburned and frozen, covered with scratches and painful, itchy bites from mosquitoes and sand fleas. They were fortunate to have broken no bones, and Jayne, who had inhaled so much water, was lucky to escape aspiration pneumonia. Photos show Jayne weeping, with a concerned Mickey hovering over her (Jack Drury, not being famous, was cropped out). Mickey comforted her: "Don't be upset, honey, sweetheart. It's all right," while Jayne was heard sobbing, "It was the sharks. That was the worst."

The three were taken to a local hospital: Mickey had a bad cut on one leg, and Jayne, said Dr. Rassin, had "quite severe exposure and many mosquito and sand flea bites." She was sedated and (wisely) kept in the hospital to make sure she did not have a respiratory infection.

Morning papers on Thursday headlined the rescue—now that the trio was alive, they were fair game. Everyone, it seems, decided that the whole episode was merely another of Jayne's hare-brained publicity stunts. "Jayne Safe—Oh, Yes, Mickey, Too," read one headline. "'Missing' Jayne Mansfield Safe" ran above a photo of her happily posing in a bathing suit on a beach.

The news coverage was jokey and leering, referring to Jayne as "the bosomy actress." The *Tampa Times* wrote that she could not have suffered from exposure: "Ridiculous! Jayne may have profited from exposure, but she never, never, never has suffered from it." The *Deadwood Pioneer-Times*: "World War III Start? Worse'n That . . . Jayne Was Missing!" The *Pittsburgh Post-Gazette*: "She took quite a chance when she fell out of that motorboat.

Any girl less endowed might have sunk immediately to the bottom." The *Springfield Journal*: "Amazing what stars will go through to get their names in headlines." The *Garden City Telegram*: "Bet Jayne Mansfield's being shipwrecked was just a Navy recruiting gag." The *Indianapolis News*: "Was buxom Jayne Mansfield in danger of being nibbled by sharks? Fear that she might be drowned gripped the world today (some of it, anyway)." The *Cincinnati Enquirer* professed itself to be worried that "Marilyn Monroe is going to arrange to get lost on top of the Empire State Building wearing only a mink coat or something, with maybe a giant sparkler in each hand." Of course, nightclub comics went to town as well, with predictable and thudding jokes, like Corbett Monica's "She swam two miles—she's got a fabulous breast stroke." (And that was quoted in newspapers as one of the *funnier* examples.)

A few columnists came to Jayne's defense, shocked by the sheer meanness of their fellow journalists. Dick Hoekstra of the *Fort Lauderdale News* stood up for his friend Jack Drury, asking, "Would any husband and father with a shred of humanity subject his wife and children to that ordeal?" The *Atlanta Constitution* took the same line, asking of Jayne, "Would she intentionally distress daughter and parents by being reported missing? It would seem to be a bad case of miscasting for Jayne Mansfield. Some critics say the fact that she posed in a bathing suit for photographers just before embarking on what turned out to be high drama at sea is indication itself that the whole thing was schemed. But Jayne Mansfield in a bathing suit, anytime, is sure to draw shutter-bugs like the mosquitos on the isle."

Even Dorothy Kilgallen, never a fan of Jayne's, admitted, "That poor girl will have to die to prove she's on the level." But she went on to chide Jayne's publicity seeking and insinuate that Jack Drury was trying to peddle his survival story to magazines. Drury responded, "Fun is fun, I don't blame some unknowing people who think it might have been a stunt. But malicious gossip like Kilgallen's item is stupid and vicious." Years later, Drury told the *Fort Lauderdale News*, "There's no way I'd freeze on a rock to get publicity for anybody. . . . Being shipwrecked with a sex symbol can be cold, rugged duty."

Columnist Mike Connolly wrote that "Jayne loves publicity, but not enough to put her folks through the agony they underwent that night. I know because I was up most of the night checking the story, talking to her mother and her secretary. If such a stunt had been arranged by her press agent Jayne would have let her family in on it beforehand."

Esther Massen, a maid at Miami's Hotel Algiers, also came to Jayne's defense: "Anybody who says that was a publicity stunt is being mean. I saw that poor girl later back at the hotel. She was suffering from sunburn, and the mosquitos had eaten her up. She had to have medical care."

Of course Jayne welcomed newsmen and photographers into her hospital room to show them her sunburn and bitten-up arms and legs, saying that she was "on top of the clouds" to be alive this morning. "I am just out of my head on sharks." The *Miami News* had a different take on the press conference, writing that the "uninhibited Jayne Mansfield hiked up her short hospital nightgown high to show reporters in Nassau how insects had feasted on her shapely haunches."

Up till now, Jayne and the press had been partners in crime, even though reporters were sometimes snarky and backstabbing. But now they saw her as The Jayne Who Cried Wolf, and Jayne and Mickey were hurt and furious. She tearfully told Hy Gardner on his TV show, "If I had twin babies, people would think it was for a publicity stunt. I never thought in my life after having gone through what we went through down there that anyone could doubt it being true." Breaking down, her voice cracking, she said, "I even don't like to discuss it, it was through the wonderful help of the dear Lord that we were saved."

She told Sheilah Graham, "I have plenty of publicity without trying to kill myself for it. The only way I can sum it up is to quote my doctor, who told me that, after Mike Todd's plane crash, he heard someone say, 'Oh, it's a publicity stunt,' and I suppose I'd have to die before people would believe what actually happened. I'd like all those people sitting before warm fires to come out to those rocks and experience what we did. I thought I was going to die."

Mickey, meanwhile, was on the phone to the *Palm Beach Post*, saying, "It's a miracle this girl is living today. She was unconscious. I thought she was dead. I love my wife very much. It would have been stupid to jeopardize her life."

Out of the hospital but still itching from her bites, Jayne flew with Mickey to Texas and the welcoming arms of the Peerses. She skipped a scheduled publicity event, the Twist Ball, in aid of Girls' Town, and rushed back to Los Angeles: "I am an actress and a mother. But first, I am a mother. We want to see our children."

❤

Jayne made her first quiz-show appearance on Groucho Marx's post–*You Bet Your Life* program, *Tell It to Groucho,* on April 19, 1962. Her guest spot, with Mickey, started out awkwardly, as Groucho leaned over to goggle directly at Jayne's breasts, saying, "I wasn't really worried about you and that escapade down in the Caribbean, Jayne, I just knew you wouldn't sink." Jayne managed to keep a rather frozen grin on her face (Mickey's reaction was not seen by the camera).

Jayne (wearing a rather out-of-date bouffant prom gown) did the ditzy blonde act very well: when asked about her pets, she said, "We have two ocelots, and two burros, but they're away at school. They're learning to be better burros." Then she and Groucho bonded. He mentioned his cameo in the film version of *Will Success Spoil Rock Hunter?,* and Jayne reached across to take his hand and said, "You were the handsomest leading man I ever had!" Groucho replied, "I think people should know you're really a bright, sentimental and understanding person. This is a whole façade of yours, that isn't based on what you actually are. This is a kind of act you do, isn't it?" Dropping her giggly demeanor, Jayne said, "The public pays money at the box office to see me a certain way, so I think it's just all part of the role I'm playing as an actress."

She plugged the American Cancer Society, where her winnings for that night would go. There weren't many winnings, though. Photos were flashed for Jayne and Mickey to identify: Jayne got Carol Channing, but they both missed Anthony Eden and Willie Mays.

For the rest of her life, Jayne would be a regular on quiz and game shows—she enjoyed them immensely. She was a guest panelist three times on the charades show *Stump the Stars* in the early '60s, and guested on the short-lived *Get the Message* in 1964 with former costars Tom Ewell and Orson Bean; she and Bean were also on *Password All-Stars* in 1964. She was a Mystery Guest ("Sign in, please!") on *What's My Line?* four times between February 1956—when she was quickly identified, since she was on Broadway in *Rock Hunter* at the time—and July 1966.

But it was *The Match Game* that became her second home; she appeared on it thirty-five times between 1964 and 1966. She was celebrity team leader opposite Orson Bean, Tom Poston, Sydney Chaplin, Bennett Cerf (five times in 1966), baseball player and announcer Joe Garagiola, and comic Milt Kamen. She appeared to be having the time of her life, not nervous or overly competitive as some celebrities could be.

Jayne's third husband, Matt Cimber, recalls that Cerf, a New York publisher and wit, found himself floored by Jayne's game-show skills. "Every time they invited Jayne to be on it, who was her opponent, but Bennett Cerf. And they thought, 'what a joke, the dumb blonde, and Bennett Cerf.' And Bennett Cerf never won." Jayne and Matt ran into Cerf at a Christmas party at Frank Sinatra's, "and Bennett Cerf said, 'You have no idea what it's like for me, all my friends are kidding me about my losing to Jayne Mansfield.' She beat him every time!"

❤

Jayne was also a favorite on talk shows, as she knew when to be ditzy and funny and when to be serious. She made her *Tonight Show* debut in April 1962, with guest host Robert Cummings and fellow guests Hedy Lamarr and Vincent Price. It was her first of six appearances on *The Tonight Show*; in the last, in 1965, she chatted with Johnny Carson alongside John and Hayley Mills, Phyllis Diller, Buddy Hackett, Steve Lawrence, and Della Reese.

"Every comedian in the world wanted her," says Matt Cimber. "Carson gave her carte blanche, he said, 'I don't care if you're walking down the street and passing our show, you don't have to be invited.' People would kill to get on Carson, all Jayne had to do was walk in the door and walk out on the set." After one appearance, says Cimber, NBC's West Coast president David Sarnoff "put out an edict that Jayne Mansfield was not allowed to wear a low-cut dress on any NBC show. That night, she went on Carson and she came out and she had a dress on that went right up to her neck, and then when she climbed the step to go sit in the chair on the platform next to him, and she had no back—it was cut right down to you-know-where. It was hysterical."

Jayne cohosted *The Mike Douglas Show* in 1963, chatting with Count Basie and singers Connee Boswell and Nancy Wilson; Merv Griffin had her as a guest three times, all in 1966. She was on Jack Paar's various shows eight times through the 1960s, her semi-friendly sparring with Zsa Zsa Gabor becoming talk-show legend. Jayne also popped up on Virginia Graham's *Girl Talk*, *The Gypsy Rose Lee Show*, and—just two weeks before her death—Joey Bishop's talk show.

Jack Paar's show was responsible for one of the funniest but at the same time most demeaning jokes about Jayne. Talk-show host Dick Cavett, working then for Paar as a writer, later told the Television Academy Foundation that "Jack was so thrilled" at getting Jayne for a guest: "I'd never seen him so excited since Noël Coward came on a couple years earlier" (as Jayne's career was already on the downslide, Paar's excitement is somewhat questionable). "Paar said, 'I gotta get the perfect introduction.'" Cavett and the other writers turned out intro after intro, all rejected. "Finally we all got sick of it, and I just went up to the typewriter and wrote, 'here they are, Jayne Mansfield,' and this became one of the most famous lines of the decade. Paar got the longest laugh I think he'd ever gotten." Cavett doesn't mention Jayne's reaction—that line was to follow her for the rest of her life, and beyond.

"Did you ever use that line yourself, in your talk shows?" the Television Academy Foundation interviewer asked. "I couldn't really, because I didn't have the opportunity," said Cavett. "I mean, it didn't apply to anybody as well as it did to Jayne Mansfield." (Cavett, over the years, interviewed Raquel Welch, Sophia Loren, Gina Lollobrigida, Ann-Margret, and Verushka, and although he did much schoolboyish ogling at them, he never had the nerve to reuse that line.)

In March 1962 Jayne returned to Fort Lauderdale for the first time since her shipwreck to attend the Jayne Mansfield Trophy Game at the new Orlando-Seminole Jai-Alai fronton, where she handed out a trophy and received an inscribed cesta. As she left the games, wrote the *Orlando Evening Star,* "a crew-cut type ran up and plucked the olive from her empty martini glass, the crowning achievement of his young life."

In 1961 Mickey was quoted as saying, "I love my wife 24 hours a day. She never gets on my nerves. Maybe that's unusual, but that's the way it is." And when Sheilah Graham talked to the couple in 1962, bringing up the current Eddie Fisher–Elizabeth Taylor–Richard Burton scandal, Mickey rather judgmentally insisted, "This won't happen to us, I'm sure. It would be impossible."

Jayne came off sounding equally prudish regarding Taylor's escapades. "There are certain laws one should obey," she told Graham. "You can't go too far wrong if you follow the Ten Commandments." Would the scandal hurt Taylor's career? "It hasn't so far," admitted Jayne. "I think true talent is never finished. Or Robert Mitchum would have been finished when he got into trouble years ago." A few months later, she said thoughtfully, "As to living with someone you are not married to, I don't approve of having affairs. But if you do have them, it's best to have them in private."

"The main thing is," said Mickey, "what do you want to get out of life—peace and serenity, or headlines and unhappiness?" He then turned to ask Jayne, "What were you doing all morning?" "Posing for photographs. But I missed you terribly." "I missed you, darling, too." Sheilah Graham noted, "I'm usually suspicious of such lovey-dovey talk. But I'm inclined to believe these two really mean it."

Then, like a bolt from the blue, in early May Jayne's attorney filed for divorce in Santa Monica Superior Court, while Jayne was "out shopping." She sneaked back home, locked herself in her bedroom, and summoned reporters. She was charging extreme mental cruelty and grievous mental suffering.

Mickey was taken completely by surprise; until the reporters showed up, he had no idea Jayne was anywhere but out shopping. "She won't say much," an obviously stunned Mickey said. "I guess she doesn't want to talk to me—or anyone. I just can't believe it. We've had misunderstandings. We've had personal problems. But nothing that I thought would ever lead to divorce court. I love her very much but she's making me madder than hell."

Jayne, seemingly just as shocked and unsure as Mickey, told reporters, "I'm no different from any other married woman. We're no different from any other married couple. We have had differences. We're not used to having them, and I guess it comes as a big shock. I'm sure we'll work it out. They really are minor but maybe because they are the only ones we have ever had they seem bigger than they are."

This quarrel came about because of Jayne's upcoming film shoot in Italy. Jayne later told her ghostwriter Leo Guild that "Mickey thought the dogs and the kids should stay at home. Mickey's viewpoint was an unselfish one. He felt I had a difficult role to play and that I would be freer without the children and pets to concentrate on my role. But I had never gone anywhere without my whole family and I wasn't going to start now. . . . All the minor differences we had over the years piled into one ogre. I was tired and unhappy—most of it having nothing to do with Mickey."

Mickey was tired and unhappy, too—mostly with being relegated to the role of baby- and dog-sitter while Jayne pursued her career. He wanted his own career, and while he didn't think Jayne should give up hers, being "Mr. Jayne Mansfield" was more wearying than he had guessed at the outset. "I don't want to be a baby-sitter in Italy," he flat-out told the UPI.

But Jayne had never been alone—she went from her childhood home to living with Paul to living with Jayne Marie to living with Mickey. The thought of being on her own in Italy terrified her, and it came out in this kind of high-handed and unreasonable behavior. No one had ever stood up to her or told her no, so now Jayne's first impulse was to call her lawyers and the press.

Jayne and Mickey made up by the next day—again, with reporters present. "Mickey, I'm your Jayne," she cooed, before an audience including James Bacon. "I always loved you, even while I was filing for divorce." She went on to explain that "Mickey and I had our first big fight. He didn't want to take the three children and four dogs to Italy while I make a picture. We compromised. We're taking the children, but only one dog."

She rationalized that "Mickey got jealous over my concern for the children. He thought I was more interested in them than him. When I filed for divorce, it brought everything to a decision. He apologized and the children will go with us. This thing is over." Jayne won and Mickey buckled—for the time being. Jayne added that she would withdraw the suit "as soon as I get around to it."

The *San Francisco Examiner* dryly noted, "Jayne Mansfield proved that for a $19 investment, it is possible to get $1,000,000's worth of free publicity." Whitney Bolton of the *Fort Myers News-Press* wrote, "It is utterly of no personal interest to me whether Jayne Mansfield is a legitimate seeker of divorce or has brooded herself into an odd publicity dodge because things haven't been too busy for her in a professional way." Bolton just wished that Jayne and Elizabeth Taylor "would go home, shut their doors and keep quiet for as long as a week." Dorothy Kilgallen managed to be insulting to both Mickey and Jayne, writing, "Jayne isn't doing much at the box office in this country, and she's worried over the future of her career. Meanwhile, she wishes Mickey would find himself a job that she could respect, instead of just working as part of her entourage." Charles McHarry of the *New York Daily News* joked that if the Pink Palace caught fire, Jayne would "first call the newspapers and then the Fire Department."

Unperturbed, Jayne said, "Every marriage needs, now and then, a 24-hour break. This enables you to have a honeymoon again."

19

A man builds only one heart-shaped pool in his life.

Mickey Hargitay

In early May Jayne, Mickey, the children, and at least one dog arrived in Rome, where Jayne was to film the screwball comedy *Panic Button*—another loan-out, produced by Seven Arts–Yankee Productions and distributed through Warner Bros. "It's a role unlike any I've ever played before. I play an intellectual," Jayne told Bob Thomas, though her appraisal was somewhat optimistic (she played a prostitute recruited to act in an indie film).

Panic Button had an impressive cast: Maurice Chevalier, a star since the 1910s, with recent hits *Gigi* and *Love in the Afternoon* behind him; forty-year-old Eleanor Parker, a star for two decades, about to step into *The Sound of Music;* rising young film and TV actor Mike Connors, who went on to star in TV's *Mannix;* reliable character actor Akim Tamiroff, who supported nearly every star in Hollywood; and Mel Welles, so great in Roger Corman's *The Little Shop of Horrors.* It was directed by George Sherman, whose thirty-year career consisted mostly of westerns and TV (*Naked City, Daniel Boone*).

Seven Arts–Yankee Productions and producer Ron Gorton had a shaky time of it in Italy. Gorton was a minor TV actor having his first fling at producing. Jayne complained to Hedda Hopper, "The production company rented me a chauffeured Cadillac and twice the insides fell out. Both times when we were driving slowly through the city—otherwise it could have been disastrous." But her biggest challenge came when she was called upon to water-ski—for the first time since her shipwreck—on Sabaudian Beach (she burst into tears after filming the scene).

Jayne—as usual—gave her producer very little grief. The real discord came from Eleanor Parker, who was not happy at being upstaged by a younger actress. "Eleanor is said to be quite disconcerted by the gallery of photographers who follow Jayne around on and off the set, obviously to see if one of her dresses is going to come apart again," wrote Dorothy Manners. "Also actor Mike Connors has been on the sidelines a couple of days with a swollen lip from a bee sting. Even cheerful Maurice Chevalier can't seem to spread too much good humor around."

Eleanor Parker told Erskine Johnson that the reports of her unhappiness were "rubbish. I hardly know [Jayne]. We had one scene together. I adore Maurice Chevalier." But then she went on to complain that "you could say I feuded plenty with the film's producer. Other than that, I'd rather not talk about working in Rome. I'm not disappointed in the picture, but I've been miserable ever since April 26. That's the day I arrived there. The working conditions were impossible." Ron Gorton told Sheilah Graham that "Eleanor Parker pulled a Marilyn Monroe and didn't show up for the first three days of filming."

Graham noted that "Eleanor is usually so cooperative that there has to be two sides heard from in this battle. Eleanor can't abide Ron," wrote Graham, "and the feeling is returned with interest. After the first day of work they have not spoken to each other and the producer communicates with his star by letter, even when the two are within a few inches of each other on the set!"

Connors—like Dan Dailey and Kenneth More before him—expressed his resentment of Jayne, complaining to Sheilah Graham that if Jayne's "clothes are tight, she doesn't bother to read the script. Also she is under the misapprehension that every man is in love with her."

Maurice Chevalier did his best to play peacemaker. "What more can an old man ask?" he said in his usual cheerful manner. "I saw Jayne Mansfield. I shouted, 'Jayne, you are beautiful!' She shouted back, 'And you are beautiful!' With a body like Jayne's, to be so absolutely innocent. Look at her face, it is absolutely innocent. . . . I play Romeo to Jayne's Juliet." Chevalier noted, "I didn't mind running up to her balcony for a dozen takes. It was coming down that tired me. This picture has been rough on me physically. I had to spend one hot day in Rome at the beach encased in bandages.

In Venice I wore the uniform of a nun and it was a hundred in the sun. I had to do the twist with Jayne and that has injured people half my age."

♥

Jayne did her level best to enjoy *la dolce vita* while in Rome. Elizabeth Taylor had been attracting most of the spotlight during her endless *Cleopatra* shoot at Rome's Cinecittà Studios, dallying with Richard Burton while husband Eddie Fisher stood by haplessly. Carlo Ponti and Sophia Loren, Audrey Hepburn, and Mel Ferrer, also shooting at Cinecittà, were pursued by paparazzi, as were other stars and locally famous gangsters, socialites, and eccentrics.

"Jayne Mansfield and Mickey Hargitay are almost stealing the thunder from Liz and Richard Burton when they stroll down the Via Veneto in Rome," wrote Dorothy Manners in May. "Jayne has to clutch her clothes to keep them on and Mickey had to clutch Jayne to keep her." They were photographed doing the twist at a Roman nightclub—some reports gleefully reported that one of Jayne's shoulder straps broke, but no photos prove it. Jayne told Donald Zec of the *Daily Mirror* that Rome was "just like being in heaven. You know why I love Rome? Because Rome loves me! They called me the Most Perfect Woman in the World and The Explosive One! It's so absolutely wunnerful. The Italians are so friendly and that's my basic character, too."

But there was a snake in the grass, at least from Mickey's viewpoint: one Enrico Bomba. Bomba was variously referred to as *Panic Button*'s associate producer or publicist—but he is listed nowhere in the film's credits, not even under his sometimes pseudonym, Henry Bay (he did produce and direct several films in the 1950s–1970s). The forty-year-old Italian was not classically handsome—no threat to Mickey in that department—but he was charming and funny and very attentive to Jayne. He was also married.

"With my husband involved in all the behind-the-scenes activity to keep us going," Jayne told Leo Guild, "I found myself bewitched by producer Bomba, who had the manners of a Walter Raleigh and was like a genie, there to see my every wish was granted." Mind you, she said this in 1963, when she and Mickey were shakily reconciled. "When Mickey was tied up, Bomba would escort me through Rome with appropriate flowery descriptions of the sights. What was a friendship was then blown up into a spectacular romance. Soon there was talk and headlines. Mickey was rightly furious. In fact, an Italian newspaper called him and offered him $5,000 to punch Enrico Bomba in the nose in front of one of his photographers. . . . Mickey and I were to the silent-treatment state, the most dangerous of all."

The blowup came in early June at a Roman nightclub, the Shaker. Most of the film's cast and crew were present, and while Jayne was doing the twist with Bomba, her dress finally came through and fell off. "It was no striptease," Jayne explained. "I just happened to be wearing a very loose-fitting dress. Occasionally it came apart. I tried to hold my dress together. I guess twisting wasn't the best thing to do in that dress."

Mickey was off in a corner chatting with producer Ron Gorton while Jayne was exiting her dress. The *New York Daily News* reported the incident: "Scowling, the brawny Mickey stalked onto the floor and tried to pull Jayne away from Bomba, but the dancers refused to be separated so easily. Mickey tugged some more until he got her away. Then he pushed and dragged her into a dark corner, where they had a heated discussion." Some of those present claimed that Mickey slapped Jayne, which both Mickey and Jayne denied. "When the party broke up at 3:30 this morning," the *News* breathlessly continued, "Jayne slipped into Bomba's car instead of Mickey's. The muscleman dashed over, pulled her out and shoved her into his own car. Then he drove off to their villa outside Rome." One Italian paper compared Jayne's goings-on to those of Nanah Kaish, the Turkish dancer whose notorious 1958 strip in a Roman nightclub was one inspiration for Fellini's *La Dolce Vita*.

"Hargitay was reported to be angry over reports that his bosomy wife Jayne has more than a passing interest in the dark, dapper Bomba," reported the *Chicago Tribune*. "One studio source reported that Mickey appeared at the set of his wife's picture *Panic Button* scowling and asking for Bomba." Dorothy Manners got her say in as well: "Despite the front she puts up, Jayne Mansfield (and I'll thank you for no cracks) may be getting ready to push a panic button of her own on *Panic Button* in Rome. Reports are her marriage to Mickey Hargitay is getting shakier and shakier. And something or someone must be bothering him about her working hours because Mickey shows up on the set every day and hangs around until finishing time. He never did that in Hollywood."

Bomba denied that he had anything but a friendly, professional interest in Jayne; he found her clever and amusing, and he hoped to work out a future film project with her. He also repeated that he was married and—as an Italian Catholic—he had no intention of getting a divorce. Jayne brushed all that off, reveling in his attentions while Mickey simmered at a low boil.

In late June the production moved to Venice for a week's location filming. Enrico Bomba—his exact job still vague—went along, but Mickey stayed in Rome with the children. A press agent tried to talk Jayne into falling out of the gondola into the Grand Canal, "but she vetoed the idea as too undignified." A good thing, too—Katharine Hepburn caught an eye infection after jumping into the filthy canal while filming *Summertime* in 1955. "I even tried to push her out of the gondola," said the press agent, "but she side-stepped and I almost went in the water."

In late July Jayne was presented with the ostentatiously named "Oscar of the Two World" award at the Villombrosa Hotel in Fiuggi, about fifty miles south of Rome. She, Ron Gorton, and actors Rossano Brazzi and Vincent Barbi drove there for the ceremony. Jayne went onstage to accept the award and, as she was coming off, a woman jumped up and screamed, "Why does she get a prize? Why don't I get one? She refused to be photographed with me." Then she attacked Jayne, slapping and scratching her. Barbi and Brazzi pulled her off. Barbi said, "I gave her a left hook. Certainly I hit women when they get out of order. She was kicking Jayne and pulling her hair and the only way to end it was by hitting her."

"I had just made a little speech and was walking back to my table when this woman knocked me down and started pulling my hair," Jayne recalled. "I had never seen her before and I don't even remember what she looked like. She claimed she had been trying to win this award 20 years, and here I walk in and win it. She also said I refused to pose for a picture with her last week, and I don't remember that at all." Jayne decided not to press charges. The attacker was identified as Alma del Rio, a forty-three-year-old cabaret entertainer. Jayne said that she still loved Italy: "The people there gave me a standing ovation that must have lasted three minutes. It was very touching."

Production on *Panic Button* wrapped midway through July. While in Italy, Jayne and Mickey starred in a commercial for Biancosarti liqueur ("halfway between a vermouth and bitter"). They dance, Jayne powders and perfumes herself before a dressing table, while they, the commercial's ostensible director and crew, enjoy sips of the product. During filming Jayne managed to slip and fall against a radiator in her dressing room, suffering a slight cut on her head.

Sheilah Graham predicted that "when Jayne and family return within a few days to California, she will reactivate her divorce against Mickey Hargitay. And his successor is already picked out—dynamic Enrique [*sic*]

212

Bomba." Jayne did pick the successor to her agent, Bill Shiffrin, dropping him in favor of Kurt Frings. Shiffrin told Martha Saxton that Jayne "wore me out. She killed all the fire in me. . . . She should have stressed her acting and not her personality. She had talent but after all her tomfoolery no one would buy her." Kurt Frings had been an artists' manager since 1941, handling such stars as Elizabeth Taylor, Richard Burton, Sophia Loren, Gloria Swanson, and Audrey Hepburn. He told Hedda Hopper that Jayne could keep working if she "starts dressing less extremely and stops all that lousy publicity. There are plenty of jobs waiting for her in Europe."

Jayne was planning another picture in Rome with Bomba, wrote Graham, and "Hargitay will not be returning to Italy with Jayne and the children. And he is so jealous of Bomba that, to appease him, Ron Gorton, producer of *Panic Button*, made the gesture of banning Bomba for two days from the set."

Panic Button was held up for two years before being released in the US; it was not seen in most of the world till 1965 (actually, it was not seen in most of the world at all). In late 1963 Louella Parsons wrote that *Panic Button* "was plagued with salary suits, etc., and Mike Connors, making *Good Neighbor Sam* at Columbia, tells me the settlement couldn't come at a better time for him. 'My residuals from *Tightrope* have run out and I can use this windfall from *Panic Button*.'" Sheilah Graham wrote in September 1963 that Ron Gorton "is planning to sue Seven Arts about the non-release of *Panic Button*, his maiden voyage into film production. 'There's going to be a lot of name-calling and quite a lot of dirt.'" Gorton also objected to the poster art, featuring Jayne in a bikini. "It's a nice, fluffy little picture to make people forget their troubles," he said. "It has no messages—and don't pay attention to the ads. They're ridiculous. They don't have anything to do with the picture. They're just to get the people in." They didn't get people in, not even when the film was released in the UK as *Let's Go Bust*.

Panic Button is indeed a nice, fluffy little picture—not at all bad—but it could and should have been much better. The plot involves a crooked businessman (Mel Welles) who needs to write off half a million dollars for tax purposes: "The surest way to lose money is to invest it in a television pilot," advises his lawyer. He sends his son Frank (Mike Connors) to Rome: Frank hires washed-up actor Philippe Fontaine (Maurice Chevalier) to star, along with Angela (Jayne), a hopeful but hopeless actress (and a high-priced call girl). Eleanor Parker plays the manager of a sketchy Roman hotel where Fontaine lives, as well as being his patient, levelheaded ex-wife.

Akim Tamiroff steals the film as the dreadful drama coach hired to direct. The collection of assorted nuts produces a supposedly so-bad-it's-good *Romeo and Juliet;* of course Frank and Angela fall in love, and of course their project is a hit (the father and son open a successful comedy studio, with Fontaine and Angela as its stars).

It is, of course, the basic plot of Mel Brooks's *The Producers,* released in 1967. But if Brooks did steal the idea, he transformed a rhinestone into a diamond. If one had never seen *The Producers, Panic Button* would be a sprightly, enjoyable film—but it suffers when compared to Mel Brooks's evil genius. The characters in *Panic Button* are essentially nice people who do the right thing; everyone in *The Producers* is gleefully, hilariously amoral. The script of *Panic Button* (by Hal Biller and Stephen Longstreet) never rises above "pleasant," either. The huge, film-killing mistake is that Chevalier and Jayne's *Romeo and Juliet* is not that bad, and not at all funny. It should have been played for real slapstick "Springtime for Hitler" laughs, but instead is seen for only a minute or so, looking like an average amateur production.

Jayne looks great, in a chic, flattering wardrobe and Jackie Kennedy bouffant (her own hair, brushed back over a hairpiece—as Jackie herself did). She also gives as good a performance as the script allows: she is mostly window dressing, but her comedy talents are wasted.

Panic Button got good reviews, despite its late and very limited release, which killed its chances of making much money or a real splash. Gee Mitchell of the *Dayton Daily News* viewed a rough cut in August 1962 and wrote that "those who saw it predict that as a result of her role in the picture, Jayne Mansfield will be emerging as one of the movies' top comediennes." But most reviews were lukewarm. Jean Walrath of the *Rochester Democrat and Chronicle* wrote that all the humor was "in the last reel. Something suddenly happens and it becomes the motion picture it should have been all the way through. . . . The humor becomes subtle, the locale and the script melt together, the actors begin to act and the reactors react and the audience joins the laughter on the screen at the film within a film. But the fun all happens rather late." Tom Rettew of the *Wilmington News Journal* was disappointed that "Miss Mansfield's most obvious assets are underplayed." The *Los Angeles Bridge News* wrote that Jayne "contributes a couple of deliciously amusing bits." And *Film Daily* called *Panic Button* "a zany comedy that . . . gallops merrily along, turning up bursts of comedy amid touches of corn."

Sophia Loren shoots Jayne the world's most famous side-eye, April 12, 1957.

Vera Jane Palmer and Paul Mansfield have a second wedding ceremony to please their families, May 10, 1950.

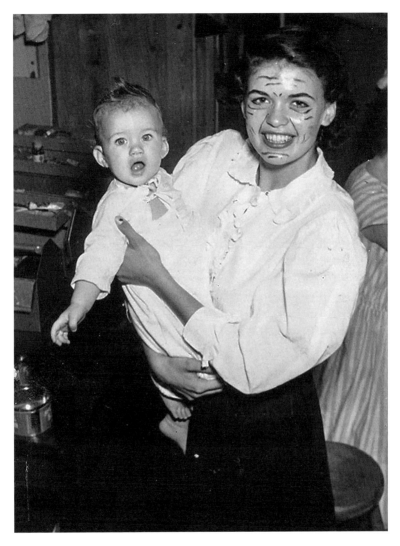

Backstage at the Austin Civic Theater's production of *The Drunkard,* Jayne (in very bad age makeup) holds baby Jayne Marie, October 1951.

(*Left*) Jayne in her first movie, *The Female Jungle,* filmed in late 1954.

(*Below*) A paparazzi goddess is born: at the *Underwater!* press event in Florida, February 1955. (Courtesy of Everett Collection.)

After costarring in *The Female Jungle,* it was back to bit parts, here in *Pete Kelly's Blues* with Jack Webb, 1955. (Courtesy of Everett Collection.)

Newly signed by Warner Bros., Jayne scored a nice supporting role in *Illegal* with (*from left*) Ellen Corby, Edward G. Robinson, and Nina Foch, 1955. (Courtesy of Everett Collection.)

(*Left*) By 1955 Jayne already knew what the press and public wanted. (Courtesy of Everett Collection.)

(*Below*) Jayne (seen here with Dan Duryea) turned in a great dramatic performance in *The Burglar,* filmed in 1955, but the movie sat on the shelf till after her *Rock Hunter* success. (Courtesy of Everett Collection.)

A Broadway star is born: with Orson Bean in *Will Success Spoil Rock Hunter?*, 1955. (Courtesy of Everett Collection.)

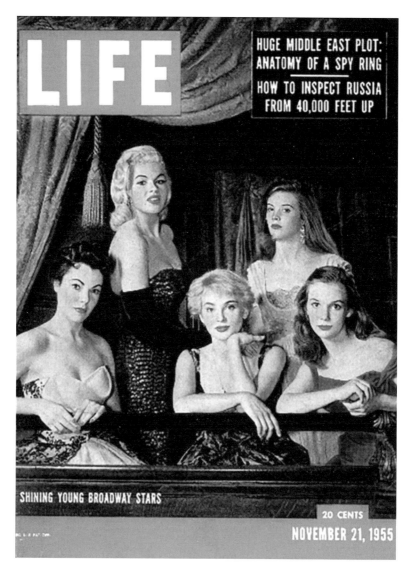

LIFE

HUGE MIDDLE EAST PLOT:
ANATOMY OF A SPY RING
_____
HOW TO INSPECT RUSSIA
FROM 40,000 FEET UP

SHINING YOUNG BROADWAY STARS

20 CENTS

NOVEMBER 21, 1955

Jayne's first *Life* cover, November 21, 1955: (*from left*) Broadway starlets Judy Tyler, Jayne, Diane Cilento, Lois Smith, and Susan Strasberg.

(*Left*) When Queens Collide: Jayne hovers nervously behind Marilyn Monroe at an Actors Studio benefit, December 1955.

(*Right*) Jayne and boyfriend Mickey Hargitay make a quiet and tasteful appearance at the press agents' Ballyhoo Ball, October 1956. (Courtesy of Everett Collection.)

Guesting on *The Jack Benny Program*, December 1956.

An example of Frank Tashlin's single-entendre humor in *The Girl Can't Help It*, 1956. (Courtesy of Everett Collection.)

"She ain't Rome—what she's got's already built!" Edmond O'Brien, Jayne, and Tom Ewell in *The Girl Can't Help It*. (Courtesy of Everett Collection.)

April 12, 1957: Jayne politely introduces herself to guest of honor
Sophia Loren at Romanoff's.

Fellow guest Rita Moreno's face says what everyone else is thinking.

"Just a perfectly normal American girl" in the film version of *Will Success Spoil Rock Hunter?*, 1957. (Courtesy of Everett Collection.)

With Tony Randall in *Will Success Spoil Rock Hunter?* (Courtesy of Everett Collection.)

Arguably Jayne's best dramatic performance was in *The Wayward Bus*, 1957. (Courtesy of Everett Collection.)

From left: Rick Jason, Dan Dailey, and Jayne in *The Wayward Bus.* (Courtesy of Everett Collection.)

Jayne and Joan Collins—both wearing the world's most fabulous sunglasses—say goodnight after a hard day's work on *The Wayward Bus*. (Courtesy of Everett Collection.)

Queen Elizabeth II pulls a Sophia Loren upon meeting Jayne in London, November 1957.

Jayne's career at Fox took a turn for the worse with *Kiss Them For Me,* 1957. *From left:* Cary Grant, Ray Walston, Jayne, Werner Klemperer, and Frank Nelson. (Courtesy of Everett Collection.)

Jayne and Bob Hope return from a USO tour, December 1957. (Courtesy of Everett Collection.)

The simple, quiet wedding of Jayne and Mickey Hargitay, January 13, 1958 (at left is Jayne's mother, Vera Peers). (Courtesy of Everett Collection.)

(*Right*) By early 1958, Jayne (with the help of Don Poynter) was promoting herself in any and every way possible.

Jayne and Mickey nightly damaged the "molten gold" dress created by David Berman during their Las Vegas revue in 1958. (Courtesy of Everett Collection.)

Portrait of Jayne from the late 1950s.

With Kenneth More in *The Sheriff of Fractured Jaw*, 1958. (Courtesy of Everett Collection.)

Jayne in her heart-shaped bathtub, ca. 1958.

In *Too Hot to Handle* with (*from left*) Christopher Lee, Leo Genn, and Sheldon Lawrence, 1959. (Courtesy of Everett Collection.)

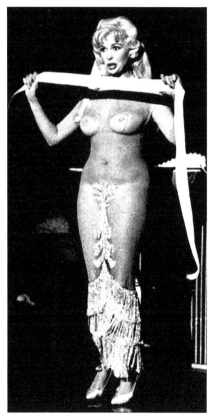

(*Left*) *Too Hot to Handle:* the costume approved for US release. (*Right*) *Too Hot to Handle:* the European version.

Portraits from *It Takes a Thief*,
made in England in 1959.

Jayne about to be done in by a killer tree in *Loves of Hercules,* 1960. (Courtesy of Everett Collection.)

Jayne's 1960–1961 act at the Dunes Hotel was immortalized on an LP.

Jayne—trying out a brown wig—shows off her heart-shaped swimming pool, 1961.

Jayne at the 1961 Berlin International Film Festival. (Courtesy of Everett Collection.)

Jayne with Ray Danton in *The George Raft Story*, 1961. (Courtesy of Everett Collection.)

Jayne hams it up with Mickey Rooney at the Golden Globes, 1961. (Courtesy of Everett Collection.)

(*Left*) Filming on location in Italy for *Panic Button,* spring 1962.

(*Below*) The very unhappy cast of *Panic Button. From left:* Jayne, Maurice Chevalier, Eleanor Parker, and Mike Connors, 1962.

Jayne with Tony Randall on *The Alfred Hitchcock Hour*, 1962.

Jayne with Enrico Bomba at the Beirut Film Festival, October 1962.
(Courtesy of Everett Collection.)

Jayne enjoyed a brief, blissful romance with singer Nelson
Sardelli in the spring of 1963. (Courtesy of Everett Collection.)

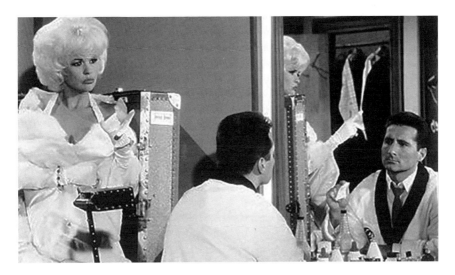

Jayne and Freddy Quinn in the German-made *Homesick for St. Pauli,* 1963. (Courtesy
of Everett Collection.)

One of Jayne's biggest career missteps was *Promises. . . . Promises!,* 1963, with (*from left*) Tommy Noonan, Marie McDonald, and Mickey Hargitay. (Courtesy of Everett Collection.)

Jayne being smacked around by Cameron Mitchell in the dark, violent crime caper *Dog Eat Dog,* 1964. (Courtesy of Everett Collection.)

(*Top*) Undoubtedly Jayne's worst film was the unwatchable *Primitive Love,* 1964, with Ciccio Ingrassia (*left*) and Franco Franchi. (Courtesy of Everett Collection.)

(*Right*) Rocking in Cannes with Rocky Roberts and the Airedales, 1964; this footage was eventually seen in the posthumous *The Wild, Wild World of Jayne Mansfield.*

On the Spanish Steps in Rome while filming *Primitive Love,* 1964; this footage was also used in *The Wild, Wild World of Jayne Mansfield.*

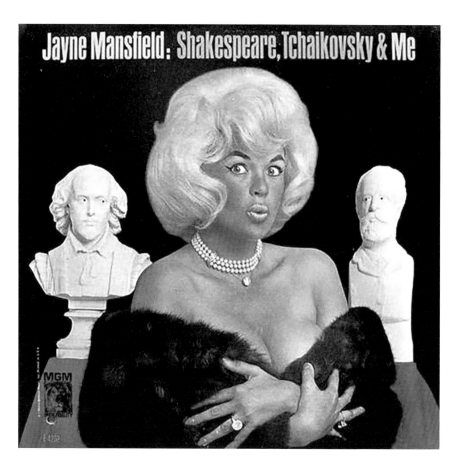

Jayne's second, inexplicable, album, released in 1964.

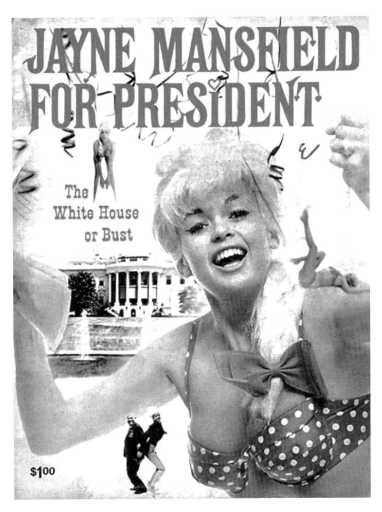

Jayne offers herself as a third-party alternative to presidential contenders
Lyndon Johnson and Barry Goldwater, 1964.

Jayne and her third husband, director Matt Cimber, ca. 1965.

Jayne (with Robert Morse) filmed a cameo for *The Loved One* in late 1964, but she was cut from the release print. (Courtesy of Everett Collection.)

Jayne with Stephen Brooks on tour in *Bus Stop*, 1964.

Jayne with Jack E. Leonard in *The Fat Spy*, 1966. (Courtesy of Everett Collection.)

One of Jayne's fleeting appearances in *Las Vegas Hillbillys,* 1966.

Jayne showing off her swimming pool to her new pal, performance artist/Satanist Anton LaVey, autumn 1966.

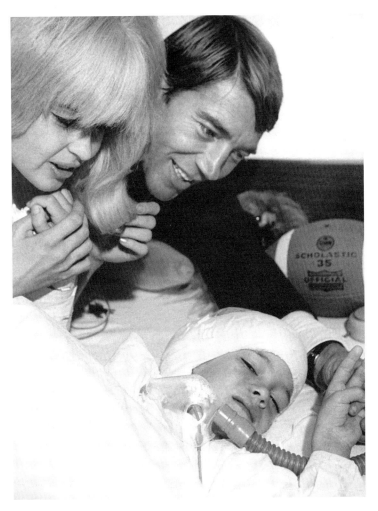

Jayne and Mickey at the bedside of their critically injured son Zoltan, who gamely gives a "V for Victory" sign, December 5, 1966. (Courtesy of Everett Collection.)

Jayne filmed *A Guide for the Married Man* (here with Terry-Thomas) in late 1966; it was released just as the news of her death hit the papers. (Courtesy of Everett Collection.)

Jayne with Walter Gregg in *Single Room Furnished,* filmed in 1965–1966.

Jayne's mod look: with Sam Brody in London, spring 1967.

Jayne and Diana Dors compare puppies, Leeds, England, May 1967. (Courtesy of Everett Collection.)

On June 28, 1967, Jayne visited Keesler Air Force Base in Biloxi. *From left:* Zoltan, Mickey Jr., Jayne, and Mariska (on the lap of Airman Second Class Johnny Burke). This may be the last photo of Jayne; twelve hours later, she was dead.

The sheet-covered body of Jayne Mansfield at the scene of the car accident that killed her, Sam Brody, and Ronald Harrison near Slidell, Louisiana, June 29, 1967. (Courtesy of Everett Collection.)

Loni Anderson and Arnold Schwarzenegger in *The Jayne Mansfield Story*, 1980. (Courtesy of Everett Collection.)

Unveiling Mariska Hargitay's Hollywood Walk of Fame star are (*from left*) Jayne's children Mickey Jr., Mariska, Zoltan, and Jayne Marie, November 8, 2013. (Courtesy of Everett Collection.)

The most cringe-making review was actually a newspaper ad for *Panic Button,* playing at the Trail Drive-In in Louisiana: "See! Scantily-Clad Jayne Mansfield in Her Usual Role!"

♥

Worse things happened during *Panic Button's* filming than Enrico Bomba and disobedient clothing. While Jayne was disporting herself in Rome and Venice, big changes were happening at 20th Century-Fox. Darryl F. Zanuck—who had co-founded the studio in 1935—had left in 1956. Since then, the studios—all studios—were suffering, due to television, the end of the block-booking system (the government had forced studios to sell their theater chains), and the rise of independent films. Spyros Skouras became president of Fox, and by 1962 the studio was being bankrupted by Elizabeth Taylor's *Cleopatra,* which cost $44 million and had been filming since 1960. Zanuck—still Fox's largest shareholder though no longer in charge—wanted to film his pet project, *The Longest Day,* for $10 million; Skouras wanted to shoot it on the cheap, which infuriated Zanuck. In June Marilyn Monroe was fired from *Something's Got to Give,* from which Jayne had already been bounced.

Zanuck raced back to Hollywood, staged a coup, and Spyros Skouras got the bum's rush. The first thing Zanuck did—after restoring *The Longest Day's* budget—was to rehire Marilyn. She was to start filming *Something's Got to Give* in the fall, and was signed to make another light comedy (which would later be shot as *What a Way to Go!,* starring Shirley MacLaine).

Zanuck's return was good news for Marilyn—but it was bad news for a lot of deadwood personnel at Fox, who were to be sacrificed in the name of *The Longest Day* and *Cleopatra.* One of the victims was Jayne Mansfield.

The story got around that Jayne was doing the twist with Maurice Chevalier on the set of *Panic Button* when she was told she'd been dropped by Fox, but it's doubtful a messenger would break into filming to tell her this. The AP reported on July 4 that Fox had announced the previous day that Jayne's "contract had expired and wasn't being renewed. A spokesman described the option dropping as routine and said the probable reason was that the studio didn't have a picture in mind for her at the moment. He noted that although Miss Mansfield has been with Fox since 1956, she has been loaned out fairly frequently for movies made elsewhere."

Jayne put on a brave face and said, "I am thrilled to death and I feel free as a bird. I had been trying for three years to get away from 20th Century-Fox. For five years I haven't done a picture on the home lot. Fox loaned me out for two or three pictures a year but I was not happy with the pictures I was doing. I have been trying to be released from the contract all along." She put out the usual kind of statement made by movie stars and politicians newly out of a job: "Jayne says she intends devoting more time to the children, thereby giving Mickey Hargitay some relief from baby-sitting." She said that she had two pictures lined up, *Operation Sevilla,* to be directed by George Stevens, and *Drink to Me Only,* with Clifton Webb, but these seem to have been wishful thinking.

She must have been terrified. As delusionally optimistic as Jayne could be about her career, she was, for the first time, without studio backing. No salary, no perks, no health insurance, not even any loan-outs. With a huge house, a growing family, and a star's lifestyle to support, she couldn't help but see the cliff in front of her. She was certainly not cheered up by the *Honolulu Star Bulletin*'s nasty report that "bovine Jayne Mansfield is no longer an employee of 20th Century-Fox Studios."

By the end of July, the family was back in the Pink Palace, but hardly settled in happily. Everyone involved had a different and contradictory tale to tell about love affairs, divorce, or marital bliss. Reynolds Packer of the *New York Daily News* reported that Mickey "was tired of being called Mr. Mansfield." When asked about Bomba, Mickey said, "I've heard about it, but it doesn't make any sense because this Bomba is a married man and has two children. And Bomba isn't the only man after Jayne. If I lose my wife I lose nothing." Jayne called Bomba "a wonderful man and a great producer," and Bomba, back in Rome, protested that "I know there's talk that Jayne and Mickey are splitting up, but I cannot believe I am the cause of it."

Jayne's secretary, Raymond Strait, claimed that Jayne would file for divorce. "This time she is really going through with it." But Ray Christina, Mickey's business manager, said, "I could be wrong. But everything seemed rosy. Jayne was laughing with Mickey, and everything seemed to be all right. But she was angry that the story of her possible divorce had been released." And the UPI chimed in with the news that Jayne had met with lawyers Greg Bautzer and Gerald Lipsky, who said, "Miss Mansfield is not filing for divorce. She is discussing the possibility of a separation with her husband." The *Tennessean*'s columnist was not impressed by all this. "Publicity, it seems, is like a narcotic. The more addicted you become, the more trouble you have to go to to get it."

In a phone interview, Mickey said, "I'm very much in love with Jayne and don't want anything to happen to our marriage." He claimed that Enrico Bomba "is trying very hard" to break them up. "I know Jayne won't go for it. She loves me." At which Jayne picked up the extension and said, "Mickey's side is very biased," and accused him of lying. Mickey: "What are lies?" Jayne: "You said I loved you."

Enrico Bomba stood up for himself, talking to the *Daily Mirror*. Mickey's accusations were "absurd," he said, "absolute nonsense. Mr. Hargitay knows perfectly well that I have never tried to sabotage his marriage. Many times I have tried to save the marriage, by pouring water on the flames when bitter arguments flared between those two. But it was obvious that their marriage was failing, anyway—even before they came to Rome. I spent a lot of time trying to calm the situation. And now he has the nerve to say this about me!"

He admitted to spending a lot of time with Jayne, "But there were always other people with us, even if her husband wasn't there. It's also true that Jayne and I spent a weekend in Venice. But that was merely for the purposes of the film. I am sincerely fond of Jayne. But I am married, and I love my wife, and I wouldn't leave her. I admire Jayne as an actress, but that's all."

On August 1 Jayne and Mickey signed a separation agreement. That same day they sat by their heart-shaped pool in bathing suits, talking to the press both in person and on the phone. "I'm not filing for immediate divorce. I am discussing a separation with my husband," said Jayne, at which point, "out of sheer embarrassment, [Mickey] got up and walked away so he wouldn't have to listen," wrote one reporter. "Never once did Jayne's attitude toward him change. All smiles—and even a certain amount of affection like a pat on the head of a friendly pooch."

On Thursday, August 2, 1962, Mickey packed up a few suitcases, flung some clothes into his car, and left the Pink Palace he had built for Jayne. "Outwardly undisturbed," reported the AP, "Hargitay stopped his red convertible momentarily as he left the home to talk with newsmen. He did not indicate his destination, but admitted he was taking with him a picture of his blonde, 29-year-old wife."

"Divorce is the worst thing that can happen to a man and his wife,"

Mickey told *Photoplay*'s Jim Hoffman the following year. "But even worse than that is staying together for the children's sake. The worst thing that can happen to kids is to see their parents unhappy. I do my kids a favor—if I can't get along with my wife—to get a divorce."

Jayne told Leo Guild that "despite Mickey's bitterness and my involvement with Bomba, we were on the phone constantly. I couldn't do without him even though it had been my decision to be apart. We talked constantly on the phone and had endless meetings. Most of the time I was in tears. I loved Mickey dearly for five years, yet Bomba had a strong romantic pull for me."

Dorothy Manners wrote a very intrusive and presumptuous article about how upset Jayne Marie was. "The day he moved out of the house the child wept bitterly. She clung to her stepfather, dissolved in tears, saying, 'You'll always be my daddy, Mickey.'" Manners claimed that Jayne Marie called Louella Parsons and begged, "Please let us come down to see you. Please talk some sense into my mother." Sheilah Graham predicted that if Jayne divorced Mickey, she'd find "he is bitterly unhappy over the break-up of his marriage and plans to fight for the partial if not complete custody of their two sons."

Decades later, Jayne Marie said that Mickey "was the backbone for her, he was able to be there for her in really difficult times. My mother always felt that she could depend on Mickey. He was pretty much the only father figure I had in my life."

❤

In 1962 Jayne was approached by Bentley Morris of Holloway House with an offer to publish her autobiography. Holloway House published such lurid paperbacks as *Ladies on Call: The Most Intimate Recollections of a Hollywood Madam* and *Honeyman: True Life Story of a B-Girl Hustler*, reprints of "naughty" classics, and biographies of such black icons as Dorothy Dandridge, Medgar Evers, Sojourner Truth, and Madame C. J. Walker. In the early '60s, it was also issuing a series of books on Hollywood personalities (for example, Barbara Payton and Jim Backus).

Jayne Mansfield's Wild, Wild World was written in early 1962 and released that August. Morris recalls today that "the book was written by Leo Guild, who was at one time an associate editor at *The Hollywood Reporter*. Leo Guild knew practically every personality in Hollywood, and we hired him as an executive editor to do a series of Hollywood books. Guild knew

Jayne personally, and she and Mickey were very pleased that he would be doing the book. She was very comfortable with Leo, who was an outstanding writer and a confidante of everybody in Hollywood. She didn't have any editorial say; but she did have extensive meetings with Leo, and I don't think she saw the book until it was published. But she was pleased with it, as was Mickey."

Years later Guild explained to the *Los Angeles Times* what makes a memoir sell: "Frankness. For example, I did a book with Liberace. Lee was averse to probing into his personal life. We had long discussions about it. I lost. The book flopped. Had Lee chosen to reveal, we would have had a best-seller." Jayne's book was compiled through interviews "while we drove around in her white Cadillac as she did her chores. She was a busy girl and couldn't take off hours at a time to be interviewed. So as she dropped the children at school, stopped at her hairdressers, saw her photographers, discussed pictures with producers at the studio and drove to bank and market openings, I sat beside her asking hundreds of questions."

He also worked from articles in her voluminous scrapbooks, but found—to no one's surprise—that these were often contradictory. "When I would appeal to her for truth she often didn't remember. Then she'd say, 'Oh make it up.'" Still, working with Jayne was a breeze compared to his collaboration with poor Barbara Payton, whose biography Guild ghosted in 1963, when she was in the last stages of alcoholism, her acting career long over. "Over and over she'd say to me, 'Let's get it all down. I want it to serve as a lesson to other actresses who try short cuts,'" Guild recalled of Payton. "We worked under the worst conditions in an apartment populated with pimps, prostitutes and rats, . . . Barbara Payton had one favor to ask when I finished her book. She didn't want to be paid in cash or check. She wanted payment in red wine."

Jayne, says Bentley Morris, "was a perfectly delightful personality, and was very pleasant to be with. And of course, she was extraordinarily attractive." Morris and Guild went to the Pink Palace before the book contract was signed to iron out details. "We showed up that morning and we were waiting for her to come down and have a little discussion with her," he says, then recalls, still somewhat stunned at the memory, "She came down with only the bottom of her body clothed. I have to admit to you, it was very difficult talking to her. It was a very unusual meeting. She of course was very proud of her body, and didn't feel it was anything that was shameful—it was quite an experience to try to talk to her."

Surprisingly, Jayne made no money from the book; she agreed to the project for publicity and the status of having her memoirs in the bookstores, says Morris. "Leo was paid [for the book]. It was good publicity for her, and of course she recognized that, and was very cooperative with Leo." As for the reliability of Jayne's first-person "autobiographical" quotes, "Whatever quotes were in the book—I don't recall intimately about the text—if she was quoted, I'd be very much assured of the integrity of Leo Guild, it's what she said." Of course, as Guild himself admitted, what she said often had little relationship with the truth.

Louis Sobol wrote with some amazement, "What do you think has just arrived at this desk? A book for review titled *Jayne Mansfield's Wild, Wild World* . . . containing startling photos of Jayne that leave little to the imagination and that's putting it mildly. Wonder just how she'll explain it to her children when they grow up." Erskine Johnson explained it to his readers with the word "Ugh!" The South African government banned *Jayne Mansfield's Wild, Wild World* as "undesirable, objectionable and obscene."

Jayne should have taken the money—*Jayne Mansfield's Wild, Wild World* got very little press, and sales were disappointing when it was released in August 1962, though it went on to become a camp collector's item. Harrison Carroll wrote that Jayne and Mickey's separation just as the book came out did not help matters, making it seem instantly outdated. "Magazines were bidding for serialization rights. They don't know quite what to do now. It was a love story in which each avowed undying affection for the other."

Harrison Carroll talked with the couple about their marital problems, and wrote that Mickey "doesn't believe that the Italian film executive [Mickey] accuses of trying to sabotage his marriage will have the nerve to come to Hollywood. 'I think he will try to persuade Jayne to go over there, I held my temper in Rome and didn't hit him,'" said Mickey. "I had plenty of chances and I had plenty of power in my arm. But I was trying to be a gentleman." Jayne claimed Bomba had nothing to do with her separation. "I have a verbal agreement to make a picture, maybe more, with him. That's all there is to it." And Bomba himself "hotly denie[d]" to Hedda Hopper that he had come between Jayne and Mickey, claiming he "actually played marriage counselor when the two battled in Rome. 'I am married, I love my wife, and wouldn't leave her.'"

By the end of August, both Jayne and Mickey were putting on a good face about moving forward. Earl Wilson wrote, "Jayne Mansfield's been skin-diving with Tony Kastner, who used to date Kim Novak." Igor Cassini (writing as Cholly Knickerbocker) claimed she was dating Brazilian billionaire Jorge Guinle, who had also been linked with Marilyn Monroe, Ava Gardner, Rita Hayworth, and Susan Hayward. "It's prestigious to have a famous woman on your arm," Guinle said in later years, "but I didn't do it for that reason. I wouldn't say I used them; I liked them and respected them. If I used them, it wasn't my intention." Kathryn Grayburn of the *Atlanta Constitution* saw Jayne in that city with "'airline man about town' Bob Christian at a local nightclub." And Dorothy Kilgallen noted that Mickey was dating actresses Jane Wald and Eva Six (he had known Six in their native Hungary).

As high profile and scandalous as Jayne's life was during August 1962, of course it was overshadowed by the big news: Marilyn Monroe's death on the night of August 4–5. Some papers were caught short: a syndicated AP story running as late as August 6 said, "It will not be a chic season for the Marilyn Monroes and the Jayne Mansfields, for Parisian designers wholeheartedly believe in the flat, or better still, no-chested woman." By August 7 that line had been rewritten as "It will not be a chic season for the Jayne Mansfields."

Rollene Saal of the *Miami News* wrote, "From everyone, the same response: 'OH, NO!' And then silence, as the news of Marilyn Monroe's death was absorbed. . . . Hollywood has plenty of sex-symbols, Jayne Mansfield, Jane Russell and all the other Janes. But they are not so real to us as Marilyn Monroe was. They're symbols all right. A symbol is something you can't touch. Marilyn Monroe had substance." A "man on the street" interview about Marilyn conducted by the *Greenville News* elicited some surprising views: one Donald Byrd said, "Personally I didn't like her. I didn't like the way she acted." Phyllis Gray added, "Of course there are a lot of her type in the world. I didn't think she was a very good actress." And one Mrs. M. G. Merck thought that "she was a beautiful woman, but she had no talent. She and Jayne Mansfield are very much alike."

In one of the many think pieces after Marilyn's death, Lloyd Shearer wrote that

> the one tangential question raised most frequently here is: who will take her place? Talent agents, studio executives, casting directors have

all studied their player lists and selfishly offered such possibilities as Jayne Mansfield, Ziva Rodann, Stella Stevens, Yvette Mimieux and Fay Spain—but for the most part such girls, while bountifully endowed in the physical sense, lack the rare, almost ineffable personality which go into the making of a universal sex symbol. They lack the "It" of Clara Bow, the "oomph" of Betty Grable, the seemingly natural sex innocence of Marilyn. They are either too rutty, too obvious, too specialized in their appeal, or deficient in the art of simultaneously arousing the libido in men and empathy in women.

Jayne herself was one of the many stars contacted for their thoughts on Marilyn. She told Kay Gardella, "I just can't believe it. I'm so sorry. I'm really so sorry."

The death of Marilyn Monroe marked a turning point in Hollywood: the comedic, sexy blonde bombshells went into slow decline. Kim Novak's white-hot career petered out by the end of the 1960s; after a few cameos and character roles, she retired to a ranch in Oregon. Swedish Anita Ekberg hit her peak with Fellini's *La Dolce Vita* and *Boccaccio '70;* she worked intermittently, but her stardom burned out. Zsa Zsa Gabor became a glittering, socialite parody of herself, while sister Eva burst forth as an unexpected comic genius on TV's *Green Acres.* Judy Holliday barely outlasted Marilyn: she made her last film in 1960 and died of cancer five years later.

Several of the B-blondes fared just as badly: Joi Lansing, Barbara Nichols, and Cleo Moore all died young of cancer, as did British Diana Dors (who, at least, had a few years as a blowzy, delightful character actress after putting on weight). Poor Belinda Lee died the same way Jayne did, but even sooner—in 1961, at the age of twenty-five. Dagmar retired from the fray and lived into her seventies, as did her British counterpart Sabrina (who, sadly, wound up as a reclusive hoarder, dying in squalor). Sheree North and Jean Carson enjoyed long careers as character actresses after their sex-symbol days ended.

Mamie Van Doren outlasted them all, through sheer force of will: she refused to acknowledge age or changing tastes. Mamie's acting work faded away in the '60s (she and Jayne would memorably cross paths in 1966), but she persisted in nightclubs, on talk shows, in summer stock, and in personal appearances, still as blonde and bosomy and glamorous in her eighties as she'd been in her twenties, a vision both terrifying and admirable. Marilyn and Jayne, she told interviewer Donald D'Haene in 2013, "are still frozen in time and I am still making my mistakes in front of God and everybody on Facebook and Twitter."

The week of Marilyn's death, one reporter pondered, "Jayne Mansfield may not make many movies, but she certainly hauls in the headlines. Some say, 'If she could only act.' Given a good director, Jayne can act. Remember her in *Wayward Bus?*" That same week, Jayne opened a Thrift City Super Discount Department Store on live TV in Atlanta.

After Marilyn's death, Jayne briefly tried to tone down her image again, as she'd done with her brown-wig flirtation the year before. Already famously bitchy designer Mr. Blackwell—of the "Worst-Dressed List"—said that "I refuse to dress her anymore. I can't go on designing for an actress who shows off my work by either having the dresses ripped off her or wrestling on the floor with them. Besides, I can't stand the shoes she wears—cheap, plastic wedges that went out long ago."

"I'm sick of the old Jayne Mansfield," Jayne told Dorothy Manners while entertaining the troops at Camp Roberts, a California National Guard post. "I feel like a new person inside—and I want that new feeling to be reflected outwardly. I feel like a person who has been going through life wearing dark glasses. And now I have taken them off. I'm seeing things in their true colors for the first time. It's so difficult to explain what has happened to me." She pleaded, "I want so much to be taken seriously, and the best way I can accomplish that is to prove in my work that I'm worthy of serious consideration. All I ask is—please give me the chance."

As if to drive her point home, she showed up for an appearance in Atlanta wearing a conservative black two-piece outfit with a loose-fitting top. She refused to talk about Mickey ("I think everything has been said about my marriage that should be said") but did reflect on Marilyn: "One of the biggest tragedies in the world," Jayne said of her death. "I think it was an accident. She was just a victim of pills." In a rare cracking of her always upbeat, wild, wild world public image, she admitted, "Show business has tremendous pressures. I feel the pressure of being in the spotlight all the time. But I make it a habit never to take those things. It isn't good."

In September Jayne gave a "New Look" cocktail party in New York. "The neckline. Haven't you been reading about it?" she asked the *New York Daily News*'s Charles McHarry. "I never did want people to see me all exposed, and now I have the courage to follow my own convictions. I may go back to my natural hair. This platinum blonde style is . . . you know, garish."

She seemed to be trying to distance herself from the whole Marilyn-clone image, now that it was shadowed by death. "I am a natural dark blonde," said Jayne. "I am not a sex symbol anymore. Well, maybe I was, but I don't like to talk about it."

Jim Bishop wrote of the "new Jayne Mansfield," complaining, "If we must have a Jayne Mansfield, what was the matter with the old one? I was on the Fox lot when Mansfield attained star status. . . . An orphan girl with a talking doll on Christmas morning could not have been happier. Jayne was ecstatic. She had nothing but a shape. Her eyes are small, her mouth large, her natural hair is dark blonde. She had nothing but the will to succeed."

Taking the long view, Bishop went on to note that Jayne's timing had been off. "Unfortunately, it happened at a time when all the great sex sirens were stepping offstage. The big Fox lot is getting smaller. The big studios are back where they started—grinding out two-reel westerns. Hollywood makes fewer pictures, and more expensive ones. Now a new Jayne Mansfield is announced. A conservative woman with a high neckline and a demure smile. Oh no, fellas. Not that."

The relentless Hedda Hopper quizzed Jayne on her new image. "It's just that I accomplished my purpose. The glamour girl was exploited," Jayne said, quite sensibly and correctly. "From now on I want to project the real thing that is inside of me, and I am getting wonderful offers for films that give me an opportunity to do it." She was not getting any such thing, but she went on: "The change in my screen personality will be reflected in my private life. The film business is universal—there's no such thing as an actor living in one place any more. However, I will never sell my pink house here."

But for all her good resolutions, Jayne was still stuck on Enrico Bomba—despite his repeated public protestations that he was not going to divorce his wife. Charles McHarry reported that Jayne "tells friends here that her current love, Italian production aid Enrico Bomba, will marry her and that they'll live happily ever after. Her friends are telling Jayne, on the other hand, that she'd better make other plans."

She flew to the Beirut Film Festival; she managed to smuggle her poodle, Soubie Wee, into Britain and on to Beirut in a bag. The customs inspector complained that "I have had this trouble at the airport before with pets belonging to film stars. Animals coming to Britain are governed by laws to prevent any spread of disease. Even a blind man's guide dog would not be allowed to land here without all the proper formalities."

Then Jayne returned to Rome to accept a Silver Mask Award as "the most popular world entertainment figure of 1962" (in 1961 it had been Elizabeth Taylor; previous winners included Sophia Loren, Anna Magnani, and Federico Fellini). She met Bomba in Rome, and the two of them planned to go to Paris. But they did not, and the stopover in Rome did not go well.

❤

Whatever happened between Jayne and Bomba, she seems to have suffered a breakdown on the way back to London, appearing tired and emotional on the plane ride. Syndicated columnist Robert Corya reported that "Jayne Mansfield arrived in London from Rome today after having cried most of the trip. An airline official said 'she was confused about her luggage and also thought she had lost her passport.' A fellow passenger, Mavis Turner, said Miss Mansfield 'collapsed in tears . . . cried for some time then appeared to go to sleep.'" Sydney businessman Dudley Osborne said that Jayne "was seen off by a man friend at Rome airport and she seemed to be very upset about the parting. She cried for a lot of the flight."

She was helped out of the plane by an airline official after all the other passengers had disembarked, and put on a New York flight; she arrived in New York looking disheveled and weak, but telling reporters "I feel fine." In New York she told Harrison Carroll, "I just couldn't keep from crying. I didn't go to Paris, I stayed in Rome all the time. I saw a lot of Enrico. Very few of the stories have mentioned that he has been separated from his wife for a number of years." Any chance she would reconcile with Mickey? "It's hard to say what will happen in the future. But I doubt that very much. Eventually, I believe I will get a divorce."

Earl Wilson wrote that Jorge Guinle "comforted and consoled" Jayne in a midtown New York hotel. When asked what went wrong with her marriage, Jayne snapped, "You marry him for two years and you tell me 'what went wrong with the marriage.'" She looked downright tragic, clutching a doll she'd bought for Jayne Marie and her Silver Mask Award. "I need an awful lot of time to think and be with my children," she said.

Back in Rome, Bomba continued to insist, "I fail to understand how anyone can suggest that our friendship is a romance. Our friendship has never gone beyond the limits of formal courtesy." The following year Jayne told *Photoplay* that "I was going to marry [Bomba]. He was forty-one, elegant, mature, with impeccable manners and taste. But suddenly I thought of Mickey and the children—and I knew my place was with them. That was the end of that."

But in September 1962 she wanted a divorce and she wanted one now. "California divorces take a year to become final, and when I make up my mind, I want to be able to move," she said, pondering a sketchy Mexican divorce.

Mickey signed the settlement, giving Jayne all their community property: the Pink Palace and their properties in Beverly Hills, Palm Springs, and the San Fernando Valley. Mickey said resignedly, "Jayne is running the show and if that's what she wants she can have it. I'll make it on my own." He bought a 1963 model sports car in white, not pink, equipped with an early car phone, and moved into a house in the Doheny Estates, in the Hollywood Hills, with sunken Roman baths and Grecian pillars.

Mickey was seen out on the town with "physical culturist" Diana Monahan, and Jayne was spotted with millionaires Mike Silverman and Bill Long. And—much to the shock of everyone—in early October Jayne and Enrico Bomba double-dated with Mickey and Jane Wald. "We're all very sophisticated people," said Jayne nonchalantly. Bomba was shopping scripts to Jayne, but her new agent, Kurt Frings, didn't like any of them and ordered her to turn them down.

For all their sophisticated double-dating, Jayne and Mickey were still on the route to divorce, and Jayne wanted that route to be via Mexico. Jayne was still delusionally sure that Enrico Bomba would marry her, even though he had never given the slightest indication that he would—indeed, he had been loudly protesting to the contrary. "It is quite possible that I will marry Enrico Bomba when I get a divorce from Mickey," Jayne insisted. "Enrico is not what people are trying to picture him—an Italian lover. He's a 41-year-old respected businessman. But Mickey doesn't want me to rush into anything. He just wants me to be sure. I admire Mickey because he's sincere in wanting me to do the right thing."

Mickey, increasingly worried about Jayne's emotional state, took the reins. "I decided that I have more of a responsibility than that to Jayne," he said (every moment in their lives, no matter how private, was shared with the press). "I don't believe she knows what she is doing. If she wants to get a divorce in California, that's all right. There would be a year's wait. I don't want anything but for Jayne to be happy. When we agreed on the property settlement, I signed away everything. But I'm not going to let Jayne rush into anything that might be foolish."

He told Vernon Scott that parting from the Pink Palace was nearly as hard as parting from Jayne and the children. "It is heartbreaking for me. I rebuilt that whole place myself, including the swimming pool. I poured my heart and soul into it. At the time of the property settlement I told Jayne it was all hers because I built it exactly as she wanted it. My new home is small by comparison—only four bedrooms. I miss her. If you love a girl once you love her forever. Just the other day she told me she loved me and thought I was a great guy. So there is still hope." Summing up their love in a way that no other love could be summed up, Mickey sighed, "I am going to build a new swimming pool, but it will not be heart-shaped. A man builds only one heart-shaped pool in his life."

Decades later, looking back from a third, happy marriage, Mickey was still struggling to figure it all out. "It's very difficult to be married to Jayne Mansfield," he said, with admirable understatement. "It wasn't easy. . . . I was tolerant. I don't know, maybe in one sense maybe I'm dominating, I don't know. Maybe I was too close to her. I don't think I could be a tough guy or demand, or be dictatorial. Maybe it was all my fault? It's possible, it may be. I tried to change, in many ways."

Getting away from Mickey and Enrico and the whole divorce mess, Jayne flew to Pittsburgh to do a cameo appearance onstage at the Carnegie Music Hall. *An Evening without Desdemona Fink* was an offbeat revue, a real change of pace for Jayne. She appeared—unannounced and unbilled— in a black dress and did the twist.

❤

Another change of pace, and a more high-profile one, came in November, when Jayne scored a real coup, costarring with Tony Randall on *The Alfred Hitchcock Hour*. This was the 1962–1965 series Hitchcock produced after his more popular *Alfred Hitchcock Presents* went off the air; still, it employed such great writers as Ray Bradbury, Richard Matheson, Patricia Highsmith, and Harlan Ellison, and directors Sydney Pollack, William Friedkin, and Hitchcock himself. Big stars, young upcomers, and respected character actors knocked each other over to obtain roles, perhaps thinking this might lead to work in one of Hitchcock's feature films. So it was a hopeful sign for Jayne to be cast, especially opposite her old *Rock Hunter* costar. Both Jayne and Randall were eager to appear in a dark drama and break loose from their comic personas.

Randall had also been suffering from typecasting—as the whiny comic sidekick—complaining that "since the *Mr. Peepers* series, no one has taken me seriously. *Mr. Peepers* almost ruined me. I decided to latch on to some serious, meaty roles, even if I had to play a deep-dyed villain. This Hitchcock drama is the gutsiest thing I've ever done, although the director [TV veteran Bernard Girard] filmed my opening scene three different ways to insure against the possibility that people would laugh at me."

A big publicity campaign was put out that Jayne had her hair cut short for the role, but she is obviously wearing a short wig over whatever was left of her own hair, and it did not flatter her. The wig was good for that one TV role, and she was brave to try it, but after a few newspaper stories publicized it, she wisely gave it up.

The episode, entitled "The Hangover," aired on December 6, with Randall as Hadley Purvis, an advertising man in denial about his alcoholism. One morning he wakes up after a binge, his wife missing, and last night's pickup, Marion (Jayne), sitting amiably in the living room (it's 1962, so after a supposed night of wild sex, the two wake up in mussed-up twin beds, separated by a large night table, Purvis wearing buttoned-up pajamas). He loses his job (the man who takes it over is named Hunter, an in-joke in an otherwise dead-serious show). Things do not end happily.

It's not one of Hitchcock's better outings: the story isn't particularly suspenseful (the "shock ending" can be guessed halfway through), and it's told in increasingly annoying flashbacks. But both Tony Randall and Jayne come through; Randall increasingly desperate and Jayne giving a quiet, unmannered performance as his sad and slightly menacing pickup.

Incidentally, Hitchcock eschewed his usual snarky sign-off for a serious public-service speech about alcoholism: "I feel that tonight's subject is an unsuitable one for humor. Alcoholism is being recognized as one of the most serious diseases of our society."

Reviews of the episode were mixed, though Jayne's performance was largely brushed off. The *Decatur Herald* wrote that "Randall, a familiar comedy face, proves his worth in this dramatic role, which is a bit more than can be said for costar Jayne Mansfield." The *Philadelphia Inquirer* hated the episode, calling it "a most unpleasant ordeal to sit through," and cruelly mentioned Jayne's "unflattering shaggy coiffure and . . . tight-fitting dress and bath towel, a bulging excess of avoirdupois." Only Herb Lyon in the *Chicago Tribune* ran a kind squib: "Jayne Mansfield's new acting image, straight from the shoulder talk, closely cropped hair, etc., as revealed via an

Alfred Hitchcock TV hour last week, is the talk of show biz. The unnerving dumb-blonde gurgling is out and Jayne's career has taken a sharp upturn."

❤

Mickey stopped by the Alfred Hitchcock set to say hello; he and Jayne went out on a friendly date to La Scala. But she still wanted that quick Mexican divorce. "Mickey asked me to wait awhile," she told the AP. "He's still hoping for a reconciliation. I may not seek the decree for a month, perhaps even two months." Mickey sighed that "Jayne called me last Monday and said she wanted to go ahead. I told her that I wouldn't oppose the idea any longer. I met her at the office of her attorney, Greg Bautzer. I signed the necessary papers."

By the end of November Jayne was sounding increasingly addled: either deeply in love or totally delusional. She told Harrison Carroll, "I just can't make up my mind what to do, whether to get a divorce or to try again with Mickey. He is a wonderful man." Two days later the UPI reported, "Jayne Mansfield announced today that she will marry an Italian film producer April 7 in Paris, where she will make her permanent home. 'I cannot name the man I will marry for legal reasons, but everything is settled. . . . I am devoting all my time to studying the Italian language, Italian literature and art. I don't go out on dates and I'm going to be in early every night. I have discovered a beautiful new world. We will live in Paris for a year or two after the wedding, and then settle down in Italy.'" Jayne was very coy about his name, but every single newspaper just came right out with "Enrico Bomba."

Bomba did arrive in New York in December, for another of their "sophisticated" get-togethers. He was stripped-searched by customs agents at Idlewild Airport, where Jayne and a Chihuahua greeted him. Earl Wilson dined with Jayne and Bomba at the Four Seasons. "Breathily, Jayne gasped of her love for Bomba. He evidently told her later that marriage was out," Wilson reported. "'Jayne does everything based on the publicity she thinks she can get,' a friend said later. 'She will try to revive the Bomba romance again in a few months. Ask Jayne if she'd like to see a movie and she'll say, Will there be any photographers there? She doesn't care what the movie is.'"

To the utter bafflement (and increasing annoyance) of the press and whatever public was still paying attention, Jayne and Mickey invited reporters to the Pink Palace on Christmas Eve to announce their reconciliation, and to reveal that she was going to make a film with Enrico Bomba called *The Italian Lover* (amusingly misprinted in one paper as *The Italian Liver*). Mickey gamely joked, "We're going to change the name of the picture to *The Hungarian Lover*." "We're still good friends," Jayne said of Bomba. "A woman has a right to change her mind, and I am a woman. I was out to dinner in New York with Mr. Bomba and some friends and I just felt like I wanted to reconcile with Mickey." Jayne gave Mickey a Chihuahua as a reconciliation and Christmas gift, because Mickey really needed another Chihuahua.

"I am throwing away my pizza and spaghetti recipes and learning how to cook goulash," Jayne exulted, and Mickey added happily, "I'm shocked! I was planning a quiet Christmas—nothing as exciting as this. When she said she was coming back, I said, 'you're kidding.'" One newsman begged, "Please don't change your mind again after our next edition."

That Christmas May Mann threw a party at her home, inviting—among many others—Jayne and seventy-seven-year-old silent-screen star Mae Murray. If anyone in Hollywood might have provided a cautionary tale for Jayne, it was Murray. A dancer in the *Ziegfeld Follies* in the 1910s, she went on to become a huge star at Universal and MGM in the 1920s. Mannered and imperious but also sweet and generous, Murray—like Jayne—lived in an oblivious pink bubble where she was the world's most beloved star and no tragedy could ever touch her.

Mae Murray was—again like Jayne—a talented actress when she had a good script and a strict director. Otherwise, she fell into posing and pouting (she went by the peculiarly unpleasant nickname the Girl with the Bee-Stung Lips). Her career and life fell apart with stunning speed: Murray walked out on her MGM contract to marry a faux prince, and by the 1930s found herself broke, homeless, and with her child taken away. When she attended May Mann's party in 1962, she was living on the kindness of strangers, still convinced she was the greatest star, still dressing and acting as if it were 1925.

Mann recalled, "Producers, directors and the various guests gathered around her. She was a super-star again, seated on a white satin chair, like a queen." Then Jayne entered, "in white fox furs over white mink, and with her diamonds glistening, stole the attention, although not intentionally, away from Mae Murray. People thoughtlessly left Mae to hover over the glamorous, younger, today star. Mae sat there, silently watching . . . wearing hand-me-down clothes of movie stars, living on charity."

20

Would you like *your* wife to go out there and take her clothes off? I didn't like it. Not at all. . . . I think that was a turning point.

Mickey Hargitay

Jayne's maternal grandmother Beatrice Palmer, eighty-two, died in a nursing home on January 9, 1963, but it was announced that Jayne would not attend the funeral, as "she is starting a new film today." She would have been well advised to go to that funeral, and bury that new film along with her grandmother.

It was at this point that Jayne made the most inexplicable, self-destructive move of her career, one that tipped her over from fading star to unemployable dirty joke. Actually, it was two moves: she agreed to star in the cheesy soft-core porn film *Promises. . . . Promises!* and to pose topless for *Playboy.*

Promises. . . . Promises! was the pet project of Tommy Noonan, a once-promising actor now in his early forties and struggling. Noonan excelled at playing weak-chinned nerds, most memorably in *Gentlemen Prefer Blondes* as Marilyn Monroe's millionaire fiancé, Gus Esmond Jr. He was also seen to great effect in *A Star Is Born,* and had a nightclub act with Peter Marshall (later a successful game-show host). But by 1963 Noonan's career was reduced to walk-ons and TV guest spots.

Nothing if not driven and ambitious, he bought a play called *Promise Her Anything,* which had to be changed to the oddly punctuated *Promises.*

. . . Promises! after the perfume company Arpège threatened to sue: "Promise Her Anything . . . but Give Her Arpège" was its highly successful advertising slogan. The play—which had never made it to Broadway—was a broad sex farce about two couples on a ship, and their attempts to get pregnant.

Noonan cowrote the script (with TV writer William Welch), co-produced (with Donald F. Taylor), and hired veteran King Donovan to direct. But the project was Noonan's all the way. He managed to raise $450,000 from countless investors: Joseph Finnigan of the UPI wrote that Noonan was "hemmed in on all side by partners, waiting for a return on their investment. . . . Tommy was long on ambition and short on dough. 'I had to get the money from individuals, friends and strangers. They've all been great. Part of the deal was that they would have no say in production as far as creativity is concerned.'" With unabashed optimism, he said, "They can't possibly lose . . . they'll have their money back 120 days after the picture is released."

Jayne was signed at $50,000; her costar was to be Mamie Van Doren. That fell apart the minute Mamie found out that Jayne was getting 2½ percent of the profits in addition to salary. "I have nothing against Jayne at all," said Mamie. "We've met several times, and I like Jayne very much. I'm sorry we won't be making the picture together, because the two of us would have been very good in the roles. I'd love to work with Jayne sometime in the future. I think it would be fun." But not 2½ percent profits' worth of fun. Jayne also proclaimed herself "disappointed we won't be working together. Mamie would have been a big plus in the picture. But if she was unhappy with the arrangements I certainly understand why she didn't accept the role. It would be wonderful if another picture came along that would be good for both of us." Tommy Noonan ducked all blame: "Mamie must have misunderstood what I told her agent."

Out with Mamie; in with Marie McDonald who, like Noonan, found her once-hot career going cold. McDonald—who would turn forty in 1963—was embarrassingly nicknamed The Body by the press ("Wasn't that awful!" she said of that tag). A band singer with Tommy Dorsey and an Earl Carroll and George White showgirl, McDonald was a 1940s pin-up girl with movie roles in such lightweight fare as *Pardon My Sarong, Getting Gertie's Garter,* and *Living in a Big Way.* A terrific comic actress in a sardonic Eve Arden manner, she said in '63 that she had done "cheesecake and leg art. Now I deserve to graduate. I've turned down a lot of parts, cheesecake, clotheshorse and other dull things. This picture is a comedy and the girl I play also sings two songs."

The husbands of Jayne and Marie would be played by Noonan and Mickey Hargitay—in a twist, Tommy Noonan would be matched with Jayne and Mickey with Marie.

The film was to be shot on the cheap, in twenty-eight days, on a set at Los Angeles's KTTV studios, with a few days of location shots on the SS *Independence,* a popular cruise ship. In a portent of major problems to come, Noonan announced to the *Los Angeles Times* that the film "includes a nude scene with Jayne Mansfield for European distribution." Did Noonan have trouble getting Jayne to agree to this scene? "Not at all. You see, she's a partner too."

Noonan was not apologetic about working on a shoestring budget, and he did have two decades of studio experience to back him up. "I just can't stand incompetence. I think that's what killed the big studios," he told the *L.A. Times.* "A picture that costs $1 million is no funnier than a picture that costs half that. I don't want to sound like a nutty gambler. I did risk everything, but before I went into this I took my package and sent out feelers as to what the picture is worth." But producing a film was one thing—getting it distributed was another matter entirely.

He told the *Times* that he hoped to make eight films a year, which even he must have known was impossible. "There's a feeling of grim earnestness" on the set, the reporter noted. "But in the midst of all this he also manages moments of calm." Noonan told the reporter, "People keep saying, 'let's make it better.' . . . Every day people come to me and say, 'we can add this or add that.' They have good ideas, but if it's not within our budget my answer has to be no."

Noonan had nothing but praise for Jayne, telling reporter Eve Starr, "She's a great comedienne. If I hadn't faith in her talent, I wouldn't have gone into debt producing this film, and given her a percentage as added inducement to play the lead." Echoing what other costars and directors would say, Noonan noted admiringly, "She's very professional in her work. She's on time, even earlier than the first call, ready with her lines, and is willing to knock herself out getting the scene right. She's worked late with no complaints." He told Herb Michelson of the *Oakland Tribune,* "When she gets out there on the set, she's simply overwhelming. All this nutty publicity of hers is really unnecessary. She could forget it, but she seems dedicated to getting her name in the papers."

Marie McDonald found herself shunted to one side as Jayne's role grew, but—like Noonan—she had enough show-business years under her belt to shrug it off. "We tried to give them equal billing. But it just didn't work out that way," Noonan said, somewhat ingenuously. "Without question, it's Mansfield's picture. For instance, both of them had song numbers. Then, we had to cut Marie's. She's a pro, though, didn't mind at all, told me the number really didn't belong in the picture."

In May 1962 Marilyn Monroe had filmed a nude swimming scene for her uncompleted *Something's Got to Give*—but the nudity was for on-set photographers only. The released film was to have shown just glimpses of her shoulders and back. Jayne, however, brandished her breasts to the cameras three times in *Promises*. Jayne's nude scenes are actually worked into the film quite naturally: she's taking a bubble bath; she's drying off afterward; she's lolling in bed post-sex. The actions are much more normal than holding up a sheet to cover her breasts in bed, as actresses still do today. But what Jayne probably did not know—and Mickey certainly didn't—is that those brief nude scenes would be shown again and again and again throughout the film in totally gratuitous flashbacks. It was shameless of Noonan, but he knew what would bring in the audiences.

Columnist Harrison Carroll was determined to be on the set for the Big Day. "There are about 20 technicians on the set and they are definitely on the qui-vive," he wrote. "There have been a few delays. When I arrive, they are still shooting the American version. Even this is a lot more interesting than a page from the telephone book. . . . Impatience is the keynote of the set. Everybody wants to get on with the scene. Naturally a little rehearsal is required. Jayne, swathed in a towel, listens carefully while director Donovan explains that she must be leaning over with her hand on the door knob as she makes her entrance."

Jayne's professionalism (and the sheer dullness of shooting a film) comes across: "'I'll try,' she says, 'but if I have to use my right hand to open the door, how am I going to hold the towel up?' But Jayne is a resourceful girl. When the camera turns, she opens the door, still maneuvers the king-size towel to cover all the strategic areas. 'Okay, print!' calls director Donovan. 'Now will everybody who isn't necessary here please clear the set?'"

At this, flats were put up to hide Jayne's portion of the set from onlookers, and assistant director Cy Roth chided the crew, "Come on, fellows, are you really needed for this shot?" Marie McDonald wandered by and— maybe not so complacent about getting her song cut after all—snarked to Carroll, "I've been called 'The Body' for years. Do you know why? Because I never show it." Roth also tossed Carroll off the set, though the columnist gamely joked, "'I have to stay. I'm an observer for the UN. And besides, what is this, the version for Europe or Mars?' So what happens? Out I go."

Mickey went, too, or so he later claimed. "I was preoccupied with other members of the cast, and it was 'shh-shh-shh,'" he said. "I felt betrayed at the time, because I knew something was going on, and it did happen. I was so pissed-off at Tommy Noonan, I literally knocked him out."

Why did Jayne agree to do nude scenes, and in such a cheap film? She was not stupid or naïve when it came to show business—she had to have known no major studio would star her after this, and that family-friendly TV would be off-limits. But she had to work, even if she was a big nude fish in a small scummy pond. "She's pushing it too much, she didn't want it to stop," said Mickey. "I kept saying to her, 'don't bother, honey, sit down, relax, choose your script.' If she'd have asked, I would have said 'no—don't do a nude scene in a bathtub.' I don't think at the time of her life it was appropriate for her."

Jayne Marie agreed, later perceptively recognizing that "the first role that pivoted her up to semi-stardom was that of a dumb blonde. And I think that, unfortunately, down the line is the downfall, because you're talking of an era that ended pretty quickly. I think she was misunderstood, but it was her own doing. She was the one that walked in there and said, 'this is what I want, and I'll take it and I'll do it,' not realizing the consequences."

And so, by February *Promises. . . . Promises!* was done, and Jayne flew to Georgia for a Cerebral Palsy telethon. The plane ran into bad weather. "I've flown thousands of miles, but never was so scared in my life," said Jayne. "The plane bobbed up and down so much I thought the seat belts would snap." She (and fellow star passengers Michael Landon and singer Molly Bee) landed safely, and Jayne played the violin on the telethon ("recognizable but a trifle flat," according to one reviewer).

Meanwhile, Tommy Noonan prepared for a fight with the Motion Picture Association of America, run by Geoffrey Shurlock since the retirement of the notorious Joseph Breen in 1954. *Promises. . . . Promises!* was to have been released in Europe with Jayne's nude scenes intact, and in the US with them cut. It's not known if this was done behind Jayne's back, but Noonan managed to get the censorship office to agree that the film could be released, complete with nude scenes, unrated in the US—but not to major theaters, and not by any reputable studio or distributor. In essence, it was to be an "art film." Or, as Neely O'Hara memorably scoffed in *Valley of the Dolls,* "Nudies, that's all they are—*nudies!*"

"There has been an unprecedented demand from the art houses to include the nude scenes," said Noonan. "So I am going to recut the picture and put them in." And with that, Jayne's career veered wildly off-track. "I think that was a turning point," Mickey said later, "when she did the film I truly believe she should not have done."

Jayne later complained—perhaps with just cause—that she had shot the nude scenes only for European release, and that she felt angry and betrayed that Noonan was releasing them in the US. But the world was shrinking by 1963: American vacationers could easily see the film in Europe, and film buffs could collect the scenes on pirated prints (as indeed happened). Her "European" scenes could be screened in stag parties and rumpus rooms from Bryn Mawr to Sacramento. Louis R. Cedrone Jr. of the *Baltimore Sun* wrote that Jayne "has reportedly given the producer permission to sell 8mm copies of her nude scenes in the film to a private company which will sell them to movie fans. Both Jayne and the producer, Tommy Noonan, will profit by the deal—artistically as well as financially since she did the film, she said, as a contribution to art."

Promises. . . . Promises! opened nationwide in August 1963, and was still playing in scattered theaters at the time of Jayne's death, in "art houses" and porn theaters, advertised as "from the pages of *Playboy:* the uncut, uncensored European version . . . (all of) Jayne Mansfield." "Barefoot to her eyebrows!" One newspaper ad featured the unfortunately accurate line "The adult comedy riot that had the whole country aghast!"

Stanley Eichelbaum of the *San Francisco Examiner* was certainly aghast, calling *Promises. . . . Promises!* "the dullest, most unpromising comedy of the year . . . the film is so confoundingly tedious that it's quite a problem staying awake long enough for Jayne's exhibition." Mickey, said Eichelbaum—rather unfairly—gave "the most atrociously wooden performance I have ever seen in a professionally-made film. A chimpanzee could have done the role with more style."

Most of the reviews were equally vicious: "This is not a movie; it's an insult. . . . Better you should buy a girlie magazine. It's cheaper, more permanent, and you can take it home with you" (Herb Michelson, the *Oakland Tribune*). Charles Moore of the *Atlanta Constitution* wrote, "It has a silly story apparently written by a 15-year-old . . . if anyone cares to see such a film, they should be permitted to—it'd serve them right."

"I laughed in what was apparently all the wrong places because the predominantly male audience (were college students given the day off?)

didn't laugh along with me," wrote Louis Cedrone Jr., adding of Jayne's bed scene, "I didn't laugh immediately because I thought she was in pain, then when I realized this was Jayne's way of getting the most out of a frame, I laughed again." Cedrone also referred to openly gay cast member T. C. Jones's character as "a deviate hairdresser," then allowed that the film "ought to do good business. . . . I had trouble finding a seat, and I saw an early morning showing."

Cedrone confronted the theater manager, who defended himself, about the appropriateness of screening the film. When angry neighbors asked him, "'Why do you show trash like this? Why don't you show more family pictures?' My answer to them is, 'where were you when we played *Mr. Limpet* at the Stanton and where were you when we played other family films?' The truth is that people don't always want family films. They want to see Sophia Loren do a strip tease and they want to see Jayne Mansfield in the nude."

The only good review appeared in the *Anniston Star*: "Jayne . . . proves without a doubt that she hasn't been getting by on her lovely face and figure alone. . . . Her performance stamp[s] Jayne as one of the bright new comediennes on the scene today." And not one mention of nudity.

By September 1963 several cities had banned *Promises. . . . Promises!*, including Detroit, Chicago, Memphis, New York, and Atlanta. No major movie company would distribute it; the producers were peddling it directly to whatever theaters would have it. In April it was ruled obscene in Cleveland, with Judge Hugh Corrigan declaring in no uncertain terms, "The producers and directors of this movie found it necessary to include three scenes in which Miss Mansfield displayed fully her elephantine charms accompanied by writhings, squirmings and gyrations."

It played on double bills at porn theaters with such fare as *Mary Had a Little*. Jayne and Mickey appeared in person at the Little Theater in Newark in early March, where *Promises. . . . Promises!* was billed as "the Colossus of Nudie Films." Noonan bragged in 1964 that "I made *Promises. . . . Promises!* for $206,000 and after the critics panned it as tasteless and vulgar, the people lined up outside the theaters. It has brought in one and a half million already and it's still going strong. We haven't even hit the foreign markets yet."

Jayne defended herself and the film, even though she may have been taken by surprise that her nude scenes appeared in the US version. "There are two scenes in which I appear nude for a brief moment," she admitted.

"The only objections I've heard is that the scenes are not long enough." When told of the Cleveland ban, she politely brushed over the "elephantine" crack and said, "I hope the police and the judges enjoyed it. They didn't ban it until they had seen it a couple of times." Even Mickey managed to loyally swallow his reservations long enough to say that the ban was "ridiculous. Anything Jayne does in movies is artistic. As far as her being nude was concerned, everybody came into the world nude. Even the policemen who closed the show were born nude. It's a shame they did it. After all, sex is here to stay."

Promises. . . . Promises! is really not that dreadful—no more painful than an episode of *The Love Boat*. The plot involves two couples on a cruise ship: Sandy and Jeff (Jayne and Tommy Noonan) and Claire and King (Marie McDonald and Mickey). Sandy and Jeff want desperately to have a baby, and the ship's doctor prescribes a placebo: zany mix-ups result in both women pregnant, and confusion about who is whose father.

Jayne gives a perfectly good performance and sings (quite nicely) "Promise Her Anything," mingling with the shipboard audience just as she would later in her nightclub act. Tommy Noonan does a Tony Randall imitation: the nervous Nellie of many a sitcom. Mickey—bless his heart—does his best. Marie McDonald is superb—looking trim and lovely, she plays Mickey's cynical, wisecracking wife with a sharp edge, stealing every scene she's in.

The film is helped out by a supporting cast of great character actors: Fritz Feld, Eddie Quillan, Marjorie Bennett; even director King Donovan's wife, comic great Imogene Coca, makes a cameo appearance; singer and vaudeville veteran Eileen Barton aces a nice bit at the film's end. Another scene-stealer is female impersonator and impressionist T. C. Jones, who plays the ship's hairdresser, Babette. In a scene that's the pinnacle of camp, he gives Sandy a box of wigs for her baby shower, and dons them for impersonations of Tallulah Bankhead (quite good), Bette Davis (hilarious), and Jayne Mansfield (terrible, but the meta-joke makes it work, as Jayne joins in: "I can do her, too!").

Tommy Noonan did not produce those eight films a year he'd hoped to. In 1964 he starred in, wrote, produced, and directed another indie sex comedy, *3 Nuts in Search of a Bolt,* with Mamie Van Doren. He tried to interest Jayne in *Jayne Mansfield Meets Frankenstein* (which actually might have been a delight), but she turned him down. Louis Cedrone Jr. joked, "If Noonan is really serious about Jaynie and the monster, and if it is successful, we'll probably have meetings between Jaynie, Dracula, the Wolf Man and The Body Snatchers."

Promises. . . . Promises!, like *Rebel without a Cause, Poltergeist,* and *The Conqueror,* acquired a reputation for being a cursed film: out of all the principals, only Mickey lived more than another decade. Marie McDonald overdosed on sleeping pills in 1965; Tommy Noonan died of a brain tumor in 1968; T. C. Jones died of cancer in 1971.

In retrospect, one wonders, what could Jayne have been thinking? Even without the nudity—and that's a big "without"—*Promises. . . . Promises!* was a cheap indie film that could do nothing but harm her career. She made a lot of money, but she could have gotten just as much from a more respectable European film, Las Vegas, or even TV. The only explanation is that Jayne *didn't* think, she just jumped in headfirst—Tommy Noonan, for all the spineless characters he played, was actually a steamroller.

❤

In 1962, wrote Louella Parsons, Publimetrix, which measures how many times a person is mentioned in the papers that year, named Bob Hope the number one celebrity—with Jayne as number two, surpassing both Elizabeth Taylor and Marilyn.

She was not mentioned in any of the New York papers from December 8, 1962, until March 31, 1963, due to that city's newspaper strike (which killed the *New York Daily Mirror*). "Talk about sour timing," wrote Walter Winchell. "Jayne Mansfield, poor thing, reconciled with her husband just as the New York papers stopped."

But still, all through January and February, while *Promises. . . . Promises!* was being shot, Jayne and Mickey used the willing press as their marriage counselors. Dave Freeman of the *Hartford Courant* dined with Jayne and shared with his readers that "there is very little hope that Jayne Mansfield's reconciliation will be a lasting one. Jayne said, 'I'm going to try real hard to work things out with Mickey. But I can't seem to get Enrico out of my mind.'" Dorothy Kilgallen felt that the whole Enrico Bomba romance was for publicity, while Earl Wilson insisted she was serious about Bomba, as Mickey was about Jane Wald.

In March Mickey beat the stuffing out of Jayne's hairdresser Lynn Hardy, who filed a $40,000 battery suit against him. Hardy claimed that on February 21 he was talking with Jayne at 3:00 a.m. after returning from a party, and Mickey pulled him out of his car and roughed him up, leaving him bleeding and semi-conscious. Mickey denied the incident had ever happened. "I've been thinking it over and weighing our problems for more than a year," said Jayne shortly after this episode. "I think it's better that we go our separate ways. Where there isn't love and affection between the parents, it's very injurious to the children."

Speaking from her engagement at Gus Stevens's Supper Club in Biloxi—where she had an appointment with destiny four years later—Jayne said that she planned to go to Juarez, Mexico, soon to get a quickie divorce. "It probably will be better if we're divorced. It's difficult for two people separated five months to adjust to circumstances. We're both intelligent people and will attempt to work this out in California next week when we get together. We both want each other to be happy and whichever way this is possible, we will choose." A week after her thirtieth birthday, while playing an engagement at Buffalo's Glen Casino, Jayne visited honeymoon haven Niagara Falls, on her own.

❤

Promises. . . . Promises! was only the first of a one-two punch to Jayne's reputation. Mickey and Harrison Carroll may have been shooed from the set during Jayne's nude scene, but photographer Bill Kobrin from *Playboy* was present, with Jayne's approval. In later years Raquel Welch, Madonna, Goldie Hawn, Sharon Stone, and other, lesser stars doffed their clothes for *Playboy.* Marilyn Monroe had appeared nude in a 1953 issue—but it was a 1949 pin-up, printed in *Playboy* over Marilyn's objections. After Jayne, it wasn't till Julie Newmar's 1968 photo spread that anyone approaching a major star became a Playmate.

With the cover teaser "The Nudest Jayne Mansfield," the article showed Jayne being primped in her dressing room and lolling about in bed, breasts and backside fully exposed (but no full-frontal nudity). For those who bought *Playboy* "for the articles," there were also pieces by Ray Bradbury, Ian Fleming, Shel Silverstein, and an interview with Billy Wilder.

The magazine—the June issue—hit newsstands in late May, but it was being talked about in shocked and disgusted tones way before then. Jayne professed herself to be blindsided, innocently batting her eyes and claiming, "I did not want these pictures published in the United States. Europeans have a much more adult outlook on nudity than Americans. I do not know how Hefner obtained those photographs. But he always gets the picture he wants." Hefner flat-out called her a liar: "That's untrue, completely untrue. The pictures were arranged with her and her agent before the motion picture began. The pictures were taken by our own people with her full consent and cooperation."

Columnist Herb Caen wrote that Jayne's friend makeup artist Ron Bygum told him that Jayne had been paid $10,000 by *Playboy* for the American rights, another $10,000 for the European rights, and that Tommy Noonan had added $30,000 to her paycheck for the additional publicity this would bring to his film (that last bit is questionable, as her whole salary for the film was $50,000). "That 'terrible' spread means my three kids will go to prep school and college and have a nest egg besides," Bygum claimed Jayne told him.

Although she denied knowing that the photos would appear in *Playboy,* Jayne took pride in them, or at least put on a good face about it. "Beauty cannot be obscene," she said, adding, "All my friends are writing to say I've never looked more beautiful."

Mickey was unable to mask his feelings. When *Photoplay*'s Jim Hoffman asked him about the *Playboy* spread, Mickey snapped, "Would you like *your* wife to go out there and take her clothes off? I didn't like it. Not at all. Am I ashamed of these pictures? No. Embarrassed? No. They're beautiful. Beautiful. That's what I finally said to myself. But if the layout had been submitted to me for my okay—I must admit I'd have torn them up."

Gossip columnists and entertainment writers agreed that Mickey should have torn them up. The always-censorious Hedda Hopper wrote, "I doubt Jayne will ever live down the nude pictures in that girly magazine that soon will be on the stands," and she was right. Louis Sobol wondered "how Jayne will explain them to her growing children, whom she claims she is trying to rear to be normal, unspoiled, non-exhibitionist individuals." Jayne contended that "right now the children think of me only as their mother, not as a movie star or glamour girl. When they grow up, I'm sure they'll understand why I've lived as I have."

Bob Freund of the *Fort Lauderdale News* was aghast: "The utter tastelessness displayed in the multi-page color layout could spell the wind-up of Jayne's somewhat frazzled career. If she had been a nobody, it would still have been in bad taste, but since she does have an international name, and a reputation as a sex symbol of sorts, wasn't it unwise of her to go practically the whole way? You've done spilled the beans." And the *Miami News* joked, "Confidential to Jayne Mansfield: I wouldn't worry too much about it. All of us from time to time get the funny feeling that everybody is looking at us."

The only people happy with the photos—besides *Playboy* readers—were Hugh Hefner and Tommy Noonan. Earl Wilson noted that "Jayne Mansfield's naked poses helped *Playboy* hit a record two million," and a Chicago newsstand operator observed, "I could have sold 50 this morning if I had them."

The courts and the government weighed in as well. That same year, publisher Ralph Ginzburg was arrested for selling *Eros* magazine through the mail: it contained nude photos of Marilyn Monroe, taken shortly before her death by Bert Stern. (*Eros* also poked fun at the Kennedys, and Attorney General Robert did not take kindly to that.) After years of battles, the Supreme Court convicted Ginzburg in 1966.

The June 1963 issue of *Playboy* was brandished on the floor of the South Carolina Senate during a debate on censorship. "Hold it higher!" yelled a senator from the rear. Senator J. B. Lawson showed the magazine to Senator James P. Stevens and shouted, "Do you think this is good for young folks?" One newspaper reported, "The question, or maybe Miss Mansfield, caught Stevens off guard. If he made any reply, it was drowned out by the chorus of senators wanting a look at what might not be good for young folks."

In early June, as the magazine was being snapped up off newsstands, Hugh Hefner was arrested. Chicago municipal judge Norman N. Elger issued an obscenity warrant after city attorney Manuel L. Port said the photos could not be considered "art," because Jayne "writhes about seductively." Hefner was released on $400 bond, after being fingerprinted and having his mug shot taken. A warrant against Hefner was also taken out in New York, though it would not be served unless he showed up there. Nassau County (New York) district attorney William Cahn said the photos showed Jayne in "obscene and provocative positions which do not appeal to the general artistic senses, but appeal primarily to the prurient (lascivious) interests."

At a late June hearing, Chicago lawyer Manuel Post waved the *Playboy* issue before Judge Nicholas J. Matkovic, calling it "filth for filth's sake . . . the most prurient kind of pornography I have ever seen." (It's safe to assume that Mr. Post did not get out much; newsstands and drugstores carried an array of such girlie mags as *Cocktail, French Follies, Daring Dolls, Busty, Highball, Bachelor Party,* and *Black Silk Stockings.*) Judge Matkovic recessed the proceeding, saying he wanted to "examine the evidence." By the end of July the case began to fizzle out: Judge Matkovic decided it was to be tried as a civil matter (they were still arguing about whether correspondence between Jayne and Hefner would be admissible as evidence).

The trial resulted in a hung jury, in December '63, with seven out of twelve voting for acquittal.

In late 1963 Jack Major of the *Akron Beacon Journal* asked Jayne about cheesecake photos, and she admitted, "I realize I never would have gotten anywhere without cheesecake, so I don't see anything wrong with continuing to pose for cheesecake pictures." She claimed—counter to Hefner's statements—that "the *Playboy* photographer visited the set on a day we were taking routine stills as part of the movie's publicity. The pictures were supposed to be used in the European campaign. I had no idea they would appear in this country." She also said, "My nude scenes in *Promises, Promises* were harmless because there was no man-woman contact in the picture. In fact, I was the only person in those scenes. What I think are obscene are movies which show men and women semi-nude in bed or where there is a hint of complete nudity with man-woman contact."

Hedda Hopper did not approve. "Our actresses who have been so anxious to take off their clothes on screen and in magazines must be crazy," she wrote. "Take Jayne Mansfield. Her career's about finished—everybody's seen everything." Hopper also took Mamie Van Doren to task and longed for the days of Florenz Ziegfeld, "who in all his years never showed a wholly naked woman." Dorothy Kilgallen, perhaps in a jab at Hedda, wrote, "Never mind what the critics say, Jayne Mansfield spells glamor and causes excitement wherever she goes. At Cavanaugh's [restaurant] she autographed menus, napkins, newspapers—anything the customers could get their hands on."

In early 1963 the public first began hearing hints that Jayne was developing a drinking problem. Like so many actresses (and nonactresses) of the day, she took sleeping pills at night, and amphetamines during the day to lose weight and for energy. Now the woman who had admitted a liking for pink champagne and the occasional cocktail was beginning to rely on liquor to hold back the panic and anxiety that were becoming part of her daily life. In March 1963 Jayne flew to Reno to be the Mystery Guest on *I've Got a Secret*, but was apparently too drunk to go on, so Carol Burnett subbed for her. Dorothy Kilgallen was coy about it: "For a couple of reasons the very patient Garry Moore became impatient with her." Eve Starr in the *Pottstown Mercury* reported that Jayne "suddenly became ill on arrival ('Probably the altitude,' she said)."

Despite their personal problems, Jayne and Mickey agreed to appear together at the Atlanta Copa, her first nightclub appearance in the South. The act would be sexy, Jayne promised: "I don't want to get away from being a sexpot. I enjoy it, as a matter of fact. I just want to add other things to it." Mickey Jr. came along on the trip. "He loves the sunshine and the blossoming of the dogwoods," said Jayne, "and of course he's a seasoned traveler already: he loves to go!" In Europe, she added, "children just naturally accompany their parents to all sorts of places, shopping, sightseeing, even to parties." The two-week engagement was a success: "Jayne Mansfield packed 'em in at the Copa," wrote the *Atlanta Constitution*. "She has completed her run and returned to Hollywood before going to Spain to begin work on her next film."

En route from Atlanta to Hollywood, though, there was a fracas in Chicago, where Jayne and Mickey were photographed yelling at each other in a nightclub. One witness claimed that Jayne slapped Mickey and flounced out. When a man offered to escort her home, Mickey grabbed her away and she fell to the pavement. He parked her in a phone booth, got their car, and drove her back to their hotel. Mickey claimed, "Jayne was in a good mood as we drove away. We played records on our car phonograph all the way home," but photos of the evening show the two glaring and yelling at each other.

They took a quick trip to Spain in April to attend Las Fallas carnival in Valencia; Jayne flew to Paris from there and met with Enrico Bomba— whether it was about a film project or something more personal, no one knew. "Mickey has been a patient man," wrote Sheilah Graham. "But Jayne seems to have completely lost her sense of values, and decorum."

Graham added rather harshly, "Jayne Mansfield, at a low ebb in her career, should really take stock of her future, privately and professionally. Jayne is pretty, not too talented, and I am sure there is a place for her in films, TV or what have you. But she has got to get back on the beam. She needs to inject some dignity into her private life."

Despite the scandals, Jayne was still a draw for crowds and in demand. In May 1963 she was named Miss American Kosher, promoting American Kosher Provision Corporation's hot dogs at McCormick Place in Chicago. She accepted roses from kosher butcher Hyman Kleinberg, while her Chihuahuas Galena and Csopy went at each other during the whole event. "When you list the attendees at this affair please put me ahead of the dogs," Jayne requested.

21

The Mickey Hargitay–Jayne Mansfield divorce cancellation
proved that he's the best friend she has.

Walter Winchell

In the spring of 1963, recovering from Enrico Bomba, at odds with
Mickey, and having just turned thirty, Jayne fell headlong for a young
man who strolled into her life while they were both playing Atlanta nightclubs.
Jayne's pinball-game romantic rebound highlights the fact that she was never
alone, never without a man, for one moment in her life. Even the multi-
married Elizabeth Taylor and Zsa Zsa Gabor had days—weeks, even—when
they could close the curtains and relax in a man-free, child-free home and
read or watch TV or chat on the phone with a friend. Not Jayne.

She was scarcely old enough to remember her birth father, so it would
be armchair psychoanalysis to attribute this need for male companionship
to his early death. But the years from 1936 to 1939 were the only ones when
Jayne was without a father, lover, or husband. From then on, it was Harry
Peers, then Paul Mansfield, Robbie Robertson, Mickey Hargitay, Enrico
Bomba, and now Nelson Sardelli. And as the years went on, she was also
surrounded by more and more children, agents, secretaries, reporters, and
a yipping pack of tiny, tiny dogs. "Blessed solitude" was a concept foreign
and horrifying to Jayne when this new man walked up to her nightclub
table.

Twenty-eight-year-old Nelson Sardelli—born in Brazil to Italian parents—was a US Army veteran who had worked as an Arthur Murray dance instructor, hospital orderly, and construction worker before discovering his real talents as a singer and comedian. His career was just building steam that spring, when he and Jayne were both playing clubs in Atlanta.

"Between shows one evening, before I even changed my tuxedo, I decided to take a walk," Sardelli remembers today. "I saw a commotion at the door of a bistro. Curiosity led me there and I was told that Jayne Mansfield was inside. Because I was dressed in a tuxedo, in Atlanta, people just moved out of my way and I went in. A young waitress saw me and came to me saying, 'Jayne Mansfield is here!' I looked at her in a matter-of-fact manner and said: 'I know; she's waiting for me.'"

Sardelli knew who Jayne was, of course, but very little else: "I knew less about her than I knew about many Hollywood personalities. I knew that she was married to Mickey Hargitay, who was once Mr. Universe, and that at one time they had some kind of trouble on a sailing boat or something like that around Bermuda, Bahamas, or who knows where. That was the extent of my Jayne Mansfield knowledge."

The helpful waitress led Sardelli through the crowd and told Jayne that "the gentleman that you are waiting for has arrived." Jayne got a look at Sardelli and he got a look at Jayne, and that was enough. His first impression of her? "She was blonde, she was pretty, and had very large boobs!" he laughs.

The two hit it off right away, chatting away in English and Italian. "She told me that she was doing a show in some hotel and by coincidence her show would start after my second show was over," says Sardelli. "She invited to come see it, so I went."

Sardelli, despite having only a few years' experience as a nightclub entertainer, was already a polished professional with high standards. "To be honest, I thought the show could use some serious help," he says of Jayne's act, but "I wasn't about to tell her that on that night. That would come later. I just waited around to tell her I was there and had enjoyed the show. I was sure that after I had said, 'Nice show, Jayne,' without any elaboration, our chapter would have come to an end."

They strolled outside to where their respective cars were waiting, and Jayne asked which one was his. "I pointed it out to her. She said, 'We will go in it.' And that was that." Sardelli draws a gentlemanly curtain over the rest of the evening, but for the next few months, Jayne had yet another Love of Her Life.

After Atlanta, Sardelli accompanied her to Canada ("I was told that more people had come to see her than the queen on her visit to the city"), Los Angeles (where they stayed in the Pink Palace), Texas (where he met Vera and Harry Peers—the press, of course, assumed he was their son-in-law to be). At the Dallas airport Sardelli was overheard to joke, "Boy, I wish Hargitay were here to help with the luggage."

Jayne decided that she couldn't wait for her California decree to become legal, so at the end of April Sardelli and Jayne (along with Galena, Jayne's most unruly Chihuahua) flew to Juarez, Mexico, where Judge Miguel Gomez Guerra granted Jayne a legally sketchy divorce from Mickey. "Things have come a long way since grandpap was a youth," wrote the pseudonymous "Dr. B. U. L. Connor" of the *El Paso Herald Post*. "It used to be that a girl never, never took her boyfriend with her when she went to get a divorce. He stayed down at the corner saloon, or else hid in the parlor."

Connor quoted Sardelli as saying, "We are very much in love. She loves me. She plays on the strings of my heart." This brings a howl of laughter from him today: "Not the style of the beast! We were a long way from connubial bliss. She did not 'play on the strings of my heart.' She also did not 'play on the drums of my ears.'"

Filing for the Mexican divorce, Jayne (who gave her age as twenty-eight, which no one let pass: "She lost two years along with Mickey") said her charge of "cruelty" was "just legal terminology. I have nothing but respect and admiration for Mickey and I wish him all the success in the world. But if you can't get along together, there is no reason for continuing the marriage." She wore a perfectly respectable yellow sheath dress, although it was described by the press as "skin-tight" and "low-cut." Questioned about her possible marriage to Sardelli, Jayne said, "I only got my divorce several hours ago. I think it's a little premature to say anything now, don't you?"

Jayne's romance with Nelson Sardelli did not always run smoothly. In early May fisticuffs broke out between him and Jayne's secretary, Raymond Strait (who also went under the names Russell Ray and Rusty Ray). While in San Francisco, Strait—sporting a black eye and bloody nose—appeared at the hotel's front desk and asked for the police to be called. He was followed by a flustered Jayne, who talked him out of it, and took him out for a calming-down dinner. Sardelli later joked to the press that the fight was over whether Willie Mays played for the Dodgers or the Giants, and the two men shook hands for the photographers. Today, Sardelli says that "there was not a 'fight.' One punch took care of the matter. At that time, Rusty hadn't yet accepted me. We have become very close friends since."

❤

At the end of May Jayne, Mickey Jr., and Zoltan flew to Hamburg, where Jayne made her first and only German film, *Heimweh nach St. Pauli* (*Homesick for St. Pauli*). Jayne Marie joined them after school let out, and in early June Nelson Sardelli completed the entourage. Jayne rented a twelve-room house with a swimming pool to keep everyone happy and out of each other's hair.

St. Pauli was directed by Werner Jacobs, whose long career included German versions of *Heidi* and *The Merry Widow;* it was based on a play by Gustav Kampendonk, who also wrote the script. Both men specialized in lightweight, whipped-cream movies, and *Heimweh nach St. Pauli* was no exception. The production company, Rapid Film, was not as squeaky-clean, with such titles as *Swinging Wives, The Resort Girls,* and *Carnal Campus* to its credit, but Jacobs and Kampendonk rose above their producers' rowdiness and made a film anyone could safely take their grandmother to see.

The film's star was singer Freddy Quinn, who was sometimes called "the German Elvis Presley"—this was inaccurate, and unfair to both singers. Quinn, who would turn thirty-two later in '63, was born in Austria and had wandered the world before becoming a pop star in Germany. As opposed to Elvis's rockabilly sound, Quinn specialized in *schlager,* a kind of modern folk music, heavy on sentiment and catchy tunes.

According to one account, Quinn was a fan of Jayne's, and put in a call to her "people" that "Mr. Quinn" would like her to costar in a film. Naturally assuming it was Anthony Quinn, Jayne picked up—fortunately for Freddy Quinn, she thought the mix-up was funny, and the two got on so well over the phone that she agreed to do the film.

Quinn was already a best-selling singer and had appeared in a dozen movies and TV shows before *Heimweh nach St. Pauli,* and was certainly a bigger name than Jayne in Germany. "Jayne adapted herself to the environment and plowed forth as she would have done anywhere else," Sardelli says of what must have been an intimidating set for Jayne, who was barely conversant in German, and who was working with an all-German cast and crew. Harrison Carroll reported that she was as on time, professional, and prepared as always, even if she did not understand a word of what was going on around her.

Heimweh nach St. Pauli—which was shot very quickly for a big-budget musical—is a silly, enjoyable film, with songs and dances crammed in approximately every five minutes. Quinn plays ex-sailor Hein, who becomes a success in New York as TV rock star Jimmy Jones. Finding himself Homesick for St. Pauli, he stows away to Germany, where he reunites with his parents, falls in love with a Nice German Girl, and gives up show business.

Jayne plays his TV costar, Evelyne (she does a very funny ad for Nofum cigarettes, "a cigarette even a four-year-old can smoke"). She looks great, with a huge but flattering wig, and a wittily designed glamour wardrobe by Anneliese Ludwig. Jayne's speaking voice is dubbed, but she sings two songs in passable German: "Snicksnack Snucklechen" (sung in a sailors' dive bar) and "Wo ist Der Mann?" (in which Nelson Sardelli makes a cameo appearance as a buckskin-clad chorus boy). Jayne also does a mean twist during a production number.

Freddy Quinn comes off more Robert Goulet than Elvis Presley, with his square-jawed looks and powerful bass-baritone voice. Quinn continued his stage, film, and TV career into the twenty-first century, but this was the only film appearance of costar Christa Schindler, who was charming as the Nice German Girl.

Heimweh nach St. Pauli opened in Germany in late August, and played in Manhattan's Yorkville section, on the Upper East Side, where there was a large German population. The *New York Daily News* was one of the few papers that noted its existence, writing, "The real scene-stealers are Erna Sellmer and Josef Albrecht, who play [Quinn's] parents so winningly that they almost upstage Miss Mansfield. And that, needless to say, is almost impossible."

When the filming was completed, Jayne and Sardelli drove to Rome, where Jayne hoped that Enrico Bomba would costar them in *The Italian Lover* (just where her children went, and with whom, was not reported). Not only did *The Italian Lover* not happen, but Jayne's brief, romantic idyll with Sardelli came to an amicable end. "Even though we had a nice time together, reality would never allow us to ever be a couple," Sardelli says. "We broke up in Rome, at the steps of the Saint Peter's Cathedral. The next day I placed her in the plane to return to America, and I closed that book and never ever saw or even talked to her, although she tried numerous times."

Jayne never badmouthed her exes unless divorce proceedings called for it, but she was particularly softhearted about Nelson Sardelli. A year after their breakup, she told *Photoplay,* "I adore Italian people. Nelson Sardelli had heart. He had soul. He's a fine person, a religious person." And for his part Sardelli has nothing but affection for Jayne: "As a person she was intelligent, a very nice, albeit misguided person, who tried to please everyone."

In late June 1963 Jayne realized that she was pregnant—within a couple of weeks, she and Mickey announced that they had called off their divorce. On July 1 Walter Winchell hinted broadly, "Jayne, they say, has quite a problem overseas." Syndicated columnist Alex Freeman wrote, "It's been rumored that Jayne is expecting, but when I asked her she just laughed it off as a silly story. She says she has no desire to ever again see singer Nelson Sardelli, whose romance with Jayne shattered her marriage in the first place." Freeman added that Jayne's lawyers "are checking—at her request— on the validity of the Mexican divorce she got from Mickey Hargitay. If they can't find a way to cancel it, she'll find some other way to marry him again."

In Toronto on July 5, Jayne said, "You just don't know what might happen. We saw each other in Washington where I just played, and he was so attentive, and we've never gotten on so well. If we could only straighten little things out."

Jayne and Mickey appeared together at the Casino Royale in Washington, DC, on July 10, and Jayne told Harrison Carroll that "things are more pleasant between me and Mickey than they have been in three years, but I don't know what's going to happen." Carroll asked about Nelson Sardelli and was told, "He's in Rome. He's doing some nightclub appearances." Have they broken up? "I don't know. I'm not sure of anything yet about my personal life. All I'm doing right now is trying to work out a schedule for my many commitments."

In late July Jayne was playing the 500 Club in Atlantic City, her interesting condition already beginning to show. Jayne and Mickey presented a swimming award on the beach and led exercises for the Junior Chamber of Commerce. Jayne wore unglamorous blue jeans, a headscarf, and a loose-fitting overblouse, to the crowd's disappointment.

By mid-August Jayne and Mickey had reconciled; Walter Winchell wrote, "The Mickey Hargitay–Jayne Mansfield divorce cancellation proved that he's the best friend she has."

Rumors have flown since 1963 that Nelson Sardelli, not Mickey, was the biological father of Jayne's new baby, future TV star Mariska Hargitay. Certainly, timing and their physical resemblance lend credence to that theory. Neither Mariska nor Mickey ever publicly went on record about the matter, and today Nelson Sardelli, in a firm but gentlemanly way, refuses to discuss the issue, merely expressing his great fondness and admiration for Jayne, Mickey, and Mariska.

The important thing is that Mickey was Mariska's father, and a very good one, too, in all the ways that matter. Whether Mickey or Nelson contributed DNA is irrelevant.

But still, Mickey had been burned more than twice by Jayne, and any illusions he had about their long-term future were over. "I couldn't help her, because I'm a great believer, everybody has to help herself," he said. "To a degree, I could tell her things, not necessarily that she would listen or do it."

He had real insight into Jayne's need for a helpmate, despite her inability to take advice. "Jaynie is the kind of person who needs a person next to her who will help her carry through her career, whether she agrees with him or not," Mickey said. "She likes my support, but she also likes to make up her own mind. Maybe, in a crazy way, my trying to help her spoiled our happiness. Then, too, I guess she began to take me for granted."

He told *Photoplay*'s Jim Hoffman in 1963—with Jayne sitting next to him—"If your wife wants to divorce you, there's no way you can hold her. I'm convinced that deep down she didn't really want to divorce me. This was just a misunderstanding between us. No real bitterness. I have no hard feelings. I don't degrade her for what happened in the past." He added— Jayne was right there, after all, and he was speaking on the record, "I love Jaynie as a girl, not a movie star. They don't make girls like her these days. Sure, she has plenty of fire, drive and ambition, but she's also very good with kids. The amazing thing about Jayne is that she is spontaneous and innocent, despite all."

While sorting out her marriage and looking for a new film—without help or interference from Fox, for a change—Jayne kept busy. "Jayne Mansfield is creating problems for her new talent agency," wrote Dorothy Kilgallen. "She's so anxious to work and start raking in money that she's okaying all kinds of café dates and letting the agency worry about overlapping and conflicting schedules."

One of these café dates, in Burlington, Ontario, went too far for police chief Kenneth Skerrett. Her nightclub routine included what producer

Paul Blane called "a satire on a strip—people will really come to see you if they think you're taking your clothes off." But Jayne's drinking was beginning to affect her professionalism—although this was rarely a problem, and one that impacted on her live appearances only, never her films. "The only problem with Jayne was," recalled Blane, "she'd take a couple of drinks, and she'd want to take it all off. I had to run onstage with her fur coat to cover her up—'wait a minute, Jayne, they're gonna put us in jail!'"

Jayne complained to the *Montreal Gazette* that the police objections were "a framed deal, a rigged setup thought up by a Burlington TV reporter. He took a film of my last number, took it to the police and tried to get them to say it was indecent. . . . My act is unbelievably tame." (Clips from this act were seen after Jayne's death in the film *Spree*).

She and Mickey flitted all around the United States that summer: doing a club act at the Iroquois Gardens in Louisville; presenting a trophy to the winner of the Junior Derby at Miles Park; appearing at the Petroleum Club's second anniversary celebration in Louisiana. In Lafayette, Louisiana, Jayne's appearance was the talk of the town: "Her high bouffant styled hair was silver blonde, highlighted with a pink spray, with a small orange ribbon in it. She wore tight white toreador pants, and a loose-fitting shirt of bright orange, with red, green and white trimming."

Jayne, invited personally by Governor W. W. Barron, served as grand marshall of the Berkeley-Martinsburg Centennial Parade in West Virginia. She was the "idol of all" at the three-mile Parade of Progress, which included bands, floats, local beauty queens, antique cars, and ninety-plus-degree heat. The most "amusing" float, according to the papers, was the Panhandle Coon Hunters, consisting of a terrified raccoon up a tree, with hunters leaping up and trying to yank its tail.

Jayne arrived in Houston wearing what looked like a ten-gallon wig and was presented with pink cowboy boots. All while carrying two Chihuahuas and wearing a sable wrap in the ninety-degree heat. When asked about John Profumo (Britain's secretary of state for war, who had been caught lying about an affair with a model connected with an attaché from the Soviet embassy), Jayne had the admirable audacity to say, "It is certainly a shame to put the bedroom antics of people we all admire on the front page and at the disposition of children."

Jayne was still haunted by *Promises. . . . Promises!* and *Playboy* wherever she went. The City Club in Cleveland booked her to talk about the *Promises* ban with the Citizens for Freedom of Mind (about a hundred

Cleveland residents attended a rally to protest the banning, along with Jayne and Mickey); in August the film was banned in Pittsburgh, along with its co-feature, *Diary of a Nudist*. The Columbus, Ohio, movie board okayed *Promises,* but made note that its main problem was "the acting is atrocious."

When the TV documentary series *Hollywood and the Stars* aired its "Sirens, Symbols & Glamour Girls" segment in October, Jayne was not mentioned. Charles Denton of the *Philadelphia Inquirer* wrote that Jayne was "deliberately left out. . . . The reason, according to the producers: 'Jayne isn't a sex symbol; she's a parody.'" Even her champion Sheilah Graham had given up on her. "I don't like to rap a girl before things have improved," wrote Graham, "but Jayne's career problem is that because of her wrong kind of publicity, she has alienated the women. And it is the women who decide which pictures to see."

❤

Then it was off to Europe to make another film before her pregnancy became too advanced (she explained, "I'm expecting twins" when asked why she was already showing). Jayne and Mickey arrived in Paris on their "second honeymoon" in mid-August, then took a trip to Budapest to visit Mickey's family before traveling on to Dubrovnik to film her next project— her third as a freelancer.

In Hungary Jayne took her mother-in-law shopping and was "admired by hundreds of goggle-eyed women in the baby linen and knitwear department." Hungarian radio and television reporters and photographers followed Jayne and the Hargitays from morning till night, until August 27, when Jayne and Mickey took off for Belgrade, Yugoslavia (at the same time as Nikita Khrushchev; they all made the front page of *Politika*). From Belgrade they flew to Dubrovnik, on the Adriatic coast, and Jayne went to work.

Jayne's next film (she signed on when Elke Sommer dropped out), produced and distributed abroad, was *Dog Eat Dog* (also released as *When Strangers Meet*). It went through a torturous route to the few theaters that eventually played it. Filmed in the fall of 1963, the film was funded by three production companies (in Italy, Germany, and Lichtenstein), and had four producers, four directors, and two screenwriters. It's a wonder the film wasn't a much bigger mess. As it is, *Dog Eat Dog* is quite an enjoyable crime caper: nihilistic, dark, and nasty.

It was filmed on one of the small islands off Dubrovnik, standing in for Greece; Mickey accompanied Jayne to the shooting locations to make sure her pregnancy wasn't threatened by any of the fight scenes and rock climbing the shoot required. (The hotel where Jayne and Mickey stayed later sued her for the $6,000 bill; Jayne told them to get it from one of the many producers.)

Dog Eat Dog is the story of $1 million and the unpleasant people who want it: three thieves, Dolph (British character actor Ivor Salter), Corbett (Cameron Mitchell, whose impressive career stretched from the 1940s to the 1990s), and Darlene (Jayne). Fleeing with the loot to an old abandoned bordello on a "Greek" island, they encounter handsome hotelier Livio (Swiss stage, screen, and TV actor Pinkas Braun), his prim sister (American actress Dodie Heath), the house's eerie, Miss Havisham–like madam (Elisabeth Flickenschildt, whose Nazi affiliations did not seem to make a dent in her later career), and her menacingly creepy servant (German Werner Peters, who excelled at played menacing creeps). As Cameron Mitchell's Corbett accurately observes, "So this is a deserted island! It's more like an Elks' Convention in Atlantic City."

The seven stranded castaways do not have nearly as much fun as their counterparts on *Gilligan's Island:* all bent on keeping the money, they turn on each other with increasing madness and violence, employing guns, knives, garrotes, and fire.

Jayne was halfway through her pregnancy and looked it; but the main affront to her appearance is a mussed wig and some truly criminal Cleopatra eyeliner. The talented cast—pros, all of them—do a good job with the overwrought characters and plot, and Jayne's Darlene is cheerfully amoral, avaricious, and eventually insane. What the cast members really have to fight is bad dubbing: the English translation is often clunky and off-kilter, and some of the voice actors are downright dreadful. Jayne lucks out with Carolyn De Fonseca, who had also voiced her in *The Loves of Hercules.* The combination of Jayne and De Fonseca results in quite a good performance, when the revolving-door directors allowed.

Jayne wrote to Sheilah Graham in late September, "We have another week in Dubrovnik on *Dog Eat Dog.* Then home to the pink palace in Hollywood to await the birth of the twins," adding that she has ordered some "motherly" wigs. When filming was completed, she and Mickey took off for a brief Roman holiday.

Dog Eat Dog didn't open till 1964 in Europe and 1965 in the US. The

Clarksville Leaf Chronicle was one of the few papers that bothered to notice it, writing that it "shows how avarice can turn a handful of people, thrown together by chance, into ravening beasts," but never actually giving an opinion on the film's quality.

By the end of October the family was back together in the Pink Palace, awaiting the "twins." Harrison Carroll wrote that it might not be twins after all, but that "the heartbeats indicate she probably can expect a daughter" (absolute nonsense medically, but Carroll turned out to be right). "I can tell you that Mickey and I really are happy," said Jayne. "We haven't selected a name for the baby, but Mickey's mother is coming up with a list." Mickey's mother flew in from Hungary to stay with them and help take care of the baby, though much of the new-baby duty generally would fall to thirteen-year-old Jayne Marie.

Walter Scott had the nerve to print a reader's questions: "Is Jayne Mansfield going to have twins or this is another of her publicity stunts? Also, who is the father?" He answered, "Miss Mansfield claims to be expecting twins which she says were fathered by Mickey Hargitay, her sometime-husband."

Jayne left her maternity bed long enough to open a Grand Tiger store in Willoughby, Ohio, in early November; she signed autographs and cut the ribbon with Mayor Gar Pierce (appearing alongside Jayne at this event were two Browns football players and "Ray Budzilek and his polka clarinet").

On November 22, 1963, President Kennedy was assassinated. The world did not grind to a halt; newspapers' entertainment sections were still full of Jayne's upcoming guest spot on the November 26 *Jack Benny Program,* as well as lurid ads for *Promises. . . . Promises!*

Jayne's skit on *Jack Benny*—filmed a few weeks earlier—was a remake of Marilyn Monroe's 1953 guest spot, in which Jack dreams of being romanced by Jayne. Of course he wakes up to reality, finding himself pursued by a homely fat lady. Veteran actress Peggy Mondo was the requisite Fat Lady (played by Maxine Gates in 1953); she and Jayne were both reduced to human punch lines because of their measurements.

TV viewers needed a release from the onslaught of shocking and depressing news that week—the assassination, Oswald's murder, the funeral—and welcomed Jack and Jayne into their homes. Fran Conklin of the *Orlando Sentinel* felt that "one can still not settle back and enjoy a silly show. . . . However, we found that good ole Jack Benny was able to take our mind off the recent tragedy."

❤

"My life is difficult," Jayne told Jim Hoffman of *Photoplay* in 1963. "Little sleep, always in front of the public. I'm a goldfish. The way to beat it is to divorce my public self from who I am. To laugh at the performing me. Jayne Mansfield, the big star, is funny to me."

One way Jayne coped with tragedy was through religion (religion, and an amazing ability to ignore anything negative or confusing in her life). Raised Methodist, she was a classic "cafeteria Christian," choosing the tenets that fit in with her own lifestyle and desires. Jayne broke a good many commandments: she made idols (a nude statue of herself in the Pink Palace certainly qualified); she was heard to take the name of the Lord her God in vain; her Sabbath days were only occasionally kept holy; she certainly committed adultery; she bore false witness against all three husbands during her divorce trials; and as for coveting, Jayne could have earned an Olympic medal for that.

During her dalliances with Enrico Bomba and Nelson Sardelli, Jayne drifted toward Catholicism. "I feel as a Catholic feels right now," she told Hoffman. "It happened when I got lost in the Bahamas. I *really* prayed—for the first time in years. I knew I *needed* something more. I *wanted* something more. I go to mass every Sunday and to church every day of the week, even if it's just kneeling on the steps." Religion, Jayne said, "governs my life. It guides my thinking and acting. It's something very nice. It gives me peace. With my crazy hours, most churches are closed when I'm up and around. But if I can just kneel on the steps and hold Someone's hand, His hand, things have a way of working out. I don't say, 'Now I'm holy, therefore I can sin.' No. I'm religious because I *need* it."

In early 1964 Harrison Carroll ran into Nelson Sardelli when they both visited the set of Tommy Noonan's latest epic, *3 Nuts in Search of a Bolt,* in Los Angeles. Carroll tried to get a rise out of Sardelli by mentioning Jayne and Mickey's reconciliation. "I wouldn't try to call them," said Sardelli. "It would be in bad taste. Besides, my girlfriend, Micki Holland, flew to California so we could spend the holidays together." Carroll noted that "Sardelli, tall, dark and handsome, used to date Micki before he met Jayne. 'She's not in the profession,' he told me. 'She's just my girlfriend, and that's fine with me.'"

On January 4—looking ready to give birth at any moment—Jayne attended the wedding of Suzanne Pleshette and Troy Donahue; the following week she was greeted with the news that Mr. Blackwell had named her the "worst undressed of the year."

Finally, on January 23, 1964, Jayne gave birth to her fourth child, an eight-pound, nine-ounce daughter. Jayne enthused, "She is the most beautiful little girl. We feel so elated. We are still planning for a family of ten. . . . The baby is named Mariska Magdolna—'Mary Magdalen' in Hungarian. But there's really nothing symbolic about it." Columnist Hy Gardner had the poor taste to make fun of Mariska Hargitay's name, writing, "Try that on your marquee." (Gardner died in 1989, before he had a chance to see that name on marquees.)

22

I spent so much time as mother's helper, I'd never experienced what it was like to be a child in my own right and have somebody look after me.

Jayne Marie Mansfield

Jayne said that she and Jayne Marie were "playing dolls" with the new baby. "We are dressing her and putting bootees on her. Mariska is such a darling. She has blue eyes and a pug nose like mine." She added that she would be leaving for Europe in February, and that "my babies always go to Europe with me. After all, they have to know what the world is like."

But as much as she loved her brothers and sister—and she did love them—Jayne Marie had not signed up to be a nursemaid. She was a teenager at one of the most exciting times to be a teenager, the 1960s. Years later, Jayne Marie told the *Pittsburgh Press,* "Despite the fact that my mother did not want me to go out with boys or wear makeup, she didn't think I was too young to take care of my half-brothers and half-sister. I raised them, and spent all my time as their nanny. I was also mother's maid—until she sent me away to boarding school. I spent so much time as mother's helper, I'd never experienced what it was like to be a child in my own right and have somebody look after me."

Being a mother was just as important to Jayne as being a star, but she was equally erratic at both jobs. Jayne loved her children, but she thought part of that love was having them around her 24/7. Bringing them with her to film shoots all over the world, to nightclub gigs and publicity trips, was part of being a "good mother." She would have been appalled to learn that her mothering skills might be looked at askance.

But they were. Years later, when trouble in the Mansfield household became public, reporter Bill Crawford would describe Jayne's disturbing behavior at a 1959 interview he'd done with her in Las Vegas. At the time none of this made it into print, perhaps because it did not seem unsettling then, or because Crawford censored himself in writing about a prominent star—although it is also possible that Crawford later exaggerated in reminiscing about the encounter. "'Jayne Marie—come here,' commanded the bikini-clad, bronze-tanned mother," Crawford would write, cruelly continuing,

> The overweight child reluctantly tumbled out of the pool, dripping wet, and shuffled toward her blonde mother's chaise longue. "Say hello to Mr. Crawford from Oklahoma," the mother requested in syrupy tones. The sad-eyed child did as commanded and muttered a greeting with a forced smile before proceeding back to the pool area. "Jayne Marie—come back here. And this time, please curtsy for the press." This was the final order barked by the mother. . . . There seemed to be little cause to interrupt Jayne Marie's swim merely to curtsy to the news media. But, it seemed important to the image-conscious Miss Mansfield that she show off her children and play the role of a mother.
>
> Later that evening I joined Miss Mansfield and Hargitay for a midnight supper in their backstage dressing room. And there was eight-year-old Jayne Marie wandering about sleepy-eyed and gorging on food. (Frustration and unhappiness in her mother's world of bright lights and show business probably were the reasons for the child's compulsive eating and overweight problem.) I thought at the time here was an extremely unhappy child. She had all the material things in the world, except a happy home. Jayne Marie probably knew her governess better than her own mother.

Bill Crawford was not the only reporter who noticed Jayne's deficient parenting skills. Italian journalist Oriana Fallaci said of Jayne, "I don't know if she was stupid or not, but I do know that she was cruel. She kept hitting her daughter. I didn't write that then, it might have hurt the child."

Actor Will Hutchins recalls that he met Jayne in the late 1950s "backstage at some celebrity gathering. She was desperately trying to be the center of attention. To me, she didn't come off as the siren, but rather as someone annoying—mostly because she had her daughter with her, and treated the girl as if she was her personal servant. It got to the point where it became embarrassing, and I left."

Jayne discussed punishments with interviewer (and fellow mother of a young daughter) Joyce Davidson in 1957. "Privileges taken away from a child is the best way to do it," Jayne said. "If my little girl disagrees with anything I agree with, I suggest that she not play for two hours, and maybe color in her room. Usually, she agrees with me after that! I don't think that physically spanking a child is good at all."

"Having children—isn't that what sex is all about?" Jayne asked Olga Curtis of the *Orlando Evening Star* in 1965 (if Olga Curtis begged to differ, she did not do so in print). "I never had any brothers or sisters and I always wanted a big family," said Jayne. "In fact, I plan to have five more children." She insisted, "My publicity doesn't affect my children. They've grown up with the idea that mama is a celebrity and what I do in public is different from what we do at home. Jayne Marie has seen me photographed since she was little, and the only effect it's had on her is that she's figure-conscious, but at her age she probably would be anyhow."

She admitted that "I'm a disciplinarian. I don't believe in spanking, but I'm pretty strict with my children. My boys get their privileges taken away if they misbehave, and I don't allow Jayne Marie to wear makeup or date, except in groups. Professionally, I suppose I shouldn't admit I have a teen-aged daughter. I kid Jayne Marie about that sometimes and tell her she better start walking around on her knees or pretending she's my sister. But I'm very proud of my children. Jayne Marie is going to be a young lady. She isn't going to repeat my mistakes and get married at 16 or be a mother at 17."

Jayne may have been kidding with Jayne Marie about pretending they were sisters, but for a young teenager it was no joke. In 1976 Jayne Marie told the *Miami Herald,* "As long as mother was alive I was never quoted as being my right age. When I was 16 I was 12. When I was 12 I was nine. I couldn't even grow my hair long because she wanted long hair—it made her look younger. When I was 13 and wanted to wear makeup and stockings, she tried to keep me in socks and patent-leather shoes. She didn't give me a bra for so long that I went straight into a size 34D."

To the *San Antonio Star,* Jayne Marie recalled, "The only time I got to go out and have a good time was when she was out of town. I never got any allowance. She believed you had to work for what you got. . . . Her image was one of looseness to a degree, and she overcompensated by keeping the children in a very strict atmosphere . . . she would not let me wear makeup or things that would make me look nice. It was a shame, because I had no intention of getting in her limelight."

But Jayne must have done something right, for Jayne Marie grew up to be a thoughtful, expressive woman with a sense of perspective and little bitterness. She recalled affectionately that "Mother loved to play jokes on people. I remember we had a birthday party and she let me put strained baby food—liver—in the cake. The guests ate it and pretended nothing was wrong. Mom and I went into a room alone and laughed so hard my sides hurt. . . . Mother put a drink in one of my hands, a cigarette in the other and let me at them. It worked. I never drank or smoked. She told me the facts of life when I was five years old. She pulled the car over on my way home from dancing lessons, and, very nervously, explained how she was going to have a baby. Then she said, 'Do you understand?' And I said, 'Yup, let's go!'"

♥

In February 1964 MGM Records released a Valentine's Day gift to the public: Jayne's album *Shakespeare, Tchaikovsky & Me*. No one, to this day, knows what to make of it. The record appears to be a camp joke: Jayne reading snippets of poetry while classical music plays in the background. Given her frequent complaints about wanting to be taken seriously as an actress, *Shakespeare, Tchaikovsky & Me* might have been interpreted as a legitimate bit of high culture—if it weren't for the album cover.

Jayne, wearing a pillowy platinum wig and a pearl choker, hefts up her cleavage with a fur stole and makes a wide-eyed kissy-face at the camera. In the background, plaster busts of Shakespeare and Tchaikovsky give each other a resigned side-eye. Jayne recites such well-worn classics as "How Do I Love Thee?" "She Walks in Beauty," "Upon the Nipples of Julia's Breast," and "Take, O, Take Those Lips Away" while a mercifully unbilled studio orchestra plays in the background. The record was directed by Milton Moss (who later helmed another LP, of Pat Carroll reading Gertrude Stein), and Earl Wilson contributed juvenile breast jokes for the liner notes.

One of the few reviewers to admit he had listened to it, Nick Jones of the *Indianapolis News*, wrote, "Jayne has done her bit for history by issuing this album. . . . Her enunciation is sloppy: she's too busy panting to let the poetry speak for itself, she bills, coos and giggles the beauty from the lines—and the album's chief value seems to be that it shows Jayne to be broader than one originally thought, if such an image can be comprehended. If the idea is a gag—then P. T. Barnum has a new rival, and more power to her. But if she's taking herself seriously, well, it's downright embarrassing." Only one loyal Texas paper felt that "she does a remarkably good job of reading 31 short love poems by Elizabeth Barrett Browning, Shelley, Lord Byron, Christopher Marlowe, Tennyson and, of course, Shakespeare."

Recovering from bronchitis, Jayne plugged the album for the *Miami News*'s Paula Breibart. Jayne wore a modest yellow sheath dress (through which Briebart managed to spot "a peek of the black bra underneath") and—veering from Shakespeare and Tchaikovsky to "Me," confided that "I try not to eat. I live on deviled eggs, steak and lemonade. I drink a little and I smoke some. But I don't inhale."

That spring Jayne guested on one of the snappiest, funniest shows on TV. *Burke's Law,* which ran from 1963 to 1966, was a police drama with a light touch of comedy—not only did it serve up baffling murders, but star Gene Barry and the show's writers often broke the fourth wall and winked at the audience (though not in a smirking way; the humor always worked).

And the list of guest stars is breathtaking: not only some of Hollywood's greats (Gloria Swanson, Mary Astor, Buster Keaton), but also a horde of hot newcomers (Tab Hunter, Rita Moreno, the Smothers Brothers, Rue McClanahan). The casting directors also had an eye out for great character bits, and episodes featured hilarious turns by Wally Cox, Carolyn Jones (who seemed to be having the time of her life), Paul Lynde, Charlie Ruggles (dressed in lederhosen and chased around by a prostitute named Girl Girl), Zsa Zsa and Eva Gabor, and Gypsy Rose Lee. Jayne's fellow blonde bombshells Diana Dors, Mamie Van Doren, and Sheree North also turned up.

Jayne's episode, "Who Killed Molly?" (aired in March 1964), is one of the better entries. The titular Molly is a housewife murdered in her shower; it develops that Molly was moonlighting as a stripper. Jayne plays Cleo Patrick, a burlesque dancer who works with a python named Buster (sadly, we never get to see this act). She has two scenes, one at the late Buster's funeral ("Did you ever go shopping for a coffin six inches wide and thirteen feet long? We finally had to settle for a fire hose"), and is sharp and funny in both.

But by the time *Burke's Law* had appeared on TV screens, Jayne had inexplicably signed to make her worst, cheesiest film. In April 1964 she and

Mickey flew to Rome, where the G.L.M. and Italian International Film production companies signed her to appear in *L'Amore Primitivo* (*Primitive Love*). The film stars the Dean Martin–Jerry Lewis–like comedy team Ciccio Ingrassia (the Dean) and Franco Franchi (the Jerry). The pair made more than one hundred movie and TV appearances together in the 1960s and '70s (their other films—translated into English—include *Oh! Those Most Secret Agents, Fistful of Knuckles,* and *The Handsome, the Ugly, and the Stupid*).

Primitive Love was Jayne's first brush with "Mondo films," shocking documentaries (both real and faked), that burst into popularity with the 1962 Italian hit *Mondo Cane* (*A Dog's World*). It showed unconnected vignettes, some amusing, some horrifying: Rudolph Valentino fanatics; animal torture; a mourning mother breast-feeding a piglet; fat ladies exercising; sex trafficking; religious fanatics; lots and lots of nude women. It was amateurish, distasteful, and a smash hit.

More Mondo films followed: *Mondo Bizarro, Mondo Hollywood,* Russ Meyer's *Mondo Topless,* and such parodies and tributes as John Waters's *Mondo Trasho* and Michael O'Donoghue's *Mr. Mike's Mondo Video.* Luigi Scattini—the director of *Primitive Love*—had only the 1963 Mondo film *Sexy Magico* to his credit, and much of that footage went into this new film.

Primitive Love stars Jayne as Dr. Jayne Mansfield, who is in Italy to present her documentary footage on "love among the primitives" to an elderly anthropologist (Carlo Kechler): "Man has actually changed very little through the centuries," propounds Dr. Jayne. "In the sphere of love, man has remained a primitive." To prove her point, she narrates racist, mildly naughty (and endless) "travelogues" of Africa, China, Brazil, the Philippines, a very fake-looking "Hawaii," and other exotic locales. Ingrassia and Franchi play lust-crazed bellhops in her hotel; they spy on Dr. Jayne's presentation, and at one point fantasize themselves as African natives and Jayne as a hoochie-coochie dancer—it's actually painful to watch. The furiously mugging Franchi in particular makes Jerry Lewis look like Buster Keaton.

To convince the unimpressed anthropologist, Jayne does a tawdry striptease for the drooling Ingrassia and Franchi; they pass out from lust, the anthropologist turns into a "cannibal" and tries to rape Jayne, who flees, and the audience dies a little inside.

While she doesn't totally strip down as in *Promises. . . . Promises!,* Jayne does appear in her bra and panties, a skimpy towel, and a bikini. She wears one of her more unfortunate mid-'60s wigs, a shoulder-length number with a large Jiffy Pop chignon plunked atop it; this wig, looking increasingly tatty, would be in service for two or three years. Jayne (again dubbed in English by Carolyn De Fonseca) appears to be medicated and embarrassed. The only person to emerge unscathed is stunning Tunisian actress Agata Flori, who plays an "African" and does a kicky dance in capri pants and an untucked blouse.

In the "Jayne's Worst Film" tournament, *Primitive Love* takes the lead. If *Promises. . . . Promises!* was a cheesy misstep, *Primitive Love* is inexcusable and inexplicable. One feels sorry for Jayne while watching it, but at the same time one cannot imagine what she was thinking in agreeing to make this childish semi-porn. Perhaps she heard "Italian Martin and Lewis" and reasoned that such respected actresses as Shirley MacLaine, Janet Leigh, and Donna Reed had swallowed their dignity and appeared with the American team. But it was a huge miscalculation.

Primitive Love was filmed in May 1964 and released in Italy that August. Over the next two or three years it skulked into US drive-ins and "adult" theaters, usually double-billed with such films as *The Farmer's Other Daughter* (featuring "star of tomorrow Judy Pennebaker" in her only film) and *That Naughty Girl,* a silly, rather innocent 1956 Brigitte Bardot sex farce. No one had the heart to review *Primitive Love.*

From *Primitive Love* to the Cannes Film Festival was quite a leap, but Jayne made it in early May. She took to the beach in a polka-dot bikini, and danced to rock group Rocky Roberts and the Airedales. Throughout May 1964 Jayne and Mickey took home movies on their travels through Europe—Cannes, Italy, France—for a proposed travelogue to be titled either *The Jayne Mansfield Report* or *Jayne Mansfield's Wild, Wild World;* these clips were to turn up after her death in her own Mondo film.

Returning to the US, Jayne signed a five-year contract with record company Original Sound, which resulted in only two recordings, "That Makes It" and "Little Things Mean a Lot," released in October 1964. "That Makes It" is a cute little number, opening with a telephone ringing and Jayne answering, "Hello . . . Yes, this is Jayne, *bay*-by," going on to sing that she wants "a man that moves, a man that grooves . . . oh, baby that *makes* it!" The background music is a catchy mid-'60s dance tune. "Little Things Mean a Lot" is a bland Connie Francis–style teen love song ("Give me your arm as we cross the street, call me at six on the dot . . . Little things mean a lot").

That same year, Jayne and Liberace recorded the novelty number "It's a Living," in which they—and Elvis impersonator Lance LeGault—humble-brag about their woes: "They don't throw us any roses, but they can't ignore our grosses, so we cry all the way to the bank!" It was done for the album *Les Poupées de Paris,* featuring the show-business caricature puppets of Sid and Marty Krofft (other celebrity voices used on the album included Gene Kelly, Pearl Bailey, and Loretta Young).

Jayne was never going to be a successful recording artist; even Marilyn Monroe and Judy Holliday—talented singers as well as actresses—cut records only as a sideline and were no threat to Doris Day or Julie London. Jayne's voice was pleasant but light and untrained; in her lower registers, she was quite good, with a full, expressive sound. But she usually relied on her higher, baby-talk voice when singing. Great for funny character songs, but not really "singing."

Over the next few years, Jayne continued to make halfhearted stabs at recording. In May 1965 she signed with Ed Chalpin's PPX Enterprises to record "As the Clouds Drift By" and "Suey," which she cut in New York that summer. "As the Clouds Drift By," sounding more 1955 than 1965, was an over-orchestrated, sappy ballad, with Jayne's voice so over-processed it sounds nothing like her. The copyright (March 1965) and recording agreement (May 1965) dates suggest that the track was most likely recorded sometime that spring.

"As the Clouds Drift By" was the B-side to her best—and most bizarre—recording. "Suey" was an excellent rock number with an instrumental backing as good as any mid-'60s dance record. According to expert John McDermott, rock icon Jimi Hendrix is playing guitar on "Suey." This leads to the irresistible mental image of Jayne Mansfield and Jimi Hendrix rocking down in the recording studio, but sadly, that was not the case. According to Niko Bauer and Doug Bell's Jimi Hendrix website, the instrumentals were probably recorded in February 1966 (possibly as early as late 1965), and Jayne added her vocals—which consisted of her squealing, "It makes my knees *freeze!*" and "It makes my liver *quiver!*" etc.—probably in March 1966, while she was appearing at the Latin Quarter in New York.

There is still a slight possibility that Jayne and Jimi passed each other in the hallways. Producer Ed Chalpin told *Straight Ahead* magazine that the two cut the record on the same day, but in different sessions: "I had to make sure he did the track without her being present 'cause, eh, you know, it might have been offensive. The way he was dressed and looked, in those days, it wasn't really in yet." The idea of Jayne Mansfield being put off by Jimi Hendrix's mod hair and clothing is highly unlikely, though, and their contracts and scheduling indicate different recording dates.

"Suey" was written by Douglas "Jocko" Henderson, who played drums on the record, and Niko Bauer suspects that he might have also written Jayne's lyrics, as they're quite similar to catchphrases he shouted on the air as a disc jockey.

"Suey" and "As the Clouds Drift By" vanished into limbo after Jayne's death, probably due to copyright difficulties—they only resurfaced decades later on Jayne Mansfield collections. Jimi Hendrix—who died in 1970—may never have known that he had played with Jayne Mansfield, and neither of them lived to hear the record released in the US (indeed, neither of them may have heard the record at all). As Jimi Hendrix didn't really rocket to international fame till the Monterey Pop Festival in June 1967—two weeks before Jayne's death—she may not even have known who he was.

❤

All through the 1960s, Jayne spoke to reporters of upcoming projects, most of which were never realized and some of which may have been manufactured out of her own imagination. She told Louella Parsons in 1962 that she was going to Rio to shoot *Act of Violence,* bankrolled by Jorge Guinle, then was off to Italy to shoot *The Midases* for Enrico Bomba, and had signed a contract to do TV for NBC.

During 1963 and '64, a parody of *Cleopatra*—no doubt a poke at Elizabeth Taylor's version—was discussed. The initial proposal was that it would be shot in Hawaii, Hollywood, and Rome, with "physical culturist Rex Ravelle" in the male lead. In 1964, while filming *Primitive Love,* Jayne was approached by Sammy Petrillo—best known for his Jerry Lewis impersonation—to film the comedy *Cleopatra Slept Here,* to be produced by Hal Roach and costarring Buster Keaton. It never happened.

Producer Dick Randall—who produced Jayne's posthumous *The Wild, Wild World of Jayne Mansfield*—bought the rights to Barbara Payton's memoirs *I Am Not Ashamed* in 1964, hoping Jayne would star as the tragic alcoholic actress. It might seem as good a showcase for her as Jessica Lange's later take on Frances Farmer, until one recalls Dick Randall's other credits: *Around the World with Nothing On, My Seven Little Bares, The Erotic Adventures of Robinson Crusoe.* Another vehicle for Jayne, *Jayne Bonne,* a James Bond parody, also failed to make it to the production stage.

In the last months of her life, Jayne told an interviewer that "I'm doing more dramatic things . . . *Fanny Hill,* which I want to do in the West End, and more dramatic pictures, but also the campy, satirical fun pictures." The *Fanny Hill* project came closer to fruition than her Frankenstein or Cleopatra movies. In January 1966 the management of the Manchester Opera House signed Jayne to make her British stage debut as the heroine in an adaptation of John Cleland's bawdy eighteenth-century novel. Successful Russian-born British theatrical producer Bernard Delfont was behind the project, so it had both pedigree and an actual chance at success, and Jayne might have been wonderful as the faux-innocent "woman of pleasure." But *Fanny Hill* was postponed time and again, and was still in ever-less-enthusiastic planning stages at the time of Jayne's death.

A persistent rumor has Jayne turning down the part of Ginger on *Gilligan's Island* in an "I don't do sitcoms" huff, but there does not seem to be any foundation for it (for one thing, Jayne rarely turned down a paying job—certainly not one that would turn into a three-year gig). Though Jayne did say in March 1963 that she did not want to do a series "because she considers herself primarily a movie actress and does not want to compete against herself."

Gilligan creator Sherwood Schwartz told the Television Academy Foundation that "I knew I wanted a gorgeous tall redhead" for the part of Ginger. "Why red, I don't know, but that's what I wanted." When the abortive pilot was filmed in November 1963, Schwartz's actress of choice, Tina Louise, was in rehearsals for the Broadway show *Fade Out—Fade In,* so redhead Kit Smythe played Ginger Grant—as a secretary, not a movie star. By the time the pilot was reshot in the summer of 1964, Louise had faded out of her show and was available—though she was furious when she found out she was to be a supporting character and not the lead, as she'd been promised.

No one thought the pilot would sell. Star Bob Denver told writer Peter Anthony Holder that Natalie Schafer—so delightful as Lovey Howell—had taken the role just for the Hawaiian vacation. "A telegram came to her table at dinner and she read it and burst into tears," Denver recalled, "and all of her friends with her on vacation said, 'Oh, Natalie, is it your mother? Is something wrong?' And she said, 'No, the pilot sold!'"

Jayne would not have been available anyway. In the summer of 1963 she was filming in Germany, and in the summer of 1964 she was in Italy, South Africa, and Yugoslavia, making films much sillier than anything Ginger Grant experienced on the uncharted desert isle.

23

She can act—but, alas, the actress in her keeps getting
stampeded by the Jayne We All Know And Love.

Mort Persky

In 1964 Jayne's career returned to its roots: live theater. She'd gotten her
training with the Austin Civic Theater, and of course became a star on
Broadway. But the movies had always been her endgame. Now, with even
the smaller film companies turning their back on her, Jayne—with Mickey
still in tow—embarked on her first of several summer-stock tours. As
Sheilah Graham wrote of Jayne's move, "Best way to remind producers you
have a following is to go on tour in a play."

Summer stock and dinner theater, or the "straw-hat circuit," sounds
like a pathetic windup to a dying career, but it was actually a thriving business from the 1930s to the 1960s. All over the country, hopeful youngsters
(Basil Rathbone, Bette Davis, Henry Fonda, and Marlon Brando started their
careers in stock), faded stars (Kay Francis, Veronica Lake, and yes, Jayne),
and still-bankable big names (Joanne Woodward and Paul Newman, Ethel
Barrymore, Angela Lansbury) toured theaters large and small—anything
from an opera house to a tent—bringing live theater to people who rarely got
to see it. The money wasn't great, and touring conditions could be rough, but
it was a chance for Jayne to work in respectable shows and do some real acting. As much as she loved being a Movie Star, she excelled at working with
live audiences, and reveled in the love emanating over the footlights.

In May 1964 Jayne signed (at $4,000 a week) to bring two of Marilyn Monroe's movie roles to the stage: the pathetic nightclub singer Cherie in *Bus Stop* (first played onstage by Kim Stanley in 1955), and wide-eyed gold digger Lorelei Lee in the 1949 musical *Gentlemen Prefer Blondes* (originated on Broadway by Carol Channing). *Bus Stop,* written by William Inge, required heavy-duty acting, and *Gentlemen Prefer Blondes* required heavy-duty singing ("A Little Girl from Little Rock" and the anthem "Diamonds Are a Girl's Best Friend," among other songs—most of which were cut from the 1953 movie version).

Jayne needed a good director; her acting ranged from brilliant to amateurish depending on the script and director she was handed. *Bus Stop* and *Gentlemen Prefer Blondes* had good scripts, so she set about interviewing potential directors. Finding a seasoned professional who was willing to do summer stock might not be easy. Jayne was lucky, finding twenty-eight-year-old New Yorker Matt Cimber on her first round of interviews.

Matt Cimber was—and is—funny, pugnacious, and no-nonsense. He already had an impressive theatrical background, having studied with acting coach Michael Chekhov, and had directed off-Broadway productions of F. Scott Fitzgerald and Jean Cocteau stories. He wasn't rich or famous, but his résumé was impressive enough to catch Jayne's eye—and his tough-guy sense of humor appealed to her.

Matt came by the Drake Hotel in New York, where Jayne was staying, for an interview. As he told writer Jim Phillips, "She was wearing jeans and didn't look like publicized images of Miss Mansfield. She was very cordial, and we went up to her room to talk. After some time, she said she had to get some rest before her flight and as I got to the door of the room I asked her what she wanted to do about *Bus Stop,* and she simply said, 'Oh, you direct it.' Then I asked about the casting and she replied, 'You can cast it too.' And that was that."

Their first show together, *Bus Stop,* had one simple set—a diner—which made things easy, and an eight-person cast. Jayne played a hopeful (and hopeless) singer who is pursued by lovestruck cowboy Bo Decker, played by Stephen Brooks, who later had a minor TV career (*Star Trek, Days of Our Lives, Medical Center*). Ann B. Davis—who was between her successful TV gigs on *The Robert Cummings Show* and *The Brady Bunch*—played the diner's owner, a role originated on Broadway by Elaine Stritch. Future

Oscar nominee (*A Patch of Blue*) Elizabeth Hartman was cast as a waitress. There was no way Mickey could carry off playing Bo, so he was cast in the supporting role of the bus driver—he was a bit hurt, but relieved at not having to play a major role. Though the two later clashed, actor Mickey and director Matt had no problems during the play's run.

Ann B. Davis did have problems, though, according to writer Richard A. Lertzman, who interviewed her in 2007. "She was a huge drunk. Bipolar. Unprofessional," said Davis about Jayne, adding that "she was about as bright as a chalkboard. Dumb as sin! She could barely read lines and was awful to the rest of the cast and crew." In case anyone was in doubt as to whether Davis maybe secretly liked Jayne, she went on: "She was vulgar, obscene and pathetic. One night, after the show and then a drinking binge, Jayne tried to pick up a local kid who was cleaning tables. I mean, he must have been like fifteen." As for Jayne's acting, said Davis, "She was awful and played it far too broad."

As for Mickey, Davis noted that he "was actually a charming gentleman who tried to clean up after Jayne. I felt badly for her children. They were lucky they had their father, Mickey. He was a gem of a guy."

Bus Stop opened at the Yonkers Playhouse on May 26, and through the spring, summer, and fall of that year the production trouped through the Midwest and the New York area.

Reviews were mixed; the *Detroit Daily Press* wrote that "Jayne Mansfield came to town to demonstrate her acting capabilities. What she revealed, however, had little to do with talent. Miss Mansfield doesn't give her 'all' to the characterization, but it was certainly all her. Her characterization was a wisp—too light, almost removed from the scene." Mort Persky in the *Detroit Free Press* went into more detail, and was a little more evenhanded in his assessment of Jayne: "The play is still there, of course," Persky wrote, "but Miss Mansfield somehow managed to turn it into more of an animal experience than a dramatic one. It might easily be deduced that she is a poor actress. She isn't. She set her sights on acting early in life and has spent a lot of time since then learning how. The result: she is a more than competent actress. . . . She can act—but, alas, the actress in her keeps getting stampeded by the Jayne We All Know And Love. . . . Consider Jayne as she makes her first entrance on the stage in a dress tight enough to make neat surgical incisions here and there. All the leg that shows is bad: knobby knee and spindle shank. . . . The dress is cut on a note of suspense: will it or will it not maintain decency and order, holding that glandular Maginot line?"

Persky also interviewed Jayne during her stay in Detroit. She told him that "I admired Kim Stanley when she did [*Bus Stop*] on Broadway. It's a role I've always wanted to do. I thought it would be fun. . . . I feel myself growing as an actress again. Right now we're trying to arrange a 15-week tour with *Cat on a Hot Tin Roof*."

She also denied again having posed for those *Playboy* photos. "I've posed for photographers who later sold the pictures to *Playboy,* but I've never taken them up on any of their offers—they keep asking me to do things like pose underwater. But I always say no." She had the gall to inno-cently claim, "I think nudity or display of the body to stimulate lascivious interest is wrong. It is against my religion. . . . I agree with the judge who said *Playboy*'s captions were written to conjure up lascivious feelings in men's minds. I think the captions put new meaning into the pictures." This at a time she was still shilling *Jayne Mansfield's Wild Wild World,* chock-full of nudie photos with lewd, winking captions.

Perksy also asked her which 1964-vintage actors she thought were sexy. Momentarily thrown, she mulled it over. "Paul Newman . . . or perhaps Alain Delon . . . would be my selection as the top masculine sex symbol. Mastroianni I think of as more of an actor than a sex symbol. Then there are George Hamilton, Raf Vallone, Curt Jurgens. . . . But I think I'd have to choose, finally, Alain Delon." Mickey, noticeably, did not make the list.

Mickey and Jayne did not make rehearsals for a New York–area run of *Bus Stop* in May, as they were flying in from Rome. The annoyed cast and crew met at the Variety Arts Studio on West 57th Street; a porter read Jayne's lines, and Matt Cimber took over Mickey's.

Matt, quite naturally, takes a more positive view of Jayne's stage per-formances. In *Bus Stop,* he says, "She didn't do an imitation of Marilyn—the only time she did an imitation of Marilyn was when she did *Rock Hunt-er,* and that was the *intention.* Once she got on a stage, and she felt all those faces looking at her, she just had herself a ball. So no matter what role she was playing, she'd follow what the plot was, and the character was, it just flowed naturally for her." Matt feels that "she was a natural onstage, that's why she was so good with comedians, she had the quick comeback, she always knew how to set up a joke."

Jayne, of course, had to bring her children, dogs, secretary, and hairdresser on tour with her. While the crew and the rest of the cast made their own arrangements, Jayne, Matt Cimber recalls, "had a friend in New England who had an agency that sold motor homes, and they gave us a motor home for the whole summer, the whole tour." The adults stayed in hotels en route (very comfortable, very clean, very well run) and the children camped out in the motor home with their nanny: "We had a ball, it was a fun thing."

Jayne certainly had fun at the Newport Jazz Festival in July, while her show was playing nearby. She donned a bikini (with a beach robe over it) and wandered about carrying a Chihuahua with red-painted claws while she grooved on Chet Baker, Max Roach, Thelonious Monk, and Sarah Vaughan. "I think jazz is just *cushy*," she enthused. "It's more cushy than any bathing suit. You can enjoy jazz everywhere, but you can only enjoy a topless bathing suit in your own home."

That summer Jayne was interviewed by extremely hostile entertainment reporter Kevin Kelly of the *Boston Globe* while dining at Dinty Moore's. Kelly described Jayne looking at her children and Matt as "Madame Pompadour estimating her court. She wore a blinding black-and-white zebra print smock over a pale skirt, and her hair rose from her head like an 18th-century peruke surrounded by a braided Baroque balcony. The coiffure was constructed by her personal 'stylist,' a wispish young Montreal Italian who sat across the table and never took his eyes off Miss Mansfield's hair, rather as though he expected the whole edifice to collapse."

"I'd like to be a serious actress, a very serious actress," Jayne told Kelly. "In fact, I consider myself a serious actress, even though I'm a happy person who loves life. I mean I really do, don't I, Mickey?" Mickey, seated next to Jayne, comes off as a buffoon, quoted by Kelly in idiotic dialect: "I buys this stew at the super in Hollyvud. Is got too many perhaps potato, but many many witamins." Jayne plowed ahead: "I've formed my own company, and I have a lot of serious pictures to do, including *The Ditch-Digger's Daughter*. I hope to get Marcello Mastroianni for it. Then there's *The Man Who Grew Younger* and *The Losers,* which is extremely dramatic and wonderful, a slice of life kind of thing."

She was also interviewed—or was supposed to have been—by Harold Stein at Danny's Hideaway in Hartford. He noted that she arrived twenty-five minutes late with Mickey Jr., Zoltan, that same hairdresser, and a small dog. She juggled her sons, fans asking for autographs, some men who claimed that they were from Fox and that Mickey had arranged an appointment with her, and a phone call from Mickey, and then dashed off to tape *The Match Game* before Stein managed to get a single question in.

❤

Jayne alternated *Bus Stop* with *Gentlemen Prefer Blondes* through the summer of 1964 (reviving the latter show in 1966). Her tour covered a lot of territory, playing at the Carousel Theater in Massachusetts, the Oakdale Music Theater in Hartford (which also featured Howard Keel in *Camelot* and John Raitt in *Oklahoma!* that summer), the Melodyland Theater in Anaheim (right between Alan Young in *Finian's Rainbow* and Juliet Prowse in *Irma La Douce*), the Melody Fair in Tonawanda, New York, and the Circle Arts Theater in Reno.

Blondes was the kind of light comedy at which Jayne excelled, but Lorelei Lee was an exhausting role, with nine songs, two of them high-voltage solos. It was also a much bigger production, with numerous set changes and a cast of nine principals plus a chorus of singers and dancers.

Kelly Brytt, cast as Lorelei's wisecracking pal Dorothy, stole the show: "With the minor exception of a girl named Kelly Brytt, who has a flair for comedy and can sing, the cast acts like a crew of Broadway rejects," wrote the acerbic Kevin Kelly of the *Boston Globe,* and Maureen B. O'Brien of the *Hartford Courant* agreed: "Kelly Brytt as Lorelei's sidekick is exuberant and in fine fettle vocally." Halfway through the run, Brytt was replaced by Patrice Wymore (Errol Flynn's widow). Mike Connolly asked Wymore "how she likes buttressing Miss Mansfield. Said she, slyly, '*Weelll,* let's say it's an experience.'"

Other players supporting Jayne were the great character comedienne Renie Riano as a hapless dowager, and western and B-movie actor Dick Foran as Lorelei's millionaire fiancé Henry Spofford. Mickey was perfectly cast as health-nut Josephus Gage. He certainly looked the part—but it called for a brash, loud actor who could sing (the health and exercise paean "I'm a-Tingle, I'm a-Glow," which could have been written for Mickey). After a few days' rehearsal, though, everyone admitted that while his acting might just get by, his singing was hopeless, and the song was dropped.

On May 6 Jayne appeared on Jack Paar's show to plug her *Blondes* tour, not impressing Louis Cedrone Jr. of the *Baltimore Sun:* "Miss Mansfield, who can be, in her own way, cute, when she engages in conversation with Mr. Paar, is still imitating the late Marilyn Monroe and ought to give it up. She sang horribly, did what I think was supposed to be dancing and was wearing what looked like a fright wig."

Reviews of *Blondes* were mixed. Some reporters (and audiences) came expecting Jayne to be Jayne, and were not disappointed. Fred Russell of the *Bridgeport Post* wrote, "Jayne gave them just what they came to see. She may not be a whiz as an actress, but she has looks, shape, personality and stage presence. She radiates warmth and sex to an extent that one, if not too critical, can overlook what failings she has and still enjoy watching her. And she can sing—and make herself heard and understood way back in the last row of the big tent. . . . She is probably at her best when she works the aisles while singing 'Diamonds Are a Girl's Best Friend.'"

The *Anaheim Bulletin*'s critic was torn. "The thousands who will be lured to this edition of *Gentlemen* will see a production that is lavish, slick, brisk and wrong. Wrong because of Lorelei's brazen misconceptions. Why, she could never be Jayne Mansfield, not for a minute. . . . But when Miss Mansfield is in vague contact with Lorelei, she asserts a vigorous comic-erotic authority as herself. The first-nighters seemed warmly appreciative of her performance in general, and of her rendition of 'Diamonds Are a Girl's Best Friend' in particular." Margaret Harford of the *Los Angeles Times* summed it up: "When Jayne's on stage, you don't watch or think of anything else, which is often a good thing." But Harford went on to add, "She has most of the lines pinned right to the target, but the show itself is a pretty slapdash affair." Harford—like so many audiences and performers—hated theater in the round: "Dialogue gets lost every time someone on the stage has his back to the audience."

Others, their knives pre-sharpened, dug in with glee. "It's a bust!" wrote Maureen B. O'Brien of the *Hartford Courant*. "Miss Mansfield shows, well, we all know what she shows, and it's still not enough to compensate for her lack of acting ability. . . . Almost all of her dialogue in the first act was inaudible, being too fast and too low. The supporting cast (and the buxom blonde needs all she can get) is good, but not strong enough to pull the show through."

The nastiest bit of work came from the *Boston Globe*'s Kevin Kelly, who wrote that "Miss Mansfield is displaying herself for what she is, a small talent with a big bust; and to keep it cozy she's brought along her husband, Mickey Hargitay, whose skill equals his wife's. The only consolation for them is that they're in the most bumbling musical production I've ever seen, Summer or Winter." He wanted "to be as kind as I can about it," which is always the prelude to a slap in the face: "It's a first-class disgrace. In the case of Miss Mansfield (let's forget Mr. Mansfield, who stalks the stage looking for the exit and doesn't sing the songs given him on the program, a large blessing, I'm sure), the expectations can't be low enough. . . . She hasn't the slightest notion of what she's doing on stage. Further, she is incapable of singing any of the Styne-Robin songs so they can be understood, and she moves through the dreadful choreography with a left-footed heft reminiscent of a series of reducing exercises which, in this case, isn't such a bad idea."

Of vicious reviews like these—which made up at least half of her notices—Matt Cimber says that the intention was mostly "intimidation. . . . They saw how much an audience loved her, and how they hated that adulation. What I was always amazed at was when some [who trashed her performance] were assigned to interview her . . . how they gushed!"

❤

Over the summer of 1964, as the *Bus Stop/Blondes* tour wound its way across the country, Jayne grew closer to Matt Cimber and more distant from Mickey. Alex Freeman of the *Hartford Courant* noted that "Jayne is living in a different motel in each town they play and has a wild romance going with a director named Matt Cimber." Jayne "made me laugh," says Matt. "I enjoyed that part of it, and I enjoyed the part of making her laugh. Many times, I tried to drive a point home with her by satirizing herself— she had a sense of humor about herself. . . . I think the only mistake in our relationship is that we got married."

On August 26 Jayne filed suit in Santa Monica to have her 1963 Mexican divorce from Mickey declared valid in California. Harrison Carroll wrote, "Jayne Mansfield and Mickey Hargitay settled everything peacefully. Mickey says he bows to Jayne's contentions that the 1963 Juarez divorce is legal. They are not married anymore. However, Mickey will fulfill his contract to go East with Jayne and do *Bus Stop*." "I love my children too much to make any trouble," said Mickey. "I don't want to fight their mother." Mickey got $70,000 in the divorce; Jayne got the Pink Palace. By this time the split made few headlines—no one really cared anymore.

Years later Mickey recalled Jayne telling him, "'I'm in love with another man, and I'm gonna marry this man.' I couldn't believe it, I heard the words, I said, 'well, if that's what you want, that's what you should do.' If you really love somebody you're always going to love this person. I loved her, but I was powerless, I couldn't do anything."

❤

Jayne had long been a fan of rock music—even before *The Girl Can't Help It,* friends and reporters had complained about rock blaring from speakers all over her house. So a chance to meet the Beatles was not to be missed, especially as she knew that where Beatles go, reporters and photographers follow.

In August 1964 the Beatles were in the midst of their first world tour; they had played the Hollywood Bowl on the 23rd and weren't due in Denver till the 26th. They were seeing the Los Angeles sights, including a day at Burt Lancaster's house, and somehow on the night of August 25, three of them wound up at the Whisky á Go-Go with Jayne, Matt Cimber, and Mamie Van Doren.

There are many stories as to how this came about. In an unverifiable *Motion Picture* magazine article, it's claimed that Paul—perhaps jokingly—said he'd like to meet Jayne, and that their press agent, Derek Taylor, took off in search of her. Jayne wanted to serve them tea poolside at the Pink Palace, but this could not be arranged because of scheduling conflicts: Jayne also had an evening performance in Anaheim, so "very early" or "very late" were their only options (Jayne was actually busier than the Beatles that week). Also, according to *Motion Picture,* the Beatles (wisely) did not trust Jayne to not have a phalanx of photographers and press on hand.

It was finally arranged for them to have late-night drinks at the Whisky á Go Go on Sunset Boulevard (it had just opened that January, and was the hippest joint in town). Jayne and Matt drove to the Bel Air home where the Beatles were staying, and found John the only band member present. They took off for the Whisky á Go Go along with Derek Taylor, reporter Bess Coleman, and Beatles' road managers Malcolm Evans and Neil Aspinall. Messages were left for George, Paul, and Ringo to join them later if they could.

According to British reporter Chris Hutchins, that Bel Air visit resulted in a nasty night. Speaking in 2015, Hutchins told the *Daily Mail* that Jayne flirtatiously tugged on John's long hair and asked, "Is this real?" John stared down at her breasts and replied, "Are *those* real?" John "hated the way the Beatles were treated as novelties, rather than real people, and he couldn't bear to be touched uninvited by strangers," said Hutchins. "This prompted him to take a horrible revenge upon Mansfield, secretly peeing into the cocktail which she had asked me to mix her and watching with delight as she drank it and pronounced it 'a real humdinger.'"

Whisky á Go Go "was indescribable," said Derek Taylor. "We had to smash our way through the crowd to get in." One in the crowd was Mamie Van Doren, who elbowed her way through to get in on the action. The small group managed to find a table to squeeze behind, and after a few moments George and Ringo showed up. In photos taken that night, Jayne looks as if she could be the Beatles' trying-to-be-hip Mom. She was only thirty-one, but in her bouffant wiglet and Cleopatra eyeliner she looked middle-aged, while the Beatles, at twenty-three (John and Ringo) and twenty-one (George), looked like teenage schoolboys. John and George, unfortunately, also acted like teenage schoolboys.

"It was a total set-up by Jayne Mansfield to have pictures taken with us," said George, with some justification. "John and I were sitting either side of her and she had her hands on our legs, by our groins—at least she did on mine." *Motion Picture* asked Jayne what she thought of George. "'Gorgeous' was her word. 'He's so composed and relaxed.' And Ringo? 'He's darling,' effervesced Jaynie. 'He has such a tremendous reserve. He doesn't say anything unless it is important.'"

The situation quickly got out of hand, as fans and photographers crowded around. "A photographer came and tried to get a picture," recalled George, "and I threw the glass of water at him." The water, unfortunately, hit Mamie Van Doren: "My dress was soaked," she later complained to Harrison Carroll. "I'm afraid I called George a nasty little boy." The party broke up quickly, and the Beatles and Jayne went their separate ways. According to Chris Hutchins, "John whispered to Jayne what had really been in the Beatle Special, as he called it, and we were forced to make a hasty and undignified exit as she went to hit him."

Less than a year later at least three of the Beatles still found Jayne to be a dirty joke. Talking with her alma mater *Playboy* magazine, they complained that "*Playboy* made her" and wasn't going to say anything bad about her. "She's a bit different, isn't she?" said Paul. "Different." "She's soft," added Ringo. "Soft and warm," agreed George. Then Paul: "She's a clot." Ringo—always the gentleman—rolled his eyes and cracked, " . . . says Paul, the god of the Beatles." But Paul was on a roll. "Actually, I haven't even met her. But you won't print that anyway, of course, because *Playboy* is very pro-Mansfield. They think she's a rave. But she really is an old bag."

The Beatles and Jayne never met again, but in 1976, long after Jayne's death, Ringo rented her Pink Palace.

❤

In the summer of 1964 the presidential primaries were heating up: incumbent Democrat Lyndon Johnson faced little opposition, while Republicans Lodge, Stassen, Rockefeller, and Margaret Chase Smith (the rare female candidate) battled with the eventual nominee, Barry Goldwater. That summer Jayne launched the Jayne Mansfield for President campaign ("The White House or Bust!"), with an accompanying book. She had her book-launch party at the Voisin Restaurant in New York; she also showed up at a Johnson rally at Toots Shor's, with copies of her book to sell.

Joke presidential candidates have thrown their fake hats into the imaginary ring since Leonard "Live-Forever" Jones (of the High Moral ticket) in 1848. Other faux candidates included Will Rogers ("I am not a member of any organized political party. I am a Democrat"), Gracie Allen (running as a Surprise Party candidate), Pogo (a million "I Go Pogo" buttons were sold), comedian Pat Paulsen ("All the problems we face in the United States today can be traced to an unenlightened immigration policy on the part of the American Indian"), Snoopy, *Mad* magazine's Alfred E. Neuman ("What, me worry?"), and Yogi Bear.

Jayne Mansfield for President was a delightfully silly little paperback crammed with photos of Jayne on Mount Rushmore ("a new bust rises"), doing the twist with Khrushchev ("Shake it a little faster, Jaynitchka, and I'll give you Albania and Cuba!"), at the Middle East trade conference ("Hi, Sheik, baby, let's trade your oil for my watermelons"), addressing a joint session ("And so I say to all you sweet Congressmen, don't make more laws—make more love!").

The inside copy proclaimed, "All right, now look down the portrait gallery of the American Presidency. What do you see there? Beards, side-whiskers, bald heads, scowls. What's missing? I'll tell you what's missing, buster—a cupid's bow smile, a false eyelash wink, a nifty cleavage. If a farmer, a clerk, a general, a Southerner can make it to the White House, why not a lady . . . better yet a WOMAN! We have a stand-out candidate in mind, and we want to show you what would happen when she rolls up her sleeves, throws out her chest and takes charge of the political scene."

It's very pre-feminist, very "a girl president? How silly!" but too light-heartedly whimsical to be offensive. Three years later a letter to the *San Bernardino County Sun* from one Violet Nimmo complained, "We now have a movie star senator [George Murphy] and a movie star governor [Ronald Reagan]. I shudder when I think what might happen if Jayne Mansfield decided to run for President of our country. Many illiterates who have never voted before will make it to the polls to vote for a movie or TV idol; therefore I am wondering why there isn't a way of testing people for common intelligence before allowing them to vote. I think it's about time we stopped exalting jerks and started thinking about the good of our country."

❤

On September 24, 1964, Jayne and Matt traveled to Baja California, Mexico, and got married. Matt was variously described in headlines as a "director," "intellectual," "ex-writer," "former college wrestler," and—writing poor Paul off completely—"Jayne's second mate." Matt said, "I was particularly attracted to her mind," which of course all the newspaper reporters found hilarious.

Jayne, maybe in a jab at Mickey, said that Matt "has the most beautiful physique I've ever seen. Our strength comes from the mind and not the body. He is very virile. He is the most wonderful person I ever met. He will be able to give me everything. Already, he's teaching me about authors and books and great plays. . . . I've never been so happy. I always dreamed about falling in love. I didn't think love existed, but I was wrong. I never knew it was possible to be so happy." If Mickey had been the athletic Joe DiMaggio to Jayne's Marilyn Monroe, Matt was her intellectual Arthur Miller.

Mickey told Earl Wilson, "I devoted eight years of my life to her and I enjoyed it." He was in Rome filming the sword-and-sandal epic *La Vendetta dei Gladiatori,* and was spotted dating California girl Gloria Wall and flight attendant Ellen Ciano (who eventually became his third wife). Ciano confirmed, "It's pretty serious between us. I'm really flipped over Mickey, but we haven't discussed marriage." She also told Harrison Carroll that Mickey "wants no more trouble with Jayne and her new husband Matt Cimber, but he will insist on seeing the children when he returns to New York." That "seeing the children" would not go smoothly.

"I certainly don't think much of Jayne's new husband, that's for sure," Mickey told the *Fort Lauderdale News.* "I just hope she brings the four children with her [to Rome]. I am dying to see them, along with Jayne." Meanwhile, Mickey's lawyer, Jerry Weber, released a statement: "We not only are going to challenge the legality of the Mexican divorce decree, but we will file an action to seek custody of the children for Mr. Hargitay."

After their marriage, Matt, Jayne, and her four children (plus dogs) moved in with Matt's parents, the Ottavianos, in Floral Park, Queens (Jayne Marie was enrolled in a school in Sag Harbor). His mother told the *New*

York Daily News, "I think it's wonderful! She's really a lovely person. . . . My Matt is a very intelligent young man, and I'm sure they'll make a go of it. Matt's pretty stubborn, too. And Jayne has a lot of things going for her." Jayne was making noises about selling the Pink Palace and using the funds to buy a New York townhouse.

Unable to let go of her dream house, she instead sold two Pen Argyl properties (those rich grandparents were gifts that kept on giving), and she and Matt bought a house at 52 East 69th Street, two blocks east of Central Park, in what is now Museum Row. The house—built in 1925—has four stories, an elevator, marble floors, and numerous fireplaces. It is adjacent to the Italian embassy; Jayne was taking up Italian cooking, and was studying to become a Roman Catholic.

Jayne should have been happy and settled; she had a husband who both loved and liked her, and who was doing his best to guide her into less appalling film and theater projects. She had loving new in-laws, a beautiful home, and a fresh start in New York. But as Jim Bishop noted in a November 1964 interview, her façade was cracking. Bishop was known to be one of the nastier gossip columnists, and at first he seemed to be going in for the kill: "Her massive vanity can only be fed by headlines and a name in lights."

But Bishop sensed and reported something sadly amiss with Jayne. "In front of the cameras, she is still a caricature of a woman," he wrote. "At home she is a cook, a dishwasher, mother, wife and sweetheart. She is loving, adoring, and impulsive. . . . Formerly, she bubbled all the time. Now she is defensive, evasive, and she will sip a little champagne and a little martini too. . . . Somewhere there is a deep hurt. Cimber treats her gently. He has faith in her talent, and Jayne needs such warmth. His family has taken the sex symbol to their hearts. Still, she receives letters from Hargitay saying, 'Come back. You belong to me,' and Jayne pretends to dismiss them with a shrug, but the message is stamped on her mind. . . . If she weeps, she does it alone."

Matt was the latest in a long line of husbands, boyfriends, agents, lawyers, and friends who tried to (figuratively) shake some sense into Jayne. It took him less than a year to discover that he had taken on an impossible task.

❤

For a moment it looked as if Jayne's career was on the upswing: she was signed for a cameo in *The Loved One,* a big-budget dark comedy from

MGM. Based on an Evelyn Waugh novel about the funeral industry, it featured brief, colorful appearances by Liberace, Milton Berle, Tab Hunter, Margaret Leighton, Barbara Nichols, and John Gielgud—Jayne might be seen only briefly, but she was in very good company.

She flew to Los Angeles in late November and put in a day's work (beautifully coiffed and made up), playing a traveler's aide at the TWA counter at International Airport, in a scene with stars Robert Morse and Jonathan Winters.

All was not well at home: when she reentered the Pink Palace for the first time in goodness knows how long, she found that the caretakers she'd hired had fallen down on the job. The home had been looted of $10,000 worth of lamps, TVs, and other furnishings. Jayne hired a twenty-four-hour guard, and let it be known via Sheilah Graham that "she knows who took the things, doesn't want to make trouble, just wants them back." By the end of the month, she had rented the house to a "store magnate from the East."

Sadly, *The Loved One* did not pan out for Jayne: the film ran way too long (four hours), and Jayne's cameo wound up on the cutting-room floor, along with Ruth Gordon's.

Still, while she was in Hollywood Jayne's press agents were doing their stuff: one of them managed to get a six-month-old story about how she owned two hundred pairs of shoes printed in more than eighty papers around the country. An interview with Russian journalists Nikolai Polianov and Alexei Adzhubei also made the rounds—in the midst of a serious discussion of political and cultural matters, they were asked whom they preferred, Jayne or Elizabeth Taylor? The Russians gamely played along. Polianov deadpanned, "I would state a preference for Miss Mansfield because her artistic arguments are most impressive," while Adzhubei countered, "I put Elizabeth Taylor higher. She is stronger in the inner portrayal of her role."

❤

The movies didn't want her; *Bus Stop* and *Gentlemen Prefer Blondes* had run their course; and now Jayne embarked on what was to be the last phase of her career: lounge singer. This was not the kind of act she had done in Vegas, with a big budget, glitzy costumes, impressive sets, and professionals writing her jokes. This was not Nat King Cole or Barbara Cook singing at the Oak Room or the Café Carlyle. Jayne's act was more like Bill Murray's

"Nick the Lounge Singer" parody on *Saturday Night Live,* or Bette Midler in her Vicky Eydie routine ("an around the world revue entitled 'Around the World in 80 Ways!'").

Jayne had reached show-biz rock bottom, but she was actually a good lounge singer, and genuinely enjoyed it: especially the one-on-one schmoozing with her audience. "She didn't have the greatest voice of all time," admits Matt Cimber. "I rewrote the lyrics to 'Put the Blame on Mame' to 'Put the Blame on Jayne,' and she would go out in the audience with a microphone and interview people. She did a hilarious bit where she'd go to some guy who was sitting with his wife, and sit in his lap and interview him. She'd look at a woman at another table and ask if that woman wasn't a better mate—it was hilarious." Jayne had a natural talent for this type of venue. "She did it all off the cuff," says Matt. "She was incredible. She had total control, she would make it real funny. She'd ask the wife, 'What's your favorite thing about him?' and she'd say, 'Oh, I like his blue eyes,' and she'd look at the husband and say, 'He doesn't have blue eyes!'"

By October 1964 Jayne was playing at the Plantation Supper Club in Greensboro, North Carolina; the *Burlington Daily Times-News* there enjoyed her act: "The famous blonde completely won over the audience with a series of wisecracks that added quite a bit of humor to the meeting," the reviewer wrote. "Jayne circulated around luncheon tables to meet and talk with each person present." While in town, she was named honorary lifetime house mother at the University of North Carolina.

❤

Matt Cimber's background was in theater, and that's what he enjoyed most. So in late October 1964 he and Jayne embarked on another show, *Champagne Complex,* by Leslie Stevens, who later wrote the more successful *The Marriage-Go-Round. Champagne Complex* had very briefly played on Broadway in 1955, starring Polly Bergen in the role Jayne played in stock, a woman who takes off her clothes every time she drinks champagne. Her fiancé (played by Douglas Marland) sends her to his uncle, a therapist, and they have an affair. The couple reunites in the last act. Matt Cimber, who directed, also played the therapist. "I'm not an actor," he says. "I only did it because it was the only convenient thing to do."

Champagne Complex ran from late October 1964 through February 1965, playing the Pabst Theater in Milwaukee and the Mineola Playhouse in Long Island, along with a few other venues, mostly on the East Coast.

The reviews were not kind. The *Milwaukee Journal* called the play "a single-joke farce which lasts nearly three yawning hours. . . . By that time, even the most avid subscriber to *Playboy* magazine is inclined to mutter '*Sheesh!* Who needs it?' and slope off to the nearest newsstand. As an actress, Miss Mansfield leaves something to be desired—namely, acting. She strides about constantly, giggles, pouts, says 'eeek!,' talks baby talk to her dog." But Sheilah Graham noted that although critics hated the play and Jayne's performance, "the show displays the standing-room-only sign, which makes you wonder how potent the critics really are."

Jayne also got terrible reviews from the Hotel Pfister in Milwaukee, which sued her for an unpaid bill of $1,049, along with $963 for damage to carpets and furniture from her ever-present dogs. Jayne's lawyer Bernard Friedman denied the charges, counter-accusing that the hotel damaged her $25,000 Bentley in the parking lot.

❤

Jayne's fashion choices shifted along with her career. The mid-1960s were a difficult transition time, style-wise: post-Kennedy era, but pre-groovy Carnaby Street. Hemlines and skirt widths varied widely; even movie stars wound up looking like slightly dowdy suburban moms. Makeup was concentrated around the eyes, with lipstick getting paler. And the hair—weird, helmet-like or floral hats were crammed over stiff bouffants and flips, with geometric Vidal Sassoon cuts just beginning to catch on.

Jayne, in her early thirties, did her best to keep up, but in 1964–1965 she struggled with tatty, back-combed wigs, and she let her dark-brown eyebrows grow back in, a look she had admitted back in the late 1950s was unflattering. She also began penciling on black Cleopatra eyeliner. The whole impression was that of an unsuccessful Jayne Mansfield impersonator, and she looked older than her years—as well as totally outside any concept of chic.

Just when Jayne was in need of new hairstyles came the Great Wig Robbery of 1965. When the US banned human-hair imports from Communist countries, wigs suddenly became worth their weight in gold. In February 1965 a band of well-organized crooks hit Wigtowne's warehouse in Brooklyn. The thieves broke in through the skylight and then through a first-floor wall and made off with $60,000 worth of goods, including four extra-fancy "nude white" wigs (worth $1,200 apiece) set aside for Jayne, and seventeen wigs that customers had left to have restyled. On their way out, the gang also pilfered an astonishing $15,000 worth of false eyelashes.

Wigtowne was not the only target in that year's hair heists. That same week salesman Alfred Averell was arrested with $111,000 worth of hot wigs and hairpieces stolen from his employer, Sylvester & Sons. He was nabbed when his getaway driver left hair hanging out the back of the truck, and police thought it was a murder or kidnapping.

By 1965 Jayne was teetering on the edge—she was seen as a washed-up has-been, but she was actually still young, lovely (when she wanted to be), and working steadily, if in sometimes dubious projects. "Jayne Mansfield jokes" still littered the variety shows and newspapers, few of them very witty. In January when Publimetrix came out with its "most-mentioned in newspapers list," Jayne had dropped from ninth place in 1963 to twenty-seventh in '64.

The soldiers still loved her: the *Army Times* asked them in the summer of 1965 what stars they'd like to have entertain them, and along with Jayne they picked Gina Lollobrigida, Paul Newman, Kim Novak, Vic Morrow, and Charlton Heston. United Aircraft Products unveiled the Jayne Mansfield Heater for survival use, thus named because it warms up your body. And she was still thought enough of a sex symbol for an Ohio real-estate development to joke, "Amy Burns lives and shops in Huber Heights. All these merchants (and more) are at her service. We'll bet you don't get the attention Amy does—unless you live in Huber Heights—or look like Jayne Mansfield. If you *don't* look like Jayne Mansfield and want the best service when you're shopping, we suggest you move to Huber Heights. If you *do* look like Jayne Mansfield, move to Huber Heights anyway. Please?"

But on the other hand, some of her publicity and career moves took on a sad, Norma Desmond quality. Jayne told Dick West of the UPI that she was going to star in a radio show—a good fifteen years after radio had turned to all-music or all-talk formats. She sent a handout to the National Association of Broadcasters reading, "This is Jayne Mansfield with a new domestic comedy radio series that I'd love to tell you about—personally. I'm available for consultation in Suite R-510 at the Sheraton Park all day today and tomorrow." West went to see her, and she told him, "*Leave It to Jayne* would also feature Matt." Asked if radio wouldn't limit her appeal, she responded: "Not at all. I feel I can project as well in oral or printed form as I can visually." She described the show as "a sort of sexy, pleasant Bicker-sons." Nothing more was heard of this project.

As her career and public profile declined, so too did the Pink Palace fall into decay, as if it were her architectural doppelgänger. In April 1965 she took out an ad in a Hollywood trade paper reading, "For lease on Millionaires Row—the fabulous 3-acre estate of Jayne Mansfield. Complete privacy, beautifully landscaped, electric gates."

Vernon Scott noticed the *Sunset Boulevard*–like eeriness of the empty house on Sunset Boulevard.

> The cavernous, empty pink mansion sits like some gingerbread tombstone. The grounds are still kept up, its rubicund glow persists; still it echoes defeat, a purposeless quest fulfilled. The house was Jayne Mansfield's monument to herself, a flamboyant, eye-catching, conversation piece . . . and empty. . . . The house and the couple lent themselves to a neo-classic tragedy. The house was never a gay, happy place. Few parties were given there; principally because the Hargitays were never part of Hollywood's social swim. . . . Never taken seriously as an actress, Jayne starred in movies on the strength of her buxom beauty and her ability to make news. . . . But still, something was lacking. There would be no Academy Awards. Her beauty could not remain intact forever. There had to be a symbol, and the pink house, wrapped in a pink cloud, was it.

Scott noted that Jayne now lived with Matt in New York "in comparative obscurity. Jayne no longer makes headlines. Perhaps she does not wish to. And her rock, her fortress, on Sunset Boulevard, stands empty."

Jayne was a rootless tumbleweed: she spent years creating the most famous home in Hollywood, but she was never really "at home" anywhere. The life of the actor or singer has always been one of travel—from the Elizabethan strolling players to traveling vaudeville troupes to bands making one-night hops. So many performers have a home base they rarely see. Jayne had a perfect ideal vision of her "House of Love," but her real homes were hotels, rented houses, dressing rooms, airplanes, and cars.

That "comparative obscurity" Vernon Scott mentioned blew up in January 1965. Mickey was back from Italy, between films, and while in New York he asked if he could see the children on January 14, to give them their late Christmas presents. It was decided best that he not stop by the Cimbers' house, so he and Jayne arranged to meet on Fifth Avenue.

Jayne and Mickey approached the corner of Fifth and 72nd Street, Jayne accompanied by Zoltan, Mickey Jr., and Matt Cimber, who had their Afghan hound on a leash. Who said what to whom is a matter of dispute, but the two men began fighting, the boys began crying, Jayne tried to comfort the children and break up the men—and the photographers (of course there were photographers) clicked away.

Mickey was holding Zoltan in his arms when Matt threw a punch at his non-Zoltan side, managing to break a bone in his own hand. The whole skirmish lasted maybe a minute, after which everyone stalked off. But both Mickey and Matt had their stories to tell. "Zoltan jumped into my arms and Cimber swung at me," said Mickey. "If I had punched him, he would have sued me for attempted murder." He told Hedda Hopper that Matt set the whole affair up for headlines and to make Mickey appear jealous. "I'm not. I walked away from a street brawl. When I go through New York I'll see my children. But not on a sidewalk."

For his part, Matt told the *Boston Globe* that "I'm not scared of that muscleman—I come from Brooklyn. I can knock his capped teeth off. He belongs in a tree." Jayne chimed in on Matt's behalf, telling Alex Freeman of the *Hartford Courant* that Mickey had brought photographers with him because he was angry at her for refusing to go on *The Tonight Show* with him to plug his new movies.

The three settled into a wary, guarded truce, although it sometimes flared up into outright aggression. Harrison Carroll reported that Mickey called the Cimbers' house asking for "Mrs. Hargitay." Jayne Marie recalled that Jayne was not innocent in the matter, either: "She would have problems with Matt, and would call Mickey, and things got stirred up." Today, Matt Cimber says, "I wasn't a great fan of Mickey, but he wasn't really a bad guy."

Shortly after the New York street fight, Mickey came by the house when Mariska was running a temperature. Jayne and Mickey began arguing over whether or not to call a doctor. "Finally I said, 'C'mon, this is ridiculous,' and I said, 'I'll call the doctor,'" says Matt. "I went over in the living room and picked up the phone. Mickey—from the other end of the living room—said, 'Put the phone down,' and he started coming at me! So I hit him with my cast, and I broke my bone all over again."

If Mickey thought he might win Jayne back, that thought ended when the Cimbers announced in March that they were expecting a baby. Matt delightedly told Louella Parsons, "Everything good is happening to us. I have interesting plans set up for Jayne's career. She's done four Jackie Glea-son shows and we're working on a TV series starring her. She'll also try to get in a film in Tokyo called *The Evasion* before the baby arrives."

Mickey returned to Italy in June to film the spaghetti western *Lo Sceriffo che non Spara*, but did not find Rome any safer than the streets of New York. While asleep in his apartment, he was clubbed on the head and stabbed by an intruder. He went unassisted to the hospital and was treated for "a pretty deep cut near the heart and a superficial cut in the abdomen." "I tell you the truth, I'm lucky to be alive," Mickey said. "I'm all mixed up and confused about this. Who did it? I don't know. It could be so many people. But honestly I don't feel I've done anybody any harm. I always try to be nice to people. I don't see why anybody would do such a thing." Producer Ralph Zucker thought the attack was over Mickey dating actress Marie Vincente, noting that he had received a threatening letter from one of her former flames.

Roman police brushed his injury off as "superficial and self-inflicted," just as Jayne's shipwreck had been called a publicity stunt. One policeman quoted Mickey as having said, "I don't know who did it, but it was probably some girl who did it with her fingernails." Another showed a master's adroitness at English: "The story has been re-dimensioned quite a bit." Earl Wilson ran a quote from Jayne on the incident that is highly dubious, as it sounds much too mean-spirited for her: "I hope for Mickey's sake it was one of his publicity stunts because I know those are nearer to his heart than the knife was."

By the time Matt married Jayne, she had so many issues that all of his good intentions were futile. Her drinking was getting out of control, though she rarely let it affect her performances. She had managed to keep this a secret until one night in June, when Alex Freeman of the *Detroit Free Press* leaked the news that "Jayne Mansfield and husband Matt Cimber made an intriguing sight as he carried her—over his shoulder—struggling and screaming up the stairs and over the threshold of their New York townhouse the other night. Her language, easily understood, however slurred, made it obvious that our Jayne had delved deeply into the grape."

In July Jayne and advice columnist and psychologist Dr. George W.

Crane guested on *The Mike Douglas Show.* Jayne, rather open and vulnerable, spoke of the tension she and other stars were under and asked him, "What else can a person use to combat insomnia and get a good night's sleep" besides pills? Crane said sleeping pills should be outlawed, like "goofballs and other stimulating drugs," and advised reading "an educational magazine or a few chapters in the Bible." Sleeping pills, he insisted, "only help you avoid facing God. So get hep!"

Jayne and Matt also had money worries (their business manager put them on an allowance of $225 a week, to be split between the two of them), and Matt had family troubles: in June his mother was rushed to Lenox Hill Hospital with a heart attack. "Momma, who had worked herself to a frazzle as Jayne's housekeeper, had decided the money wasn't worth it and was going to quit," wrote the ever-gossipy Alex Freeman, "but after she got out of the hospital, Jayne promised to be more considerate and Fanny may return to her employ." Matt, today, brushes that off as "nonsense!"

There were more problems at the Cimber house than Jayne's drinking or Mrs. Ottaviano's health. On Mother's Day, Matt's father was visiting his wife at Lenox Hill Hospital while Matt, Jayne, and the children enjoyed the nice seventy-degree-ish day to go boating in Central Park. When they returned home at 6:20, they found their house had been broken into, via a rear, ground-floor window accessible through an alley, and $51,000 worth of jewelry had been taken from Jayne's bedroom jewel box.

Jayne had always worked during the early stages of her pregnancies, and she did not want to just sit around the townhouse getting bigger through the summer of 1965. "She said, 'I can't spend the whole summer doing nothing, I'll go crazy,'" Matt recalls. "So we found this wonderful play about this pregnant girl, *Nature's Way.* So we went out on the summer-stock circuit, and it was hugely successful. Everyplace she went, she sold out."

Nature's Way was written by Herman Wouk (*The Caine Mutiny, Marjorie Morningstar*), but it was far from his best work. It had played—briefly—on Broadway in 1957, starring Betsy von Furstenberg and Orson Bean as young marrieds expecting their first baby and dealing with a mother-in-law, taxes, and jealousy.

Matt directed and costarred in the show. "The new laff-riot," as it was billed, played in the Veterans' Memorial Auditorium in Columbus, Ohio; the Ivorytown Playhouse in Hartford (which was soon to feature Shelley

Winters in *Who's Afraid of Virginia Woolf?*); Eddie Rich's Colonie Summer Theater in Latham, New York; the Town and Country Playhouse, Rochester, New York; and Guy Palmerston's Lake Whalom Playhouse in Fitchburg, Massachusetts, among other venues.

As ever, hotels dreaded her approach. Jayne and her entourage were asked to leave the Christmas Island Motel in New Hampshire, due mostly to the seven dogs that accompanied them. "Seven dogs are six too many," said owner Philip Roux. "Miss Mansfield is a fine person, but she's no different from any other guest when it comes to this kind of problem." Jean Walrath of the *Rochester Democrat and Chronicle* numbered the crowd as Jayne and Matt, all the kids, a secretary, a bodyguard/moving man, two Afghans, one Great Dane, three Chihuahuas, and one Pomeranian. "It's wonderful we can have our family together with us. I try to see good in everything," said Jayne.

As usual, interviewers loved her; she always provided good copy. Charles Marland of the *Hartford Courant* wrote, "Aside from being a great-looking lady, she is also very nice. No airs. No phony. Polite. Regular. And if you've seen her pictures and think she's a little soft upstairs, she's not. Smart. Bright. Sense of humor." She enthusiastically told Ken Echard of the *Troy Times Record* about her pregnancy diet: porterhouse steaks and her own salads. "I throw in everything. Well, you know—hard-boiled eggs, scallions, radishes, carrots and an oil vinegar dressing—and oh yes, don't forget the salami!" Echard pondered, "What does the future hold for Jayne? No one really knows. Not even Jayne herself. But one thing is for certain. With all the warmth, charm and lovingness she has, she will never lose the success she has attained."

She told the *Fitchburg Sentinel* about several films in the works, none of which panned out: her Bond parody; *What a Mother!* at Fox; *Honorary House Mother at a Boy's Fraternity*; and a Broadway show called *Vanessa— Forty-Eight Hours in Feathers*. Jayne spoke of her "13-year-old daughter" Jayne Marie (who was actually fifteen), and said with unintentional irony that today's teens should "not grow up too fast . . . there is a right time to do the right thing." Her advice to young actors? "Get . . . experience in your own home town, and in college. When you feel you have enough to back you up, then go on to Hollywood and New York."

Love Jayne the critics did; love *Nature's Way* they did not. Jean Walrath wrote, "Jayne Mansfield made her entrance on stage at the Town and Country Playhouse last night wearing a billowing turquoise negligee with white fur cuffs. She made her exit in an ice blue lace dress with ice blue ostrich feathers around the hem. Between those two gowns—and there were eight others—[was] something that could be called a play. . . . Besides wearing gowns, the temporarily plump Miss Mansfield did some acting that wasn't at all bad. All the cast did every bit as well as could be expected."

Walrath also interviewed Barry Tuttle, who managed the theater in which *Nature's Way* was playing. "Jayne Mansfield came to town and while hundreds clustered around her motel to get a look, the theater starved. . . . Rochesterians will look at but not buy a carnival-type attraction." Though by the end of the run, Tuttle had to admit that "few of his shows did well that summer: *A Funny Thing Happened on the Way to the Forum, Stop the World, I Want to Get Off,* Cesar Romero in *Strictly Dishonorable* and Dorothy Lamour in *Du Barry Was a Lady* also bombed. Only *Gigi* and *Mary, Mary* did well." Walrath concluded that "a summer theater crowd will take almost anything—anything but Jayne Mansfield, that is—for laughter."

Howard Healy of the *Troy Times Record* also liked Jayne better than he liked the show: "It is hard to imagine another comedy that is as low-keyed. This comedy rambles over more subjects than an encyclopedia and fails to tie even two of them together. Nothing jells. Everything is sprawling. . . . The performance, however, is professional down to the smallest character part. And with Miss Mansfield playing her part in a knowingly soft-toned way, there were frequent bright spots in the production."

For her part, Jayne was one of the few performers who enjoyed theater in the round, which she had to deal with at Eddie Rich's Colonie Summer Theater: "I think you can reach everybody that way," she told a radio interviewer. "You're practically against the audience."

24

I know we both did it for the money. It wasn't that much in those days. She was trying to survive, and she had a family.

Mamie Van Doren

Jayne's next project was a quickie musical comedy filmed in Cape Coral, Florida, in June 1965. Producer Patrick Pleven predicted hopefully, "It won't be just another one of those beach movies, but an unusual picture that adults can enjoy, too. It's a fast-moving, breezy sort of movie with a nice feeling to it and full of exciting visual effects."

The Fat Spy may not be Jayne's worst film, but it is certainly in the bottom five. It is a "kooky" '60s comedy in the style of *The Monkees* (whose TV series debuted a year later). The plot revolves around two competing cosmetics companies searching for the Fountain of Youth: one run by George Wellington (aging movie star Brian Donlevy, of *The Great McGinty* and *Beau Geste,* in a role originally meant for George Raft), the other by Camille Salamander (Phyllis Diller). Insult comic Jack E. Leonard, a kind of second-string Don Rickles, plays Irving, the childlike, incompetent fat spy, and also his scheming twin brother, Herman. Jayne is "Junior," the daughter and second-in-command of Wellington (Junior is madly in love with Irving, to her father's understandable disgust).

Producer Pleven wanted to appeal to the teen market, so he threw in a group of vacationing beach-party youngsters, played by inexpensive pop singers Jordan Christopher, Lauree Berger, and Johnny Tillotson (their lip-synching is so inept that they appear to be mouthing completely different songs from those on the soundtrack). The only genuinely funny moments come with Leonard's anti-love ballad to Diller ("I kissed you and in my heart there was a panic—kissing you was just like kissing Darryl F. Zanuck").

Jayne, in the middle of her pregnancy, wears maternity clothes (and in one scene nothing more than a tiny towel wrapped around her—when she bends over, she exposes nearly as much as she did in *Promises. . . . Promises!*). Her wig is a helmet-like pageboy, and her acting appropriately cartoonish for the film's style, though next to Jack E. Leonard's wild over-acting, she comes off as a mistress of understated comedy. Attempting to disguise Jayne's pregnancy, "they photographed her behind anything they could find," recalled Diller. "And frankly, poor girl, *I* looked *good* next to her." Diller added, "We get along great together. When I talk to her she doesn't know what I'm talking about, but I can't understand her either."

Dick Sayers, the local press office director, called *The Fat Spy* "a bomb, a real turkey. I believe it was set to show in Fort Myers for two weeks and was pulled after one. Jack E. Leonard had a chronic allergy to mosquitoes and he was miserable most of the time. Phyllis Diller was a real character. She'd order pizza at night and save it to eat cold for breakfast in the morning. She used to carry around this huge satchel filled with thick joke books that she kept consulting."

As usual, Jayne was professional and pleasant to all. Local reporter Phil Keys saw her at Page Field, "besieged by autograph hunters," chatting with fans. The *Tampa Tribune* admiringly noted that she'd been filming in ninety-five-degree heat in an aviation jacket and helmet (and wig): "She has been out there for six hours, and always ready to pose with any tourist who had nerve enough to ask her to stand beside him. 'You better take another, honey,' she said to a woman, 'I think I blinked the first time.'"

The Fat Spy did not appeal to teens, their parents, or pretty much anyone else. It was released in Los Angeles on May 11, 1966, and played around the country at drive-ins for the next few years. Fans of Phyllis Diller and Jack E. Leonard's talent have not "reckoned with the total lack of it in the movie's director Joseph Cates and writer Matthew Andrews," wrote the merciless Kevin Thomas in the *Los Angeles Times*. "The result is a waste of monumental proportions. . . . Innate professionalism keeps [Diller], Leonard and Donlevy from losing their dignity entirely, but Miss Mansfield is grotesque in appearance and manner. . . . All told, *The Fat Spy* is about as funny as a funeral."

Jayne's life continued to be rocky as she awaited the birth of her fifth baby. Mickey was consulting with a Hollywood attorney to see if he could get partial or even full custody of his children with Jayne. Sheilah Graham reported that he had not seen them since that January fight, though in September he and Jayne came to a visitation agreement and he picked up the kids for the day.

Not helping matters was a trashy 1965 tell-all paperback, ostensibly written by Mickey, called *My Marriage to Jayne*. Dorothy Kilgallen panned it as "truly a shameful and sordid publication." The book's cover copy promoted it as "the never before published intimate details of the world's most shocking marriage told by the only man who could tell it." Walter Scott reported that Jayne's now-former secretary Russell Ray (aka Raymond Strait) was planning a book with a "wild title" about his eight years working for Jayne (it finally came out in 1974, the wild title being Dick Cavett's old joke, *Here They Are: Jayne Mansfield*).

The very pregnant but always restive Jayne performed at the "all new elegant Ambassador Restaurant and Supper Club" in Hamden, Connecticut, in which she and Matt owned a share. She spoke to Alex Freeman while in Connecticut, offering "novel advice to expectant mothers. Jayne says she goes on the wagon in her fourth month. She adds: 'If you feel like a pick-me-up after that, ask your doctor to give you some kind of a pill.'"

The Pink Palace was untenanted by this time, looked after only by "an old retainer." The *New York Daily News* said it was up for sale at $1 million for the house and property. In September Jayne and Matt (after a ten-day vacation in the Catskills) moved back in to await the arrival of their baby. Antonio "Tony" Raphael Ottaviano Cimber was born on Sunday, October 18, at Cedars of Lebanon Hospital, just three hours after Jayne checked in. He was ten days late, Jayne told Louella Parsons. "I guess he was waiting for our doctor, Dr. Red Krohn, to get back from Europe." Jayne was photographed with perfect hair and makeup (including Cleopatra eyeliner) shortly after the birth. Headlines variously called Tony Jayne's third, fourth, or fifth child, and when Jayne Marie was remembered, she was reported as thirteen, fourteen, or fifteen years old.

Jayne spent most of November at home looking after Tony and straightening up the Pink Palace, though she did cut the ribbon at the White Front Store in South San Francisco. Carol Channing and Jayne's *Wayward Bus* costar Rick Jason also attended, along with Beatles lookalikes the Liverpool Five.

❤

While Jayne was preparing to give birth, Matt was hard at work on her next touring show, ironically about an ex-chorus girl who marries a scientist and cannot get pregnant. *The Rabbit Habit* was written by Rex Carlton, who also wrote the wonderfully awful horror movie *The Brain That Wouldn't Die*. Matt directed, and the producer was Dick Randall, who later produced Jayne's posthumous "documentary." *The Rabbit Habit* had an impressive supporting cast: Hugh Marlowe (*All about Eve*), Alex D'Arcy (*How to Marry a Millionaire*), Joan Shawlee (*Some Like It Hot*), and raucous character actress Marjorie Bennett (who had been briefly seen in *Promises. . . . Promises!*).

The show opened on December 1 in Denver and played a week before moving on to the Oriental Theater in Portland—where co-producer Lee Hewitt cancelled it. He claimed that he refused to hire three union stage-hands he didn't need; theater manager Harry Hanson said the number of stagehands was set at eleven, and the eight assigned to the show simply would not suffice. Hanson also said advance sales were not good. The company packed up and left for Seattle; their San Francisco date was cancelled before they even got there.

Jayne told Olga Curtis of the *Orlando Evening Star* that the show was a comedy "in which I play a flighty wife who can't have a baby, which is a pretty funny part for me." The *Rocky Mountain News* called *The Rabbit Habit* "un-funny and un-sexy. What is worse, it is unprofessional. The two-act play has too many faults—primarily with the script. Opening night found actors falling over sets, doorbells ringing before anyone was at the door, and the prompter emerging as the star of the show." *Variety* agreed that "though Jayne Mansfield has comic possibilities, the show is poor . . . woefully written and misdirected."

"Some of the cast members are mumbling, but so far no open rebellion," wrote Dorothy Manners, and Harrison Carroll added, "It's been a little hectic but *The Rabbit Habit* will make it to Broadway. They are due to open on Valentine's Day at the Hudson Theater. Jayne will take a week off on the Northwest tour to spend the holidays at her pink stucco mansion here."

No such luck. The Broadway run was cancelled, at a loss of $60,000. Jayne decided not to continue the tour, as she had club dates and yet another terrible, terrible movie to make.

♥

Jayne's next film started life as *Country Music USA,* but due to the popularity of TV's *The Beverly Hillbillies* it was saddled with the title *Las Vegas Hillbillys* (that inexplicable spelling was often rendered in ads and reviews as "Hillbillies" or "Hill Billies"). It was shot in December 1965; Jayne's few scenes were filmed late that month.

Las Vegas Hillbillys tells the story of Woody Wetherby (singer Ferlin Husky, in one of his few acting roles), who inherits a rundown Vegas saloon from his uncle, along with $40,000 in debt and the contract of singer/waitress Boots Malone (Mamie Van Doren). There's not much suspense: Woody quickly makes the business a success, with the help of his no-nonsense Aunt Clem (veteran character actress Billie Bird) and Vegas star Tawny Downs (Jayne, floating in and out of the film like a somewhat detached, benevolent spirit, wearing a series of loose-fitting clothes—two months after giving birth to Tony, she had not lost all of her baby weight). Aunt Clem gets all her country-star friends to perform, and Tawny handles the gambling concession (this consists of Jayne—smothered in ostrich feathers—standing next to a roulette wheel looking vaguely interested). The film doesn't really end, it just stops—there's a pie fight, Woody and Boots kiss, and it's over.

The "Hillbillys" are written and acted as condescending *Li'l Abner* caricatures, though Billie Bird and Don Bowman—as Woody's pal Jeepers—manage to surmount the script with their engaging performances. Even country-music fans will be overwhelmed by the endless numbers, featuring stars lip-synching to their hits, with varying degrees of comfort. There is certainly a banquet of great singers on display: Ferlin Husky had passed his 1950s peak, but he was still hugely popular; Del Reeves sings two of his catchy novelty numbers; Connie Smith—just breaking through to stardom—does a terrific "Nobody but a Fool," and "Southern Gentleman" Sonny James does three numbers. Mamie Van Doren belts out two non-country tunes and does herself proud. Jayne's only number (in a dream sequence) is her 1964 recording "That Makes It!," which she lip-synchs into a telephone while doing the twist and lap-dancing on a chorus boy.

Las Vegas Hillbillys was directed by Arthur C. Pierce (*Women of the Prehistoric Planet, The Human Duplicators*), written by Larry Jackson (*Cottonpickin' Chickenpickers*), and produced by Bernard and Lawrence Woolner (*Attack of the 50 Foot Woman, Mutiny in Outer Space*), and it ranks low even on their résumés. Years later Mamie Van Doren admitted of herself and Jayne, "I know we both did it for the money. It wasn't that much in those days. She was trying to survive, and she had a family."

The publicity men tried to play up a big feud between Jayne and Mamie, and it's true the two fading bombshells were leery of one another. Van Doren later wrote, "We only had one argument—top billing" (Jayne won, although Van Doren had by far the larger role). "Jayne and I didn't speak half a dozen words [to each other]. We simply refused to be in the same room with each other if we could possibly avoid it."

The few critics who even deigned to notice *Las Vegas Hillbillys* when it had its May 1966 premiere in Fresno brushed it off. "If you go for this type of music, this should be your dish," wrote *Motion Picture Exhibitor;* though *Box-Office Magazine* hopefully (and incorrectly) predicted that "with good promotional backing [it] will garner excellent box-office grosses."

Kevin Thomas in the *Los Angeles Times* unleashed his fury on everyone but Mamie. Ferlin Husky is "funny only as a man who thinks he's handsome can be when he really isn't. The effect has to be seen to be believed." Of Jayne, "the less said the kinder," but then he goes ahead and says it: "She's the same old caricature of her former self, and, as usual, her gowns look like she got them through a mail order ad in a movie magazine." Thomas did cheer on Mamie, though: "No matter what the circumstances, Miss Van Doren always knows how to take care of herself, holds on to her sense of humor and looks great."

Impossible to discourage, the Woolner brothers planned the follow-up *Hawaiian Hillbillys,* which failed to launch. They did get Husky and Joi Lansing, taking over Mamie's role of Boots Malone, to star in *Hillbillys in a Haunted House* (1967), which mercifully put an end to the series.

❤

In January 1966 Jayne got a high-profile, high-paying gig at New York's Latin Quarter. She played there for six weeks, wearing a gown by Walt Emeson that "costs $1,000 an ounce (whole gown cost $1500)," as per Earl Wilson. "She has four costume changes in the show, which, if laid end to end, would make some other girl half a costume. Jayne's necklines set a new low."

The reviews weren't good or bad; they were resigned to what Jayne's act had become. "She may not win any Oscars, but she wins a lot of other guys and gals with her act," wrote Frank Ross of the *New York Daily News,* and Mel Heimer of the *Evening Independent* described her "doing her customary wide-eyed, breathy imitation of a dumb blonde. She does it skillfully and I commend her—but the one time I met her years back, she had brown hair and was an intelligent, level-headed performer who apparently had decided to fashion a character somewhere between Marie Wilson and Marilyn Monroe and stick with it."

Barbara Holliday of the *Detroit Free Press* called Jayne "that heart-shaped, all-American Valentine," and reported one audience member favorably assessing the show as "no corny overblown, serious songs, no 100 chorus boys to cover up. Jayne does what comes naturally." Holliday described Jayne "playing at being Jayne Mansfield for the benefit and edification of the boys in the front row. So we get the flimsy negligee, the rainbow, the mile-long cigarette holder, the plunging gown with the laced sides gaping, the Mansfield giggle and the Mansfield jiggle. Jayne's stint is hokey, harmless and fun, a double-barreled jape with Jayne having the best laugh of all."

Disaster nearly struck during this run, when toddler Mariska, in the Hotel Americana suite, swallowed a hundred-milligram sleeping pill. Fortunately, Matt saw her do it and called a doctor. "Jayne didn't feel up to going on the second show—but she did," said Matt.

Not many of her gigs were as high-rent as the Latin Quarter. Jayne had the habit of saying yes to every offer, and she hired too many agents, business managers, and assistants, some of them capable, some of them incompetent or crooked, and all working at cross-purposes. She sometimes found herself booked for two jobs at the same time on opposite ends of the country.

And the joking about her had become less the affectionate "the Jayne we all know and love" and more vicious. Jack O'Brian wrote in 1966 of a Legion of Decency monsignor remarking of one of her films that although he "had no moral resistance to the story nor its treatment," he couldn't approve of "Jayne's topography"; but, he sighed resignedly, "You can't do much about a freak, can you?" An ad for one of her guest spots on *The Mike Douglas Show* that year read, "Jayne Mansfield Sings (?)"

That spring Matt booked Jayne to do a southern college campus tour, ostensibly to read Shakespeare. Auburn University in Alabama, the University of Georgia, and the University of North Carolina at Chapel Hill signed up for *Jayne Go-Goes to College,* and a rock band and go-go girls were hired to supplement the Shakespeare. "'The evil that men do is oft interred in their bones,'" Jayne explained. "That means that men are born that way. The evil is just in their bones."

The tour fizzled out after the University of Miami said, "No, thank you." Student government president Tom Spenser noted that they "can find something better to do with $3,000 than listen to Jayne Mansfield murder Shakespeare." By March 8 Jayne had abandoned the project, complaining, "People have always said I have a head on my shoulders—but hardly anybody ever seems to look up that high."

She booked a week at the Three Rivers Inn in Syracuse (others playing there that season included Tony Bennett, Rosemary Clooney, and Sammy Davis Jr.). She also subbed for an ailing Zsa Zsa Gabor for four "adults-only" shows at the Valley Music Theater with Sid and Marty Krofft's puppet show. The daytime Krofft kiddie show was *Instant Fairy Tales for Children;* Jayne appeared in the nighttime version, *Instant Fairy Tales for Adults.*

❤

Jayne's next tour sprang from *Las Vegas Hillbillys,* and turned out to be as big a misstep as the film itself had been. Her professed love for country music seems convenient and contrived, but she grew up in Texas in the 1940s—along with big-band music, country provided the soundtrack to her coming-of-age. Radio stations and jukeboxes in Texas during Jayne's teen years familiarized her with the Carter family, Bill Monroe, Hank Williams—so it's not odd that Jayne, who always had a radio or record on, would genuinely enjoy the music of the *Las Vegas Hillbillys,* if not its script.

She signed on for a twenty-two-day tour through the South with the *Country Music Spectacular,* providing unlikely support for Minnie Pearl, Hank Snow, Sonny James, Johnny Paycheck, and Tommy Cash (Johnny's brother). Ads promised Jayne would be "singing, dancing, playing the 'Fiddle' and doing humorous sketches." The *Spectacular* played St. Petersburg, Orlando, and Tampa, and was not a success. Country-music fans did not want precious time taken up by a Hollywood poseur like Jayne, and whatever Jayne fans showed up got to see precious little of her.

Reviews were vicious; only Everett Parker of the *Orlando Sentinel* held his fire: "Hank Snow brought down the house. . . . Johnny Paycheck's articulate voice filled the entire auditorium and the audience registered their approval with applause and cheers. . . . The Duke of Paducah [Benjamin 'Whitey' Ford] added to the amusement by offering a solid half-hour's worth of jokes and comedy skits. . . . Jayne Mansfield, hostess of the jamboree, appeared infrequently throughout the show. She sang a couple of songs near the end, changing costumes as often as a chameleon changes its color."

Jack McDavitt Jr. of that same paper came by to interview her, as she balanced Chihuahuas Popsicle and Momsicle on her knees, which she had skinned horseback riding ("It happened in Syracuse. The horse started to gallop. He kept going and I didn't"). "She was dressed in a white sweater and skirt and go-go boots, but she still didn't look like the girl next door," McDavitt related. "Not in my neighborhood, anyway." She told him how much she loved country music, that her new record "As the Clouds Roll By" was country style (it totally wasn't). "It all started when I appeared in *Las Vegas Hill Billies* [*sic*]. Ferlin Huskey is in the movie and I liked the way he sang."

Jim Pigdeon of the *Tampa Tribune* showed no mercy, beginning with Jayne's sad, tawdry dressing room: "Cigarette butts are smashed on the concrete floor. Here Miss Mansfield is sitting on a folding chair waiting on her cue, as they say in show bizz. She sips on a soft drink in a paper cup and smokes." He moved on from there to skewer her personal appearance: "'Do you wear a wig? Your hair looks funny.' 'A wig? Of course not,' Miss Mansfield says. (Her hair DID look funny. It had the texture of, say, cotton candy, and the color of a banana popsicle.) . . . She wears no jewelry other than a wedding band set with small diamonds. Her fingernails are short and not polished. She is dressed in this gold-lamé, cowgirl-like outfit, impractical for roundup time, to be sure, but it, well, does things for Miss Mansfield's figure."

Of course, Pigdeon was not content to rest there, but produced a merciless critique of her performance. "And there, up on the stage, she stands, fingers in belt-loops, chest forward, and starts to sing. What's this, she can't sing a lick! She tries, to be sure, but she talks her way through it and when she tries for a high note it misses, and, well, it is embarrassing. Now she is walking across the stage, an unnatural walk it is, too hippy, you know? And she's laughing—an unnatural laugh, forced. Miss Mansfield did a comic routine in the show and tried a couple of songs out. It was disappointing. There were even usherettes at that center who, well, let's face it, had better physiques . . . it felt like it must have felt when I learned the Easter Bunny was not for real."

Don Sider of the *Tampa Bay Times* provided accompaniment to Pigdeon's venom. "It was . . . well . . . surrealistic, like a crazy painting by Salvador Dalí set to music," he wrote.

> About three hours of country music and about six minutes of Jayne. The country music was good for those who appreciate it. Jayne was awful. She opened the show in a gold leather cowgirl suit that made her look, for all the world, like a sexy French poodle. . . . In the second act she came back on in a white skirt and yellow sweater. You know how the guys in the Fraternal Order of Ostriches look when they have to dress like girls for a lodge skit, and they stuff their sweaters with wool sox and rolls of paper? Well, that's how she looked. She did a pretty terrible skit about milking a cow and then sang a terrible song about how a country girl can do fine in the city if she turns to organized vice. Jayne's third appearance—ah, in a red dress cut low enough to tell the world that the REAL Jayne Mansfield had stood up—was to say goodbye and thank St. Petersburghers for being such a won-der-ful audience, m-m-m-m-yuh!

Sider admitted, "There have been times, on television and in clubs, when Jayne Mansfield has exhibited some talent besides her hyperbolic physique. The Bayfront audience saw none of it though."

On May 11 Jayne dropped out of the *Country Music Spectacular,* her spokesman explaining that "she is filming another movie." (She wasn't.)

25

The most astounding fact about Miss Mansfield is that in reality she really hasn't done very much recently, . . . yet she still has an enthusiastic following.

Richard Lebherz

Matt was determined to get Jayne's career back on some kind of upward track—if not financially, then at least toward something more respectable and artistically rewarding. Touring shows and nightclubs did not seem to be working out, and the only films she was being offered were C-level trash. So he took matters into his own hands.

In 1961 he had directed a four-act play, *Walk-Up,* at Greenwich Village's Provincetown Playhouse. It was a dark kitchen-sink drama about the residents of a New York apartment building. Written by Gerald Sanford (who went on to write for *Knight Rider, ChiPs,* and *Barnaby Jones*), it got good reviews ("fascinating and always interesting"), as did Matt's direction. The three female leads were played by Carol Guilford (an unhappy teen bride), Mary Tagmin (a pregnant, unmarried woman), and Sheila Barry (a prostitute at the end of her rope).

Matt bought the rights and signed on with producers Hugo Grimaldi and Michael Musto (not to be confused with the New York gossip columnist of the same name). This Musto had written for Abbott and Costello and the Three Stooges, which did not bode well for a kitchen-sink drama. And indeed, Matt had trouble with him from the start. Matt told Musto, "'Look, if you give me the rights, we're gonna make it in a small studio in

301

Hollywood, I think we can make something really good.' I promised him that I would stay true to the play. 'The only thing is you gotta open it up a little bit,'" says Cimber. "But in any event, this guy goes ahead, and he's got Walter Winchell, he's got his wife [actress Dorothy Keller] in it, he's got things happening in it, and I felt terrible. He ruined the picture."

The film—retitled *Single Room Furnished*—was shot sporadically through 1965 and into early '66, whenever Jayne had the time, and whenever studios, crew, and actors were available. Jayne played all three female leads, as the same person during different intervals in her life: the teenage bride, the young pregnant woman, the broken-down prostitute.

It was a good idea: low-budget indie films were a springboard for many directors and performers in the 1960s, and Andy Warhol, George and Mike Kuchar, and Herschell Gordon Lewis got their start on little or no budgets. Such shoestring character studies as *The Pawnbroker, The Leather Boys,* and *Killer's Kiss* eventually got critical acclaim, if not box-office success. Even Jayne's early *Female Jungle* and *The Burglar* turned out to be great showcases for her.

The film version of *Single Room Furnished* was a drama about life in a cheap New York apartment house—particularly the life of Jayne's character, told mostly in flashback. She's first seen as teen bride Johnny; she and her young husband have a dialogue on the fire escape, which comes off rather like an acting-school exercise. Martin Horsey, as her husband, looks younger than his twenty-one years and Jayne, in a voluminous waist-length blonde wig, makes a very unconvincing teen. And red suspenders over a white T-shirt was *not* a good look on Jayne.

Johnny's husband runs off to sea and Jayne's character returns a few years later as Mae, well on the Downward Path. This second segment—a romantic triangle between three drab, lonely people—is much better, especially as Fabian Dean and Musto's wife Dorothy Keller, as the other sides of the triangle, are quite talented and lift Jayne to their level. Wearing an un-flattering plaid shirt, little makeup, and a brown wig, Jayne plays a pregnant, unwed, and desperate character, giving quite a respectable performance.

But it's in the third segment that she really shines—Johnny/Mae returns to the same apartment house as Eileen, a sad, broken prostitute in a tight dress and bouffant blonde wig (actually one wig and two hairpieces, all pinned precariously together). She flirts with a janitor and fends off a lovesick sailor and an obnoxious john (played by Bruno VeSota, who had directed Jayne in *Female Jungle*), and she gives her best dramatic performance since *The Wayward Bus.* Her Eileen wears a thin shell of cheer over hopelessness, and in her last scene, where she dares the sailor to kill her, Jayne gives as brave and honest a performance as she ever had.

Single Room Furnished had a very limited release in late 1966. Says Matt Cimber, "It was amazing how people flipped for Jayne! Which bothered [Michael Musto]—so he took it and put it on the shelf. She's wonderful in it, she'd never done anything really like that. She worked so well, in her whole approach to the role. We had a great cinematographer, he went on to win Academy Awards [László Kovács, later of *Easy Rider, Five Easy Pieces,* and *Paper Moon*]. Terrific fellow."

The film finally had an official release shortly after Jayne's death, with a tacked-on intro by Walter Winchell, himself in a personal and career downward spiral. Whatever his previous reservations about the film, Michael Musto now said that "Jayne proved she was really a fine dramatic actress in this picture. All she needed was a chance to prove her ability. Nobody was willing to give her an opportunity. She gives a warm, moving performance."

Musto also gave an inaccurate and self-serving account of the production, never once mentioning Matt Cimber: "Jayne began the picture with me in September of 1966. But she had another commitment in October. We stopped shooting until February of 1967. There were problems and we had to stop production again with five key scenes to film. She died in June before we could finish the picture. . . . I had to rewrite and reorganize the picture so it would make sense without the missing scenes." None of this was true; she had been shooting with Matt since 1965, and the film was completed by the time she died.

Only the *San Francisco Examiner* deigned to review *Single Room Furnished,* writing, "This may be—quite seriously—the worst film to go into general first-run release. The late Jayne Mansfield, who deserved better, is the only name in the cast."

❤

With the collapse of the *Country Music Spectacular* and *Jayne Go-Goes to College,* it was back to *Gentlemen Prefer Blondes,* which Jayne revived in the summer of 1966, performing at the Music Fair Theater in Long Island, the Painters Mill Music Fair in Pikesville, the Valley Forge Music Fair, the Storrowtown Music Fair in Massachusetts, and the Westbury Music Fair on Long Island.

At the Camden County Music Fair, she shared the summer season with Liza Minnelli in *The Boy Friend,* Shirley Jones in *The Sound of Music,* and Howard Keel in *Carousel,* so this was no cut-rate tour. Though Mary-ellen Lake of the *Hartford Courant* did note that "the feminine costumes, unfortunately, seem to have seen better days. Their somewhat rag-tag condition gave the whole thing an air of a traveling medicine show . . . it is hoped that by now Miss Mansfield's second-act costume has been mended."

As usual, hotels dreaded her approach—well, not all hotels. At the Warren House motel she wandered around the lobby in a bathing suit, but "nobody was calling the manager. No one had to. He was standing right behind Miss Mansfield, grinning broadly."

Jayne and her retinue were as good as a show themselves. Leonard H. Gashel of the *Philadelphia Inquirer* spotted seven-year-old Mickey Jr. selling memorabilia outside the tent: autographed photos, rocks, frogs, and turtles. "Miklós is fascinated with small animals and rocks and he thinks they are worth a lot of money," said Jayne. "I normally pass out my autographed pictures free to persons desiring them but I suspect that Miklós is selling them behind my back." Gashel reported, "She wants to travel with the children and thinks it is 'very educational' for them. On Monday night [two-year-old] Mariska stopped the show by running down the aisle during 'Little Rock' and jumping into Jayne's arms." Jayne explained, "She sleeps through most of my performances but she probably woke up just as I was coming on stage and had a sudden urge to join me."

Otto Dekom of the *Wilmington Morning News* joined the long line of reporters who were unimpressed by Jayne professionally but who found her a charmer in person. "While one expects the private and public image of an entertainment star to be different, the contrast presented by Jayne Mansfield is surprisingly great. Off stage, she is quiet, unassuming, and charming." In her dressing room, "two boys were on her flank and her teenage daughter—who physically takes after her—stood behind the chair. Obviously, the tableau was arranged for the photographers. Nevertheless, even after the pictures were taken, the boys clung to their mother. Only when she sent them to kiss the hand of the lady sitting next to me did they let go. During our conversation, the younger boy climbed on his mother's lap, beside a tiny dog."

Dekom found it rather sad that "Jayne talks as though she still had a thriving career, studios bidding for her—was she trying to convince her interviewer, or herself? Or did she really believe her own PR? 'My husband manages me and we discuss what I'm going to do—sometimes we agree. I try to balance everything, the dramatic role, the glamorous role, the nightclub appearances, how many motion pictures I do, and records. None of us is beyond taking lessons. I hope when I'm 100 years old, I'm still taking lessons.'"

Jayne enjoyed playing Lorelei Lee: "It's so kicky and fun and bubbly. I adore the role, really I do, and believe me, you can grow in it. There are all kinds of new things I find in every performance."

Patti Karr got unanimous raves as Dorothy. Karr was a veteran Broadway gypsy (*Bells Are Ringing, Redhead, Once upon a Mattress*) who was later seen on TV in *Sex and the City* and *The Sopranos*.

Opening night was challenging. The prop crew dropped a piece of scenery into the orchestra pit during the first act, props were dropped and broken during scene changes, and just as Jayne went into "Diamonds Are a Girl's Best Friend," a very loud train passed by the theater.

Reviews were even less kind than they'd been on her previous *Gentlemen Prefer Blondes* tour. Lowell E. Sunderland of the *Baltimore Sun* praised Jayne's castmates Patti Karr, Isabelle Farrell, Camila Ashland, and Alan North, then closed with, "Miss Mansfield just isn't a singer. Somehow 'Diamonds Are a Girl's Best Friend' and 'Gintlemin Prifur Blahns,' as Miss Mansfield sings it, aren't meant to be pouted. But that's her style, and so goes the show." The always captious Louis R. Cedrone Jr. of the *Baltimore Sun* wrote that "the nicest thing you can say about it is that it was ragged. Timing was off, Miss Mansfield had difficulty sticking with the orchestra at times, the dancing, ambitious as it was for a tent production, was rough, and the sound seemed unusually bad. . . . Miss Mansfield, of course, has her own special talent, but while it is evident here, it doesn't do much for Lorelei. . . . I am being especially kind, and it hasn't been easy."

"Jayne Mansfield can play a dumb but beautiful blonde like Lorelei Lee without really trying, and that's just what she did last night," wrote George Beezer of the *Philadelphia Bulletin*.

But some critics saw past the increasingly lax performances and Jayne's fading vocal skills and recognized that—beyond "star power"— there was something essentially lovable about her. "The most astounding fact about Miss Mansfield is that in reality she really hasn't done very much recently either in films or on Broadway, and not since *Will Success Spoil Rock Hunter* has she had a hit, yet she still has an enthusiastic following," wrote reporter Richard Lebherz. "Whether this is due to good publicity or due to her winning personality, I don't know. I would suspect a little of both. . . . As Lorelei, she is a lovely pink fluffy kitten, and an inner touch of kindness and humor . . . plays constantly across her adorable face. You could tell, as there most always is, that there was a certain resentment in the audience against her, because after all, for goodness sakes, she is a Big Star, and she's known all over the world, so let's just see, shall we, if she lives up to her reputation." He noted that "Miss Mansfield will autograph your program after the show, that is, if you want to wait in a line that looks like it might extend from Shady Grove to the Capitol Steps."

Otto Dekom likewise recognized that "Miss Mansfield may not be the most accomplished actress, but she is an accomplished entertainer. What she may lack in technique she makes up for by the weight of her personality—not to speak of other assets. One thing particularly helped Miss Mansfield: She was trying to do her best. Many 'name' stars come to summer theater because it pays well, not to share an experience with the audience. For instance, José Ferrer last year was completely bored—and so was his audience. . . . The dumb blonde part, which made Jayne Mansfield famous, is carried off well and even her singing turns out to be pleasing, although she has neither a strong nor an unusually good voice."

The only glimpse we get of Jayne in *Gentlemen Prefer Blondes* is from her July 15, 1966, appearance on *The Merv Griffin Show,* during which she sang "Diamonds Are a Girl's Best Friend." And it's hardly a fair viewing: she brought along Mickey Jr. and Zoltan (both very embarrassed), Mariska (giggling and hamming it up), and baby Tony, as well as four yappy dogs. "Would you like to do something for the kids?" asked Merv, and guest Henny Youngman shouts, "How about feeding them in front of us?" which the audience let him know was over the line. Jayne got up and sang "Diamonds" in an affected but strong and on-key voice (though she was upstaged by Mariska, who jumped out of her chair and ran to sit next to co-host Arthur Treacher). One can't tell, of course, if this is how Jayne sang as Lorelei, or if she was just being herself that night—but it's all we have of her *Gentlemen Prefer Blondes.*

Wonderfully eccentric singer Monti Rock III was also a guest that night, and he and Jayne obviously hit it off, trading friendly chatter while Griffin, Youngman, and Treacher had no idea what to make of either of them. Rock held one of the dogs in his lap, which won Jayne over—when he sang a rockabilly version of "The Tennessee Waltz," Jayne got up and danced with him, to the audience's delight—Jayne and Rock were obviously having a ball.

After *Blondes* closed, it was back to the nightclubs and dinner the-aters (the Three Rivers Inn, "Central New York's Only Theatre Restaurant") and ribbon-cuttings (Topps Family Discount Store in Baltimore). Three Rivers Inn owner Dom Bruno told the *Syracuse Post Standard* that "it promises to be a real bang-up opening. They say the reservations have been coming in fast for the past several days. No wonder! You can bet Jayne will wow 'em with her large repertoire of comedy skits, recitations and um-m-m-m glamour."

Jayne (wearing a mesh bikini) was given the Golden Driller Award at the International Petroleum Exposition in Tulsa; she was supposed to per-form, along with Henny Youngman, Dinah Shore, and Jerry Colonna, but the American Guild of Variety Artists wouldn't let them go on for free, and the angry audience demanded its money back.

She earned $10,000 a week doing a return appearance at Gus Ste-vens's Supper Club in Biloxi. Stevens was having problems of his own: he told the *Delta Democrat-Times* that the new Mississippi liquor law, under which he was able to sell only beer, was costing him business. "I'll lose $100,000. I've got shows booked in here, obligations. Jerry van Dyke—the TV star—$7,000 a week. Jayne Mansfield. . . . I've got 200 people on my payroll. If business drops off too badly I'm going to start cutting the payroll Monday. So will everyone else." But he invited Jayne to return the following summer, if he was still in business.

May Mann threw Jayne a thirty-third birthday party at Mann's Los Angeles home, featuring a five-month-old elephant named Jumboette, painted pink (Jayne wanted to take it home, but Mayor Sam Yorty's secre-tary, Dorothy More, a guest, said it would not be legal). They served pink lemonade, and actress Sue Ane Langdon arrived with her hair streaked in twelve colors.

In San Francisco Jayne greeted returning Vietnam veterans (Squad-ron VA-85, fresh from seven months' action in the South China Sea), along with "a band, throngs of relatives and several cases of champagne." As much as Jayne loved the troops, the reciprocal feeling was fading with the years. Vernon Scott reported that the favorite Vietnam pin-up girls were Ann-Margret, Angie Dickinson, Lana Wood (Natalie's younger sister), and Dorothy Provine. "Such long-time sex symbols as Jayne Mansfield and Ma-mie Van Doren aren't creating a stir at all." Jayne was, after all, nearly old enough to be the mother of some of the eighteen-year-old soldiers. As an extra jab she didn't need, hairstylist Andre de Paul issued his list of "besttressed women," topped by the Duchess of Windsor, Babe Paley, Joan Crawford, and Grace Kelly; the "worst" list was headed by Jayne.

"The more success you meet with, the more problems you have, there is no doubt about it," Jayne admitted to Otto Dekom of the *Wilmington Morning News* that summer. Her usual sunny and optimistic demeanor had dimmed. "We all have personal problems. I think my life is the most complicated I know of. There are many forces that play against each other—having five children, having a reputation of being a sex symbol." Still, she insisted, "I enjoy handling my problems."

26

"Was I any good?" she kept asking. No matter what was being
discussed, she kept interrupting with: "Was I really any good?"

Al Forrest

By midsummer 1966, both Matt and Jayne realized their brief marriage
had been an impulsive misstep. "Mean old gossips are trying to claim
there's trouble in the Jayne Mansfield ménage," reported Earl Wilson in late
June, adding that there had been "loud quarrels" at the City Squire Motel.
The UPI reported in mid-July that "Jayne Mansfield and her husband of
less than two years, Matt Cimber, have agreed to a trial separation." Jayne
told the press, "It's because of personal problems. We'll be living under the
terms of separate maintenance but he'll continue to travel with me as my
manager. I have all the respect in the world for him as a manager and he
has handled my career wonderfully and intelligently and will continue to
do so." The *Bridgeport Telegram* could not resist going with the headline
"Jayne Mansfield Busts Up with Latest Hubby."

Jayne dined with Earl Wilson at Jilly's Saloon in New York, accompanied by four dogs. She was looking forward to seeing Mickey again, she
told Wilson: "I've given up marriage to concentrate on my career, but need
all the friends I can get." Wilson got Mickey on the phone and was told,
"Jayne needs me now. I never felt I wasn't married to her. I've never been
out of love with her."

Matt took Tony back to Los Angeles, while Mickey stayed at the Garden City Hotel—with his future wife, Ellen. "Although Jayne has made it clear she has no further romantic interest in Mickey," predicted Alex Freeman, "her pals are betting she won't care for the idea of his being around with another girl. They expect a violent explosion when Jayne returns and finds Mickey and his playmate."

The split with Matt started out amicably. Jayne and Matt would "still be together, for Matt is continuing as my manager," she told Harrison Carroll. "You know, he is one of the best in the business. We are going to try hard to work out our problems, but a legal separation seems the best answer right now." But of course these things always blow up once child custody comes into it.

Today, Matt Cimber has nothing derogatory to say about Jayne. "I got to the point where I felt like I was living my life for her, totally. I just felt like my career was going out the door, and I said, 'Look, you know, this is not working.'" Matt was friends with Jayne's sometimes-lawyer Greg Bautzer, who told him, "'Look, Matt, you guys get along so well,' he wanted me to continue helping her, and I said, 'Greg, I can't do it. I gotta move out.' And she was very upset. She said, 'We can live our lives and have our personal things and you can stay here,' and I just couldn't do it. So I took this apartment behind the Chinese Theater, I took my car, and I left. I said, 'Look, wherever I can help, I'll help.'"

Matt had found his own career stalled as he tried to help Jayne's. "I came from the theater," he says. "I was trained in the theater, and when we got married, I wanted her to do more theater. Unfortunately, we were in Hollywood, where back in the '60s there was literally no theater."

And then there was Jayne's increasing drinking problem, her use of downers to sleep and uppers to wake, her ever more contentious relationship with Jayne Marie, and her pining over her ex, Mickey—that cannot have been easy for the present husband. "She would never face the fact that she had a drinking problem," Matt recalls. "If she could have done that, I would have stuck it out. But because she totally denied it, I knew it would be a very long time before she ever would be ready, if ever, to try to do something about it. If I were a little more mature, then I might have been able to deal with the situation a little differently. But at the time, that was how I saw it had to be, that I would just leave, and enough was enough."

❤

Jayne left all her husbands behind in late July and August 1966, embarking on a performing tour of Bogotá, Colombia, and Caracas, Venezuela. For once she also left the children at home, "because you never know when a revolution is going to break out in one of those countries."

She held a press conference in Bogotá, telling reporters that she opposed contraceptives, loved bikinis, wanted the war in Vietnam to end, would rather marry an intelligent man than a rich one ("but he should at least have some money"), and would pose in the nude only if ordered to do so by a movie studio. Her nightclub shows went well, and she met not one but two handsome young love interests. Twenty-six-year-old Dutch writer Jan Cremer had written *I, Jan Cremer* in 1964; in this partly fictionalized memoir he claimed, "I've been in love with Jayne Mansfield for years." Cremer "wooed her ardently," according to Louis Sobol, during her South American tour, later "advising intimates that he and Jayne were not at all 'sympatico.'"

More sympatico was twenty-year-old student Douglas Olivares; when Jayne prepared to leave Caracas in mid-August, he had a ticket to accompany her back to Los Angeles. But Jayne found herself under "virtual house arrest" as Venezuelan authorities combed over her earnings to make sure she wasn't trying to cheat them out of taxes for her shows in Caracas and Maracaibo. Jayne bizarrely claimed that she had only been on vacation at a resort hotel and hadn't earned any money during her stay. "I think they're just playing a little game with me," she told reporters.

This did not go over well: she spent forty-five minutes with Judge Enrique Farias in his chambers, and he ordered her to be detained. Her lawyer, Ted Sifo, noted that "The [tax] offices are closed over the weekend, of course, and Monday is a holiday here. So we can't get into the tax office until Tuesday morning."

By August 17 Jayne had gone through three court appearances, was still stranded in Venezuela, and was about to miss a club date in Memphis. "I love the place and the people and everyone is doing his best to sort it out," she said, "but it's no holiday for me." Court officials declared that her documents had been "adulterated," and she was fined a rather modest $220 for irregularities in her tax-clearance papers.

By August 20 the situation was getting intimidating; she was held pending yet another hearing. "I've fallen in love with Venezuela," Jayne claimed, sounding a bit Stockholm-syndromed. Harrison Carroll noted that the $220 fine had been upped to $12,000.

It was the end of August before Jayne and her new companion Douglas Olivares flew to Las Vegas, where she was scheduled to play the Fremont Hotel. "She doesn't even have an act ready," reported Alex Freeman. Jayne did manage to cobble together a solo routine, playing two weeks at the Fremont (after her death the hotel billed her estate $7,047 for costumes they had supplied). Olivares accompanied Jayne back to the Pink Palace—the close proximity of thirty-three-year-old Jayne, her twenty-year-old lover, and her sixteen-year-old daughter was, to put it mildly, socially awkward.

Around this time her place in the pantheon of camp and pop art was affirmed by her appearance in the short film *Poem Posters,* by experimental director Charles Henri Ford. Clips and images of Jayne, Andy Warhol, Edie Sedgwick, Roy Lichtenstein, William S. Burroughs, Robert Indiana, Claes Oldenburg, and James Rosenquist were seen by the very few people who caught a showing.

Jayne also had her last encounter with her first husband in 1966, while playing a date in Tulsa, Oklahoma. "I was attending an oil show," Paul Mansfield recalled sadly years later. "She was there in town, performing in a nightclub. And it was . . . umm . . . I'm glad they didn't turn the lights up, it was a bad-looking place. So, yes, I was disappointed that it had come to that. Back in the teeny-tiny little dressing room she was selling pictures of herself for fifty cents apiece. That was a real shocker. She gave me one free."

The end of Jayne's marriage to Matt Cimber propelled her into one last great love, with attorney Sam Brody. He was just shy of his fortieth birthday when Jayne hired him in September 1966 to represent her in what would become a very nasty custody fight with Matt—most of the nastiness being generated by Brody, who was a ferocious and merciless lawyer. A partner of famed (and controversial) San Francisco–based attorney Melvin Belli, Sam had worked on the defense of Jack Ruby before veering into entertainment and divorce law.

Jayne's friend May Mann, though she did not approve of Sam, recognized his magnetism: "Sam turned on real charm from gray-blue steel eyes set in a smooth face, with a rugged jaw and sparse light hair. He had a trim, athletic build in spite of his short stature. He walked with the air of a Napoleon." Sam was also married—he and his wife, Beverly, had two children: Keith, eight, and Elizabeth, two.

Jayne's effect on Sam Brody was little short of electric. One can speculate about what was going on in his life—the state of his marriage (his wife was in failing health), his feelings about his career and turning forty—but whatever the reason, as Matt says today, "He really was in love with her, like a madman. Like this guy who never had a good-looking woman in his life, and now he's going out of his mind."

Matt has every reason to think of Sam Brody as "kind of a slime," considering what was about to happen in his custody fight. "It wasn't just Jayne, it was his reputation in town," says Matt, adding, "He wasn't the most horrible guy in the world, but he abandoned a wife who was in a wheelchair, his wife used to call me late at night and cry on the phone, I didn't know what the hell to say to her." But Matt admits that Jayne was not the best romantic partner herself by 1966. "Brody was the wrong guy at the wrong time. But I'm not so sure *any* guy could have really dealt with it at the time. The only person who could have dealt with it was Jayne herself. I really feared at the time that something would happen."

Jayne and Matt's separation had started out friendly and congenial— to the extent that any separation can. But with Sam Brody acting on Jayne's behalf, things got very ugly very quickly. Jayne flew from Los Angeles to New York to pick up baby Tony, only to find that Matt had taken him to stay with his sister in Floral Park, not wanting the baby to be looked after by Jayne and Sam. "Matt has promised to return the baby," Jayne said hopefully. "I'm sure that there will be no custody battle when we get our divorce."

But a custody battle there was. Alex Freeman of the *Detroit Free Press* reported that Matt "said that Jayne could have the baby back when she agreed to a rational discussion with him, her lawyer, and business manager Charles Goldring. Apparently Jayne has agreed to the meeting and they'll try to work out an equitable custody agreement. Matt wants to keep Tony six months of the year and let Jayne have him the remaining six months."

On September 17 Matt was ordered by a Santa Monica court to turn the baby over to Jayne; she said he was in violation of a custody agreement they had signed in July. A week later Judge William Murray of Orange County Superior Court, saying he needed more time to consider the case, continued it until October 6. But Jayne and Sam appeared before Judge Murray, claiming that Matt was using Tony as a "pawn or wedge to obtain a money settlement, or that he will bring the child back if she drops the divorce action."

Sam told the court that Jayne supported Matt and his whole family, buying him clothes and paying his medical bills. Sam dropped dark hints that he could spill some dirty details on Matt that "I feel are quite shocking and disgusting and not proper to relate at this time." The most unforgivable act in the drama came when, according to the UPI, "the bosomy actress claimed in her suit that Cimber threatened to kill the child if Miss Mansfield did not give him $50,000."

This was obviously a malicious and outlandish claim, and it's hard to believe that Jayne knew Sam was going to go this route, let alone that she could believe the allegation herself. She never had a bad word to say about Matt—even after their split—and accusing him of endangering their son was a shocking bit of character assassination, even for a shark of a lawyer like Sam Brody. No one credited the claim, and Matt somehow swallowed his fury and did not sue for libel.

Jayne's battle plan, said columnist Florabel Muir, "is the securing of depositions from Hollywood stars to bolster her claim to be a good and devoted mother. Wherever she goes, Jayne usually has her brood of five in tow. . . . Jayne asserts that Matt is willing to give her a divorce for a price." "The struggle between Jayne Mansfield and estranged Matt Cimber for the custody of their small son is getting rougher," said Sheilah Graham in an admirable understatement, "with each side promising to tell all. I had imagined we knew all. I hear that Jayne regrets having given Mickey Hargitay the old heave-ho. He was a good husband for her. You sometimes don't know what you have until you have thrown it out."

Then sixteen-year-old Jayne Marie was dragged into the case, stating in court that Sam and Jayne were perfectly capable of looking after Tony. She later admitted that "I was asked to lie, and I did it under coercion and recanted my statements, because I came to a crossroads in my life at sixteen that I had to do what I felt was right in my heart, even if she was my mother." Matt's lawyer hammered away at the teenager about Sam and Jayne's private carryings-on "until Jayne Marie made several damaging statements about mommy's drinking and use of barbiturates." Alex Freeman reported that "Jayne Mansfield says she'll never forgive estranged husband Matt Cimber's ploy of having her daughter Jayne Marie testify against Jayne during the couple's custody battle for their infant son, Tony."

Judge Allen T. Lynch awarded Jayne temporary custody of Tony, with Matt allowed one hour twice a week for visitation, pending further hearings.

❤

That unpleasantness behind her, at least for now, Jayne and Sam took off for the San Francisco Film Festival, which was held October 20–30. Whether baby Tony accompanied them or stayed with his father was not, oddly, reported in the press, despite all the recent drama. The festival's general manager, David Sacks, complained that Jayne had not been invited and he feared she would make a spectacle of herself. Jayne produced her invitation, which a sharp-eyed AP reporter noticed had the name of Polly Bergen crossed out and Jayne's typed over it.

The *San Francisco Examiner* optimistically wrote, "Playne Jayne Mansfield is said to be plotting to conceal her outgoing personality at the Film Festival and do the Grand Dame bit, thereby putting down the detractors who wanted to dis-invite her." Jayne put those hopes to rest by showing up at an event in a black dress split along its entire length down both sides, held together by crisscrossed bits of material and sheer will power. Local dowagers glared haughtily at her through their metaphorical lorgnettes: "I feel so unchic in my Norell," complained Mrs. George Dyer, whose pale blue coat was banded by sequins at hem and wrists. And Mrs. Walter Haas Jr. echoed her sentiments with, "I feel absolutely square."

Jayne's final "look" debuted in this last year of her life: Groovy Jayne. In her early thirties, she still had the baby face of a twenty-year-old, and her figure was remarkably trim for a mother of five. She ditched the bouffant wigs for long, straight ones (often topped by large bows or headbands), lightened her makeup, and wore minidresses and go-go boots. She was perhaps a tad old for the Peggy Lipton/Michelle Phillips look, but it was her most flattering since the very early '60s. Sheilah Graham observed, "She is wearing her hair like a thick flaxen cape and her mini-dresses come miles above her boot-clad legs. It is quite startling to see Jayne emerging from her tiny European sports car, always accompanied by her best friend and admirer, lawyer Sam Brody."

Her costumes became more and more of less and less as she and Sam hit all the cocktail parties and screenings she could "Polly Bergen" her way into. At a Chamber of Commerce Film Festival party, Jayne appeared "mainly in a G-string and backless skirt and covering her breasts with two Chihuahua dogs." She was turned away at the door. At another party, she was demurely covered up in silver lamé pants and jacket accessorized with purple suede boots and pale lavender kid gloves.

Four days into the San Francisco Film Festival, David Sacks had had quite enough and went to the press. "She was not invited," Sacks said. "She came anyway, she was not welcome. I finally approached her and said, 'Madame, I do not know how much a pound you are charging, but whatever it is I will pay it if you will leave.' I suppose it would be nice to have sexy starlets at the Film Festival, as they do at Cannes. In my opinion, Miss Mansfield does not meet the standard."

David Sacks was not the only person fed up with Jayne. Susie Strauss, public relations head of the Fairmount Hotel, complained, "I've been trying for two days to evict Jayne Mansfield, and do you think we can get her out of that room? I should say not. We told her she could have it for only one night, at the opening of the film festival, and she is still there with her two Chihuahua dogs. Thank goodness she didn't bring her four children as she threatened to do."

"I was invited and I'm going to many other events," Jayne retorted from the Russian Hill apartment of a friend, Mrs. Lucia Halse (Susie Strauss had finally gotten her booted out of the Fairmount). "I don't ever remember meeting Mr. Sacks. We're trying to reach Mr. Sacks now but we understand he's awfully hard to reach." As for her sideless dress, Jayne disputed the description, saying it showed "very little cleavage" and that she had indeed gotten into the Chamber of Commerce party. "My dresses are provocative," she admitted, "but they certainly are not obscene. It certainly wasn't my intention to cause an uproar. I was upset by everything that happened." Sam added, "Carroll Baker wore a dress that was a more apparent exposure of anatomy. But of course, Miss Mansfield has more anatomy to expose."

Jayne, on a roll, put David Sacks firmly in his place: "It's my contention that Mr. Sacks said all those things because he wanted to read about himself in print. I think he is a victim of bad public relations advice. So I've offered to do his public relations in the future."

Guy Wright of the *San Francisco Examiner* had the last word, calling the whole debacle "a tempest in a D-cup."

♥

After the embarrassing disaster of the San Francisco Film Festival, Jayne and Sam decided to see the town's sights—and, for good and bad, San Francisco was vibrating with energy in '66. The Compton's Cafeteria Riot had taken place in August—a pre-Stonewall LGBTQ civil-rights protest that has faded in retrospect but was quite a sensation at the time. There was also a race riot in Hunter's Point after a police officer fatally shot an unarmed black teen. In October Golden Gate Park hosted the Love Pageant Rally, featuring the Grateful Dead, Janis Joplin, and lots of drugs. The famed Summer of Love didn't take place till the following year, but San Francisco was already a gathering place for hippies, runaways, fashion innovators, artists, and rock groups (Joplin joined Big Brother and the Holding Company that year).

Although Sam was a San Francisco native, Jayne latched onto the delightfully named Ron Bygum, described by the *San Francisco Examiner* as "a handsome 6'4" local art student," as her tour guide (he later founded Ron Bygum's Fabulous Faces, a popular skincare salon).

Jayne caught a topless all-girl band at Tipsy's, and clips of them later wound up in her posthumous *Wild, Wild World* film. "Robin, leader of the group, stopped the show to introduce her," reported one paper, "then got back to the act. Jayne quipped later that she was just checking the competition."

One of the town's entertainingly colorful figures was thirty-six-year-old Anton LaVey, who in 1966 founded his Church of Satan in his tiny, black-painted Edwardian house on California Street. LaVey conducted Satanic rituals (with nude altar girls and chalices of "blood"); shaved his head, grew a goatee, and was photographed in cheesy Halloween capes and horned hoods; and kept a pet lion, till the city quite wisely made him relocate it to an animal refuge.

LaVey was no more a Satanist than Bela Lugosi was a vampire, and he was about as terrifying as Herman Munster. Chicago-born Howard Stanton Levey dropped out of high school and literally ran away to join the circus. He worked a variety of odd jobs (some odder than others) before forming his Church of Satan in the best possible place: the craziness of 1966 San Francisco. He had as much fun being a parody of a Satanist as Jayne did being a parody of a movie star. LaVey barely kept a straight face in some of his interviews, sometimes letting the mask slip and actually laughing.

Intelligent, loquacious, and well versed in religion (and human nature), LaVey told writer John Godwin, "Our religion is the only one, I think, in complete accordance with human nature. It is based on indulgence. Instead of commanding our members to repress their natural urges, we teach that they should follow them. . . . That's how most of them live already, in any case." His infamous home was, Godwin said, "wildly sinister or high camp, depending on your attitude. . . . [It is] rather like a cross between a chapel, an arsenal, and the clubhouse of a juvenile gang."

LaVey's *Satanic Bible* (published in 1969) and his interviews reveal a mixture of anti-religious homilies ("Satanism has been frequently misrepresented as 'devil worship,' when in fact it constitutes a clear rejection of all forms of worship as a desirable component of the personality. . . . I detest the sanctimonious attitude of people toward violence, always saying 'it's God's will'") and good common sense ("Stupidity—the top of the list for Satanic Sins. It's too bad that stupidity isn't painful. Ignorance is one thing, but our society thrives increasingly on stupidity").

It's not known whose idea it was for Jayne and LaVey to get together. It may have been Ron Bygum's. In late October he spent a very busy day with Jayne and Sam: she had her horoscope read by astrologer Gavin Chester Arthur, then met LaVey and his lion; they somehow sneaked back into the film festival to catch *Night Games,* and then went on to dinner at Trader Vic's.

Not surprisingly, Jayne and LaVey got on like a house afire. They were both performance artists, publicity hounds, and possessors of a sense of high camp; they found each other a great deal of fun. Although she was a Christian (lately making noises about converting to Judaism for Sam's sake), Jayne good-naturedly posed for photos at LaVey's home, holding a skull, drinking from a chalice, while LaVey loomed over her in his devil getup, trying to look menacing. The cult-like creepiness is somewhat undercut by glimpses of Sam in the background of uncropped photos, talking on the phone or slumped in a chair looking bored.

Jayne and LaVey became friends, going out on the town, talking religion and philosophy (Jayne was delighted to find someone who took her opinions seriously and wanted to discuss something other than her measurements). Another set of considerably less Satanic photos was taken on LaVey's visit to the Pink Palace—he looks like friendly Uncle Anton, hanging out by the pool, lazing around the kitchen with Sam, Jayne, and the kids, cuddling one of her Chihuahuas.

Jayne believed in religion and was mildly superstitious: "Now, if there was a ladder directly in front of me and I had a choice of going under it or around it, I'd take the latter," she said. "But if I had no choice and had to go under the blame thing, well—I don't think I'd be scared or superstitious—I just don't believe in black magic." She did believe in astrology, or at least was amused by it, and was good friends with astrologer Sidney Omar. But "Jayne's a realist," Matt Cimber said in 1965.

By the end of October Jayne was off to Vancouver. As soon as Jayne was out of the country, Anton LaVey started claiming her as a convert. "No one buys it," wrote Jack O'Brian of the *Philadelphia Daily News*. Columnist Marilyn Beck may not have bought it, but she knew a good item when she saw one, and in February 1967 gave the eager LaVey an interview: "The wizard told me that quite a few Hollywood personalities are now following Satanism," she wrote. "I can't mention their names," LaVey said, "because most are afraid for their reputations. Some even belong to other churches as a means of cover in order to maintain their respectability, but have given up believing in the hypocritical things that are preached there."

Beck added, "I couldn't ask Jayne Mansfield about it because she is traveling . . . but I'll talk to her as soon as I can get her on the phone." The very next day Beck did reach her on the phone, and Jayne laid to rest rumors of her Satanism, although the legend still crops up: "Anton is a good friend of mine and we have had some fascinating discussions concerning his religion," Jayne said. "The man is a genius, and I enjoy tremendously talking with anyone who is an intellectual. But I am not on the verge of converting, and can't understand [why] Anton said I was. I am a staunch Catholic, and I always will be."

❤

In October and November Jayne and Sam traveled north to British Columbia, where she played club dates in Vancouver and Victoria. She expressed an interest in visiting the famous Oakalla Prison Farm east of Vancouver: "I am tremendously interested in prisons and I want to visit one here," she said. "I'd also like to watch a magistrate's court in session from the public gallery. I want to visit orphanages and meet the children. I'm interested, too, in the care of the insane." As to what dresses she would wear in her shows, Jayne teased, "I will wear all the dresses that caused the furor at the San Francisco Film Festival—and lots more that are much more fun."

Jack Wasserman of the *Vancouver Sun* admired Jayne's self-promotional skills, which she had been exercising for well over a decade. "She says outrageous things in a pleasant way," he wrote. "It's easy to see why she has been the darling of the headline writers and the picture editors down through the years. It requires a rare talent to remain newsworthy on the tenuous basis that Miss Mansfield has achieved and retained her measure of fame. It is undoubtedly her greatest talent. Her nightclub act is exactly what you'd expect. Her first night was a sellout, proving the power of positive slinking." "It was a demonstration of a massive put-on," wrote the *Van-*

couver Province, "where Miss Mansfield, who knows the value of publicity, satirized her image as a sex bomb."

Jayne did indeed see all the local sights she'd wanted to tour, but managed to make a spectacle of herself in the process, garnering a lot of bad press and ill feelings among the local officials. Mickey and Matt had been steadying influences on Jayne and at least tried to rein in her zanier impulses. Sam only egged her on—after years as a buttoned-down lawyer, he seemed to enjoy the hijinks as much as she did.

She showed up late for her engagements, keeping Mayor Alfred Toone waiting so long he finally left. "A spokesman at her hotel said she'd been unwell and required medical attention," claimed the *Times Colonist,* adding sarcastically that "even if she was two hours late arriving at the Protestant Orphanage Home for children from broken homes, she was polite and motherly, wasn't she? And those two lovable little Chihuahuas she carried. She had them dressed up in knitted suits with pom-poms, didn't she, so they wouldn't be cold?"

Sam and Jayne visited Vancouver's Central Criminal Court on a Sunday, and Jayne charmed assistant city engineer William Jorgenson into letting them inside. She and Sam held a mock trial for one of her Chihuahuas (whether Momsicle or Popsicle was in the dock was not noted) for "sexual impropriety." Though they were just kidding around in an empty (except for reporters) room, Vancouver officials blew it hugely out of proportion and gave Jayne exactly the kind of publicity she didn't want. When senior magistrate William Oslter heard of it, he hit the roof, and city employee John Marshall called it an "obvious mockery of the courts."

It seemed to hit aldermen particularly hard. Alderman Hugh Stephen thundered, "I am mad. The whole dignity of British justice and municipal institutions have been brought into flagrant disrepute. This was obviously done to further the personal publicity program of a movie star. In order that we may not be faced with this type of ridiculous incident in the future an exhaustive examination of the actions and decisions leading up to this affair should be undertaken." He added that Jayne should not have been received at city hall, and that personally "I wouldn't cross the street to see her." Alderman Michael Griffin was "too disgusted to be quoted fully. But you can say that this kind of exhibitionism is an insult to all the people of Greater Victoria. If Miss Mansfield never sets foot on Vancouver Island again it will suit me fine." Jayne protested that she "only sat in the magistrate's chair for a few minutes, and then only because the deputy chief of police invited me to. I never said a word." Deputy police chief Ray Maitland agreed that "nothing of impropriety went on in my presence."

Another fluffy publicity appearance went wrong when Jayne was to be named a Musqueam princess (Inamet Quassin, or "Beautiful Star") at the tribe's community hall at 6:00 p.m. Jayne and Sam were two and a half hours late; she claimed she'd been scouring her hotel for blankets to steal and donate to the tribe, and then her car had broken down, *and* she cut her thumb on her makeup case. "I've been bleeding all day and I feel faint," she said. Jayne retired to the ladies' room with a bottle of cognac and Sam asked if the ceremony could be held the next day instead. Willard Sparrow snapped, "It's over. Not later tonight, not tomorrow." But around 11:00 Jayne was finally made a princess, and then headed for the Cave club for her 10:15 show. Hotel manager Peter Hudson said that Jayne owed him for those blankets, and for her bill of $2,700 (including long-distance calls to Acapulco). Jayne sent the hotel a check for $2,200 and considered it payment in full.

The University of British Columbia invited Jayne to speak about "obscenity and the law." One law student said to her, "We understand one of your films—*Promises, Promises*—received a C-rating from the censors here and was banned. Can you tell us why it was banned here?" Jayne coolly replied, "Well, I really don't know. Maybe it's because Mickey Hargitay appeared in one scene naked from the waist up." A "roar of applause" came from the students. Jayne added that there is a difference between pornography and "clean, wholesome sex." Student: "What, then, Miss Mansfield, is your personal definition of 'clean, wholesome sex?'" "Me." The students loved her and presented her with a law faculty sweatshirt.

Of course, Jayne also sat for numerous interviews during her British Columbia stay; some were light and silly, some shockingly revealing. She spoke of sports: "I hate bullfights. They're so cruel. But I just adore bullfighters. I'm just mad about soccer. I mean soccer is, well, so utterly graceful. And I love cricket. I went to a game in England and I autographed the bat. It was so sweet. But the sport I am really wild about is polo. It's so very exciting and high class. I want all my boys to play polo."

She and Sam talked of fast cars, a chat that seems prophetically eerie in hindsight. Jayne loved sports cars, she said. "I mean real fast sports cars. Right now I've got my Bentley, the one we brought up from San Francisco. It goes pretty fast. We were doing 100 coming up out of Los Angeles and the policemen stopped us. It was real fun." Sam corrected her: "We were doing 120. And you wouldn't even know it. She loves fast driving." Jayne added, "I love it for the kicks. Just like dear Porfirio," a reference to much-married playboy Porfirio Rubirosa, who had died in a car crash the year before.

The saddest and most revealing moment came in Vancouver when Al Forrest of the *Times Colonist* interviewed Jayne in her dressing room. "She made an unforgettable portrait sitting there half-dressed," he recalled, "with drink near her hand, huddled in a corner of the dressing room fretting and twisting her fingers. She drank a lot when she worked. Nerves. 'Was I any good?' she kept asking. No matter what was being discussed, she kept interrupting with: 'Was I really any good?' Onstage she was a swaggering, no-talent blonde bombshell. Backstage she was a terrified little girl. Half-drunk and pitiful."

❤

After all that aggravation and drama, Jayne needed a pleasant vacation day with her children when she returned to Los Angeles in late November. She took Mickey Jr., Zoltan, and Mariska (along with Sam, May Mann, and a handful of reporters and photographers) to Jungleland USA in Thousand Oaks. Opened in 1926, Jungleland was a zoo and theme park, which also supplied (supposedly) trained animals to movie and TV shoots.

On November 27 Jayne—who had already met Anton LaVey's lion— posed with a large male specimen, then moved on to pose with a lioness. The animals were all on chains with seven-foot leads. While everyone else was concentrating on Jayne's shoot, Zoltan wandered back to the male lion—which attacked. Dave Payne, a freelance photographer, recalled, "I don't know whether he was conscious or not but I don't think so. . . . The lion jumped him, knocking him down on his stomach and then got him by the neck." Two nearby men struggled to free Zoltan; Payne said that "Miss Mansfield was crying, but she wasn't in hysterics or anything. She was pretty well shaken up. I sure was."

The *Los Angeles Times* quoted one of Zoltan's rescuers, Murray Banks, a psychology professor at the New York Institute of Technology: "It was the most terrifying moment of my life. The lion had Zoltan face-down, holding him with its paws, while it gnawed at his head. It bit him at least twice. I could see the blood gushing and his skull was bared to the bone. I don't know what made the animal let go. In one more second the boy would certainly have been dead."

The *New York Daily News* reported, "Doctors will not know for four days whether [Zoltan] will survive. The youngster underwent five hours of surgery by five doctors who removed a piece of bone from his skull. . . . Zoltan is reported to be lying in bed with 25 to 30 open wounds which must drain for four days to prevent infection." Jayne, weeping uncontrollably, was sedated at the hospital.

The day after the attack Zoltan was awake and asking Jayne for a snake and a kangaroo rat. "His eyes lit up when I promised to get them," she said hopefully. "That shows that he can get his mind off his injuries." The following day he underwent surgery to have his punctured spleen removed.

Mickey, of course, sped from Rome to California as quickly as he could. "I have not slept for the last three days, because it is night time here when it is daytime over there," he said. Frustratingly, his flight was diverted to Phoenix because Los Angeles was fogged in. It was December 1 before he made it to the hospital, bringing a toy racing car. Zoltan's condition was "improved but still guarded." Unable to talk because of a tracheotomy tube, he gamely made a "V for Victory" sign for his parents.

The press was on Jayne's side for once, brushing aside her bringing her children within pouncing range of wild animals. "Jayne Mansfield has sometimes done some silly things," wrote Dorothy Manners, "but not being a good mother isn't one of them. The hand of the town is on her shoulder."

On December 6 Zoltan took a downward turn, developing spinal meningitis. A hospital spokesman told the press, "The original head wound was wide open when he was on the ground at the animal compound. It apparently picked up foreign matter such as dirt, straw and manure that has infected the spinal fluid. It was thoroughly cleaned out at the hospital, of course, but the doctors have been watching him closely for such a development. He complained of a headache last night, and was running a temperature of 102 degrees."

Jayne herself developed viral pneumonia, with a temperature of 103, and was ordered to go to a hospital or home to bed. "I'm not going to a hospital because if my son Zoltan's condition changes, I wouldn't be able to rush to his side," she said. "The whole ordeal has been a nightmare from which I haven't awakened." Jayne gratefully added that Zoltan had received thousands of cards, flowers, and gifts from fans, some sent to the hospital and some to their home. When fan Vivian Gilmore of San Francisco, a total stranger, sent Zoltan a get-well card, she got a handwritten note back from Jayne: "Dear Mrs. Gilmore: I want to personally thank you for your heartwarming concern for Zoltan. Thank God he's recovering fully. Now that the doctors have given me the wonderful news this is truly a beautiful earth to live upon again."

On December 9 Zoltan's temperature was down and his tracheotomy tube was removed, allowing him to eat. But an X-ray showed a piece of bone pressing on the covering of his spinal canal: if not removed, it could cause brain damage—so more surgery was needed.

Thanks to the quick action of onlookers at the scene of the attack and doctors later, Zoltan recovered with amazing rapidity and was able to go home for Christmas. Jayne put up a twenty-foot tree, and his gifts included a robot and a baseball bat and balls. Jayne, "full of shots and vitamins" to recover from her pneumonia, said that Zoltan's recovery was "the most beautiful Christmas present in the world." Of course she had photographers there as the children unwrapped their presents. Zoltan's bandages were off, though he looked weak and frail. "It's the best Christmas present any mother could have. He's alive, and he's well, and he's getting better every day," said Jayne. "The doctors say he's going to make a good recovery." A reporter asked him what he wanted to be when he grew up, and Zoltan—his mother's son when it came to a good quip—told him, "A lion tamer."

Jayne had been booked for a January tour of Manila, Tokyo, Bangkok, and Hong Kong, "but that depends of course on Zoltan's condition. The doctor thinks that a month's recuperation will be enough. If any complications develop, though, I have an out clause in my contract." She was also heading to the United Kingdom in March, both to play nightclubs and for her proposed West End *Fanny Hill* show ("It's a very funny satire of the *Tom Jones* type. And it's just funny, not risqué. Otherwise, I wouldn't do it").

In the midst of all this trauma—and still suffering from pneumonia—Jayne reported to her alma mater, 20th Century-Fox, for work. It was a major film, but only a cameo role. On December 21 she began what would be a few days' work (for $10,000) on the smirking sex comedy *A Guide for the Married Man*, directed by dancer Gene Kelly.

Columnist Harold Heffernan guessed that Fox had given her the role out of compassion, but the deal had already been finalized before Zoltan's accident. "Sympathy of the entire show world, both here and abroad, went to Jayne Mansfield over the tragic holiday season," he wrote. Jayne said, "I never knew people could be so thoughtful. So sympathetic. We've had cards from Malaya, South Africa, Australia—and they're still coming in."

A Guide for the Married Man's plot revolves around sad-sack Walter

Matthau, bored with his marriage to sweet and gorgeous Inger Stevens. His smarmy pal, played by Robert Morse in his best boyish satyr mode, outlines the titular guide to Matthau: how to cheat on your wife, avoiding the various ways one might get caught. Like Morse's *The Loved One,* this film is packed with guest cameos by major and minor stars: in addition to Jayne, there are fleeting adultery skits starring Lucille Ball, Jack Benny, Sid Caesar, Art Carney, Carl Reiner, Phil Silvers, and Polly Bergen. Jayne's costar is British comic Terry-Thomas, playing a man who brings her home for a daytime fling, only to discover afterward that her bra has gone missing. Screenwriter Frank Tarloff said that "this actually happened to a friend of his, and the man, beside himself, is now thinking of burning his house down before his wife comes across the missing bra." The joke, of course, being that Jayne Mansfield's bra could not possibly be explained away as anyone else's.

The *Oakland Tribune* felt that Jayne's was "the funniest of these stories, designed to illustrate the cardinal rule 'never bring her to your home.'" The *New York Daily News* called *Guide* "a truly adult farce. . . . The racy game is played, for the most part, with a flourish, and without offense to anyone." Today the entire film comes off as cringingly unpleasant, the awfulness of the characters not offset by any real wit or humor.

At the end of the year Barbara Flanagan of the *Minneapolis Star* reported that Jayne, amazingly, had received an honorable mention in the Gallup poll of the Year's Most Admirable Women. "How about that?" marveled Flanagan. "Miss Mansfield's nomination is heartwarming. I've considered her a true homebody—she was Brownie leader and a Sunday school teacher, by the way—ever since I visited the pink house in Beverly Hills with the heart-shaped pool, heart-shaped bed and heart-shaped bathtub. She even had pink lights in the kitchen and every woman knows how flattering they are. Miss Mansfield also showed her thrifty nature to me when she said she had saved seven and a half books of trading stamps for a bassinet. And then spent only $200 to cover it in baby blue tulle."

What would turn out to be Jayne's last Christmas card showed her (in pink dress and white boots) in front of the Pink Palace with all five children. Inscribed at the bottom: "May the blessings of this glorious holiday season be bestowed upon you and yours."

27

She doesn't earn her living by entertaining, but by threatening to.

Harry Karns

Before Jayne left on her next tour, she and Matt Cimber had to meet in court to hash out custody of their son. "Matt will insist that the court be open to the public," said one report. "Cimber plans to make some startling charges, all of which will indicate that Jayne is unfit to take care of their baby. Miss Mansfield's attorney will be Sam Brody, who has his own marital troubles since coming under Jayne's magic spell." Jayne told Herb Kelly of the *Miami News* that she and Sam would marry as soon as they got their respective divorces; Sam presented her with a diamond ring and a foreign sports car to prove his devotion, much to his current wife's indignation.

Jayne's Asian tour would take her through nightclubs in Tokyo and Bangkok—but, most important from her standpoint, she would be entertaining the troops in Vietnam. Ever since her early USO tours with Bob Hope (and before that, when she was a military wife arguing with majors' wives), Jayne had been antiwar but pro-troops. Like many Americans in 1967, she wondered if the war in Vietnam would ever end, or be "won," but she still supported the fighting men and women. This tour would shake Jayne in a way her Bob Hope excursions had not.

At the end of January Jayne—with Sam accompanying her—kicked off her tour playing Tokyo's new Latin Quarter, arriving in the city in a leopard coat that she flung off to reveal a silver miniskirt, white sweater, black tights, and go-go boots. Her itinerary included Hong Kong, Bangkok, Manila, Taipei, and Okinawa, she said, and she wanted to live in Asia forever: "American men are in kindergarten, European men are post-graduates, but Asian men—they are the best." She also noted that she wanted to talk to Zen priests "in my search for the truth"—and possibly to counteract the Anton LaVey publicity.

In Manila she was presented with a male water buffalo, and hoped to find a female one to go with it. "I own several dogs, cats, a mynah bird and a full-grown ocelot. I just love animals." As far as her visits to the troops, Jayne said, "I'll do everything I possibly can to help raise their morale and their spirits." She also suggested that the military allow "marvelous long hair for military men when they are not in combat and very mod clothes, to pep up enlistment."

Jayne arrived in Vietnam on Valentine's Day, landing in Saigon's Tan Son Nhut airbase, wearing that silver miniskirt with a brown sweater and black boots, drawing "a chorus of whistles from GI camera bugs." When Jayne was asked if she would entertain the enemy Viet Cong, her answer was more thoughtful and controversial than the interviewer was expecting: "I feel that soldiers anywhere in any army are acting upon the orders of their superiors," she said. "They don't make the decisions. I would do almost anything to initiate world peace, because I believe war is a foolish, childish, animalistic, unthinking, unintelligent way of trying to accomplish a purpose."

On February 17 she journeyed into the Mekong Delta, which would soon see some of the heaviest battles of that year. But the mood that day was light, as Jayne took to an improvised stage on the back of a truck for songs and comedy. One officer climbed up alongside and told her, "We wanted to give you a flak jacket, but we couldn't find one to fit, so we devised this." He handed her a jacket made from two pink-painted helmets fastened together with khaki straps. Jayne doubled up with laughter and gamely strapped on the twin helmets to the roars of cheering infantrymen of the Third Brigade, Ninth Infantry Division. Later Jayne donned a colonel's helmet and brandished a pair of .45-caliber pistols for picture-snapping soldiers.

She visited the Dong Tam base camp, Marines at Da Nang, and infantrymen at Pleiku in the central highlands, where "battles raged a few miles east along the Cambodian border." Her most distressing but rewarding visit was to a hospital at Bien Hoa, northwest of Saigon. Openly crying, she told a reporter, "I just cannot leave them. I want to stay as long as I can. I wish I could convey some sort of message to the rest of the American people, to give some idea of what our men are going through in this war." The reporter noted, "At each bedside, the blonde star spoke softly to the patients and stroked their hair. One paratrooper told her, 'You can stay here as long as you want. You sure are great for us here.'"

On February 19 Jayne met with South Vietnamese prime minister Nguyễn Cao Kỳ and his wife Đặng Tuyết Mai at the Continental Hotel in Saigon. The party was given by the Associated Press for writer Ed White, but in the next room Jayne heard a more boisterous gathering taking place. Accompanied by a "bearded beatnik escort," she sneaked over to the Vietnamese students' bash and sang a few songs with them.

Not all soldiers were happy to see Jayne. Not that they would have preferred a younger, hipper star—the whole idea of Hollywood descending upon them in the midst of war sat badly with Specialist Don Drumm, a New Jersey native and newsman. He wrote, "A touch of artificial Hollywood seemed strange to the troops, who had been 'in country' only two weeks and hadn't yet been exposed to the terrors of war—only the boredom. Jayne Mansfield was remembered not as a goddess or a Florence Nightingale in a bikini, but as yesterday's dumb-blonde movie star who could fill an hour or a two-piece bathing suit equally well." Drumm brought up Zoltan's recent mauling, noting that Jayne was suing Jungleland for what he saw as her carelessness: "'Typical of California,' said the Easterners, and the California troops, for once, shut up. It's for sure none of us would pose for pictures with a live hand grenade, but maybe Jayne will turn the trick. Then she can sue the Army for a million, provided she goes through the chain of command. Come to think of it, this might not be a bad show at all—if they let us go."

The US press treated Jayne's trip as a joke, of course. Allis Spackman of the *San Bernardino County Sun* sarcastically called her Defense Secretary McNamara's secret weapon, a new Joan of Arc: "After our boys get charged up by Jayne, they are apt to go zooming right though Hanoi and on into China before they run out of steam. . . . Imagine the consternation of Comrade Ho Chi Minh when he hears the tumult and shouting outside his palace and in rides Jayne, platinum tresses waving in the breeze, it will be enough to curl his wispy beard. And when she says, 'Ho, honey, how about a little negotiating? You know, just the two of us, somewhere away from the crowd?' What will Ho say? Well what would you say?"

Jayne finally got to meet her Buddhist monk, in Bangkok. "Her questions were confusing and the answers she received from the polite, orange-robed Buddhist were ambiguous," wrote Thomas Thompson of the *Amarillo Globe-Times*. "Why did you become a monk? How can you smoke cigarettes, which are a stimulant, and not drink? What kind of peace do you monks find? What kind of god or gods do you pray to? Are you the kind of monks who burn themselves?" Frustratingly, Thompson did not record the monk's replies to Jayne's queries.

Jayne did a three-night show at Bangkok's Sani Chateau, probably the most expensive nightspot in town. Reporter Thomas Thompson and embassy employee Billy Cox took in the show and were not overwhelmed. "We were told there were no more tables, but we kept standing around as though we couldn't understand," Thompson wrote. "Finally, we were led to a rather remote table from which we watched as Miss Mansfield moved her remarkable person around and cooed her improbable baby talk. There was a scattering of Americans, but the audience was mainly Oriental men: Chinese, Indians, Thai types and Japanese. . . . The younger men all had eyes for Jayne, but the older Nipponese gentlemen soon dozed off to sleep."

On February 20 an exhausted, disheveled, and emotionally overwrought Jayne, physically supported by Sam, who hovered protectively, returned to the US via Travis Air Force Base in California. She was ambushed by a KRON-TV reporter and camera crew. Jayne wore oversized military pants, a ratty, unwashed wig, and her face was red and swollen from crying.

Tearfully, her voice shaky, she told the reporter, "There's no front line in Vietnam. The fighting is everywhere, everywhere. Everywhere I was, people were brought in, dead, or half-dead, either right before, or during, or after there were mortar attacks. . . . If you feel you could make someone happy, add something, you feel happy. But really, I got very broken up about this. They're lying there, without limbs, and there's *no one,* there's no one there to hold their hand and say 'I love you, everything's going to be fine.' This one person in particular"—Jayne lost her composure and began crying at this point—"he just got to me, he lost his leg, he was very beautiful—they're *all* beautiful—but he was 25 years old, and the thing that upset me most is that they're so proud of what they did. There is no bitterness at all."

❤

Jayne found nothing but aggravation waiting for her when she got back to the US in late February. Beverly Brody accused Jayne of adultery with Sam in a complaint added to one she had already filed on July 7, 1966. The *San Francisco Examiner* reported that Jayne's children had walked in on Sam and Jayne in bed; Beverly said the two had been having an affair since November 15, and had bedded down together in Los Angeles, San Francisco, British Columbia, Japan, and Acapulco. "In one conversation with Miss Mansfield, Mrs. Brody reported the actress told her Brody had struck her in the mouth, requiring three stitches to close a cut lip." And Jayne also filed a $345,000 suit against Matt, charging that he struck and bit her; "using his fists and mouth, [he] kicked and stomped" her "about the face and body in a fit of rage."

"Miss Mansfield has called me on a number of occasions," said an understandably annoyed and confused Beverly, "and has very freely discussed with me her current love affair with my husband. The children of Jayne Mansfield have also witnessed the fact that she and my husband have occupied the same bed together in the Jayne Mansfield home on a number of occasions." "We are dealing with a brazen and arrogant woman," said Beverly's lawyer, Benjamin Reinhardt. Upon which, Jayne filed a $60,000 damage suit against both Beverly and Matt, charging that they had been harassing her with phone calls at all hours of the night, interfering with her "mental and emotional tranquility" and causing her "emotional distress."

Jayne, having won temporary custody of Tony, was given permission to take him on her tour of England for nine weeks. "Outside the court with her lawyer, Samuel Brody, Miss Mansfield denied accusations that she committed adultery with Brody," said the press. "In Los Angeles Monday, Mrs. Brody filed a petition asking [for] a temporary restraining order to keep Miss Mansfield away from the Brody children." Beverly contended that "because of [Jayne's] attitude about commonly accepted standards of decency and conduct, I believe our children's best interest would be endangered by permitting our children to be in her presence." Beverly also said her son Keith "has been allowed to play with Miss Mansfield's pet ocelot while unsupervised by an adult," a rather shocking accusation after what had happened to Zoltan.

"What's next for Jayne?" asked Harrison Carroll. "She's not sure. She was supposed to leave in March for a European singing tour, and then go to England to appear in a satirical stage version of *The Memoirs of Fanny Hill*. But she's wanted immediately for a picture in Manila." That picture in Manila—if it ever existed—failed to pan out, and Jayne prepared for her exhausting March–April tour of towns large and small throughout Great Britain: London, York, Richmond, Newcastle-upon-Tyne, Batley, Blackpool, Westhoughton, Latchford, Tralee, Weston, Bartley, Leeds, and Bristol, as well as other hastily scheduled one-night stands.

The trip started out on a low-comedy note—like many celebrities, Jayne thought she could bypass England's strict quarantine rules and sneak her Chihuahuas Popsicle and Momsicle past airport security. Rather than sedating them inside her carry-on or stuffing them down the front of her dress, she convinced Sam to put on her leopard-skin coat and hold the dogs under his arms. He looked as convincing as three small children perched on one another's shoulders in a trench coat. Popsicle and Momsicle were confiscated and crated up to be shipped back to L.A.

Jayne wept her tale of woe at the Hotel Savoy, explaining that Popsicle was so upset she had to chew his food for him. "I've been crying all the way in from the airport. I'm terribly upset because I'm afraid that Popsicle won't eat unless I'm with him. I also want to contact a British lawyer to see if there is anything we can do for him. Otherwise the dogs will spend a couple of days in quarantine and then be returned to the United States."

Sam claimed that "I told the airline people I had them, but they didn't tell me there were any quarantine regulations. If we had known that, we would have sent the dogs on to Jayne's home in Los Angeles instead of bringing them here." It's conceivable—though not likely—that a world traveler like Jayne might not know of the UK's strict animal-quarantine rules, but there is no way a lawyer like Sam would be so ignorant. Sam was fined $140 for dog smuggling. Prosecutor Lord Stormont deadpanned, "An airport official saw Brody wearing a leopard-skin coat which was obviously not his because it fitted in all the wrong places. He was very bulky." Brody pleaded "technically guilty" and said, "I do apologize for the inconvenience I have given the government of England. I had no intention of breaking the law."

Jayne and Sam made a dashing couple at the York Press Ball, but on the way back to Richmond, their taxi broke down. The two thumbed a ride and were picked up by a lorry driver, who was, said Sam, "a helluva nice guy. He offered to let Jayne have a turn at steering the truck." The driver later found a diamond-covered watch in his truck and returned it to Jayne's hotel; he refused the reward she offered him (they kept his name mum, as his company forbade giving lifts).

Jayne's primary employer for this tour was Don Arden, the father of future rock star Ozzy Osbourne's wife Sharon. Arden handled many big acts—Jerry Lee Lewis, Little Richard, Black Sabbath—and was known as a cutthroat, no-nonsense businessman. Jayne was lucky to be booked by him, but she was soon to realize that he was no fatherly, understanding manager.

On April 8 Arden fired her from her $8,400-a-week, eight-week tour of British clubs for breach of contract; he claimed that she failed to show up for rehearsals and kept audiences waiting for up to an hour. Arden sent a telegram to her Newcastle-upon-Tyne hotel cutting her loose; she was about midway through the tour when this happened. "I intend to take legal action against Miss Mansfield for breach of contract," said Arden, to which Jayne replied, "I just don't understand it. I have not walked out. I am here ready to perform. I thought I was doing great."

She continued, "I've been sacked. But it was not my fault. Once my hairdresser did not turn up on time. I thought I was doing great, but so far I've not been paid a penny." Arden said, through Contemporary Record Company spokesman David Jacobs, that there had been a number of complaints about Jayne, including her appearing onstage in street clothes. "Customers at the clubs have been kept waiting for as long as an hour for her to arrive for her performance," Jacobs told the *Sydney Morning Herald*. "There can be no excuses for that." Jayne failed to appear at two Teeside clubs and had to be replaced by a pop group. "Miss Mansfield's withdrawal is a shock," said Jayne's lawyers. "We know that she has been late arriving for performances on certain occasions, but just recently her punctuality has improved."

For the first time in her career, Jayne's drinking was interfering with her professionalism. Jacobs claimed that Jayne "drank too much, was frequently late for shows, poorly rehearsed, wearing the wrong clothes and appeared onstage with bruised legs." Sam Brody, it was apparent, was not good for her, personally or professionally. A heavy drinker himself, he enabled Jayne's increasing problem; this was also the first public hint that he may have been hitting her. Sam said the charges were "untrue, comical, ludicrous and diabolical," and he and Jayne filed a $90,000 suit against

Contemporary Record Company, saying she had received neither her security deposit nor a single paycheck.

To be fair to Sam, Jayne's bruises might have been caused by bumping into furniture while drunk, or by her many leaping dogs. But this excuse wears thin as more witnesses claimed that the couple's fights were violent. "Those who appear in spotlights should not acquire bruises," wrote the *New York Daily News*'s Jon Gladstone. "Jayne's lucrative cabaret schedule, which was to have lasted two months, hadn't even reached its quarter-mark before it was canceled . . . the announced reason: 'Disfiguring black and blue marks from the knees up.'" David Jacobs charged that the ugly bruises made it impossible for her to wear the miniskirts that her appearances called for. He also said she had been doing some drinking and was frequently late for rehearsals. "What caused the blemishes on Miss Mansfield's lily-white epidermis?" asked Gladstone. "They could be anybody's guess, of course, except that a further company contention was that she had a public slugging match with her constant companion, 39-year-old Los Angeles attorney Sam Brody, and then 'cried for him' when he flew back to the States for three days."

On April 10, shortly after she was cut loose by Don Arden, Sam officially proposed to Jayne. "Sam's a marvelous man and I love him," said Jayne. "We've been through thick and thin together. You can draw your own conclusions on whether I am going to accept." Sam added, "Our divorces come through at the same time in July. That means we can marry then."

Jayne's tour continued without Don Arden's bookings. She signed an $11,200-a-week contract for appearances in Blackpool and South Yorkshire, but was left on her own when Sam had to fly back to the US to attend to business. Back in London, she was not lonely for male companionship for long: Timothy Kitson, a member of Parliament for Richmond, in North Yorkshire, invited her to visit the Speaker's Gallery in the House of Commons. Jayne shimmied to her viewing place in a low-cut micro-minidress, and the Speaker, Horace King, had to call for order. Jayne took the seat usually occupied by Mary Wilson, Prime Minister Harold's wife. The *Guardian* reported that "Dennis Healey was droning on about biological weapons in the House yesterday; meanwhile, wriggling in the Gallery sat Jayne Mansfield, her biological weapons well displayed in plunging mini kit. Tories facing began to buzz; Labour men with their backs to her front started craning around."

From Parliament she journeyed to Westhoughton, a history-packed town in Greater Manchester, and then to the smaller town of Latchford Without, a parish of Latchford in Cheshire. "The big names are more and more learning to hunt down the big money where it is to be made," wrote the *Guardian,* "but Latchford Without must be reckoned a bit off the beaten track, even by today's standards of touring." Losing Don Arden was obviously a blow to Jayne's tour.

Sam was back at her side when scandal struck in Ireland. Jayne was booked to play the Mount Brandon Hotel, a recently opened showcase in Tralee. But the Most Reverend Denis Moyinhan, Roman Catholic bishop of County Kerry, was having none of it. In his sermons he urged the faithful to stay home, and the dean of Kerry, Monsignor John Lane, jumped in to call Jayne "a goddess of lust," characterizing her show as "an attempt to besmirch the name of our town for filthy gain." This, of course, was the best publicity Jayne could have had, and customers would have been lined up around the block at the Mount Brandon had management not caved in and cancelled her show.

Jane and Sam promptly called a press conference. Jayne looked adorable in her long wig, minidress, and boots, and Sam hovered protectively by her side, jumping in with comments every minute or two. "It must have been a misunderstanding," said Jayne, sweetly baffled and not at all angry. "The bishop has never seen my act. My act is not dirty. I am not a sex symbol, I am a motion picture actress. I am also a Catholic, and I contribute very heavily to the church's funds. I worked hard for my money and out of every $2,800 I earn the church gets a generous portion. I also support five children and make regular contributions to charities."

Harry Karns of the *Long Beach Independent* sarcastically remarked, "Jayne Mansfield's sexy performance is cancelled in Ireland, but she gets her fee anyway. She doesn't earn her living by entertaining, but by threatening to."

At least one Brit stood up for Jayne in print: one Mrs. M. Hooton of Wigan wrote to the *Daily Mirror,* "I can't understand the remarks made by the Dean of Kerry about Jayne Mansfield. My husband and I saw Miss Mansfield's act in Westhoughton, Lanca., last week and as she says, there's nothing sexy or immoral in it. Her act is just good fun. Why, she even plays the violin."

The reliably vituperative Donald Zec of the *Detroit Free Press* was—unfortunately for Jayne—in town to witness one of the British performances. Even for Zec, the review was insolent. "If I had not seen the whole quivering absurdity with my own bruised eyeballs I would not have believed it," he wrote. "Correction. I did see it, and I still don't believe it. . . . Unhampered by anything approaching talent; blithely indifferent to such musical oddities as flats and sharps; dispensing the lyrics with a mixture of two parts hot breath to one part gurgle, our bosomy heroine gave a display which must qualify her as a candidate for the worst performance on any stage anywhere."

Zec tried to laugh off his vitriol in an affectionate way, but failed:

> And I wouldn't have missed one bouncing moment of it. . . . Miss Mansfield slides into the limelight, one leg crossed over the other, all bosom, black sequins and bows. She is leaning against the wall—or maybe the wall is leaning against her—and it is clear that for what we are about to receive she hopes we will be truly grateful. Thirty seconds of sound and movement is sufficient to indicate that Marilyn Monroe and Mae West figure prominently in Miss Mansfield's scheme of things. But whereas Marilyn and Mae had poise, humor, subtlety, style and gaiety, the Sequined One did not. As with Mae West, she—our Jayne—was assisted by four dancing youths looking like mini–George Rafts in black shirts, tight slacks and pretty light on muscle. How they succeeded, at the end of one number, in lifting this outsized sugar plum fairy above their heads and come back smiling shows what good troupers they are.

Zec did raise some germane points. "Jayne has never been more than a fair-to-good singer, but even the best must keep their instrument in tune: coaching, warm-ups, exercises." Jayne did none of this, so by now her singing voice—even miked—was a breathy whisper, sometimes veering off-key. Still, even audiences and critics who jeered at her enjoyed her shows. Even at her lowest, she exuded such joy and love—and a need for love—that it was like watching a puppy or baby chick. In a micro-mini and go-go boots.

Without her children, and with her club dates falling apart, Jayne had no one and nothing to stabilize her. She was swept away by Sam, but his own drinking and unrealistic pushiness only exacerbated her instability. Mickey and Matt had tried to rein her in; Sam couldn't even rein himself in. Their disastrous *folie à deux* became more obvious. Jayne's bruises, her lateness, her unprofessionalism—a first for her—and her wild personality swings, from thoughtful social critic to dizzy go-go girl, fascinated and appalled onlookers.

There's something riveting about seeing a celebrity fall apart in public. John Barrymore, Judy Garland, Anna Nicole Smith, Amy Winehouse: one watches the self-destructive fireworks with a mixture of sadness and schadenfreude, hoping their family or friends will save them, but knowing how this is all going to turn out. By 1967 Jayne was in obvious trouble. Her drinking and pill popping were public knowledge, her relationship with Sam Brody was increasingly ugly, her performances becoming more slipshod and desperate. Yet the press and most of the public just pointed and laughed, as they tend to do in these situations. No one in 1967 would suggest that Jayne needed rehab or a battered women's shelter; those were simply not options then. And Jayne was so cheerfully dismissive of any problems in her life: upbeat and bubbly in interviews, talking about her great plans, emphasizing how happy and lucky she was.

"The point has now been reached where, if I pick up a newspaper and find no mention of Miss Mansfield, I assume a page must be missing and start looking for it," wrote Art Evans of the *Edmonton Journal.* Jayne visited a small London dress boutique, and some fifty photographers, newsreel cameramen, and reporters followed her in. "It must have been mighty crowded in there but such are the perils faced daily by intrepid London newsmen assigned to cover film celebrities," wrote Evans. "One sees editors calling for volunteers for this dangerous work, and every male in the office (including copy boys) gallantly stepping forward. The morale must be terrific."

On her Stockholm stop, wrote reporter Hendrick Rechendorff, "Jayne Mansfield drew more attention on the dance floor last night than she got in her opening night club act here. First nighters called the night club act a flop, but the police called the spat she later had with her escort, Los Angeles attorney Samuel S. Brody, a scandal." In a particularly ugly scene that showed just how bad she and Sam were for each other, "he boxed her ears and she told him to 'go to hell forever,' witnesses said." Reporter Robert Sylvester thought it was hilarious: "She must have two-timed as she one-stepped," he weakly joked.

While in England, Jayne hobnobbed with local celebrities. Diana Dors, at thirty-six, was also several years past her prime. Like Jayne, she had always bristled at being compared with Marilyn Monroe: Dors had proved herself a talented dramatic actress in 1956's *Yield to the Night* (loosely based on the controversial conviction and hanging of Ruth Ellis; Ellis had actually been an extra in Dors's 1951 film *Lady Godiva Rides*

Again). But by 1967 Dors was overweight and washed up; from being "the British Marilyn Monroe" she'd become "the British Jayne Mansfield."

Diana Dors was also smart and funny and eventually became a delightful character actress and bawdy comic (her 1970s sitcom *Queenie's Castle* showed her to be a fusion of Mollie Sugden in *Are You Being Served?* and Divine in *Hairspray*). Jayne and Diana met backstage at one of Jayne's nightclub shows and posed together for photos, both brandishing Chihuahuas. "In all the time I knew Jayne, she never let her mask fall once," said the insightful Dors. "Until, at the end, I really believe she did think and speak like a Kewpie doll."

Jayne also met thirty-one-year-old singer Engelbert Humperdinck, who himself was often dismayed at being compared with Tom Jones. Humperdinck recalled in his memoirs that Jayne "had been performing in cabaret in a club in Bristol where I was on tour, and she had accepted an invitation to sit down and have dinner with us." Like many, he was happily amazed by her genuine friendliness. "Jayne was bright and vivacious and very interested in me and my background and we talked for a long time. Before she left, she said to me, 'You must come to visit my home in Los Angeles.' 'I'd love to come to America,' I said, as she wrote down her address and her telephone number for me, 'and I'd certainly love to see this pink palace you live in.' I knew I could never afford to go then, but it was a nice thought!"

Sam was back at Jayne's side by late April, but he found he had some competition in Alan Wells, a young promoter and owner of the Webbington Club, a converted Edwardian manor near Weston-super-Mare. He booked Jayne for a week at the club (at $8,400), supported by TV comic Ken Wilson and "exotic dancer" Jojo Jagoo.

The press was all over the possible romance, and Jayne and Wells gave them lots of material. "Only a few days ago she announced that she would marry Brody as soon as his divorce came through," wrote the *Detroit Free Press*. "Brody returned Friday ready to accompany Jayne to her next club date at Bartley, near Leeds." Wells threw a lavish going-away party for Jayne, with champagne and a huge cake with "Farewell to Jayne, love from Alan" written across it, and all hell, predictably, broke loose. "About 3:00 a.m. things finally flared between Wells and Brody," according to the *Free Press*. "Wells pushed the lawyer onto a tray of champagne glasses that crashed to the floor." Jayne also crashed to the floor, and photographers angled for an upskirt shot. "A jealous old flame of Wells had to be restrained as she tried to claw Wells. Someone sat on the cake, and Jayne, weeping hysterically, was taken out of harm's way to another room." Sam seemed ready to throw in the towel, saying sadly that "although he still loved Jayne, he knew it was all over. . . . And a triumphant Wells, declaring his great love for Jayne—who was snuggling at his side—flew off to Leeds with her in a chartered plane."

In Leeds Jayne gave a bizarre, off-kilter TV interview, with a baffled, embarrassed Wells hovering in the background. She was very affected, calling the interviewer "lover" and "darling," a faux British accent sneaking in ("I dahnce"), wearing kicky disco-ball earrings: "I do a satire on sex—don't you?" she asks the flummoxed interviewer, who says, "It sounds a very fair reply." Asked what her act would be like if she went to West Cornwall, which was very Methodist, Jayne laughed, "Well, I guess I would be very Methodist." Englishmen are "just the grooviest, they're out of sight, I dig them!" Her groovy Englishman, Alan Wells, backed slowly out of camera range—and soon backed out of Jayne's life.

In addition to hospitals, Jayne visited prisons: on April 30 she took a plane to Leeds and a Rolls-Royce to Armley Prison. She sat atop the Rolls and signed autographs for guards before heading inside, where she was joined by American dance team Steve and Jimmy Clark, and Halifax band Dino and the Travellers. Les Piggen, the guitarist for the Travellers, recalls that Jayne opened her act with some readings from Shakespeare, to the audible disappointment of the audience. She took their cue and flirtatiously asked, "Would you like to see my Chihuahuas?" The prisoners made it quite clear that yes, they would like to see her Chihuahuas. Jayne sang several songs (including "This Queen Has Her Aces in All the Right Places"), and proved to be a huge hit with the inmates.

Back in London Jayne gave a rambling interview to Sheilah Graham. "To say that Jayne Mansfield is trouble-prone is understating the case by approximately one million miles," Graham sighed, adding with ill-disguised amusement, "You won't believe the latest." It was rumored that a young suitor from Stockholm slit his wrists when Jayne refused to go home with him. "I stayed with him all night in the hospital," claimed Jayne. As for the photo of her knocked to the floor during the Sam Brody/Alan Wells fight? "But I was wearing panties!"

Jayne also bemoaned other woes: "In Germany I sprained my back.

The sink in my dressing room fell on my head." She was suing an airline for losing three bright-pink suitcases with $39,200 worth of gowns and jewels when she and Sam flew from New York to Stockholm. She was "frightened" to go back to the US and face Matt's custody hearing. "Remember Enrico Bomba, the Italian I was so much in love with? Well, he's just come into a fortune from an uncle who died. I was never as much in love with anyone as I was with Enrico." As for Mickey, "He's a wonderful friend. He'll testify for me at the divorce trial." She was still planning on her stage version of *Fanny Hill,* "and I'll come back to Europe to make more personal appearances. I made more money in Stockholm than Sammy Davis." "She's like a child," wrote Graham, "a child who is well-developed physically, but who is not very grown-up elsewhere. . . . Meanwhile, Jayne keeps on working and waiting for the next catastrophe."

The next catastrophe—the next series of catastrophes—came swiftly after Jayne's return to the US in May. Beverly Brody had already named Jayne as "the 41st other woman" in her divorce suit against Sam Brody. Jayne sued Beverly for harassment; she also sued Don Arden for breach of contract and Matt Cimber for harassment, assault, and battery; Matt counter-sued for back fees as her manager.

"No one seems to be quite sure which fiancé Jayne Mansfield has brought back from Britain," wrote Sheilah Graham. "This dear girl can walk into a room engaged to one man and come out married to another. To read about her or look at the way she dresses, you'd think she was someone from outer space. But when you talk with her, no one is more charming. It's a puzzlement."

Bob Crane, who had interviewed Jayne when he was a radio deejay and who was now starring in TV's *Hogan's Heroes,* gave a vicious interview to Marilyn Beck in April 1967, insulting just about every actress in Hollywood. Jayne, he said, "does nothing to me. There is nothing subtle about her. It's almost a commercial type of sex." He also attacked Raquel Welch and Ursula Andress ("They look mad instead of sexy"), Carroll Baker ("tries too terribly hard to look sexy, and fails so completely"), Mamie Van Doren ("too obvious"), Brigitte Bardot ("doesn't have as perfect a figure as she should"), Mia Farrow ("Nothing! And especially with that boy's haircut, she turns me off"), and Joan Collins ("Baby, if you knew how ridiculous you look!"). Crane then went on to slag nonfamous women, saying that only about 1 percent of women look good in miniskirts, "and that one percent is under the age of 20!"

Not all of Jayne's fellow performers were as mean-spirited. When Leonard Lyons was talking to Geraldine Page about her being one of the most respected film and theater actresses, and the topic of Jayne came up, Page very nicely said, "One difference between Jayne Mansfield and me is that she went to college and I didn't."

❤

Throughout May and early June, Jayne and Sam became one of the most colorful couples in Hollywood and New York, but not in a good way. Sheilah Graham "saw them together at the Brown Derby in Hollywood with Jayne in her miniest mini. When they walked out, even the blasé used-to-everything waiters at this starry restaurant stood still to stare." Harrison Carroll spotted them at La Scala with three of Jayne's children, Jayne "wearing a patent leather dress." Carroll also saw Jayne and Sam in New York, dining with Mickey "at the Voison in New York, no doubt discussing the divorce." Whether Jayne was legally married to Mickey or Matt would soon become a sticky legal issue. Judge Allen Lynch awarded Jayne custody of Tony, now a toddler; Lynch planned a hearing to finalize Matt's visitation rights later that summer.

Sam threw an engagement party for Jayne in late May featuring flowers, champagne, a gold charm bracelet, and a necklace with a jeweled drop and thirteen diamonds. Earl Wilson reported that Jayne was consulting with Rabbi Max Nussbaum of the Temple Israel of Hollywood, who had converted Elizabeth Taylor to Judaism when she married Mike Todd. "I've had some serious talks about it with Rabbi Nussbaum," said Jayne, who only recently had insisted, "I am a staunch Catholic, and I always will be."

Jayne was, of course, still a joke to most of the public: in early June 1967 up-and-coming comic Joan Rivers wisecracked, "Put Jayne Mansfield and Twiggy together and what have you got? Jayne Mansfield!"

❤

By her mid-thirties, Jayne had survived many of the misfortunes that plague most people during a lifetime—her father's death, romantic disasters, financial worries, career disappointments. But in June 1967 she suffered the worst trauma that could come to someone whose identity centered around being a good mother: sixteen-year-old Jayne Marie fled the Pink Palace and applied for protective custody at the West Los Angeles police station.

According to Earl Wilson, Jayne Marie had been telling her friends that she was going to leave home as soon as she turned eighteen. It was hard enough living with Jayne: "They had intercoms through the whole house," she later recalled, "and she would get on and scream my name, 'Jayne Marie, come here, Jayne Marie, come here.' . . . I would water down the liquor and get rid of the pills, and do whatever I could to try to keep her away from it." Jayne Marie's relationship with her mother may have been tense—more so than most teens and their moms experience—but the addition of Sam Brody to the household was explosive. It is impossible to make any excuses for Sam—Jayne's previous husbands and lovers may have had their faults, but Sam Brody had developed into a world-class heel.

On June 17 the *Washington Post* reported that Jayne Marie had arrived at the West Los Angeles police station the day before, "claiming a male friend of her mother beat her with a belt and slapped and hit her. Young Jayne had slipped out of the pink Sunset Boulevard home she shared with her mother. . . . She arrived at the police station with attorney Bernard Cohen." Cohen requested that Jayne Marie be placed in the custody of William Pigue (Paul Mansfield's uncle) in Huntington Beach. Instead, police sergeant Shirley Maxwell took her to McLaren Hall, a police protective facility for juveniles. "The girl apparently didn't need any medical treatment," said a spokesman at McLaren Hall. "She had welts and bruises on her mouth and hips. She spent the night in a dormitory with six other girls and had breakfast with them this morning. She seems well enough today. She seems to be getting along well with the girls."

Predictably, Jayne fell apart and Sam went on the attack. He said that the police had no right to take Jayne Marie to a juvenile facility. Jayne tearfully agreed to let Jayne Marie live with the Pigues: "I want her to find herself." Astonishingly, despite the fact that photos showed Jayne Marie's bruises, Deputy District Attorney Mark McDonald said, "We feel there is insufficient evidence for a felony complaint against Miss Mansfield or Mr. Brody."

A preliminary court hearing about Jayne Marie's situation was held during the third week of June; Jayne's friend and biographer May Mann claimed to have court transcripts, though these have never been verified. William Pigue told Sam Brody's co-counsel Don Caruso that he had called to speak to Jayne Marie, but Jayne had told him that she was grounded: "You know I am a very strict mother, and Jayne Marie had been a very naughty girl. She is not being allowed privileges." Jayne told Judge Lynch that Jayne Marie had been smoking pot, having boyfriends over to the house, and taking diet pills. When asked why Jayne Marie should not live with William Pigue, according to May Mann's account, Jayne dropped a bombshell, replying, "The child is not the blood relation of the Pigues," and went on to name Jayne Marie's supposed biological father.

Sam Brody was allowed to question Jayne, who testified tearfully (again, according to May Mann), "I don't want my child smoking marijuana and drinking booze until five in the morning. Call the maid and ask what she does in my bedroom when I'm out of town. I say it is not possible to have the child back here."

Jayne Marie told Judge Lynch that the breaking point came the night she fled: "Mr. Brody had never touched me or struck me in any way. But that night he literally beat me."

As of June 20 Jayne Marie was living with William Pigue and his wife Mary, and the abuse and neglect charges were held over till later that summer, after Jayne had fulfilled her date at Gus Stevens's Supper Club. The AP referred to it as "a vacation trip to Biloxi," where she and Sam could relax with Mickey Jr., Zoltan, and Mariska, while Tony stayed with his father Matt in Los Angeles.

Decades later, Jayne Marie was able to look back on the ordeal with admirable grace. "I don't know if it was the depression, maybe, where her career was going," she said. "I mean, who wants to work in a nightclub in Biloxi? That was not her choice. There really wasn't any help from men, and it was her that did it. I don't want to blame her. I believe a lot of it was her surroundings—she used to trust me and listen to me. At the very end, she wouldn't do that. And at that point in time, I had to throw in the towel. . . . It was a terrible mess, and a heartbreaking moment for me and her."

Mickey, too, with the passing of the years, was sad and resigned. "Her life at that time was very much in a turmoil. I hadn't seen her at that time for maybe five, six months. And I think the change was quite severe. It's not the Jayne I used to know. I took off her sunglasses and her eyes were all red—bloodshot, and blue. I said, 'what happened?' She said 'Sam beat me up.' It seemed that something very severe had to happen."

Sam and Jayne couldn't even get out of Los Angeles without calamity. During the Jayne Marie hearing, they were driving home from a late dinner at La Scala. Jayne had stopped, waiting to turn left on Sunset Boulevard, when another driver rear-ended her car. The crash threw Jayne against the windshield and she suffered cuts and bruises on her face, arms, and chest. Sam was injured only slightly.

Much worse was to occur that week. Jayne and Sam were at the intersection of Sunset Boulevard and Whittier Drive in Beverly Hills when their car was struck again—this time, Jayne wasn't hurt, but Sam was taken to UCLA Medical Center with a broken right leg. He was put in a lower-leg cast, and of course was unable to drive, which would prove disastrous on their upcoming trip to Biloxi.

In late June Jayne gave extensive interviews to Ivor Davis of the *London Express* and Peter McDonald of the North American Newspaper Alliance (NANA). She told Davis, "Trouble follows me everywhere. It's always around the corner trying to jinx me. But I think I've managed to shake it off. . . . My career is just beginning again. I have the children, and there's so many offers of films and TV I need the time to think it all over." A producer had pitched her a five-minute "Dear Jayne" TV segment for humorous love and sex advice. Sam jumped into the conversation: "Great, great. She'll be beautiful. Can you see it, Jayne? You're the love goddess—it's for you, baby." Jayne planned out the show: "How about a keyhole view of life in the Jayne Mansfield household—I mean all sorts of funny things happen here. No one would believe it. My boy got me to sign 50 pictures. Then I discovered he sold them off for 50 cents apiece in school—what a business brain, that boy." Sam admitted, "We've had a tough time lately. Jayne falls into trouble easy—it chases her." Jayne agreed. "We've both been losers lately, like there's been a jinx.

She became reflective with Peter McDonald, telling him, "All my husbands have been completely different, but the mistake, I think, has been in my own mind." It also sounded as though Jayne had begun to realize that Sam Brody was a bad lot. "If you want something badly enough, you go searching for it, trying to fit your mental image to the man rather than seeing if the man fits your image. . . . Do you know what life is? It's a whole equation, a series of balances! Who you happen to be with, your mental attitude at a moment can tip the balance and change your own direction."

Jayne, asked earlier in 1967 if she was happy, replied, "No. I have wonderful happy moments, I consider myself tremendously fortunate, having five children. But I think a person who is tremendously complicated, and involved, I don't think that person would ever be a contented, happy person. But as long as there are enough happy moments to overbalance the unhappy ones . . ."

28

Jayne Mansfield will probably not be remembered as a great actress. I think, though, that she will be best remembered for her sportsmanship. . . . If she brought about some unhappiness, I believe she balanced the scale through the happiness she created. I am glad that I met her.

Bill Soberanes

Jayne was booked to play Gus Stevens's Supper Club from June 23 to July 4, but she and Sam arrived a day late, due to Sam's broken leg. An ad featuring a late 1950s glamour shot of Jayne promised patrons that they would see "the most publicized and beautiful TV and movie star setting the pace for the low neckline-miniskirt." Also on the bill was Brenda Bynes, "blond songstress, guitarist, and former Miss Pepsi Cola." Later that month Mamie Van Doren "with her dancing partner and strip act" would be following Jayne.

Jayne and Sam flew into Keesler Air Force Base in Biloxi, then bought a Rolls-Royce—paying by check—so Jayne could chauffeur Sam and the kids around for the rest of the trip. Jayne, Sam, and the three children registered at the Broadwater Beach Hotel in Biloxi, a 1930s Art Moderne resort (they quickly shifted to the Edgewater Gulf Hotel—perhaps because of too many dogs and children, again). The Rolls-Royce check failed to clear, leaving the troupe stranded between the Edgewater Gulf and Gus Stevens's club, dependent on whoever could give them a lift.

On Wednesday, June 28, Jayne revisited Keelser Air Force Base and its hospital, sitting by the bedside of the injured, signing casts, holding hands, and doing what she did best—showing a genuine interest in others, asking questions, and offering encouragement. The children came along, and photos show Mickey Jr. and Zoltan growing into skinny pre-teens, and three-and-a-half-year-old Mariska sitting on the lap of Airman Second Class Johnny Burke.

That night Jayne did the 9:00 and 11:00 shows at Gus Stevens's ("No need to dress up, come as you are," read the ads). She had very little to drink, so the shows—while not up to her early Vegas standards—would have been a pleasant mix of funny, breathy songs and Jayne kidding and flirting with the customers.

According to the *Biloxi Gulfport Daily Herald,* at the 9:00 show Jayne asked one male customer why he was all alone. He had just arrived from Denver, he told Jayne, who sat on his lap and cooed that she loved Denver: "It's so Colorado-ish." A woman took a photo of Jayne with her arm around her husband—where is that photo now? one wonders—and reporter Billy Ray Quave wrote that "she left a happy audience. The people had not only spent a pleasant 30 minutes, but they felt that they had personally met someone who was not only internationally famous, but pretty and a real person."

There was to be no rest that night, though: Jayne was due in New Orleans for a noon interview on WDSU radio with local personality Al Shea; it was about a ninety-mile late-night drive, and Jayne was stuck without a car; the Edgewater Gulf refused to provide a limo. Gus Stevens offered his wife's 1966 Buick Electra. The silver, four-door hardtop sedan had air-conditioning, so Sam didn't have to struggle out of his suit on a hot June night, and Jayne wore a light-blue minidress, boots, and stockings. Stevens supplied Jayne and Sam with a bottle of whiskey, a bottle of scotch, a Coke, and some sandwiches in case they got caught short in New Orleans. After the WDSU interview, Jayne was booked to entertain Seabees at the naval mobile construction battalion training center in Gulfport.

Someone had to drive the car. Jayne didn't want to, Sam's leg was in a cast, Gus Stevens and his club manager, Tony Picillo, had other business to attend to—the unlucky driver drafted was nineteen-year-old Ronnie Harrison (Jayne slipped him a $20 tip). Generally brushed off as just "the driver," Ronald Bernard Harrison was a University of Mississippi student with a day job at Koury's Men's Store in Gulfport; he was working nights at Gus Stevens's for the summer. He was also the fiancé of the Stevenses' daughter Elaine—in fact, they were expecting a baby. "We were planning to be married in 72 hours," Elaine told Fox News in 2018. "We went to high school together. We graduated together. It was young first love. My sweetheart."

Before leaving for New Orleans, Jayne called Mickey. "We had a very sweet, very kind, very loving conversation," he said years later, perhaps romanticizing a bit in hindsight. "She said to me, the last thing I heard, 'honey, the kids will be asleep, don't worry about them, I'll put them in the back seat. I'll talk to you later. I gotta go.' That was the end."

According to Gus Stevens, Ronnie Harrison played a trick on Jayne, in the cause of safety. Stevens had told Harrison that Jayne wanted to leaf through newspapers and fan magazines on the ride, but he knew that having overhead lights on inside the car would make nighttime driving more dangerous. Before setting out Harrison unscrewed all the interior lights and hid them, telling Jayne they had burned out.

Zoltan, who was just shy of seven years old, later recalled, "We knew we had to go somewhere in the nighttime, and it was a big rush to go to another place. We were tired, my brother and me and my sister, we were all tired. We got in the car, and basically, probably just fell asleep."

Elaine Stevens enacted a real-life 1960s teen tragedy song: she recalled that Ronnie "was pulling out of the driveway. They wouldn't let him come in. He looked at me and said, 'Will you always love me?' I said, 'Of course I will always love you. I will always love you.' And he took off. That was the last time I saw him."

Harrison was familiar with the road between Biloxi and New Orleans, having driven Elaine to H. Sophie Newcomb Memorial College along that route several times. He'd also made sure to take a two-hour nap as soon as he knew he'd have a long drive that night. They took US 90, a two-lane road called the Old Spanish Trail that stretched from San Diego to St. Augustine. It was a notorious death trap, particularly in the Louisiana section. Senator Francis Romero had been lobbying to have the road ("Blood Alley") widened. "State police rush to accidents on it daily," wrote one local paper. "And south Louisiana residents advise that a person takes his life in his hands to drive down it. But there are no plans to widen some of the most dangerous sections of narrow, treacherous US Highway 90. 'We really need the highway widened bad,' State Police Sgt. HA Pontiff of Franklin said. 'We have accidents all day long.'"

At 12:45 on the morning of Thursday, June 29, according to Gus

Stevens, the party took off. Mickey Jr., Zoltan, and Mariska were in the front seat alongside Harrison, and Jayne and Sam took the back, where Sam could stretch out his painful leg. The four Chihuahuas were crated to keep them from snuggling under the gas or brake pedals.

They made two stops along the way—one at Jimmy's Texaco Service Station to get those inside lights fixed—worker Harold Riden explained (probably with some prodding from Harrison) that Jimmy's did not carry the right size. Riden witnessed a life-changing moment during this stop: seeing how sleepy the kids were, Jayne shifted them into the back seat, while she and Sam crammed themselves into the front with Harrison. Sam sat in the middle—no doubt repositioning his cast-bound leg in a vain attempt to find a comfortable position—while Jayne sat in the right-hand passenger's seat, her lap full of fan magazines and newspapers, which she pored through even in the relative darkness, seeking clippings for her scrapbooks.

They next stopped at an all-night diner called the White Kitchen in Slidell, about sixty miles from Biloxi. It was around 2:00 a.m. Jayne used the ladies' room and bought some cookies and Cokes. A startled patron and her son asked her for her autograph, which Jayne happily gave.

Motorist Mava Fountain told police that as she was traveling at fifty-five to sixty miles per hour on that stretch of road, two cars passed her; one of them must have been Jayne's. Another driver, John Beck, traveling at fifty to sixty miles per hour, said that Harrison passed him "like a streak of lightning." Driving at that speed on a badly lighted road at night seems suicidal, but judging from the testimony of other motorists that night, it seemed to be typical.

They crossed the Fort Pike Bridge over the Rigolets, a strait connecting the Gulf of Mexico to Lake Pontchartrain. About two miles after the bridge, Harrison was cruising along at sixty miles per hour, according to police estimates. Sam was—one hopes—asleep, and Jayne was concentrating on rifling through fan magazines.

Then, at 2:25 a.m., as quick as that, all three were dead.

❤

How did the accident happen, and who—if anyone—was to blame? That question would wend its way through the courts for years, never to be satisfactorily answered.

Three vehicles were involved. In front was a mosquito-fogging truck

347

owned by the City of New Orleans, driven by James T. McLelland. Following behind was a Johnson Motors Freight Lines trailer rig driven by Richard Rambo. The tractor and trailer combined weighed 25,700 pounds, and was filled with 28,000 pounds of "miscellaneous freight." And behind Rambo's rig was the Buick—which plowed at full speed into the truck. The front end of the car wedged violently under the trailer, crushing the three front-seat passengers.

McLelland's fogging truck was not actually on the road, but traveling at five miles per hour on the shoulder. McClelland and other witnesses stated that at the time of the accident, he had turned his fogging machine off, so it was the dark, unlit road, not the fog, that made the situation so dangerous. Richard Rambo told the police that "there was no fog on or near the highway . . . the fog from the fog machine was in the marsh area off the highway and it was drifting away."

Rambo told police he thought he had been going at about fifty to sixty miles per hour after crossing the Fort Pike Bridge, but when he noticed the red blinking lights on the back of McLelland's truck, he slowed down to about twenty—though Rambo did not have his foot on the brakes; those brake lights would have given Ronnie Harrison a few extra seconds of warning.

Damage to the Buick—and the injuries of the three killed—show that Harrison, at the very last second, saw Rambo's truck and swerved to the left to avoid it. He thus hit it diagonally, which is why the right front of his car—where Jayne was seated—took the brunt of the impact.

Rambo was, amazingly, uninjured. He stopped immediately and ran back to the Buick, which was rammed several feet under his truck—he could hear screaming coming from the back seat. Rambo opened the rear door and—with the help of Thomas Landry (passing motorist Mava Fountain's passenger)—pulled the children from the tumble of luggage and upholstery, and carried them to the side of the road. Mickey Jr. was the most badly injured of the children, suffering a broken right arm and right leg, as well as lacerations. Zoltan had cuts and bruises, and Mariska had nearly been suffocated, "her head jammed between the door post and the back seat," before one of her brothers screamed for Richard Rambo to go back and search for her; she had a serious cut on her face that required plastic surgery. Two of the four Chihuahuas in the car were killed.

Fountain and Landry took the children to Charity Hospital in New

Orleans. Landry drove, while Fountain sat in the back seat with them, trying to staunch the blood and comfort them. "I don't remember anything else but just waking up in the back seat," Zoltan later said. "It was kind of an eerie, weird feeling. I knew we were in an accident, but it almost seemed like we were in a dream."

Rambo lit a flare to warn off approaching cars, and ran up to McLelland's fogging truck—he had not even heard the crash—and asked him to call the police from a nearby fishing camp. McLelland also called his boss, George Carmichael, head of the New Orleans mosquito-control unit, who came to the scene of the accident: "It was the most dreadful thing I've ever seen."

Rambo was able to pull Jayne out of the car and drag her to the side of the road, but Sam and Ronnie were jammed in too tightly to be extricated. The police report states that "a large deposit of brains" and "a large portion of skull" were scattered on the roadway as Rambo carried Jayne away from the wreckage. Examining the underside of Rambo's truck, police found "a small portion of brain matter along with particles of blonde hair, and slightly to the left, "brain matter with small patches of black hair" on the truck and its mud flap. Jayne's voluminous wig was caught in the shards of the windshield, leading to still-current decapitation rumors.

Ronnie Harrison, being on the left side of the car, was the least disfigured: he was pinned between the seat and the steering wheel, the top of his skull split open. Sam, seated in the center, had his face crushed to the point of unrecognizability against the dashboard.

Jayne was not decapitated: She suffered "scalp avulsion combined with an open skull avulsion fracture and open craniocerebral injury." It's a difference of seven inches, but "decapitation" sells more papers—also, those wig-in-the-windshield photos made up people's minds. Graphic police photos show the left side of Jayne's dress drenched in blood; her eyes and mouth are open—her teeth still intact—and her skull sliced off just above the eyebrows.

All three died instantly, and due to the severe brain injuries, they suffered no pain. But there had been a second or two of warning, accounting for Ronnie's swerve to the left, and Jayne's "closed fractures of right humerus," revealed in her autopsy. Joanna Campbell comments on Scott Michaels's Find a Death website that this "is a very common injury in car accidents, it happens when people's reaction is to put their hand out to stop them from flying forward in the car." So while Jayne had a brief moment of panic, it cannot have been long enough for her to fully comprehend what was happening.

At 4:45 all three bodies and their belongings (Jayne's bright-pink "leatherette" suitcases, jewelry, money, ID, and—oddly—a St. Christopher medal found on Sam Brody)—were taken to the city morgue. Assistant coroner Ignacio Medina said the bodies were "pretty well torn up. Miss Mansfield lay dead in her blue boots, blue stockings and blue dress that was shredded to bits." None of the drivers involved—nor Sam—had any alcohol in their system. Jayne tested positive for .08 percent, "which is not indicative according to present legal standards as a level of intoxication" (and, of course, she was not driving, anyway).

In the aftermath of the accident, Glenn Stokes, director of the Jefferson Parish Mosquito Control Unit, said ground fogging would be immediately suspended because of the "extreme safety hazard involved," and that the parish would probably switch to aerial spraying (which sounds equally unhealthy to residents, but one shouldn't judge unless one has dealt with Louisiana mosquitoes).

❤

Jayne Marie found out about her mother's death in an unnecessarily brutal way. "I looked out the window and I saw a *Monseigneur* from the Catholic church walking up," she recalled, "and right as he hit the door my aunt handed me a newspaper and the headlines were 'Jayne Mansfield decapitated.' Which isn't really what happened, but that's the way I found out." Jayne Marie's uncle said, "She took it like the little trouper she is," that she "cried softly for a long time, but was relieved that earlier this week she had dropped a battery complaint made against her mother and Sam Brody." Mickey, even decades later unable to talk about Jayne's death without crying, said, "I went into the funeral home, I said, 'can I see her?' 'Yes.' I saw her, the last time. It wasn't really her anymore. You know, the soul was gone, the spirit was gone, it was just a machine. It wasn't her." He told Mickey Jr. that his mother had "'a date with God.' He is a smart boy. He understood."

Criminal district judge Bernard J. Bagert ordered Jayne's body to be released jointly to Mickey and her parents. Matt asked for a court order to name him administrator of her estate. All three children were released from the hospital and into Mickey's care on July 5. "I have to look after them now," said Mickey. "I planned to meet Jaynie here in New Orleans. I was supposed to come to New Orleans today or tomorrow to see the kids."

June 1967 also saw the deaths of Spencer Tracy, Claude Rains, Dorothy Parker, director G. W. Pabst, and jazz great Billy Strayhorn. Just a few days before Jayne's death, twenty-five-year-old French actress Françoise Dorléac died when her Renault crashed, flipped, and burned near Nice. But Jayne's death was the one that made the front page and the TV news breaks: Tracy, Rains, and Parker were old and their deaths not unexpected; Pabst and Dorléac were more famous overseas; and only jazz fans knew who Strayhorn was. Jayne was the lead story on a day when other news included particularly bloody fighting in Saigon and Jerusalem, twenty-four people dying in a Hong Kong plane crash, and two of the Rolling Stones being arrested on drug charges.

A Guide for the Married Man was in theaters in June 1967, and Herb Kelly of the *Miami News* cynically noted that Jayne's death probably helped the box office. George McKinnon of the *Boston Globe* was more thoughtful: "Midway through the film the laughter of the audience abruptly stopped on opening night," his review read. "This was when the late Jayne Mansfield suddenly appeared on the screen in a cameo role with Terry-Thomas. What normally should have been one of the more hilarious episodes was greeted with a hush as if the spectre of death flashed across the screen."

Jayne's pal Anton LaVey saw an opportunity for publicity and jumped in feet-first, claiming that he'd been responsible for Sam Brody's death, but that Jayne and Ronnie Harrison had just been collateral damage. It was reported that Jayne "had sought [LaVey's] help allegedly to stop harassment by her boyfriend, attorney Steve [*sic*] Brody. To oblige her, LaVey claims he put a hex on him. LaVey 'reluctantly' takes credit for his demise. . . . 'When lightning strikes, sometimes the innocent also are killed.'"

The decapitation rumors started the day after Jayne's death and were often featured in newspaper headlines (at least three papers added a subhead, "Two Chihuahuas Killed," which must have felt like an extra slap to Sam Brody's and Ronnie Harrison's loved ones).

Along with the obituaries and news stories came the think pieces and what would ordinarily be called appreciations. But depressingly few of them were appreciative, and even those were tepid and backhanded. The *Tampa Times* started out with, "Jayne Mansfield was not a great actress. She was hardly what you'd call an inspiration for modern youth." But the paper went on to admit that "she brought a wealth of humor to the many phases of show business where her talents were displayed. Show business will miss Miss Mansfield and the brand of humor which was her stock in trade. And so will the rest of us who found moments of pleasant relaxation chuckling at this young lady who rarely took herself seriously and could kid the dickens out of some of our more stodgy institutions."

Bill Soberanes of the *Petaluma Argus-Courier* echoed the *Tampa Times*: "Jayne Mansfield will probably not be remembered as a great actress," but added that "she will be best remembered for her sportsmanship—she was a wonderful person to interview, to work with. . . . If she brought about some unhappiness, I believe she balanced the scale through the happiness she created. I am glad that I met her." Geoffrey Cooper of the *Tennessean* called her "the last of her breed—an honest, straight-forward sex symbol."

Whitney Bolton of the *Fort Myers News-Press* called Jayne "one of the most colorful women ever in films. She did not summon dignity to her occasions, yet she meant well at all times. . . . The simplest way to put it is the one that is most painful—she was a woman people never took seriously. Is that a dreadful thing to say about her? Perhaps, but it is true. She kindled more mockery than respect, yet I think that respect in many, many ways should have been her portion."

But many of the articles following Jayne's death were shockingly vicious. Jayne's old antagonist the Reverend Billy Graham came right out of the gate, according to Yorkshire vicar Peter Mullen, crowing that "her death, including the grotesque form of it, was a direct punishment meted out by God."

Many gossip columnists and entertainment reporters—who had been making a living off Jayne for more than a decade, and who had sat down for long, friendly chats with her—all but spat on her grave. Leonard Lyons called Jayne "a pathetic parody. . . . When she decided that 'it takes uncoverage to get coverage,' she'd uncover anyplace where photographers were present." Jim Bishop went poetic: "Miss Mansfield was 80 different faces in a mirror on the headboard of her bed. She had it made of bits of pink glass, and when she luxuriated in the big couch, she could swing over on her stomach and stare at all those vapid blondes and murmur, 'You're a star.'"

Jack Wasserman of the *Vancouver Sun* wrote on the day the news of her death broke that "Jayne Mansfield was a tragic, no talent woman. She couldn't sing, she couldn't dance, she couldn't act. . . . She came out of obscurity as a Hollywood studio's answer to Marilyn Monroe, who was also an emotional mess but who had a certain talent." Wasserman noted that at the advanced age of thirty-four, Jayne "was fighting the ravages of time and dissipation and the certain knowledge that this was the last time around the circuit. If there's any consolation to be taken from the sudden violent and tragic death of any human being, it might be that Jayne can stop pushing now. Today her name will be in all the papers, which would have appealed to her deep need." One reader—Betty Bruce, bless her heart—wrote in to the *Vancouver Sun* to say that Wasserman's article was "about the poorest taste of anything I have ever read. If he had to be despicable, he should have been so when the person was alive."

Robert Kistler of the *Des Moines Register* put forth that Jayne "isn't much mourned. . . . Perhaps she wasn't ever a star because she couldn't act. To most women, Mansfield was grotesque. But to me, her comedy, her image and her silly sexiness were the poor trappings of an outdated clown hopelessly roaming a super-sophisticated world." Roger Ebert, in his first year writing for the *Chicago Sun-Times,* called Jayne "almost a caricature of the dumb blonde, bigger, blonder, dumber, more publicity-conscious than any who had gone before. . . . But she wasn't really very good as an actress. She didn't have comic timing and the natural warmth of Monroe, and, truth to tell, she was never as sexy, either. . . . She had the props, but she never found the secret."

❤

Unmourned and jeered at by the press, Jayne was nonetheless a huge loss to her fans and her family, and funeral arrangements were carefully planned. Mickey's lawyer, Jerome Weber, won his argument that "at the time of her demise, Mr. Hargitay was her legal husband. Any subsequent attempts at marriage would be unsuccessful because of a prior undissolved marriage." Matt said he would not fight the decision: "That would be an extremely morbid thing. Jayne will probably be buried in Dallas, and that's the way it is."

In fact, Jayne's sealed bronze casket was flown to John F. Kennedy International Airport and taken by hearse to the Pullis Funeral Home in Pen Argyl. Undertaker Clyde Pullis said the funeral in Fairview Cemetery would be "strictly private"; the Reverend Charles Montgomery, pastor of the Zion Methodist Church in Pen Argyl, would conduct the service. The town's only florist was on vacation, so businesses in neighboring towns were kept busy with orders, including Mickey's thirteen red roses with the message, "For ever and ever, I love you Jayne, Mickey." "I always sent her constantly 13 red roses," he explained. "I never had to sign it. She knew it was from me. It was our unspoken love message, even when we were apart."

The AP was prepared for a circus. "There were crowds of nearly 1,000 both in front of the Pullis Funeral Home and at the Fairview Cemetery about two miles away." Many went to the cemetery early, hours before the 2 p.m. service on Monday, July 3, and had their lunch picnic-style while waiting for the sixteen-car procession to arrive. Spectators broke through police lines and ran across graves to snap photographs of the bronze casket with its blanket of pink roses. "We just wanted a little privacy," said Mickey. "Why couldn't the people have left us to weep in peace?" The AP scoffed at the local trash: "Adults and children, many dressed in bathing suits and in shorts, sat on curbstones or on their porches." But news photos taken that day actually show women in crisp cotton dresses and men in shirts and long pants, many wearing neckties.

Jayne Marie looked the picture of grief—her mother's death could not have come at a worse time for her—as did Vera and Harry Peers. Jayne's children by Mickey were still hospitalized, and Tony remained in California with Matt. The press said that Paul Mansfield did not attend, but Jayne Marie recalled seeing him there: "My father, Paul Mansfield, was at my mother's funeral," she said in the 1970s. "It was the last time I've seen or heard from him."

Mickey dropped a small note and piece of jewelry into the grave before it was filled in.

Several local papers printed the announcement, "Please accept our sincere thanks for your love, co-operation, assistance and consideration during our recent tragedy. It was an honor and a privilege to bring our girl home.—The Family of Jayne Mansfield."

While Jayne's body rested in Pen Argyl, her spirit and aura remained in Hollywood. "She liked a lot of publicity and she should be allowed to be buried that way," said Matt Cimber. "I know she would have wanted a Hollywood funeral in a grand manner. No one loved Hollywood more than she did." On July 6 there was a memorial service at All Saints Church in Beverly Hills, with the Reverend Herbert J. Smith presiding. Pat Boone and Peter Palmer sang; Cesar Romero and Fox executives were among the ushers. Both Mickey and Matt attended, shaking hands in a show of cordiality. Matt asked, "How are the children?" and Mickey said, "Fine," then turned and walked away. Deputy Mayor Joseph Quinn called Jayne a "grand person" who had "a knack for having a lot of fun."

The Jayne Mansfield Fan Club placed a stone in the Hollywood Forever Cemetery reading, "WE LIVE TO LOVE YOU MORE EACH DAY," and misdating her birth year as 1938 (to which Jayne would not have objected). Hollywood Forever, founded in 1899 as the Hollywood Cemetery, contains the remains of fellow stars Rudolph Valentino, Judy Garland, Marion Davies, Valerie Harper, Douglas Fairbanks Sr. and Jr., Tyrone Power, and the Talmadge sisters, among many others.

Ronald Bernard "Ronnie" Harrison was buried on July 1 at the Southern Memorial Park in Biloxi. "But the greatest of these is love," from the New Testament, is carved on his gravestone. His fiancée Elaine Stevens was naturally shattered by Ronnie's death; her parents made her give up their baby for adoption. She was also angry that Ronnie was brushed off as merely "the driver" whenever Jayne's death was mentioned. "We were considered collateral damage," she told Fox News. "He was just some vagabond young man who parked cars for dad. An unknown. Without a name. Without a face."

Sam Brody was not buried until August 2, in Hillside Memorial Park, Los Angeles. A brass plaque on his crypt reads, "Our Beloved," though the thoughts of his wheelchair-bound wife Beverly, dressed in black and wearing dark glasses at his funeral, can only be imagined.

In April 1968 Mickey took Mickey Jr., Zoltan, and Mariska to visit Jayne's grave, where a white Italian marble, heart-shaped tombstone had been erected. "I thought it would be nice to bring the children down to Pen Argyl to see Jaynie's grave," Mickey said. "The children were all hurt in the crash and couldn't attend their mother's funeral."

❤

And then the lawsuits started, growing over the decades to resemble Dickens's *Jarndyce vs. Jarndyce* from *Bleak House*. Controversy over wills, divorce authenticity, child custody, real estate, jewelry, and insurance policies, as well as suits against every conceivable party who might have been responsible in all three deaths—it all played out in Los Angeles and Louisiana until Jayne's children were adults.

Mickey filed more than $1 million worth of suits against the City of New Orleans, Johnson Motors Freight Lines, Richard Rambo, James T.

McLelland, Gus Stevens, and the estate of Ronnie Harrison (he charged that Harrison, Rambo, and McLelland "operated their vehicles in a negligent manner"). Matt Cimber and William Pigue filed $4.8 million suits against the three drivers as well; a jury eventually decided that Ronnie Harrison, not Rambo or McLelland, was negligent through speeding.

Then it was discovered that Sam Brody had made a new will leaving everything to Jayne, cutting his ailing wife and young children out ("I hereby bequeath and give all my estate, whether personal, real or otherwise, to the only person in the world I love, Jayne Mansfield"). Beverly demanded that his previous will, dated October 15, 1958, be declared valid. Her lawyer pointed out that since Sam and Jayne died simultaneously, his bequest to Jayne was invalid. Beverly filed a suit against Jayne's estate, saying Sam had "lavished $150,000 worth of community property funds on Miss Mansfield." She also sought $50,000 for Sam's legal services to Jayne, $25,000 for his services as manager of her career, and $100,000 for money Brody allegedly loaned to Jayne. A court eventually awarded $185,000 to Beverly and her children.

Lawyers, administrators, and advisors got busy. Mickey, as expected, was appointed guardian of Mickey Jr., Zoltan, and Mariska, and Matt of Tony. Jayne Marie's fate was somewhat vague, as Jayne had implied that Paul Mansfield was not her biological father, and Paul Mansfield showed no enthusiasm for taking her in anyway. William and Mary Pigue were eventually appointed her guardians. All those guardians needed money for childcare: Mickey petitioned for $257,533 from Jayne's estate, and a Superior Court judge approved $5,131 to William Pigue for Jayne Marie's expenses, plus $230 a month.

The cases dragged on through the late 1960s and on into the '70s. Jayne's business manager Charles Goldring estimated that she had left $35,000 in cash, $163,000 in stocks, and $250,000 in property. Matt's attorney, Richard Meyer, testified that Mickey had gotten $10,000 and two parcels of land when he and Jayne divorced in 1964. In 1968 some of Jayne's art and jewelry was auctioned off, including a 11.89-carat diamond ring, a watch set with 520 diamonds, a diamond and ruby clip, and a diamond bracelet, as well as paintings, porcelains, silver, period furniture, and Oriental rugs (Sophie Tucker's estate sale was combined with Jayne's— Soph had died in 1966).

By 1969 the estate was dwindling, but there were still many claimants. Los Angeles judge Arthur Marshall ruled that Jayne's five children would receive $22,000 each, and the three children who'd been injured in the crash received an additional $5,000 each from the Gus Stevens club. In 1978 Stevens said that "the death of Jayne was just about the death of me in the nightclub business. Things went downhill after that. Her ex-husbands sued me and her boyfriend's wife sued me. Sued me for $4 million. Forty lawyers were involved, the city of New Orleans was involved, Johnson Motor Freight Lines was involved. I paid all court and funeral expenses." Gus Stevens's club closed in 1975 and was demolished in 2000. Stevens died in 1998.

In 1971 estate attorney Irwin Briscoe said that all the expensive litigation meant that creditors "would be lucky to get 30 percent of what they claim," and there might not be a single cent left to divide. Probate judge Neil Lake found that Jayne's estate wound up with assets of $75,000 and debts of $53,000, plus accountants' and lawyers' fees—leaving nothing. Mickey said, "It's a little unfair to leave the children without any money whatsoever." The *Des Moines Register* came through with the headline "Treasure Chest Empty."

As soon as they were out of the hospital, Mickey took Mickey Jr., Zoltan, and Mariska back to the Pink Palace and tried to give them as "normal" a childhood as possible. Neighbor Tony Curtis kindly invited them all over for his daughter Alexandra's third birthday party on July 19. In August all three children came down with the mumps, because that's just the kind of summer they were having.

Matt moved Jayne's menagerie to a pet shop and put all the animals up for sale: an ocelot, two Afghans, a Venezuelan terrier, five kittens, a talking mynah bird, and two Chihuahuas, Dorothy and Cow (so apparently it was Popsicle and Momsicle who had perished with Jayne).

29

Forget the Kardashians, she was completely so good at selling
herself. Jayne created a monster and then she couldn't get rid of
it. . . . If she had only given up her façade, and let herself go
deeper than that. I think she got frightened, the façade was so
successful.

Loni Anderson

Jayne had two films released posthumously in addition to *Single Room
Furnished*—but these featured years-old clips of her. *Spree* (released in
November 1967) was basically an advertisement for Las Vegas, though it
was so trashy that Juliet Prowse and Vic Damone sued to have their
segments deleted. The *New York Daily News* agreed that "no one would
want his or her name linked with this tacky promotion film for Las Vegas.
It is nothing more than very dated footage of those lavish Vegas revues, to
which has been added an overbearing narrative, and some obviously staged
girl-picks-up-boy sequences. Compounding the felony with incredible bad
taste, someone has included a bit from a routine of the late Jayne Mansfield."

A Spokane paper wrote, "There's really nothing in *Spree* to offend
anyone, except perhaps the Chamber of Commerce at Las Vegas . . . nothing naughtier than the late Jayne Mansfield grappling awkwardly and pa-
thetically with some loose clothing in a nightclub." Don Morrison of the
Minneapolis Star described one of the debauched "docudrama" segments
involving an innocent young woman meeting a Vegas habitué: "He is a nice
looking chap (I pegged him for a vacationing supermarket manager), but
the depths of his depravity is revealed when he puts his arm around the girl
in a crowded night club. She leaves in mortal outrage."

But the most high-camp and jaw-droppingly on-the-nose tribute came with *The Wild, Wild World of Jayne Mansfield,* possibly the most deliriously, enjoyably bad film of her career. In the spring and summer of 1968, the "documentary" began playing at drive-ins and sketchier theaters around the country (it was rated X for its ubiquitous tits-and-ass footage). One of the four credited producers, Dick Randall, had already inflicted *Primitive Love* upon the public. Writer Charles Ross penned the films *Nympho: A Woman's Urge* and *The Sexperts.* So this was not going to be a Ken Burns documentary.

Wild, Wild World is an hour and a half of pure godawful joy, beginning with the jingly theme music by Marcello Gigante, which enters one's head and *never leaves.* The film starts with Jayne's voice welcoming us: "Hi—I'm Jayne Mansfield. For the next couple of hours, I'd like you to come along with me. I want you to share some of the wild, way-out experiences I had during my last trip around the world." Except it's not Jayne, it's her frequent dubber Carolyn De Fonseca, doing such an expert impersonation that several documentaries have used sound clips from *Wild, Wild World* under the impression that they were actually Jayne.

The film whisks us through Rome ("where the men have *hand* problems"), Paris ("a city of *sin,* of vice, and unashamed *love*"), Cannes (where your typical girl "is able to make a bikini out of a midget's handkerchief"), the nudist Isle of Levant ("I hope nobody was *watching* me—I'm basically very shy"), and Los Angeles ("I saw the wildest topless things you could imagine").

About twenty minutes of the footage is really Jayne: sometimes wearing her awful *Primitive Love* wig and hairpiece, sometimes a flattering, tousled bouffant (occasionally the wigs change mid-scene; the fact that no editor is credited is unsurprising). The footage of Jayne was taken in 1964 for a proposed travelogue series variously called *Jayne Mansfield Reports* or *Mansfield by Night.* But many of the Jaynes seen in the film are doubles, shot from behind and wearing wigs that don't match the actual Jayne footage.

We also get badly acted vignettes of girl-watchers and peeping toms, prostitution, pickups (straight and gay), a Roman statue turning into a very embarrassed and unhappy Mickey Hargitay, topless shoeshine girls and window-washers, and striptease lessons. Along the way, Jayne—Chihuahua always in tow—encounters Rocky Roberts and the Airedales (the only class act in the film, performing "The Bird Is the Word" in Cannes while Jayne twists along, her Chihuahua looking up in undisguised terror), a topless female rock band, a "Bust Stop" contest, and various nightclub dancers, clothed and unclothed. We also get clips from *Primitive Love* and *Loves of Hercules,* with De Fonseca explaining them away as "silly, wicked, little daydreams."

Two of the more historically interesting segments take place at a gay nightclub in Paris and the Miss All-America Camp Beauty Pageant in New York (several clips are lifted from the 1967 short *Queens at Heart*). "Jayne's" narration is condescending, but no more so than would be expected in 1968. ("The boy-girls were all twittering and giggling, laughing nervously, poor dears. I could almost imagine some guy falling for one of these . . . 'girls.' It sure is a mixed-up world!") But the real Jayne is shown dancing and chatting happily with the Paris club habitués, which takes some of the sting out.

Charles Ross's script is packed with so many bubbleheaded quotes it's hard to choose a favorite: "Saturday night in old Rome must have been just the living end," "That dog was eying my Chu-Chu—but no French romance for him," "Midgets and dwarfs need sex, too"—all breathily uttered by De Fonseca in perfect Jaynese. The film ends jarringly with Jayne's fatal car wreck (in the reenactment she crashes into a tree), photos of Jayne's and Sam's corpses, and the bereft Mickey, Mickey Jr., and Zoltan wandering around the now-empty Pink Palace.

The Wild, Wild World of Jayne Mansfield got very few reviews. Jean Walrath of the *Rochester Democrat and Chronicle* called it "an unnerving spectacle for certain males, but for any woman who has to be begged to go along, it's for catching up on sleep. It fails to live up to the billing of 'the true life story of the real Jayne, never before seen on the screen,' unless that's a put-on." The *Wilmington Morning News* characterized it as "a monuments [*sic*] of ineptness."

Newspaper ads and posters tried their best: "Uninhibited! Unbeliev-able! Unforgettable! The real Jayne Mansfield in her mad, mad world! Never before seen on any screen! Jayne sees all—shows all—tells all!" But *The Wild, Wild World of Jayne Mansfield* sank quickly from sight, resurfacing as a cult favorite only with the advent of VCRs and DVDs.

❤

Jayne was gone but never forgotten: indeed, to this day she has one of the most loyal and protective fan bases of any of the Golden Age stars, rivaling Marilyn Monroe and James Dean. In 1970 newspapermen presented

Raquel Welch with the "Jayne Mansfield Award, given annually to the actress getting the most publicity." Welch told reporter Hal Boyle, "Being thought of as nothing but a glamour girl is my biggest hate right now. It seems to be synonymous with being empty-headed. My reception heretofore has been based on glamour, physical appearance and comedy. Now I like to show I have other dimensions." Boyle of course riposted, "The dimensions that have contributed largely to her present fame can be summarized: 37-22½-35½." In 1972 the *Windsor Star* wrote of curvaceous sexpots, "As far as movies are concerned the whole thing came to a thankful end with the death of Jayne Mansfield. Tragic and violent as her death was it signaled the end of the line for her kind of looks."

For years after Jayne's death, columnist Jim Bishop managed to be both inaccurate and vicious: "I knew her well. . . . She couldn't act, but she did everything everyone told her—and I mean everything. Fox pinned a gold star on her dressing room and gave her a piano she couldn't play. . . . Then she hurried from Mobile to New Orleans to keep a cheap nightclub date and ran under the tailgate of a truck. She was decapitated. Tragically, she had lost her head years before." In 1980 Bishop added that "Jayne Mansfield was an imposter. . . . As an actress, she couldn't pass as a spear carrier in a high school play."

Three biographies of Jayne were published in the mid-1970s, all high profile and widely reviewed. Two were by Jayne's associates, one by a professor of history and women's studies.

Hollywood columnist May Mann was a longtime friend of Jayne's (indeed, she was an adoring fan-girl of many a star). Her *Jayne Mansfield* (1973) is a loopy "memoir" told in Jayne's voice as channeled through Mann's self-described psychics: "Then came her call from the spirit world asking me . . . to complete the Jayne Book! 'Tell the truth, May! When May passes to this plane we will be together and will seek adventure and life here and will come back together.'" May Mann passed to that plane in 1995. Her book is completely unreliable, except for the few interviews Mann conducted with Jayne's associates.

In 1974 Raymond Strait—formerly "Rusty Ray" or "Russell Ray," one of Jayne's many secretaries—published *The Tragic, Secret Life of Jayne Mansfield* (later reissued as *Here They Are: Jayne Mansfield,* and yet again under its original title). It dwelt mainly on Jayne's scandals and misconduct, giving short shrift to her career.

The most professional of the lot was Martha Saxton's *Jayne Mansfield and the American Fifties,* published in 1975. Saxton actually interviewed many of Jayne's family and coworkers, cited her sources, and did her homework on Jayne's acting career, as well as the tribulations of a 1950s–1960s sex symbol.

Since then, numerous books about Jayne have been published (some, recently, as ebooks). Such writers as Richard Koper, Jocelyn Faris, Frank Ferruccio, Guus Luijters, Michael Feeney Callan, and others have had their say, and all of their books are worth investigating. The most high-profile book involving Jayne was Kenneth Anger's notorious *Hollywood Babylon,* a 1959 compilation of scandals, gossip, innuendo, and inaccuracies, featuring a cover shot of her at her Jayniest—from the 1957 Sophia Loren party. The first time most of the reading public saw photos of Jayne's death was in this book, which also featured a photo of one of her Chihuahua's corpses.

Jayne's significance seemed to pick up steam through the celebrity-mad 1970s and '80s. In 1976 Andy Warhol said that Jayne was his "patron saint. Her life may not have been spotless, but she always made copy— she was the poet of publicity." Three years later Joe Judd and David Brothers registered the Church of Jayne Mansfield of the New Atomic Age in Utah, under the premise that "the present laws of physics are passing away."

Jayne became a rock muse beginning in the 1980s, especially in the punk and New Wave worlds, and continuing well into the 2010s. Numerous songs have referred to her, or have even been written about her:

The Chills' "16 Heart-Throbs" (1988)
Sigue Sigue Sputnik's "Hey Jane Mansfield Superstar!" (1988) ("Cha-cha heels and patent bra")
The Bates' "The Lips of Jayne Mansfield" (1990) ("I don't want to die without knowing the pleasure of kissing the lips of Jayne Mansfield")
L.A. Guns' "The Ballad of Jayne" (1990)
The Moldy Dogs' "Bring Me Jayne's Head" (1991)
Siouxsie and the Banshees' "Kiss Them for Me" (1991) ("No party she'd not attend; No invitation she wouldn't send")
The 5.6.7.8's irrepressible Japanese rockabilly "I Walk Like Jayne Mansfield" (1994)
The Cramps' "Confessions of a Psycho Cat" (1997)
The Masons' "Bombshell" (2000)

Katy Rose's "Overdrive" (2004) ("Diamonds where there once were
stars, I'm sitting in Jayne Mansfield's car")
The Mansfields' "Jayne Mansfield Was a Punk" (2005)
Robbie Williams's "The Actor" (2006)
The Montecristos' "Jayne Mansfield" (2015)
Sharon Needles' "Hollywouldn't" (2015) ("You can sell your soul for a
two-bit role, like Jayne Mansfield you can lose control")
Kid Pariah's "Jayne Mansfield" (2018)

Jayne's death influenced more than pop culture; those red-and-white
reflective strips on the rear of tractors, trailers, and trucks are called
"Mansfield bars." Days after the deaths of Jayne, Sam, and Ronnie, auto
designer Leopold Garcia told the *Albuquerque Journal,* "'Rear safety
bumpers would have saved them.' Last December Garcia recommended to
the National Safety Council that the government should require rear
bumpers at the level of auto bumpers on trucks with rear overhanging beds
or frames. 'My recommendation was praised and pigeonholed,'" Garcia
complained.

In 1971 the *Washington Post* reported, "The National Highway Traffic
Safety Administration proposed a standard that would require that the rear
ends of heavy trucks and trailers be designed to prevent what is called 'underride' when a car strikes from behind. An energy-absorbing device
would hang down from the frame of the truck to break the impact of an
in-crashing car and thus prevent the car's top—its passenger compart-
ment—from being shorn off."

Mansfield bars are meant to warn drivers, not actually stop cars—
though at slow enough speeds, they can save lives. The Insurance Institute for
Highway Safety released a report in 2011 stating that the majority of Mansfield bars would fail in underride crashes, and that structural guidelines were
inadequate (the institute has a "Toughguard" award for companies producing the strongest bars). In 2017 Senators Kirsten Gillibrand and Marco Rubio
proposed a bill that would require guards on the sides and front of all trucks;
it has been blocked by the Truck Trailer Manufacturers Association, which
cites added cost, added weight, and technical challenges.

While Jayne may have bestowed her name on Mansfield bars, it is
Jennifer Tierney, who lost her father to a 1983 underride crash, who has
done the most effective lobbying. Her work eventually required all North

Carolina truck trailers to be equipped with reflective tape. "While there is still much work to be done in improving truck underride protections—like passing the Stop Underrides Act—ensuring that rear underride guards be inspected annually is a step in the right direction," Tierney said in 2019.

❤

In 1980 show business's leading blonde bombshell was Loni Anderson, a breakout star on TV's *WKRP in Cincinnati.* She'd already had a brush with Jayne: in her University of Minnesota play *The Great Git-Away,* a reviewer said that she "brought Jayne Mansfield style to sexy Sarah and was beautifully distracting in her brief swimsuit." "That was the first time I ever wore a blonde wig," laughs Anderson.

For her first starring role in a TV movie, Anderson was asked by Alan Landsburg Productions to bring a bio-pic of Jayne to the small screen. "I related to her so much because we were both teenage moms, both brunettes who found fame as blondes," she says today. "When I researched her, I felt such a kinship with her," she adds. "What made me sad was I kept thinking, today she would have been—forget the Kardashians, she was completely so good at selling herself. Jayne created a monster and then she couldn't get rid of it. Marilyn was always trying to hide and was vulnerable, and Jayne was out there looking for every opportunity. If she had only given up her façade, and let herself go deeper than that. I think she got frightened, the façade was so successful. She needed the right director, she needed someone to say, 'Drop that persona and be the character.'"

Anderson had say regarding casting and insisted on Arnold Schwarzenegger—who up till then had shown no aptitude as an actor—to play Mickey Hargitay. "Everybody kept saying, 'We can't have Arnold in the movie, Arnold's not an actor, nobody will understand a word he says,'" recalls Anderson. "I said, 'No, I think you need Arnold.' Arnold was so cute, because he wanted so desperately to be good. He's smart, he's so interesting, he has a sense of humor in two languages—he's just a smart guy, I enjoyed working with him, and I really liked how hard he worked."

Anderson desperately wanted to shoot at the Pink Palace—"The outdoor scenes, anyway; where else could one find a heart-shaped swimming pool?" But the home was now owned by singer Engelbert Humperdinck, and "we kept getting stonewalled by Engelbert Humperdinck's manager," she recalls. Then—during pre-production—Anderson and Humperdinck both happened to be guests on *The Tonight Show.* "I was talking about the fact that I was doing Jayne Mansfield, and he said, 'You know, I own Jayne Mansfield's house,' and I said, 'We have been dying to get your heart-shaped swimming pool, and so far your people have said no to us.' I turned and looked at the audience and said, 'Wouldn't you love to see us in that heart-shaped swimming pool?' And the audience cheered, so I *shamed* him," Anderson laughs. "The next day they called and said, 'Of course you can use it!'"

She recalls that the location shooting was a bit odd: Humperdinck "wouldn't let anyone in the house but me. We were in the pool and I needed to take a shower and get redone for the next scene. There was a guard at the door. . . . I had a little map to the shower."

If she was nervous about Jayne's family's reaction to the movie, Anderson's worries were put to rest when "Mariska came to visit me on the set of *WKRP* and said, 'I never knew my mom and I just wanted to come over and meet you.' It was so, so sweet. Eventually my daughter and Mariska were in the same sorority at UCLA." Years later, in 1994, when Anderson and Mariska costarred in the TV movie *Gambler V: Playing for Keeps,* "she said, 'I have a surprise for you,' and in the door came Mickey and his wife. We took all kinds of pictures together, and Mickey finally told me how much he loved my portrayal [in *The Jayne Mansfield Story*], and as we all gathered around, he said, 'It's like having the family together.' Took my breath away."

The Jayne Mansfield Story—aired on October 29, 1980, on CBS—is better than most biographical TV movies: it hits the necessary marks, takes several understandable liberties with the facts for dramatic effect, and telescopes events because of time limitations; it invents some characters and combines others (a loyal agent, a best gal-pal). It also makes salient points about Jayne's image, her career missteps, Fox's businesslike heartlessness about her, and her steely ambition. What comes through is Anderson's performance. Not only was she the only real blonde bombshell in 1980, she facially resembled Jayne, and she didn't mind letting herself be seen ragged and makeup-free.

The movie got great ratings, tons of publicity, and mixed reviews. The *Baltimore Evening Sun* called it "an effective drama. Loni Anderson proves that she is a very serious actress. She becomes Jayne Mansfield with a strong display of acting range." What's really amazing is that the hopelessly wooden Arnold Schwarzenegger of *The Jayne Mansfield Story* so quickly went on to become the versatile talent of *Twins, Total Recall,* and the *Terminator* and *Expendables* movies. Anderson herself has maintained an active career, most recently as a hilariously dissipated mother on Amazon Prime's *My Sister Is So Gay.*

One person who was not charmed by *The Jayne Mansfield Story* is Matt Cimber, who says, "They asked me to use my name, and I said, 'If you can get Robert De Niro to play me, I'll say okay.' And they said, 'I guess you don't want us to do it,' and I said, 'I guess I don't.' The day that show was premiering, I'm shooting *Fake-Out* with Telly Savalas. He and I went up to my suite and turned it on. We saw a scene where she comes walking into an agent's office wearing this gigantic hat, dressed like she's going to go watch a polo match, and she goes up to the secretary and says, 'Hi! I'm Jayne Mansfield, and I want to be a movie star.' Telly and I looked at each other, and we said, 'Let's get the fuck outta here.'"

Jayne's family moved on, as is only healthy; each member had different coping mechanisms. Paul Mansfield had remarried in 1957. His new wife "brought to our marriage a son, and we've had three together," he said. Paul Mansfield died in 2013, aged eighty-three.

"After the tragedy, I didn't like the image of being seen as 'Jayne Mansfield's ex-husband,'" says Matt Cimber. "I really didn't like that identity, so I cut her out of my realm of work. Maybe it was unfair, I don't know." But Matt never bad-mouthed Jayne or regretted his years with her. "I did a play with John Steinbeck, *Burning Bright*," he says, "and he adored Jayne; so did Tennessee Williams. She never was unkind to anybody, she was always polite, she was always giving." He says today that "I married a wonderful girl who adopted Tony and has been a wonderful mother to him." Matt Cimber has two children in addition to Tony.

Nelson Sardelli went on to become a popular mainstay in Las Vegas, also acting in such films as *Myra Breckinridge* and *The Professionals.* He married Micki (Fledia Fay) Holland, "the mother of my two daughters, Giovanna Francesca Maria Amelia Fay and Pietra Domenica Isolina Graziella Fay," he says. "Micki taught me integrity and decency. She deserved better than the husband she got." After Micki's death in 2012, Nelson married Lorraine Marie Thompson, "who has filled all the voids in my life."

Mickey remarried, too, shortly after Jayne's death. "Ellen was a friend of Jaynie's and the kids all love her," Mickey said shortly before their wedding. "When we began to think about marriage, I asked the kids first if it was all right with them. Little Zoltan said, 'now we'll have two mommies, one with God and one with us.'" It was a happy marriage, lasting till Mickey's death in 2006 at the age of eighty. Mickey and Ellen were excellent parents to Mickey Jr., Zoltan, and Mariska. Mickey appeared in a handful of films, as well as a 2003 episode of his daughter's TV series *Law & Order: Special Victims Unit.*

All of Jayne's children have done well for themselves, though some have struggled with her legacy and her early death. Mickey would be delighted that his namesake owns Mickey Hargitay Plants in Hollywood, a thriving "full service plant nursery and garden shop" that caters to locals and stars. "It was my chore when I was a kid growing up to water the plants," said Mickey Jr. "I didn't know that was what I was going to end up doing. I probably hated it at the time, but you end up loving what you sometimes don't as a child. I'd probably make more money if I built a four-story apartment building and sat around collecting rent. But that's just not me."

Zoltan Hargitay, who has worked as a carpenter on several films, and Tony Cimber, who has produced and directed several TV documentaries, stay out of the spotlight. They decline to talk about their mother.

Mariska Hargitay attended the UCLA School of Theater Film and Television, and the Groundlings Theatre and School in Los Angeles. She began acting professionally in the early '80s. Mariska struggled through years of small roles in big projects and big roles in small projects (*Falcon Crest, Baywatch, Tequila and Bonetti, Seinfeld, Can't Hurry Love*) before hitting the jackpot playing Detective Olivia Benson on *Law & Order: Special Victims Unit.* Mariska's character is the longest running on that series; she debuted in 1999 and has since been promoted to lieutenant and commanding officer. Affected by some of the story lines on her show, Mariska started the Joyful Heart Foundation, which helps victims of sexual assault, domestic violence, and child abuse.

She spoke to *People* magazine in 2018 about her mother: "The way I've lived with loss is to lean into it. . . . She was just so ahead of her time. She was an inspiration, she had this appetite for life, and I think I share that with her. . . . Someone once said about [remembering] my mother: 'All you have to do is look in the mirror.' She's with me still."

Jayne Marie Mansfield struggled through the 1970s with financial, career, and romantic challenges. "When mother died, I had virtually no money," she said in 1975. "I became a secretary first, but I wasn't very good at that. I did much better in the hairdressing field. I already had lots of experience, since I used to do mother's hair all the time. Being a hairdresser gave me the financial security I needed, while I tried to put the pieces of my life back together." She was briefly married in the late 1970s: "We rushed it, both too young really. He went his way, I went mine, no hard feelings." In 1976 she posed for *Playboy* and in 1978 acted in the Katharine Hepburn movie *Olly, Olly, Oxen Free*.

"To this day I hear from women, I think almost more than I hear from men, how much they admired Jayne Mansfield," Jayne Marie said decades after her mother's death. "They remember her as a very smart, loving, intelligent woman who cared a lot about her family, about people. She was taken very young, but she gave a lot while she was here. You probably can't remember any of the movies that she made, but you know darn well that she existed."

❤

Jayne Mansfield's Death Car has had it own fate and fame. The vehicles in which President Kennedy, Bonnie and Clyde, Archduke Franz Ferdinand, Hank Williams, General Patton, and Tom Mix met their deaths are all on display, in museums large or small.

In 1975 Jayne's crushed, still-bloodied Buick turned up on the midway at the Indiana State Fair, a mannequin's head lying in the front seat providing an extra jolt of bad taste (one paper even noted the "Max Factor blood dripping out of the corner of the mouth"). Billboards outside the display tent ballyhooed, "Was she a sorceress? Part saint, part sinner, she WAS ALL WOMAN!"

This sort of thing did not sit well with Scott Michaels, who is genially obsessed with both death and celebrities ("When I was young, I would thumb directly to the end of any biography, to find out how and where they died. If there were photos—even better"). He moved to Los Angeles and became the darkly funny guide of Dearly Departed Tours (an informative drive around Hollywood's death and scandal sites), also opening the Artifact Museum, of which Jayne's car is the star attraction. Other displays include Mae West's dental plate, Rock Hudson's Rolodex, Karen Carpenter's bathroom sink, and Lana Turner's cigarette lighter and perfume bottle. Many of his exhibits have been rescued from dumpsters and demolition sites. Michaels also runs the hugely informative Find a Death website.

For all his dark humor, Michaels has a genuine love and respect for celebrities and for Hollywood history. "I've always loved Jayne Mansfield," he says. He stresses that "something very important to me is respecting the dead. . . . You will not see any gory or gruesome photographs in my museum. We take what we do very seriously."

Michaels explains that Jayne's Death Car "has had several owners. Mostly collectors who wanted to make sure it wasn't destroyed. But after you save something like that, what can you do with it? It's not something that you can throw open your backyard to the public and show. It attracts a very specific type of person."

Michaels met with Mickey Jr. to give him a heads-up that the car was going to be put on display. "I explained who I was and he was understandably taken aback. He questioned the morbid nature of the display. I explained that we loved his mother, and this is a part of Hollywood history. Our Dealey Plaza, if you will. He was very kind and made clear I do not have his approval, but appreciated the fact that I introduced myself and let him know ahead of time. We left with a smile and a handshake. That was one of the worst conversations I had to work myself up to have."

In 2012 Billy Bob Thornton and Tom Epperson's film *Jayne Mansfield's Car* opened, featuring an impressive cast (Thornton, Robert Duvall, John Hurt, Kevin Bacon). It was a Southern Gothic drama set in 1969 about a wildly unhappy Alabama family burying their runaway matriarch. Her new British family shows up for the awkward funeral. Car-wreck-obsessed patriarch Duvall bonds with rival Hurt at a traveling exhibit of the titular car. There's a particularly sweet moment when a boy at the exhibit, after everyone leaves, walks up to a poster of Jayne and gives her a kiss on the cheek.

More lastingly famous than her car was Jayne's house: her image lived on in the Pink Palace. It was sold to an unidentified client in 1968 for $180,000 in a court-ordered auction. A 1973 episode of *Barnaby Jones* ("Sing a Song of Murder") was filmed there, featuring a rock star found dead in the heart-shaped pool. In 1976 Ringo Starr—the only Beatle not to have bad-mouthed Jayne—rented the Pink Palace, now toned down to white.

The following year singer Engelbert Humperdinck—finally having reached stardom in the US—was in the market for a large home for himself, his wife, and their growing family. In his memoirs, Humperdinck recalled Realtor Bea Heath showing him some Polaroids of a house for sale:

"I said, 'That's some home. It's really nice. Did you say who it belonged to?' 'It's called the Pink Palace,' she replied, 'and at one time, it belonged to Jayne Mansfield.'"

Shocked and delighted at the coincidence of finally "visiting" Jayne ten years after their only meeting, Humperdinck "bought it and fixed it up at an expense that totaled $1.9 million—and we went on to live in the Pink Palace for 27 years." In the 1970s, he recalled,

> the Pink Palace was beautiful, but very dilapidated and a little on the dark side. The Pink Palace was our first, glamorous American home and we loved bringing it back to its former glory. . . . On the wall, going down the stairs, there were framed pin-up pictures of Jayne in all her glory, and I also inherited a naked bust of her, but unfortunately the statuette was so badly damaged, she was missing her left nipple! When the builders were taking down a wall in the house, they came across a lot of memorabilia and personal stuff that Jayne had stuck to the walls, which made it a fantastic piece of film history. The ceiling in Jayne's office was covered in red leather pads. Once, when there was an earthquake, one of the pads came off, and underneath it, we discovered a hand-painted ceiling from years before.

The house also came with a tenant, Humperdinck discovered. "We used to come downstairs in the morning and find dried, green leaves scattered everywhere. As it turned out, . . . we had a guest—a tramp, who was living in the attic. Apparently, he used to come down at night to help himself to the contents of our refrigerator and, as an animal lover, he always left a sprinkling of dry catnip leaves behind him for our cat, Tommy Dorsey. . . . At first we thought the herb on the floor was some kind of drug and we were somewhat rattled. . . . It wasn't until a builder came to repair the roof that our tramp was discovered and scared off into finding himself another attic in which to live."

The Humperdincks moved out when their son Jason was old enough to drive, as "in our 27-year tenure on the winding Sunset Boulevard, there were 49 fatal car accidents. The roads around the mansion were full of curved, treacherous bends, and we were appalled at the number of accidents that seemed to happen almost every day." In 1981 Monaco-based businessman Ghazi Aita bought the Pink Palace.

Los Angeles has a shameful history when it comes to architectural preservation. The Brown Derby, the Ambassador Hotel, the Garden of Allah, Pickfair—all have fallen to dust. Owlwood, the estate next to Jayne's, was owned by Tony Curtis, and then Sonny and Cher, and then was bought by Ameriquest Capital Corporation founder Roland Arnall. He also bought the Pink Palace, which he demolished in November 2002. Jayne's children were not even given enough notice to collect mementos.

Jayne would not have resigned herself philosophically to her death—no matter how tawdry and overwhelming her life became, she loved every minute of it, and lived every minute to the utmost. The only thing about her death she'd have welcomed was that it happened to her instead of her children—she never would have survived the death of Mickey Jr., Zoltan, and Mariska, and would gladly have given up her life for them. No matter how wildly off-kilter her mothering skills were, she loved her children.

Jayne loved her life, and she loved love. Mickey is usually thought of as "the love her of life," but she had many of those. Paul, Robbie, Mickey, Enrico, Nelson, Matt, and Sam were all genuinely the loves of her life when she was with them. She was never "between men."

Her unexpected, gruesome death was a shocking and life-altering sorrow to her family and friends, but it really was a "Jayne Mansfield ending." "The death of a beautiful woman is, unquestionably, the most poetical topic in the world," said Edgar Allan Poe, and we idolize Jayne, Marilyn, Carole Lombard, Jean Harlow, and such breathtaking men as Rudolph Valentino, James Dean, and River Phoenix partly because they were snatched away so young while they were still red-hot. Death can be an excellent career move.

Reporter Hobe Mission recalled interviewing Jayne during her early Broadway days. "Repeatedly during the meal, Miss Mansfield mentioned her determination to be a movie star. . . . Miss Mansfield never once mentioned the word actress or mentioned her wish to act. To her, quite obviously, stardom was everything, and the idea of acting had never been a serious consideration. . . . Despite what must have been frustrations and difficulties of a spotty career, Jayne Mansfield invariably seemed a nice person. Perhaps she wouldn't have thought so, but that's not a bad alternative to being a star."

Acknowledgments

I'd particularly like to thank Loni Anderson, the late Orson Bean, Matt Cimber, Bentley Morris, Don Poynter, and Nelson Sardelli for granting me what turned out to be informative, funny, and candid interviews.

For DVDs and VHS tapes, books, photographs, and documentary information, many thanks to Michael Barnes, Cynthia Brideson, Jon Darby, Karen Gershenhorn, Larry Harnisch, Richard Lertzman, Donna Lethal, Scott Michaels, Troy Musgrave, Mel Neuhaus, Stephen "Tad" O'Brien, James Robert Parish, Steven Rosen, Martha Saxton, Bettina Uhlich, Laura Wagner, Nancy Winter, and James Zeruk Jr.

As always, I am indebted to my ruthless, obsessive editors, Richard Kukan and Robin DuBlanc, who caught an embarrassing amount of errors and clunky writing.

Notes

Chapter 1

"I'm so frightened" (*Entertainment Weekly*, Nov. 5, 2014).

Chapter 2

"I shielded her from every unpleasantness" (*This Is Your Life*, Dec. 18, 1960).
"The doctor said, 'Jump on this foot, now jump on that foot'" (Matt Cimber to author, Mar. 22, 2019).
"I wasn't shy long" (*Los Angeles Times*, Nov. 11, 1956).
"It's a good thing I'm not a writer" (*This Is Your Life*, Dec. 18, 1960).
"a real snob school" (Saxton, *Jayne Mansfield*, 14).
"upper-class and upper-middle-class" (ibid., 15).
"She would come over to our house" (ibid., 17).
"Jaynie was crazy about him" (ibid., 25).
"a real vision of loveliness" (*Arena Blondes: Jayne Mansfield*, Illuminations Films, aired BBC 2, Dec. 24, 1999).
"My parents were very strict" (Ray Parker, syndicated column, Jan. 2, 1957).
"I feel very strongly about that college bit" (ibid.).
"someday she'd be going to Hollywood" (*Blonde Ambition: Jayne Mansfield*, Prometheus Entertainment, *A&E Biography*, aired Feb. 9, 2004).
"We took Jayne Marie to chemistry class" (*Boston Globe*, Oct. 6, 1955).
"she was going to get married" (Saxton, *Jayne Mansfield*, 33).
"She kind of came into her own" (ibid., 30).
"People used to bring dogs to be destroyed" (Ray Parker, syndicated column, Jan. 2, 1957).
"because I insisted on studying dramatics" (ibid.).
"I think she was a good mother" (*Blonde Ambition*, 2004).
"Paul could have been a marvelous entertainer" (John T. McCullough, syndicated column, Jan. 15, 1956).
"tears the piano apart" (*Austin-American*, Oct. 2, 1951).

"He promised to take me to Hollywood" (Ray Parker, syndicated column, Jan. 2, 1957).

"I took ballet and seven singing lessons a week" (ibid.).

"Another call from another major's wife" (ibid.).

"I kept nine hamsters" (ibid.).

"That is not true" (ibid.).

"We weren't living very high on the hog" (*Boston Globe,* Oct. 6, 1955).

"put his foot down" (Ray Parker, syndicated column, Jan. 2, 1957).

"a student of psychology" (*Boston Globe,* Aug. 3, 1958).

"I used to think, 'this is terrible!'" (*Boston Globe,* Oct. 6, 1955).

"She was quiet in those days" (*Edmonton Journal,* Oct. 27, 1966).

"I said, okay" (*Arena Blondes*).

"We had a combined income of about $150 a month" (Ray Parker, syndicated column, Jan. 2, 1957).

"Within a couple of weeks" (*Blonde Ambition,* 2004).

"She talked about it constantly" (*Louisville Courier-Journal,* July 25, 1976).

"I knew it wasn't going to work" (Ray Parker, syndicated column, Jan. 2, 1957).

"I had begun to not like what I saw" (*Arena Blondes*).

Chapter 3

"I have a pink mink stole" (*Los Angeles Times,* Nov. 11, 1956).

"A rather handsome young man met Jayne on the street" (Guild, *Jayne Mansfield's Wild, Wild World,* 24).

A director who promised me a bit part" (ibid., 37).

"I haven't met the wolf I couldn't handle" (Ray Parker, syndicated column, Jan. 2, 1957).

"I was asked if I were a member of the Screen Actors' Guild" (Guild, *Jayne Mansfield's Wild, Wild World,* 35).

"I called Paramount Studios" (*Tabloid* [Toronto TV show], Aug. 1957).

"I don't know why I picked Paramount" (Ray Parker, syndicated column, Jan. 2, 1957).

"Don't hold me responsible" (*Boston Globe,* Oct. 8, 1965).

"I wanted, needed and had to succeed" (Guild, *Jayne Mansfield's Wild, Wild World,* 61).

"I was learning painfully" (ibid., 39).

"I had ten lines" (*Bergen Evening Record,* July 11, 1956).

"In the cast of characters" (Guild, *Jayne Mansfield's Wild, Wild World,* 61).

"sounded easy but it wasn't" (ibid., 40).

"It was made in a very poor section of Los Angeles" (Earl Wilson, syndicated column, Sept. 1, 1956).

Notes

"It wasn't *Gone with the Wind*" (Guild, *Jayne Mansfield's Wild, Wild World*, 42).
"On the last day of shooting" (ibid., 43).
"took Miss Mansfield to the bookkeeper" (Mann, *Jayne Mansfield*, 27).
"I saw myself on the screen" (Guild, *Jayne Mansfield's Wild, Wild World*, 42).
"In her own right" (Koper, *Affectionately*, 155).
"As a jaded good-time girl" (ibid.).
"If you'll gamble, I'll gamble" (Guild, *Jayne Mansfield's Wild, Wild World*, 45).
"She never refused the press" (Saxton, *Jayne Mansfield*, 46).
"promised me the star treatment" (*Des Moines Tribune*, Dec. 31, 1956).
"Some inferred" (Gladstone, *The Man Who Seduced Hollywood*, 268).
"The quality of making everyone stop in their tracks" (Sheilah Graham, syndicated column, Oct. 7, 1956).
"wasn't even my own suit" (unidentified newspaper article, Dec. 9, 1956).
"On the planes" (*Arizona Republic,* Oct. 30, 1955).
"almost unnoticed at first" (*Orlando Sentinel,* undated article).
"I wouldn't like to see my daughter do cheesecake pictures" (Earl Wilson, syndicated column, Sept. 1, 1956).
"the 18-year-old actor" (Warner Bros. press release, Feb. 20, 1955).
"Out at the Austin Civic Theater" (*Austin-American,* Feb. 24, 1955).
"I want to be known as an actress" (James Bacon, syndicated column, Apr. 2, 1955).
"gorgeous Jayne Mansfield" (*Boston Globe,* undated article).
"Miss Mansfield is splendid" (*New York Daily News,* undated article).
"what her sisters, Monroe and Russell, have she also has abundantly" (*Capital Times* Oct. 21, 1955).
"You'll see, briefly, Jayne Mansfield" (*Indianapolis News,* Nov. 17, 1955).
"I thought you were just another blonde" (*Los Angeles Times,* Dec. 6, 1955).
"just the usual murders, mayhems and intrigues" (Koper, *Affectionately*, 145).
"a jazzed-up version of *Dragnet*" (ibid., 143).
"*Dragnet* with a trumpet" (*Photoplay,* July 1959).
"I think the only thing I ever turned down was Miss Roquefort Cheese" (Saxton, *Jayne Mansfield*, 48).
"I want to be known for my acting, not my bust" (*Long Beach Independent,* Apr. 14, 1955).
"My dog's name is Byron" (Vernon Scott, syndicated column, Mar. 27, 1955).
"A diet is no good if it makes you feel so hungry" (Lydia Lane, syndicated column, May 31, 1955).
"God always sent me help" (Mann, *Jayne Mansfield*, 40).
"He tried to back her in it" (*Blonde Ambition: Jayne Mansfield,* Prometheus Entertainment, *A&E Biography,* aired Feb. 9, 2004).
"was not a dumb blonde" (ibid.).

"the best thing I've ever done" (*Bergen Evening Record,* July 11, 1956).

"It's a quietly effective portrayal" (*Box Office,* May 11, 1957).

"There's a sufficient talent" (*Motion Picture Herald,* June 8, 1957).

"competent" (Koper, *Affectionately,* 153).

Chapter 4

"My problem was whether to get an actress to play a broad" (*Ottawa Citizen,* Apr. 3, 1965).

"My movie career didn't seem to be hitting out too well" (*Austin-American,* Dec. 20, 1955).

"Jayne took her big chance" (*Ottawa Citizen,* Apr. 3, 1965).

"she'd get up early in the morning" (Saxton, *Jayne Mansfield,* 58).

"was always late and had no discipline" (ibid., 53).

"I got up and said she could leave" (ibid.).

"a cast which hardly could be improved upon" (*Philadelphia Inquirer,* Sept. 13, 1955).

"a fast and racy comedy" (*Boston Globe,* Sept. 25, 1955).

"talented actress" (Walter Winchell, syndicated column, Oct. 21, 1955).

"Jayne Mansfield Outdoes Marilyn in Latest Show" (International News Service [INS] release, Oct. 14, 1955).

"a masterpiece of architecture" (*New York Daily News,* Oct. 23, 1955).

"mighty slim" (Bob Thomas, Associated Press [AP] release, Nov. 11, 1955).

"the buxom Jayne Mansfield" (*Life,* Sept. 11, 1955).

"Since displaying her limited but appealing talents" (*Austin-American,* Oct. 4, 1955).

"There is absolutely no chance" (*Life,* Apr. 23, 1956).

"I loved Jayne" (Orson Bean to author, Jan. 17, 2019).

"a sweet, simple girl" (ibid.).

"is a little naïve" (*Paterson News,* Oct. 5, 1955).

"I haven't had a chance" (Louella Parsons, syndicated column, Nov. 21, 1955).

"With brown hair" (*New York Herald Tribune,* Nov. 26, 1955).

"It's my responsibility" (Dorothy Kilgallen, syndicated column, Dec. 8, 1955).

"It's nothing, really nothing" (*New York Herald Tribune,* Nov. 26, 1955).

"Miss Mansfield should not let Manhattan scribblers' reporters" (Kaspar Monahan, syndicated column, Dec. 15, 1955).

"It's great, it's just great" (*Los Angeles Times,* Dec. 6, 1955).

"but I'd like good, solid, meaty roles" (Joan Hanauer, INS release, Dec. 11, 1955).

"Mel Pape—is he still the director?" (*Austin-American,* Dec. 20, 1955).

"Buddy Adler has flown to New York" (Louella Parsons, syndicated column, Oct. 24, 1955).

Notes

"Dore Schary of MGM" (*Austin-American,* Oct. 31, 1955).

"Jayne to be tested for a Harlow bio-pic" (*New York Daily News,* Nov. 1, 1955).

"Jayne had a meeting at MGM's New York offices" (Walter Winchell, syndicated column, Nov. 2, 1955).

"Four studios are after her for movies" (*San Mateo Times,* Nov. 8, 1955).

"Whether Marilyn will see her attorneys about it all" (Erskine Johnson, Newspaper Enterprise Association (NEA) release, Aug. 21, 1955).

"She is as beautiful as Marilyn Monroe" (Walter Winchell, syndicated column, Oct. 18, 1955).

"the rich man's Marilyn Monroe" (KBWD radio, Dec. 15, 1955).

"Jayne Mansfield Outdoes Marilyn in Latest Show" (INS release, Oct. 14, 1955).

"No. It's a composite of all the glamour girls" (Earl Wilson, syndicated column, Sept. 25, 1955).

"Marilyn and I are completely different" (Aline Mosby, UP).

"I've always thought" (Mel Heimer, syndicated column, Mar. 2, 1956).

"how to cut down the ranks of bachelors" (*Indianapolis Star,* Jan. 4, 1956).

"the toast of Broadway" (Louella Parsons, syndicated column, Jan. 1, 1956).

"The whole town's talking about her" (*Hartford Courant,* Nov. 12, 1955).

"the most amazing phenomenon on Broadway" (*Los Angeles Times,* Nov. 10, 1955).

"the Broadway Gal of the Year" (Earl Wilson, syndicated column, Dec. 31, 1955).

"receives fan letters with cash enclosed" (*New York Daily News,* Jan. 17, 1956).

"'Jayne Mansfield,' someone shouted" (Ed Reardon, syndicated column, Oct. 1955).

"I always rush home" (Dick Kleiner, syndicated column, Mar. 26, 1956).

"We get up around eight" (Dick Kleiner, syndicated column, Mar. 26, 1956).

"only in what might be called the larval stage" (*Life,* Apr. 23, 1956).

"friendly and frank" (ibid.).

"Jayne Mansfield didn't pose for a picture all day" (Earl Wilson, syndicated column, Mar. 23, 1956).

"fed up with Jayne Mansfield" (*Davenport Daily Times,* Mar. 23, 1956).

"making snide, lofty remarks" (Mel Heimer, syndicated column, Apr.12, 1956).

"The newest cocktail is the Jayne Mansfield" (*New York Daily News,* Apr. 13, 1956).

"the retiring little woodland flower" (*New York Daily News,* Apr. 22, 1956).

"steak, mink" (Walter Winchell, syndicated column, Jan. 11, 1956).

"a good dramatic actress" (*New York Daily News,* Feb. 17, 1956).

"My personality is entirely different from the pictures" (Claire Cox, United Press (UP) release, May 15, 1956).

"It's *divoon*" (*New York Daily News,* Mar. 2, 1956).

"Jayne Mansfield does get around" (*Philadelphia Inquirer,* Mar. 3, 1956).

"sparse crowd" (*Passaic Herald News,* May 4, 1956).

"one of her rare public appearances" (*New York Daily News,* May 17, 1956).

"shiny-faced, wind-blown and rather unappealing" (Alice F. Keegan, syndicated column, July 11, 1956).

"If Jayne Mansfield doesn't watch her step" (*New York Daily News,* June 15, 1956).

"They're all very high on Jayne" (Louella Parsons, syndicated column, Feb. 15, 1956).

"Unless people are prepared for what's coming" (*Life,* Apr. 23, 1956).

"I'm a full-fledged star now" (Louella Parsons, syndicated column, July 7, 1956).

"My whole career has been revamped" (Charles Mercer, AP release, July 8, 1956).

"A girl needs mink" (Claire Cox, UP release, May 15, 1956).

Chapter 5

"a perfect gentleman" (Earl Wilson, syndicated column, Mar. 22, 1956).

"serious" (Louella Parsons, syndicated column, Mar. 3, 1955).

"rare combination of brawn, brains and achievement" (*Sydney Morning Herald,* Mar. 11, 1956).

"freaked out" (Mel Neuhaus to author, Feb. 14, 2019).

"He is a strong, powerful man" (*Sydney Morning Herald,* Mar. 11, 1956).

"I took one look at him and swooned" (John T. McCullough, syndicated column, Jan. 15, 1956).

"My beau, Robbie Robertson" (*Boston Globe,* Oct. 6, 1955).

"I rather don't think I will" (Sheilah Graham, syndicated column, May 4, 1956).

"I liked him" (Saxton, *Jayne Mansfield,* 63).

"very sweet, very courtly and refreshing" (*New York Daily News,* May 1, 1956).

"This guy talked me into entering a weight-lifting contest" (*Oakland Tribune,* Jan. 3, 1961).

"I was singing a song" (*Arena Blondes: Jayne Mansfield,* Illuminations Films, aired BBC 2, Dec. 24, 1999).

"Jayne Mansfield admits she's found her dream man" (Dorothy Kilgallen, syndicated column, May 22, 1956).

"phones Jayne three times a day" (Earl Wilson, syndicated column, May 22, 1956).

"Rather than embrace the relationship we had" (*Blonde Ambition: Jayne Mansfield,* Prometheus Entertainment, *A&E Biography,* aired Feb. 9, 2004).

"Mae West is furious" (Dorothy Kilgallen, syndicated column, June 5, 1956).

"We don't have so much fun dancing" (Harrison Carroll, syndicated column, Oct. 4, 1956).

"I had heard the rumors" (*Los Angeles Times,* Sept. 3, 1958).

"I was knocked out for a minute" (*New York Daily News,* June 8, 1956).

"emotionally involved with Miss West" (ibid.).

"No, but not in public before" (ibid.).

"I am an actor" (Harley Murray, INS release, June 7, 1956).

"She's a dangerous publicity seeker" (Leonard, *Mae West*, 307).

"There is no truth that I'm having a feud" (*Bergen Evening Record,* July 11, 1956).

"Mae's muscle-man show needed business" (unidentified newspaper article, 1964).

"We haven't seen each other for five days" (*New York Daily News,* June 9, 1956).

"The vomans vait for you" (Earl Wilson, syndicated column, June 15, 1956).

"colorful real estate millionaire Henry Epstein" (Dorothy Kilgallen, syndicated column, Oct. 22, 1955).

"I never met her but once in my life" (Louella Parsons, INS release, Aug. 25, 1955).

"All I have now is a Great Dane, a Chihuahua, three cats" (ibid.).

"an insult to animal lovers" (Earl Wilson, syndicated column, Sept. 15, 1955).

"so she hopes the ASPCA'll lay off" (Earl Wilson, syndicated column, Oct. 24, 1955).

"He's so attached to me" (Earl Wilson, syndicated column, Nov. 5, 1955).

"contrary to the general belief" (*Tabloid* [Toronto TV show], Aug. 1957).

"She cautioned me about Chihuahuas" (Bill Soberanes, unidentified newspaper article, 1983).

"did not have fits of temperament" (ibid.).

"Blimey, what a dumbell!" (*Petaluma Argus-Courier,* May 9, 1956).

"This is the first time I'll be singing in public" (*Philadelphia Inquirer,* July 11, 1956).

"I've had to turn down lots of shows" (*Bergen Evening Record,* July 11, 1956).

"among the best demonstrations" (*Baltimore Sun,* July 17, 1956).

"a diverting 90 minutes" (*Chicago Tribune,* July 16, 1956).

"attacked their targets" (Jack O'Brian, INS release, July 16, 1956).

"shone in her portrayal of the traditional dumb blonde" (*New York Times,* July 16, 1956).

"Biggest scene-stealer and laugh-getter" (*Syracuse Post-Standard,* July 18, 1956).

"as a visitor from outer space" (Dick Kleiner, NEA release, Aug. 1, 1956).

"its writing was cheap" (Jack O'Brian, INS release, Aug. 14, 1956).

"It was richly rewarding" (*Boston Globe,* July 27, 1956).

"disillusioning many" (*New York Daily News,* July 19, 1956).

"Television is fabulous!" (*Philadelphia Inquirer,* Apr. 26, 1956).

Chapter 6

"I feel you have boosted my career" (*Philadelphia Inquirer,* Sept. 5, 1956).

"To get ahead these days" (*Hartford Courant,* Sept. 8, 1956).

"It's exactly what I want to do" (Louella Parsons, syndicated column, May 4, 1956).

"the storm was over" (Mel Heimer, syndicated column, Sept. 26, 1956).

"Until a few years ago" (Bob Thomas, syndicated column, Oct. 8, 1956).

"Everything was hunky-dory" (*Arena Blondes: Jayne Mansfield,* Illuminations Films, aired BBC 2, Dec. 24, 1999).

"I haven't got a dime in the bank" (Olga Curtis, INS release, June 17, 1956).

"It's wonderful to come back as an established actress" (*Los Angeles Times,* Sept. 17, 1956).

"This has been the happiest, most exciting week of my life" (Jack Gaver, UP drama editor, Sept. 17, 1956).

"I won't even have a breathing spell" (ibid.).

"I like rock 'n' roll" (Ray Parker, syndicated column, Jan. 2, 1957).

"all the reviewers—Truffaut, and Godard, and all these people" (Johnston and Willemen, *Frank Tashlin,* 159).

"could look out of proportion" (Louella Parsons, syndicated column, Sept. 18, 1956).

"You should see the rushes of a scene" (*Hollywood Today,* Oct. 6, 1956).

"I thought maybe my costumes might be designed" (*Los Angeles Times,* Sept. 30, 1956).

"This girl can handle a five-page scene of dialogue" (Harrison Carroll, syndicated column, Nov. 1, 1956).

"She always arrived on the set on time" (Mann, *Jayne Mansfield,* 52).

"my acting gave him goose pimples" (*Hollywood Today,* Oct. 6, 1956).

"I could try my whole life" (John Waters, https://www.youtube.com/watch?v=-n3vyvEPgOw, from the British DVD of *The Girl Can't Help It*).

"I don't think you can work with Jerry Lewis and Jayne Mansfield" (ibid.).

"Imagine a statue with breasts like Mansfield's" (Johnston and Willemen, *Frank Tashlin,* 57).

"Gene Vincent was *scary*" (John Waters, https://www.youtube.com/watch?v=-n3vyvEPgOw, from the British DVD of *The Girl Can't Help It*).

"After all, the censors can't condemn a girl" (*Hollywood Today,* Oct. 6, 1956).

"is just liable to be a big star" (Dorothy Kilgallen, syndicated column, Dec. 13, 1956).

"I burn my critical boats" (*News Chronicle,* Aug. 19, 1957).

"Grade A quality" (*Los Angeles Times,* Feb. 9, 1957).

"Who wants her to act?" (*Birmingham Daily Post,* Mar. 11, 1957).

"I was rockin' and rollin' with Princess Margaret" (Robert Musel, United Press International (UPI) release, Feb. 15, 1957).

"Any doubts about the permanency of shimmering Jayne Mansfield" (Harold

Heffernan, North American Newspaper Alliance [NANA] release, Dec. 27, 1956).

"Her endowments" (*Capital Times,* Dec. 29, 1956).

"walks like Marilyn Monroe" (*London Evening News,* Feb. 2, 1957).

"the basketball king" (Guild, *Jayne Mansfield's Wild, Wild World,* 22).

"If I want to look happy" (ibid., 26).

"she has so many offers and requests for her time" (unidentified newspaper article, Nov. 15, 1956).

"I could afford to send her to a private school" (Ray Parker, syndicated column, Jan. 2, 1957).

"She was a delight to work with" (unidentified syndicated article, Nov. 24, 1963).

"I was offered $75,000 a picture" (Sheilah Graham, syndicated column, Oct. 7, 1956).

"to feel satisfied with myself" (ibid.).

"Princess Grace will have a boy" (John Crosby, syndicated column, Jan. 2, 1957).

"You'll be amazed" (*Tampa Bay Times,* Oct. 31, 1957).

"billed as 'good for the grouchy boss'" (*Petaluma Argus Courier,* Nov. 1, 1957).

"a manufacturer offered me a $20,000 advance" (Harrison Carroll, syndicated column, June 20, 1957).

"She got involved with the rotgut of Hollywood" (Saxton, *Jayne Mansfield,* 48).

"I think she eventually got more than that" (Don Poynter to author, Nov. 4, 2019).

"Fox was opposed to this" (ibid.).

"Mickey Hargitay was out spraying the lawn" (ibid.).

"She was very straightforward" (ibid.).

"are not compatible to our marriage" (unidentified newspaper article, Feb. 8, 1955).

"When I married Paul" (*New York Daily News,* Nov. 24, 1956).

"No man wants to be second choice" (*New York Daily News,* Mar. 16, 1956).

"I'm a very stainless character" (AP release, Mar. 22, 1956).

"pain, anguish and distress" (AP release, Jan. 4, 1957).

"I hope he eventually finds the type of wife he wants" (Ray Parker, syndicated column, Jan. 2, 1957).

"I want a husband and six children" (Aline Mosby, undated UP release).

"I'm just an average guy" (ibid.).

Chapter 7

"When I left Hollywood" (*Los Angeles Times,* Nov. 11, 1956).

"My hair is a different color" (ibid.).

"I don't wear a girdle" (ibid.).

"I never let my eating get out of hand" (ibid.).

"I like you people" (*Los Angeles Times,* Dec. 11, 1956).

"This could ruin my whole evening" (unidentified newspaper article, Jan. 8, 1957).

"most promising newcomers" (Bob Thomas, AP release, Dec. 24, 1956).

"Joan Crawford has always acted like a star should act" (*Chicago Tribune,* Dec. 8, 1956).

"The movie people pose too much" (Aline Mosby, syndicated column, Jan. 25, 1957).

"I didn't encounter anybody" (*Minneapolis Star Tribune,* Jan. 30, 1957).

"in a sepulchral whisper" (John Crosby, syndicated column, Feb. 3, 1957).

"the Jayne Mansfield thing" (*New York Times,* Feb. 5, 1957).

"beautiful, luscious cashmere cardigans" (unidentified Indiana, PA, newspaper, Feb. 21, 1957).

"Let it be stated for the record" (Ray Parker, syndicated column, Jan. 2, 1957).

"After work I go home" (*Chicago Tribune,* Nov. 25, 1956).

"Jayne Mansfield Covered with Bumps" (AP release, Feb. 28, 1957).

"Oh, Joan, you English are so prudish!" (Collins, *Past Imperfect*).

"It was the kiss of death" (Sheilah Graham, syndicated column, Jan. 25, 1957).

"rock-n-roll star Jayne Mansfield" (*Anniston Star,* June 2, 1957).

"Miss Mansfield can do little" (*Pittsburgh Press,* May 31, 1957).

"Although Miss Mansfield contributes a capable acting job" (*Fairbanks Daily News-Miner,* June 15, 1957).

"as Mansfield performances go" (*Pittsburgh Post-Gazette,* May 31, 1957).

"All things considered" (*Baltimore Evening Sun,* June 1, 1957).

"All the persons involved strike me as shallow" (*Pittsburgh Post-Gazette,* May 31, 1957).

"was one of my favorite pictures" (Louella Parsons, syndicated column, July 6, 1958).

"Jack Warner was impressed" (Sheilah Graham, syndicated column, Mar. 5, 1957).

"maintains a Jayne Mansfield-ish publicity pace" (Hy Gardner, syndicated column, Mar. 25, 1957).

"The movie business at mid-century" (Bob Thomas, AP release, Mar. 10, 1957).

"For all their publicity-madness" (Erskine Johnson, syndicated column, May 2, 1957).

"The real truth is that Jayne" (*People,* May 28, 1961).

"Isn't that what this picture is all about?" (*Los Angeles Times,* Apr. 12, 1957).

"a little page" (ibid.).

"Luckily she didn't bring the Great Dane" (*Los Angeles Times,* Apr. 17, 1957).

"cut so dangerously low" (*Philadelphia Inquirer,* Apr. 14, 1957).

"She undulated over to the bar" (*Daily Herald,* Apr. 15, 1957).
"the photographers who wanted solo pictures of Sophia" (Louella Parsons, syndicated column, Apr. 16, 1957).
"Undaunted, Jayne came back to the bar" (*Daily Herald,* Apr. 15, 1957).
"I have been one of Jayne's best boosters" (Louella Parsons, syndicated column, Apr. 16, 1957).
"Jayne has two obvious gimmicks" (*Los Angeles Times,* Apr. 18, 1957).
"She doesn't lend herself to spectacular publicity" (*Wall Street Journal,* Apr. 28, 1957).
"Pish-tush!" (Bob Thomas, AP release, Apr. 22, 1957).
"wins by a neckline" (*Philadelphia Inquirer,* Apr. 14, 1957).
"I chose to wear a gown that was low cut in front" (Guild, *Jayne Mansfield's Wild, Wild World,* 80).
"If you're a Bernhardt or a Shakespeare" (unidentified newspaper article, 1957).
"no more semi-nudes" (Earl Wilson, syndicated column, May 4, 1957).
"When I saw the photographs" (Louella Parsons, syndicated column, Apr. 25, 1957).
"I am normally a very quiet, home-loving girl" (Louella Parsons, syndicated column, May 7, 1957).
"But when I came to Hollywood" (ibid.).
"Tell me, what's wrong with me?" (ibid.).
"dropped her mink coat" (AP release, Apr. 29, 1957).

Chapter 8

"My day starts at 5 a.m." (Ray Parker, syndicated column, Jan. 2, 1957).
"I don't always agree with her studio" (Barbara Rabin, World News Service (WNS) release, Nov. 14, 1957).
"carries her everywhere" (Dick Kleiner, NEA release, Aug. 19, 1957).
"People keep saying" (Weaver, *I Talked with a Zombie,* 300).
"the difference between living and *earning* a living" (*Film Culture,* 1962).
"hilarious" (*Los Angeles Times,* Aug. 9, 1957).
"increased skill as a comedienne" (*Akron Beacon Journal,* Aug. 18, 1957).
"shrill, gurgly squeal" (*Boston Globe,* Sept. 6, 1957).
"Up to now" (*Atlanta Constitution,* Oct. 11, 1957).
"Miss Mansfield is a good 'straight' woman" (*El Paso Herald-Post,* Aug. 9, 1957).
"Miss Mansfield, with a wiggle here and a waggle there" (*San Francisco Examiner,* Aug. 17, 1957).
"I felt as though I'd go mad" (*Pittsburgh Press,* Aug. 12, 1957).
"silly, sloppy and smutty" (*San Francisco Examiner,* Aug. 17, 1957).
"What 20th Century-Fox has done" (*Oakland Tribune,* Aug. 19, 1957).

"I know men are always making eyes at Jayne" (Lee Belser, INS release, Apr. 8, 1957).

"Until next October 21, I am a married woman" (UP release, Mar. 19, 1957).

"We have a lot of things in common" (Lee Belser, INS release, Apr. 8, 1957).

"Miss Mansfield on film" (*Star Tribune,* Feb. 8, 1959).

"When she's dressed properly" (*Miami News,* Feb. 4, 1961).

"The press and photographers have put me where I am" (*Minneapolis Tribune,* July 21, 1957).

"She would do anything for the press" (*Arena Blondes: Jayne Mansfield,* Illuminations Films, aired BBC 2, Dec. 24, 1999).

"I can remember when I had all sorts of time to myself" (*Minneapolis Tribune,* July 21, 1957).

Some of them, they actually build their lives around me" (*Boston Globe,* Aug. 3, 1958).

"Every time she did a play" (Matt Cimber to author, Mar. 22, 2019).

"A few times we almost missed a plane" (Nelson Sardelli to author, Mar. 25, 2019).

"She's not only intelligent but she talks directly to you" (*Montreal Gazette,* Oct. 27, 1962).

"She didn't talk about herself" (*Orlando Sentinel,* Feb. 17, 1963).

"It was a friendly, captivating face" (*Arlington Heights Herald,* Mar. 8, 1962).

"she remembered me" (*Munster Times,* Mar. 27, 1966).

"The staff of a hotel" (*Rocky Mountain Telegram,* May 30, 1965).

Chapter 9

"What could have been a tawdry part" (AP release, Mar. 24, 1945).

"They wanted me to costar with Cary Grant" (Matt Cimber to author, Mar. 22, 2019).

"They were building the other girl up" (ibid.).

"swished into the Blue Fox" (*San Francisco Examiner,* May 7, 1957).

"made four movies for $60,000" (Sheilah Graham, syndicated column, July 11, 1957).

"is charming and youngish" (*New York Daily News,* Sept. 1, 1957).

"I was lousy in my first picture" (Bob Thomas, syndicated column, Nov. 28, 1961).

"Has looks and poise" (*New York Daily News,* Nov. 9, 1957).

"The reviews of Suzy's emoting" (Vernon Scott, syndicated column, Dec. 7, 1957).

"is allowed, or probably encouraged" (*New York Daily News,* Nov. 9, 1957).

"the platinum-haired and over-sized woman" (*Miami News,* Nov. 27, 1957).

"giggling nymphomaniac" (*Louisville Courier-Journal,* undated article).

Notes

"an inept female impersonator" (Walter Winchell, syndicated column, Dec. 4, 1959).

"laugh-minded audiences" (*Detroit Free Press,* Nov. 13, 1957).

"proves herself not only exceedingly lovely to look at" (*Valley Morning Star,* undated article).

"What I want to do more than anything else" (Louella Parsons, syndicated column, May 7, 1957).

"She did prove that she can do more than just stand around" (*Los Angeles Times,* May 28, 1957).

"She's better than Jack Benny" (*Orlando Evening Star,* May 27, 1957).

"Nobody expects her to have talent" (*Ottawa Citizen,* May 27, 1957).

"Her piano playing" (*San Diego Examiner,* May 28, 1957).

liked her violin recital (*New York Daily News,* May 27, 1957).

"violin and piano playing" (*Vancouver Sun,* May 27, 1957).

"With that mannequin-like hair" (*Cincinnati Enquirer,* May 28, 1957).

"I feel so vitriolic" (Golden, *The Brief, Madcap Life of Kay Kendall,* 114).

"A fashion model can't be voluptuous" (AP release, Apr. 22, 1958).

"I'm not the Marilyn Monroe type" (Vernon Scott, syndicated column, Jan. 5, 1956).

"I don't wiggle" (Ray Parker, syndicated column, Jan. 2, 1957).

"From now on I want to be the real me" (*Baltimore Sun,* Aug. 11, 1957).

"Sex appeal made me famous" (*Philadelphia Inquirer,* May 29, 1957).

"They promise me more money" (Sheilah Graham, syndicated column, May 14, 1957).

"*The Girl Can't Help It* is making a fortune" (Earl Wilson, syndicated column, Aug. 1, 1957).

"has swimsuits in nearly all sizes" (*Philadelphia Inquirer,* July 1, 1957).

"Two years ago if I had met Spyros Skouras" (*Philadelphia Inquirer,* Aug. 13, 1957).

"Everyone should try to be the best" (*Lubbock Avalanche-Journal,* July 14, 1957).

"chubby Jack King" (AP release, July 18, 1957).

"it's green and has a cute shape" (*Minneapolis Tribune,* July 21, 1957).

"Hollywood is a very good influence on Jayne Marie" (ibid.).

"I really love to bathe in pink champagne" (ibid.)

"The only negative thing about me is that I'm slightly nervous" (ibid.).

"I see Jayne Mansfield over there" (*Desert Sun,* July 13, 1957).

"I may make a movie in Paris" (*Desert Sun,* July 16, 1957).

"There's no feud with Jayne Mansfield" (UP release, Aug. 16, 1957).

"This Jayne Mansfield" (Erskine Johnson, syndicated column, Feb. 7, 1958).

"Zsa Zsa Gabor was always trying to be her big buddy" (Matt Cimber to author, Mar. 22, 2019).

"When he calls you out there" (ibid.).

"I enjoyed it" (*Pittsburgh Press,* Nov. 19, 1962).

"grossly unfunny" (*Democrat & Chronicle,* Jan. 5, 1962).

"the chatter stressed double and, with Paar's crafty help, triple entendres" (*Philadelphia Inquirer,* Jan. 7, 1962).

"have the advantage of being inflated" (UPI release, July 16, 1957).

"Daggie proved to be the most entertaining" (*New York Daily News,* Aug. 12, 1957).

"hubby-snatching" (AP release, Aug. 15, 1957).

"Jayne Mansfield's Overnight Mickey!" (*Whisper,* June 1957).

"I know nothing about it" (AP release, Aug. 20, 1957).

"the average teenager knows Jayne Mansfield's statistics" (syndicated release, Aug. 17, 1957).

"I can't help it if I'm on their minds" (UPI release, June 9, 1958).

Chapter 10

"Hollywood's greatest natural acting talent since Lassie" (AP, Jan. 8, 1957).

"a caricature from a forgotten era" (Erskine Johnson, NEA release, Aug. 3, 1958).

"would love to know why every editor" (*Arizona Daily Star,* Mar. 21, 1958).

"one of the world's best photographers and a big coward" (*Los Angeles Times,* Aug. 14, 1962).

"Miss Mansfield is a member of that falling shoulder strap school of acting" (Lee Belser, INS release, June 21, 1962).

"Men who gape at the likes of Miss Mansfield" (*Tennessean,* Mar. 2, 1958).

"Jayne Mansfield—you call that charm?" (*Philadelphia Inquirer,* Mar. 25, 1956).

"Jayne Mansfield's appearance" (*Philadelphia Inquirer,* Aug. 9, 1962).

"Given to giggling and squealing" (Michael Sean O'Shea, syndicated column, July 21, 1958).

"stars like Jayne Mansfield, Marilyn Monroe" (James Bacon, AP release, Jan. 13, 1957).

"American males form the most susceptible group" (NANA release, Nov. 12, 1957).

"dull" (*New York Daily News,* July 14, 1957).

"I now rate Mansfield as the cleverest woman I have ever met" (*Daily Herald,* April 27, 1957).

"I still think—don't we all?—that Jayne is a terrible actress" (*Akron Beacon Journal,* Dec. 15, 1963).

"In my world, Jayne Mansfield is the ultimate movie star" (John Waters, https://www.youtube.com/watch?v=-n3vyvEPgOw, from the British DVD of *The Girl Can't Help It*).

"I never got over Jayne Mansfield" (ibid.).

"I have light weight barbells" (*Los Angeles Times,* May 31, 1959).

"I think eating can get to be a habit" (ibid.).

"It does wonderful things to a face" (ibid.).

"I think most men find big bosoms exciting" (ibid.).

"It's bad to kill to eat" (*Springfield News-Leader,* Feb. 9, 1959).

"perfect as a cooing parody" (*Detroit Free Press,* Aug. 1, 1957).

"High necklines" (Joan Hanauer, INS release, Aug. 7, 1957).

"a tight blue sweater and pink skirt" (UP release, Aug. 7, 1957).

"Thank you very much, ma'am" (AP release, Aug. 7, 1957).

"grinned like a schoolboy" (ibid.).

"Don't you think it was terrible" (NEA release, Sept. 7, 1957).

"The Mansfield face" (*Montgomery Advertiser,* Aug. 4, 1957).

"hundreds of persons of all ages" (*Boston Globe,* Aug. 8, 1957).

"I would love to go back to Bryn Mawr" (AP release, Aug. 8, 1957).

"The personality I portray" (*Tabloid* [Toronto TV show], Aug. 1957).

"No. No, I really haven't" (ibid.).

"instead of being the marvelous marbled mansion" (*Los Angeles Times,* Sept. 20, 1957).

"I just love you English" (INS release, Sept. 26, 1957).

"I think London and British people are wonderful" (UP release, Sept. 26, 1957).

"She was crushed and bruised" (*Sydney Morning Herald,* Sept. 28, 1957).

"Whisper it softly" (*People,* Sept. 30, 1957).

"scared of the competition" (ibid.).

"The British press did its best" (Sheilah Graham, syndicated column, Oct. 9, 1957).

"a gentle, sympathetic, shy, very human person" (Godley, *Moscow Gatecrash,* 12).

"strange, unexpected closeness" (ibid.).

"The Eiffel tower is most impressive" (INS release, Oct. 2, 1957).

"Jayne and I have talked many times on the phone" (Harrison Carroll, syndicated column, Oct. 14, 1957).

"I hope this is not going to start still another rumor" (AP release, Oct. 21, 1957).

"I think so" (VARA television interview, Oct. 11, 1957, https://www.youtube.com/watch?v=xHHfsRrsXTo).

"The near riot" (*Windsor Star,* Oct. 24, 1957).

"but I never thought for a moment it would be possible" (UP release, Oct. 2, 1957).

"Buckingham Palace officials" (Leonard Lyons, syndicated column, Oct. 23, 1957).

"I have just come back from your country" (AP release, Nov. 5, 1957).

"The Queen is beautiful" (AP release, Nov. 6, 1957).

"on the basis of audience response" (*Londonderry Sentinel,* Jan. 4, 1958).

"Vulgar and over-busted" (*El Paso Herald-Post,* Nov. 14, 1957).

Chapter 11

"I saw the man I love" (James Bacon, syndicated column, Dec. 1, 1957).

"If people are going to call me Mr. Mansfield" (Wambly Bald, NANA release, Dec. 8, 1957).

"I didn't think anything would top meeting Queen Elizabeth" (UP release, Nov. 7, 1957).

"we were driving back from the airport" (Harrison Carroll, syndicated column, Nov. 16, 1957).

"Will rock spoil success hunter?" (James Bacon, syndicated column, Dec. 1, 1957).

"Most of it was rigorously routine" (*Philadelphia Inquirer,* Nov. 18, 1957).

"Jayne Mansfield overcame her histrionic shortcomings" (*San Francisco Examiner,* Nov. 20, 1957).

"She displayed about as much talent as a rock" (*San Mateo Times,* Nov. 17, 1957).

"a rip-roaring audience" (*Honolulu Star-Bulletin,* Dec. 17, 1957).

"autographed photo hangs next to M-1 carbines" (INS release, Dec. 24, 1957).

"Somebody should have asked me first" (AP release, Dec. 20, 1957).

"stood in the rain for the photogs" (*Los Angeles Times,* Dec. 21, 1957).

"Oh, for God's sake, Jayne" (*Honolulu Star-Bulletin,* Mar. 6, 1966).

"Jayne Mansfield doesn't require a passport" (*Oakland Tribune,* Jan. 27, 1958).

"It was a joy to share in the laughter of the marines" (*New York Daily News,* Jan. 18, 1958).

"most of the time she isn't dressed" (*Salt Lake Tribune,* Jan. 4, 1958).

"We are going to have a very quiet wedding" (Louella Parsons, syndicated column, Jan. 4, 1958).

"This is one time I don't want a lot of publicity" (AP release, Jan. 8, 1958).

"I said, 'honey, I don't want 100 people'" (*Blonde Ambition: Jayne Mansfield,* Prometheus Entertainment, *A&E Biography,* aired Feb. 9, 2004).

"I want the ceremony to be serious and serene" (*Troy Record,* Jan. 10, 1958).

"with some slight irreverence" (*Daily Herald,* Apr. 25, 1957).

"But through it all, Jayne was the perfect bride" (*Los Angeles Times,* Jan. 14, 1958).

"Did you see Jayne Mansfield in her wedding gown?" (*Opelousas Daily World,* Jan. 14, 1958).

"I wanted the reception to be in my home town" (*Los Angeles Times,* Jan. 14, 1958).

"just a little old white mink" (*Boston Globe,* Jan. 14, 1958).

Notes

"I was not prepared to do so" (AP release, Apr. 15, 1958).

"She is too new" (Jim Bishop, syndicated column, Feb. 7, 1958).

"80-year honeymoon" (INS release, Jan. 20, 1958).

"Mickey has fixed my present home up" (Harrison Carroll, syndicated column, Dec. 31, 1956).

"mulling construction of a heart-shaped house" (Bob Thomas, AP release, Mar. 10, 1957).

"She wanted nostalgia" (*Arena Blondes: Jayne Mansfield,* Illuminations Films, aired BBC 2, Dec. 24, 1999).

"We're going to decorate the house" (Vernon Scott, syndicated column, Jan. 14, 1958).

"never a shy one" (Dorothy Kilgallen, syndicated column, Dec. 3, 1957).

"The studio's going to flip!" (Earl Wilson, syndicated column, Aug. 1, 1957).

"It's no longer necessary" (*Los Angeles Times,* Feb. 16, 1958).

"A lotta people are gonna come up here to laugh at her" (*Philadelphia Inquirer,* Feb. 10, 1958).

"surround her with a big show" (James Bacon, syndicated column, May 11, 1958).

"I just don't know what to say" (Harrison Carroll, syndicated column, Feb. 11, 1958).

"I told her she could walk and turn around in it" (*Los Angeles Times,* Nov. 7, 1982).

"Jayne Mansfield's Las Vegas act is a hit" (Earl Wilson, syndicated column, Feb. 28, 1958).

"mop-up" (*Philadelphia Inquirer,* Aug. 22, 1958).

"a jolly early-morning open house" (*Boston Globe,* Mar. 3, 1958).

"Oh, I'm sure God is against gambling" (ibid.).

"It just comes out as a dumb blonde" (Bob Thomas, AP release, Feb. 15, 1960).

"It's always in a child's best interest" (AP release, Apr. 17, 1958).

"having eight years difference" (*Blonde Ambition*).

"came like a stab in the back" (*Indianapolis Star,* Apr. 20, 1958).

"We spend about $45 to $50 a month on food" (AP release, Sept. 24, 1958).

"If they have so many rooms in that house" (UPI release, Oct. 3, 1958).

"Attention all officers" (*Los Angeles Times,* Sept. 25, 1958).

"palatial hardship mansion" (*New York Daily News,* Sept. 24, 1958).

"He is more interested in his own pursuits" (UPI release, Sept. 26, 1958).

"it became apparent" (UPI release, Sept. 28, 1958).

"It's so—oh, so *regal*" (AP release, Oct. 2, 1958).

"It seems terrible that we are sending all that money overseas" (*Scranton Tribune,* Oct. 1, 1958).

Chapter 12

"I want to do the picture" (Sheilah Graham, syndicated column, Feb. 28, 1958).

"I don't think the sack dress is here to stay" (*Indianapolis News,* Apr. 19, 1958).

"I'm so happy" (AP release, Apr. 26, 1958).

"She has become a kind of Pied Piper" (*Liverpool Echo,* May 23, 1958).

"Gee! Those people!" (ibid.).

"The trouble is, every so often you get kinda human" (ibid.).

"Spain looks so *American*" (*Indianapolis Star,* Apr. 20, 1958).

"The bulk of the Indians were Spanish gentlemen" (AP release, July 11, 1958).

"Kenneth is such a sweetie" (*Sydney Morning Herald,* July 13, 1958).

"Her talent is very limited" (UPI release, Dec. 1, 1958).

"Raoul Walsh, putting Jayne Mansfield through her paces" (Hedda Hopper, syndicated column, June 7, 1958).

"Jayne Mansfield has one big advantage" (Sheilah Graham, syndicated column, June 10, 1958).

"I wore wasp-waisted dresses" (*New York Daily News,* July 30, 1958).

"It would be as ridiculous to criticise" (*London Observer,* Nov. 9, 1958).

"just a series of exaggerated events" (*Pittsburgh Press,* Jan. 9, 1959).

"Jayne looks more like a caricature of Jayne Mansfield" (*St. Louis Post-Dispatch,* Jan. 9, 1959).

"Jayne Mansfield also is in the film" (*Chicago Tribune,* Jan. 16, 1959).

"A caricature of Marilyn Monroe is permissible" (*New York Daily News,* Mar. 14, 1959).

"Jayne Mansfield, pretty and pink" (*Pasadena Independent,* Jan. 16, 1959).

"Whether you like her acting or not is beside the point" (*Daily American,* June 8, 1959).

"splendid" (*Coventry Evening Telegraph,* Jan. 13, 1959).

"It's a wonderful time in the life of woman" (*Pasadena Independent Star-News,* Aug. 10, 1959).

"are delighted" (AP release, July 10, 1958).

"Texas may be smaller, but we're louder" (AP release, July 22, 1958).

"a large girl" (*Pittsburgh Press,* Aug. 8, 1958).

"It's all very beautiful and artistic" (ibid.).

"No, I think they're old-fashioned" (ibid.).

"I'm a very religious person" (ibid.).

"I have spoken with almost every star of importance" (*Philadelphia Inquirer,* Aug. 4, 1958).

"has forced Hollywood queens" (*Life,* July 29, 1958).

"If I made a picture outside of Fox" (*Boston Globe,* Aug. 3, 1958).

"It's ridiculous" (UPI release, Oct. 4, 1958).

"the Jayne Mansfield of Japan" (*Honolulu Advertiser,* Dec. 24, 1958).

"makes Jayne Mansfield look like a boy!" (*Marion Star,* Dec. 19, 1958).

"If, for example, a journalist asks me who wrote *Othello*" (UPI release, Dec. 8, 1958).

"Marilyn's blue eyes are wary" (Vernon Scott, UPI release, Aug. 26, 1958).

"Marilyn carefully steers the conversation" (ibid.).

"Mostly I want to rest until the baby comes" (AP release, Aug. 17, 1958).

"We were walking along a steep garden path" (*Daily Mirror,* Dec. 17, 1958).

"They gave me a spinal so I could watch" (*Springfield News-Leader,* Feb. 9, 1959).

Chapter 13

"Texas-sized—that's bigger than king-sized" (Bob Thomas, AP release, Feb. 27, 1959).

"The front door with its pink Christmas wreath" (*Star Tribune,* Feb. 8, 1959).

"It makes you feel you were being hugged by teddy bears" (*Honolulu Star-Bulletin,* Jan. 18, 1961).

"Sex appeal has nothing to do with bodily proportions" (unidentified newspaper article, February 1959).

"I had these little red roses on the bosom of my dress" (UPI release, Feb. 9, 1959).

"I'm black and blue all over" (ibid.).

"They meant well" (AP release, Feb. 13, 1959).

"Nah, it's never happened" (*Oakland Tribune,* Jan. 3, 1961).

"Jayne Mansfield had a bad scare" (Walter Winchell, syndicated column, Feb. 11, 1959).

"Isn't it great to have Jayne Mansfield back in the news again?" (*Arizona Daily Star,* Feb. 11, 1959).

"where men are men" (AP release, Feb. 13, 1959).

"Jayne Mansfield's headlines out of Rio de Janeiro" (Dorothy Kilgallen, syndicated column, Feb. 13, 1959).

"The top comes down in a crowd" (*Daily Press,* Feb. 18, 1959).

"The front page story describing Jayne Mansfield's disgraceful conduct" (*Minneapolis Star Tribune,* Feb. 18, 1959).

"She was asking for it" (*Vancouver Province,* Feb. 20, 1959).

"Jayne had everything" (Mann, *Jayne Mansfield,* 53).

"her darling Mickey Hargitay" (Dorothy Kilgallen, syndicated column, spring [undated] 1959).

"All the studio can see me in is comedies" (Bob Thomas, AP release, Mar. 6, 1959).

"I go to all the PTA meetings" (*New York Daily News,* Mar. 7, 1959).

"like a tousled well-developed teenager" (*Fort Lauderdale News,* Feb. 16, 1959).

"I love being dominated" (ibid.).
"Jayne Mansfield showed up to play a violin" (*Orlando Evening Star,* Mar. 2, 1959).
"Jayne Mansfield also appeared" (*New York Daily News,* Mar. 2, 1959).
"Rock 'n' roll music blared into all the rooms" (UPI release, Mar. 1959).
"solicit free loot for their new house" (Dorothy Kilgallen, syndicated column, Dec. 2, 1958).
"Three weeks' salary" (*Blonde Ambition: Jayne Mansfield,* Prometheus Entertainment, *A&E Biography,* aired Feb. 9, 2004).
"That woman doesn't even exist" (unidentified newspaper article, 1959).
"stage actors have learned" (*Philadelphia Inquirer,* May 14, 1959).
"brought a gasp from first-nighters" (James Bacon, AP release, May 15, 1959).
"Jayne Mansfield's Las Vegas costume" (*Star Press,* May 25, 1959).
"She is no Dinah Shore" (James Bacon, AP release, May 15, 1959).
"I'm getting $25,000 a week" (Rick Du Brow, UPI release, May 10, 1959).
"I'd rather pose for a six-year-old boy than for *Life* magazine" (*Lawton Constitution and Morning Press,* June 28, 1959).
"It's a real swingin' show" (Erskine Johnson, syndicated column, May 7, 1959).

Chapter 14

"The role will be a dramatic one" (Russ Leadabrand, syndicated column, Aug. 3, 1959).
"The butler will double as a chauffeur" (Sheilah Graham, syndicated column, Aug. 11, 1959).
"Who? You had better ask my wife" (UPI release, Aug. 7, 1959).
"By British law" (Sheilah Graham, syndicated column, July 28, 1961).
"When I showed up" (AP release, Sept. 17, 1961).
"It took Jayne Mansfield only a few minutes" (Windsor, *The Autobiography of a Cockney Sparrow*).
"She was non-communicative with almost everyone" (ibid.).
"although she had been a big star" (ibid.).
"You couldn't blame Jayne" (Harrison Carroll, syndicated column, July 19, 1961).
"a particular scene" (*Harrow Observer,* Aug. 23, 1962).
"Perhaps the least uncomplimentary thing" (*Guardian,* Sept. 24, 1960).
"critics agreed it was so terrible" (*Sydney Morning Herald,* Dec. 4, 1960).
"When the British make an American-type movie" (*Indianapolis Star,* Sept. 27, 1962).
"wobbled through the picture" (*Age,* June 15, 1962).
"has better proportions as a person than as an actress" (*Philadelphia Inquirer,* Sept. 14, 1962).

"nine out of ten for her work" (*People,* Sept. 15, 1960).

"we bumped into each other on a plane" (*Daily Mirror,* Dec. 28, 1960).

"She's got every blue ribbon in Europe" (Hedda Hopper, syndicated column, Oct. 1, 1959).

"neither a realist nor a gentleman" (*Indianapolis Star,* Sept. 23, 1959).

"It is an insult" (UPI release, Sept. 30, 1959).

"I'm going to have a plaque made" (*Daily Mirror,* Sept. 25, 1959).

"Cheer me up" (*People,* Nov. 29, 1959).

"Sol Lesser and Cy Weintraub are producing" (Louella Parsons, syndicated column, Sept. 3, 1959).

"I feel that a star owes it to her public" (1959 British TV interview).

"babies always like to see their mothers in simple, fresh clothes" (UPI release, Aug. 24, 1959).

"The singularly untalented Jayne Mansfield" (*New York Times,* Aug. 15, 1963).

"Jayne Mansfield who, confronted with a part" (*Coventry Evening Telegraph,* July 19, 1960).

"The sight of Jayne Mansfield as the brains" (unidentified newspaper article).

"Miss Mansfield emerges as a dramatic actress" (*Motion Picture Herald,* undated review).

"talked to the writers and reporters of the cheaper press" (Sheilah Graham, syndicated column, Aug. 11, 1959).

"Lancashire folks love kiddies" (*Stage,* Sept. 19, 1959).

"The baby blinked in the glare of TV lights" (Reuters release, Sept. 7, 1959).

"If that Blackpool bluenose is going to start interfering" (*Moline Dispatch,* Sept. 10, 1959).

"Everybody thinks being a celeb is fun" (Walter Winchell, syndicated column, Sept. 13, 1959).

"There were hundreds of children" (*Tampa Tribune,* Sept. 8, 1959).

"I've had a very nasty trick played on me" (AP release, Oct. 12, 1959).

"the Soviets have photographed the reverse side of the moon" (UPI release, Oct. 29, 1959).

"monumental bad taste" (*Daily Telegraph,* Oct. 1959).

"I checked with 20th Century-Fox" (Sheilah Graham, syndicated column, Dec. 1, 1959).

"I've changed my whole approach to acting" (Joe Finnegan, AP release, Dec. 21, 1959).

"When it was that warm" (*Pittsburgh Press,* Dec. 29, 1959).

"good, familiar fun" (*Paducah Sun,* Jan. 19. 1960).

"somewhat sweeter than a howling coyote" (*San Francisco Examiner,* Jan. 15, 1960).

"Jayne Mansfield toured the Far East" (*Oakland Tribune,* Jan. 21, 1960).

Chapter 15

"will be photographed all over" (Earl Wilson, syndicated column, Jan. 2, 1960).

"a decade colored by Kim Novak's lavender" (Bob Thomas, syndicated column, Jan. 2, 1960).

"one hopes Miss Jayne Mansfield will call a press conference" (Joseph Alsop, syndicated column, Jan. 5, 1960).

"They take good care of me" (unidentified newspaper article, Jan. 2, 1960).

"Her Junoesque figure" (*Pittsburgh Press,* Mar. 16, 1960).

"I wish him luck" (Pat Herman, UPI release, Jan. 29, 1960).

"You can't hide the fact that we have bosoms" (ibid.).

"I love avant-garde fashion" (*Lancaster Sunday News,* July 26, 1964).

"with a gay disregard for nature" (*New York Daily News,* Feb. 8, 1956).

"orchid, frosted and tutti-frutti" (*Zaneseville Times Recorder,* Nov. 4, 1964).

"Wigs are only chic when they are undetectable" (Dariaux, *Elegance,* 277).

"My fans don't want it" (*New York Daily News,* Aug. 24, 1961).

"When I am on personal appearance tours" (*South Bend Tribune,* Mar. 18, 1962).

"So the next thing I know" (Matt Cimber to author, Mar. 22, 2019).

The excitement Jayne Mansfield puts into her voice" (Louella Parsons, syndicated column, Jan. 2, 1960).

"I just love to bathe in stereophonic sound" (*Pasadena Times,* Jan. 14, 1960).

"*Everything* was pink" (*Blonde Ambition: Jayne Mansfield,* Prometheus Entertainment, *A&E Biography,* aired Feb. 9, 2004).

"In the mammoth living room" (James Bacon, syndicated column, Feb. 14, 1960).

"The whole place has a rather recreational atmosphere" (*Vancouver Sun,* Dec. 15, 1960).

"We're getting a beauty parlor" (Rick Du Brow, UPI release, Oct. 31, 1961).

"bold of pink paint on the house" (*Indiana Gazette,* Mar. 26, 1962).

"The town frowns on the antics of Jayne Mansfield" (James Bacon, syndicated column, June 5, 1960).

"I love this house" (James Bacon, syndicated column, Feb. 14, 1960).

Chapter 16

"When I first read the script" (Joe Finnegan, AP release, Dec. 21, 1959).

"there's never a dull moment" (Sheilah Graham, syndicated column, May 20, 1960).

"struck dumb over curvaceous Jayne Mansfield's preoccupations" (*Indianapolis Star,* June 5, 1960).

"The bull was given a sleeping pill" (*Miami News,* Feb. 4, 1961).

"will never be seen as a picture in this country" (Sheilah Graham, syndicated column, Apr. 24, 1964).

Notes

"Mickey and I were invited to as many as three parties a night" (AP release, May 27, 1960).

"just great. We were like a couple of kids" (*Indianapolis News,* May 28, 1961).

"blond (?) movie star (?) Jayne Mansfield" (*Republic,* June 1, 1960).

"obviously pleased with their assignment" (*Los Angeles Times,* June 12, 1960).

"Many newsmen, who are probably the hard-boiled type" (*Mexia Daily News,* June 20, 1960).

"I have my political convictions" (Vernon Scott, syndicated column, July 13, 1960).

"awfully uncomfortable and worried" (UPI release, July 24, 1960).

"Ninety-five percent of all women" (CNS release, July 27, 1960).

"All we can do is pray" (UPI release, July 28, 1960).

"I'm so thrilled" (UPI release, Aug. 2, 1960).

"I've never won an Oscar" (Mike Connolly, syndicated column, Aug. 11, 1960).

"We want to have a bunch more kids" (Harrison Carroll, syndicated column, Aug. 30, 1960).

"The latest ideas in plumbing, heating and air conditioning" (*Albuquerque Journal,* Sept. 18, 1960).

"Why all this fuss over an ordinary Joe?" (*Boston Globe,* Sept. 2, 1960).

"which looked pink even in black and white" (unidentified newspaper article, Oct. 1960).

"The visit with Jayne Mansfield" (*Oakland Tribune,* Oct. 7, 1960).

"I don't want to return to Europe" (Harrison Carroll, syndicated column, Sept. 12, 1960).

"This particular Greek actress I play" (Joe Hyams, syndicated column, Oct. 23, 1960).

"This actress is different" (ibid.).

"I research all day long" (ibid.).

"It's in the nude" (Harrison Carroll, syndicated column, Nov. 21, 1960).

"It was a monstrous affair" (*Sydney Morning Herald,* Dec. 4, 1960).

"As far as acting is concerned" (Joe Hyams, syndicated column, Oct. 23, 1960).

"Of course I would" (*Sydney Morning Herald,* Dec. 4, 1960).

"20th Century-Fox is ready to release a dozen films" (Dorothy Kilgallen, syndicated column, Nov. 17, 1960).

"a brassiere for Jayne Mansfield" (*New York Daily News,* July 21, 1963).

"Mickey and I miss our lovely home" (Dorothy Manners, syndicated column, Oct. 31, 1960).

"After the savage mauling" (*Sydney Morning Herald,* Dec. 4, 1960).

"I know in my last film" (ibid.).

"I'm not unhappy about my career" (ibid.).

"Jayne's appearances in the film" (*Daily Oklahoman,* July 15, 1962).

"Mickey and I want to have a bunch of kids" (Harrison Carroll, syndicated column, Nov. 22, 1960).

"I'm really looking forward to it" (*Desert Sun,* Nov. 29, 1960).

Chapter 17

"There will be a proper amount of clothing" (*Philadelphia Daily News,* Dec. 9, 1960).

"Tonight I learned a lesson" (UPI release, Dec. 30, 1960).

"two-year-old Mickey, Jr." (*Philadelphia Daily News,* Feb. 3, 1961).

"Eyef got to go to me ahfice" (*Honolulu Star-Bulletin,* Jan. 18, 1961).

"We have a remote control [TV] set" (Hy Gardner, syndicated column, May 1, 1961).

"busy in the yard sloshing cement around" (*Province,* June 16, 1961).

"probably the most spectacular home in Hollywood history" (UPI release, Oct. 31, 1961).

"In front Mickey has created a scene of Roman ruins" (ibid.).

"Our living room is 50 feet long" (UPI release, March 29, 1961).

"She wore a loose-fitting coat" (*Miami News,* Feb. 4, 1961).

"I can't stand to see anything hurt" (ibid.).

"I really don't like meat" (Arlene Dahl, syndicated column, Oct. 2, 1961).

"It's strictly a family show" (UPI release, Apr. 24, 1961).

"Mickey's syndicated exercise series is catching on" (Eve Starr, syndicated column, Jan. 25, 1963).

"I like fresh fruit, fresh vegetables and fresh meat" (*Oakland Tribune,* Jan. 3, 1962).

"I'm not a fanatic" (UPI release, Oct. 6, 1962).

"Just the other day on the show" (Vernon Scott, syndicated column, Oct. 16, 1962).

"tried to please both male and female physical culture fans" (*Los Angeles Times,* May 10, 1966).

"She seems to turn up at everything new" (AP release, Oct. 7, 1961).

"Somebody hollered, 'here she comes!'" (*Tucson Daily Citizen,* Sept. 15, 1961).

"telling her just what to do" (ibid.).

"a new low" (*Atlanta Constitution,* Aug. 17, 1962).

"She handled questions with the skill of a diplomat" (*Montreal Gazette,* Aug. 30, 1962).

"in some respects she was very thrifty" (*Blonde Ambition: Jayne Mansfield,* Prometheus Entertainment, *A&E Biography,* aired Feb. 9, 2004).

"urchins" (*Los Angeles Times,* Sept. 12, 1958).

"reviewing the contributions of the motion picture industry" (*Desert Sun,* Jan. 27, 1962).

Notes

"as throughout her career she assisted these organizations" (AP release, July 2, 1967).

"a pair of American private eyes" (*Los Angeles Times,* Aug. 30, 1961).

"Jayne would rather make movies" (Mike Connolly, syndicated column, Feb. 22, 1961).

"an entertaining enough mystery" (*Paducah Sun,* Aug. 30, 1961).

"The only thing left out was a good script" (*Victoria Advocate,* Aug. 30, 1961).

"Jayne says about a dozen words" (*Atlanta Constitution,* Aug. 30, 1961).

"a girl who is thought of as dumb" (UPI release, Jan. 9, 1962).

"The studio has put an OK on a Mickey Hargitay–Jayne Mansfield comedy series" (*Philadelphia Inquirer,* Feb. 2, 1962).

"I don't know who's playing who" (Lloyd Shearer, syndicated column, Sept. 3, 1961).

"We say, 'Georgie,' and he says, 'Baby'" (UPI release, July 23, 1961).

"The film is made well enough" (*Indianapolis Star,* Mar. 2, 1962).

"clearing out all their expendable people" (Sheilah Graham, syndicated column, Aug. 26, 1961).

"George Cukor is a perfectionist" (Mike Connolly, syndicated column, Sept. 2, 1961).

"I've got an old aunt in Vienna" (George Stevens, Jr., *Conversations with the Great Moviemakers of Hollywood's Golden Age,* [New York: Knopf, 2016], 312).

"Being an international sex symbol is fine" (Bob Thomas, syndicated column, July 24, 1961).

"Elsa bawled her out" (Dorothy Kilgallen, syndicated column, June 1, 1961).

"she obliged photographers" (*Montreal Gazette,* June 22, 1961).

"After all, Berlin is not Cannes" (UPI release, June 26, 1961).

"I didn't even notice the others" (Harrison Carroll, syndicated column, July 19, 1961).

"I love you both, Mama and Papa" (AP release, June 29, 1961).

"although Mickey is now an American citizen" (Harrison Carroll, syndicated column, July 19, 1961).

"It's nothing you haven't seen before" (*Minneapolis Star,* Sept. 27, 1961).

"It had to happen" (*Lompoc Record,* Dec. 4, 1961).

"She is gentle but firm" (*Weekend Magazine,* Sept. 16, 1961).

"The one strange thing about the Mansfield home" (ibid.).

"When was the last time you saw Jayne Mansfield" (*Allentown Morning Call,* Dec. 3, 1961).

"my husband and I shared two-family cottages" (Dorothy Kilgallen, syndicated column, Aug. 13, 1965).

"protects the gals as much as he can" (*Marion Ohio Star,* Jan. 19, 1966).

Chapter 18

"I doubt if we'll go to the beach" (*Fort Lauderdale News,* Jan. 28, 1962).

"It was terrible" (*Blonde Ambition: Jayne Mansfield,* Prometheus Entertainment, *A&E Biography,* aired Feb. 9, 2004).

"about two blocks" (*Fort Lauderdale News,* Feb. 7, 1978).

"The water kept getting higher and higher" (UPI release, Feb. 10, 1962).

"All I can remember is the cold" (*Fort Lauderdale News,* Feb. 7, 1978).

"dragged her into the water" (ibid.).

"Movie Beauty Missing at Sea" (*Montgomery Advertiser,* Feb. 8, 1962).

"Jayne Mansfield Missing—Lost off Nassau" (*Hackensack Record,* Feb. 8, 1962).

"Jayne Mansfield Feared Lost in Boating Mishap" (*Pasadena Independent,* Feb. 8, 1962).

"Jayne Mansfield Lost at Sea" (*Springfield News-Leader,* Feb. 8, 1962).

"Self-Made Bombshell Loved Her Publicity" (James Bacon, syndicated column, Feb. 8, 1962).

"Don't be upset, honey" (Ben Funk, AP release, 1962).

"quite severe exposure" (*Orlando Evening Star,* Feb. 8, 1962).

"Jayne Safe—Oh, Yes, Mickey, Too" (*Colton Courier,* Feb. 9, 1962).

"'Missing' Jayne Mansfield Safe" (*Sunbury Daily Item,* Feb. 8, 1962).

"the bosomy actress" (*La Crosse Tribune,* Feb. 8, 1962).

"Ridiculous!" (*Tampa Times,* Feb. 9, 1962).

"World War III Start?" (*Deadwood Pioneer-Times,* Feb. 8, 1962).

"She took quite a chance" (*Pittsburgh Post-Gazette,* Feb. 10, 1962).

"Amazing what stars will go through" (*Springfield Journal,* Mar. 22, 1962).

"Bet Jayne Mansfield's being shipwrecked" (*Garden City Telegram,* Feb. 10, 1962).

"Was buxom Jayne Mansfield in danger of being nibbled by sharks?" (*Indianapolis News,* Feb. 8, 1962).

"Marilyn Monroe is going to arrange to get lost" (*Cincinnati Enquirer,* Feb. 10, 1962).

"She swam two miles" (Earl Wilson, syndicated column, Feb. 13, 1962).

"Would any husband and father with a shred of humanity" (*Fort Lauderdale News,* Feb. 10, 1962).

"Would she intentionally distress daughter and parents" (*Atlanta Constitution,* Feb. 11, 1962).

"That poor girl will have to die" (Dorothy Kilgallen, syndicated column, Feb. 12, 1962).

"Fun is fun" (*Fort Lauderdale News,* Feb. 25, 1962).

"There's no way I'd freeze on a rock to get publicity" (*Fort Lauderdale News,* Feb. 7, 1978).

"Jayne loves publicity" (Mike Connolly, syndicated column, Feb. 17, 1962).

"Anybody who says that was a publicity stunt" (*Rocky Mountain Telegram,* May 30, 1965).

"on top of the clouds" (UPI release, Feb. 9, 1962).

"uninhibited Jayne Mansfield" (*Miami News,* Feb. 9, 1962).

"If I had twin babies" (*Hy Gardner Calling,* October 21, 1962).

"I have plenty of publicity" (Sheilah Graham, syndicated column, Mar. 25, 1962).

"It's a miracle this girl is living today" (*Palm Beach Post,* Feb. 9, 1962).

"I am an actress and a mother" (AP release, Feb. 11, 1962).

"Every time they invited Jayne" (Matt Cimber to author, Mar. 22, 2019).

"Every comedian in the world wanted her" (ibid.).

"Jack was so thrilled" (Television Academy Foundation interview, Dec. 12, 2008, https://interviews.televisionacademy.com/interviews/dick-cavett).

"Did you ever use that line yourself" (ibid.).

"a crew-cut type ran up" (*Orlando Evening Star,* Mar. 29, 1962).

"I love my wife 24 hours a day" (*St. Louis Post Dispatch,* May 21, 1961).

"This won't happen to us" (Sheilah Graham, syndicated column, Mar. 26, 1962).

"There are certain laws one should obey" (ibid.).

"As to living with someone you are not married to" (UPI release, May 17, 1962).

"The main thing is" (Sheilah Graham, syndicated column, Mar. 26, 1962).

"She won't say much" (AP release, May 4, 1962).

"I'm no different from any other married woman" (ibid.).

"Mickey thought the dogs and the kids should stay at home" (Guild, *Jayne Mansfield's Wild, Wild World,* 92).

"I don't want to be a baby-sitter in Italy" (UPI release, May 5, 1962).

"Mickey, I'm your Jayne" (James Bacon, AP release, May 5, 1962).

"Mickey got jealous" (ibid.).

"Jayne Mansfield proved" (*San Francisco Examiner,* May 5, 1962).

"It is utterly of no personal interest to me" (*Fort Myers News-Press,* May 9, 1962).

"Jayne isn't doing much at the box office" (Dorothy Kilgallen, syndicated column, May 11, 1962).

"first call the newspapers and then the Fire Department" (*New York Daily News,* June 7, 1962).

"Every marriage needs" (*Des Moines Register,* May 12, 1962).

Chapter 19

"It's a role unlike any I've ever played before" (Bob Thomas, syndicated column, May 4, 1962).

"The production company rented me a chauffeured Cadillac" (Hedda Hopper, syndicated column, June 25, 1962).

"Eleanor is said to be quite disconcerted" (Dorothy Manners, syndicated column, June 25, 1962).

"rubbish" (Erskine Johnson, syndicated column, Sept. 14, 1962).

"Eleanor Parker pulled a Marilyn Monroe" (Sheilah Graham, syndicated column, July 25, 1962).

"Eleanor is usually so cooperative" (ibid.).

"clothes are tight" (Sheilah Graham, syndicated column, Mar. 25, 1964).

"What more can an old man ask?" (Sheilah Graham, syndicated column, Oct. 20, 1962).

"Jayne Mansfield and Mickey Hargitay are almost stealing the thunder" (Dorothy Manners, syndicated column, May 16, 1962).

"just like being in heaven" (*Daily Mirror,* June 4, 1962).

"With my husband" (Guild, *Jayne Mansfield's Wild, Wild World,* 118).

"When Mickey was tied up" (ibid., 119).

"It was no striptease" (AP release, June 8, 1962).

"Scowling, the brawny Mickey stalked onto the floor" (*New York Daily News,* June 9, 1962).

"Hargitay was reported to be angry" (*Chicago Tribune,* July 8, 1962).

"Despite the front she puts up" (Dorothy Manners, syndicated column, July 19, 1962).

"but she vetoed the idea" (Erskine Johnson, syndicated column, Sept. 14, 1962).

"Why does she get a prize?" (AP release, July 26, 1962).

"I had just made a little speech" (UPI release, July 26, 1962).

"when Jayne and family return" (Sheilah Graham, syndicated column, July 19, 1962).

"wore me out" (Saxton, *Jayne Mansfield,* 120).

"starts dressing less extremely" (Hedda Hopper, *New York Daily News,* Aug. 13, 1962).

"Hargitay will not be returning to Italy" (Sheilah Graham, syndicated column, July 19, 1962).

"was plagued with salary suits" (Louella Parsons, syndicated column, Dec. 19, 1963).

"is planning to sue Seven Arts" (Sheilah Graham, syndicated column, Sept. 10, 1963).

"those who saw it" (*Dayton Daily News,* Aug. 16, 1962).

"in the last reel" (*Rochester Democrat and Chronicle,* Nov. 7, 1964).

"Miss Mansfield's most obvious assets" (*Wilmington News Journal,* Nov. 19, 1964).

"contributes a couple of deliciously amusing bits" (*Los Angeles Bridge News,* Apr. 16, 1964).

"a zany comedy" (*Film Daily,* undated review, 1964).

Notes

"See! Scantily-Clad Jayne Mansfield in Her Usual Role!" (*Crowley Post-Signal,* Jan. 23, 1965).

"contract had expired" (AP release, July 4, 1962).

"I am thrilled to death" (ibid.).

"Jayne says she intends devoting more time to the children" (*Philadelphia Daily News,* July 13, 1962).

"bovine Jayne Mansfield" (*Honolulu Star Bulletin,* July 6, 1962).

"was tired of being called Mr. Mansfield" (*New York Daily News,* July 28, 1962).

"This time she is really going through with it" (AP release, July 30, 1962).

"I could be wrong" (AP release, July 31, 1962).

"Miss Mansfield is not filing for divorce" (UPI release, July 31, 1962).

"Publicity, it seems, is like a narcotic" (*Tennessean,* July 29, 1962).

"I'm very much in love with Jayne" (UPI release, Aug. 1, 1962).

"absurd" (*Daily Mirror,* Aug. 3, 1962).

"But there were always other people with us" (ibid.).

"I'm not filing for immediate divorce" (Dorothy Manners, syndicated column, Aug. 2, 1962).

"Outwardly undisturbed" (AP release, Aug. 2, 1962).

"Divorce is the worst thing that can happen" (*Photoplay,* Dec. 1963).

"despite Mickey's bitterness" (Guild, *Jayne Mansfield's Wild, Wild World,* 119).

"The day he moved out of the house" (Dorothy Manners, syndicated column, Aug. 9, 1962).

"he is bitterly unhappy" (Sheilah Graham, syndicated column, Aug. 11, 1962).

"was the backbone for her" (*Blonde Ambition: Jayne Mansfield,* Prometheus Entertainment, *A&E Biography,* aired Feb. 9, 2004).

"the book was written by Leo Guild" (Bentley Morris to author, Mar. 27, 2019).

"Frankness" (*Los Angeles Times,* Nov. 5, 1967).

"When I would appeal to her for truth" (ibid.).

"was a perfectly delightful personality" (Bentley Morris to author, Mar. 27, 2019).

"Leo was paid" (ibid.).

"What do you think has just arrived at this desk?" (Louis Sobol, syndicated column, Jan. 10, 1964).

"Ugh!" (Erskine Johnson, syndicated column, Jan. 14, 1964).

"undesirable, objectionable and obscene" (Reuters, Aug. 7, 1964).

"Magazines were bidding" (Harrison Carroll, syndicated column, Aug. 13, 1962).

"doesn't believe that the Italian film executive" (ibid.).

"hotly denie[d]" (Hedda Hopper, syndicated column, Aug. 14, 1962).

"Jayne Mansfield's been skin-diving" (Earl Wilson, syndicated column, Aug. 17, 1962).

"It's prestigious to have a famous woman" (*New York Times,* Oct. 3, 1982).

"'airline man about town' Bob Christian" (*Atlanta Constitution,* Aug. 24, 1962).

"It will not be a chic season" (AP release, Aug. 6, 1962).

"From everyone, the same response" (*Miami News,* Aug. 7, 1962).

"Personally I didn't like her" (*Greenville News,* Aug. 12, 1962).

"the one tangential question" (Lloyd Shearer, syndicated column, Oct. 14, 1962).

"I just can't believe it" (Kay Gardella, syndicated column, Aug. 6, 1962).

"are still frozen in time" (*Beat Magazine,* 2013).

"Jayne Mansfield may not make many movies" (*Valley Times Today,* Aug. 7, 1962).

"I refuse to dress her anymore" (AP release, Aug. 18, 1962).

"I'm sick of the old Jayne Mansfield" (Dorothy Manners, syndicated column, Aug. 16, 1962).

"I think everything has been said" (*Atlanta Constitution,* Aug. 16, 1962).

"The neckline" (*New York Daily News,* Sept. 27, 1962).

"new Jayne Mansfield" (Jim Bishop, syndicated column, Oct. 12, 1962).

"Unfortunately, it happened at a time" (ibid.).

"It's just that I accomplished my purpose" (Hedda Hopper, syndicated column, Oct, 23, 1962).

"tells friends here that her current love" (*New York Daily News,* Aug. 16, 1962).

"I have had this trouble at the airport" (AP release, Oct. 19, 1962).

"the most popular world entertainment figure" (Harrison Carroll, syndicated column, Sept. 5, 1962).

"Jayne Mansfield arrived in London" (Robert Corya, syndicated column, Sept. 18, 1962).

"was seen off by a man friend" (UPI release, Sept, 18, 1962).

"I feel fine" (*New York Daily News,* Sept. 19, 1962).

"I just couldn't keep from crying" (Harrison Carroll, syndicated column, Sept. 26, 1962).

"comforted and consoled" (Earl Wilson, syndicated column, Sept. 24, 1962).

"You marry him for two years and you tell me" (UPI release, Sept. 19, 1962).

"I need an awful lot of time to think" (Harrison Carroll, syndicated column, Oct. 9, 1962).

"I fail to understand" (AP release, Sept. 19, 1962).

"I was going to marry [Bomba]" (*Photoplay,* Dec. 1963).

"California divorces take a year to become final" (*Paducah Sun,* Sept. 26, 1962).

"Jayne is running the show" (Mike Connolly, syndicated column, Oct. 3, 1962).

"We're all very sophisticated people" (Mike Connolly, syndicated column, Oct. 10, 1962).

"It is quite possible that I will marry Enrico Bomba" (AP release, Oct. 13, 1962).

"I decided that I have more of a responsibility" (ibid.).

"It is heartbreaking for me" (Vernon Scott, syndicated column, Oct. 16, 1962).

"It's very difficult to be married to Jayne Mansfield" (*Arena Blondes: Jayne Mansfield,* Illuminations Films, aired BBC 2, Dec. 24, 1999).

"since the *Mr. Peepers* series" (*Troy Record,* Nov. 28, 1962).
"Randall, a familiar comedy face" (*Decatur Herald,* Dec. 6, 1962).
"a most unpleasant ordeal" (*Philadelphia Inquirer,* Dec. 7, 1962).
"Jayne Mansfield's new acting image" (*Chicago Tribune,* Dec. 9, 1962).
"Mickey asked me to wait awhile" (AP release, Nov. 24, 1962).
"Jayne called me last Monday" (ibid.).
"I just can't make up my mind" (Harrison Carroll, syndicated column, Nov. 27, 1962).
"Jayne Mansfield announced today" (UPI release, Nov. 29, 1962).
"Breathily, Jayne gasped of her love for Bomba" (Earl Wilson, syndicated column, Dec. 26, 1962).
"We're going to change the name of the picture" (AP release, Dec. 24, 1962).
"I am throwing away my pizza and spaghetti recipes" (UPI release, Dec. 25, 1962).
"Producers, directors and the various guests gathered around her" (Mann, *Jayne Mansfield,* 109).

Chapter 20

"she is starting a new film today" (AP release, Jan. 11, 1963).
"hemmed in on all sides" (Joseph Finnigan, UPI release, Jan. 24, 1963).
"I have nothing against Jayne at all" (Vernon Scott, syndicated column, Jan. 23, 1963).
"Mamie must have misunderstood" (Harrison Carroll, syndicated column, Jan. 24, 1963).
"Wasn't that awful!" (UPI release, Mar. 8, 1963).
"includes a nude scene with Jayne Mansfield" (*Los Angeles Times,* Feb. 3, 1963).
"I just can't stand incompetence" (ibid.)
"There's a feeling of grim earnestness" (ibid.).
"She's a great comedienne" (Eve Starr, syndicated column, Mar. 6, 1963).
"When she gets out there on the set" (*Oakland Tribune,* Aug. 23, 1963).
"We tried to give them equal billing" (ibid.).
"There are about 20 technicians" (Harrison Carroll, syndicated column, Feb. 7, 1963).
"'I'll try,' she says" (ibid.).
"Come on, fellows" (ibid.).
"I was preoccupied with other members of the cast" (*Arena Blondes: Jayne Mansfield,* Illuminations Films, aired BBC 2, Dec. 24, 1999).
"She's pushing it too much" (ibid.).
"the first role that pivoted her up to semi-stardom" (ibid.).
"I've flown thousands of miles" (Harrison Carroll, syndicated column, Feb. 2, 1963).

Notes

"recognizable but a trifle flat" (*Progress-Index,* Feb. 9, 1963).

"There has been an unprecedented demand" (Harrison Carroll, syndicated column, June 28, 1963).

"I think that was a turning point" (*Arena Blondes,* BBC 2, 1999).

"has reportedly given the producer permission" (*Baltimore Sun,* Jan. 10, 1964).

"the dullest, most unpromising comedy" (*San Francisco Examiner,* Aug. 23, 1963).

"This is not a movie" (*Oakland Tribune,* Sept. 5, 1963).

"It has a silly story" (*Atlanta Constitution,* Nov. 25, 1963).

"I laughed in what was apparently all the wrong places" (*Baltimore Sun,* Apr. 23, 1964).

"Why do you show trash like this?" (ibid.).

"Jayne . . . proves without a doubt" (*Anniston Star,* Feb. 2, 1964).

"The producers and directors of this movie" (AP release, Apr. 10, 1964).

"I made *Promises. . . . Promises!* for $206,000" (*San Francisco Examiner,* June 30, 1964).

"There are two scenes in which I appear nude" (UPI release, Nov. 11, 1963).

"I hope the police and the judges enjoyed it" (*Pittsburgh Press,* Nov. 11, 1963).

"ridiculous. Anything Jayne does in movies is artistic" (*Austin-American,* Nov. 11, 1963).

"If Noonan is really serious about Jaynie" (*Baltimore Sun,* June 22, 1964).

"Talk about sour timing" (Walter Winchell, syndicated column, Jan, 14, 1963).

"there is very little hope" (*Hartford Courant,* Jan. 10, 1963).

"I've been thinking it over" (AP release, Apr. 18, 1963).

"It probably will be better if we're divorced" (unidentified newspaper article, Feb. 9, 1963).

"I did not want these pictures published" (UPI release, June 6, 1963).

"That 'terrible' spread" (Herb Caen, syndicated column, Aug. 11, 1963).

"Beauty cannot be obscene" (UPI release, June 6, 1963).

"Would you like *your* wife to go out there and take her clothes off?" (*Photoplay,* Dec. 1963).

"I doubt Jayne will ever live down the nude pictures" (Hedda Hopper, syndicated column, May 3, 1963).

"how Jayne will explain them" (Louis Sobol, syndicated column, May 19, 1963).

"right now the children think of me only as their mother" (*Akron Beacon Journal,* Dec. 15, 1963).

"The utter tastelessness displayed" (*Fort Lauderdale News,* June 2, 1963).

"Confidential to Jayne Mansfield" (*Miami News,* June 5, 1963).

"Jayne Mansfield's naked poses" (Earl Wilson, syndicated column, June 3, 1963).

"Hold it higher!" (AP release, May 22, 1963).

"writhes about seductively" (AP release, June 5, 1963).

"obscene and provocative positions" (AP release, June 15, 1963).

"filth for filth's sake" (UPI release, July 26, 1963).
"I realize I never would have gotten anywhere" (*Akron Beacon Journal,* Dec. 15, 1963).
"Our actresses who have been so anxious to take off their clothes" (Hedda Hopper, syndicated column, Sept. 26, 1964).
"Never mind what the critics say" (Dorothy Kilgallen, syndicated column, Sept. 26, 1964).
"For a couple of reasons the very patient Garry Moore" (Dorothy Kilgallen, syndicated column, Mar. 4, 1963).
"suddenly became ill on arrival" (Eve Starr, syndicated column, Mar. 6, 1963).
"I don't want to get away from being a sexpot" (*Atlanta Constitution,* Mar. 12, 1963).
"He loves the sunshine" (*Atlanta Constitution,* Apr. 3, 1963).
"Jayne was in a good mood" (*Chicago Tribune,* Mar. 16, 1963).
"Mickey has been a patient man" (Sheilah Graham, syndicated column, Mar. 19, 1963).
"Jayne Mansfield, at a low ebb in her career" (ibid.).
"When you list the attendees at this affair" (UPI release, May 6, 1963).

Chapter 21

"Between shows one evening" (Nelson Sardelli to author, Mar. 25, 2019).
"I knew less about her than I knew about many Hollywood personalities" (ibid.).
"the gentleman that you are waiting for has arrived" (ibid.).
"She told me that she was doing a show" (ibid.).
"To be honest, I thought the show could use some serious help" (ibid.).
"I pointed it out to her" (ibid.).
"I was told that more people had come to see her" (ibid.).
"Boy, I wish Hargitay were here" (*Atlanta Constitution,* May 1, 1963).
"Things have come a long way" (*El Paso Herald Post,* May 1, 1963).
"We are very much in love" (ibid.).
"Not the style of the beast!" (Nelson Sardelli to author, Mar. 25, 2019).
"She lost two years" (*Atlanta Constitution,* May 1, 1963).
"I only got my divorce several hours ago" (UPI release, May 1, 1963).
"there was not a 'fight'" (Nelson Sardelli to author, Mar. 25, 2019).
Quinn was a fan of Jayne's (*Bild,* July 30, 2019).
"Jayne adapted herself" (ibid.).
"The real scene-stealers are Erna Sellmer and Josef Albrecht" (*New York Daily News,* Jan. 2, 1965).
"Even though we had a nice time together" (Nelson Sardelli to author, Mar. 25, 2019).

Notes

"I adore Italian people" (*Photoplay,* Dec. 1963).

"As a person she was intelligent" (Nelson Sardelli to author, Mar. 25, 2019).

"Jayne, they say, has quite a problem overseas" (Walter Winchell, syndicated column, July 1, 1963).

"It's been rumored that Jayne is expecting" (Alex Freeman, syndicated column, Aug. 16, 1963).

"You just don't know what might happen" (*Calgary Herald,* July 5, 1963).

"things are more pleasant" (Harrison Carroll, syndicated column, July 10, 1963).

"The Mickey Hargitay–Jayne Mansfield divorce cancellation" (Walter Winchell, syndicated column, Sept. 9, 1963).

"I couldn't help her" (*Blonde Ambition: Jayne Mansfield,* Prometheus Entertainment, *A&E Biography,* aired Feb. 9, 2004).

"Jaynie is the kind of person" (*Photoplay,* Dec. 1963).

"If your wife wants to divorce you" (ibid.).

"Jayne Mansfield is creating problems" (Dorothy Kilgallen, syndicated column, May 28, 1963).

"The only problem with Jayne" (UPI release, July 6, 1963).

"she'd take a couple of drinks" (*Arena Blondes: Jayne Mansfield,* Illuminations Films, aired BBC 2, Dec. 24, 1999).

"a framed deal" (*Montreal Gazette,* July 8, 1963).

"Her high bouffant styled hair" (*Lafayette Advertiser,* Aug. 2, 1963).

"idol of all" (*Hagerstown Morning Herald,* July 1, 1963).

"amusing" (ibid.).

"It is certainly a shame" (UPI release, July 30, 1963).

"the acting is atrocious" (AP release, Nov. 16, 1963).

"deliberately left out" (*Philadelphia Inquirer,* Sept. 8, 1963).

"I don't like to rap a girl" (Sheilah Graham, syndicated column, Oct. 1, 1963).

"I'm expecting twins" (*Daily Mirror,* Aug. 27, 1963).

"admired by hundreds of goggle-eyed women" (AP release, Aug. 26, 1963).

"We have another week in Dubrovnik" (Sheilah Graham, syndicated column, Oct. 1, 1963).

"shows how avarice can turn a handful of people" (*Clarksville Leaf Chronicle,* May 8, 1966).

"the heartbeats indicate" (Harrison Carroll, syndicated column, Oct. 30, 1963).

"Is Jayne Mansfield going to have twins" (Walter Scott, syndicated column, Oct. 19, 1963).

"one can still not settle back" (*Orlando Sentinel,* Nov. 27, 1963).

"My life is difficult" (*Photoplay,* Dec. 1963).

"I feel as a Catholic feels" (ibid.).

"I wouldn't try to call them" (Harrison Carroll, syndicated column, Jan. 6, 1964).

"worst undressed of the year" (*Long Beach Independent,* Jan. 17, 1964).

"She is the most beautiful little girl" (AP release, Jan. 23, 1964).

"Try that on your marquee" (Hy Gardner, syndicated column, Feb. 24, 1964).

Chapter 22

"playing dolls" (Harrison Carroll, syndicated column, Feb. 7, 1964).

"Despite the fact that my mother did not want me to go out" (*Pittsburgh Press,* Nov. 23, 1975).

"Jayne Marie—come here" (*Lawton Constitution and Morning Press,* June 25, 1967).

"Later that evening I joined Miss Mansfield" (ibid.).

"I don't know if she was stupid or not" (NEA release, Apr. 3, 1977).

"backstage at some celebrity gathering" (Will Hutchins to author, Apr. 23, 2019).

"Privileges taken away from a child" (*Tabloid* [Toronto TV show], Aug. 1957).

"Having children—isn't that what sex is all about?" (*Orlando Evening Star,* Dec. 7, 1965).

"I'm a disciplinarian" (ibid.).

"As long as mother was alive" (*Miami Herald,* Feb. 28, 1976).

"The only time I got to go out" (*San Antonio Star,* Oct. 19, 1975).

"Mother loved to play jokes" (*Louisville Courier-Journal,* July 25, 1976).

"Jayne has done her bit for history" (*Indianapolis News,* Apr. 16, 1964).

"she does a remarkably good job" (*San Antonio Express and News,* June 28, 1964).

"a peek of the black bra underneath" (*Miami News,* Apr. 22, 1964).

According to expert John McDermott (John E. McDermott, *Hendrix: Setting the Record Straight* [New York: Grand Central, 1992]).

"I had to make sure he did the track" (Earlyhendrix.com).

"physical culturist Rex Ravelle" (AP release, Sept. 1, 1963).

"I'm doing more dramatic things" (*Arena Blondes: Jayne Mansfield,* Illuminations Films, aired BBC 2, Dec. 24, 1999).

"because she considers herself primarily a movie actress" (*Atlanta Constitution,* Mar. 12, 1963).

"I knew I wanted a gorgeous tall redhead" (Sherwood Schwartz interview, the Television Academy Foundation, Sept. 17, 1997, https://interviews. televisionacademy.com/interviews/sherwood-schwartz).

"A telegram came to her table" (Bob Denver to Peter Anthony Holder, CJAD 800 AM, Montreal, Jan. 6, 1994, https://www.peteranthonyholder.com/ Archives/2016/cjad27.htm).

Chapter 23

"Best way to remind producers" (Sheilah Graham, syndicated column, Apr. 26, 1964).

Notes

"She was wearing jeans" (*Gorilla Position,* Oct. 23, 2018).

"She was a huge drunk" (interview by Richard A. Lertzman, *The Life and Times of Hollywood* blog, https://thelifeandtimesofhollywood.com/featured-content/).

"was actually a charming gentleman" (ibid.).

"Jayne Mansfield came to town" (*Detroit Daily Press,* Sept. 10, 1964).

"The play is still there" (*Detroit Free Press,* Nov. 29, 1964).

"I admired Kim Stanley" (ibid.).

"I've posed for photographers" (ibid.).

"Paul Newman . . . or perhaps Alain Delon" (ibid.).

"She didn't do an imitation of Marilyn" (Matt Cimber to author, Mar. 22, 2019).

"had a friend in New England" (ibid.).

"I think jazz is just *cushy*" (UPI release, July 5, 1964).

"Madame Pompadour estimating her court" (*Boston Globe,* June 28, 1964).

"I'd like to be a serious actress" (ibid.).

"With the minor exception of a girl named Kelly Brytt" (ibid.).

"Kelly Brytt as Lorelei's sidekick is exuberant" (*Hartford Courant,* July 8, 1964).

"how she likes buttressing Miss Mansfield" (Mike Connolly, syndicated column, Sept. 2, 1964).

"Miss Mansfield, who can be, in her own way, cute" (*Baltimore Sun,* May 6, 1964).

"Jayne gave them just what they came to see" (*Bridgeport Post,* July 8, 1964).

"The thousands who will be lured to this edition" (*Anaheim Bulletin,* Aug. 19, 1964).

"When Jayne's on stage" (*Los Angeles Times,* Aug. 20, 1964).

"It's a bust!" (*Hartford Courant,* July 8, 1964).

"Miss Mansfield is displaying herself for what she is" (*Boston Globe,* June 23, 1964).

"intimidation" (Matt Cimber to author, Mar. 22, 2019).

"Jayne is living in a different motel in each town" (*Hartford Courant,* Aug. 28, 1964).

"made me laugh" (Matt Cimber to author, Mar. 22, 2019).

"Jayne Mansfield and Mickey Hargitay settled everything peacefully" (Harrison Carroll, syndicated column, Aug. 29, 1964).

"'I'm in love with another man'" (*Arena Blondes: Jayne Mansfield,* Illuminations Films, aired BBC 2, Dec. 24, 1999).

"Is this real?" (*Daily Mail,* May 8, 2015).

"was indescribable" (Meet the Beatles for Real, http://www.meetthebeatlesforreal.com/).

"It was a total set-up by Jayne Mansfield" (The Beatles Bible, https://www.beatlesbible.com/).

"A photographer came and tried to get a picture" (ibid.).

Notes

"My dress was soaked" (Harrison Carroll, syndicated column, Sept. 5, 1964).

"John whispered to Jayne" (*Daily Mail,* May 8, 2015).

"*Playboy* made her" (*Playboy,* Feb. 1965).

Jayne Mansfield for President: The White House or Bust (Incorporated Books, 1964).

"We now have a movie star senator" (*San Bernardino County Sun,* Mar. 3, 1967).

"I was particularly attracted to her mind" (*New York Daily News,* Sept. 30, 1964).

"has the most beautiful physique" (ibid.).

"I devoted eight years of my life to her" (Earl Wilson, syndicated column, Oct. 30, 1964).

"It's pretty serious between us" (*Hartford Courant,* Feb. 25, 1965).

"wants no more trouble with Jayne" (Harrison Carroll, syndicated column, Feb. 1, 1965).

"I certainly don't think much of Jayne's new husband" (*Fort Lauderdale News,* Nov. 13, 1964).

"We not only are going to challenge the legality" (Harrison Carroll, syndicated column, Oct. 8, 1964).

"I think it's wonderful!" (*New York Daily News,* Sept. 30, 1964).

"Her massive vanity can only be fed by headlines" (Jim Bishop, syndicated column, Nov. 30, 1964).

"In front of the cameras" (ibid.).

"she knows who took the things" (Sheilah Graham, syndicated column, Dec. 23, 1964).

"I would state a preference for Miss Mansfield" (*Tampa Bay Times,* Nov. 1, 1964).

"She didn't have the greatest voice" (Matt Cimber to author, Mar. 22, 2019).

"The famous blonde completely won over the audience" (*Burlington Daily Times-News,* Oct. 17, 1964).

"I'm not an actor" (Matt Cimber to author, Mar. 22, 2019).

"a single-joke farce" (*Milwaukee Journal,* Oct. 28, 1964).

"the show displays the standing-room-only sign" (Sheilah Graham, syndicated column, Feb. 2, 1965).

"Amy Burns lives and shops in Huber Heights" (*Dayton Daily News,* Apr. 4, 1965).

"This is Jayne Mansfield" (UPI release, Mar. 24, 1965).

"For lease on Millionaires Row" (Vernon Scott, syndicated column, Apr. 17, 1965).

"The cavernous, empty pink mansion" (ibid.).

"in comparative obscurity" (ibid.).

"Zoltan jumped into my arms" (*Boston Globe,* Jan. 15, 1965).

"I'm not. I walked away from a street brawl" (Hedda Hopper, syndicated column, Feb. 9, 1965).

"I'm not scared of that muscleman" (*Boston Globe,* Jan. 15, 1965).

Mickey had brought photographers (*Hartford Courant,* Jan. 15, 1965).

"Mrs. Hargitay" (Harrison Carroll, syndicated column, Jan. 28, 1965).

"She would have problems with Matt" (*Blonde Ambition: Jayne Mansfield,*
    Prometheus Entertainment, *A&E Biography,* aired Feb. 9, 2004).

"I wasn't a great fan of Mickey" (Matt Cimber to author, Mar. 22, 2019).

"Finally I said, 'C'mon, this is ridiculous'" (ibid.).

"Everything good is happening to us" (Louella Parsons, syndicated column, Mar.
    11, 1965).

"a pretty deep cut near the heart" (AP release, June 3, 1965).

"superficial and self-inflicted" (*Quad City Times,* June 5, 1965).

"I don't know who did it" (AP release, June 10, 1965).

"I hope for Mickey's sake" (Earl Wilson, syndicated column, June 10, 1965).

"Jayne Mansfield and husband Matt Cimber" (*Detroit Free Press,* June 3, 1965).

"What else can a person use to combat insomnia" (*Ogden Standard-Examiner,*
    July 31, 1965).

"Momma, who had worked herself to a frazzle" (*Detroit Free Press,* June 11,
    1965).

"nonsense!" (Matt Cimber to author, Mar. 22, 2019).

"She said, 'I can't spend the whole summer doing nothing'" (ibid.).

"Seven dogs are six too many" (*Portsmith Herald,* June 23, 1965).

"It's wonderful we can have our family together" (*Rochester Democrat and
    Chronicle,* July 20, 1965).

"Aside from being a great-looking lady" (*Hartford Courant,* July 15, 1965).

"I throw in everything" (*Troy Times Record,* Aug. 19, 1965).

"13-year-old daughter" (*Fitchburg Sentinel,* July 23, 1965).

"Jayne Mansfield made her entrance on stage" (*Rochester Democrat and
    Chronicle,* July 21, 1965).

"Jayne Mansfield came to town" (*Rochester Democrat and Chronicle,* Aug. 1,
    1965).

"It is hard to imagine another comedy" (*Troy Times Record,* Aug. 18, 1965).

"I think you can reach everybody that way" (Aug. 1965 radio interview, https://
    www.youtube.com/watch?v=JDAwwC5Trdc).

Chapter 24

"It won't be just another one of those beach movies" (*Fort Myers News-Press,* May
    25, 1965).

"they photographed her behind anything they could find" (*San Francisco
    Examiner,* Dec. 11, 1965).

"a bomb, a real turkey" (*Fort Myers News-Press,* Sept. 5, 1976).

Notes

"besieged by autograph hunters" (*Fort Myers News-Press*, June 14, 1965).

"reckoned with the total lack of it" (*Los Angeles Times*, May 13, 1966).

he had not seen them since that January fight (Sheila Graham, syndicated column, Sept. 3, 1965).

"truly a shameful and sordid publication" (Dorothy Kilgallen, syndicated column, May 25, 1965).

"wild title" (Walter Scott, syndicated column, Mar. 15, 1960).

"all new elegant Ambassador Restaurant and Supper Club" (*Hartford Courant*, Aug. 6, 1965).

"novel advice to expectant mothers" (Alex Freeman, syndicated column, Aug. 12, 1965).

"an old retainer" (Sheilah Graham, syndicated column, Sept. 8, 1965).

said it was up for sale (*New York Daily News*, May 24, 1965).

"I guess he was waiting for our doctor" (Louella Parsons, syndicated column, Nov. 3, 1965).

"in which I play a flighty wife" (*Orlando Evening Star*, Dec. 7, 1965).

"un-funny and un-sexy" (*Rocky Mountain News*, Dec. 2, 1965).

"though Jayne Mansfield has comic possibilities" (*Variety*, Dec. 8, 1965).

"Some of the cast members are mumbling" (Dorothy Manners, syndicated column, Dec. 17, 1965).

"It's been a little hectic" (Harrison Carroll, syndicated column, Dec. 17, 1965).

"I know we both did it for the money" (*Blonde Ambition: Jayne Mansfield*, Prometheus Entertainment, *A&E Biography*, aired Feb. 9, 2004).

"We only had one argument" (Van Doren, *Playing the Field*, 227).

"If you go for this type of music" (*Motion Picture Exhibitor*, May 11, 1966).

"with good promotional backing" (*Box-Office*, May 16, 1966).

"funny only as a man who thinks he's handsome" (*Los Angeles Times*, Sept. 23, 1966).

"costs $1,000 an ounce" (Earl Wilson, syndicated column, Jan. 13, 1966).

"She may not win any Oscars" (*New York Daily News*, Jan. 21, 1966).

"doing her customary wide-eyed, breathy imitation" (*Evening Independent*, Feb. 8, 1966).

"that heart-shaped, all-American Valentine" (*Detroit Free Press*, Feb. 11, 1966).

"Jayne didn't feel up to going on the second show" (Earl Wilson, syndicated column, Jan. 21, 1966).

"had no moral resistance to the story" (Jack O'Brian, syndicated column, Feb. 25, 1966).

"Jayne Mansfield Sings (?)" (*Scranton Times-Tribune*, Mar. 14, 1966).

"The evil that men do is oft interred in their bones" (NANA release, Feb. 23, 1966).

"can find something better to do with $3,000" (AP release, Feb. 24, 1966).

"People have always said I have a head on my shoulders" (*Pittsburgh Press,* Mar. 8, 1966).

"singing, dancing, playing the 'Fiddle'" (*Tampa Tribune,* Apr. 24, 1966).

"Hank Snow brought down the house" (*Orlando Sentinel,* May 8, 1966).

"It happened in Syracuse" (*Orlando Sentinel,* May 6, 1966).

"Cigarette butts are smashed on the concrete floor" (*Tampa Tribune,* May 9, 1966).

"And there, up on the stage" (ibid.).

"It was . . . well . . . surrealistic" (*Tampa Bay Times,* May 9, 1966).

Chapter 25

"Look, if you give me the rights, we're gonna make it" (Matt Cimber to author, Mar. 22, 2019).

"It was amazing how people flipped" (ibid.).

"Jayne proved she was really a fine dramatic actress" (Vernon Scott, syndicated column, July 30, 1967).

"Jayne began the picture with me in September" (ibid.).

"This may be—quite seriously—the worst film" (*San Francisco Examiner,* Nov. 10, 1968).

"the feminine costumes" (*Hartford Courant,* July 13, 1966).

"nobody was calling the manager" (*Baltimore Sun,* June 15, 1966).

"Miklós is fascinated with small animals" (*Philadelphia Inquirer,* July 7, 1966).

"While one expects the private and public image" (*Wilmington Morning News,* July 1, 1966).

"Jayne talks as though she still had a thriving career" (ibid.).

"It's so kicky and fun and bubbly" (ibid.).

"Miss Mansfield just isn't a singer" (*Baltimore Sun,* June 16, 1966).

"the nicest thing you can say about it" (ibid.).

"Jayne Mansfield can play a dumb but beautiful blonde" (*Philadelphia Bulletin,* July 1, 1966).

"The most astounding fact" (*Frederick News,* June 23, 1966).

"Miss Mansfield may not be the most accomplished actress" (*Wilmington Morning News,* June 29, 1966).

"it promises to be a real bang-up opening" (*Syracuse Post Standard,* Apr. 22, 1966).

"I'll lose $100,000" (*Delta Democrat-Times,* July 3, 1966).

"a band, throngs of relatives and several cases of champagne" (*San Francisco Examiner,* June 4, 1966).

"Such long-time sex symbols as Jayne Mansfield" (Vernon Scott, UPI release, Apr. 25, 1966).

"The more success you meet with" (*Wilmington Morning News,* July 1, 1966).

Chapter 26

"Mean old gossips" (Earl Wilson, syndicated column, June 24, 1966).

"Jayne Mansfield and her husband" (UPI release, July 14, 1966).

"Jayne Mansfield Busts Up with Latest Hubby" (*Bridgeport Telegram,* July 14, 1966).

"I've given up marriage" (Earl Wilson, syndicated column, July 19, 1966).

"Although Jayne has made it clear" (*Hartford Courant,* Aug. 9, 1966).

"still be together" (Harrison Carroll, syndicated column, July 23, 1966).

"I got to the point" (Matt Cimber to author, Mar. 22, 2019).

"I came from the theater" (ibid.).

"She would never face the fact" (ibid.).

"because you never know when a revolution" (*Philadelphia Inquirer,* July 7, 1966).

"but he should at least have some money" (UPI release, July 29, 1966).

"I've been in love with Jayne Mansfield for years" (Cremer, *I, Jan Cremer,* 303).

"wooed her ardently" (Louis Sobol, syndicated column, Sept. 14, 1966).

"virtual house arrest" (UPI release, Aug. 12, 1966).

"The [tax] offices are closed" (ibid.).

"I love the place and the people" (UPI release, Aug. 17, 1966).

"I've fallen in love with Venezuela" (UPI release, Aug. 20, 1966).

"She doesn't even have an act ready" (*Hartford Courant,* Aug. 23, 1966).

"I was attending an oil show" (*Arena Blondes: Jayne Mansfield,* Illuminations Films, aired BBC 2, Dec. 24, 1999).

"Sam turned on real charm" (Mann, *Jayne Mansfield,* 183).

"He really was in love with her" (Matt Cimber to author, Mar. 22, 2019).

"kind of a slime" (ibid.).

"Matt has promised to return the baby" (Harrison Carroll, syndicated column, Sept. 9, 1966).

"said that Jayne could have the baby back" (*Detroit Free Press,* Sept. 11, 1966).

"pawn or wedge" (*Indianapolis Star,* Sept. 24, 1966).

"I feel are quite shocking and disgusting" (ibid.).

"the bosomy actress claimed" (UPI release, Oct. 15, 1966).

"is the securing of depositions" (Florabel Muir, syndicated column, Sept. 30, 1966).

"The struggle between Jayne Mansfield" (Sheilah Graham, syndicated column, Oct. 17, 1966).

"I was asked to lie" (*Blonde Ambition: Jayne Mansfield,* Prometheus Entertainment, *A&E Biography,* aired Feb. 9, 2004).

"until Jayne Marie made several damaging statements" (*Detroit Free Press,* Nov. 20, 1966).

"Playne Jayne Mansfield is said to be plotting" (*San Francisco Examiner,* Oct. 10, 1966).

Notes

"I feel so unchic in my Norell" (*San Francisco Examiner,* Oct. 21, 1966).
"She is wearing her hair" (Sheilah Graham, syndicated column, Jan. 17, 1967).
"mainly in a G-string and backless skirt" (*San Francisco Examiner,* Oct. 24, 1966).
"She was not invited" (*Miami News,* Oct. 25, 1966).
"I've been trying for two days to evict Jayne Mansfield" (*Akron Beacon Journal,* Oct. 26, 1966).
"I was invited" (*Miami News,* Oct. 25, 1966).
"Carroll Baker wore a dress" (*Vancouver Province,* Oct. 26, 1966).
"It's my contention that Mr. Sacks" (ibid.).
"a tempest in a D-cup" (*San Francisco Examiner,* Oct. 26, 1966).
"a handsome 6'4" local art student" (*San Francisco Examiner,* Oct. 19, 1966).
"Robin, leader of the group" (*San Francisco Examiner,* Nov. 5, 1966).
"Our religion is the only one" (Wilcox, *Religion in Today's World,* 387).
"Satanism has been frequently misrepresented" (LaVey, *Satanic Bible*).
"Now, if there was a ladder directly in front of me" (Sidney Omar, unidentified newspaper column, 1965).
"No one buys it" (*Philadelphia Daily News,* Feb. 21, 1967).
"The wizard told me" (Marilyn Beck, syndicated column, Feb. 28, 1967).
"I couldn't ask Jayne Mansfield about it" (ibid.).
"I am tremendously interested in prisons" (*Vancouver Sun,* Oct. 26, 1966).
"She says outrageous things in a pleasant way" (*Vancouver Sun,* Oct. 27, 1966).
"It was a demonstration of a massive put-on" (*Vancouver Province,* Oct. 27, 1966).
"A spokesman at her hotel" (*Times Colonist,* Oct. 31, 1966).
"sexual impropriety" (*Times Colonist,* Nov. 1, 1966).
"I am mad" (ibid.).
"only sat in the magistrate's chair" (*Times Colonist,* Nov. 2, 1966).
"I've been bleeding all day" (*Vancouver Sun,* Nov. 2, 1966).
"We understand one of your films" (*Vancouver Sun,* Nov. 5, 1966).
"I hate bullfights" (*Province,* Nov. 2, 1966).
"I mean real fast sports cars" (ibid.).
"She made an unforgettable portrait" (*Times Colonist,* Dec. 30, 1966).
"I don't know whether he was conscious or not" (AP release, Nov. 27, 1966).
"It was the most terrifying moment of my life" (*Los Angeles Times,* Nov. 27, 1966).
"Doctors will not know for four days" (*New York Daily News,* Nov. 28, 1966).
"His eyes lit up" (AP release, Nov. 28, 1966).
"I have not slept for the last three days" (AP release, Nov. 30, 1966).
"improved but still guarded" (UPI release, Dec. 2, 1966).
"Jayne Mansfield has sometimes done some silly things" (*San Francisco Examiner,* Dec. 2, 1966).

"The original head wound was wide open" (AP release, Dec. 6, 1966).

"I'm not going to a hospital" (ibid.).

"Dear Mrs. Gilmore" (*San Francisco Examiner,* July 5, 1967).

"full of shots and vitamins" (*Los Angeles Times,* Dec. 25, 1966).

"It's the best Christmas present any mother could have" (*Los Angeles Times,* Dec. 26, 1966).

"but that depends of course on Zoltan's condition" (Harrison Carroll, syndicated column, Jan. 13, 1967).

"Sympathy of the entire show world" (Harold Heffernan, NANA release, Jan. 4, 1967).

"this actually happened to a friend of his" (*Oakland Tribune,* May 8, 1967).

"the funniest of these stories" (ibid.).

"a truly adult farce" (*New York Daily News,* May 26, 1967).

"How about that?" (*Minneapolis Star,* Dec. 30, 1966).

Chapter 27

"Matt will insist that the court be open to the public" (*Hartford Courant,* Jan. 9, 1967).

"American men are in kindergarten" (Reuters release, Feb. 6, 1967).

"I own several dogs, cats, a mynah bird" (*Sydney Morning Herald,* Feb. 12, 1967).

"I'll do everything I possibly can" (AP release, Feb. 2, 1967).

"a chorus of whistles" (AP release, Feb. 14, 1967).

"I feel that soldiers anywhere in any army" (Reuters release, Feb. 14, 1967).

"We wanted to give you a flak jacket" (AP release, Feb. 17, 1967).

"battles raged a few miles east" (ibid.).

"I just cannot leave them" (AP release, Feb. 18, 1967).

"bearded beatnik escort" (UPI release, Feb. 19, 1967).

"A touch of artificial Hollywood" (*Courier-News,* Feb. 23, 1967).

"After our boys get charged up" (*San Bernardino County Sun,* Feb. 20, 1967).

"Her questions were confusing" (*Amarillo Globe-Times,* Feb. 23, 1967).

"We were told there were no more tables" (ibid.).

"There's no front line in Vietnam" (KRON-TV newsreel, https://www.youtube.com/watch?v=wHvkeZeTCTo&t=17s).

"In one conversation with Miss Mansfield" (*San Francisco Examiner,* Feb. 23, 1967).

"using his fists and mouth" (UPI release, Mar. 28, 1967).

"Miss Mansfield has called me" (*San Francisco Examiner,* Feb. 23, 1967).

"We are dealing with a brazen and arrogant woman" (AP release, Mar. 10, 1967).

"mental and emotional tranquility" (ibid.).

"Outside the court with her lawyer" (AP release, Mar. 7, 1967).

Notes

"What's next for Jayne?" (Harrison Carroll, syndicated column, Mar. 9, 1967).

"I've been crying all the way in from the airport" (AP release, Mar. 24, 1967).

"I told the airline people I had them" (ibid.).

"An airport official saw Brody" (AP release, Apr. 28, 1967).

"a helluva nice guy" (*Reading Evening Post,* Apr. 8, 1967).

"I intend to take legal action" (UPI release, Apr. 8, 1967).

"I've been sacked" (AP release, Apr. 8, 1967).

"Customers at the clubs have been kept waiting" (*Sydney Morning Herald,* Apr. 9, 1967).

"drank too much" (AP release, Apr. 10, 1967).

"Those who appear in spotlights" (*New York Daily News,* May 7, 1967).

"Sam's a marvelous man" (*Baltimore Evening Sun,* Apr. 10, 1967).

"Dennis Healey was droning on" (*Guardian,* Apr. 13, 1967).

"The big names are more and more learning to hunt" (*Guardian,* Apr. 15, 1967).

"a goddess of lust" (AP release, Apr. 22, 1967).

"It must have been a misunderstanding" (*Orlando Sentinel,* Apr. 25, 1967).

"Jayne Mansfield's sexy performance" (*Long Beach Independent,* May 2, 1967).

"I can't understand the remarks made" (*Daily Mirror,* Apr. 27, 1967).

"If I had not seen the whole quivering absurdity" (*Detroit Free Press,* Apr. 30, 1967).

"And I wouldn't have missed one bouncing moment of it" (ibid.).

"Jayne has never been more than a fair-to-good singer" (ibid.).

"The point has now been reached" (*Edmonton Journal,* Mar. 30, 1967).

"Jayne Mansfield drew more attention" (*New York Daily News,* May 25, 1967).

"She must have two-timed as she one-stepped" (*New York Daily News,* May 26, 1967).

"In all the time I knew Jayne" (Diana Dors interview, https://www.youtube.com/watch?v=Yi3cFn_2JL4).

"had been performing in cabaret" (Humperdinck, *What's in a Name?* 151).

"Only a few days ago she announced" (*Detroit Free Press,* May 1, 1967).

"I do a satire on sex—don't you?" (1967 newsreel, https://www.youtube.com/watch?v=hmRGfpvJS_s).

"Would you like to see my Chihuahuas?" (*Daily Mail,* July 2019).

"To say that Jayne Mansfield is trouble-prone" (Sheila Graham, syndicated column, June 10, 1967).

"In Germany I sprained my back" (ibid.).

"No one seems to be quite sure" (Sheila Graham, syndicated column, May 16, 1967).

"does nothing to me" (Marilyn Beck, syndicated column, Apr. 10, 1967).

"One difference between Jayne Mansfield and me" (Leonard Lyons, syndicated column, Apr. 2, 1962).

"saw them together at the Brown Derby" (Sheilah Graham, syndicated column, May 19, 1967).

"wearing a patent leather dress" (Harrison Carroll, syndicated column, May 20, 1967).

"I've had some serious talks about it" (Earl Wilson, syndicated column, June 7, 1967).

"Put Jayne Mansfield and Twiggy together" (unidentified newspaper article).

"They had intercoms through the whole house" (*Blonde Ambition: Jayne Mansfield,* Prometheus Entertainment, *A&E Biography,* aired Feb. 9, 2004).

"claiming a male friend of her mother beat her" (*Washington Post,* June 18, 1967).

"I want her to find herself" (*Boston Globe,* June 25, 1967).

"We feel there is insufficient evidence" (UPI release, June 25, 1967).

"You know I am a very strict mother" (Mann, *Jayne Mansfield,* 248).

"The child is not the blood relation of the Pigues" (ibid., 250).

"I don't want my child smoking marijuana" (ibid.).

"Mr. Brody had never touched me" (ibid., 252).

"a vacation trip to Biloxi" (AP release, June 25, 1967).

"I don't know if it was the depression" (*Arena Blondes: Jayne Mansfield,* Illuminations Films, aired BBC 2, Dec. 24, 1999).

"Her life at that time was very much in a turmoil" (ibid.).

"Trouble follows me everywhere" (*San Francisco Examiner,* June 29, 1967).

"All my husbands have been completely different" (NANA release, July 5, 1967).

"No. I have wonderful happy moments" (*Arena Blondes*).

Chapter 28

"the most publicized and beautiful" (*Clarion-Ledger,* June 11, 1967).

"It's so Colorado-ish" (*Biloxi Gulfport Daily Herald,* June 30, 1967).

"We were planning to be married in 72 hours" (Fox News, Feb. 2, 2018).

"We had a very sweet, very kind, very loving conversation" (*Blonde Ambition: Jayne Mansfield,* Prometheus Entertainment, *A&E Biography,* aired Feb. 9, 2004).

"We knew we had to go somewhere in the nighttime" (*Arena Blondes: Jayne Mansfield,* Illuminations Films, aired BBC 2, Dec. 24, 1999).

"was pulling out of the driveway" (Fox News, Feb. 2, 2018).

"State police rush to accidents on it daily" (*Monroe Star-News,* Apr. 17, 1968).

"like a streak of lightning" (New Orleans Police Department report no. F-20607-67).

"miscellaneous freight" (ibid.).

"there was no fog on or near the highway" (ibid.).

"her head jammed" (ibid.).

"I don't remember anything else" (*Arena Blondes,* 1999).

"It was the most dreadful thing I've ever seen" (AP release, June 29, 1967).

"a large deposit of brains" (New Orleans Police Department report no. F-20607-67).

"scalp avulsion combined with an open skull avulsion" (City of New Orleans certificate of death, no. 670004357).

"closed fractures of right humerus" (ibid.).

"is a very common injury in car accidents" (Joanna Campbell, Findadeath.com, https://findadeath.com/jayne-mansfield/).

"pretty well torn up" (*Boston Globe,* June 29, 1967).

"which is not indicative" (New Orleans Police Department report no. F-20607-67).

"extreme safety hazard involved" (UPI release, June 30, 1967).

"I looked out the window" (*Blonde Ambition,* 2004).

"She took it like the little trouper she is" (UPI release, June 30, 1967).

"I went into the funeral home" (*Arena Blondes,* 1999).

"a date with God" (AP release, June 30, 1967).

"I have to look after them now" (UPI release, June 30, 1967).

cynically noted that Jayne's death (*Miami News,* July 1, 1967).

"Midway through the film" (*Boston Globe,* July 13, 1967).

"had sought [LaVey's] help" (*Danville Register,* Sept. 22, 1967).

"Two Chihuahuas Killed" (*Reno Evening Gazette,* June 28, 1967).

"Jayne Mansfield was not a great actress" (*Tampa Times,* June 30, 1967).

"Jayne Mansfield will probably not be remembered as a great actress" (*Petaluma Argus-Courier,* June 30, 1967).

"the last of her breed" (*Tennessean,* July 2, 1967).

"one of the most colorful women ever" (*Fort Myers News-Press,* July 7, 1967).

"her death, including the grotesque form of it" (*Guardian,* Feb. 5, 1979).

"a pathetic parody" (Leonard Lyons, syndicated column, July 1, 1967).

"Miss Mansfield was 80 different faces" (Jim Bishop, syndicated column, July 3, 1967).

"Jayne Mansfield was a tragic, no talent woman" (*Vancouver Sun,* June 29, 1967).

"about the poorest taste of anything I have ever read" (*Vancouver Sun,* July 6, 1967).

"isn't much mourned" (*Des Moines Register,* July 10, 1967).

"almost a caricature of the dumb blonde" (*Chicago Sun-Times,* July 2, 1967).

"at the time of her demise" (*Arizona Republic,* July 1, 1967).

"That would be an extremely morbid thing" (*Austin-American,* July 1, 1967).

"strictly private" (AP release, July 1, 1967).

"I always sent her constantly 13 red roses" (*New York Daily News,* July 4, 1967).

"There were crowds of nearly 1,000" (AP release, July 4, 1967).

"My father, Paul Mansfield" (*Pittsburgh Press,* Nov. 23, 1975).

"Please accept our sincere thanks" (*Allentown Morning Call,* July 24, 1967).

"She liked a lot of publicity" (*Allentown Morning Call,* July 1, 1967).

"How are the children?" (AP release, July 7, 1967).

"We were considered collateral damage" (Fox News, Feb. 2, 2018).

"I thought it would be nice" (*Allentown Morning Call,* Apr. 11, 1968).

"operated their vehicles in a negligent manner" (UPI release, Apr. 23, 1968).

"I hereby bequeath" (AP release, Aug. 1, 1967).

"the death of Jayne" (*Greenville News,* Oct. 25, 1978).

"would be lucky to get 30 percent" (AP release, Feb. 2, 1971).

"It's a little unfair" (*Los Angeles Times,* Sept. 29, 1977).

"Treasure Chest Empty" (*Des Moines Register,* Oct. 3, 1977).

Chapter 29

"no one would want his or her name" (*New York Daily News,* Nov. 30, 1967).

"There's really nothing in *Spree*" (*Semi-weekly Spokesman,* Dec. 8, 1967).

"He is a nice looking chap" (*Minneapolis Star,* Dec. 16, 1967).

"an unnerving spectacle for certain males" (*Rochester Democrat and Chronicle,* May 11, 1968).

"a monuments [*sic*] of ineptness" (*Wilmington Morning News,* Jan. 31, 1969).

"Being thought of as nothing but a glamour girl" (Vernon Scott, syndicated column, Mar. 1, 1970).

"The dimensions that have contributed largely to her present fame" (AP release, Mar. 3, 1970).

"As far as movies are concerned" (*Windsor Star,* 1972).

"I knew her well" (Jim Bishop, syndicated column, Oct. 6, 1972).

"Jayne Mansfield was an imposter" (Jim Bishop, syndicated column, Sept. 18, 1980).

"Then came her call from the spirit world" (Mann, *Jayne Mansfield,* vi).

"patron saint" (*San Antonio Press,* Feb. 1, 1976).

"the present laws of physics" (*Palm Beach Post,* Oct. 4, 1979).

"Rear safety bumpers would have saved them" (*Albuquerque Journal,* July 1, 1967).

"The National Highway Traffic Safety Administration" (*Washington Post,* Dec. 15, 1971).

"While there is still much work to be done" (Truck Safety Coalition press release, May 24, 2019).

"brought Jayne Mansfield style" (*Minneapolis Star Tribune,* May 27, 1966).

"That was the first time I ever wore a blonde wig" (Loni Anderson to author, Aug. 2, 2019).

"I related to her so much" (ibid.).

"Everybody kept saying" (ibid.).

"The outdoor scenes, anyway" (ibid.).

"wouldn't let anyone in the house but me" (ibid.).

"Mariska came to visit me on the set" (ibid.).

"an effective drama" (*Baltimore Evening Sun,* Oct. 29, 1980).

"They asked me to use my name" (Matt Cimber to author, Mar. 22, 2019).

"brought to our marriage a son" (*Arena Blondes: Jayne Mansfield,* Illuminations Films, aired BBC 2, Dec. 24, 1999).

"After the tragedy" (Matt Cimber to author, Mar. 22, 2019).

"the mother of my two daughters" (Nelson Sardelli to author, Mar. 25, 2019).

"Ellen was a friend of Jaynie's" (*Allentown Morning Call,* Apr. 11, 1968).

"It was my chore when I was a kid" (*Los Angeles Times,* Dec. 9, 2016).

"The way I've lived with loss" (*People,* Mar. 28, 2018).

"When mother died" (*Pittsburgh Press,* Nov. 23, 1975).

"We rushed it" (*Louisville Courier-Journal,* July 25, 1976).

"To this day I hear from women" (*Blonde Ambition: Jayne Mansfield,* Prometheus Entertainment, *A&E Biography,* aired Feb. 9, 2004).

"Max Factor blood" (*Muncie Star Press,* Aug. 24, 1975).

"When I was young" (Scott Michaels to author, Nov. 20, 2019).

"I've always loved Jayne Mansfield" (ibid.).

"has had several owners" (ibid.).

"I explained who I was" (ibid.)

"I said, 'That's some home'" (Humperdinck, *What's in a Name?* 151).

"bought it and fixed it up" (ibid.).

"We used to come downstairs" (ibid., 152).

"in our 27-year tenure" (ibid., 153).

"The death of a beautiful woman" (Edgar Allan Poe, "The Philosophy of Composition," *Graham's Magazine,* Apr. 4, 1846).

"Repeatedly during the meal" (*Hackensack Record,* July 10, 1967).

Selected Bibliography

Collins, Joan. *Past Imperfect: An Autobiography.* New York: Simon & Schuster, 1984.

Dariaux, Genevieve Antoine. *Elegance.* Garden City, NY: Doubleday, 1964.

Faris, Jocelyn. *Jayne Mansfield: A Bio-Bibliography.* Westport, CT: Greenwood, 1994.

Gladstone, James. *The Man Who Seduced Hollywood: The Life and Loves of Greg Bautzer.* Chicago: Chicago Review, 2013.

Godley, John. *Moscow Gatecrash: A Peer behind the Curtain.* Boston: Houghton Mifflin, 1959.

Godwin, John. *Occult America.* New York: Doubleday, 1972.

Golden, Eve. *The Brief, Madcap Life of Kay Kendall.* Lexington: University Press of Kentucky, 2002.

Guild, Leo. *Jayne Mansfield's Wild, Wild World.* Los Angeles: Holloway House, 1963.

Humperdinck, Engelbert. *What's in a Name?* London: Virgin Books, 2004.

Jason, Rick. *Scrapbooks of My Mind: A Hollywood Autobiography.* Sarasota, FL: Strange New Worlds, 2000.

Johnston, Claire, and Paul Willemen. *Frank Tashlin.* Colchester, UK: Vineyard, 1973.

Koper, Richard. *Affectionately, Jayne Mansfield.* Albany, GA: BearManor Media, 2012.

LaVey, Anton. *The Satanic Bible.* New York: Avon, 1969.

Leonard, Maurice. *Mae West: Empress of Sex.* London: HarperCollins, 1992.

Mann, May. *Jayne Mansfield: A Biography.* New York: Drake, 1973.

More, Kenneth. *More or Less.* London: Hodder & Stoughton, 1978.

Saxton, Martha. *Jayne Mansfield and the American Fifties.* New York: Houghton Mifflin, 1975.

Steinbeck, John. *The Wayward Bus.* New York: Viking, 1947.

Taylor, Theodore. *Jule: The Story of Composer Jule Styne.* New York: Random House, 1979.

Selected Bibliography

Van Doren, Mamie. *Playing the Field—My Story.* New York: G. P. Putnam's Sons, 1987.

Weaver, Tom. *I Talked with a Zombie: Interviews with 23 Veterans of Horror and Sci-Fi Films and Television.* Jefferson, NC: McFarland, 2009.

Wilcox, Melissa M. *Religion in Today's World.* Abingdon-on-Thames, UK: Routledge, 2012.

Windsor, Barbara: *The Autobiography of a Cockney Sparrow.* London: Arrow Books, 1991.

Index

423

Index

Index

Index

Index

Screen Classics

Screen Classics is a series of critical biographies, film histories, and analytical studies focusing on neglected filmmakers and important screen artists and subjects, from the era of silent cinema through the golden age of Hollywood to the international generation of today. Books in the Screen Classics series are intended for scholars and general readers alike. The contributing authors are established figures in their respective fields. This series also serves the purpose of advancing scholarship on film personalities and themes with ties to Kentucky.

Series Editor

Patrick McGilligan

Books in the Series

He's Got Rhythm: The Life and Career of Gene Kelly
    Cynthia Brideson and Sara Brideson
Ziegfeld and His Follies: A Biography of Broadway's Greatest Producer
    Cynthia Brideson and Sara Brideson
The Marxist and the Movies: A Biography of Paul Jarrico
    Larry Ceplair
Dalton Trumbo: Blacklisted Hollywood Radical
    Larry Ceplair and Christopher Trumbo
Warren Oates: A Wild Life
    Susan Compo
Improvising Out Loud: My Life Teaching Hollywood How to Act
    Jeff Corey with Emily Corey
Crane: Sex, Celebrity, and My Father's Unsolved Murder
    Robert Crane and Christopher Fryer
Jack Nicholson: The Early Years
    Robert Crane and Christopher Fryer
Anne Bancroft: A Life
    Douglass K. Daniel
Being Hal Ashby: Life of a Hollywood Rebel
    Nick Dawson
Bruce Dern: A Memoir
    Bruce Dern with Christopher Fryer and Robert Crane
Intrepid Laughter: Preston Sturges and the Movies
    Andrew Dickos
Miriam Hopkins: Life and Films of a Hollywood Rebel
    Allan R. Ellenberger
Vitagraph: America's First Great Motion Picture Studio
    Andrew A. Erish
Jayne Mansfield: The Girl Couldn't Help It
    Eve Golden
John Gilbert: The Last of the Silent Film Stars
    Eve Golden
Stuntwomen: The Untold Hollywood Story
    Mollie Gregory
Saul Bass: Anatomy of Film Design
    Jan-Christopher Horak
Hitchcock Lost and Found: The Forgotten Films
    Alain Kerzoncuf and Charles Barr
Pola Negri: Hollywood's First Femme Fatale
    Mariusz Kotowski
Sidney J. Furie: Life and Films
    Daniel Kremer
Albert Capellani: Pioneer of the Silent Screen
    Christine Leteux
Ridley Scott: A Biography
    Vincent LoBrutto
Mamoulian: Life on Stage and Screen
    David Luhrssen

Maureen O'Hara: The Biography
  Aubrey Malone
My Life as a Mankiewicz: An Insider's Journey through Hollywood
  Tom Mankiewicz and Robert Crane
Hawks on Hawks
  Joseph McBride
Showman of the Screen: Joseph E. Levine and His Revolutions in Film Promotion
  A. T. McKenna
William Wyler: The Life and Films of Hollywood's Most Celebrated Director
  Gabriel Miller
Raoul Walsh: The True Adventures of Hollywood's Legendary Director
  Marilyn Ann Moss
Veit Harlan: The Life and Work of a Nazi Filmmaker
  Frank Noack
Harry Langdon: King of Silent Comedy
  Gabriella Oldham and Mabel Langdon
Charles Walters: The Director Who Made Hollywood Dance
  Brent Phillips
Some Like It Wilder: The Life and Controversial Films of Billy Wilder
  Gene D. Phillips
Ann Dvorak: Hollywood's Forgotten Rebel
  Christina Rice
Mean...Moody...Magnificent!: Jane Russell and the Marketing of a Hollywood Legend
  Christina Rice
Fay Wray and Robert Riskin: A Hollywood Memoir
  Victoria Riskin
Lewis Milestone: Life and Films
  Harlow Robinson
Michael Curtiz: A Life in Film
  Alan K. Rode
Arthur Penn: American Director
  Nat Segaloff
Film's First Family: The Untold Story of the Costellos
  Terry Chester Shulman
Claude Rains: An Actor's Voice
  David J. Skal with Jessica Rains
Barbara La Marr: The Girl Who Was Too Beautiful for Hollywood
  Sherri Snyder
Buzz: The Life and Art of Busby Berkeley
  Jeffrey Spivak
Victor Fleming: An American Movie Master
  Michael Sragow
Hollywood Presents Jules Verne: The Father of Science Fiction on Screen
  Brian Taves
Thomas Ince: Hollywood's Independent Pioneer
  Brian Taves
Picturing Peter Bogdanovich: My Conversations with the New Hollywood Director
  Peter Tonguette